K price

Dictionary
Spanish – English
English – Spanish

Diccionario
Español – Inglés
Inglés – Español

Berlitz Publishing
Union, NJ · Munich · Singapore

Edited by the Berlitz Editorial Staff

Cover photo by ID Image Direkt CD-ROM GmbH, Germany

Neither the presence nor the absence of a designation
that any entered word constitutes a trademark should be
regarded as affecting the legal status of any trademark.

Berlitz Publishing
95 Progress Street
Union, NJ 07083
USA

Printed in Austria
ISBN 981-246-375-5

Contents

Indice

Preface

In selecting the vocabulary and phrases for this dictionary, the editors have had the traveller's needs foremost in mind. This book will prove a useful companion to casual tourists and business travellers alike who appreciate the reassurance a small and practical dictionary can provide. It offers them — as well as beginners and students — all the basic vocabulary they will encounter and have to use, giving the key words and expressions to allow them to cope in everyday situations.

Like our successful phrase books and travel guides, these dictionaries — created with the help of a computer data bank — are designed to slip into your pocket or purse, and thus have a role as handy companions at all times.

Besides just about everything you normally find in dictionaries, there are these Berlitz bonuses:

• simplified pronunciation after each foreign-word entry, making it easy to read and enunciate words whose spelling may look forbidding

• a unique, practical glossary to simplify reading a foreign restaurant menu and to take the mystery out of complicated dishes and indecipherable names on bills of fare

• useful information on how to tell the time and how to count, on conjugating irregular verbs, commonly seen abbreviations and converting to the metric system, in addition to basic phrases.

While no dictionary of this size can pretend to completeness, we are confident this dictionary will help you get most out of your trip abroad.

Berlitz Publishing

Prefacio

Al seleccionar las entradas de este diccionario, los redactores han tenido especialmente en cuenta las necesidades del viajero. Este diccionario, pequeño y práctico, ofrece no solo el vocabulario básico, sino también las expresiones más frecuentes del lenguaje diario. Por ello, resulta una obra indispensable para viajeros, turistas y hombres de negocios.

Al igual que nuestros conocidos manuales de conversación y guías turísticas, este diccionario ha sido ideado para llevarse encima, ya sea en el bolsillo o en un bolso de mano, asumiendo de este modo su papel de compañero disponible en todo momento.

Además de la información que de ordinario se ofrece en un diccionario, esta obra proporciona:

- Una transcripción fonética sencilla, que facilita la pronunciación sin necesidad de conocimientos específicos

- un léxico gastronómico inédito, que le permitirá "descifrar" los menús en un restaurante y acceder al secreto de los platos complicados y a los misterios de la cuenta

- Apéndices prácticos que le ayudarán a comunicar la hora y a contar, así como a utilizar los verbos irregulares, las abreviaturas más comunes y algunas expresiones útiles.

Este diccionario, pequeño, ligero y práctico, no pretende ser completo sino proporcionar a quien lo emplee un medio para enfrentarse al viaje en el extranjero.

Berlitz Publishing

Spanish-English

Español-Inglés

Introduction

This dictionary has been designed to take account of your practical needs. Unnecessary linguistic information has been avoided. The entries are listed in alphabetical order regardless of whether the entry word is printed in a single word or in two or more separate words. When an entry is followed by sub-entries, such as expressions and locutions, these, too, have been listed in alphabetical order.

Each main-entry word is followed by a phonetic transcription (see guide to pronunciation). Following the transcription is the part of speech of the entry word whenever applicable. When an entry word may be used as more than one part of speech, the translations are grouped together after the respective part of speech.

Spanish feminine headwords are shown as follows:

abonado ... *m*, **-a** *f* subscriber

ciudadano ... *m*, **-a** *f* citizen

comediante ... *m*, **-a** *f* actor; comedian

The feminine forms of these headwords are: **abonada** (pl ~s), **ciudadana** (pl ~s), **comedianta** (pl ~s).

Whenever an entry word is repeated in sub-entries a tilde (~) is used to represent the full entry word.

An asterisk (*) in front of a verb indicates that the verb is irregular. For details you may refer to the lists of irregular verbs.

The dictionary is based on Castilian Spanish. All words and meanings of words that are exclusively Mexican have been marked as such (see list of abbreviations used in the text).

Abbreviations

adj	adjective	*n*	noun
adv	adverb	*nAm*	noun (American)
Am	American	*num*	numeral
art	article	*p*	past tense
conj	conjunction	*pl*	plural
f	feminine	*plAm*	plural (American)
fMe	feminine (Mexican)	*pp*	past participle
fpl	feminine plural	*pr*	present tense
fplMe	feminine plural (Mexican)	*pref*	prefix
L.Am.	Latin America	*prep*	preposition
m	masculine	*pron*	pronoun
Me	Mexican	*v*	verb
mMe	masculine (Mexican)	*vAm*	verb (American)
mpl	masculine plural	*vMe*	verb (Mexican)
mplMe	masculine plural (Mexican)		

Guide to Pronunciation

Each main entry in this part of the dictionary is followed by a phonetic transcription which shows you how to pronounce the words. This transcription should be read as if it were English. It is based on Standard British pronunciation, though we have tried to take account of General American pronunciation also. Below, only those letters and symbols are explained which we consider likely to be ambiguous or not immediately understood.

The syllables are separated by hyphens, and stressed syllables are printed in *italics*.

Of course, the sounds of any two languages are never exactly the same, but if you follow carefully our indications, you should be able to pronounce the foreign words in such a way that you'll be understood. To make your task easier, our transcriptions occasionally simplify slightly the sound system of the language while still reflecting the essential sound differences.

Consonants

bh	a rather indecisive **b**, i.e. one verging on **v**
dh	like **th** in **th**is, often rather indecisive, possibly quite like **d**
g	always hard, as in **g**o
g	a **g**-sound where the tongue doesn't quite close the air passage between itself and the roof of the mouth, so that the escaping air produces audible friction; it is also on occasions pronounced as an indecisive **g**
kh	like **g**, but based on a **k**-sound; therefore hard and voiceless, like **ch** in Scottish lo**ch**
lʸ	like **lli** in mi**lli**on
ñ	as in the Spanish se**ñ**or, or like **ni** in o**ni**on
r	slightly rolled in the front of the mouth
rr	strongly rolled **r**
s	always hard, as in **s**o

Vowels and Diphthongs

ah a short version of the **a** in c**a**r, i.e. a sound between **a** in c**a**t and **u** in c**u**t
igh as in s**igh**
ou as in l**ou**d

1) Raised letters (e.g. **ay**^{oo}, ^{y}**ah**) should be pronounced only fleetingly.
2) Spanish vowels (i.e. not diphthongs) are pure and fairly short. Therefore, you should try to read a transcription like **oa** without moving tongue or lips while pronouncing the sound.

Latin-American Pronunciation

Our transcriptions reflect the pronunciation of Castilian, the official language of Spain. In Latin America, two of the Castilian sounds are practically unknown:
1) **ll** as in the word ca**ll**e (which we represent by **l^{y}**) is usually pronounced like Spanish **y** (as in English **y**et); in the Río de la Plata region, though, both **ll** and **y** are pronounced like **s** in plea**s**ure.
2) The letters **c** (before **e** and **i**) and **z** are pronounced like **s** in **s**o instead of **th** as in **th**in.

A

a (ah) *prep* to, on; at; **a las ...** at ... o'clock

abacería (ah-bhah-thay-*ree*-ah) *f* grocer's

abacero (ah-bhah-*thay*-roa) *m* grocer

abadía (ah-bhah-*dhee*-ah) *f* abbey

abajo (ah-*bhah*-khoa) *adv* downstairs; down; **hacia ~** downwards

abandonar (ah-bhahn-doa-*nahr*) *v* abandon

abanico (ah-bhah-*nee*-koa) *m* fan

abarrotería (ah-bhah-rroa-tay-*ree*-ah) *f Me* grocer's

abarrotero (ah-bhah-rroa-*tay*-roa) *m Me* grocer

abastecimiento (ah-bhahss-tay-thee-*m^yayn*-toa) *m* supply

abatido (ah-bhah-*tee*-dhoa) *adj* down

abecedario (ah-bhay-thay-*dah*-r^yoa) *m* alphabet

abedul (ah-bhay-*dhool*) *m* birch

abeja (ah-*bhay*-khah) *f* bee

abertura (ah-bhayr-*too*-rah) *f* opening

abeto (ah-*bhay*-toa) *m* fir tree

abierto (ah-*bh^yayr*-toa) *adj* open

abismo (ah-*bhee*-zmoa) *m* abyss

ablandador (ah-bhlahn-dah-*dhoar*) *m* water softener

ablandar (ah-bhlahn-*dahr*) *v* soften

abogado (ah-bhoa-*gah*-dhoa) *m*, **-a** *f* barrister, lawyer, attorney; solicitor; advocate

abolir (ah-bhoa-*leer*) *v* abolish

abolladura (ah-bhoa-l^yah-*dhoo*-rah) *f* dent

abonado (ah-bhoa-*nah*-dhoa) *m*, **-a** *f* subscriber

abono (ah-*bhoa*-noa) *m* subscription

aborto (ah-*bhoar*-toa) *m* miscarriage; abortion

abrazar (ah-bhrah-*thahr*) *v* embrace; hug

abrazo (ah-*bhrah*-thoa) *m* hug; embrace

abrecartas (ah-bhray-*kahr*-tahss) *m* paper knife, *Am* letter opener

abrelatas (ah-bhray-*lah*-tahss) *m* tin opener, can opener *Am*

abreviatura (ah-bhray-bh^yah-*too*-rah) *f* abbreviation

abrigar (ah-bhree-*gahr*) *v* shelter

abrigo (ah-*bhree*-goa) *m* coat, overcoat; **~ de pieles** fur coat

abril (ah-*bhreel*) April

abrir (ah-*bhreer*) *v* open; unlock; turn on

abrochar (ah-bhroa-*chahr*) *v* button

abrupto (ah-*bhroop*-toa) *adj* steep

absceso (ahbhs-*thay*-soa) *m* abscess

absolutamente (ahbh-soa-loo-tah-*mayn*-tay) *adv* absolutely

absoluto (ahbh-soa-*loo*-toa) *adj* sheer; total

abstemio (ahbhs-*tay*-m^yoa) *m* teetotaller

*abstenerse de (ahbhs-tay-*nayr*-say) abstain from

abstracto (ahbhs-*trahk*-toa) *adj* abstract

absurdo (ahbh-*soor*-dhoa) *adj* absurd; foolish

abuela (ah-*bhway*-lah) *f* grandmother

abuelo (ah-*bhway*-loa) *m* grandfather, granddad; **abuelos** *mpl* grandparents *pl*

abundancia (ah-bhoon-*dahn*-th^yah) *f* abundance, plenty

abundante (ah-bhoon-*dahn*-tay) *adj* abundant, plentiful

aburrido (ah-bhoo-*rree*-dhoa) *adj* boring, dull

aburrir (ah-bhoo-*rreer*) *v* bore, annoy

abusar de (ah-bhoo-*sahr*) exploit

abuso (ah-*bhoo*-soa) *m* misuse, abuse

acá (ah-*kah*) *adv* here

acabar (ah-kah-*bhahr*) *v* end;
acabado finished; over

academia (ah-kah-*dhay*-m^yah) *f*
academy; ~ **de bellas artes** art
school

acampador (ah-kahm-pah-*dhoar*) *m*
camper

acampar (ah-kahm-*pahr*) *v* camp

acantilado (ah-kahn-tee-*lah*-dhoa) *m*
cliff; *adj* steep

acariciar (ah-kah-ree-th^y*ahr*) *v* caress

acaso (ah-*kah*-soa) *adv* perhaps

accesible (ahk-thay-*see*-bhlay) *adj*
accessible

acceso (ahk-*thay*-soa) *m* entrance,
access; approach

accesorio (ahk-thay-soa-r^yoa) *adj*
additional; **accesorios** *mpl*
accessories *pl*

accidental (ahk-thee-dhayn-*tahl*) *adj*
accidental

accidente (ahk-thee-*dhayn*-tay) *m*
accident; ~ **aéreo** plane crash

acción (ahk-th^y*oan*) *f* action; deed;
stock; **acciones** *fpl* stocks and shares

acechar (ah-thay-*chahr*) *v* watch for

aceite (ah-*thay*-tay) *m* oil; ~
bronceador suntan oil; ~ **de oliva**
olive oil; ~ **lubricante** lubrication oil

aceitoso (ah-thay-*toa*-soa) *adj* oily

aceituna (ah-thay-*too*-nah) *f* olive

acelerador (ah-thay-lay-rah-*dhoar*) *m*
accelerator

acelerar (ah-thay-lay-*rahr*) *v*
accelerate

acento (ah-*thayn*-toa) *m* accent

acentuar (ah-thayn-*twahr*) *v*
emphasize, stress

aceptar (ah-thayp-*tahr*) *v* accept

acera (ah-*thay*-rah) *f* pavement;
sidewalk *Am*

acerca de (ah-*thayr*-kah day) about

acercarse (ah-thayr-*kahr*-say) *v*
approach

acero (ah-*thay*-roa) *m* steel; ~
inoxidable stainless steel

***acertar** (ah-thayr-*tahr*) *v* *hit; guess
right

acidez (ah-thee-*dhayth*) *f* acidity

ácido (*ah*-thee-dhoa) *m* acid

aclamar (ah-klah-*mahr*) *v* cheer

aclaración (ah-klah-rah-th^y*oan*) *f*
explanation

aclarar (ah-klah-*rahr*) *v* clarify

acné (ahk-*nay*) *m* acne

acogida (ah-koa-*khee*-dhah) *f*
reception

acomodación (ah-koa-moa-dhah-
th^y*oan*) *f* accommodation

acomodado (ah-koa-moa-*dhah*-
dhoa) *adj* well-to-do

acomodador (ah-koa-moa-dhah-
dhoar) *m* usher

acomodadora (ah-koa-moa-dhah-
dhoa-rah) *f* usherette

acomodar (ah-koa-moa-*dhahr*) *v*
accommodate

acompañar (ah-koam-pah-*ñahr*) *v*
accompany; conduct

aconsejar (ah-koan-say-*khahr*) *v*
recommend, advise

***acontecer** (ah-koan-tay-*thayr*) *v*
occur

acontecimiento (ah-koan-tay-thee-
m^y*ayn*-toa) *m* event; happening,
occurrence

***acordar** (ah-koar-*dhahr*) *v* agree;
***acordarse** *v* remember, recollect,
recall

acortar (ah-koar-*tahr*) *v* shorten,
reduce

***acostar** (ah-koass-*tahr*) *v* *lay down;
***acostarse** *v* *go to bed

acostumbrado (ah-koass-toom-*brah*-
dhoa) *adj* accustomed; customary;
***estar** ~ **a** *be used to

acostumbrar (ah-koass-toom-*brahr*)

v accustom

*acrecentarse (ah-kray-thayn-*tahr*-say) *v* increase

acreditar (ah-kray-dhee-*tahr*) *v* credit

acreedor (ah-kray-ay-*dhoar*) *m* creditor

acta (*ahk*-tah) *f* certificate; **actas** minutes

actitud (ahk-tee-*toodh*) *f* attitude; position

actividad (ahk-tee-bhee-*dhahdh*) *f* activity

activo (ahk-*tee*-bhoa) *adj* active

acto (*ahk*-toa) *m* act, deed

actor (ahk-*toar*) *m* actor

actriz (ahk-*treeth*) *f* actress

actual (ahk-*twahl*) *adj* present; current

actualmente (ahk-twahl-*mayn*-tay) *adv* now

actuar (ahk-*twahr*) *v* act

acuarela (ah-kwah-*ray*-lah) *f* watercolo(u)r

acuerdo (ah-*kwayr*-dhoa) *m* approval; agreement, settlement; **¡de acuerdo!** all right!, okay!; ***estar de ~ con** approve of

acumulador (ah-koo-moo-lah-*dhoar*) *m* battery

acusación (ah-koo-sah-*th*ᵛ*oan*) *f* charge

acusado (ah-koo-*sah*-dhoa) *m*, **-a** *f* accused

acusar (ah-koo-*sahr*) *v* accuse; charge

adaptador (ah-dhahp-tah-*dhoar*) *m* adaptor

adaptar (ah-dhahp-*tahr*) *v* adapt; suit

adecuado (ah-dhay-*kwah*-dhoa) *adj* adequate; convenient, appropriate

adelantar (ah-dhay-lahn-*tahr*) *v* *get on; **por adelantado** in advance; **prohibido ~** no overtaking

adelante (ah-dhay-*lahn*-tay) *adv* ahead, onwards, forward

adelanto (ah-dhay-*lahn*-toa) *m* advance

adelgazar (ah-dhayl-gah-*thahr*) *v* lose weight

además (ah-dhay-*mahss*) *adv* moreover, furthermore, besides; **~ de** beyond, besides

adentro (ah-*dhayn*-troa) *adv* inside, in; **hacia ~** inwards

aderezo (ah-dhee-*ray*-thoa) *m* salad dressing

adeudado (ah-dhay°°-*dhah*-dhoa) *adj* due

adición (ah-dhee-*th*ᵛ*oan*) *f* addition

adicional (ah-dhee-th*ᵛ*oa-*nahl*) *adj* additional

adicionar (ah-dhee-th*ᵛ*oa-*nahr*) *v* add; count

¡adiós! (ah-*dh*ᵛ*oass*) good-bye!

adivinar (ah-dhee-bhee-*nahr*) *v* guess

adjetivo (ahdh-khay-*tee*-bhoa) *m* adjective

administración (ahdh-mee-neess-trah-*th*ᵛ*oan*) *f* administration; direction

administrativo (ahdh-mee-neess-trah-*tee*-bhoa) *adj* administrative

admirable (ahdh-mee-*rah*-bhlay) *adj* admirable

admiración (ahdh-mee-rah-*th*ᵛ*oan*) *f* admiration

admirador (ahdh-mee-rah-*dhoar*) *m*, **-a** *f* fan

admirar (ahdh-mee-*rahr*) *v* admire

admisión (ahdh-mee-*s*ᵛ*oan*) *f* admission; admittance

admitir (ahdh-mee-*teer*) *v* admit; acknowledge

adolescente (ah-dhoa-layss-*thayn*-tay) *m/f* teenager

adonde (ah-*dhoan*-day) *adv* where

adoptar (ah-dhoap-*tahr*) *v* adopt

adorable (ah-dhoa-*rah*-bhlay) *adj* adorable

adorar (ah-dhoa-*rahr*) *v* worship

adorno (ah-*dhoar*-noa) *m* ornament

adquirible (ahdh-kee-*ree*-bhlay) *adj* obtainable, available

*adquirir (ahdh-kee-*reer*) *v* acquire; *buy

adquisición (ahdh-kee-see-th^y*oan*) *f* acquisition

aduana (ah-*dwah*-nah) *f* Customs *pl*

adulto (ah-*dhool*-toa) *adj* grown-up, adult; *m*, **-a** *f* grown-up, adult

adverbio (ahdh-*bhayr*-bh^yoa) *m* adverb

advertencia (ahdh-bhayr-*tayn*-th^yah) *f* warning

adversario (ahdh-bhayr-*sah*-r^yoa) *m*, **-a** *f* opponent, adversary

*advertir (ahdh-bhayr-*teer*) *v* caution, warn; notice

aerolínea (ah-ay-roa-*lee*-nay-ah) *f* airline

aeropuerto (ah-ay-roa-*pwayr*-toa) *m* airport

aerosol (ah-ay-roa-*soal*) *m* atomizer

afamado (ah-fah-*mah*-dhoa) *adj* noted

afección (ah-fayk-th^y*oan*) *f* affection

afectado (ah-fayk-*tah*-dhoa) *adj* affected

afectar (ah-fayk-*tahr*) *v* affect; feign

afeitadora eléctrica (ah-fay-tah-*dhoa*-rah ay-*layk*-tree-kah) electric razor

afeitarse (ah-fay-*tahr*-say) *v* shave; **máquina de afeitar** safety-razor; shaver

afición (ah-fee-th^y*oan*) *f* hobby

aficionado (ah-fee-th^yoa-*nah*-dhoa) *m* supporter

afilar (ah-fee-*lahr*) *v* sharpen; **afilado** sharp

afiliado (ah-fee-l^y*ah*-dhoa) *adj* affiliated

afirmación (ah-feer-mah-th^y*oan*) *f* statement

afirmar (ah-feer-*mahr*) *v* claim

afirmativo (ah-feer-mah-*tee*-bhoa) *adj* affirmative

afligido (ah-flee-*khee*-dhoa) *adj* sad; ***estar ~** grieve

afluente (ah-*flwayn*-tay) *m* tributary

afortunado (ah-foar-too-*nah*-dhoa) *adj* fortunate, lucky

África (*ah*-free-kah) *f* Africa

África del Sur (*ah*-free-kah dayl soor) South Africa

africano (ah-free-*kah*-noa) *adj* African; *m* African

afuera (ah-*fway*-rah) *adv* outside, outdoors; **hacia ~** outwards

afueras (ah-*fway*-rahss) *fpl* outskirts *pl*

agarradero (ah-gah-rrah-*dhay*-roa) *m* handle

agarrar (ah-gah-*rrahr*) *v* grasp, seize; **agarrarse** *v* *hold on

agarre (ah-*gah*-rray) *m* grip, grasp

agencia (ah-*khayn*-th^yah) *f* agency; **~ de viajes** travel agency

agenda (ah-*khayn*-dah) *f* diary

agente (ah-*khayn*-tay) *m* agent; **~ de policía** policeman; **~ de viajes** travel agent

ágil (*ah*-kheel) *adj* supple

agitación (ah-khee-tah-th^y*oan*) *f* excitement; bustle

agitar (ah-khee-*tahr*) *v* stir up

agosto (ah-*goass*-toa) August

agotado (ah-goa-*tah*-dhoa) *adj* sold out

agotar (ah-goa-*tahr*) *v* use up

agradable (ah-grah-*dhah*-bhlay) *adj* agreeable; enjoyable, pleasing, pleasant; nice

*agradecer (ah-grah-dhay-*thayr*) *v* thank

agradecido (ah-grah-dhay-*thee*-dhoa) *adj* grateful, thankful

agrario (ah-*grah*-r^yoa) *adj* agrarian

agresivo (ah-gray-*see*-bhoa) *adj* aggressive

agrícola (ah-*gree*-koa-lah) *adj* agrarian

agricultura (ah-gree-kool-*too*-rah) *f* agriculture

agrio (*ah*-gr^yoa) *adj* sour

agua (*ah*-gwah) *f* water; **~ corriente** running water; **~ de mar** seawater; **~ de soda** soda-water; **~ dulce** fresh water; **~ helada** iced water; **~ mineral** mineral water; **~ potable** drinking-water

aguacate (ah-gwah-*kah*-tay) *m* avocado

aguacero (ah-gwah-*thay*-roa) *m* shower; downpour

aguafuerte (ah-gwah-*fwayr*-tay) *f* etching

aguanieve (ah-gwah-n^y*ay*-bhay) *f* slush

aguantar (ah-gwahn-*tahr*) *v* *bear

aguardar (ah-gwahr-*dahr*) *v* expect

aguardiente (ah-gwahr-d^y*ayn*-tay) *m* brandy; fruit-based alcoholic spirit

agudo (ah-*goo*-dhoa) *adj* keen; acute

águila (*ah*-gee-lah) *m* eagle

aguja (ah-*goo*-khah) *f* needle; spire; **labor de ~** needlework

agujero (ah-goo-*khay*-roa) *m* hole

ahí (ah-*ee*) *adv* there

ahogar (ah-oa-*gahr*) *v* drown; **ahogarse** *v* *be drowned

ahora (ah-*oa*-rah) *adv* now; **de ~ en adelante** henceforth; **hasta ~** so far

ahorrar (ah-oa-*rrahr*) *v* save

ahorros (ah-*oa*-rroass) *mpl* savings *pl*; **caja de ~** savings bank

ahuyentar (ou-^y*ayn*-*tahr*) *v* chase away

aire (*igh*-ray) *m* air; sky; breath; **~ acondicionado** air-conditioning; **cámara de ~** inner tube; ***tener aires de** look

airear (igh-ray-*ahr*) *v* air, ventilate

airoso (igh-*roa*-soa) *adj* airy

aislado (ighz-*lah*-dhoa) *adj* isolated

aislador (ighz-lah-*dhoar*) *m* insulator

aislamiento (ighz-lah-m^y*ayn*-toa) *m* isolation; insulation

aislar (ighz-*lahr*) *v* isolate; insulate

ajedrez (ah-khay-*dhrayth*) *m* chess

ajeno (ah-*khay*-noa) *adj* foreign

ajetrearse (ah-khay-tray-*ahr*-say) *v* labo(u)r

ajo (*ah*-khoa) *m* garlic

ajustar (ah-khooss-*tahr*) *v* adjust

ala (*ah*-lah) *f* wing

alabar (ah-lah-*bhahr*) *v* praise

alambre (ah-*lahm*-bray) *m* wire

alargar (ah-lahr-*gahr*) *v* lengthen; renew; hand to

alarma (ah-*lahr*-mah) *f* alarm; **~ de incendio** fire alarm

alarmante (ah-lahr-*mahn*-tay) *adj* alarming

alarmar (ah-lahr-*mahr*) *v* alarm

alba (*ahl*-bhah) *f* dawn

albañil (ahl-bhah-*ñeel*) *m* bricklayer

albaricoque (ahl-bhah-ree-*koa*-kay) *m* apricot

albornoz (ahl-bhoar-*noath*) *m* bathrobe

alboroto (ahl-bhoa-*roa*-toa) *m* noise, racket

álbum (*ahl*-bhoom) *m* album

alcachofa (ahl-kah-*choa*-fah) *f* artichoke

alcalde (ahl-*kahl*-dhay) *m* mayor

alcance (ahl-*kahn*-thay) *m* reach, range

alcanzable (ahl-kahn-*thah*-bhlay) *adj* attainable

alcanzar (ahl-kahn-*thahr*) *v* achieve, reach

alce (*ahl*-thay) *m* moose

alcohol (ahl-*koal*) *m* alcohol; **~ de quemar** methylated spirits

alcohólico (ahl-*koa*-lee-koa) *adj* alcoholic

aldea (ahl-*day*-ah) *f* hamlet

alegrar (ah-lay-*grahr*) *v* cheer up

alegre (ah-*lay*-gray) *adj* cheerful, merry, joyful; glad, gay

alegría (ah-lay-*gree*-ah) *f* gaiety; gladness

alejar (ah-lay-*khahr*) *v* move away

alemán (ah-lay-*mahn*) *adj* German; *m* German

Alemania (ah-lay-*mah*-nʸah) *f* Germany

***alentar** (ah-layn-*tahr*) *v* encourage

alergia (ah-*layr*-khʸah) *f* allergy

alérgico (ah-*layr*-khee-koa) *adj* allergic

alfiler (ahl-fee-*layr*) *m* pin

alfombra (ahl-*foam*-brah) *f* carpet

alfombrilla (ahl-foam-*bree*-lʸah) *f* rug

alga (*ahl*-gah) *f* alga; seaweed

álgebra (*ahl*-gay-bhrah) *f* algebra

algo (*ahl*-goa) *pron* something; *adv* somewhat

algodón (ahl-goa-*dhoan*) *m* cotton; **de ~** cotton-wool; **de ~** cotton

alguien (*ahl*-gʸayn) *pron* someone, somebody

alguno (ahl-*goo*-noa) *adj* any; **algunos** *adj* some; *pron* some

alhaja (ah-*lah*-khah) *f* gem

aliado (ah-*lʸah*-dhoa) *m* associate

alianza (ah-*lʸahn*-thah) *f* alliance

alicates (ah-lee-*kah*-tayss) *mpl* pliers *pl*

alienado (ah-lʸah-*nah*-dhoa) *m* lunatic

aliento (ah-*lʸayn*-toa) *m* breath

alimentar (ah-lee-mayn-*tahr*) *v* *feed

alimento (ah-lee-*mayn*-toa) *m* fare; food; **alimentos naturales** health food

alivio (ah-*lee*-bhʸoa) *m* relief

alma (*ahl*-mah) *f* soul

almacén (ahl-mah-*thayn*) *m* depot, warehouse, depository, store house; store; **~ de licores** off-licence; liquor store *Am*; **grandes almacenes** department store

almacenaje (ahl-mah-thay-*nah*-khay) *m* storage

almacenar (ahl-mah-thay-*nahr*) *v* store

almeja (ahl-*may*-khah) *f* clam

almendra (ahl-*mayn*-drah) *f* almond

almirante (ahl-mee-*rahn*-tay) *m* admiral

almohada (ahl-moa-*ah*-dhah) *f* pillow; **~ eléctrica** heating pad

almohadilla (ahl-moa-ah-*dhee*-lʸah) *f* pad

almohadón (ahl-moa-ah-*dhoan*) *m* cushion; pillow

almorzar (ahl-moar-*thahr*) *v* have lunch; have a mid-morning snack

almuerzo (ahl-*mwayr*-thoa) *m* lunch, luncheon

alojamiento (ah-loa-khah-*mʸayn*-toa) *m* accommodation, lodgings *pl*

alojar (ah-loa-*khahr*) *v* lodge

alondra (ah-*loan*-drah) *f* lark

alquilar (ahl-kee-*lahr*) *v* hire; rent, lease, *let

alquiler (ahl-kee-*layr*) *m* rent; **~ de coches** car hire; **de ~** for hire

alrededor de (ahl-ray-dhay-*dhoar* day) around, round; about

alrededores (ahl-ray-dhay-*dhoa*-rayss) *mpl* environment, surroundings *pl*

altar (ahl-*tahr*) *m* altar

altavoz (ahl-tah-*bhoath*) *m* loudspeaker

alteración (ahl-tay-rah-*thʸoan*) *f* alteration

alterar (ahl-tay-*rahr*) *v* alter

alternar con (ahl-tayr-*nahr*) mix with

alternativa (ahl-tayr-nah-*tee*-bhah) *f* alternative

alternativo (ahl-tayr-nah-*tee*-bhoa) *adj* alternate

altiplano (ahl-tee-*plah*-noa) *m* high plateau *pl*

altitud (ahl-tee-*toodh*) *f* altitude

alto (*ahl*-toa) *adj* high, tall; **en ~** overhead

¡alto! (*ahl*-toa) stop!

altura (ahl-*too*-rah) *f* height

alubia (ah-*loo*-bh^yah) *f* kidney bean

aludir a (ah-loo-*dheer*) allude to

alumbrado (ah-loom-*brah*-dhoa) *m* lighting

alumna (ah-*loom*-nah) *f* schoolgirl

alumno (ah-*loom*-noa) *m* pupil; schoolboy

alzar (ahl-*thahr*) *v* raise

allá (ah-l^y*ah*) *adv* over there; **más ~** beyond; **más ~ de** past, beyond

allí (ah-l^y*ee*) *adv* there

ama (*ah*-mah) *f* owner; **~ de casa** housewife, homemaker; **~ de llaves** housekeeper; **~ de leche, ~ de cría** L.Am. wetnurse

amable (ah-*mah*-bhlay) *adj* kind, friendly

amado (ah-*mah*-dhoa) *adj* beloved

amaestrar (ah-mah-ayss-*trahr*) *v* train

amamantar (ah-mah-mahn-*tahr*) *v* nurse

amanecer (ah-mah-nay-*thayr*) *m* sunrise, daybreak

amante (ah-*mahn*-tay) *m/f* lover

amapola (ah-mah-*poa*-lah) *f* poppy

amar (ah-*mahr*) *v* love

amargo (ah-*mahr*-goa) *adj* bitter

amarillo (ah-mah-*ree*-l^yoa) *adj* yellow

ámbar (*ahm*-bahr) *m* amber

ambicioso (ahm-bee-th^y*oa*-soa) *adj* ambitious

ambiental (ahm-b^yayn-*tahl*) *adj* environmental

ambiente (ahm-b^y*ayn*-tay) *m* atmosphere; **medio ~** environment

ambiguo (ahm-*bee*-gwoa) *adj* ambiguous

ambos (*ahm*-boass) *adj* both; either

ambulancia (ahm-boo-*lahn*-th^yah) *f* ambulance

ambulante (ahm-boo-*lahn*-tay) *adj* itinerant

amenaza (ah-may-*nah*-thah) *f* threat

amenazador (ah-may-nah-thah-*dhoar*) *adj* threatening

amenazar (ah-may-nah-*thahr*) *v* threaten

ameno (ah-*may*-noa) *adj* nice

América (ah-*may*-ree-kah) *f* America; **~ Latina** Latin America

americana (ah-may-ree-*kah*-nah) *f* jacket

americano (ah-may-ree-*kah*-noa) *adj* American; *m* American

amiga (ah-*mee*-gah) *f* friend

amígdalas (ah-*meeg*-dhah-lahss) *fpl* tonsils *pl*

amigdalitis (ah-meeg-dhah-*lee*-teess) *f* tonsilitis

amigo (ah-*mee*-goa) *m* friend

amistad (ah-meess-*tahdh*) *f* friendship

amistoso (ah-meess-*toa*-soa) *adj* friendly

amnistía (ahm-neess-*tee*-ah) *f* amnesty

amo (*ah*-moa) *m* master

amoníaco (ah-moan-*nee*-ah-koa) *m* ammonia

amontonar (ah-moan-toa-*nahr*) *v* pile

amor (ah-*moar*) *m* love; darling, sweetheart

amorío (ah-moa-*ree*-oa) *m* affair, romance

amoroso (ah-moa-*roa*-soa) *adj* amorous

amortiguador (ah-moar-tee-gwah-*dhoar*) *m* shock absorber

amortizar (ah-moar-tee-*thahr*) *v* *pay off

amotinamiento (ah-moa-tee-nah-*m^yayn*-toa) *m* mutiny

ampliación (ahm-pl^yah-th^y*oan*) *f* enlargement; extension

ampliar (ahm-*pl^yahr*) *v* enlarge; extend

amplio (*ahm*-pl^yoa) *adj* broad

ampolla (ahm-*poa*-l^yah) *f* blister

amueblar (ah-mway-*bhlahr*) *v* furnish

analfabeto (ah-nahl-fah-*bhay*-toa) *m* illiterate

analgésico (ah-nahl-*khay*-see-koa) *m* painkiller

análisis (ah-*nah*-lee-seess) *f* analysis

analista (ah-nah-*leess*-tah) *m* analyst

analizar (ah-nah-lee-*thahr*) *v* analyse; *break down

análogo (ah-*nah*-loa-goa) *adj* similar

anarquía (ah-nahr-*kee*-ah) *f* anarchy

anatomía (ah-nah-toa-*mee*-ah) *f* anatomy

anciano (ahn-*th^yah*-noa) *adj* aged; elderly

ancla (*ahng*-klah) *f* anchor

ancho (*ahn*-choa) *adj* broad; wide; *m* breadth

anchoa (ahn-*choa*-ah) *f* anchovy

anchura (ahn-*choo*-rah) *f* width

***andar** (ahn-*dahr*) *v* walk

andén (ahn-*dayn*) *m* platform

anemia (ah-*nay*-m^yah) *f* anaemia

anestesia (ah-nayss-*tay*-s^yah) *f* anaesthesia

anexar (ah-nayk-*sahr*) *v* annex

anexo (ah-*nayk*-soa) *m* annex, enclosure

anfiteatro (ahn-fee-tay-*ah*-troa) *m* amphitheater *Am*, amphitheatre; dress circle

anfitrión (ahn-fee-*tr^yoan*) *m* host

ángel (*ahng*-khayl) *m* angel

angosto (ahng-*goass*-toa) *adj* narrow, tight

anguila (ahng-*gee*-lah) *f* eel

ángulo (*ahng*-goo-loa) *m* angle

angustioso (ahng-gooss-*t^yoa*-soa) *adj* afraid

anhelar (ah-nay-*lahr*) *v* desire, long for

anhelo (ah-*nay*-loa) *m* longing

anillo (ah-*nee*-l^yoa) *m* ring; **~ de boda** wedding ring; **~ de esponsales** engagement ring

animado (ah-nee-*mah*-dhoa) *adj* crowded; lively; animated

animal (ah-nee-*mahl*) *m* beast, animal; **~ de presa** beast of prey; **~ doméstico** pet

animar (ah-nee-*mahr*) *v* encourage, inspire; animate

ánimo (*ah*-nee-moa) *m* mind; courage

aniversario (ah-nee-bhayr-*sah*-r^yoa) *m* anniversary; jubilee

anoche (ah-*noa*-chay) *adv* last night

anónimo (ah-*noa*-nee-moa) *adj* anonymous

anormal (ah-noar-*mahl*) *adj* abnormal

anotación (ah-noa-tah-*th^yoan*) *f* entry

anotar (ah-noa-*tahr*) *v* *write down

ansia (*ahn*-s^yah) *f* anxiety

ansioso (ahn-*s^yoa*-soa) *adj* anxious, eager

ante (*ahn*-tay) *prep* in front of

anteayer (ahn-tay-ah-*^yayr*) *adv* the day before yesterday

antecedentes (ahn-tay-thay-*dhayn*-tayss) *mpl* background

antemano (ahn-tay-*mah*-noa): **de ~** beforehand

antena (ahn-*tay*-nah) *f* aerial

anteojos (ahn-tay-*oa*-khoass) *mpl* glasses, spectacles

antepasado (ahn-tay-pah-*sah*-dhoa) *m*, **-a** *f* ancestor

anterior (ahn-tay-*r^yoar*) *adj* former, prior, previous

antes (*ahn*-tayss) *adv* before; formerly; at first; **~ de** before; **~ de que** before

antibiótico (ahn-tee-*bh^{y}oa*-tee-koa) *m* antibiotic

anticipar (ahn-tee-thee-*pahr*) *v* advance

anticipo (ahn-tee-*thee*-poa) *m* advance

anticonceptivo (ahn-tee-koan-thayp-*tee*-bhoa) *m* contraceptive

anticongelante (ahn-tee-koang-khay-*lahn*-tay) *m* antifreeze

anticuado (ahn-tee-*kwah*-dhoa) *adj* old-fashioned; ancient, out of date, quaint

anticuario (ahn-tee-*kwah*-r^{y}oa) *m*, **-a** *f* antique dealer

Antigüedad (ahn-tee-gway-*dhahdh*) *f* antiquity

antigüedades (ahn-tee-gway-*dhah*-dhayss) *fpl* antiquities *pl*

antiguo (ahn-*tee*-gwoa) *adj* ancient, antique; former

antipatía (ahn-tee-pah-*tee*-ah) *f* antipathy, dislike

antipático (ahn-tee-*pah*-tee-koa) *adj* nasty, unpleasant

anticipado (ahn-tee-thee-*pah*-dhoa) *adj* advance; early; **por ~** in advance

antirrobo (ahn-tee-*roa*-bhoa) *m* antitheft device

antojarse (ahn-toa-*khahr*-say) *v* fancy, *feel like

antojo (ahn-*toa*-khoa) *m* fad, whim

antología (ahn-toa-loa-*khee*-ah) *f* anthology

antorcha (ahn-*toar*-chah) *f* torch

anual (ah-*nwahl*) *adj* annual, yearly

anuario (ah-*nwah*-ree-oa) *m* annual

anudar (ah-noo-*dhahr*) *v* tie; knot

anular (ah-noo-*lahr*) *v* cancel

anunciar (ah-noon-*th^{y}ahr*) *v* announce

anuncio (ah-*noon*-th^{y}oa) *m* announcement; advertisement

anzuelo (ahn-*thway*-loa) *m* fishing hook

añadir (ah-ñah-*dheer*) *v* add

año (*ah*-ñoa) *m* year; **al ~** per annum; **~ bisiesto** leap year; **~ nuevo** New Year

apagado (ah-pah-*gah*-dhoa) *adj* mat

apagar (ah-pah-*gahr*) *v* extinguish; *put out, switch off

aparato (ah-pah-*rah*-toa) *m* appliance, apparatus; machine

aparcamiento (ah-pahr-kah-*m^{y}ayn*-toa) *m* parking; **zona de ~** parking zone

aparcar (ah-pahr-*kahr*) *v* park; shelve

***aparecer** (ah-pah-ray-*thayr*) *v* appear

aparente (ah-pah-*rayn*-tay) *adj* apparent

aparición (ah-pah-ree-*th^{y}oan*) *f* apparition

apariencia (ah-pah-r^y*ayn*-th^{y}ah) *f* appearance, semblance

apartado (ah-pahr-*tah*-dhoa) *adj* remote; *m* post office box

apartamento (ah-pahr-tah-*mayn*-toa) *m* suite; apartment *Am*

apartar (ah-pahr-*tahr*) *v* separate

aparte (ah-*pahr*-tay) *adv* aside; *adj* individual

apasionado (ah-pah-s^{y}oa-*nah*-dhoa) *adj* passionate

apearse (ah-pay-*ahr*-say) *v* *get off

apelación (ah-pay-lah-*th^{y}oan*) *f* appeal

apelmazado (ah-payl-mah-*thah*-dhoa) *adj* lumpy; compacted

apellido (ah-pay-*l^{y}ee*-dhoa) *m* family name, surname; **~ de soltera** maiden name

apenado (ah-pay-*nah*-dhoa) *adj* sorry, sad

apenas (ah-*pay*-nahss) *adv* hardly, barely, scarcely; just

apéndice (ah-*payn*-dee-thay) *m* appendix

apendicitis (ah-payn-dee-*thee*-teess) *f* appendicitis

aperitivo (ah-pay-ree-*tee*-bhoa) *m* aperitif, drink

apertura (ah-payr-*too*-rah) *f* opening

apestar (ah-payss-*tahr*) *v* *stink

apetito (ah-pay-*tee*-toa) *m* appetite

apetitoso (ah-pay-tee-*toa*-soa) *adj* appetizing

apio (*ah*-p^yoa) *m* celery

aplaudir (ah-plou-*dheer*) *v* clap

aplauso (ah-*plou*-soa) *m* applause

aplazar (ah-plah-*thahr*) *v* postpone, adjourn, *put off

aplicación (ah-plee-kah-s^yoan) *f* application

aplicar (ah-plee-*kahr*) *v* apply; **aplicarse a** apply, *be valid for

apodo (ah-*poa*-dhoa) *m* nickname

apogeo (ah-poa-*khayoa*) *m* height; zenith

***apostar** (ah-poass-*tahr*) *v* *bet

apoyar (ah-poa-*^yahr*) *v* support; **apoyarse** *v* *lean

apoyo (ah-*poa*-^yoa) *m* support; assistance

apreciar (ah-pray-*th^yahr*) *v* appreciate

aprecio (ah-*pray*-th^yoa) *m* appreciation

aprender (ah-prayn-*dayr*) *v* *learn; **aprenderse de memoria** memorize

aprendiz (ah-prayn-*dheeth*) *m*, **-a** *f* apprentice, trainee

apresar (ah-pray-*sahr*) *v* hijack

apresurarse (ah-pray-soo-*rahr*-say) *v* hasten, hurry

apretado (ah-pray-*tah*-dhoa) *adj* tight

***apretar** (ah-pray-*tahr*) *v* press; tighten

apretón (ah-pray-*toan*) *m* clutch; **~ de manos** handshake

aprobación (ah-proa-bhah-*th^yoan*) *f* approval

***aprobar** (ah-proa-*bhahr*) *v* approve; pass

apropiado (ah-proa-*p^yah*-dhoa) *adj* appropriate, suitable, proper; fit

aprovechar (ah-proa-bhay-*chahr*) *v* profit, benefit

aproximadamente (ah-proak-see-mah-dhah-*mayn*-tay) *adv* about, approximately

aproximado (ah-proak-see-*mah*-dhoa) *adj* approximate

aptitud (ahp-tee-*toodh*) *f* qualification; faculty

apto (*ahp*-toa) *adj* suitable; ***ser ~ para** qualify

apuesta (ah-*pwayss*-tah) *f* bet

apuntar (ah-poon-*tahr*) *v* aim at; point out

apunte (ah-*poon*-tay) *m* note; memo; **libreta de apuntes** notebook

aquel (ah-*kayl*) *adj*, **-la** *f* that; **aquellos, aquellas** *pl* those

aquél (ah-*kayl*) *pron*, **-la** *f* that (one); **aquéllos** *pl* those (ones)

aquello *pron* that

aquí (ah-*kee*) *adv* here

árabe (*ah*-rah-bhay) *adj* Arab; *m* Arab

Arabia Saudí (ah-*rah*-bh^yah sou-*dhee*) Saudi Arabia

arado (ah-*rah*-dhoa) *m* plough

arancel (ah-rahn-*thayl*) *m* tariff; duty

araña (ah-*rah*-ñah) *f* spider; **tela de ~** cobweb

arar (ah-*rahr*) *v* plough

arbitrario (ahr-bhee-*trah*-r^yoa) *adj* arbitrary

árbitro (*ahr*-bhee-troa) *m* referee; umpire; arbitrator

árbol (*ahr*-bhoal) *m* tree; **~ de levas** camshaft

arbusto (ahr-*bhooss*-toa) *m* shrub

arca (*ahr*-kah) *f* chest

arcada (ahr-*kah*-dhah) *f* arcade

arce (*ahr*-thay) *m* maple

arcén (ahr-*thayn*) *m* shoulder; hard shoulder

arcilla (ahr-*thee*-lʸah) *f* clay

arco (*ahr*-koa) *m* arch, bow; **~ iris** rainbow

archivo (ahr-*chee*-bhoa) *m* archives *pl*

arder (ahr-*dhayr*) *v* *burn

ardilla (ahr-*dhee*-lʸah) *f* squirrel

área (*ah*-ray-ah) *f* area; are

arena (ah-ray-nah) *f* sand

arenoso (ah-ray-*noa*-soa) *adj* sandy

arenque (ah-*rayng*-kay) *m* herring

Argelia (ahr-*khay*-lʸah) *f* Algeria

argelino (ahr-khay-*lee*-noa) *adj* Algerian; *m* Algerian

Argentina (ahr-khayn-*tee*-nah) *f* Argentina

argentino (ahr-khayn-*tee*-noa) *adj* Argentinian; *m* Argentinian

argumentar (ahr-goo-mayn-*tahr*) *v* argue

argumento (ahr-goo-*mayn*-toa) *m* argument

árido (*ah*-ree-dhoa) *adj* arid

arma (*ahr*-mah) *f* weapon, arm

armador (ahr-mah-*dhoar*) *m* shipowner

armadura (ahr-mah-*dhoo*-rah) *f* frame; armour

armar (ahr-*mahr*) *v* arm

armario (ahr-mah-rʸoa) *m* cupboard; closet

armonía (ahr-moa-*nee*-ah) *f* harmony

aroma (ah-*roa*-mah) *m* aroma

arpa (*ahr*-pah) *f* harp

arqueado (ahr-kay-*ah*-dhoa) *adj* arched

arqueología (ahr-kay-oa-loa-*khee*-ah) *f* arch(a)eology

arqueólogo (ahr-kay-*oa*-loa-goa) *m*, **-a** *f* arch(a)eologist

arquitecto (ahr-kee-*tayk*-toa) *m* architect

arquitectura (ahr-kee-tayk-*too*-rah) *f* architecture

arrancar (ah-rrahng-*kahr*) *v* uproot, pull out; start off

arrastrar (ah-rrahss-*trahr*) *v* haul, drag; *draw; **arrastrarse** *v* crawl

arrecife (ah-rray-*thee*-fay) *m* reef

arreglar (ah-rray-*glahr*) *v* settle; tidy up; repair, fix; **arreglarse con** *make do with

arreglo (ah-*rray*-gloa) *m* arrangement; settlement; **con ~ a** in accordance with

arrendamiento (ah-rrayn-dah-mʸayn-toa) *m* lease; **contrato de ~** lease

*arrendar (ah-rrayn-*dahr*) *v* lease

arrepentimiento (ah-rray-payn-tee-mʸayn-toa) *m* regret, repentance

arrepentirse (ah-rray-payn-*teer*-say) *v* be sorry; change one's mind; **~ de** regret

arrestar (ah-rrayss-*tahr*) *v* arrest

arresto (ah-*rrayss*-toa) *m* arrest

arriba (ah-*rree*-bhah) *adv* above; upstairs; up

arriesgado (ah-rryayz-gah-dhoa) *adj* risky

arriesgar (ah-rrʸayz-*gahr*) *v* venture, risk

arrodillarse (ah-rroa-dhee-lʸahr-say) *v* *kneel

arrogante (ah-rroa-*gahn*-tay) *adj* arrogant

arrojar (ah-rroa-*khahr*) *v* *throw

arroyo (ah-*rroa*-ʸoa) *m* stream, brook

arroz (ah-*rroath*) *m* rice

arruga (ah-*rroo*-gah) *f* wrinkle

arrugar (ah-rroo-*gahr*) *v* wrinkle

arruinar (ah-rrwee-*nahr*) *v* ruin; **arruinado** broke

arte (*ahr*-tay) *m/f* art; **artes industriales** arts and crafts; **bellas artes** fine arts

arteria (ahr-*tay*-rʸah) *f* artery; **~ principal** thoroughfare

artesanía (ahr-tay-sah-*nee*-ah) *f* handicraft

artesano (ahr-tay-*sah*-noa) *m* craftsman

articulación (ahr-tee-koo-lah-*th*ʸ*oan*) *f* joint

artículo (ahr-*tee*-koo-loa) *m* article

artificial (ahr-tee-fee-*th*ʸ*ahl*) *adj* artificial

artificio (ahr-tee-*fee*-th*ʸ*oa) *m* artifice

artista (ahr-*teess*-tah) *m/f* artist

artístico (ahr-*teess*-tee-koa) *adj* artistic

arzobispo (ahr-thoa-*bheess*-poa) *m* archbishop

asa (*ah*-sah) *f* handle

asamblea (ah-sahm-*blay*-ah) *f* assembly, meeting

asado (ah-*sah*-doa) *adj* roasted, baked; *m* roast meat

asalto (ah-*sahl*-toa) *m* attack; robbery, raid; round

asar (ah-*sahr*) *v* roast; **~ en parrilla** roast

asbesto (ahdh-*bhayss*-toa) *m* asbestos

ascensor (ah-thayn-*soar*) *m* lift; elevator *Am*

asco (*ahss*-koa) *m* disgust; **me da ~** I find it disgusting; **¡qué asco!** how revolting, how disgusting!

aseado (ah-say-*ah*-dhoa) *adj* tidy

asegurar (ah-say-goo-*rahr*) *v* assure, insure; **asegurarse de** ascertain

asesinar (ah-say-see-*nahr*) *v* murder

asesinato (ah-say-see-*nah*-toa) *m* murder, assassination

asesino (ah-say-*see*-noa) *m*, **-a** *f* murderer

asfalto (ahss-*fahl*-toa) *m* asphalt

así (ah-*see*) *adv* thus, so; **~ que** so that

Asia (*ah*-sʸah) *f* Asia

asiático (ah-sʸ*ah*-tee-koa) *adj* Asian; *m* Asian

asiento (ah-sʸ*ayn*-toa) *m* seat

asignación (ah-seeg-nah-*th*ʸ*oan*) *f* allowance

asignar (ah-seeg-*nahr*) *v* allot; **~ a** assign to

asilo (ah-*see*-loa) *m* asylum

asimismo (ah-see-*meez*-moa) *adv* also, likewise

***asir** (ah-*seer*) *v* grip

asistencia (ah-seess-*tayn*-thʸah) *f* attendance; assistance

asistente (ah-seess-*tayn*-tay) *m* assistant

asistir (ah-seess-*teer*) *v* assist, aid; **~ a** assist at, attend

asma (*ahz*-mah) *f* asthma

asociación (ah-soa-thʸah-*th*ʸ*oan*) *f* association; club, society

asociado (ah-soa-*th*ʸ*ah*-dhoa) *m* associate

asociar (ah-soa-*th*ʸ*ahr*) *v* associate; **asociarse a** join

asombrar (ah-soam-*brahr*) *v* amaze, astonish

asombro (ah-*soam*-broa) *m* amazement; wonder

asombroso (ah-soam-*broa*-soa) *adj* astonishing

aspecto (ahss-*payk*-toa) *m* aspect; appearance, look; sight

áspero (*ahss*-pay-roa) *adj* harsh; rough

aspiración (ahss-pee-rah-*th*ʸ*oan*) *f* inhalation; aspiration

aspirador (ahss-pee-rah-*dhoar*) *m* vacuum cleaner; **pasar el ~** hoover, vacuum *Am*

aspirar (ahss-pee-*rahr*) *v* aspire; **~ a** aim at

aspirina (ahss-pee-*ree*-nah) *f* aspirin

asqueroso (ahss-kay-*roa*-soa) *adj* disgusting

astilla (ahss-*tee*-lʸah) *f* splinter; chip

astillero (ahss-tee-lʸ*ay*-roa) *m* shipyard

astronauta (ahss-troa-no*u*-tah) *m/f* astronaut

astronomía (ahss-troa-noa-*mee*-ah) *f* astronomy

astucia (ahss-*too*-th^yah) *f* ruse

astuto (ahss-*too*-toa) *adj* cunning; clever, sly

asunto (ah-*soon*-toa) *m* affair, matter; concern, business; topic

asustado (ah-sooss-*tah*-dhoa) *adj* afraid

asustar (ah-sooss-*tahr*) *v* scare; **asustarse** *v* *be frightened

atacar (ah-tah-*kahr*) *v* attack, assault; *strike

atadura (ah-tah-*dhoo*-rah) *f* binding

atajo (ah-*tah*-khoa) *m* L.Am. short cut

atañer (ah-tah-*ñayr*) *v* concern

ataque (ah-*tah*-kay) *m* attack, fit; stroke; **~ cardíaco** heart attack

atar (ah-*tahr*) *v* tie, *bind; fasten; bundle

atareado (ah-tah-ray-*ah*-dhoa) *adj* busy

atardecer (ah-*tahr*-de-*thayr*) *v* get dark; *m* dusk

atasco (ah-*tahss*-koa) *m* traffic jam

atención (ah-tayn-th^yoan) *f* attention; consideration, notice; **prestar ~** *pay attention, look out

***atender a** (ah-tayn-*dayr*) attend to, see to; nurse

atentamente (ah-tayn-tah-*mayn*-tay) *adv* attentively; (Yours) sincerely

atento (ah-*tayn*-toa) *adj* attentive; thoughtful

ateo (ah-*tay*-oa) *m* atheist

aterido (ah-tay-*ree*-dhoa) *adj* numb

aterrador (ah-tay-rrah-*dhoar*) *adj* terrifying

aterrizaje (ah-tay-rree-*thah*-khay) *m* landing; **~ forzoso, ~ de emergencia** emergency landing

aterrizar (ah-tay-rree-*thahr*) *v* land

aterrorizar (ah-tay-rroa-ree-*thahr*) *v* terrify

Atlántico (aht-*lahn*-tee-koa) *m* Atlantic

atleta (aht-*lay*-tah) *m* athlete

atletismo (aht-lay-*teez*-moa) *m* athletics *pl*

atmósfera (aht-*moass*-fay-rah) *f* atmosphere

atómico (ah-*toa*-mee-koa) *adj* atomic

átomo (*ah*-toa-moa) *m* atom

atónito (ah-*toa*-nee-toa) *adj* speechless

atormentar (ah-toar-mayn-*tahr*) *v* torment

atornillar (ah-toar-nee-*l^yahr*) *v* screw

atracar (ah-trah-*kahr*) *v* dock

atracción (ah-trahk-th^yoan) *f* attraction

atraco (ah-*trah*-koa) *m* hold-up

atractivo (ah-trahk-*tee*-bhoa) *adj* attractive

***atraer** (ah-trah-*ayr*) *v* attract

atrapar (ah-trah-*pahr*) *v* ensnare; trap

atrás (ah-*trahss*) *adv* back

atrasado (ah-trah-*sah*-dhoa) *adj* overdue; delayed

atraso (ah-*trah*-soa) *m* backwardness; **atrasos** arrears

***atravesar** (ah-trah-bhay-*sahr*) *v* cross, pass through

atreverse (ah-tray-*bhayr*-say) *v* dare

atrevido (ah-tray-*bhee*-dhoa) *adj* daring

***atribuir a** (ah-tree-*bhweer*) assign to

atropellar (ah-troh-phay-*l^yahr*) *v* knock down

atroz (ah-*troath*) *adj* atrocious

atún (ah-*toon*) *m* tuna

audacia (ou-*dhah*-th^yah) *f* audacity

audaz (ou-*dhahth*) *adj* audacious; bold

audible (ou-*dhee*-bhlay) *adj* audible

audiencia (ou- *dh^yayn*-th^yah) *f* audience; court; **índice de ~** ratings *pl*

auditorio (ou-dhee-*toa*-r^yoa) *m* audience

aula (*ou*-lah) *f* auditorium; lecture hall

aumentar (ou-mayn-*tahr*) *v* increase, raise

aumento (ou-*mayn*-toa) *m* increase; rise; raise *Am*

aun (ah-*oon*) *adv* (aún) yet; even

aunque (*oung*-kay) *conj* although, though

auricular (ou-ree kou-*lahr*) *m* receiver; **auriculares** headphones, earphones

aurora (ou-*roa*-rah) *f* dawn

ausencia (ou-*sayn*-th^yah) *f* absence

ausente (ou-*sayn*-tay) *adj* absent

Australia (ouss-*trah*-l^yah) *f* Australia

australiano (ouss-trah-*l'ah*-noa) *adj* Australian; *m* Australian

Austria (*ouss*-tr^yah) *f* Austria

austríaco (ouss-*tree*-ah-koa) *adj* Austrian; *m* Austrian

auténtico (ou-*tayn*-tee-koa) *adj* authentic; true, original

auto (*ou*-toa) *m* car

autoadhesivo (ou-toa-ahdhea-*seeh*-boa) *adj* self-adhesive

autobús (ou-toa-*bhooss*) *m* coach, bus

autocar (ou-toa-*kahr*) *m* bus

autocaravana (ou-toa-kahrah-*bahna*) *f* camper van

autoestopista (ou-toa-ayss-toa-*peess*-tah) *m/f* hitchhiker

automático (ou-toa-*mah*-tee-koa) *adj* automatic

automóvil (ou-toa-*moa*-bheel) *m* motor-car, automobile; **~ club** automobile club

automovilismo (ou-toa-moa-bhee-*leez*-moa) *m* motoring

automovilista (ou-toa-moa-bhee-*leess*-tah) *m* motorist

autonomía (ou-toa-noa-*mee*-ah) *f* self-government

autónomo (ou-*toa*-noa-moa) *adj* independent, autonomous

autopista (ou-toa-*peess*-tah) *f* motorway; highway *Am*; **~ de peaje** turnpike *Am*

autopsia (ou-*toap*-s^yah) *f* autopsy

autor (ou-*toar*) *m* author

autoridad (ou-toa-ree-*dhahdh*) *f* authority

autoritario (ou-toa-ree-*tah*-r^yoa) *adj* authoritarian

autorización (ou-toa-ree-thah-*th'oan*) *f* authorization; permission

autorizar (ou-toa-ree-*thahr*) *v* allow; license

autoservicio (ou-toa-sayr-*bhee*-th^yoa) *m* self-service

autostop: *hacer ~ (ah-*thayr* ou-toa-*stoap*) hitchhike

auxiliar (ouk-see-*l'ahr*) *adj* auxiliary; *m/f* assistant; **~ de vuelo** stewardess, flight attendant; *v* help

auxilio (ouk-*see*-l^yoa) *m* assistance; **primeros auxilios** first aid

avance (ah-*bhan*-thay) *m* advance

avalancha (ah-bhah-*lahn*-chah) *f* avalanche

avanzar (ah-bhahn-*thahr*) *v* advance

avaro (ah-*bhah*-roa) *adj* avaricious

ave (*ah*-bhay) *f* bird; S.Am. chicken; **~ de presa, ~ de rapiña** bird of prey

avefría (ah-bhay-*free*-ah) *f* pewit

avellana (ah-bhay-*l'ah*-nah) *f* hazelnut

avena (ah-*bhay*-nah) *f* oats *pl*

avenida (ah-bhay-*nee*-dhah) *f* avenue

aventura (ah-bhayn-*too*-rah) *f* adventure

*avergonzarse (ah-bhayr-goan-*thahr*-say) *v* *be ashamed

avería (ah-bhay-*ree*-ah) *f* breakdown

averiarse (ah-bhay-r^y*ahr*-say) *v* *break down; **averiado** *adj* out of order

aversión (ah-bhayr-s^yoan) *f* aversion, dislike

avestruz (ah-bhayss-*trooth*) *m* ostrich

avión (ah-bh^yoan) *m* aeroplane; aircraft, plane; airplane *Am*; ~ **a reacción** jet; ~ **turborreactor** turbojet

avisar (ah-bhee-*sahr*) *v* inform

aviso (ah-*bhee*-soa) *m* notice

avispa (ah-*bheess*-pah) *f* wasp

ayer (ah-^yayr) *adv* yesterday

ayuda (ah-^yoo-dhah) *f* help; relief; ~ **de cámara** valet

ayudante (ah-^yoo-*dhahn*-tay) *m/f* helper

ayudar (ah-^yoo-*dhahr*) *v* aid, help

ayuntamiento (ah-^yoon-tah-m^yayn-toa) *m* town hall

azada (ah-*thah*-dhah) *f* spade

azafata (ah-thah-*fah*-tah) *f* hostess; stewardess

azar (ah-*thahr*) *m* chance, luck

azor (ah-*thoar*) *m* hawk

azote (ah-*thoa*-tay) *m* whip

azotea (ah-thoa-*tay*-ah) *f* flat roof; **estar mal de la ~** *colloquial* be crazy

azúcar (ah-*thoo*-kahr) *m/f* sugar; **terrón de ~** lump of sugar

azucena (ah-thoo-*thay*-nah) *f* lily

azul (ah-*thool*) *adj* blue

azulejo (ah-thoo-*lay*-khoa) *m* tile

B

babor (bah-*bhoar*) *m* port

bacalao (bah-kah-*lah*-oa) *m* cod

bacteria (bahk-*tay*-r^yah) *f* bacterium

bache (*bah*-chay) *m* pothole

bahía (bah-*ee*-ah) *f* bay

bailar (bigh-*lahr*) *v* dance

baile (*bigh*-lay) *m* dance

baja (*bah*-khah) *f* slump

bajada (bah-*khah*-dhah) *f* descent

bajamar (bah-khah-*mahr*) *f* low tide

bajar (bah-*khahr*) *v* lower; **bajarse** *v* *bend down

bajo (*bah*-khoa) *adj* low; short; *prep* under, below; *m* bass

bala (*bah*-lah) *f* bullet

baladí (bah-lah-*dhee*) *adj* insignificant

balance (bah-*lahn*-thay) *m* balance

balanza (bah-*lahn*-thah) *f* scales *pl*

balbucear (bahl-bhoo-thay-*ahr*) *v* falter

balcón (bahl-*koan*) *m* balcony; circle

balde (*bahl*-day) *m* pail, bucket

balneario (bahl-nay-*ah*-r^yoa) *m* spa

ballena (bahl-^yay-nah) *f* whale

ballet (bah-*lay*) *m* ballet

baloncesto (bah-loan-*thayss*-toa) *m* basketball

balonmano (bah-loan-*mah*-noa) *m* handball

bambú (bahm-*boo*) *m* bamboo

banca (*bahng*-kah) *f* banking; banks *pl*; bank; *Méx* bench

bancario (bahng-*kah*- r^yoa) *adj* bank

banco (*bahng*-koa) *m* bank; bench

banda (*bahn*-dah) *f* band; gang

bandeja (bahn-*day*-khah) *f* tray

bandera (bahn-*day*-rah) *f* flag; banner

bandido (bahn-*dee*-dhoa) *m* bandit

banquete (bahng-*kay*-tay) *m* banquet

bañador (bah-ñah-*dhoar*) *m* swim(ming) trunks, swimsuit

bañarse (bah-*ñahr*-say) *v* bathe

baño (*bah*-ñoa) *m* bath; *mMe* bathroom; ~ **turco** Turkish bath;

calzón de ~ swim(ming) trunks;
traje de ~ swimsuit
bar (bahr) *m* bar; saloon, café
baranda (bah-*rahn*-dah) *f* banisters *pl*
barandilla (bah-rahn-*dee*-lʸah) *f* rail;
railing
barato (bah-*rah*-toa) *adj* inexpensive,
cheap
barba (*bahr*-bhah) *f* beard
barbacoa (bahr-bhah-*koa*-ah) *f*
barbecue
barbero (bahr-*bhay*-roa) *m* barber
barbilla (bahr-*bhee*-lʸah) *f* chin
barca (*bahr*-kah) *f* boat
barco (*bahr*-koa) *m* boat
barítono (bah-*ree*-toa-noa) *m*
baritone
barman (*bahr*-mahn) *m* bartender,
barman
barniz (bahr-*neeth*) *m* varnish; **~ para
las uñas** nail polish
barómetro (bah-*roa*-may-troa) *m*
barometer
barquillo (bahr-*kee*-lʸoa) *m* waffle
barra (*bah*-rrah) *f* bar, rod; counter
barrer (bah-*rrayr*) *v* *sweep
barrera (bah-*rray*-rah) *f* barrier, rail; **~
de protección** crash barrier
barril (bah-*rreel*) *m* barrel, cask
barrio (*bah*-rrʸoa) *m* quarter, district;
~ bajo slum
barroco (bah-*rroa*-koa) *adj* baroque
barrote (bah-*rroa*-tay) *m* thick bar;
rung
basar (bah-*sahr*) *v* base
báscula (*bahss*-koo-lah) *f* scales,
weighing machine
base (*bah*-say) *f* basis, base
basílica (bah-*see*-lee-kah) *f* basilica
bastante (bahss-*tahn*-tay) *adv*
enough, sufficient; fairly, rather,
quite
bastar (bahss-*tahr*) *v* suffice
bastardo (bahss-*tahr*-dhoa) *m* bastard

bastón (bahss-*toan*) *m* cane; walking
stick; **bastones de esquí** ski sticks
basura (bah-*soo*-rah) *f* trash, rubbish,
garbage; **cubo de la ~** rubbish bin
bata (*bah*-tah) *f* dressing gown; **~ de
baño** bathrobe; **~ suelta** negligee
batalla (bah-*tah*-lʸah) *f* battle
batería (bah-tay-*ree*-ah) *f* battery
batido (bah-*tee*-dhoa) *adj* well-
trodden; *m* milkshake
batidora (bah-tee-*dhoa*-rah) *f* mixer
batir (bah-*teer*) *v* *beat, whip
baúl (bah-*ool*) *m* trunk
bautismo (bou-*teez*-moa) *m* baptism
bautizar (bou-tee-*thahr*) *v* christen,
baptize
bautizo (bou-*tee*-thoa) *m* christening,
baptism
baya (*bah*-ʸah) *f* berry
bebé (bay-*bhay*) *m* baby
beber (bay-*bhayr*) *v* *drink
bebida (bay-*bhee*-dhah) *f* drink,
beverage; **~ no alcohólica** soft drink;
bebidas espirituosas spirits
beca (*bay*-kah) *f* grant, scholarship
beige (*bay*-khay) *adj* beige
béisbol (*bayz*-bhoal) *m* baseball
belga (*bayl*-gah) *adj* Belgian; *m*
Belgian
Bélgica (*bayl*-khee-kah) *f* Belgium
belleza (bay-*lʸay*-thah) *f* beauty;
salón de ~ beauty salon
bello (*bay*-lʸoa) *adj* fine
bellota (bay-*lʸoa*-tah) *f* acorn
***bendecir** (bayn-day-*theer*) *v* bless
bendición (bayn-dee-*thʸoan*) *f*
blessing
beneficio (bay-nay-*fee*-thʸoa) *m*
profit, benefit
berenjena (bay-rayng-*khay*-nah) *f*
eggplant
berro (*bay*-rroa) *m* watercress
besar (bay-*sahr*) *v* kiss
beso (*bay*-soa) *m* kiss

betún (bay-*toon*) *m* shoe polish

biblia (bee-bhl^yah) *f* bible

biblioteca (bee-bhl^yoa-*tay*-kah) *f* library

bicho (*bee*-choa) *m* bug; creepy-crawly; creature; **¿qué ~ te ha picado?** what's eating you?

bici (*bee*-thee) *f* , **bicicleta** (bee-thee-*klay*-tah) *f* cycle, bicycle

bien (b^yayn) *adv* well; **¡bien!** all right!; **bien ... bien** either ... or

bienes (b^yay-nayss) *mpl* goods *pl*; possessions

bienestar (b^yay-nayss-*tahr*) *m* ease; welfare

bienvenida (b^yayn-bhay-*nee*-dhah) *f* welcome; ***dar la ~** welcome

bienvenido (b^yayn-bhay-*nee*-dhoa) *adj* welcome

biftec (beef-*tayk*) *m* steak

bifurcación (bee-foor-kah-*th*^y*oan*) *f* fork in road

bifurcarse (bee-foor-*kahr*-say) *v* fork

bigote (bee-*goatay*) *m* moustache

bilingüe (bee-*leeng*-gway) *adj* bilingual

bilis (*bee*-leess) *f* gall, bile

billar (bee-l^y*ahr*) *m* billiards *pl*

billete (bee-l^y*ay*-tay) *m* ticket; **~ de andén** platform ticket; **~ de banco** banknote; **~ gratuito** free ticket

biología (b^yoa-loa-*khee*-ah) *f* biology

biológico (b^yoa-*loa*-khee-koa) *adj* biological

bisagra (bee-*sah*-grah) *f* hinge

bizco (*beeth*-koa) *adj* cross-eyed

bizcocho (beeth-*koa*-choa) *m* sponge cake

blanco¹ (*blahng*-koa) *adj* white; blank

blanco² (*blahng*-koa) *m* mark, target

blando (*blahn*-doa) *adj* soft

blanquear (blahng-kay-*ahr*) *v* bleach

bloc (bloak) *mMe* writing-pad

bloque (*bloa*-kay) *m* block; writing pad

bloquear (bloa-kay-*ahr*) *v* block

blusa (*bloo*-sah) *f* blouse

bobina (boa-*bhee*-nah) *f* spool; **~ del encendido** ignition coil

bobo (*boa*-bhoa) *adj* silly; foolish

boca (*boa*-kah) *f* mouth

bocadillo (boa-kah-*dhee*-l^yoa) *m* sandwich

bocado (boa-*kah*-dhoa) *m* bite

bocina (boa-*thee*-nah) *f* horn, hooter; **tocar la ~** hoot, honk *Am*

boda (*boa*-dhah) *f* wedding

bodega (boa-*dhay*-gah) *f* hold

bofetada (boa-fay-*tah*-dhah) *f* smack, slap

boina (*boi*-nah) *f* beret

bola (*boa*-lah) *f* ball; ball bearing; scoop; fib; **~ de nieve** snowball; **no dar pie con ~** get everything wrong

bolera (boa-*lay*-rah) *f* bowling alley

boletín meteorológico (boa-lay-*teen* may-tay-oa-roa-*loa*-khee-koa) weather forecast

boleto (boa-*lay*-toa) *mMe* ticket

bolígrafo (boa-*lee*-grah-foa) *m* ballpoint pen, Biro®

Bolivia (boa-lee-bh^yah) *f* Bolivia

boliviano (boa-lee-bh^y*ah*-noa) *adj* Bolivian; *m* Bolivian

bolsa (*boal*-sah) *f* bag; stock market, stock exchange; purse; **~ de hielo** ice bag; **~ de papel** paper bag

bolsillo (boal-*see*-l^yoa) *m* pocket

bolso (*boal*-soa) *m* handbag; bag

bollo (*boa*-l^yoa) *m* bun

bomba (*boam*-bah) *f* pump; bomb; **~ de agua** water pump; **~ de gasolina** petrol pump; fuel pump *Am*

bombardear (boam-bahr-dhay-*ahr*) *v* bomb

bombear (boam-bay-*ahr*) *v* pump

bomberos (boam-*bay*-roass) *mpl* fire brigade, fire department *Am*

bombilla (boam-*bee*-lʸah) *f* light bulb; **~ de flash** flash bulb

bombón (boam-*boan*) *m* chocolate; candy *Am*

bondad (boan-*dahdh*) *f* goodness

bondadoso (boan-dah-*dhoa*-soa) *adj* good-natured, kind

bonito (boa-*nee*-toa) *adj* pretty; fair, nice, lovely

boquilla (boa-*kee*-lʸah) *f* cigarette holder

bordado (boar-*dhah*-dhoa) *m* embroidery

bordar (boar-*dhahr*) *v* embroider

borde (*boar*-dhay) *m* edge, border; verge, rim, brim; **~ del camino** wayside

bordillo (boar-*dhee*-lʸoa) *m* curb

bordo: a ~ (ah *boar*-doa) aboard

borracho (boa-*rrah*-choa) *adj* drunk

borrar (boa-*rrahr*) *v* erase

borrascoso (boa-rrahss-*koa*-soa) *adj* gusty

borrón (boa-*rroan*) *m* blot

bosque (*boass*-kay) *m* wood, forest

bosquejar (boass-kay-*khahr*) *v* sketch

bosquejo (boass-*kay*-khoa) *m* sketch

bostezar (boass-tay-*thahr*) *v* yawn

bota (*boa*-tah) *f* boot; **botas de esquí** ski boots

botadura (boa-tah-*dhoo*-rah) *f* launching

botánica (boa-*tah*-nee-kah) *f* botany

bote (*boa*-tay) *m* row(ing) boat; **~ a motor** motorboat

botella (boa-*tay*-lʸah) *f* bottle

botón (boa-*toan*) *m* button; knob, push-button; **~ del cuello** collar stud

botones (boa-*toa*-nayss) *mpl* bellboy

bóveda (*boa*-bhay-dhah) *f* vault, arch

boxear (boak-say-*ahr*) *v* box

boya (*boa*-ʸah) *f* buoy

braga (*brah*-gah) *f* briefs *pl*; panties *pl*

bragueta (brah-*gay*-tah) *f* fly

branquia (*brahng*-kʸah) *f* gill

Brasil (brah-*seel*) *m* Brazil

brasileño (brah-see-*lay*-ñoa) *adj* Brazilian; *m* Brazilian

braza (*brah*-thah) *f* breaststroke; **~ de mariposa** butterfly stroke

brazalete (brah-thah-*lay*-tay) *m* bracelet; armband

brazo (*brah*-thoa) *m* arm; **del ~** arm-in-arm

brea (*bray*-ah) *f* tar

brecha (*bray*-chah) *f* breach

bregar (bray-*gahr*) *v* labo(u)r

breve (*bray*-bhay) *adj* brief; **en ~** soon

brezal (bray-*thahl*) *m* moor

brezo (*bray*-thoa) *m* heather

brillante (bree-lʸ*ahn*-tay) *adj* brilliant

brillar (bree-lʸ*ahr*) *v* glow, *shine

brillo (*bree*-lʸoa) *m* glow, gloss

brincar (breeng-*kahr*) *v* hop; skip

brindar (breen-*dahr*) *v* offer; *v* drink a toast

brindis (*breen*-deess) *m* toast

brisa (*bree*-sah) *f* breeze

británico (bree-*tah*-nee-koa) *adj* British; *m* Briton

brocha (*broa*-chah) *f* brush; **~ de afeitar** shaving brush

broche (*broa*-chay) *m* brooch

broma (*broa*-mah) *f* joke

bronca (*broang*-kah) *f* row

bronce (*broan*-thay) *m* bronze; **de ~** bronze

bronceado (broan-thay-*ah*-doa) *adj* tanned; *m* suntan

bronquitis (broang-*kee*-teess) *f* bronchitis

brotar (broa-*tahr*) *v* bud

bruja (*broo*-khah) *f* witch

brújula (*broo*-khoo-lah) *f* compass

brumoso (broo-*moa*-soa) *adj* foggy; hazy

brutal (broo-*tahl*) *adj* brutal

bruto (*broo*-toa) *adj* gross

bucear (boo-thay-*ahr*) *v* dive

bueno (*bway*-noa) *adj* good; kind; sound; **¡bueno!** well!

buey (bway) *m* ox

bufanda (boo-*fahn*-dah) *f* scarf

buffet (boof-*fayt*) *m* buffet

buhardilla (bwahr-*dee*-lᵞah) *f* attic

buho (*boo*-oa) *m* owl

buitre (*bwee*-tray) *m* vulture

bujía (boo-*khee*-ah) *f* spark(ing) plug

Bulgaria (bool-*gah*-rᵞah) *f* Bulgaria

búlgaro (*bool*-gah-roa) *adj* Bulgarian; *m* Bulgarian

bulto (*bool*-toa) *m* bulk

bulla (*boo*-lᵞah) *f* fuss

buque (*boo*-kay) *m* ship; vessel; ~ **a motor** launch; ~ **cisterna** tanker; ~ **de guerra** man-of-war; ~ **velero** sail(ing) boat

burbuja (boor-*boo*-khah) *f* bubble

burdel (boor-*dhayl*) *m* brothel

burdo (*boor*-dhoa) *adj* coarse

burgués (boor-*gayss*) *adj* middleclass, bourgeois

burla (*boor*-lah) *f* mockery

burlarse de (boor-*lahr*-say) mock

burocracia (boo-roa-*krah*-thᵞah) *f* bureaucracy

burro (*boo*-rroa) *m* donkey

buscar (booss-*kahr*) *v* look for; look up, *seek, search; hunt for; *ir a ~ *get, pick up, fetch

búsqueda (*booss*-kay-dhah) *f* search

busto (*booss*-toa) *m* bust

butaca (boo-*tah*-kah) *f* armchair, easy chair; orchestra seat *Am*

buzón (boo-*thoan*) *m* pillar box, letter box; mailbox *Am*

C

caballero (kah-bhah-*lᵞay*-roa) *m* gentleman; knight

caballitos (kah-bhah-*lᵞee*-toass) *mpl* merry-go-round

caballo (kah-*bhah*-lᵞoa) *m* horse; ~ **de carrera** racehorse; ~ **de vapor** horsepower

cabaña (kah-*bhah*-ñah) *f* cabin, hut

cabaret (kah-bhah-*rayt*) *m* cabaret

cabecear (kah-bhay-thay-*ahr*) *v* nod

cabeceo (kah-bhay-*thay*-oa) *m* nod

cabello (kah-*bhay*-lᵞoa) *m* hair; **suavizante de ~** conditioner

cabelludo (kah-bhay-*lᵞoo*-dhoa) *adj* hairy

caber (kah-*bhayr*) *v* fit; **caben tres litros** it holds three litres (*Am* liters); **cabemos todos** there's room for all of us; **no cabe duda** there's no doubt; **no me cabe en la cabeza** I just don't understand

cabeza (kah-*bhay*-thah) *f* head; ~ **de turco** scapegoat; **dolor de ~** headache

cabezudo (kah-bhay-*thoo*-dhoa) *adj* headstrong, stubborn

cabina (kah-*bhee*-nah) *f* cabin; booth; ~ **telefónica** telephone booth

cable (*kah*-bhlay) *m* cable

cabo (*kah*-bhoa) *m* cape

cabra (*kah*-bhrah) *f* goat

cabritilla (kah-bhree-*tee*-lᵞah) *f* kid

cabrón (kah-*bhroan*) *m* goat

cacahuate (kah-kah-*wah*-tay) *mMe* peanut

cacahuete (kah-kah-*way*-tay) *m* peanut

cacerola (kah-thay-*roa*-lah) *f*

saucepan

cachear (kah-chay-*ahr*) *v* search

cachivache (kah-chee-*bhah*-chay) *m* junk

cada (*kah*-dhah) *adj* every, each; ~ **uno** everyone

cadáver (kah-*dhah*-bhayr) *m* corpse

cadena (kah-*dhay*-nah) *f* chain

cadera (kah-*dhay*-rah) *f* hip

caducado (kah-dhoo-*kah*-dhoa) *adj* expired

*****caer** (kah-*ayr*) *v* *fall; **dejar** ~ drop

café (kah-*fay*) *m* coffee; coffee shop

cafeína (kah-fay-*ee*-nah) *f* caffeine

cafetera (kah-fay-*tay*-rah) *f* coffee maker; coffee pot; ~ **filtradora** percolator

cafetería (kah-fay-tay-*ree*-ah) *f* snack bar, cafeteria

caída (kah-*ee*-dhah) *f* fall

caja (*kah*-khah) *f* box; crate; pay desk; cashier *Am*; ~ **de ahorros** savings bank; ~ **de cartón** carton; ~ **de caudales** safe, vault; ~ **de cerillas** matchbox; ~ **de colores** paintbox; ~ **de velocidades** gearbox; ~ **fuerte** safe; ~ **metálica** canister

cajero (kah-*khay*-roa) *m* cashier; ~ **automático** cash dispenser, ATM

cajón (kah-*khoan*) *m* drawer

cal (kahl) *f* lime

calabacín (kah-lah-bah-*theen*) *m* squash

calamar (kah-lah-*mahr*) *m* squid

calambre (kah-*lahm*-bray) *m* cramp

calamidad (kah-lah-mee-*dhahdh*) *f* disaster

calcetín (kahl-thay-*teen*) *m* sock

calcio (*kahl*-th^{y}oa) *m* calcium

calculadora (kahl-koo-lah-*dhoa*-rah) *f* calculator

calcular (kahl-koo-*lahr*) *v* reckon, calculate

cálculo (*kahl*-koo-loa) *m* calculation;

~ **biliar** gallstone

caldo (*kahl*-doa) *m* stock; ~ **de cultivo** breeding ground

calefacción (kah-lay-fahk-*th^{y}oan*) *f* heating

calefactor (kah-lay-fahk-*toar*) *m* heater

calendario (kah-layn-*dah*-r^{y}oa) *m* calendar

calentador (kah-layn-tah-*dhoar*) *m* heater; ~ **de agua** water heater

*****calentar** (kah-layn-*tahr*) *v* warm, heat

calidad (kah-lee-*dhahdh*) *f* quality; **de primera** ~ first-class

caliente (kah-*l^{y}ayn*-tay) *adj* warm, hot

calificado (kah-lee-fee-*kah*-dhoa) *adj* qualified

calina (kah-*lee*-nah) *f* haze

calinoso (kah-lee-*noa*-soa) *adj* hazy

calma (*kahl*-mah) *f* calm

calmante (kahl-*mahn*-tay) *m* tranquillizer, sedative

calmar (kahl-*mahr*) *v* calm down; **calmarse** *v* calm down

calor (kah-*loar*) *m* warmth, heat

caloría (kah-loa-*ree*-ah) *f* calorie

calorífero (kah-loa-*ree*-fay-roa) *m* hotwater bottle

calvo (*kahl*-bhoa) *adj* bald

calzada (kahl-*thah*-dhah) *f* carriageway, causeway; drive

calzado (kahl-*thah*-dhoa) *m* footwear

calzoncillos (kahl-thoan-*thee*-l^{y}oass) *mpl* pants *pl*, briefs *pl*, drawers; shorts *plAm*

callado (kah-*l^{y}ah*-dhoa) *adj* silent, quiet

callarse (kah-*l^{y}ar*-say) *v* *be silent

calle (*kah*-l^{y}ay) *f* street; road; ~ **lateral** side street; ~ **mayor** main street

callejón (kah-l^{y}ay-*khoan*) *m* alley, lane; ~ **sin salida** cul-de-sac

callo (*kah*-l^{y}oa) *m* callus; corn

cama (*kah*-mah) *f* bed; **~ de tijera** camp-bed; cot *Am*; **camas gemelas** twin beds; **~ y desayuno** bed and breakfast

cámara (*kah*-mah-rah) *f* camera; **~ fotográfica** camera

camarada (kah-mah-*rah*-dhah) *m* comrade

camarera (kah-mah-*ray*-rah) *f* waitress

camarero (kah-mah-*ray*-roa) *m* waiter; steward; **jefe de camareros** head waiter

camarón (kah-mah-*roan*) *m* shrimp

cambiar (kahm-*b*ʸ*ahr*) *v* alter, change; vary; exchange, switch; **~ de marcha** change gear

cambio (*kahm*-bʸoa) *m* change, variation; turn; alteration; exchange; exchange rate; **oficina de ~** money exchange

camello (kah-*may*-lʸoa) *m* camel

caminar (kah-mee-*nahr*) *v* *go; hike

caminata (kah-mee-*nah*-tah) *f* walk

camino (kah-*mee*-noa) *m* way; road; **a mitad de ~** halfway; **borde del ~** roadside; **~ de** bound for; **~ en obras** road up; **~ principal** main road

camión (kah-*m*ʸ*oan*) *m* lorry; truck *Am*

camioneta (kah-mʸoa-*nay*-tah) *f* van

camisa (kah-*mee*-sah) *f* shirt

camiseta (kah-mee-*say*-tah) *f* undershirt; vest

camisón (kah-mee-*soan*) *m* nightdress

campamento (kahm-pah-*mayn*-toa) *m* camp

campana (kahm-*pah*-nah) *f* bell

campanario (kahm-pah-*nah*-rʸoa) *m* steeple

campaña (kahm-*pah*-ñah) *f* campaign; **catre de ~** camp bed

campeón (kahm-pay-*oan*) *m* champion

campesino (kahm-pay-*see*-noa) *m* peasant

camping (*kahm*-peeng) *m* camping site, camping

campo (*kahm*-poa) *m* countryside, country; field; **~ de aviación** airfield; **~ de golf** golf course; **~ de tenis** tennis court; **día de ~** picnic

Canadá (kah-nah-*dhah*) *m* Canada

canadiense (kah-nah-*dh*ʸ*ayn*-say) *adj* Canadian; *m* Canadian

canal (kah-*nahl*) *m* canal; channel; **Canal de la Mancha** English Channel

canario (kah-*nah*-rʸoa) *m* canary

cancelación (kahn-thay-lah-*th*ʸ*oan*) *f* cancellation

cancelar (kahn-thay-*lahr*) *v* cancel

cáncer (*kahn*-thayr) *m* cancer

canción (kahn-*th*ʸ*oan*) *f* song

cancha (*kahn*-chah) *f* tennis court

candado (kahn-*dah*-dhoa) *m* padlock

candelabro (kahn-day-*lah*-bhroa) *m* candelabrum

candidato (kahn-dee-*dhah*-toa) *m* candidate

canela (kah-*nay*-lah) *f* cinnamon

cangrejo (kahng-*gray*-khoa) *m* crab

canguro (kahng-*goo*-roa) *m* kangaroo

canica (kah-*nee*-kah) *f* marble

canoa (kah-*noa*-ah) *f* canoe

cansancio (kahn-*sahn*-thʸoa) *m* fatigue

cansar (kahn-*sahr*) *v* tire; **cansado** tired, weary

cantadora (kahn-tah-*dhoa*-rah) *f* singer

cantante (kahn-*tahn*-tay) *m* singer

cantar (kahn-*tahr*) *v* *sing

cántaro (*kahn*-tah-roa) *m* pitcher; jug

cantera (kahn-*tay*-rah) *f* quarry

cantidad (kahn-tee-*dhahdh*) *f* amount, quantity; number; lot

cantina (kahn-*tee*-nah) f canteen; fMe saloon

canto (*kahn*-toa) m singing; edge

caña (*kah*-ñah) f cane; **~ de pescar** fishing rod

cañada (kah-*ñah*-dhah) f glen; gully, ravine

cáñamo (*kah*-ñah-moa) m hemp

cañón (kah-*ñoan*) m gun; gorge

caos (*kah*-oass) m chaos

caótico (kah-*oa*-tee-koa) adj chaotic

capa (*kah*-pah) f cloak, cape; layer, deposit

capacidad (kah-pah-thee-*dhahdh*) f capacity

capaz (kah-*pahth*) adj able; capable; ***ser ~ de** *be able to; qualify

capellán (kah-pay-*l*ʸ*ahn*) m chaplain

capilla (kah-*pee*-lʸah) f chapel

capital (kah-pee-*tahl*) m capital; adj capital

capitalismo (kah-pee-tah-*leez*-moa) m capitalism

capitán (kah-pee-*tahn*) m captain

capitulación (kah-pee-too-lah-thʸ*oan*) f capitulation

capítulo (kah-*pee*-too-loa) m chapter

capó (kah-*poa*) m bonnet; hood Am

capricho (kah-*pree*-choa) m fancy, whim

cápsula (*kahp*-soo-lah) f capsule

captura (kahp-*too*-rah) f capture

capturar (kahp-too-*rahr*) v capture

capucha (kah-*poo*-chah) f hood

capullo (kah-*poo*-lʸoa) m bud

caqui (*kah*-kee) m khaki

cara (*kah*-rah) f face

caracol (kah-rah-*koal*) m snail; **~ marino** winkle

carácter (kah-*rahk*-tayr) m character

característica (kah-rahk-tay-*reess*-tee-kah) f characteristic, feature; quality

característico (kah-rahk-tay-*reess*-tee-koa) adj typical, characteristic

caracterizar (kah-rahk-tay-ree-*thahr*) v characterize, mark

caramelo (kah-rah-*may*-loa) m caramel, toffee, sweet

caravana (kah-rah-*bhah*-nah) f caravan; trailer Am

carbón (kahr-*bhoan*) m coal; **~ de leña** charcoal

carburador (kahr-bhoo-rah-*dhoar*) m carburet(t)or

cárcel (*kahr*-thayl) f jail, gaol

carcelero (kahr-thay-*lay*-roa) m jailer

cardenal (kahr-dhay-*nahl*) m cardinal

cardinal (kahr-dhee-*nahl*) adj cardinal

cardo (*kahr*-dhoa) m thistle

*carecer (kah-ray-*thayr*) v lack

carencia (kah-*rayn*-thʸah) f want, shortage

carga (*kahr*-gah) f charge; cargo, freight, load; batch

cargar (kahr-*gahr*) v charge; load

cargo (*kahr*-goa) m office; freight

caridad (kah-ree-*dhahdh*) f charity

carillón (kah-ree-*l*ʸ*oan*) m chimes pl

cariño (kah-*ree*-ñoa) m affection; pet

cariñoso (kah-ree-*ñoa*-soa) adj affectionate

carmesí (kahr-may-*see*) adj crimson

carnaval (kahr-nah-*bhahl*) m carnival

carne (*kahr*-nay) f meat; flesh; **~ de cerdo** pork; **~ de gallina** goose flesh; **~ de ternera** veal; **~ de vaca** beef

carné (kahr-*nay*) m card

carnero (kahr-*nay*-roa) m mutton

carnet (kahr-*nayt*) m card; **~ de conducir** driver's license Am, driving licence; **~ de identidad** identity card

carnicero (kahr-nee-*thay*-roa) m butcher

caro (*kah*-roa) adj expensive, dear

carpa (*kahr*-pah) f carp

carpintero (kahr-peen-*tay*-roa) *m* carpenter

carrera (kah-*rray*-rah) *f* career; race; ~ **de caballos** horserace; **pista para carreras** racetrack

carrete (kah-*rray*-tay) *m* (roll of) film; ~ **de hilo** reel of thread

carretera (kah-rray-*tay*-rah) *f* highway

carretilla (kah-rray-*tee*-lᵛah) *f* wheelbarrow

carril (kah-*rreel*) *m* lane; **carril-bici** cycle lane; **carril-bus** bus lane

carro (*kah*-rroa) *m* cart; wagon; cartload; *Me* car

carrocería (kah-rroa-thay-*ree*-ah) *f* coachwork

carroza (kah-*rroa*-thah) *f* coach; carriage

carta (*kahr*-tah) *f* map; letter; menu; playing card; ~ **certificada** registered letter; ~ **de crédito** letter of credit; ~ **de recomendación** letter of recommendation; ~ **de vinos** wine list; ~ **marina** chart

cartel (kahr-*tayl*) *m* poster, placard

cárter (*kahr*-tayr) *m* crankcase

cartera (kahr-*tay*-rah) *f* bag; satchel; wallet

cartero (kahr-*tay*-roa) *m* postman; mailman

cartón (kahr-*toan*) *m* cardboard; carton; **de ~** cardboard

cartucho (kahr-*too*-choa) *m* cartridge

casa (*kah*-sah) *f* house; home; **a ~** home; **ama de ~** housewife; ~ **de campo** cottage; ~ **de correos** post-office; ~ **del párroco** vicarage; ~ **de pisos** block of flats; apartment house *Am*; ~ **de reposo** rest home; ~ **flotante** houseboat; ~ **señorial** manor house; **en ~** at home; indoors, indoor, home; **gobierno de la ~** housekeeping

casado (kah-*sah*-doah) *adj* married;

recién ~ newly-wed

casarse (kah-*sahr*-say) *v* marry

cascada (kahss-*kah*-dhah) *f* waterfall

cascanueces (kahss-kah-*nway*-thayss) *m* nutcrackers *pl*

cáscara (*kahss*-kah-rah) *f* shell; skin; ~ **de nuez** nutshell

casco (*kahss*-koa) *m* helmet; hoof

casero (kah-*say*-roa) *adj* homemade; homeloving; domestic

casi (*kah*-see) *adv* almost, nearly

casino (kah-*see*-noa) *m* casino

caso (*kah*-soa) *m* event; case; instance; ~ **de urgencia** emergency; **en ~ de** in case of; **en ningún ~** by no means; **en tal ~** then; **en todo ~** at any rate, anyway

caspa (*kahss*-pah) *f* dandruff

casquillo (kahss-*kee*-lᵛoa) *m* socket

castaña (kahss-*tah*-ñah) *f* chestnut

castellano (kahss-tay-*lᵛah*-noa) *adj* Castilian; *m* Castilian

castigar (kahss-tee-*gahr*) *v* punish

castigo (kahss-*tee*-goa) *m* penalty, punishment

castillo (kahss-*tee*-lᵛoa) *m* castle

casto (*kahss*-toa) *adj* chaste; pure

castor (kahss-*toar*) *m* beaver

casualidad (kah-swah-lee-*dhahdh*) *f* chance; coincidence; **por ~** by chance

catacumba (kah-tah-*koom*-bah) *f* catacomb

catálogo (kah-*tah*-loa-goa) *m* catalogue

catarro (kah-*tah*-rroa) *m* cold, catarrh

catástrofe (kah-*tahss*-troa-fay) *f* disaster, catastrophe, calamity

catedral (kah-tay-*dhrahl*) *f* cathedral

catedrático (kah-tay-*dhrah*-tee-koa) *m* professor

categoría (kah-tay-goa-*ree*-ah) *f* category

católico (kah-*toa*-lee-koa) *adj* catholic, Roman Catholic

catorce (kah-*toar*-thay) *num* fourteen

caucho (*kou*-choa) *m* rubber

causa (*kou*-sah) *f* cause, reason; case; lawsuit; **a ~ de** because of, on account of, for, owing to

causar (kou-*sahr*) *v* cause

cautela (kou-*tay*-lah) *f* caution

cautivar (kou-tee-*bhahr*) *v* fascinate

cava (*kah*-bah) *m* cava, sparkling wine

cavar (kah-*bhahr*) *v* *dig

caviar (kah-*bh*ʸ*ahr*) *m* caviar

cavidad (kah-bhee-*dhahdh*) *f* cavity

caza (*kah*-thah) *f* chase, hunt; game; **apeadero de ~** lodge

cazador (kah-thah-*dhoar*) *m*, **-a** *f* hunter

cazar (kah-*thahr*) *v* hunt; chase; **~ en vedado** poach

cazo (*kah*-thoa) *m* saucepan

cazuela (ka-*thoo*-ay-lah) *f* pan

cebada (thay-*bhah*-dhah) *f* barley

cebo (*thay*-bhoa) *m* bait

cebolla (thay-*bhoa*-lʸah) *f* onion

cebollino (thay-bhoa-*lʸee*-noa) *m* chives *pl*

cebra (*thay*-bhrah) *f* zebra

ceder (thay-*dhayr*) *v* indulge; *give in

***cegar** (thay-*gahr*) *v* blind

ceja (*thay*-khah) *f* eyebrow

celda (*thayl*-dah) *f* cell

celebración (thay-lay-bhrah-*thʸoan*) *f* celebration

celebrar (thay-lay-*bhrahr*) *v* celebrate

célebre (*thay*-lay-bhray) *adj* famous

celebridad (thay-lay-bhree-*dhahdh*) *f* celebrity

celeste (thay-*layss*-tay) *adj* heavenly; celestial

celibato (thay-lee-*bhah*-toa) *m* celibacy

celo (*thay*-loa) *m* zeal; **celos** jealousy

celofán (thay-loa-*fahn*) *m* cellophane

celoso (thay-*loa*-soa) *adj* zealous; envious, jealous

célula (*thay*-loo-lah) *f* cell

cementerio (thay-mayn-*tay*-rʸoa) *m* churchyard, graveyard, cemetery

cemento (thay-*mayn*-toa) *m* cement

cena (*thay*-nah) *f* dinner, supper

cenar (thay-*nahr*) *v* dine, *eat

cenicero (thay-nee-*thay*-roa) *m* ashtray

cenit (thay-*neet*) *m* zenith

ceniza (thay-*nee*-thah) *f* ash

censura (thayn-*soo*-rah) *f* censorship

centelleante (thayn-tay-lʸay-*ahn*-tay) *adj* sparkling

centígrado (thayn-*tee*-grah-dhoa) *adj* centigrade

centímetro (thayn-*tee*-may-troa) *m* centimetre, centimeter *Am*

central (thayn-*trahl*) *adj* central; **~ eléctrica** power station; **~ telefónica** telephone exchange

centralizar (thayn-trah-lee-*thahr*) *v* centralize

centro (*thayn*-troa) *m* centre, center *Am*; **~ comercial** shopping centre, mall; **~ de la ciudad** town centre; **~ de recreo** recreation centre

cepillar (thay-pee-*lʸahr*) *v* brush

cepillo (thay-*pee*-lʸoa) *m* brush; **~ de dientes** toothbrush; **~ de la ropa** clothes brush; **~ para el cabello** hairbrush; **~ para las uñas** nailbrush

cera (*thay*-rah) *f* wax

cerámica (thay-*rah*-mee-kah) *f* ceramics *pl*; crockery, pottery

cerca (*thayr*-kah) *f* fence

cerca de (*thayr*-kah day) near, by; almost

cercano (thayr-*kah*-noa) *adj* close, nearby, near

cercar (thayr-*kahr*) *v* encircle, surround

cerdo (*thayr*-dhoa) *m* pig

cereales (thay-ray-*ah*-layss) *mpl*

cereals, grain

cerebro (thay-*ray*-bhroa) *m* brain; **conmoción cerebral** concussion

ceremonia (thay-ray-*moa*-n^yah) *f* ceremony

cereza (thay-*ray*-thah) *f* cherry

cerilla (thay-*ree*-l^yah) *f* match

cerillo (thay-*ree*-l^yoa) *mMe* match

cero (*thay*-roa) *m* zero, nought

cerrado (thay-*rrah*-dhoa) *adj* closed; narrow-minded; introverted; overcast; **curva cerrada** tight curve

cerradura (thay-rrah-*dhoo*-rah) *f* lock; **ojo de la ~** keyhole

*cerrar (thay-*rrahr*) *v* close, *shut; fasten; turn off; **~ con llave** lock

cerrojo (thay-*rroa*-khoa) *m* bolt

certificación (thayr-tee-fee-kah-th^yoan) *f* certificate

certificado (thayr-tee-fee-*kah*-dhoa) *m* certificate; **~ de salud** health certificate

certificar (thayr-tee-fee-*kahr*) *v* register

cervecería (thayr-bhay-thay-*ree*-ah) *f* brewery

cerveza (thayr-*bhay*-thah) *f* beer; ale

cesar (thay-*sahr*) *v* cease, quit, stop, discontinue

césped (*thayss*-paydh) *m* lawn; grass

cesta (*thayss*-tah) *f* basket

cesto (*thayss*-toa) *m* hamper; **~ para papeles** wastepaper basket

chabacano (chah-bhah-*kah*-noa) *mMe* apricot

chal (chahl) *m* shawl

chaleco (chah-*lay*-koa) *m* waistcoat; vest *Am*; **~ salvavidas** lifebelt

chalet (chah-*layt*) *m* chalet

champán (chahm-*pahn*) *m* champagne

champú (chahm-*poo*) *m* shampoo

chantaje (chahn-*tah*-khay) *m* blackmail; *hacer **~** blackmail

chapa (*chah*-pah) *f* plate, sheet

chaparrón (chah-pah-*rroan*) *m* cloudburst

chapucero (chah-poo-*thay*-roa) *adj* sloppy

chaqueta (chah-*kay*-tah) *f* jacket; **~ de lana** cardigan; **~ ligera** blazer

charanga (chah-*rahng*-gah) *f* brass band

charco (*chahr*-koa) *m* puddle; pool

charla (*chahr*-lah) *f* chat

charlar (chahr-*lahr*) *v* chat

chasis (chah-*seess*) *m* chassis

checo (*chay*-koa) *adj* Czech; *m* Czech

cheque (*chay*-kay) *m* cheque; check *Am*; **~ de viajero** traveller's cheque

chicle (*chee*-klay) *m* chewing gum

chica (*chee*-kah) *f* girl

chico (*chee*-koa) *m* boy; kid

chichón (chee-*choan*) *m* lump

Chile (*chee*-lay) *m* Chile

chileno (chee-*lay*-noa) *adj* Chilean; *m* Chilean

chillar (chee-*l^yahr*) *v* scream, shriek

chillido (chee-*l^yee*-dhoa) *m* scream, shriek

chimenea (chee-may-*nay*-ah) *f* chimney; fireplace

China (*chee*-nah) *f* China

chinche (*cheen*-chay) *f* bug; drawing pin; thumbtack *Am*

chino (*chee*-noa) *adj* Chinese; *m* Chinese; *adjMe* curly

chiringuito (chee-reen-*gee*-toa) *m* beach bar

chisme (*cheez*-may) *m* gossip; *contar **chismes** gossip

chispa (*cheess*-pah) *f* spark

chiste (*cheess*-tay) *m* joke

chistoso (cheess-*toa*-soa) *adj* witty, humorous

chocante (choa-*kahn*-tay) *adj* revolting, shocking

chocar (choa-*kahr*) *v* collide, crash,

bump; shock; **~ contra** knock against

chocolate (choa-koa-*lah*-tay) *m* chocolate

chófer (*choa*-fayr) *m* chauffeur

choque (*choa*-kay) *m* crash; shock

chorizo (choa-*ree*-thoa) *m* chorizo; *colloquial* thief; rump steak

chorro (*choa*-rroa) *m* spout, jet

chubasco (choo-*bahs*-koa) *m* shower

chuleta (choo-*lay*-tah) *f* chop, cutlet

chulo (*choo*-loa) *colloquial adj* fantastic, great; *adj Me* attractive; cocky; *m* pimp

chupar (choo-*pahr*) *v* suck

churro (*choo*-rroa) *m* fritter; botched job

cicatriz (thee-kah-*treeth*) *f* scar

ciclista (thee-*kleess*-tah) *m* cyclist

ciclo (*thee*-kloa) *m* cycle

ciego (th^y*ay*-goa) *adj* blind

cielo (th^y*ay*-loa) *m* heaven; sky; **~ raso** ceiling

ciencia (*th^{y}ayn*-th^{y}ah) *f* science

científico (th^{y}ayn-*tee*-fee-koa) *adj* scientific; *m*, **-a** *f* scientist

ciento (*th^{y}ayn*-toa) *num* hundred; **por ~** percent

cierre (*th^{y}ay*-rray) *m* fastener; **~ relámpago** zipper

cierto (*th^{y}ayr*-toa) *adj* certain; **por ~** indeed

ciervo (*th^{y}ayr*-bhoa) *m* deer

cifra (*thee*-frah) *f* number, figure

cigarrillo (thee-gah-*rree*-l^{y}oa) *m* cigarette

cigüeña (thee-*gway*-ñah) *f* stork

cigüeñal (thee-gway-*ñahl*) *m* crankshaft

cilindro (thee-*leen*-droa) *m* cylinder; **culata del ~** cylinder head

cima (*thee*-mah) *f* top, summit; hilltop

cinc (theengk) *m* zinc

cincel (theen-*thayl*) *m* chisel

cinco (*theeng*-koa) *num* five

cincuenta (theeng-*kwayn*-tah) *num* fifty

cine (*thee*-nay) *m* pictures

cinematógrafo (thee-nay-mah-*toa*-grah-foa) *m* cinema

cinta (*theen*-tah) *f* ribbon, tape; **~ adhesiva** scotch tape, adhesive tape; **~ de goma** elastic band; **~ métrica** tape-measure

cintura (theen-*too*-rah) *f* waist

cinturón (theen-too-*roan*) *m* belt; bypass; **~ de seguridad** seat belt

circo (*theer*-koa) *m* circus

circulación (theer-koo-lah-*th^{y}oan*) *f* circulation

circular (theer-koo-*lahr*) *v* circulate

círculo (*theer*-koo-loa) *m* circle, ring; club

circundante (theer-koon-*dahn*-tay) *adj* surrounding

circundar (theer-koon-*dahr*) *v* circle

circunstancia (theer-koons-*tahn*-th^{y}ah) *f* circumstance, condition

ciruela (thee-*rway*-lah) *f* plum; **~ pasa** prune

cirujano (thee-roo-*khah*-noa) *m* surgeon

cisne (*theez*-nay) *m* swan

cistitis (theess-*tee*-teess) *f* cystitis

cita (*thee*-tah) *f* date, appointment; meeting; quotation

citar (thee-*tahr*) *v* make an appointment with; quote

ciudad (th^{y}oo-*dhahdh*) *f* city, town

ciudadanía (th^{y}oo-dhah-dhah-*nee*-ah) *f* citizenship

ciudadano (th^{y}oo-dhah-*dhah*-noa) *m*, **-a** *f* citizen

cívico (*thee*-bhee-koa) *adj* civic

civil (thee-*bheel*) *adj* civilian, civil

civilización (thee-bhee-lee-thah-*th^{y}oan*) *f* civilization

civilizado (thee-bhee-lee-*thah*-dhoa) *adj* civilized

claridad (klah-ree-*dhahdh*) f clarity

clarificar (klah-ree-fee-*kahr*) v clarify

claro (*klah*-roa) adj clear; plain, distinct; serene, bright; m clearing

clase (*klah*-say) f class; sort; form; classroom; ~ **media** middle class; ~ **turista** tourist class; **de primera** ~ first-rate; **toda** ~ **de** all sorts of

clásico (*klah*-see-koa) adj classical

clasificar (klah-see-fee-*kahr*) v classify, assort, sort, arrange

cláusula (*klou*-soo-lah) f clause

clavar (klah-*bhahr*) v pin

clavicémbalo (klah-bhee-*thaym*-bah-loa) m harpsichord

clavícula (klah-*bhee*-koo-lah) f collarbone

clavo (*klah*-bhoa) m nail

clemencia (klay-*mayn*-th^{y}ah) f mercy

clérigo (*klay*-ree-goa) m clergyman, minister

cliente (kl^y*ayn*-tay) m client, customer

clima (*klee*-mah) m climate

climatizado (klee-mah-tee-*thah*-dhoa) adj air-conditioned

clínica (*klee*-nee-kah) f clinic

cloro (*kloa*-roa) m chlorine

club de yates yacht club

cobarde (koa-*bhahr*-dhay) adj cowardly; m coward

cobertizo (koa-bhayr-*tee*-thoa) m shed

cobrador (koa-bhrah-*dhoar*) m conductor

cobrar (koa-*bhrahr*) v cash

cobre (*koa*-bhray) m copper, brass; **cobres** mpl brassware

cocaína (koa-kah-*ee*-nah) f cocaine

cocer (koa-*thayr*) v cook; boil; bake; **cocerse** cook; boil; bake; colloquial be roasting

cocido (koa-*thee*-doa) adj boiled; m stew

cocina (koa-*thee*-nah) f kitchen; cooker, stove; ~ **de gas** gas cooker

cocinar (koa-thee-*nahr*) v cook

cocinero (koa-thee-*nay*-roa) m cook

coco (*koa*-koa) m coconut

cocodrilo (koa-koa-*dhree*-l^{y}oa) m crocodile

cóctel (*koak*-tayl) m cocktail

coche (*koa*-chay) m car; carriage; ~ **cama** sleeping-car; ~ **comedor** dining-car; ~ **de carreras** sports-car; ~ **Pullman** Pullman

cochecillo (koa-chay-*thee*-l^{y}oa) m pram; baby carriage Am

cochinillo (koa-chee-*nee*-l^{y}oa) m piglet

codicioso (koa-dhee-*th^{y}oa*-soa) adj greedy

código (*koa*-dhee-goa) m code; ~ **postal** zip code Am

codo (*koa*-dhoa) m elbow

codorniz (koa-dhoar-*neeth*) f quail

coger (koa-*khayr*) v *catch; *take; **llegar a** ~ *catch

coherencia (koa-ay-*rayn*-th^{y}ah) f coherence

cohete (koa-*ay*-tay) m rocket

coincidencia (koa-een-thee-*dhayn*-th^{y}ah) f concurrence

coincidir (koa-een-thee-*dheer*) v coincide

cojear (koa-khay-*ahr*) v limp

cojo (*koa*-khoa) adj lame

col (koal) m cabbage; ~ **de Bruselas** Brussels sprouts pl

cola (*koa*-lah) f queue, file, line; tail; gum, glue; *hacer ~ queue

colaboración (koa-lah-bhoa-rah-*th^{y}oan*) f cooperation

colcha (*koal*-chah) f bedspread

colchón (koal-*choan*) m mattress

colección (koa-layk-*th^{y}oan*) f collection; ~ **de arte** art collection

coleccionar (koa-layk-th^{y}oa-*nahr*) v gather

coleccionista (koa-layk-th^yoa-*neess*-tah) *m* collector

colectivo (koa-layk-*tee*-bhoa) *adj* collective

colector (koa-layk-*toar*) *m* collector

colega (koa-*lay*-gah) *m* colleague

colegio (koa-*lay*-kh^yoa) *m* college

cólera (*koa*-lay-rah) *f* anger, passion, temper

colérico (koa-*lay*-ree-koa) *adj* hot-tempered

*colgar (koal-*gahr*) *v* *hang

coliflor (koa-lee-*floar*) *f* cauliflower

colina (koa-*lee*-nah) *f* hill

colisión (koa-lee-s^y*oan*) *f* collision

colmena (koal-*may*-nah) *f* beehive

colmo (*koal*-moa) *m* height

colocar (koa-loa-*kahr*) *v* lay, place, *put

Colombia (koa-*loam*-b^yah) *f* Colombia

colombiano (koa-loam-b^y*ah*-noa) *adj* Colombian; *m* Colombian

colonia (koa-*loa*-n^yah) *f* colony; **~ veraniega** holiday camp

color (koa-*loar*) *m* colo(u)r; **~ de aguada** watercolo(u)r; **de ~** colo(u)red

colorado (koa-loa-*rah*-dhoa) *adj* colo(u)rful

colorante (koa-loa-*rahn*-tay) *m* colo(u)rant

colorete (koa-loa-*ray*-tay) *m* blush

columna (koa-*loom*-nah) *f* column, pillar; **~ del volante** steering column

columpiarse (koa-loom-p^y*ahr*-say) *v* *swing

columpio (koa-*loom*-p^yoa) *m* swing; seesaw

collar (koa-l^y*ahr*) *m* beads *pl*, necklace; collar

coma (*koa*-mah) *f* comma; *m* coma

comadrona (koa-mah-*dhroa*-nah) *f* midwife

comandante (koa-mahn-*dahn*-tay) *m* commander; captain

comarca (koa-*mahr*-kah) *f* district

comba (*koam*-bah) *f* bend

combate (koam-*bah*-tay) *m* combat, battle, struggle, fight; **~ de boxeo** boxing match

combatir (koam-bah-*teer*) *v* combat, battle, *fight

combinación (koam-bee-nah-th^y*oan*) *f* combination; slip

combinar (koam-bee-*nahr*) *v* combine

combustible (koam-booss-*tee*-bhlay) *m* fuel; **~ líquido** fuel oil

comedia (koa-*may*-dh^yah) *f* comedy; **~ musical** musical

comediante (koa-may-*dh^yahn*-tay) *m*, **-a** *f* actor; comedian

comedor (koa-may-*dhoar*) *m* dining room

comentar (koa-mayn-*tahr*) *v* comment

comentario (koa-mayn-*tah*-r^yoa) *m* comment

*comenzar (koa-mayn-*thahr*) *v* commence, *begin

comer (koa-*mayr*) *v* *eat

comercial (koa-mayr-*th^yahl*) *adj* commercial

comerciante (koa-mayr-*th^yahn*-tay) *m/f* merchant; trader, dealer; **~ al por menor** retailer

comerciar (koa-mayr-*th^yahr*) *v* trade

comercio (koa-*mayr*-th^yoa) *m* commerce, trade, business; **~ al por menor** retail trade

comestible (koa-mayss-*tee*-bhlay) *adj* edible

comestibles (koa-mayss-*tee*-bhlayss) *mpl* groceries *pl*; **tienda de ~ finos** delicatessen

cometer (koa-may-*tayr*) *v* commit

cómico (*koa*-mee-koa) *adj* comic,

funny; *m* comedian; entertainer

comida (koa-*mee*-dhah) *f* food; meal; ~ **principal** dinner

comidilla (koa-mee-*dhee*-lʸah) *f* hobby-horse

comienzo (koa-*mʸayn*-thoa) *m* beginning, start

comillas (koa-*mee*-lʸahss) *fpl* quotation marks

comisaría (koa-mee-sah-*ree*-ah) *f* police station

comisión (koa-mee-*sʸoan*) *f* committee, commission

comité (koa-mee-*tay*) *m* committee

comitiva (koa-mee-*tee*-bhah) *f* group

como (*koa*-moa) *adv* as, like, like; **así** ~ as well as; ~ **máximo** at most; ~ **si** as if

cómo (*koa*-moa) *adv* how

cómoda (*koa*-moa-dhah) *f* chest of drawers; bureau *Am*

comodidad (koa-moa-dhee-*dhahdh*) *f* comfort, leisure

cómodo (*koa*-moa-dhoa) *adj* convenient, easy

compacto (koam-*pahk*-toa) *adj* compact

compadecerse de (koam-pah-dhay-*thayr*-say) pity

compañero (koam-pah-*ñay*-roa) *m*, -**a** *f* companion; partner; associate; ~ **de clase** classmate

compañía (koam-pah-*ñee*-ah) *f* company; society

comparación (koam-pah-rah-*thʸoan*) *f* comparison

comparar (koam-pah-*rahr*) *v* compare

compartimento (koam-pahr-tee-*mayn*-toa) *m* compartment; ~ **para fumadores** smoking compartment

compartir (koam-pahr-*teer*) *v* share

compasión (koam-pah-*sʸoan*) *f* compassion; sympathy

compasivo (koam-pah-*see*-bhoa) *adj* compassionate, sympathetic

compatriota (koam-pah-*trʸoa*-tah) *m* countryman

compeler (koam-pay-*layr*) *v* compel

compensación (koam-payn-sah-*thʸoan*) *f* compensation

compensar (koam-payn-*sahr*) *v* compensate; *make good

competencia (koam-pay-*tayn*-thʸah) *f* competition, rivalry; competence

competente (koam-pay-*tayn*-tay) *adj* expert, qualified, competent

competidor (koam-pay-tee-*dhoar*) *m*, -**a** *f* competitor, rival

***competir** (koam-pay-*teer*) *v* compete

compilar (koam-pee-*lahr*) *v* compile

***complacer** (koam-plah-*thayr*) *v* please; *give satisfaction

complejo (koam-*play*-khoa) *adj* complex; *m* complex

completamente (koam-play-tah-*mayn*-tay) *adv* completely, quite

completar (koam-play-*tahr*) *v* complete; fill in; fill out *Am*

completo (koam-*play*-toa) *adj* complete; whole, total, utter; full up

complicado (koam-plee-*kah*-dhoa) *adj* complicated

cómplice (*koam*-plee-thay) *m* accomplice

complot (koam-*ploat*) *m* plot

***componer** (koam-poa-*nayr*) *v* compose

comportarse (koam-poar-*tahr*-say) *v* behave, act

composición (koam-poa-see-*thʸoan*) *f* composition; essay

compositor (koam-poa-see-*toar*) *m*, -**a** *f* composer

compra (*koam*-prah) *f* purchase; ***ir de compras** shop, go shopping; **saco de compras** shopping bag

comprador (koam-prah-*dhoar*) *m*, -**a**

f purchaser, buyer

comprar (koam-*prahr*) *v* purchase, *buy

comprender (koam-prayn-*dayr*) *v* *understand; *see, *take; comprise, contain

comprensión (koam-prayn-*s^yoan*) *m* understanding

compresa (koam-*pray*-sah) *f* sanitary towel, sanitary napkin *Am*

comprimido (koam-pree-*mee*-doa) *m* pill

comprobante (koam-proa-*bhahn*-tay) *m* voucher

***comprobar** (koam-proa-*bhahr*) *v* ascertain, diagnose, establish, note; prove

comprometerse (koam-proa-may-*tayr*-say) *v* engage

compromiso (koam-proa-*mee*-soa) *m* compromise; engagement

compuerta (koam-*pwayr*-tah) *f* sluice

computadora (koam-poo-tah-*doa*-rah) *f L.Am* computer; ~ **portátil** laptop

común (koa-*moon*) *adj* common; ordinary; **en ~** joint

comuna (koa-*moo*-nah) *f* commune

comunicación (koa-moo-nee-kah-*th^yoan*) *f* communication

comunicado (koa-moo-nee-*kah*-dhoa) *m* communiqué, information

comunicar (koa-moo-nee-*kahr*) *v* communicate, inform

comunidad (koa-moo-nee-*dhahdh*) *f* congregation

comunismo (koa-moo-*neez*-moa) *m* communism

comunista (koa-moo-*neess*-tah) *m* communist

con (koan) *prep* with; by

***concebir** (koan-thay-*bheer*) *v* conceive

conceder (koan-thay-*dhayr*) *v* extend, grant; award

concentración (koan-thayn-trah-*th^yoan*) *f* concentration

concentrarse (koan-thayn-*trahr*-say) *v* concentrate

concepción (koan-thayp-*th^yoan*) *f* conception

concepto (koan-*thayp*-toa) *m* idea

***concernir** (koan-thayr-*neer*) *v* touch, concern; **concerniente a** concerning

concesión (koan-thay-*s^yoan*) *f* concession

conciencia (koan-*th^yayn*-th^yah) *f* conscience; consciousness

concierto (koan-*th^yayr*-toa) *m* concert

conciso (koan-*thee*-soa) *adj* concise

***concluir** (koang-*klweer*) *v* conclude, finish; infer

conclusión (koang-kloo-*s^yoan*) *f* conclusion; ending

***concordar** (koang-koar-*dhahr*) *v* agree

concreto (koang-*kray*-toa) *adj* concrete

concurrido (koang-koo-*rree*-dhoa) *adj* busy

concurrir (koang-koo-*rreer*) *v* coincide; concur

concurso (koang-*koor*-soa) *m* competition, contest; quiz

concha (*koan*-chah) *f* shell; seashell

condado (koan-*dah*-dhoa) *m* county

conde (*koan*-day) *m* count, earl

condena (koan-*day*-nah) *f* conviction

condenado (koan-day-*nah*-dhoa) *m* convict

condenar (koan-day-*nahr*) *v* sentence; condemn

condesa (koan-*day*-sah) *f* countess

condición (koan-dee-*th^yoan*) *f* condition, term

condicional (koan-dee-th^yoa-*nahl*) *adj* conditional

condimentado (koan-dee-mayn-*tah*-dhoa) *adj* spiced

*****conducir** (koan-doo-*theer*) *v* *lead, carry, conduct; *drive

conducta (koan-*dook*-tah) *f* behavio(u)r, conduct

conducto (koan-*dook*-toa) *m* pipe

conductor (koan-*dook*-toar) *m* driver; *mMe* conductor

conectar (koa-nayk-*tahr*) *v* connect

conejo (koa-*nay*-khoa) *m* rabbit; **conejillo de Indias** guinea pig

conexión (koa-nayk-$s^y oan$) *f* connection

confeccionado (koan-fayk-th^{y}oa-nah-dhoa) *adj* ready-made

confederación (koan-fay-day-rah-th^{y}oan) *f* union

conferencia (koan-fay-*rayn*-th^{y}ah) *f* conference; lecture; ~ **interurbana** long-distance call

*****confesarse** (koan-fay-*sahr*-say) *v* confess

confesión (koan-fay-$s^y oan$) *f* confession

confiable (koan-f^yah-bhlay) *adj* trustworthy

confianza (koan-f^yahn-thah) *f* faith, trust, confidence; **indigno de** ~ untrustworthy

confiar (koan-f^yahr) *v* commit; ~ **en** trust

confidencial (koan-fee-dhayn-th^{y}ahl) *adj* confidential

confirmación (koan-feer-mah-th^{y}oan) *f* confirmation

confirmar (koan-feer-*mahr*) *v* confirm, acknowledge

confiscar (koan-feess-*kahr*) *v* confiscate, impound

confitería (koan-fee-tay-*ree*-ah) *f* sweetshop; candy store *Am*

confitero (koan-fee-*tay*-roa) *m* confectioner

confitura (koan-fee-*too*-rah) *f* marmalade

conflicto (koan-*fleek*-toa) *m* conflict

conforme (koan-*foar*-may) *adj* alike; in agreement; ~ **a** according to, in agreement with

conformidad (koan-foar-mee-*dhahdh*) *f* agreement

confort (koan-*foart*) *m* comfort

confortable (koan-foar-*tah*-bhlay) *adj* comfortable; cosy

confundir (koan-foon-*deer*) *v* *mistake, confuse

confusión (koan-foo-$s^y oan$) *f* confusion; disturbance

confuso (koan-*foo*-soa) *adj* confused

congelado (koang-khay-*lah*-dhoa) *adj* frozen; **alimento** ~ frozen food

congelador (koang-khay-lah-*dhoar*) *m* deep-freeze

congelar (koang-khay-*lahr*) *v* *freeze

congestión (koang-khayss-$t^y oan$) *f* congestion

congregación (koang-gray-gah-th^{y}oan) *f* congregation

congreso (koang-*gray*-soa) *m* congress

conjetura (koang-khay-*too*-rah) *f* guess

conjuración (koang-khoo-rah-th^{y}oan) *f* plot, conspiracy

conmemoración (koan-may-moa-rah-th^{y}oan) *f* commemoration

conmovedor (koan-moa-bhay-*dhoar*) *adj* touching; moving

*****conmover** (koan-moa-*bhayr*) *v* move

*****conocer** (koa-noa-*thayr*) *v* *know

conocido (koa-noa-*thee*-dhoa) *m* acquaintance

conocimiento (koa-noa-thee-m^yayn-toa) *m* knowledge

conquista (koang-*keess*-tah) *f* conquest, capture

conquistador (koang-keess-tah-

dhoar) m conqueror

conquistar (koang-keess-*tahr) v* conquer, capture

consciente (koan-*th*ʸ*ayn*-tay) *adj* conscious, aware

consecuencia (koan-say-*kwayn*-th*ʸ*ah) *f* consequence, result; issue

***conseguir** (koan-say-*geer) v* *get; *make, obtain

consejero (koan-say-*khay*-roa) *m* counsel(l)or; council(l)or

consejo (koan-*say*-khoa) *m* advice, counsel; council, board

consentimiento (koan-sayn-tee-*m*ʸ*ayn*-toa) *m* consent; approval

***consentir** (koan-sayn-*teer) v* agree, consent

conserje (koan-*sayr*-khay) *m* concierge, janitor

conservación (koan-sayr-bhah-th*ʸ*oan) *f* preservation

conservador (koan-sayr-bhah-*dhoar) adj* conservative

conservar (koan-sayr-*bhahr) v* preserve

conservas (koan-*sayr*-bhahss) *fpl* tinned food, canned food *Am*

conservatorio (koan-sayr-bhah-*toa*-rʸoa) *m* music academy

considerable (koan-see-dhay-*rah*-bhlay) *adj* considerable

consideración (koan-see-dhay-rah-th*ʸ*oan) *f* consideration

considerado (koan-see-dhay-*rah*-dhoa) *adj* considerate

considerar (koan-see-dhay-*rahr) v* regard, consider; *think over; count, reckon

consigna (koan-*seeg*-nah) *f* left luggage office, baggage check *Am*

consiguiente: por ~ (poar koan-see-g*ʸ*ayn-tay) consequently

consistir en (koan-seess-*teer*) consist of

***consolar** (koan-soa-*lahr) v* comfort

consorcio (koan-*soar*-th*ʸ*oa) *m* concern

conspirar (koans-pee-*rahr) v* conspire

constante (koans-*tahn*-tay) *adj* even, constant; steadfast

constar de (koans-*tahr*) consist of

constitución (koans-tee-too-th*ʸ*oan) *f* constitution

***constituir** (koans-tee-*tweer) v* constitute; represent

construcción (koans-trook-th*ʸ*oan) *f* construction

***construir** (koans-*trweer) v* construct, *build

consuelo (koan-*sway*-loa) *m* comfort

cónsul (*koan*-sool) *m* consul

consulado (koan-soo-*lah*-dhoa) *m* consulate

consulta (koan-*sool*-tah) *f* consultation

consultar (koan-sool-*tahr) v* consult

consultorio (koan-sool-*toa*-rʸoa) *m* surgery; doctor's office *Am*

consumidor (koan-soo-mee-*dhoar) m*, **-a** *f* consumer

consumir (koan-soo-*meer) v* use up; consume; eat; eat away at

contacto (koan-*tahk*-toa) *m* contact; touch

contador (koan-tah-*dhoar) m* meter

contagioso (koan-tah-*kh*ʸ*oa*-soa) *adj* infectious, contagious

contaminación (koan-tah-mee-nah-th*ʸ*oan) *f* pollution

***contar** (koan-*tahr) v* count; relate, *tell; **~ con** rely on

contemplar (koan-taym-*plahr) v* contemplate

contemporáneo (koan-taym-poa-*rah*-nay-oa) *adj* contemporary; *m* contemporary

contenedor (koan-tay-nay-*dhoar) m* container

*contener (koan-tay-*nayr*) *v* contain; restrain

contenido (koan-tay-*nee*-dhoa) *m* contents *pl*

contentar (koan-tayn-*tahr*) *v* satisfy

contento (koan-*tayn*-toa) *adj* happy, glad, content, joyful; pleased

contestar (koan-tayss-*tahr*) *v* answer

contienda (koan-t^y*ayn*-dah) *f* dispute

contiguo (koan-*tee*-gwoa) *adj* neighbo(u)ring; adjacent

continental (koan-tee-nayn-*tahl*) *adj* continental

continente (koan-tee-*nayn*-tay) *m* continent

continuación (koan-tee-nwah-th^y*oan*) *f* sequel; continuation

continuamente (koan-tee-nwah-*mayn*-tay) *adv* all the time, continually

continuar (koan-tee-*nwahr*) *v* *go on, *go ahead; carry on, continue, *keep on; *keep

continuo (koan-*tee*-nwoa) *adj* continuous, continual

contorno (koan-*toar*-noa) *m* outline, contour

contra (*koan*-trah) *prep* against, versus

contrabandear (koan-trah-bhahn-day-*ahr*) *v* smuggle

*contradecir (koan-trah-dhay-*theer*) *v* contradict

contradictorio (koan-trah-dheek-*toa*-r^yoa) *adj* contradictory

contrahecho (koan-trah-*ay*-choa) *adj* deformed

contralto (koan-*trahl*-toa) *m* alto

contrario (koan-*trah*-r^yoa) *adj* opposite, contrary; *m* contrary, reverse; **al ~** on the contrary

contraste (koan-*trahss*-tay) *m* contrast

contratiempo (koan-trah-t^y*aym*-poa) *m* misfortune

contratista (koan-trah-*teess*-tah) *m* contractor

contrato (koan-*trah*-toa) *m* agreement, contract

contribución (koan-tree-bhoo-th^y*oan*) *f* contribution

*contribuir (koan-tree-*bhweer*) *v* contribute

contrincante (koan-treeng-*kahn*-tay) *m/f* opponent

control (koan-*troal*) *m* inspection, control

controlar (koan-troa-*lahr*) *v* check, control

controvertible (koan-troa-bhayr-*tee*-bhlay) *adj* controversial

controvertido (koan-troa-bhayr-*tee*-dhoa) *adj* controversial

convencer (koam-bayn-*thayr*) *v* convince, persuade; convict

convencimiento (koam-bayn-thee-m^y*ayn*-toa) *m* conviction

conveniente (koam-bay-n^y*ayn*-tay) *adj* adequate, proper; convenient

convenio (koam-*bay*-n^yoa) *m* settlement

*convenir (koam-bay-*neer*) *v* agree; fit, suit

convento (koam-*bayn*-toa) *m* cloister, convent

conversación (koam-bayr-sah-th^y*oan*) *f* conversation, talk, discussion

*convertir (koam-bayr-*teer*) *v* convert; ***convertirse en** turn into

convicción (koam-beek-th^y*oan*) *f* conviction; persuasion

convidar (koam-bee-*dhahr*) *v* invite

convulsión (koam-bool-s^y*oan*) *f* convulsion

cónyuges (*koan*-^yoo-khayss) *mpl* married couple

coñac (koa-*ñahk*) *m* cognac

cooperación (koa-oa-pay-rah-*th^yoan*) f co-operation

cooperador (koa-oa-pay-rah-*dhoar*) adj cooperative

cooperativa (koa-oa-pay-rah-*tee*-bhah) f cooperative

cooperativo (koa-oa-pay-rah-*tee*-bhoa) adj cooperative

coordinación (koa-oar-dhee-nah-*th^yoan*) f coordination

coordinar (koa-oar-dhee-*nahr*) v coordinate

copa (*koa*-pah) f cup

copia (*koa*-p^yah) f copy, carbon copy

copiar (koa-p^y*ahr*) v copy

coraje (koa-*rah*-khay) m courage, bravery

coral (koa-*rahl*) m coral

corazón (koa-rah-*thoan*) m heart; core

corbata (koar-*bhah*-tah) f tie, necktie; ~ **de lazo** bow tie

corbatín (koar-bhah-*teen*) m bow tie

corcino (koar-*thee*-noa) m fawn

corcho (*koar*-choa) m cork

cordel (koar-*dhayl*) m string

cordero (koar-*dhay*-roa) m lamb

cordial (koar-*dh^yahl*) adj cordial, hearty, sympathetic

cordillera (koar-dhee-*l^yay*-rah) f mountain range

cordón (koar-*dhoan*) m cord, line; lace, shoe-lace; ~ **de extensión** extension cord; ~ **flexible** flex

cornamenta (koar-nah-*mayn*-tah) f antlers pl

corneja (koar-*nay*-khah) f crow

coro (*koa*-roa) m choir

corona (koa-*roa*-nah) f crown

coronar (koa-roa-*nahr*) v crown

coronel (koa-roa-*nayl*) m colonel

corpulento (koar-poo-*layn*-toa) adj corpulent, stout

corral (koa-*rrahl*) m yard; **aves de ~** poultry

correa (koa-*rray*-ah) f leash, strap; ~ **del ventilador** fan belt; ~ **de reloj** watch-strap

corrección (koa-rrayk-*th^yoan*) f correction

correcto (koa-*rrayk*-toa) adj correct; right

corredor (koa-rray-*dhoar*) m, -a f runner; agent; ~ **de apuestas** bookmaker; ~ **de bolsa** stockbroker; ~ **de casas** house agent

***corregir** (koa-rray-*kheer*) v correct

correo (koa-*rray*-oa) m post, mail; ~ **aéreo** airmail; **enviar por ~** mail; **sello de correos** postage stamp

correr (koa-*rrayr*) v *run; dash; flow

correspondencia (koa-rrayss-poan-*dayn*-th^yah) f correspondence

corresponder (koa-rrayss-poan-*dayr*) v correspond; **corresponderse** v correspond

corresponsal (koa-rrayss-poan-*sahl*) m/f correspondent

corrida de toros (koa-*rree*-dhah day *toa*-roass) bullfight

corriente (koa-*rr^yayn*-tay) adj current; regular, customary; plain; f current; stream; ~ **alterna** alternating current; ~ **continua** direct current; ~ **de aire** draught, draft *Am*

corromper (koa-rroam-*payr*) v corrupt

corrupción (koa-rroop-*th^yoan*) f corruption

corrupto (koa-*rroop*-toa) adj corrupt

corsé (koar-*say*) m corset

cortado (koar-tah-doa) adj cut; closed; curdled; shy; **quedarse ~** be embarrassed; m coffee with a dash of milk

cortadura (koar-tah-*dhoo*-rah) f cut

cortaplumas (koar-tah-*ploo*-mahss) m penknife

cortar (koar-*tahr*) v *cut; chip, *cut off

corte (*koar*-tay) f court

cortés (koar-*tayss*) adj civil, courteous, polite

corteza (koar-*tay*-thah) f bark; crust

cortijo (koar-*tee*-khoa) m farmhouse

cortina (koar-*tee*-nah) f curtain

corto (*koar*-toa) adj short

cortocircuito (koar-toa-theer-*kwee*-toa) m short circuit

cosa (*koa*-sah) f thing; **entre otras cosas** among other things

cosecha (koa-*say*-chah) f harvest, crop

coser (koa-*sayr*) v sew

cosméticos (koaz-*may*-tee-koass) mpl cosmetics pl

cosquillear (koass-kee-l'*ahr*) v tickle

costa (*koass*-tah) f coast

*costar (koass-*tahr*) v *cost

coste (*koass*-tay) m cost

costilla (koass-*tee*-l'ah) f rib

costoso (koass-*toa*-soa) adj expensive

costumbre (koass-*toom*-bray) f custom; **costumbres** morals

costura (koass-*too*-rah) f seam; **sin ~** seamless

cotidiano (koa-tee-*dh'ah*-noa) adj everyday

cráneo (*krah*-nay-oa) m skull

cráter (*krah*-tayr) m crater

creación (kray-ah-*th'oan*) f creation

crear (kray-*ahr*) v create

*crecer (kray-*thayr*) v *grow

crecimiento (kray-thee-*m'ayn*-toa) m growth

crédito (*kray*-dhee-toa) m credit

crédulo (*kray*-dhoo-loa) adj credulous

creencia (kray-*ayn*-th'ah) f belief

*creer (kray-*ayr*) v believe; guess, reckon

crema (*kray*-mah) f cream; **~ de afeitar** shaving cream; **~ de base**

foundation cream; **~ de noche** night cream; **~ facial** face cream; **~ hidratante** moisturizing cream; **~ para la piel** skin cream; **~ para las manos** hand cream

cremallera (kray-mah-*l'ay*-rah) f zip, zipper Am

cremoso (kray-*moa*-soa) adj creamy

crepúsculo (kray-*pooss*-koo-loa) m twilight, dusk

crespo (*krayss*-poa) adj curly

cresta (*krayss*-tah) f ridge

creta (*kray*-tah) f chalk

criada (kr'ah-dhah) f (house)maid

criado (kr'ah-dhoa) m servant

criar (kr'ahr) v rear; raise

criatura (kr'ah-*too*-rah) f creature; infant

crimen (*kree*-mayn) m crime

criminal (kree-mee-*nahl*) adj criminal; m criminal

criminalidad (kree-mee-nah-lee-*dhahdh*) f criminality

crisis (*kree*-seess) f crisis

cristal (kreess-*tahl*) m crystal; pane; **de ~** crystal

cristiano (kreess-*t'ah*-noa) adj Christian; m Christian

Cristo (*kreess*-toa) Christ

criterio (kree-*tay*-r'oa) m criterion

crítica (*kree*-tee-kah) f criticism

criticar (kree-tee-*kahr*) v criticize

crítico (*kree*-tee-koa) adj critical; m, **-a** f critic

cromo (*kroa*-moa) m chromium

crónica (*kroa*-nee-kah) f chronicle

crónico (*kroa*-nee-koa) adj chronic

cronológico (kroa-noa-*loa*-khee-koa) adj chronological

cruce (*kroo*-thay) m crossroads; **~ para peatones** pedestrian crossing; crosswalk Am

crucero (kroo-*thay*-roa) m cruise

crucificar (kroo-thee-fee-*kahr*) v

crucify

crucifijo (kroo-thee-*fee*-khoa) *m* crucifix

crucifixión (kroo-thee-feek-s^y*oan*) *f* crucifixion

crudo (*kroo*-dhoa) *adj* raw

cruel (krwayl) *adj* harsh, cruel

crujido (kroo-*khee*-dhoa) *m* crack

crujiente (kroo-kh^y*ayn*-tay) *adj* crisp

crujir (kroo-*kheer*) *v* creak, crack

cruz (krooth) *f* cross

cruzada (kroo-*thah*-dhah) *f* crusade

cruzar (kroo-*thahr*) *v* cross

cuaderno (kwah-*dhayr*-noa) *m* notebook; exercise book

cuadrado (kwah-*dhrah*-dhoa) *adj* square; *m* square

cuadriculado (kwah-dhree-koo-*lah*-dhoa) *adj* chequered

cuadro (*kwah*-dhroa) *m* cadre; picture; **a cuadros** chequered; **~ de distribución** switchboard

cuál (kwahl) *pron* which

cualidad (kwah-lee-*dhahdh*) *f* property

cualquiera (kwahl-k^y*ay*-rah) *pron* anyone, anybody; whichever; **cualquier cosa** anything

cuando (*kwahn*-doa) *conj* when; **~ quiera que** whenever

cuándo (*kwahn*-doa) *adv* when

cuánto (*kwahn*-toa) *adv* how much; how many; **cuanto más ... más** the ... the; **en cuanto a** as regards

cuarenta (kwah-*rayn*-tah) *num* forty

cuarentena (kwah-rayn-*tay*-nah) *f* quarantine

cuartel (kwahr-*tayl*) *m* barracks *pl*; **~ general** headquarters *pl*

cuarto¹ (*kwahr*-toa) *num* fourth; *m* quarter; **~ de hora** quarter of an hour

cuarto² (*kwahr*-toa) *m* chamber; **~ de aseo** lavatory; washroom *Am*; **~ de baño** bathroom; **~ de niños** nursery;

~ para huéspedes spare room

cuatro (*kwah*-troa) *num* four

Cuba (*koo*-bhah) *f* Cuba

cubano (koo-*bhah*-noa) *adj* Cuban; *m* Cuban

cubierta (koo-*bh^yayr*-tah) *f* cover; deck

cubierto (koo-*bh^yayr*-toa) *adj* cloudy

cubiertos (koo-*bh^yayr*-toass) *mpl* cutlery

cubo (*koo*-bhoa) *m* cube; **~ de la basura** dustbin

cubrir (koo-*bhreer*) *v* cover

cuclillo (koo-*klee*-l^yoa) *m* cuckoo

cuchara (koo-*chah*-rah) *f* spoon; tablespoon

cucharada (koo-chah-*rah*-dhah) *f* spoonful

cucharadita (koo-chah-rah-*dhee*-tah) *f* teaspoonful

cucharilla (koo-chah-*ree*-l^yah) *f* teaspoon

cuchillo (koo-*chee*-l^yoa) *m* knife

cuello (*kway*-l^yoa) *m* neck; collar; **~ de botella** bottleneck

cuenta (*kwayn*-tah) *f* account; bill; check *Am*; bead; **~ de banco** bank account; ***darse ~** *see

cuento (*kwayn*-toa) *m* story, tale

cuerda (*kwayr*-dhah) *f* cord; string; ***dar ~** *wind

cuerno (*kwayr*-noa) *m* horn

cuero (*kway*-roa) *m* leather; **~ vacuno** cowhide

cuerpo (*kwayr*-poa) *m* body

cuervo (*kwayr*-bhoa) *m* raven

cuestión (kwayss-t^y*oan*) *f* matter, issue, question

cueva (*kway*-bhah) *f* cavern, cave; wine cellar

cuidado (kwee-*dhah*-dhoa) *m* care; ***tener ~** watch out, look out

cuidadoso (kwee-dhah-*dhoa*-soa) *adj* careful; diligent

cuidar de (kwee-*dahr*) attend to, look after, tend, *take care of

cuidarse (kwee-*dahr*-say) look after oneself, take care of oneself; **~ de hacer** take care to do

culebra (koo-*lay*-bhrah) f snake

culo (*koo*-loa) m *vulgar* ass, arse; *colloquial* butt, bum; **ser ~ de mal asiento** *colloquial* be restless

culpa (*kool*-pah) f guilt, fault, blame

culpable (kool-*pah*-bhlay) adj guilty

culpar (kool-*pahr*) v blame, accuse

cultivar (kool-tee-*bhahr*) v cultivate; *grow, raise

cultivo (kool-*tee*-bhoa) m cultivation

culto (*kool*-toa) adj cultured; m worship

cultura (kool-*too*-rah) f culture

cultural (kool-too-*rahl*) adj cultural

cumbre (*koom*-bray) f peak

cumpleaños (koom-play-*ah*-ñoass) m birthday

cumplimentar (koom-plee-mayn-*tahr*) v compliment

cumplimiento (koom-plee-*mᵞayn*-toa) m compliment

cumplir (koom-*pleer*) v comply, carry out

cuna (*koo*-nah) f cradle; **~ de viaje** carrycot

cuneta (koo-*nay*-tah) f ditch; gutter

cuña (*koo*-ñah) f wedge

cuñada (koo-*ñah*-dhah) f sister-in-law

cuñado (koo-*ñah*-dhoa) m brother-in-law

cuota (*kwoa*-tah) f quota

cupón (koo-*poan*) m coupon

cúpula (*koo*-poo-lah) f dome

cura (*koo*-rah) m priest; f cure

curación (koo-rah-*thᵞoan*) f cure, recovery

curandero (koo-rahn-*day*-roa) m quack

curar (koo-*rahr*) v cure, heal; **curarse** v recover

curato (koo-*rah*-toa) m parsonage

curiosidad (koo-rᵞoa-see-*dhahdh*) f curiosity; sight; curio

curioso (koo-rᵞoa-soa) adj curious; inquisitive; quaint

cursi (*koor*-see) adj *colloquial* affected

cursiva (koor-*see*-bhah) f italics pl

curso (*koor*-soa) m course; lecture; **~ intensivo** intensive course

curva (*koor*-bhah) f turn, curve, bend

curvado (koor-*bhah*-dhoa) adj curved

curvo (*koor*-bhoa) adj crooked, bent

custodia (kooss-*toa*-dhᵞah) f custody

cuyo (*koo*-ᵞoa) pron whose; of which

D

dadivoso (dah-dhee-*bhoa*-soa) adj lavish with gifts

dado[1] (*dah*-doa) m dice

dado[2] (*dah*-doa) adj given

daltoniano (dahl-toa-nᵞah-noa) adj colo(u)r-blind

dama (*dah*-mah) f lady

danés (dah-*nayss*) adj Danish; m Dane

dañar (dah-*ñahr*) v damage; *hurt

daño (*dah*-ñoa) m mischief; harm; *hacer ~ *hurt

dañoso (dah-*ñoa*-soa) adj harmful

***dar** (dahr) v *give; **dado que** supposing that

dátil (*dah*-teel) m date

dato (*dah*-toa) *m* data *pl*

de (day) *prep* of; out of, from, off; with

debajo (day-*bhah*-khoa) *adv* underneath, beneath, below; ~ **de** under, beneath, below

debate (day-*bhah*-tay) *m* debate, discussion

debatir (day-bhah-*teer*) *v* discuss

deber (day-*bhayr*) *m* duty; *v* *have to, need to, need; owe; ~ **de** *be bound to

debido (day-*bhee*-dhoa) *adj* due; proper; ~ **a** owing to

débil (*day*-bheel) *adj* faint, weak, feeble

debilidad (day-bhee-lee-*dhahdh*) *f* weakness

decencia (day-*thayn*-thʸah) *f* decency

decente (day-*thayn*-tay) *adj* decent

decepcionar (day-thayp-thʸoa-*nahr*) *v* *let down, disappoint

decidir (day-thee-*dheer*) *v* decide; **decidido** resolute

décimo (*day*-thee-moa) *num* tenth

decimoctavo (day-thee-moak-*tah*-bhoa) *num* eighteenth

decimonono (day-thee-moa-*noa*-noa) *num* nineteenth

decimoséptimo (day-thee-moa-*sayp*-tee-moa) *num* seventeenth

decimosexto (day-thee-moa-*sayks*-toa) *num* sixteenth

*decir (day-*theer*) *v* *say, *tell; ***querer** ~ *mean

decisión (day-thee-sʸoan) *f* decision

decisivo (day-thee-*see*-bhoa) *adj* decisive

declaración (day-klah-rah-*thʸoan*) *f* statement, declaration

declarar (day-klah-*rahr*) *v* state, declare

decoración (day-koa-rah-*thʸoan*) *f* decoration

decorativo (day-koa-rah-*tee*-bhoa) *adj* decorative

decreto (day-*kray*-toa) *m* decree

dedal (day-*dhahl*) *m* thimble

dédalo (*day*-dhah-loa) *m* muddle

dedicar (day-dhee-*kahr*) *v* devote, dedicate

dedo (*day*-dhoa) *m* finger; ~ **auricular** little finger; ~ **del pie** toe

*deducir (day-dhoo-*theer*) *v* infer, deduce; deduct

defecto (day-*fayk*-toa) *m* fault

defectuoso (day-fayk-*twoa*-soa) *adj* defective, faulty

*defender (day-fayn-*dayr*) *v* defend

defensa (day-*fayn*-sah) *f* defence, defense *Am*; plea; *Me* fender

defensor (day-fayn-*soar*) *m* defender, proponent; champion

déficit (*day*-fee-theet) *m* deficit

definición (day-fee-nee-*thʸoan*) *f* definition

definir (day-fee-*neer*) *v* define; **definido** definite

definitivo (day-fee-nee-*tee*-bhoa) *adj* definitive

deforme (day-*foar*-may) *adj* deformed

dejar (day-*khahr*) *v* *let, *leave; *leave behind, desert; ~ **de** stop

del (dayl) *contraction of* de el

delantal (day-lahn-*tahl*) *m* apron

delante de (day-*lahn*-tay day) before, in front of, ahead of

delegación (day-lay-gah-*thʸoan*) *f* delegation

delegado (day-lay-*gah*-dhoa) *m* delegate

deleite (day-*lay*-tay) *m* delight

deleitoso (day-lay-*toa*-soa) *adj* delightful

deletrear (day-lay-tray-*ahr*) *v* *spell

deletreo (day-lay-*tray*-oa) *m* spelling

delgado (dayl-*gah*-dhoa) *adj* thin

deliberación (day-lee-bhay-rah-*thʸoan*) *f* deliberation

deliberar (day-lee-bhay-*rahr*) v
deliberate; **deliberado** adj deliberate
delicado (day-lee-*kah*-dhoa) adj
delicate, tender
delicia (day-*lee*-th^{y}ah) f joy, delight
delicioso (day-lee-*th^{y}oa*-soa) adj
wonderful, delightful, delicious,
lovely
delincuente (day-leeng-*kwayn*-tay) m
criminal
delito (day-*lee*-toa) m crime
demanda (day-*mahn*-dah) f request;
application; demand
demás (day-*mahss*) adj other;
remaining; **lo ~** the rest; **los ~** the
others
demasiado (day-mah-s^y*ah*-dhoa) adv
too
democracia (day-moa-*krah*-th^{y}ah) f
democracy
democrático (day-moa-*krah*-tee-koa)
adj democratic
*****demoler** (day-moa-*layr*) v demolish
demolición (day-moa-lee-th^y*oan*) f
demolition
demonio (day-*moa*-n^{y}oa) m devil
demostración (day-moass-trah-
th^y*oan*) f demonstration
*****demostrar** (day-moass-*trahr*) v
demonstrate, *show, prove
*****denegar** (day-nay-*gahr*) v deny
denominación (day-noa-mee-nah-
th^y*oan*) f denomination
denso (*dayn*-soa) adj thick, dense
dentadura postiza (dayn-tah-*dhoo*-
rah poass-*tee*-thah) false teeth,
dentures
dentista (dayn-*teess*-tah) m dentist
dentro (*dayn*-troa) adv inside; **de ~**
within; **~ de** inside, within; into; in
departamento (day-pahr-tah-*mayn*-
toa) m department; section, division
depender de (day-payn-*dayr*) depend
on

dependiente (day-payn-*d^{y}ayn*-tay)
adj dependant; m, **-a** f sales clerk Am,
shop assistant
deporte (day-*poar*-tay) m sport;
conjunto de ~ sportswear; **chaqueta
de ~** sports jacket
deportista (day-poar-*teess*-tah) m
sportsman
depositar (day-poa-see-*tahr*) v bank
depósito (day-*poa*-see-toa) m
deposit; **~ de gasolina** petrol tank,
gas tank Am
depresión (day-pray-s^y*oan*) f
depression
deprimente (day-pree-*mayn*-tay) adj
depressing
deprimir (day-pree-*meer*) v depress;
deprimido blue, depressed, low
derecha (day-*ray*-chah) f right; **la ~** the
right(-hand); **a la ~** on the right; to
the right
derecho (day-*ray*-choa) m right; law,
right, justice, straight; adj upright;
right-hand; **~ administrativo**
administrative law; **~ civil** civil law; **~
comercial** commercial law; **~
electoral** franchise, suffrage; **~ penal**
criminal law
derivar de (day-ree-*bhahr*) *be
derived from
derramar (day-rrah-*mahr*) v *shed
derribar (day-rree-*bhahr*) v knock
down
derrochador (day-rroa-chah-*dhoar*)
adj wasteful
derrota (day-*rroa*-tah) f defeat
derrotar (day-rroa-*tahr*) v defeat
derrumbarse (day-rroom-*bahr*-say) v
collapse
desabotonar (day-sah-bhoa-toa-
nahr) v unbutton
desacelerar (day-sah-thay-lay-*rahr*) v
slow down
desacostumbrado (day-sah-koass-

toom-*brah*-dhoa) *adj* unaccustomed

desacostumbrar (day-sah-koass-toom-*brahr*) *v* unlearn

desafiar (day-sah-*f*'*ahr*) *v* dare; challenge

desafilado (day-sah-fee-*lah*-dhoa) *adj* blunt

desafortunado (day-sah-foar-too-*nah*-dhoa) *adj* unlucky, unfortunate

desagradable (day-sah-grah-*dhah*-bhlay) *adj* nasty, disagreeable, unpleasant; unkind

desagradar (day-sah-grah-*dhahr*) *v* displease

desagüe (day-*sah*-gway) *m* sewer, drain

desaliñado (day-sah-lee-*ñah*-doa) *adj* untidy

desánimo (day-*sah*-nee-moa) *m* depression, discouragement

***desaparecer** (day-sah-pah-ray-*thayr*) *v* disappear; vanish

desaparecido (day-sah-pah-ray-*thee*-dhoa) *adj* lost; *m* missing person

desapasionado (day-sah-pah-s'oa-*nah*-dhoa) *adj* matter-of-fact; dispassionate

***desaprobar** (day-sah-proa-*bhahr*) *v* disapprove

desarrollar (day-sah-rroa-*l*'*ahr*) *v* develop; unfold; unwind

desarrollo (day-sah-*rroa*-l'oa) *m* development; unfolding

desasosiego (day-sah-soa-s'ay-goa) *m* unrest

desastre (day-*sahss*-tray) *m* disaster, calamity

desastroso (day-sahss-*troa*-soa) *adj* disastrous

desatar (day-sah-*tahr*) *v* *undo, untie, unfasten

desautorizado (day-sou-toa-ree-*thah*-dhoa) *adj* unauthorized

desayunar (day-sah-'oo-*nahr*) *v* have breakfast

desayuno (day-sah-'*oo*-noa) *m* breakfast

descafeinado (dayss-kah-fay-*nah*-dhoa) *adj* decaffeinated

descansar (dayss-kahn-*sahr*) *v* rest; relax

descanso (dayss-*kahn*-soa) *m* rest; break; half-time

descarado (dayss-kah-*rah*-dhoa) *adj* bold, impertinent

descargar (dayss-kahr-*gahr*) *v* discharge, unload

descendencia (day-thayn-*dayn*-th'ah) *f* origin; descendants

***descender** (day-thayn-*dhayr*) *v* *fall

descendiente (day-thayn-*d*'*ayn*-tay) *m/f* descendant; *adj* descending

descolorido (dayss-koa-loa-*ree*-dhoa) *adj* discolo(u)red

descompostura (dayss-koam-poass-*too*-rah) *fMe* breakdown

***desconcertar** (dayss-koan-thayr-*tahr*) *v* overwhelm, embarrass

desconectar (dayss-koa-nayk-*tahr*) *v* disconnect

desconfiado (dayss-koan-*f*'*ah*-dhoa) *adj* suspicious; distrusting

desconfianza (dayss-koan-*f*'*ahn*-thah) *f* suspicion; distrust

desconfiar de (dayss-koan-*f*'*ahr*) *v* distrust

descongelarse (dayss-koang-khay-*lahr*-say) *v* thaw

***desconocer** (dayss-koa-noa-*thayr*) *v* not to *know, fail to recognize

desconocido (dayss-koa-noa-*thee*-dhoa) *adj* unknown; unfamiliar

descontento (dayss-koan-*tayn*-toa) *adj* discontented

descorchar (dayss-koar-*chahr*) *v* uncork

descortés (dayss-koar-*tayss*) *adj* impolite

describir (dayss-kree-*bheer*) *v* describe

descripción (dayss-kreep-*th*ʸ*oan*) *f* description

descubierto (dayss-koo-*bh*ʸ*ayr*-toa) *m* overdraft

descubrimiento (dayss-koo-bhree-*m*ʸ*an*-toa) *m* discovery

descubrir (dayss-koo-*bhreer*) *v* discover, detect

descuento (dayss-*kwayn*-toa) *m* discount; ~ **bancario** bank rate

descuidar (dayss-kwee-*dhahr*) *v* neglect; **descuidado** careless, negligent, slovenly

descuido (dayss-*kwee*-dhoa) *m* carelessness, negligence; oversight

desde (*dayz*-dhay) *prep* from; since; ~ **entonces** since; ~ **que** since

desdén (dayz-*dhayn*) *m* disdain

desdichado (dayz-dhee-*chah*-dhoa) *adj* unhappy

deseable (day-say-*ah*-bhlay) *adj* desirable

desear (day-say-*ahr*) *v* desire; wish, want

desecar (day-say-*kahr*) *v* drain

desechable (day-say-*chah*-bhlay) *adj* disposable

desechar (day-say-*chahr*) *v* discard

desecho (day-*say*-choa) *m* refuse

desembarcar (day-saym-bahr-*kahr*) *v* disembark; land

desembocadura (day-saym-boa-kah-*dhoo*-rah) *f* mouth

desempaquetar (day-saym-pah-kay-*tahr*) *v* unpack

desempeñar (day-saym-pay-*ñahr*) *v* perform

desempleo (day-saym-*play*-oa) *m* unemployment

desengaño (day-sayng-*gah*-ñoa) *m* disappointment

desenvoltura (day-saym-boal-*too*-rah) *f* ease; eloquence

*desenvolver (day-saym-boal-*bhayr*) *v* unwrap; expound

deseo (day-*say*-oa) *m* wish, desire

desertar (day-sayr-*tahr*) *v* desert

desesperación (day-sayss-pay-rah-*th*ʸ*oan*) *f* despair

desesperado (day-sayss-pay-*rah*-dhoa) *adj* hopeless, desperate; ***estar** ~ despair

desfavorable (dayss-fah-bhoa-*rah*-bhlay) *adj* unfavo(u)rable

desfile (dayss-*fee*-lay) *m* parade

desgarrar (dayz-gah-*rrahr*) *v* *tear

desgracia (dayz-*grah*-th*yah*) *f* misfortune

desgraciadamente (dayz-grah-th*yah*-dhah-*mayn*-tay) *adv* unfortunately

*deshacer (day-sah-*thayr*) *v* *undo; **deshacerse de** get rid of

deshielo (day-*s*ʸ*ay*-loa) *m* thaw

deshonesto (day-soa-*nayss*-toa) *adj* dishonest

deshonor (day-soa-*noar*) *m* dishonor; disgrace

deshonra (day-*soan*-rah) *f* dishonor; shame

deshuesar (day-sway-*sahr*) *v* bone

desierto (day-s*ʸayr*-toa) *adj* desert; *m* desert

designar (day-seeg-*nahr*) *v* designate; appoint

desigual (day-see-*gwahl*) *adj* unequal, uneven

desinclinado (day-seeng-klee-*nah*-dhoa) *adj* unwilling

desinfectante (day-seen-fayk-*tahn*-tay) *m* disinfectant

desinfectar (day-seen-fayk-*tahr*) *v* disinfect

desinteresado (day-seen-tay-ray-sah-dhoa) *adj* unselfish

desliz (dayz-*leeth*) *m* slide; slip

deslizarse (dayz-lee-*thahr*-say) *v*

*slide; slip

deslucido (dayz-loo-*thee*-dhoa) *adj*
dim

desmayarse (dayz-mah-*y ahr*-say) *v*
faint

desnudarse (dayz-noo-*dhahr*-say) *v*
undress

desnudo (dayz-*noo*-dhoa) *adj* naked,
nude, bare; *m* nude

desnutrición (dayz-noo-tree-*th y oan*) *f*
malnutrition

desocupado (day-soa-koo-*pah*-dhoa)
adj unoccupied; unemployed

desodorante (day-soa-dhoa-*rahn*-tay)
m deodorant

desolador (day-soa-lah-*doar*) *adj*
bleak

desorden (day-*soar*-dayn) *m* disorder;
mess

despachar (dayss-pah-*chahr*) *v*
dispatch, despatch, *send off

despacho (dayss-*pah*-choa) *m* study;
office

despedida (dayss-pay-*dhee*-dhah) *f*
parting; departure

***despedir** (dayss-pay-*dheer*) *v*
dismiss; fire; ***despedirse** *v* check
out

despegar (dayss-pay-*gahr*) *v* *take off

despegue (dayss-*pay*-gay) *m* take-off

despensa (dayss-*payn*-sah) *f* pantry,
larder

desperdicio (dayss-payr-*dhee*-th y oa)
m litter; waste

despertador (dayss-payr-tah-*dhoar*)
m alarm clock

***despertar** (dayss-payr-*tahr*) *v* *wake,
*awake; ***despertarse** *v* wake up

despierto (dayss-*p y ayr*-toa) *adj*
awake; vigilant

***desplegar** (dayss-play-*gahr*) *v*
unfold; expand

desplomarse (dayss-ploa-*mahr*-say) *v*
collapse

despreciar (dayss-pray-*th y ahr*) *v*
scorn, despise

desprecio (dayss-*pray*-th y oa) *m* scorn,
contempt

despreocupado (dayss-pray-oa-koo-
pah-dhoa) *adj* carefree

después (dayss-*pwayss*) *adv*
afterwards; then; ~ **de** after; ~ **de que**
after

destacado (dayss-tah-*kah*-dhoa) *adj*
outstanding

destacarse (dayss-tah-*kahr*-say) *v*
*stand out

destapar (dayss-tah-*pahr*) *v* uncover

destello (dayss-*tay*-l y oa) *m* glare

***desteñirse** (dayss-tay-*ñeer*-say) *v*
fade, discolo(u)r; **no destiñe** fast-
dyed

destinar (dayss-tee-*nahr*) *v* destine;
address

destinatario (dayss-tee-nah-*tah*-r y oa)
m, **-a** *f* addressee

destino (dayss-*tee*-noa) *m* fate,
destiny, lot; destination

destornillador (dayss-toar-nee-l y ah-
dhoar) *m* screwdriver

destornillar (dayss-toar-nee-*l y ahr*) *v*
unscrew

destrucción (dayss-trook-*th y oan*) *f*
destruction

***destruir** (dayss-*trweer*) *v* destroy;
wreck

desvalorización (dayz-bhah-loa-ree-
thah-*th y oan*) *f* devaluation

desvalorizar (dayz-bhah-loa-ree-
thahr) *v* devalue

desvelado (dayz-bhay-*lah*-dhoa) *adj*
sleepless

desventaja (dayz-bhayn-*tah*-khah) *f*
disadvantage

desviar (dayz-*bh y ahr*) *v* avert;
desviarse *v* deviate

desvío (dayz-*bhee*-oa) *m* detour;
diversion

detallado (day-tah-lʲah-dhoa) *adj*
detailed

detalle (day-tah-lʲay) *m* detail; **vender
al ~** sell retail

detective (day-tayk-*tee*-bhay) *m/f*
detective

detención (day-tayn-thʲoan) *f* custody

*detener (day-tay-*nayr*) *v* detain

detergente (day-tayr-*khayn*-tay) *m*
detergent

determinar (day-tayr-mee-*nahr*) *v*
define, determine; **determinado**
definite

detestar (day-tayss-*tahr*) *v* hate,
dislike

detrás (day-*trahss*) *adv* behind; **~ de**
behind, after

deuda (*day*ᵒᵒ-dhah) *f* debt

*devolver (day-bhoal-*bhayr*) *v* *bring
back; *send back

día (*dee*-ah) *m* day; **¡buenos días!**
hello!; **de ~** by day; **~ de trabajo**
working day; **~ laborable** weekday;
el otro ~ recently

diabetes (dʲah-*bhay*-tayss) *f* diabetes

diabético (dʲah-*bhay*-tee-koa) *m*, **-a** *f*
diabetic

diablo (dʲah-bhloa) *m* devil

diagnosis (dʲahg-*noa*-seess) *m*
diagnosis

diagnosticar (dʲahg-noass-tee-*kahr*)
v diagnose

diagonal (dʲah-goa-*nahl*) *adj*
diagonal; *f* diagonal

dialecto (dʲah-*layk*-toa) *m* dialect

diamante (dʲah-*mahn*-tay) *m*
diamond

diapositiva (dʲah-poa-see-*tee*-bhah) *f*
slide

diario (dʲah-*rʲ*oa) *adj* daily; *m* daily,
newspaper; diary; **a ~** per day; **~
matutino** morning paper

diarrea (dʲah-*rray*-ah) *f* diarrh(o)ea

dibujar (dee-bhoo-*khahr*) *v* sketch,
*draw

dibujo (dee-*bhoo*-khoa) *m* sketch,
drawing; **dibujos animados** cartoon

diccionario (deek-thʲoa-*nah*-rʲoa) *m*
dictionary

diciembre (dee-thʲaym-bray) *m*
December

dictado (deek-*tah*-dhoa) *m* dictation

dictador (deek-tah-*dhoar*) *m* dictator

dictadura (deek-tah-*dhoo*-rah) *f*
dictatorship

dictáfono (deek-*tah*-foa-noa) *m*
dictaphone

dictar (deek-*tahr*) *v* dictate

dichoso (dee-*choa*-soa) *adj* happy

diecinueve (dʲay-thee-*nway*-bhay)
num nineteen

dieciocho (dʲay-thʲoa-choa) *num*
eighteen

dieciséis (dʲay-thee-*sayss*) *num*
sixteen

diecisiete (dʲay-thee-*sʲay*-tay) *num*
seventeen

diente (dʲayn-tay) *m* tooth; **~ de león**
dandelion

diesel (*dee*-sayl) *m* diesel

diestro (dʲayss-troa) *adj* skil(l)ful

diez (dʲayth) *num* ten

diferencia (dee-fay-*rayn*-thʲah) *f*
difference; contrast, distinction

diferente (dee-fay-*rayn*-tay) *adj*
different; unlike

*diferir (dee-fay-*reer*) *v* vary, differ;
delay

difícil (dee-*fee*-theel) *adj* hard,
difficult

dificultad (dee-fee-kool-*tahdh*) *f*
difficulty

difteria (deef-*tay*-rʲah) *f* diphtheria

difunto (dee-*foon*-toa) *adj* deceased;
dead

difuso (dee-*foo*-soa) *adj* dim; diffused

digerible (dee-khayss-*tee*-bhlay) *adj*
digestible

*digerir (dee-khay-*reer*) *v* digest

digestión (dee-khayss-*t^yoan*) *f* digestion

digital (dee-khee-*tahl*) *adj* digital

dignidad (deeg-nee-*dhahd*) *f* dignity

digno de (*dee*-ñoa day) worthy of

dilación (dee-lah-*th^yoan*) *f* delay, respite

diligencia (dee-lee-*khayn*-th^yah) *f* diligence

diligente (dee-lee-*khayn*-tay) *adj* diligent

dimensión (dee-mayn-*s^yoan*) *f* extent, size

Dinamarca (dee-nah-*mahr*-kah) *f* Denmark

dínamo (*dee*-nah-moa) *f* dynamo

dinero (dee-*nay*-roa) *m* money; ~ **contante** cash

dios (d^yoass) *m* god

diosa (d^y*oa*-sah) *f* goddess

diploma (dee-*ploa*-mah) *m* diploma, certificate

diplomático (dee-ploa-*mah*-tee-koa) *m* diplomat

diputado (dee-poo-*tah*-dhoa) *m* Member of Parliament

dirección (dee-rayk-*th^yoan*) *f* direction; way; address; leadership, lead; ~ **de escena** direction; ~ **única** one-way traffic

directamente (dee-rayk-tah-*mayn*-tay) *adv* straight; straight away

directo (dee-*rayk*-toa) *adj* direct

director (dee-rayk-*toar*) *m*, -**a** *f* director, manager; conductor; ~ **de escuela** head teacher, headmaster; principal

dirigir (dee-ree-*kheer*) *v* head; direct

disciplina (dee-thee-*plee*-nah) *f* discipline

discípulo (deess-*thee*-poo-loa) *m* disciple; pupil

disco (*deess*-koa) *m* disc; record

disco compacto (*deess*-koa koam-*pahk*-toa) *m* compact disc; **reproductor de ~s ~s** CD player

discreto (deess-*kray*-toa) *adj* discreet; inconspicuous

disculpa (deess-*kool*-pah) *f* apology

disculpar (deess-kool-*pahr*) *v* excuse; **disculparse** *v* apologize; **¡disculpe!** sorry!

discurso (deess-*koor*-soa) *m* speech

discusión (deess-koo-*s^yoan*) *f* discussion, argument

discutir (deess-koo-*teer*) *v* discuss, deliberate, argue

*disentir (dee-sayn-*teer*) *v* disagree

diseñar (dee-say-*ñahr*) *v* design

diseño (dee-say-*ñoa*) *m* design; pattern; **cuaderno de ~** sketch-book

disfraz (deess-*frahth*) *m* disguise

disfrazarse (deess-frah-*thahr*-say) *v* disguise

disfrutar (deess-froo-*tahr*) *v* enjoy

disgustar (deez-gooss-*tahr*) *v* displease

disimular (dee-see-moo-*lahr*) *v* conceal

dislocar (deez-loa-*kahr*) *v* dislocate

disminución (deez-mee-noo-*th^yoan*) *f* decrease

*disminuir (deez-mee-*nweer*) *v* reduce, lessen, decrease

*disolver (dee-soal-*bhayr*) *v* dissolve

disparar (deess-pah-*rahr*) *v* fire

disparo (deess-*pah*-roa) *m* shot

dispensar (deess-payn-*sahr*) *v* exempt; ~ **de** discharge of; **¡dispense usted!** sorry!

dispensario (deess-payn-*sah*-r^yoa) *m* health centre (center *Am*)

*disponer (deess-poa-*nayr*) *v* sort; ~ **de** dispose of

disponible (deess-poa-*nee*-bhlay) *adj* available; spare

disposición (deess-poa-see-*th^yoan*) *f*

disposal

dispuesto (deess-*pwayss*-toa) *adj*
inclined, willing

disputa (deess-*poo*-tah) *f* dispute,
argument, quarrel

disputar (deess-poo-*tahr*) *v* argue,
quarrel; dispute

distancia (deess-*tahn*-thʸah) *f*
distance; space, way

distinción (deess-teen-thʸoan) *f*
distinction, difference

distinguido (deess-teeng-gee-dhoa)
adj distinguished, dignified

distinguir (deess-teeng-*geer*) *v*
distinguish; **distinguirse** *v* excel

distinto (deess-*teen*-toa) *adj* distinct

distracción (deess-trahk-*thʸoan*) *f*
distraction; amusement

*distraer (deess-trah-*ayr*) *v* distract

distribuidor (deess-tree-bhwee-
dhoar) *m* distributor

*distribuir (deess-tree-*bhweer*) *v*
distribute; issue

distrito (deess-*tree*-toa) *m* district; ~
electoral constituency

disturbio (deess-*toor*-bhʸoa) *m*
disturbance

disuadir (dee-swah-*dheer*) *v* dissuade
from

diversión (dee-bhayr-sʸoan) *f*
pleasure, fun; diversion,
entertainment

diverso (dee-*bhayr*-soa) *adj* diverse

divertido (dee-bhayr-*tee*-dhoa) *adj*
amusing, entertaining

*divertir (dee-bhayr-*teer*) *v* amuse,
entertain

dividir (dee-bhee-*dheer*) *v* divide

divino (dee-*bhee*-noa) *adj* divine

división (dee-bhee-sʸoan) *f* division;
section

divorciado (dee-bhoar-*thʸah*-doa)
adj divorced; *m*, **-a** (dee-bhoar-
thʸah-dah) *f* divorcee

divorciar (dee-bhoar-*thʸahr*) *v* divorce

divorcio (dee-*bhoar*-thʸoa) *m* divorce

doblar (doa-*bhlahr*) *v* *bend; fold

doble (*doa*-bhlay) *adj* double

doce (*doa*-thay) *num* twelve

docena (doa-*thay*-nah) *f* dozen

doctor (doak-*toar*) *m* doctor

doctrina (doak-*tree*-nah) *f* doctrine

documento (doa-koo-*mayn*-toa) *m*
document

*doler (doa-*layr*) *v* ache

dolor (doa-*loar*) *m* ache, pain; grief;
dolores *mpl* labo(u)r; **sin ~** painless

dolorido (doa-loa-*ree*-dhoa) *adj*
painful

doloroso (doa-loa-*roa*-soa) *adj* sore

domesticado (doa-mayss-tee-*kah*-
dhoa) *adj* tame

domesticar (doa-mayss-tee-*kahr*) *v*
tame

doméstico (doa-*mayss*-tee-koa) *adj*
domestic; **faenas domésticas**
housework

domicilio (doa-mee-*thee*-lʸoa) *m*
domicile

dominación (doa-mee-nah-*thʸoan*) *f*
domination

dominante (doa-mee-*nahn*-tay) *adj*
leading

dominar (doa-mee-*nahr*) *v* dominate;
master

domingo (doa-*meeng*-goa) *m* Sunday

dominio (doa-*mee*-nʸoa) *m* dominion,
rule

don (doan) *m* talent; ability

donación (doa-nah-*thʸoan*) *f* donation

donante (doa-*nahn*-tay) *m* donor

donar (doa-*nahr*) *v* donate

donde (*doan*-day) *conj* where; **en ~
sea** anywhere

dónde (*doan*-day) *adv* where

dondequiera (doan-day-*kʸay*-rah)
adv anywhere; **~ que** wherever

dorado (doa-*rah*-dhoa) *adj* gilt;

golden
dormido (doar-*mee*-dhoa) *adj* asleep;
  quedarse ~ *oversleep
*****dormir** (doar-*meer*) *v* *sleep
dormitorio (doar-mee-*toa*-r^yoa) *m*
  bedroom; dormitory
dos (doass) *num* two; **~ veces** twice
dosis (*doa*-seess) *f* dose
dotado (doa-*tah*-dhoa) *adj* talented
dragón (drah-*goan*) *m* dragon
drama (*drah*-mah) *m* drama
dramático (drah-*mah*-tee-koa) *adj*
  dramatic
drenar (dray-*nahr*) *v* drain
droga (*droa*-ghah) *f* drug; **~ de
  diseño** designer drug
droguería (droa-gay-*ree*-ah) *f*
  chemist's, pharmacy; drugstore *Am*
ducha (*doo*-chah) *f* shower
ducharse (doo-*chahr*-say) *v* have a
  shower, shower
duda (*doo*-dhah) *f* doubt; *****poner en ~**
  query; **sin ~** undoubtedly, without

doubt
dudar (doo-*dhahr*) *v* doubt
dudoso (doo-*dhoa*-soa) *adj* doubtful
duelo (*dway*-loa) *m* duel; grief
duende (*dwayn*-dhay) *m* elf
dueña (*dway*-ñah) *f* landlady, owner
dueño (*dway*-ñoa) *m* landlord, owner
dulce (*dool*-thay) *adj* sweet; smooth;
  m sweet; **dulces** cake; sweets; candy
  Am
duna (*doo*-nah) *f* dune
duodécimo (dwoa-*day*-thee-moa)
  num twelfth
duque (*doo*-kay) *m* duke
duquesa (doo-*kay*-sah) *f* duchess
duración (doo-rah-th^y*oan*) *f* duration
duradero (doo-rah-*dhay*-roa) *adj*
  permanent, lasting
durante (doo-*rahn*-tay) *prep* for,
  during
durar (doo-*rahr*) *v* last; continue
duro (*doo*-roa) *adj* hard; tough

E

ébano (*ay*-bhah-noa) *m* ebony
eclipse (ay-*kleep*-say) *m* eclipse
eco (*ay*-koa) *m* echo
economía (ay-koa-noa-*mee*-ah) *f*
  economy
económico (ay-koa-*noa*-mee-koa) *adj*
  economic; thrifty, economical; cheap
economista (ay-koa-noa-*meess*-tah)
  m economist
economizar (ay-koa-noa-mee-*thahr*)
  v economize
Ecuador (ay-kwah-*dhoar*) *m* Ecuador
ecuador (ay-kwah-*dhoar*) *m* equator
ecuatoriano (ay-kwah-toa-r^y*ah*-noa)
  m Ecuadorian

eczema (ayk-*thay*-mah) *m* eczema
echar (ay-*chahr*) *v* toss, throw; **~ abajo**
  demolish; **~ al correo** post; **~ a
  perder** *spoil; **~ la culpa** blame;
  echarse lie down
edad (ay-*dhahdh*) *f* age; **mayor de ~** of
  age; **menor de ~** under age
Edad Media (ay-*dhahdh* may-dh^yah)
  Middle Ages
edición (ay-dhee-th^y*oan*) *f* issue,
  edition; **~ de mañana** morning
  edition
edificar (ay-dhee-fee-*kahr*) *v*
  construct
edificio (ay-dhee-*fee*-th^yoa) *m*

construction, building

editor (ay-dhee-*toar*) *m*, **-a** *f* publisher

edredón (ay-dhray-*dhoan*) *m* eiderdown

educación (ay-dhoo-kah-*th*ᵞ*oan*) *f* education

educar (ay-dhoo-*kahr*) *v* educate, *bring up, raise

efectivamente (ay-fayk-tee-bhah-*mayn*-tay) *adv* as a matter of fact, in fact

efectivo (ay-fayk-*tee*-bhoa) *m* cash; ***hacer** ~ cash

efecto (ay-*fayk*-toa) *m* effect

efectuar (ay-fayk-*twahr*) *v* effect; implement

eficacia (ay-fee-*kah*-th*ᵞ*ah) *f* effectiveness; efficacy

eficaz (ay-fee-*kahth*) *adj* effective

eficiente (ay-fee-*th*ᵞ*ayn*-tay) *adj* efficient

egipcio (ay-*kheep*-th*ᵞ*oa) *adj* Egyptian; *m* Egyptian

Egipto (ay-*kheep*-toa) *m* Egypt

egoísmo (ay-goa-*eez*-moa) *m* ego(t)ism, selfishness

egoísta (ay-goa-*eess*-tah) *adj* ego(t)istic, selfish

eje (*ay*-khay) *m* axle; axis; main point

ejecución (ay-khay-koo-th*ᵞ*oan) *f* execution

ejecutar (ay-khay-koo-*tahr*) *v* perform, execute

ejecutivo (ay-khay-koo-*tee*-bhoa) *adj* executive; *m*, **-a** *f* executive

ejemplar (ay-khaym-*plahr*) *m* copy

ejemplo (ay-*khaym*-ploa) *m* instance, example; **por** ~ for instance, for example

ejercer (ay-khayr-*thayr*) *v* exercise; to practice; to manage

ejercicio (ay-khayr-*thee*-th*ᵞ*oa) *m* exercise

ejercitar (ay-khayr-thee-*tahr*) *v* exercise

ejército (ay-*khayr*-thee-toa) *m* army

el (ayl) *art* (f la; pl los, las) the *art*

él (ayl) *pron* he

elaborar (ay-lah-boa-*rahr*) *v* elaborate

elasticidad (ay-lahss-tee-thee-*dhahdh*) *f* elasticity

elástico (ay-*lahss*-tee-koa) *adj* elastic; *m* rubber band

elección (ay-layk-th*ᵞ*oan) *f* choice, pick, selection; election

electricidad (ay-layk-tree-thee-*dhahdh*) *f* electricity

electricista (ay-layk-tree-*theess*-tah) *m/f* electrician

eléctrico (ay-*layk*-tree-koa) *adj* electric

electrónico (ay-layk-*troa*-nee-koa) *adj* electronic

elefante (ay-lay-*fahn*-tay) *m* elephant

elegancia (ay-lay-*gahn*-th*ᵞ*ah) *f* elegance

elegante (ay-lay-*gahn*-tay) *adj* elegant, stylish

***elegir** (ay-lay-*kheer*) *v* elect, select

elemental (ay-lay-mayn-*tahl*) *adj* primary

elemento (ay-lay-*mayn*-toa) *m* element

elevador (ay-lay-bhah-*dhoar*) *m*Me lift; elevator *Am*

elevar (ay-lay-*bhahr*) *v* elevate

eliminar (ay-lee-mee-*nahr*) *v* eliminate

elogio (ay-*loa*-kh*ᵞ*oa) *m* praise, glory

ella (*ay*-l*ᵞ*ah) *pron* she

ello (*ay*-l*ᵞ*oa) *pron* it

ellos (*ay*-l*ᵞ*oass) *pron* they

emancipación (ay-mahn-thee-pah-th*ᵞ*oan) *f* emancipation

embajada (aym-bah-*khah*-dhah) *f* embassy

embajador (aym-bah-khah-*dhoar*) *m* ambassador

embalaje (aym-bah-*lah*-khay) *m* packing

embalar (aym-bah-*lahr*) *v* pack

embalse (aym-*bahl*-say) *m* reservoir

embarazada (aym-bah-rah-*thah*-dhah) *adj* pregnant

embarazoso (aym-bah-rah-*thoa*-soa) *adj* embarrassing, awkward; puzzling

embarcación (aym-bahr-kah-th^y*oan*) *f* vessel; embarkation

embarcar (aym-bahr-*kahr*) *v* embark

embargar (aym-bahr-*gahr*) *v* confiscate

embargo (aym-*bahr*-goa) *m* embargo; **sin ~** yet, however, though, still

emblema (aym-*blay*-mah) *m* emblem

embotellamiento (aym-boa-tay-l^{y}ah-m^y*ayn*-toa) *m* traffic jam

embrague (aym-*brah*-gay) *m* clutch

embriagado (aym-br^{y}ah-*gah*-dhoa) *adj* intoxicated

embrollar (aym-broa-*l^{y}ahr*) *v* muddle

embrollo (aym-broa-*l^{y}oa*) *m* muddle

embromar (aym-broa-*mahr*) *v* tease, kid

embudo (aym-*boo*-dhoa) *m* funnel

emergencia (ay-mayr-*khayn*-th^{y}ah) *f* emergency

emigración (ay-mee-*grah*-th^{y}oan) *f* emigration

emigrante (ay-mee-*grahn*-tay) *m* emigrant

emigrar (ay-mee-*grahr*) *v* emigrate

eminente (ay-mee-*nayn*-tay) *adj* eminent; outstanding

emisión (ay-mee-*s^{y}oan*) *f* issue

emisor (ay-mee-*soar*) *m* transmitter

emitir (ay-mee-*teer*) *v* *broadcast; utter

emoción (ay-moa-*th^{y}oan*) *f* emotion

empalme (aym-*pahl*-may) *m* junction

empanada (aym-pah-*nah*-dah) *f* pie

empapar (aym-pah-*pahr*) *v* soak

empaquetar (aym-pah-kay-*tahr*) *v* pack up

emparedado (aym-pah-ray-*dhah*-dhoa) *m* sandwich

emparentado (aym-pah-rayn-*tah*-dhoa) *adj* related

empaste (aym-*pahss*-tay) *m* filling

empeñar (aym-pay-*ñahr*) *v* pawn

empeño (aym-*pay*-ñoa) *m* pawn; determination

emperador (aym-pay-rah-*dhoar*) *m* emperor

emperatriz (aym-pay-rah-*treeth*) *f* empress

***empezar** (aym-pay-*thahr*) *v* *begin, start

empleado (aym-play-*ah*-dhoa) *m*, **-a** *f* employee; **~ de oficina** clerk

emplear (aym-play-*ahr*) *v* employ; engage

empleo (aym-*play*-oa) *m* job, employment

emprender (aym-prayn-*dayr*) *v* *undertake

empresa (aym-*pray*-sah) *f* undertaking, enterprise; concern, business

empujar (aym-poo-*khahr*) *v* push; press

empujón (aym-poo-*khoan*) *m* push

en (ayn) *prep* at, in; inside, to

enamorado (ay-nah-moa-*rah*-dhoa) *adj* in love

enamorarse (aynah-moa-*rahr*-say) *v* *fall in love

encaje (ayn-kah-khay-) *m* lace

enano (ay-*nah*-noa) *m* dwarf

encantado (ayng-kahn-*tah*-dhoa) *adj* delighted; pleased

encantador (ayng-kahn-tah-*dhoar*) *adj* glamorous; charming, enchanting

encantar (ayng-kahn-*tahr*) *v* delight; bewitch

encanto (ayng-*kahn*-toa) *m* glamour, charm; spell

encarcelamiento (ayng-kahr-thay-lah-m^yayn-toa) *m* imprisonment

encarcelar (ayng-kahr-thay-*lahr*) *v* imprison

encargarse de (ayng-kahr-*gahr*-say) *take over, *take charge of

encargo (ayng-*kahr*-goa) *m* assignment

encariñado con (ayng-kah-ree-*ñah*-dhoa koan) attached to

encendedor (ayn-thayn-day-*dhoar*) *m* cigarette lighter

*encender** (ayn-thayn-*dayr*) *v* *light; turn on, switch on

encendido (ayn-thayn-*dee*-dhoa) *m* ignition

*encerrar** (ayn-thay-*rrahr*) *v* *shut in; encircle

encía (ayn-*thee*-ah) *f* gum

enciclopedia (ayn-thee-kloa-*pay*-dh^yah) *f* encyclop(a)edia

encima (ayn-*thee*-mah) *adv* above; over; ~ **de** over, above, on top of

encinta (ayn-*theen*-tah) *adj* pregnant

encogerse (ayng-koa-*khayr*-say) *v* *shrink; **no encoge** shrinkproof

*encontrar** (ayng-koan-*trahr*) *v* *come across, *find; *encontrarse con** *meet, encounter, run into

encorvado (ayng-koar-*bhah*-dhoa) *adj* curved

encuentro (ayng-*kwayn*-troa) *m* meeting, encounter

encuesta (ayng-*kwayss*-tah) *f* survey

encurtidos (ayng-koor-*tee*-dhoass) *mpl* pickles *pl*

enchufar (ayn-choo-*fahr*) *v* plug in

enchufe (ayn-*choo*-fay) *m* plug

endosar (ayn-doa-*sahr*) *v* endorse

endulzar (ayn-dool-*thahr*) *v* sweeten

enemigo (ay-nay-*mee*-goa) *m*, **-a** *f* enemy

energía (ay-nayr-*khee*-ah) *f* energy; power; zest; ~ **nuclear** nuclear

energy

enérgico (ay-*nayr*-khee-koa) *adj* energetic

enero (ay-*nay*-roa) January

enfadado (ayn-fah-*dhah*-dhoa) *adj* angry, cross

énfasis (*ayn*-fah-seess) *m* emphasis, stress

enfatizar (ayn-fah-tee-*thahr*) *v* emphasize

enfermedad (ayn-fayr-may-*dhahdh*) *f* disease; ailment, sickness, illness; ~ **venérea** venereal disease

enfermera (ayn-fayr-*may*-rah) *f* nurse

enfermo (ayn-*fayr*-moa) *adj* sick, ill

enfoque (ayn-*foa*-kay) *m* approach

enfrentarse con (ayn-frayn-*tahr*-say) confront; face up to

enfrente de (ayn-*frayn*-tay day) facing, opposite

engañar (ayng-gah-*ñahr*) *v* cheat, deceive; fool

engaño (ayng-*gah*-ñoa) *m* deceit

engrasar (ayng-grah-*sahr*) *v* grease

enhorabuena (ayn-oa-rah-*bway*-nah) *f* congratulations *pl*; **dar la ~** congratulate

enigma (ay-*neeg*-mah) *m* mystery, enigma, puzzle

enjuagar (ayng-khwah-*gahr*) *v* rinse

enjugar (ayng-khoo-*gahr*) *v* wipe

enlace (ayn-*lah*-thay) *m* connection, link

enlazar (ayn-lah-*thahr*) *v* link

enojado (ay-noa-*khah*-doa) *adj* angry, cross

enojo (ay-*noa*-khoa) *m* anger

enorme (ay-*noar*-may) *adj* huge, enormous, immense

enrollar (ayn-roa-*l^yahr*) *v* *wind

ensaimada (ayn-say-*mah*-dhah) *f* pastry in the form of a spiral

ensalada (ayn-sah-*lah*-dhah) *f* salad

ensaladilla (ayn-sah-lah-*dee*-l^yah) *f*:

~ rusa Russian salad

ensamblar (ayn-sahm-*blahr*) v join

ensayar (ayn-sah-^y*ahr*) v test; rehearse; **ensayarse** v practise

ensayo (ayn-*sah*-^yoa) m test; rehearsal; essay

ensenada (ayn-say-*nah*-dhah) f inlet, creek

enseñanza (ayn-say-*ñahn*-thah) f tuition; teachings pl

enseñar (ayn-say-*ñahr*) v *teach; *show

ensueño (ayn-*sway*-ñoa) m day-dream

entallar (ayn-tah-*l^yahr*) v carve

*entender (ayn-tayn-*dayr*) v conceive; *take

entendimiento (ayn-tayn-dee-*m^yayn*-toa) m insight; conception

enteramente (ayn-tay-rah-*mayn*-tay) adv completely, entirely, quite

enterar (ayn-tay-*rahr*) v inform; **~se de** find out about

entero (ayn-*tay*-roa) adj whole, entire

*enterrar (ayn-tay-*rrahr*) v bury

entierro (ayn-*t^yay*-rroa) m burial

entonces (ayn-*toan*-thayss) adv then; **desde ~** since then

entrada (ayn-*trah*-dhah) f entry, entrance, way in; admission; appearance; entrance-fee; **prohibida la ~** no admittance

entrañas (ayn-*trah*-ñahss) fpl insides

entrar (ayn-*trahr*) v *go in, enter

entre (*ayn*-tray) prep among, amid; between

entreacto (ayn-tray-*ahk*-toa) m intermission

entrega (ayn-*tray*-gah) f delivery

entregar (ayn-tray-*gahr*) v *give; deliver; commit; extradite

entremeses (ayn-tray-*may*-sayss) mpl hors-d'œuvre

entrenador (ayn-tray-nah-*dhoar*) m,

-a f trainer, coach

entrenamiento (ayn-tray-nah-*m^yayn*-toa) m training

entrenar (ayn-tray-*nahr*) v train, drill

entresuelo (ayn-tray-*sway*-loa) m mezzanine

entretanto (ayn-tray-*tahn*-toa) adv meanwhile, in the meantime

*entretener (ayn-tray-tay-*nayr*) v amuse, entertain

entretenido (ayn-tray-tay-*nee*-dhoa) adj entertaining

entretenimiento (ayn-tray-tay-nee-*m^yayn*-toa) m amusement, entertainment

entrevista (ayn-tray-*bheess*-tah) f interview

entrometido (ayn-troa-may-*tee*-dhoa) adj interfering; nosy

entusiasmo (ayn-too-*s^yahz*-moa) m enthusiasm

entusiasta (ayn-too-*s^yahss*-tah) adj enthusiastic, keen

envase (aym-*bah*-say) m container; (empty) bottle; **~ de cartón** carton; **~ no retornable** nonreturnable bottle

envenenar (aym-bay-nay-*nahr*) v poison

enviado (aym-*b^yah*-dhoa) m envoy

enviar (aym-*b^yahr*) v dispatch, *send

envidia (aym-*bee*-dh^yah) f envy

envidiar (aym-bee-*dh^yahr*) v envy, grudge

envidioso (aym-bee-*dh^yoa*-soa) adj envious

envío (aym-*bee*-oa) m expedition, consignment

*envolver (aym-boal-*bhayr*) v wrap; involve

epidemia (ay-pee-*dhay*-m^yah) f epidemic

epilepsia (ay-pee-*layp*-s^yah) f epilepsy

epílogo (ay-*pee*-loa-goa) m epilogue

episodio (ay-pee-*soa*-dheoa) m

episode

época (*ay*-poa-kah) *f* period

equilibrio (ay-kee-*lee*-bhr^{y}oa) *m* balance

equipaje (ay-kee-*pah*-khay) *m* baggage, luggage; ~ **de mano** hand luggage; hand baggage *Am*; **furgón de equipajes** luggage van

equipar (ay-kee-*pahr*) *v* equip

equipo (ay-*kee*-poa) *m* outfit, equipment; gang; team; crew; soccer team

equitación (ay-kee-tah-*th^{y}oan*) *f* riding

equivalente (ay-kee-bhah-*layn*-tay) *adj* equivalent

equivocación (ay-kee-bhoa-kah-*th^{y}oan*) *f* misunderstanding, mistake

equivocado (ay-kee-bhoa-*kah*-dhoa) *adj* mistaken

equivocarse (ay-kee-bhoa-*kahr*-say) *v* *be mistaken

equívoco (ay-*kee*-bhoa-koa) *adj* ambiguous

era (*ay*-rah) *f* era

erguido (ayr-*gee*-dhoa) *adj* erect

erigir (ay-ree-*kheer*) *v* erect

erizo (ay-*ree*-thoa) *m* hedgehog; ~ **de mar** sea-urchin

***errar** (ay-*rrahr*) *v* err; wander

erróneo (ay-*rroa*-nay-oa) *adj* wrong

error (ay-*rroar*) *m* mistake, error

erudito (ay-roo-*dhee*-toa) *m*, **-a** *f* scholar

esbelto (ayz-*bhayl*-toa) *adj* slim, slender

escala (ayss-*kah*-lah) *f* scale; ~ **de incendios** fire escape; ~ **musical** scale

escalar (ayss-kah-*lahr*) *v* ascend

escalera (ayss-kah-*lay*-rah) *f* stairs *pl*, staircase; ~ **de mano** ladder; ~ **móvil** escalator

escalofrío (ayss-kah-loa-*free*-oa) *m*

chill, shiver

escalope (ayss-kah-*loa*-pay) *m* escalope

escama (ayss-*kah*-mah) *f* scale

escándalo (ayss-*kahn*-dah-loa) *m* scandal; offence, offense *Am*

Escandinavia (ayss-kahn-dee-*nah*-bh^{y}ah) *f* Scandinavia

escandinavo (ayss-kahn-dee-*nah*-bhoa) *adj* Scandinavian; *m* Scandinavian

escapar (ayss-kah-*pahr*) *v* escape

escaparate (ayss-kah-pah-*rah*-tay) *m* shopwindow

escape (ayss-*kah*-pay) *m* exhaust; **gases de ~** exhaust gases

escarabajo (ayss-kah-rah-*bhah*-khoa) *m* beetle, bug

escarcha (ayss-*kahr*-chah) *f* frost

escarnio (ayss-*kahr*-n^{y}oa) *m* scorn

escasez (ayss-kah-*sayth*) *f* scarcity, shortage

escaso (ayss-*kah*-soa) *adj* scarce; minor

escena (ay-*thay*-nah) *f* scene; setting

escenario (ayss-thay-*nah*-r^{y}oa) *m* stage

esclavo (ayss-*klah*-bhoa) *m* slave

esclusa (ayss-*kloo*-sah) *f* lock

escoba (ayss-*koa*-bhah) *f* broom

escobilla (ayss-koa-*bee*-l^{y}ah) *f* small brush; wiper blade

escocés (ayss-koa-*thayss*) *adj* Scottish, Scotch; *m* Scot

Escocia (ayss-koa-th^{y}ah) *f* Scotland

escoger (ayss-koa-*khayr*) *v* *choose, pick

escolta (ayss-*koal*-tah) *f* escort

escoltar (ayss-koal-*tahr*) *v* escort

escombro (ayss-*koam*-broa) *m* mackerel

esconder (ayss-koan-*dayr*) *v* *hide

escribano (ayss-kree-*bhah*-noa) *m* clerk

escribir (ayss-kree-*bheer*) *v* *write; **~ a máquina** type; **papel de ~** notepaper; **por escrito** written, in writing

escrito (ayss-*kree*-toa) *m* writing

escritor (ayss-kree-*toar*) *m* writer

escritorio (ayss-kree-*toa*-rʸoa) *m* desk, bureau

escritura (ayss-kree-*too*-rah) *f* handwriting

escrupuloso (ayss-kroo-poo-*loa*-soa) *adj* careful

escuchar (ayss-koo-*chahr*) *v* listen; **~ a escondidas** eavesdrop

escuela (ayss-*kway*-lah) *f* school; **director de ~** head teacher, headmaster; **~ secundaria** secondary school

escultor (ayss-kool-*toar*) *m*, **-a** *f* sculptor

escultura (ayss-kool-*too*-rah) *f* sculpture

escupir (ayss-koo-*peer*) *v* *spit

ese (*ay*-say) *adj* that; **ése** *pron* that

esencia (ay-*sayn*-thʸah) *f* essence

esencial (ay-sayn-*thʸahl*) *adj* essential; vital

esfera (ayss-*fay*-rah) *f* sphere; atmosphere

*esforzarse (ayss-foar-*thahr*-say) *v* try, bother

esfuerzo (ayss-*fwayr*-thoa) *m* effort; strain; stress

eslabón (ayz-lah-*bhoan*) *m* link

esmaltar (ayz-mahl-*tahr*) *v* glaze

esmalte (ayz-*mahl*-tay) *m* enamel

esmeralda (ayz-may-*rahl*-dah) *f* emerald

esnórquel (ayz-*noar*-kayl) *m* snorkel

eso (*ay*-soa) *pron* that

espaciar (ayss-pah-*thʸahr*) *v* space

espacio (ayss-*pah*-thʸoa) *m* room; space

espacioso (ayss-pah-*thʸoa*-soa) *adj* spacious, roomy, large

espada (ayss-*pah*-dah) *f* sword

espalda (ayss-*pahl*-dah) *f* back; **dolor de ~** backache

espantado (ayss-pahn-*tah*-dhoa) *adj* frightened

espantar (ayss-pahn-*tahr*) *v* frighten

espanto (ayss-*pahn*-toa) *m* fright; horror

espantoso (ayss-pahn-*toa*-soa) *adj* dreadful

España (ayss-*pah*-ñah) *f* Spain

español (ayss-pah-*ñoal*) *adj* Spanish; *m*, **-a** *f* Spaniard; **los Españoles** the Spanish

esparadrapo (ayss-pah-rah-*dhrah*-poa) *m* adhesive tape, plaster

esparcir (ayss-pahr-*theer*) *v* scatter, *shed

espárrago (ayss-*pah*-rrah-goa) *m* asparagus

especia (ayss-*pay*-thʸah) *f* spice

especial (ayss-pay-*thʸahl*) *adj* special; peculiar, particular

especialidad (ayss-pay-thʸah-lee-*dhahdh*) *f* speciality

especialista (ayss-pay-thʸah-*leess*-tah) *m/f* specialist

especializarse (ayss-pay-thʸah-lee-*thahr*-say) *v* specialize; **especializado** skilled

especialmente (ayss-pay-thʸahl-*mayn*-tay) *adv* especially

especie (ayss-*paythʸay*) *f* species, breed

específico (ayss-pay-*thee*-fee-koa) *adj* specific

espécimen (ayss-*pay*-thee-mayn) *m* specimen

espectáculo (ayss-payk-*tah*-koo-loa) *m* spectacle, show; **~ de variedades** floor show

espectador (ayss-payk-tah-*dhoar*) *m* spectator

espectro (ayss-*payk*-troa) *m* ghost; spectrum

especular (ayss-pay-koo-*lahr*) *v* speculate

espejo (ayss-*pay*-khoa) *m* mirror, looking-glass

espera (ayss-*pay*-rah) *f* waiting, wait

esperanza (ayss-pay-*rahn*-thah) *f* hope; expectation

esperar (ayss-pay-*rahr*) *v* hope; wait; expect, await

espesar (ayss-pay-*sahr*) *v* thicken

espeso (ayss-*pay*-soa) *adj* thick

espesor (ayss-pay-*soar*) *m* thickness

espía (ayss-*pee*-ah) *m* spy

espiar (ayss-p*ʸahr*) *v* peep

espina (ayss-*pee*-nah) *f* thorn; fishbone; ~ **dorsal** backbone

espinacas (ayss-pee-*nah*-kahss) *fpl* spinach

espinazo (ayss-pee-*nah*-thoa) *m* spine

espirar (ayss-pee-*rahr*) *v* expire

espíritu (ayss-*pee*-ree-too) *m* spirit; ghost

espiritual (ayss-pee-ree-*twahl*) *adj* spiritual

espléndido (ayss-*playn*-dee-dhoa) *adj* splendid; glorious, enchanting, magnificent

esplendor (ayss-playn-*doar*) *m* splendo(u)r

esponja (ayss-*poang*-khah) *f* sponge

esposa (ayss-*poa*-sah) *f* wife; **esposas** *fpl* handcuffs *pl*

esposo (ayss-*poa*-soa) *m* husband

espuma (ayss-*poo*-mah) *f* froth, foam, lather

espumante (ayss-poo-*mahn*-tay) *adj* sparkling

espumar (ayss-poo-*mahr*) *v* foam

espumoso (ayss-poo-*moa*-ssoa) *adj* frothy, foamy; sparkling

esputo (ayss-*poo*-toa) *m* spit

esqueleto (ayss-kay-*lay*-toa) *m* skeleton

esquema (ayss-*kay*-mah) *m* diagram; scheme

esquí (ayss-*kee*) *m* ski; skiing; ~ **acuático** water ski; **salto de ~** ski jump

esquiador (ayss-k*ʸ*ah-*dhoar*) *m* skier

esquiar (ayss-k*ʸahr*) *v* ski

esquina (ayss-*kee*-nah) *f* corner

esquivo (ayss-*kee*-bhoa) *adj* shy

estable (ayss-*tah*-bhlay) *adj* permanent, stable

*establecer (ayss-tah-bhlay-*thayr*) *v* establish

establo (ayss-*tah*-bhloa) *m* stable

estación (ayss-tah-th*ʸoan*) *f* season; station; depot *Am*; ~ **central** central station; ~ **de servicio** filling station; ~ **terminal** terminal

estacionamiento (ayss-tah-th*ʸ*oa-nah-*m*ʸ*ayn*-toa) *m* parking lot *Am*; **derechos de ~** parking fee

estacionar (ayss-tah-th*ʸ*oa-*nahr*) *v* park; **prohibido estacionarse** no parking

estadio (ayss-*tah*-dh*ʸ*oa) *m* stadium

estadística (ayss-tah-*dheess*-tee-kah) *f* statistics *pl*

Estado (ayss-*tah*-doa) *m* state

estado (ayss-*tah*-dhoa) *m* state, condition

Estados Unidos (ayss-*tah*-dhoass oo-*nee*-dhoass) the States, United States

estafa (ayss-*tah*-fah) *f* swindle

estafador (ayss-tah-fah-*dhoar*) *m*, -**a** *f* swindler

estafar (ayss-tah-*fahr*) *v* cheat, swindle

estallar (ayss-tah-*lʸahr*) *v* explode

estampa (ayss-*tahm*-pah) *f* engraving

estampilla (ayss-tahm-*pee*-l*ʸ*ah) *fMe* stamp

estancia (ayss-*tahn*-th*ʸ*ah) *f* stay

estanco (ayss-*tahng*-koa) *m* cigar

shop, tobacconist's

estanque (ayss-*tahng*-kay) *m* pond

estanquero (ayss-tahng-*kay*-roa) *m* tobacconist

estante (ayss-*tahn*-tay) *m* shelf

estaño (ayss-*tah*-ñoa) *m* tin; pewter

*estar (ayss-*tahr*) *v* *be

estatua (ayss-*tah*-twah) *f* statue

estatura (ayss-tah-*too*-rah) *f* figure

este[1] (*ayss*-tay) *m* east

este[2] (*ayss*-tay) *adj* this; **éste** *pron* this

estera (ayss-*tay*-rah) *f* mat

estéril (ayss-*tay*-reel) *adj* sterile

esterilizar (ayss-tay-ree-lee-*thahr*) *v* sterilize

estético (ayss-*tay*-tee-koa) *adj* aesthetic

estiércol (ayss-*tyayr*-koal) *m* dung

estilo (ayss-*tee*-loa) *m* style

estilográfica (ayss-tee-loa-*grah*-fee-kah) *f* fountain pen

estima (ayss-*tee*-mah) *f* esteem

estimación (ayss-tee-mah-*th*^y*oan*) *f* respect; estimate

estimar (ayss-tee-*mahr*) *v* esteem; estimate

estimulante (ayss-tee-moo-*lahn*-tay) *m* stimulant

estimular (ayss-tee-moo-*lahr*) *v* stimulate; urge

estímulo (ayss-*tee*-moo-loa) *m* impulse

estipulación (ayss-tee-poo-lah-*th*^y*oan*) *f* stipulation

estirar (ayss-tee-*rahr*) *v* stretch

estirón (ayss-tee-*roan*) *m* tug

esto (*ayss*-toa) *adj* this

estola (ayss-*toa*-lah) *f* stole

estómago (ayss-*toa*-mah-goa) *m* stomach; **dolor de ~** stomachache

estorbar (ayss-toar-*bhahr*) *v* disturb, embarrass

estornino (ayss-toar-*nee*-noa) *m* starling

estornudar (ayss-toar-noo-*dhahr*) *v* sneeze

estrangular (ayss-trahng-goo-*lahr*) *v* choke, strangle

estrato (ayss-*trah*-toa) *m* layer

estrechar (ayss-tray-*chahr*) *v* tighten

estrecho (ayss-*tray*-choa) *adj* narrow; tight

estrella (ayss-*tray*-l^yah) *f* star

estremecimiento (ayss-tray-may-thee-*m*^y*ayn*-toa) *m* shudder

estreñido (ayss-tray-*ñee*-dhoa) *adj* constipated

estreñimiento (ayss-tray-ñee-*m*^y*ayn*-toa) *m* constipation

estrés (ay-*strayss*) *m* stress

estribor (ayss-tree-*bhoar*) *m* starboard

estricto (ayss-*treek*-toa) *adj* strict

estrofa (ayss-*troa*-fah) *f* stanza

estropeado (ayss-troa-pay-*ah*-dhoa) *adj* broken; crippled

estropear (ayss-troa-pay-*ahr*) *v* mess up

estructura (ayss-trook-*too*-rah) *f* structure; fabric

estuche (ayss-*too*-chay) *m* case

estudiante (ayss-too-*dh*^y*ahn*-tay) *m* student

estudiar (ayss-too-*dh*^y*ahr*) *v* study

estudio (ayss-*too*-dh^yoa) *m* study

estufa (ayss-*too*-fah) *f* stove; **~ de gas** gas stove

estupendo (ayss-too-*payn*-doa) *adj* wonderful

estúpido (ayss-*too*-pee-dhoa) *adj* stupid; dumb

etapa (ay-*tah*-pah) *f* stage

etcétera (ayt-*thay*-tay-rah) and so on, etcetera

eternidad (ay-tayr-nee-*dhahdh*) *f* eternity

eterno (ay-*tayr*-noa) *adj* eternal

etíope (ay-*tee*-oa-pay) *adj* Ethiopian;

m Ethiopian

Etiopía (ay-t^yoa-p^yah) *f* Ethiopia

etiqueta (ay-tee-*kay*-tah) *f* tag

Europa (ay^{oo}-*roa*-pah) *f* Europe

europeo (ay^{oo}-roa-*pay*-oa) *adj*
European; *m* European

evacuar (ay-bhah-*kwahr*) *v* evacuate

evaluar (ay-bhah-*lwahr*) *v* evaluate,
estimate

evaporar (ay-bhah-poa-*rahr*) *v*
evaporate

evasión (ay-bhayn-*s^yoan*) *f* escape

eventual (ay-bhayn-*twahl*) *adj*
eventual; possible

evidente (ay-bhee-*dhayn*-tay) *adj*
evident; self-evident

evidentemente (ay-bhee-dhayn-tay-
mayn-tay) *adv* apparently

evitar (ay-bhee-*tahr*) *v* avoid

evolución (ay-bhoa-loo-*th^yoan*) *f*
evolution

exactamente (ayk-sahk-tah-*mayn*-
tay) *adv* exactly

exactitud (ayk-sahk-tee-*toodh*) *f*
correctness

exacto (ayk-*sahk*-toa) *adj* precise,
exact, accurate

exagerar (ayk-sah-khay-*rahr*) *v*
exaggerate

examen (ayk-*sah*-mayn) *m*
examination

examinar (ayk-sah-mee-*nahr*) *v*
examine

excavación (ayks-kah-bhah-*th^yoan*) *f*
excavation

exceder (ayk-thay-*dhayr*) *v* exceed

excelencia (ayk-thay-*layn*-th^yah) *f*
excellence

excelente (ayk-thay-*layn*-tay) *adj*
excellent, fine

excéntrico (ayk-*thayn*-tree-koa) *adj*
eccentric

excepción (ayk-thayp-*th^yoan*) *f*
exception

excepcional (ayk-thayp-th^yoa-*nahl*)
adj exceptional

excepto (ayk-*thayp*-toa) *prep* except

excesivo (ayk-thay-*see*-bhoa) *adj*
excessive

exceso (ayk-*thay*-soa) *m* excess; ~ **de
velocidad** speeding

excitación (ayk-thee-tah-*th^yoan*) *f*
excitement

excitante (ayk-thee-*tahn*-tay) *adj*
exciting

excitar (ayk-thee-*tahr*) *v* excite

exclamación (ayks-klah-mah-*th^yoan*)
f exclamation

exclamar (ayks-klah-*mahr*) *v* exclaim

*excluir (ayks-*klweer*) *v* exclude

exclusivamente (ayks-kloo-see-
bhah-*mayn*-tay) *adv* exclusively,
solely

exclusivo (ayks-kloo-*see*-bhoa) *adj*
exclusive

excursión (ayks-koor-*s^yoan*) *f* trip,
excursion

excusa (ayks-*koo*-sah) *f* apology,
excuse

excusar (ayks-koo-*sahr*) *v* excuse

exento (ayk-*sayn*-toa) *adj* exempt; ~
de impuestos duty-free

exhausto (ayk-*souss*-toa) *adj*
exhausted

exhibir (ayk-see-*bheer*) *v* exhibit,
display

exigencia (ayk-see-*khayn*-th^yah) *f*
demand; requirement

exigente (ayk-see-*khayn*-tay) *adj*
demanding; particular

exigir (ayk-see-*kheer*) *v* demand

exiliado (ayk-see-l^y*ah*-dhoa) *m* exile

exilio (ayk-*see*-l^yoa) *m* exile

eximir (ayk-see-*meer*) *v* exempt

existencia (ayk-seess-*tayn*-th^yah) *f*
existence; **existencias** *fpl* supply,
stock; ***tener en ~** stock

existir (ayk-seess-*teer*) *v* exist

éxito (*ayk*-see-toa) *m* success, luck; hit; **de ~** successful; ***tener ~** manage, succeed

exorbitante (ayk-soar-bhee-*tahn*-tay) *adj* prohibitive

exótico (ayk-*soa*-tee-koa) *adj* exotic

expansión (ayks-pahn-s^y*oan*) *f* expansion

expedición (ayks-pay-dhee-th^y*oan*) *f* expedition; shipment

expediente (ayks-pay-dh^y*ayn*-tay) *m* file; means; record

expedir (ayks-pay-*deer*) *v* issue; send, dispatch

experiencia (ayks-pay-r^y*ayn*-th^{y}ah) *f* experience

experimentar (ayks-pay-ree-mayn-*tahr*) *v* experiment; experience

experimentado experienced

experimento (ayks-pay-ree-*mayn*-toa) *m* experiment

experto (ayks-*payr*-toa) *m* expert

expirar (ayks-pee-*rahr*) *v* expire

explicable (ayks-plee-*kah*-bhlay) *adj* explainable

explicación (ayks-plee-kah-th^y*oan*) *f* explanation

explicar (ayks-plee-*kahr*) *v* explain; account for

explícito (ayks-*plee*-thee-toa) *adj* express, explicit

explorador (ayks-ploa-rah-*dhoar*) *m* explorer; scout; boy scout

exploradora (ayks-ploa-rah-*dhoa*-rah) *f* girl guide; scout *Am*

explorar (ayks-ploa-*rahr*) *v* explore

explosión (ayks-ploa-s^y*oan*) *f* explosion, blast; outbreak

explosivo (ayks-ploa-*see*-bhoa) *adj* explosive; *m* explosive

explotar (ayks-ploa-*tahr*) *v* exploit

*exponer (ayks-poa-*nayr*) *v* exhibit

exportación (ayks-poar-tah-th^y*oan*) *f* exportation, export

exportar (ayks-poar-*tahr*) *v* export

exposición (ayks-poa-see-th^y*oan*) *f* exposition, exhibition, display, show; exposure; **~ de arte** art exhibition

exposímetro (ayks-poa-*see*-may-troa) *m* exposure meter

expresar (ayks-pray-*sahr*) *v* express

expresión (ayks-pray-s^y*oan*) *f* expression

expresivo (ayks-pray-*see*-bhoa) *adj* expressive

expreso (ayks-*pray*-soa) *adj* explicit; express; **por ~** special delivery

expulsar (ayks-pool-*sahr*) *v* expel; eject

exquisito (ayks-kee-*see*-toa) *adj* exquisite; delicious

éxtasis (*ayks*-tah-seess) *m* ecstasy

*extender (ayks-tayn-*dayr*) *v* *spread, expand

extenso (ayks-*tayn*-soa) *adj* comprehensive, extensive

extenuar (ayks-tay-*nwahr*) *v* exhaust; weaken

exterior (ayks-tay-r^y*oar*) *adj* external, exterior; *m* exterior, outside

externo (ayks-*tayr*-noa) *adj* outward

extinguir (ayks-teeng-*geer*) *v* extinguish

extintor (ayks-teen-*toar*) *m* fire-extinguisher

extorsión (ayks-toar-s^y*oan*) *f* extortion

extorsionar (ayks-toar-s^{y}oa-*nahr*) *v* extort

extra (*ayks*-trah) *adj* extra

extracto (ayks-*trahk*-toa) *m* excerpt

*extraer (ayks-trah-*ayr*) *v* extract

extranjero (ayks-trahng-*khay*-roa) *adj* alien, foreign; *m*, **-a** *f* alien, foreigner; stranger; **en el ~** abroad

extrañar (ayks-trah-*ñahr*) *v* amaze, surprise; banish

extraño (ayks-*trah*-ñoa) *adj* strange; peculiar, queer, funny, foreign

extraoficial (ayks-trah-oa-fee-*th*ᵞ*ahl*) *adj* unofficial

extraordinario (ayks-trah-oar-dhee-*nah*-rᵞoa) *adj* extraordinary, exceptional

extravagante (ayks-trah-bhah-*gahn*-tay) *adj* extravagant

extraviar (ayks-trah-*bh*ᵞ*ahr*) *v* *mislay

extremo (ayks-*tray*-moa) *adj* extreme; very, utmost; *m* extreme; end

exuberante (ayk-soo-bhay-*rahn*-tay) *adj* exuberant

F

fábrica (*fah*-bhree-kah) *f* factory; works *pl*, mill; ~ **de gas** gasworks

fabricante (fah-bhree-*kahn*-tay) *m* manufacturer

fabricar (fah-bhree-*kahr*) *v* manufacture

fábula (*fah*-bhoo-lah) *f* fable

fácil (*fah*-theel) *adj* easy

facilidad (fah-thee-lee-*dhahdh*) *f* ease; facility

facilitar (fah-thee-lee-*tahr*) *v* facilitate

factor (fahk-*toar*) *m* factor

factura (fahk-*too*-rah) *f* invoice

facturar (fahk-too-*rahr*) *v* invoice; bill

facultad (fah-kool-*tahdh*) *f* faculty

fachada (fah-*chah*-dhah) *f* façade

faisán (figh-*sahn*) *m* pheasant

falda (*fahl*-dah) *f* skirt

fallo (*fah*-lᵞoa) *m* mistake; fault; judg(e)ment; ~ **cardiaco** heart failure

falsificación (fahl-see-fee-kah-*th*ᵞ*oan*) *f* fake

falsificar (fahl-see-fee-*kahr*) *v* forge, counterfeit

falso (*fahl*-soa) *adj* false; untrue

falta (*fahl*-tah) *f* error; want, lack; offence; **sin** ~ without fail

faltar (fahl-*tahr*) *v* fail

fallar (fah-*l*ᵞ*ahr*) *v* fail

*fallecer (fah-lᵞay-*thayr*) *v* die, pass away

fama (*fah*-mah) *f* fame; **de** ~ **mundial**

world-famous; **de mala** ~ notorious

familia (fah-*mee*-lᵞah) *f* family

familiar (fah-mee-*l*ᵞ*ahr*) *adj* familiar

famoso (fah-*moa*-soa) *adj* famous

fanático (fah-*nah*-tee-koa) *adj* fanatical

fantasía (fahn-tah-*see*-ah) *f* fantasy

fantasma (fahn-*tahz*-mah) *m* spook, phantom, ghost

fantástico (fahn-*tahss*-tee-koa) *adj* fantastic

farallón (fah-rah-*l*ᵞ*oan*) *m* cliff, bluff

farmacéutico (fahr-mah-*thay*ᵒᵒ-tee-koa) *m* chemist, pharmacist *Am*

farmacia (fahr-*mah*-thᵞah) *f* chemist's, pharmacy; drugstore *Am*

faro (*fah*-roa) *m* headlight; lighthouse

farol trasero (fah-*roal* trah-*say*-roa) taillight

farsa (*fahr*-sah) *f* farce

fascismo (fah-*theez*-moa) *m* fascism

fascista (fah-*theess*-tah) *adj* fascist; *m* fascist

fase (*fah*-say) *f* stage, phase

fastidiar (fahss-tee-*dh*ᵞ*ahr*) *v* annoy, bother

fastidioso (fahss-tee-*dh*ᵞ*oa*-soa) *adj* annoying, bothersome

fatal (fah-*tahl*) *adj* fatal; mortal

fatigar (fah-tee-*gahr*) *v* tire; **fatigarse** get tired

favor (fah-*bhoar*) *m* favo(u)r; **a** ~ **de**

on behalf of; **por ~** please

favorable (fah-bhoa-*rah*-bhlay) *adj* favo(u)rable

*favorecer (fah-bhoa-ray-*thayr*) *v* favo(u)r

favorecido (fah-bhoa-ray-*thee*-dhoa) *m*, **-a** *f* payee

favorito (fah-bhoa-*ree*-toa) *adj* pet; *m*, **-a** *f* favo(u)rite

fax (fahks) *m* fax; **enviar un ~** send a fax

fe (fay) *f* faith

febrero (fay-*bhray*-roa) February

febril (fay-*bhreel*) *adj* feverish, hectic

fecundo (fay-*koon*-doa) *adj* fertile

fecha (*fay*-chah) *f* date

federación (fay-dhay-rah-*th^y oan*) *f* federation

federal (fay-dhay-*rahl*) *adj* federal

felicidad (fay-lee-thee-*dhahdh*) *f* happiness

felicitación (fay-lee-thee-tah-*th^y oan*) *f* congratulation

felicitar (fay-lee-thee-*tahr*) *v* congratulate

feliz (fay-*leeth*) *adj* happy

femenino (fay-may-*nee*-noa) *adj* feminine; female

fenómeno (fay-*noa*-may-noa) *m* phenomenon

feo (*fay*-oa) *adj* ugly

feria (*fay*-r^y ah) *f* fair

fermentar (fayr-mayn-*tahr*) *v* ferment

feroz (fay-*roath*) *adj* wild

ferretería (fay-rray-tay-ree-ah) *f* hardware store

ferrocarril (fay-rroa-kah-*rreel*) *m* railway; railroad *Am*

fértil (*fayr*-teel) *adj* fertile

fertilidad (fayr-tee-lee-*dhahdh*) *f* fertility

festival (fayss-tee-*bhahl*) *m* festival

festivo (fayss-*tee*-bhoa) *adj* festive

feudal (fay^oo-*dhahl*) *adj* feudal

fiable (f^y *ah*-bhlay) *adj* reliable

fianza (f^y *ahn*-thah) *f* security; bail; deposit

fiasco (f^y *ahss*-koa) *m* failure

fibra (*fee*-bhrah) *f* fibre

ficción (feek-*th^y oan*) *f* fiction

ficha (*fee*-chah) *f* chip, token

fiebre (f^y *ay*-bhray) *f* fever; **~ del heno** hay fever

fiel (f^y ayl) *adj* faithful, true

fieltro (f^y *ayl*-troa) *m* felt

fiero (f^y *ay*-roa) *adj* fierce

fiesta (f^y *ayss*-tah) *f* feast; party; holiday

figura (fee-*goo*-rah) *f* figure

figurarse (fee-goo-*rahr*-say) *v* imagine

fijador (fee-khah-*dhoar*) *m* setting lotion, hair gel, hair spray

fijar (fee-*khahr*) *v* attach; **fijarse en** mind

fijo (*fee*-khoa) *adj* fixed; permanent

fila (*fee*-lah) *f* row, rank

Filipinas (fee-lee-*pee*-nahss) *fpl* Philippines *pl*

filipino (fee-lee-*pee*-noa) *adj* Philippine; *m* Filipino

filmar (feel-*mahr*) *v* film

filme (*feel*-may) *m* film

filosofía (fee-loa-soa-*fee*-ah) *f* philosophy

filósofo (fee-*loa*-soa-foa) *m*, **-a** *f* philosopher

filtrar (feel-*trahr*) *v* strain

filtro (*feel*-troa) *m* filter; **~ de aire** air-filter; **~ del aceite** oil filter

fin (feen) *m* end; aim, purpose; **a ~ de** so that; **al ~** at last

final (fee-*nahl*) *adj* eventual, final; *m* end; **al ~** at last

financiar (fee-nahn-*th^y ahr*) *v* finance

financiero (fee-nahn-*th^y ay*-roa) *adj* financial

finanzas (fee-*nahn*-thahss) *fpl* finances *pl*

finca (*feeng*-kah) *f* country estate; property

fingir (feeng-*kheer*) *v* pretend

finlandés (feen-lahn-*dayss*) *adj* Finnish; *m* Finn

Finlandia (feen-*lahn*-d^{y}ah) *f* Finland

fino (*fee*-noa) *adj* delicate, fine; sheer

firma (*feer*-mah) *f* signature; firm

firmar (feer-*mahr*) *v* sign

firme (*feer*-may) *adj* steady, firm; secure

física (*fee*-see-kah) *f* physics

físico (*fee*-see-koa) *adj* physical; *m* physicist

flaco (*flah*-koa) *adj* thin

flamenco (flah-*mayng*-koa) *m* flamingo

flan (flahn) *m* crème caramel

flauta (*flou*-tah) *f* flute

flecha (*flay*-chah) *f* arrow

flexible (flayk-*see*-bhlay) *adj* flexible; supple, elastic

flojo (*floa*-khoa) *adj* weak

flor (floar) *f* flower

florista (floa-*reess*-tah) *m/f* florist

floristería (floa-reess-tay-*ree*-ah) *f* flower-shop

flota (*floa*-tah) *f* fleet

flotador (floa-tah-*dhoar*) *m* float

flotar (floa-*tahr*) *v* float

fluido (*floo*-ee-dhoa) *adj* fluid; *m* fluid

*fluir (flweer) *v* flow, stream

foca (*foa*-kah) *f* seal

foco (*foa*-koa) *m* focus; spotlight; *mMe* light bulb

folklore (foal-*kloa*-ray) *m* folklore

folleto (foa-l^y*ay*-toa) *m* brochure

fondo (*foan*-doa) *m* background; ground, bottom; *mMe* slip; **fondos** *mpl* fund

fontanero (foan-tah-*nay*-roa) *m* plumber

footing (*foo*-teengh) *m* jogging; **hacer ~** go jogging, jog

forastero (foa-rahss-*tay*-roa) *m*, **-a** *f* foreigner; stranger

forma (*foar*-mah) *f* form, shape

formación (foar-mah-th^y*oan*) *f* formation

formal (foar-*mahl*) *adj* formal

formalidad (foar-mah-lee-*dhahdh*) *f* formality

formar (foar-*mahr*) *v* form, shape; educate

formato (foar-*mah*-toa) *m* size

formidable (foar-mee-*dhah*-bhlay) *adj* huge

fórmula (*foar*-moo-lah) *f* formula

formulario (foar-moo-*lah*-r^{y}oa) *m* form; **~ de matriculación** registration form

forro (*foa*-rroa) *m* lining

fortaleza (foar-tah-*lay*-thah) *f* fortress, fort

fortuna (foar-*too*-nah) *f* fortune; good luck

forúnculo (foa-*roong*-koo-loa) *m* boil

*forzar (foar-*thahr*) *v* force; strain

forzosamente (foar-thoa-sah-*mayn*-tay) *adv* by force

foso (*foa*-soa) *m* moat

foto (*foa*-toa) *f* photo

fotocopia (foa-toa-*koa*-p^{y}ah) *f* photocopy

fotocopiar (foa-toa-koa-*p^{y}ahr*) *v* photocopy

fotografía (foa-toa-grah-*fee*-ah) *f* photograph; photography; **~ de pasaporte** passport photograph

fotografiar (foa-toa-grah-*f^{y}ahr*) *v* photograph

fotógrafo (foa-*toa*-grah-foa) *m* photographer

fracasado (frah-kah-*sah*-dhoa) *adj* unsuccessful

fracaso (frah-*kah*-soa) *m* failure

fracción (frahk-th^y*oan*) *f* fraction

fractura (frahk-*too*-rah) *f* fracture,

break

fracturar (frahk-too-*rahr*) v fracture

frágil (*frah*-kheel) adj fragile

fragmento (frahg-*mayn*-toa) m fragment, piece; extract

frambuesa (frahm-*bway*-sah) f raspberry

francés (frahn-*thayss*) adj French; m Frenchman

Francia (*frahn*-th^yah) f France

franco (*frahng*-koa) adj postage paid, post-paid

francotirador (frahng-koa-tee-rah-*dhoar*) m sniper

franela (frah-*nay*-lah) f flannel

franja (*frahng*-khah) f fringe; trimming

franqueo (frahng-*kay*-oa) m postage

frasco (*frahss*-koa) m flask

frase (*frah*-say) f sentence; phrase

fraternidad (frah-tayr-nee-*dhahdh*) f fraternity

fraude (*frou*-dhay) m fraud

frecuencia (fray-*kwayn*-th^yah) f frequency

frecuentar (fray-kwayn-*tahr*) v associate with

frecuente (fray-*kwayn*-tay) adj frequent

frecuentemente (fray-kwayn-tay-*mayn*-tay) adv frequently, often

***fregar** (fray-*gahr*) v wash up; scrub

***freír** (fray-*eer*) v fry

frenar (fray-*nahr*) v slow down

freno (*fray*-noa) m brake; ~ **de mano** handbrake; ~ **de pie** foot brake

frente (*frayn*-tay) f forehead; m front

fresa (*fray*-sah) f strawberry

fresco (*frayss*-koa) adj fresh; chilly, cool

fricción (freek-*th^yoan*) f friction

frigorífico (free-goa-*ree*-fee-koa) m refrigerator

frío (*free*-oa) adj cold; m cold

frito (*free*-toa) (p freír); adj fried; **fritos** fried food

frontera (froan-*tay*-rah) f frontier, border; boundary

frotar (froa-*tahr*) v rub

fruta (*froo*-tah) f fruit

fruto (*froo*-toa) m fruit, result, consequence

fuego (*fway*-goa) m fire

fuente (*fwayn*-tay) f source, fountain; dish

fuera (*fway*-rah) adv out; off, away; ~ **de** outside, out of; ~ **de lugar** misplaced; ~ **de temporada** off season

fuerte (*fwayr*-tay) adj powerful, strong; mighty; loud

fuerza (*fwayr*-thah) f force; power, might, energy; strength; ~ **de voluntad** will-power; ~ **motriz** driving force; **fuerzas armadas** military force, armed forces

fugarse (foo-*gahr*-say) v run away; escape

fugitivo (foo-khee-*tee*-bhoa) m runaway

fumador (foo-mah-*dhoar*) m smoker; **compartimento para fumadores** smoker

fumar (foo-*mahr*) v smoke; **prohibido** ~ no smoking

función (foon-*th^yoan*) f function

funcionamiento (foon-th^yoa-nah-m^yayn-toa) m working, operation

funcionar (foon-th^yoa-*nahr*) v work, operate

funcionario (foon-th^yoa-nah-r^yoa) m civil servant

funda (*foon*-dah) f case, cover; ~ **de almohada** pillowcase

fundación (foon-dah-*th^yoan*) f foundation

fundamentado (foon-dah-mayn-*tah*-dhoa) adj well-founded

fundamental (foon-dah-mayn-*tahl*) *adj* fundamental, basic

fundamento (foon-dah-*mayn*-toa) *m* basis, base

fundar (foon-*dahr*) *v* found

fundir (foon-*deer*) *v* melt

funerales (foo-nay-*rah*-layss) *mpl* funeral

furgoneta (foor-goa-*nay*-tah) *f* delivery van

furioso (foo-rᵛ*oa*-soa) *adj* furious

furor (foo-*roar*) *m* anger, rage

fusible (foo-*see*-bhlay) *m* fuse

fusil (foo-*seel*) *m* gun

fusión (foo-sᵛ*oan*) *f* merger

fútbol (*foot*-bhoal) *m* soccer; football

futuro (foo-*too*-roa) *adj* future

G

gabinete (gah-bhee-*nay*-tay) *m* cabinet

gafas (*gah*-fahss) *fpl* glasses, spectacles *pl*; ~ **de sol** sunglasses *pl*; ~ **submarinas** goggles *pl*

gaitero (gigh-*tay*-roa) *adj* gaudy

galería (gah-lay-*ree*-ah) *f* gallery; ~ **de arte** art gallery

galgo (*gahl*-goa) *m* greyhound

galope (gah-*loa*-pay) *m* gallop

galleta (gah-lᵛ*ay*-tah) *f* biscuit, cookie *Am*

gallina (gah-lᵛ*ee*-nah) *f* hen

gallo (*gah*-lᵛoa) *m* cock; ~ **de bosque** grouse

gamba (*gahm*-bah) *f* prawn

gamuza (gah-*moo*-thah) *f* suede

gana (*gah*-nah) *f* desire; appetite

ganador (gah-nah-*dhoar*) *adj* winning

ganancia (gah-*nahn*-thᵛah) *f* gain, profit

ganar (gah-*nahr*) *v* gain; *make, earn

ganas (*gah*-nahss) *fpl* desire; **tener ~ de** want to

gancho (*gahn*-choa) *m* hook

ganga (*gahng*-gah) *f* bargain

garaje (gah-*rah*-khay) *m* garage; **dejar en ~** garage

garante (gah-*rahn*-tay) *m* guarantor

garantía (gah-rahn-*tee*-ah) *f* guarantee

garantizar (gah-rahn-tee-*thahr*) *v* guarantee

garganta (gahr-*gahn*-tah) *f* throat; **dolor de ~** sore throat

garra (*gah*-rrah) *f* claw

garrafa (gah-*rrah*-fah) *f* carafe

garrote (gah-*rroa*-tay) *m* club, cudgel

garza (*gahr*-thah) *f* heron

gas (gahss) *m* gas; **cocina de ~** gas cooker

gasa (*gah*-sah) *f* gauze

gasolina (gah-soa-*lee*-nah) *f* petrol; gasoline *Am*, gas *Am*; ~ **sin plomo** unleaded petrol; **puesto de ~** petrol station, gas station *Am*

gasolinera (gah-soa-*lee*-nayh-rah) *f* gas station *Am*, petrol station

gastado (gahss-*tah*-dhoa) *adj* worn-out, worn, threadbare

gastar (gahss-*tahr*) *v* *spend; wear out

gasto (*gahss*-toa) *m* expense, expenditure; **gastos de viaje** fare, travel(l)ing expenses

gástrico (*gahss*-tree-koa) *adj* gastric

gastrónomo (gahss-*troa*-noa-moa) *m*, **-a** *f* gourmet

gatear (gah-tay-*ahr*) *v* *creep, crawl

gato (*gah*-toa) *m* cat; jack

gaviota (gah-*bh^yoa*-tah) *f* gull, seagull

gemelos (khay-*may*-loass) *mpl* twins *pl*; binoculars *pl*; cuff links *pl*; **~ de campaña** field glasses

***gemir** (khay-*meer*) *v* groan, moan

generación (khay-nay-rah-*th^yoan*) *f* generation

generador (khay-nay-rah-*dhoar*) *m* generator

general (khay-nay-*rahl*) *adj* general; universal, public, broad; *m* general; **en ~** in general

generalmente (khay-nay-rahl-*mayn*-tay) *adv* mostly, as a rule

generar (khay-nay-*rahr*) *v* generate

género (*khay*-nay-roa) *m* gender; kind

generosidad (khay-nay-roa-see-*dhahdh*) *f* generosity

generoso (khay-nay-*roa*-soa) *adj* generous, liberal

genial (khay-*n^yahl*) *adj* genial

genio (*khay*-n^yoa) *m* genius

genital (khay-nee-*tahl*) *adj* genital

gente (*khayn*-tay) *f* folk; people; nation *pl*

gentil (khayn-*teel*) *adj* polite, genteel, charming

genuino (khay-*nwee*-noa) *adj* genuine

geografía (khay-oa-grah-*fee*-ah) *f* geography

geográfico (khay-oa-*grah*-fee-koa) *adj* geographical

geología (khay-oa-loa-*khee*-ah) *f* geology

geometría (khay-oa-may-*tree*-ah) *f* geometry

gerencial (khay-rayn-*th^yahl*) *adj* administrative

germen (*khayr*-mayn) *m* germ; source

gesticular (khayss-tee-koo-*lahr*) *v* gesticulate

gestión (khayss-*t^yoan*) *f* administration, management

gesto (*khayss*-toa) *m* sign; gesture; grimace

gigante (khee-*gahn*-tay) *m* giant

gigantesco (khee-gahn-*tayss*-koa) *adj* enormous, gigantic

gimnasia (kheem-*nah*-s^yah) *f* gymnastics *pl*

gimnasio (kheem-*nah*-s^yoa) *m* gymnasium

gimnasta (kheem-*nahss*-tah) *m* gymnast

ginecólogo (khee-nay-*koa*-loa-goa) *m*, **-a** *f* gyn(a)ecologist

girar (khee-*rahr*) *v* turn, twist, swivel

giro (*khee*-roa) *m* draft; **~ postal** postal order

glaciar (glah-*th^yahr*) *m* glacier

glándula (*glahn*-doo-lah) *f* gland

globo (*gloa*-bhoa) *m* globe; balloon

gloria (*gloa*-r^yah) *f* glory

glorieta (gloa-r^y*ay*-tah) *f* roundabout, traffic circle

glosario (gloa-*sah*-r^yoa) *m* vocabulary

gobernador (goa-bhayr-nah-*dhoar*) *m* governor

gobernante (goa-bhayr-*nahn*-tay) *m* ruler

***gobernar** (goa-bhayr-*nahr*) *v* reign, rule

gobierno (goa-*bh^yayr*-noa) *m* government; rule; **~ de la casa** housekeeping

goce (*goa*-thay) *m* enjoyment

gol (goal) *m* goal

golf (goalf) *m* golf; **campo de ~** golf links, golf course *Am*

golfo (*goal*-foa) *m* gulf

golondrina (goa-loan-*dree*-nah) *f* swallow

golosina (goa-loa-*see*-nah) *f* delicacy; **golosinas** sweets; candy *Am*

golpe (*goal*-pay) *m* blow; knock, bump; ***dar golpes** bump

golpear (goal-pay-*ahr*) *v* *beat,

knock, *strike; thump, tap

golpecito (goal-pay-*thee*-toa) *m* tap

gollerías (goa-l^yay-*ree*-ahss) *fpl*
delicacies

goma (*goa*-mah) *f* gum; ~ **de borrar**
eraser, rubber; ~ **de mascar** chewing
gum; ~ **espumada** foam rubber

góndola (*goan*-doa-lah) *f* gondola

gordo (*goar*-dhoa) *adj* big; fat, stout

gorra (*goa*-rrah) *f* cap

gorrión (goa-rr^y*oan*) *m* sparrow

gorro (*goa*-rroa) *m* cap; ~ **de baño**
bathing cap

gota (*goa*-tah) *f* drop; gout

gotear (goa-tay-*ahr*) *v* leak

goteo (goa-*tay*-oa) *m* leak

gótico (*goa*-tee-koa) *adj* Gothic

gozar (goa-*thahr*) *v* enjoy

grabación (grah-bhah-th^y*oan*) *f*
recording

grabado (grah-*bhah*-dhoa) *m*
engraving; picture, print

grabador (grah-bhah-*dhoar*) *m*
engraver

grabar (grah-*bhahr*) *v* engrave

gracia (*grah*-th^yah) *f* grace; **de ~** free,
gratis

gracias (*grah*-th^yahss) thank you

gracioso (grah-th^y*oa*-soa) *adj* funny,
humorous; graceful

grado (*grah*-dhoa) *m* degree; grade; **a
tal ~** so

gradual (grah-*dhwahl*) *adj* gradual

graduar (grah-*dhwahr*) *v* grade;
classify; **graduarse** *v* graduate

gráfico (*grah*-fee-koa) *adj* graphic; *m*
graph, chart, diagram

gramática (grah-*mah*-tee-kah) *f*
grammar

gramatical (grah-mah-tee-*kahl*) *adj*
grammatical

gramo (*grah*-moa) *m* gram

Gran Bretaña (grahn bray-*tah*-ñah)
Great Britain

grande (*grahn*-day) *adj* big; great,
large, major

grandeza (grahn-*day*-thah) *f*
greatness; grandness

grandioso (grahn-d^y*oa*-soa) *adj*
superb, magnificent

granero (grah-*nay*-roa) *m* barn

granito (grah-*nee*-toa) *m* granite

granizo (grah-*nee*-thoa) *m* hail

granja (*grahng*-khah) *f* farm

granjera (grahng-*khay*-rah) *f* farmer's
wife

granjero (grahng-*khay*-roa) *m* farmer

grano (*grah*-noa) *m* grain; corn;
pimple

grapa (*grah*-pah) *f* clamp; staple

grasa (*grah*-sah) *f* fat, grease; *fMe*
shoe polish

grasiento (grah-s^y*ayn*-toa) *adj* fatty,
greasy

graso (*grah*-soa) *adj* fat

grasoso (grah-*soa*-soa) *adj* greasy

gratis (*grah*-teess) *adv* free of charge

gratitud (grah-tee-*toodh*) *f* gratitude

grato (*grah*-toa) *adj* enjoyable

gratuito (grah-*twee*-toa) *adj* gratis,
free of charge, free

grava (*grah*-bhah) *f* gravel

grave (*grah*-bhay) *adj* grave; bad

gravedad (grah-bhay-*dhahdh*) *f*
gravity

Grecia (*gray*-th^yah) *f* Greece

griego (gr^y*ay*-goa) *adj* Greek; *m*
Greek

grieta (gr^y*ay*-tah) *f* cleft, chasm; cave

grifo (*gree*-foa) *m* tap; faucet *Am*

grillo (*gree*-l^yoa) *m* cricket

gripe (*gree*-pay) *f* influenza, flu

gris (greess) *adj* grey

gritar (gree-*tahr*) *v* cry; yell, scream,
shout

grito (*gree*-toa) *m* cry; yell, scream,
shout

grosella (groa-*say*-l^yah) *f* currant; ~

espinosa gooseberry; **~ negra** black-currant

grosero (groa-*say*-roa) *adj* gross; coarse, rude, impertinent

grotesco (groa-*tayss*-koa) *adj* ludicrous

grúa (*groo*-ah) *f* crane

gruesa (*grway*-sah) *f* gross

grueso (*grway*-soa) *adj* corpulent

grumo (*groo*-moa) *m* lump

***gruñir** (groo-*ñeer*) *v* growl

grupo (*groo*-poa) *m* group; party, set, bunch

gruta (*groo*-tah) *f* grotto

guante (*gwahn*-tay) *m* glove

guapo (*gwah*-poa) *adj* handsome

guarda (gwahr-dhah) *m* custodian

guardabarros (gwahr-dhah-*bhah*-rroass) *m* mudguard

guardabosques (gwahr-dhah-*bhoass*-kayss) *m* forester

guardar (gwahr-*dhahr*) *v* *keep, *put away; guard; **~ con llave** lock up; **guardarse** *v* beware

guardarropa (gwahr-dhah-*rroa*-pah) *m* wardrobe; cloakroom; checkroom

Am

guardería (gwahr-dhay-*ree*-ah) *f* nursery

guardia (*gwahr*-dh^yah) *f* guard; *m* policeman; **~ personal** bodyguard

guardián (gwahr-*dh^yahn*) *m* attendant, warden; caretaker

guateque (gwah-*tay*-kay) *m* party

guerra (*gay*-rrah) *f* war; **~ mundial** world war

guía (*gee*-ah) *m* guide; *f* guidebook; **~ telefónica** telephone directory; telephone book *Am*

guiar (g^yahr) *v* guide

guión (g^yoan) *m* dash; hyphen

guisante (gee-*sahn*-tay) *m* pea

guisar (gee-*sahr*) *v* cook

guiso (*gee*-soa) *m* stew, casserole

guitarra (gee-*tah*-rrah) *f* guitar

gusano (goo-*sah*-noa) *m* worm

gustar (gooss-*tahr*) *v* care for, like; fancy

gusto (*gooss*-toa) *m* taste; **con mucho ~** with pleasure

gustosamente (gooss-toa-sah-*mayn*-tay) *adv* willingly, gladly

H

***haber** (ah-*bhayr*) *v* *have

hábil (*ah*-bheel) *adj* able, skilful, skilled

habilidad (ah-bhee-lee-*dhahdh*) *f* ability; skill, art

habitable (ah-bhee-*tah*-bhlay) *adj* inhabitable, habitable

habitación (ah-bhee-tah-*th^yoan*) *f* room; **~ para huéspedes** guest room

habitante (ah-bhee-*tahn*-tay) *m* inhabitant

habitar (ah-bhee-*tahr*) *v* inhabit

hábito (*ah*-bhee-toa) *m* habit

habitual (ah-bhee-*twahl*) *adj* habitual

habitualmente (ah-bhee-twahl-*mayn*-tay) *adv* usually

habla (*ah*-bhlah) *f* speech; language

hablar (ah-*bhlahr*) *v* *speak, talk

***hacer** (ah-*thayr*) *v* act; *do; *have, cause to, *make; **hace** ago; ***hacerse** *v* *become; *grow, *go, *get

hacia (*ah*-th^yah) *prep* at, towards, to; about; **~ abajo** down; **~ adelante** forward; **~ arriba** upwards, up; **~**

atrás backwards

hacienda (ah-*th*^y*ayn*-dah) f estate

hacha (ah-*chah*) f axe

hada (ah-dhah) f fairy; **cuento de hadas** fairytale

halcón (ahl-*koan*) m hawk

halibut (ah-lee-*bhoot*) m halibut

hallar (ah-*l*^y*ahr*) v *come across

hallazgo (ah-*l*^y*ahdh*-goa) m finding

hamaca (ah-*mah*-kah) f hammock

hambre (*ahm*-bray) f hunger

hambriento (ahm-*br*^y*ayn*-toa) adj hungry

harina (ah-*ree*-nah) f flour

harto de (*ahr*-toa day) fed up with, tired of

hasta (*ahss*-tah) prep to, till, until; **~ ahora** so far; **~ que** till

hay (ah^y) there is; there are; **~ que** it is necessary

haya (ah-^yah) f beech

hebilla (ay-*bhee*-l^yah) f buckle

hebreo (ay-*bhray*-oa) m Hebrew

hechizar (ay-chee-*thahr*) v bewitch

hecho (ay-choa) m fact

*heder (ay-*dhayr*) v *smell

hediondo (ay-*dh*^y*oan*-doa) adj smelly

helado (ay-*lah*-dhoa) adj freezing; m ice-cream

*helar (ay-*lahr*) v *freeze

hélice (*ay*-lee-thay) f propeller

hemorragia (ay-moa-*rrah*-kh^yah) f h(a)emorrhage; **~ nasal** nosebleed

hemorroides (ay-moa-*rroi*-dhayss) fpl h(a)emorrhoids pl, piles pl

hendidura (ayn-dee-*dhoo*-rah) f chink, crack

heno (ay-noa) m hay

heredar (ay-ray-*dhahr*) v inherit

hereditario (ay-ray-dhee-*tah*-r^yoa) adj hereditary

herencia (ay-rayn-*th*^yah) f inheritance, legacy

herida (ay-*ree*-dhah) f injury, wound

herido (ay-*ree*-doa) adj wounded; injured; m wounded man; injured man

*herir (ay-*reer*) v injure, wound

hermana (ayr-*mah*-nah) f sister

hermano (ayr-*mah*-noa) m brother

hermético (ayr-*may*-tee-koa) adj airtight

hermoso (ayr-*moa*-soa) adj beautiful

hernia (*ayr*-n^yah) f hernia; **~ intervertebral** slipped disc

héroe (*ay*-roa-ay) m hero

heroico (ay-*roi*-koa) adj heroic

heroísmo (ay-roa-*eez*-moa) m heroism

herradura (ay-rrah-*dhoo*-rah) f horseshoe

herramienta (ay-rrah-*m*^y*ayn*-tah) f tool, utensil, implement; **bolsa de herramientas** tool kit

herrería (ay-rray-*ree*-ah) f ironworks

herrero (ay-*rray*-roa) m smith, blacksmith

herrumbre (ay-*rroom*-bray) f rust

*hervir (ayr-*bheer*) v boil

heterosexual (ay-tay-roa-sayk-*swahl*) adj heterosexual

hidalgo (ee-*dhahl*-goa) m nobleman

hidrógeno (ee-*dhroa*-khay-noa) m hydrogen

hiedra (^yay-dhrah) f ivy

hielo (^yay-loa) m ice

hierba (^yayr-bhah) f herb; **brizna de ~** blade of grass; **mala ~** weed

hierro (^yay-rroa) m iron; **de ~** iron; **~ fundido** cast iron

hígado (ee-gah-dhoa) m liver

higiene (ee-*kh*^yay-nay) f hygiene

higiénico (ee-*kh*^yay-nee-koa) adj hygienic; **papel ~** toilet paper

higo (ee-goa) m fig

hija (ee-khah) f daughter

hijastra (ee-*khahss*-trah) f stepdaughter

hijastro (ee-*khahss*-troa) *m* stepchild

hijo (*ee*-khoa) *m* son

hilar (ee-*lahr*) *v* *spin

hilo (*ee*-loa) *m* yarn, thread; **~ de zurcir** darning wool

himno (*eem*-noa) *m* hymn; **~ nacional** national anthem

hinchar (een-*chahr*) *v* inflate; **hincharse** *v* *swell

hinchazón (een-chah-*thoan*) *f* swelling

hipo (*ee*-poa) *m* hiccup

hipocresía (ee-poa-kray-*see*-ah) *f* hypocrisy

hipócrita (ee-*poa*-kree-tah) *adj* hypocritical; *m* hypocrite

hipódromo (ee-*poa*-dhroa-moa) *m* race-course

hipoteca (ee-poa-*tay*-kah) *f* mortgage

hispanoamericano (eess-pah-noa-ah-may-ree-*kah*-noa) *adj* Spanish-American

histérico (eess-*tay*-ree-koa) *adj* hysterical

historia (eess-*toa*-rʸah) *f* history; **~ de amor** love story; **~ del arte** art history

histórico (eess-*toa*-ree-koa) *adj* historical, historic

hocico (oa-*thee*-koa) *m* mouth, snout

hogar (oa-*gahr*) *m* hearth

hoja (*oa*-khah) *f* leaf; sheet; blade; **~ de afeitar** razor blade; **~ de pedido** order form; **hojas de oro** gold leaf

¡hola! (*oa*-lah) hello!

Holanda (oa-*lahn*-dah) *f* Holland

holandés (oa-lahn-*dayss*) *adj* Dutch; *m* Dutchman

hombre (*oam*-bray) *m* man

hombro (*oam*-broa) *m* shoulder

homenaje (oa-may-*nah*-khay) *m* tribute, homage

homosexual (oa-moa-sayk-*swahl*) *adj* homosexual

hondo (*oan*-doa) *adj* deep

honesto (oa-*nayss*-toa) *adj* honest; honourable, straight

hongo (*oang*-goa) *m* mushroom; toadstool

honor (oa-*noar*) *m* hono(u)r; glory

honorarios (oa-noa-*rah*-rʸoass) *mpl* fee

honra (*oan*-rrah) *f* honour

honradez (oan-rah-*dhayth*) *f* honesty

honrado (oan-*rrah*-dhoa) *adj* honest

honrar (oan-*rahr*) *v* honour

hora (*oa*-rah) *f* hour; **~ de llegada** time of arrival; **~ de salida** time of departure; **~ punta** rush hour; **horas extraordinarias** overtime; **horas de consulta** consultation hours; **horas de oficina** office hours, business hours; **horas de visita** visiting hours; **horas hábiles** business hours

horario (oa-*rah*-rʸoa) *m* schedule; timetable; **~ comercial** business hours *pl*; **~ de verano** summer time

horca (*oar*-kah) *f* gallows *pl*

horizontal (oa-ree-thoan-*tahl*) *adj* horizontal

horizonte (oa-ree-*thoan*-tay) *m* horizon

hormiga (oar-*mee*-gah) *f* ant

hormigón (oar-mee-*goan*) *m* concrete

hornear (oar-nay-*ahr*) *v* bake

horno (*oar*-noa) *m* oven; furnace; **~ de microonda** microwave oven

horquilla (oar-*kee*-lʸah) *f* hairpin, hair-grip; bobby pin *Am*

horrible (oa-*rree*-bhlay) *adj* horrible; hideous

horror (oa-*rroar*) *m* horror

horticultura (oar-tee-kool-*too*-rah) *f* horticulture

hospedar (oass-pay-*dhahr*) *v* entertain; **hospedarse** *v* stay

hospedería (oass-pay-dhay-*ree*-ah) *f* hostel

hospicio (oass-*pee*-thʸoa) *m* home

hospital (oass-pee-*tahl*) *m* hospital

hospitalario (oass-pee-tah-*lah*-r^{y}oa) *adj* hospitable

hospitalidad (oass-pee-tah-lee-*dhahdh*) *f* hospitality

hostal (oass-*tahl*) *m* hostel

hostil (oass-*teel*) *adj* hostile

hotel (oa-*tayl*) *m* hotel

hoy (oi) *adv* today; ~ **en día** nowadays

hoyo (oa-^{y}oa) *m* pit

hueco (*way*-koa) *adj* hollow; *m* gap

huelga (*wayl*-gah) *f* strike; ***estar en ~ *strike**

huella (*way*-l^{y}ah) *f* trace

huérfano (*wayr*-fah-noa) *m* orphan

huerto (*wayr*-toa) *m* kitchen garden

hueso (*way*-soa) *m* bone; stone

huésped (*wayss*-paydh) *m* guest; lodger, boarder

hueva (*way*-bhah) *f* roe

huevera (*way*-*bhay*-rah) *f* egg-cup

huevo (*way*-bhoa) *m* egg; **yema de ~** egg yolk

*huir (weer) *v* escape

hule (*oo*-lay) *mMe* rubber

humanidad (oo-mah-nee-*dhahdh*) *f* humanity, mankind

humano (oo-*mah*-noa) *adj* human

humedad (oo-may-*dhahdh*) *f* moisture, humidity, damp

*humedecer (oo-may-dhay-*thayr*) *v* moisten, damp

húmedo (*oo*-may-dhoa) *adj* moist, humid, damp; wet

humilde (oo-*meel*-day) *adj* humble, meek

humo (*oo*-moa) *m* smoke, steam, vapo(u)r

humor (oo-*moar*) *m* spirit, mood; humo(u)r; **de buen ~** good-tempered, good-humo(u)red

humorístico (oo-moa-*reess*-tee-koa) *adj* humorous

hundirse (oon-*deer*-say) *v* *sink; collapse

húngaro (*oong*-gah-roa) *adj* Hungarian; *m* Hungarian

Hungría (oong-*gree*-ah) *m* Hungary

huracán (oo-rah-*kahn*) *m* hurricane

hurtar (oor-*tahr*) *v* *steal

hurto (*oor*-toa) *m* theft

I

ibérico (ee-*bhay*-ree-koa) *adj* Iberian

icono (ee-*koa*-noa) *m* icon

ictericia (eek-tay-*ree*-th^{y}ah) *f* jaundice

ida (*ee*-dah) *f* outward journey; **(billete de) ~ y vuelta** round trip (ticket), return (ticket)

idea (ee-*dhay*-ah) *f* idea

ideal (ee-dhay-*ahl*) *adj* ideal; *m* ideal

idéntico (ee-*dhayn*-tee-koa) *adj* identical

identidad (ee-dhayn-tee-*dhahdh*) *f* identity; **carnet de ~** identity card

identificación (ee-dhayn-tee-fee-kah-*th^{y}oan*) *f* identification

identificar (ee-dhayn-tee-fee-*kahr*) *v* identify

idioma (ee-*dh^{y}oa*-mah) *m* language

idiomático (ee-dh^{y}oa-*mah*-tee-koa) *adj* idiomatic

idiota (ee-*dh^{y}oa*-tah) *adj* idiotic; *m* idiot, fool

ídolo (*ee*-dhoa-loa) *m* idol

iglesia (ee-*glay*-s^{y}ah) *f* church

ignorancia (eeg-noa-*rahn*-th^{y}ah) *f*

ignorance
ignorante (eeg-noa-*rahn*-tay) *adj*
ignorant
ignorar (eeg-noa-*rahr*) *v* ignore
igual (ee-*gwahl*) *adj* equal, alike; level,
even; **sin ~** unsurpassed
igualar (ee-gwah-*lahr*) *v* level,
equalize; equal
igualdad (ee-gwahl-*dahdh*) *f* equality
igualmente (ee-gwahl-*mayn*-tay) *adv*
alike; equally
ilegal (ee-lay-*gahl*) *adj* illegal,
unlawful
ilegible (ee-lay-*khee*-bhlay) *adj*
illegible
ileso (ee-*lay*-soa) *adj* unhurt
ilimitado (ee-lee-mee-*tah*-dhoa) *adj*
unlimited
iluminación (ee-loo-mee-nah-*th^{y}oan*)
f illumination
iluminar (ee-loo-mee-*nahr*) *v*
illuminate
ilusión (ee-loo-*s^{y}oan*) *f* illusion
ilustración (ee-looss-trah-*th^{y}oan*) *f*
illustration; picture
ilustrar (ee-looss-*trahr*) *v* illustrate
ilustre (ee-*looss*-tray) *adj* illustrious
imagen (ee-*mah*-khayn) *f* image,
picture; **~ reflejada** reflection
imaginación (ee-mah-khee-nah-
th^{y}oan) *f* imagination
imaginar (ee-mah-khee-*nahr*) *v*
imagine; conceive; **imaginarse** *v*
fancy, imagine
imaginario (ee-mah-khee-*nah*-r^{y}oa)
adj imaginary
imbécil (eem-*bay*-theel) *adj* stupid;
m/f idiot, imbecile
imitación (ee-mee-tah-*th^{y}oan*) *f*
imitation
imitar (ee-mee-*tahr*) *v* imitate, copy
impaciente (eem-pah-*th^{y}ayn*-tay) *adj*
eager, impatient
impar (eem-*pahr*) *adj* odd

imparcial (eem-pahr-*th^{y}ahl*) *adj*
impartial
impecable (eem-pay-*kah*-bhlay) *adj*
faultless
impedimento (eem-pay-dhee-*mayn*-
toa) *m* impediment
***impedir** (eem-pay-*dheer*) *v* hinder,
impede; restrain, prevent
impeler (eem-pay-*layr*) *v* propel
imperdible (eem-payr-*dhee*-bhlay) *m*
safety pin
imperfección (eem-payr-fayk-*th^{y}oan*)
f fault
imperfecto (eem-payr-*fayk*-toa) *adj*
imperfect
imperial (eem-pay-r^y*ahl*) *adj* imperial
imperio (eem-*pay*-r^{y}oa) *m* empire
impermeable (eem-payr-may-*ah*-
bhlay) *adj* waterproof, rainproof; *m*
raincoat, mackintosh
impersonal (eem-payr-soa-*nahl*) *adj*
impersonal
impertinencia (eem-payr-tee-*nayn*-
th^{y}ah) *f* impertinence
impertinente (eem-payr-tee-*nayn*-
tay) *adj* bold, impertinent
impetuoso (eem-pay-*twoa*-soa) *adj*
impetuous; violent; hasty
implicar (eem-plee-*kahr*) *v* implicate,
imply
imponente (eem-poa-*nayn*-tay) *adj*
grand, imposing
importación (eem-poar-tah-*th^{y}oan*) *f*
import
importador (eem-poar-tah-*dhoar*) *m*
importer
importancia (eem-poar-*tahn*-th^{y}ah) *f*
importance; ***tener ~** matter
importante (eem-poar-*tahn*-tay) *adj*
important; considerable, capital, big
importar (eem-poar-*tahr*) *v* import
importuno (eem-poar-*too*-noa) *adj*
annoying
imposible (eem-poa-*see*-bhlay) *adj*

impossible

impotencia (eem-poa-*tayn*-th^{y}ah) f
impotence

impotente (eem-poa-*tayn*-tay) adj
powerless; impotent

impresora (eem-pray-*soah*-rah.) f
printer

impresión (eem-pray-s^{y}oan) f
impression; ~ **digital** fingerprint

impresionante (eem-pray-s^{y}oa-*nahn*-
tay) adj impressive; striking

impresionar (eem-pray-s^{y}oa-*nahr*) v
*strike, impress

impreso (eem-*pray*-soa) m printed
matter

imprevisto (eem-pray-*bheess*-toa) adj
unexpected, incidental

***imprimir** (eem-pree-*meer*) v print

improbable (eem-proa-*bhah*-bhlay)
adj unlikely, improbable

impropio (eem-*proa*-p^{y}oa) adj
improper; wrong

improvisar (eem-proa-bhee-*sahr*) v
improvise

imprudente (eem-proo-*dhayn*-tay)
adj imprudent; unwise, indiscreet

impudente (eem-poo-*dhayn*-tay) adj
impudent; shameless

impuesto (eem-*pwayss*-toa) m
taxation, tax; Customs duty; ~ **de
aduana** Customs duty; **impuestos
de importación** import duty; **libre
de impuestos** tax-free

impulsivo (eem-pool-*see*-bhoa) adj
impulsive

impulso (eem-*pool*-soa) m urge,
impulse

inaccesible (ee-nahk-thay-*see*-bhlay)
adj inaccessible

inaceptable (ee-nah-thayp-*tah*-bhlay)
adj unacceptable

inadecuado (ee-nah-dhay-*kwah*-
dhoa) adj inadequate; unfit,
unsuitable

inapreciable (ee-nah-pray-*th^{y}ah*-
bhlay) adj priceless; imperceptible

incapaz (eeng-kah-*pahth*) adj unable,
incapable

incendio (een-*thayn*-d^{y}oa) m fire

incidente (een-thee-*dhayn*-tay) m
incident

incienso (een-th^{y}ayn-soa) m incense

incierto (een-th^{y}ayr-toa) adj uncertain

incineración (een-thee-nay-rah-
th^{y}oan) f cremation

incinerar (een-thee-nay-*rahr*) v
cremate

incisión (een-thee-s^{y}oan) f cut

incitar (een-thee-*tahr*) v incite

inclinación (eeng-klee-nah-th^{y}oan) f
tendency, inclination; incline

inclinar (eeng-klee-*nahr*) v bow;
inclinado inclined; sloping, slanting;
inclinarse v *be inclined to; slope,
slant

***incluir** (eeng-*klweer*) v include;
enclose; count; **todo incluido** all in

incluso (eeng-*kloo*-soa) adj inclusive,
included

incombustible (eeng-koam-booss-
tee-bhlay) adj fireproof

incomodidad (eeng-koa-moa-dhee-
dhahdh) f inconvenience

incómodo (eeng-*koa*-moa-dhoa) adj
uncomfortable

incompetente (eeng-koam-pay-*tayn*-
tay) adj incompetent; unqualified

incompleto (eeng-koam-*play*-toa) adj
incomplete

inconcebible (eeng-koan-thay-*bhee*-
bhlay) adj inconceivable

incondicional (eeng-koan-dee-th^{y}oa-
nahl) adj unconditional

inconsciente (eeng-koan-*th^{y}ayn*-tay)
adj unaware; unconscious

inconveniencia (eeng-koam-bay-
n^y*ayn*-th^{y}ah) f inconvenience

incorrecto (eeng-koa-*rrayk*-toa) adj

incorrect

increíble (eeng-kray-*ee*-bhlay) *adj*
incredible

incrementar (eeng-kray-mayn-*tahr*) *v*
increase

inculto (eeng-*kool*-toa) *adj*
uncultivated; uneducated

incurable (eeng-koo-*rah*-bhlay) *adj*
incurable

indagación (een-dah-gah-*th*ᵛ*oan*) *f*
inquiry

indecente (een-day-*thayn*-tay) *adj*
indecent

indefenso (een-day-*fayn*-soa) *adj*
unprotected

indefinido (een-day-fee-*nee*-dhoa) *adj*
indefinite

indemnización (een-daym-nee-thah-
*th*ᵛ*oan*) *f* compensation, indemnity

independencia (een-day-payn-*dayn*-
th*ᵛ*ah) *f* independence

independiente (een-day-payn-*d*ᵛ*ayn*-
tay) *adj* independent; self-employed,

indeseable (een-day-say-*ah*-bhlay)
adj undesirable

India (*een*-dᵛah) *f* India

indicación (een-dee-kah-*th*ᵛ*oan*) *f*
indication

indicador (een-dee-kah-*dhoar*) *m*
trafficator, indicator, blinker *Am*

indicar (een-dee-*kahr*) *v* indicate;
declare

indicativo (een-dee-kah-*tee*-bhoa) *m*
indicative

índice (*een*-dee-thay) *m* index, table of
contents; index finger

indiferencia (een-dee-fay-*rayn*-thᵛah)
f indifference

indiferente (een-dee-fay-*rayn*-tay) *adj*
indifferent; careless

indígena (een-*dee*-khay-nah) *m* native

indigestión (een-dee-khayss-tᵛ*oan*) *f*
indigestion

indignación (een-deeg-nah-*th*ᵛ*oan*) *f*

indignation

indio (*een*-dᵛoa) *adj* Indian; *m* Indian

indirecto (een-dee-*rayk*-toa) *adj*
indirect

indispensable (een-deess-payn-*sah*-
bhlay) *adj* essential

indispuesto (een-deess-*pwayss*-toa)
adj unwell

individual (een-dee-bhee-*dhwahl*) *adj*
individual

individuo (een-dee-*bhee*-dhwoa) *m*
individual

Indonesia (een-doa-*nay*-sᵛah) *f*
Indonesia

indonesio (een-doa-*nay*-sᵛoa) *adj*
Indonesian; *m* Indonesian

indudable (een-doo-*dhah*-bhlay) *adj*
undoubtable; unquestionable

indulto (een-*dool*-toa) *m* pardon

industria (een-*dooss*-trᵛah) *f* industry;
ingenuity

ineficiente (ee-nay-fee-*th*ᵛ*ayn*-tay) *adj*
inefficient

inesperado (ee-nayss-pay-*rah*-dhoa)
adj unexpected

inestable (ee-nayss-*tah*-bhlay) *adj*
unsteady, unstable

inevitable (ee-nay-bhee-*tah*-bhlay)
adj unavoidable, inevitable

inexacto (ee-nayk-*sahk*-toa) *adj*
incorrect, inaccurate; false

inexperto (ee-nayks-*payr*-toa) *adj*
inexperienced

inexplicable (ee-nayks-plee-*kah*-
bhlay) *adj* unaccountable

infancia (een-*fahn*-thᵛah) *f* infancy

infantil (een-fahn-*teel*) *adj* childlike

infección (een-fayk-*th*ᵛ*oan*) *f* infection

infectar (een-fayk-*tahr*) *v* infect;
infectarse *v* *become infected

inferior (een-fay-rᵛ*oar*) *adj* inferior;
bottom

infiel (een-fᵛ*ayl*) *adj* unfaithful

infierno (een-fᵛ*ayr*-noa) *m* hell

infinidad (een-fee-nee-*dhahdh*) f
infinity

infinitivo (een-fee-nee-*tee*-bhoa) m
infinitive

infinito (een-fee-*nee*-toa) adj endless,
infinite

inflable (een-*flah*-bhlay) adj inflatable

inflación (een-flah-*th^yoan*) f inflation

inflamable (een-flah-*mah*-bhlay) adj
inflammable

inflamación (een-flah-mah-*th^yoan*) f
inflammation

influencia (een-*flwayn*-th^yah) f
influence

*influir (een-*flweer*) v influence

influjo (een-*floo*-khoa) m influence

influyente (een-floo-*^yayn*-tay) adj
influential

información (een-foar-mah-*th^yoan*) f
enquiry, information; **oficina de
informaciones** inquiry office

informal (een-foar-*mahl*) adj informal;
casual

informar (een-foar-*mahr*) v report,
inform; **informarse** v inquire

informe (een-*foar*-may) m report;
informes mpl information; ***pedir
informes** inquire

infrarrojo (een-frah-*rroa*-khoa) adj
infra-red

ingeniero (eeng-khay-*n^yay*-roa) m
engineer

ingenio (eeng-khay-nyoa) n wit

ingenioso (eeng-khay-*n^yoa*-soa) adj
ingenious; witty

ingenuo (eeng-*khay*-nwoa) adj naïve;
simple

Inglaterra (eeng-glah-*tay*-rrah) f
England; Britain

ingle (*eeng*-glay) f groin

inglés (eeng-*glayss*) adj English; m
Englishman; Briton

ingrato (eeng-*grah*-toa) adj ungrateful

ingrediente (eeng-gray-*dh^yayn*-tay) m
ingredient

ingresar (eeng-gray-*sahr*) v deposit

ingreso (eenggray-soa) m entry

ingresos (eeng-*gray*-soass) mpl
revenue, earnings pl; income;
impuesto sobre los ~ income tax

inhabitable (ee-nah-bhee-*tah*-bhlay)
adj uninhabitable

inhabitado (ee-nah-bhee-*tah*-dhoa)
adj uninhabited

inhalar (ee-nah-*lahr*) v inhale

inicial (ee-nee-*th^yahl*) adj initial; f
initial

iniciar (ee-nee-*th^yahr*) v initiate

iniciativa (ee-nee-th^yah-*tee*-bhah) f
initiative

ininterrumpido (ee-neen-tay-rroom-
pee-dhoa) adj continuous

injusticia (eeng-khooss-*tee*-th^yah) f
injustice

injusto (eeng-*khooss*-toa) adj unfair,
unjust

inmaculado (een-mah-koo-*lah*-dhoa)
adj immaculate; stainless, spotless

inmediatamente (een-may-dh^yah-
tah-*mayn*-tay) adv instantly,
immediately

inmediato (een-may-*dh^yah*-toa) adj
immediate, prompt; **de ~**
immediately

inmenso (een-*mayn*-soa) adj
immense

inmigración (een-mee-grah-*th^yoan*) f
immigration

inmigrante (een-mee-*grahn*-tay) m
immigrant

inmigrar (een-mee-*grahr*) v
immigrate

inmodesto (een-moa-*dhayss*-toa) adj
immodest

inmueble (een-*mway*-bhlay) m
building

inmunidad (een-moo-nee-*dhahdh*) f
immunity

inmunizar (een-moo-nee-*thahr*) *v* immunize

innato (een-*nah*-toa) *adj* innate; natural

innecesario (een-nay-thay-*sah*-r^{y}oa) *adj* unnecessary

innumerable (een-noo-may-*rah*-bhlay) *adj* innumerable

inocencia (ee-noa-*thayn*-th^{y}ah) *f* innocence

inocente (ee-noa-*thayn*-tay) *adj* innocent

inoculación (ee-noa-koo-lah-*th^{y}oan*) *f* inoculation

inocuo (ee-*noa*-kwoa) *adj* harmless

inoportuno (ee-noa-poar-*too*-noa) *adj* inconvenient; misplaced

inquietarse (eeng-k^{y}ay-*tahr*-say) *v* worry

inquieto (een-*k^{y}ay*-toa) *adj* restless; uneasy, worried

inquietud (eeng-k^{y}ay-*toodh*) *f* unrest; worry

inquilino (eeng-kee-*lee*-noa) *m* tenant

insalubre (een-sah-*loo*-bhray) *adj* unhealthy

insatisfecho (een-sah-teess-*fay*-choa) *adj* dissatisfied

inscribir (eens-kree-*bheer*) *v* enter, book, list; **inscribirse** *v* register, check in; enro(l)l

inscripción (eens-kreep-*th^{y}oan*) *f* inscription; registration

insecticida (een-sayk-tee-*thee*-dhah) *m* insecticide

insecto (een-*sayk*-toa) *m* insect; bug *Am*

inseguro (een-say-*goo*-roa) *adj* unsafe; doubtful

insensato (een-sayn-*sah*-toa) *adj* senseless

insensible (een-sayn-*see*-bhlay) *adj* insensitive; heartless

insertar (een-sayr-*tahr*) *v* insert

insignificante (een-seeg-nee-fee-*kahn*-tay) *adj* unimportant, petty, insignificant

insípido (een-*see*-pee-dhoa) *adj* insipid; tasteless

insistir (een-seess-*teer*) *v* insist

insolación (een-soa-lah-*th^{y}oan*) *f* sunstroke

insolencia (een-soa-*layn*-th^{y}ah) *f* insolence

insolente (een-soa-*layn*-tay) *adj* insolent

insólito (een-*soa*-lee-toa) *adj* uncommon, unusual

insomnio (een-*soam*-n^{y}oa) *m* insomnia

insonorizado (een-soa-noa-ree-*thah*-dhoa) *adj* soundproof

insoportable (een-soa-poar-*tah*-bhlay) *adj* intolerable

inspección (eens-payk-*th^{y}oan*) *f* inspection; **~ de pasaportes** passport control

inspeccionar (eens-payk-th^{y}oa-*nahr*) *v* inspect

inspector (eens-payk-*toar*) *m*, **-a** *f* inspector

inspirar (een-spee-*rahr*) *v* inspire

instalación (eens-tah-lah-*th^{y}oan*) *f* installation; plant

instalar (eens-tah-*lahr*) *v* install; furnish

instantánea (eens-tahn-*tah*-nay-ah) *f* snapshot

instantáneamente (eens-tahn-tah-nay-ah-*mayn*-tay) *adv* instantly

instante (eens-*tahn*-tay) *m* instant; second; **al ~** instantly

instinto (een-*steen*-toa) *m* instinct

institución (eens-tee-too-*th^{y}oan*) *f* institution, institute

*instituir (eens-tee-*tweer*) *v* institute

instituto (eens-tee-*too*-toa) *m* institution, institute

instrucción (eens-trook-*th*ʸoan) *f*
instruction; direction

instructivo (eens-trook-*tee*-bhoa) *adj*
instructive

instructor (eens-trook-*toar*) *m*, **-a** *f*
instructor

***instruir** (eens-*trweer*) *v* instruct

instrumento (eens-troo-*mayn*-toa) *m*
instrument; **~ músico** musical
instrument

insuficiente (een-soo-fee-*th*ʸayn-tay)
adj insufficient

insufrible (een-soo-*free*-bhlay) *adj*
unbearable

insultante (een-sool-*tahn*-tay) *adj*
offensive, insulting

insultar (een-sool-*tahr*) *v* insult

insulto (een-*sool*-toa) *m* insult

intacto (een-*tahk*-toa) *adj* intact;
unbroken, whole

integral (een-tay-*grahl*) *adj* integral

integrar (een-tay-*grahr*) *v* integrate

intelecto (een-tay-*layk*-toa) *m*
intellect

intelectual (een-tay-layk-*twahl*) *adj*
intellectual

inteligencia (een-tay-lee-*khayn*-
th ʸah) *f* intelligence, brain

inteligente (een-tay-lee-*khayn*-tay)
adj intelligent; clever, smart

intención (een-tayn-*th*ʸoan) *f*
intention, purpose; ***tener la ~ de**
intend to

intencionado (een-tayn-th ʸoa-*nah*-
dhoa) *adj* on purpose

intencional (een-tayn-th ʸoa-*nahl*) *adj*
intentional

intensidad (een-tayn-see-*dhahdh*) *f*
intensity

intenso (een-*tayn*-soa) *adj* intense

intentar (een-tayn-*tahr*) *v* attempt, try;
intend

intercambiar (een-tayr-kahm-*b*ʸ*ahr*) *v*
exchange

interés (een-tay-*rayss*) *m* interest

interesado (een-tay-ray-*sah*-dhoa) *adj*
interested; concerned; *m* candidate

interesante (een-tay-ray-*sahn*-tay) *adj*
interesting

interesar (een-tay-ray-*sahr*) *v* interest

interferencia (een-tayr-fay-*rayn*-
th ʸah) *f* interference

interferir (een-tayr-fay-*reer*) *v*
interfere

ínterin (*een*-tay-reen) *m* interim

interior (een-tay-r ʸ*oar*) *adj* inside,
inner; domestic; *m* interior, inside

intermediario (een-tayr-may-*dh*ʸ*ah*-
r ʸoa) *m* intermediary

intermedio (een-tayr-*may*-dh ʸoa) *m*
interlude

intermitente (een-tayr-mee-*tayn*-tay)
adj intermittent; *m* turn signal,
indicator

internacional (een-tayr-nah-th ʸoa-
nahl) *adj* international

internado (een-tayr-*nah*-dhoa) *m*
boarding school

interno (een-*tayr*-noa) *adj* internal

interpretar (een-tayr-pray-*tahr*) *v*
interpret

intérprete (een-*tayr*-pray-tay) *m*
interpreter

interrogar (een-tay-rroa-*gahr*) *v*
interrogate

interrogativo (een-tay-rroa-gah-*tee*-
bhoa) *adj* interrogative

interrogatorio (een-tay-rroa-gah-*toa*-
r ʸoa) *m* interrogation, examination

interrumpir (een-tay-rroom-*peer*) *v*
interrupt

interrupción (een-tay-rroop-*th*ʸoan) *f*
interruption

interruptor (een-tay-rroop-*toar*) *m*
switch

intersección (een-tayr-sayk-*th*ʸoan) *f*
intersection

intervalo (een-tayr-*bhah*-loa) *m*

interval

intervención (een-tayr-bhayn-*th*ʸ*oan*) *f* intervention

*intervenir (een-tayr-bhay-*neer*) *v* intervene

intestino (een-tayss-*tee*-noa) *m* intestine, gut; **~ recto** rectum; **intestinos** intestines *pl*, bowels *pl*

intimidad (een-tee-mee-*dhahdh*) *f* privacy; intimacy

íntimo (*een*-tee-moa) *adj* intimate

intoxicación alimentaria (een-toak-see-kah-*th*ʸ*oan* ah-lee-mayn-*tah*-rʸah) food poisoning

intransitable (een-trahn-see-*tah*-bhlay) *adj* impassable

intriga (een-*tree*-gah) *f* intrigue

introducción (een-troa-dhook-*th*ʸ*oan*) *f* introduction

*introducir (een-troa-dhoo-*theer*) *v* introduce; *bring up

intruso (een-*troo*-soa) *m* intruder; trespasser

inundación (ee-noon-dah-*th*ʸ*oan*) *f* flood

inusitado (ee-noo-see-*tah*-dhoa) *adj* unusual

inútil (ee-*noo*-teel) *adj* useless

inútilmente (ee-noo-teel-*mayn*-tay) *adv* in vain

invadir (eem-bah-*dheer*) *v* invade

inválido (eem-*bah*-lee-dhoa) *adj* invalid, disabled; *m* invalid

invasión (eem-bah-sʸ*oan*) *f* invasion

invención (eem-bayn-*th*ʸ*oan*) *f* invention

inventar (eem-bayn-*tahr*) *v* invent

inventario (eem-bayn-*tah*-rʸoa) *m* inventory

inventivo (eem-bayn-*tee*-bhoa) *adj* inventive

inventor (eem-bayn-*toar*) *m* inventor

invernadero (eem-bayr-nah-*dhay*-roa) *m* greenhouse

inversión (eem-bayr-sʸ*oan*) *f* investment

inversionista (eem-bayr-sʸoa-*neess*-tah) *m* investor

inverso (eem-*bayr*-soa) *adj* reverse

*invertir (eem-bayr-*teer*) *v* invert; invest

investigación (eem-bayss-tee-gah-*th*ʸ*oan*) *f* research; investigation, enquiry

investigador (eem-bhayss-tee-gah-*dhoar*) *m* research worker

investigar (eem-bayss-tee-*gahr*) *v* investigate, enquire

invierno (eem-*b*ʸ*ayr*-noa) *m* winter; **deportes de ~** winter sports

invisible (eem-bee-*see*-bhlay) *adj* invisible

invitación (eem-bee-tah-*th*ʸ*oan*) *f* invitation

invitado (eem-bee-*tah*-dhoa) *m* guest

invitar (eem-bee-*tahr*) *v* invite; ask

inyección (een-ʸayk-*th*ʸ*oan*) *f* shot, injection

inyectar (een-ʸayk-*tahr*) *v* inject

*ir (eer) *v* *go; **~ por** fetch; ***irse** *v* *go away

Irak (ee-*rahk*) *m* Iraq

Irán (ee-*rahn*) *m* Iran

iraní (ee-rah-*nee*) *adj* Iranian; *m* Iranian

iraquí (ee-rah-*kee*) *adj* Iraqi; *m* Iraqi

irascible (ee-rahss-*thee*-bhlay) *adj* irascible, quick-tempered

Irlanda (eer-*lahn*-dah) *f* Ireland

irlandés (eer-lahn-*dayss*) *adj* Irish; *m* Irishman

ironía (ee-roa-*nee*-ah) *f* irony

irónico (ee-*roa*-nee-koa) *adj* ironical

irrazonable (ee-rrah-thoa-*nah*-bhlay) *adj* unreasonable

irreal (ee-rray-*ahl*) *adj* unreal

irreflexivo (ee-rray-flayk-*see*-bhoa) *adj* rash, impetuous

irregular (ee-rray-goo-*lahr*) *adj*
irregular; uneven

irrelevante (ee-rray-lay-*bhahn*-tay)
adj insignificant

irreparable (ee-rray-pah-*rah*-bhlay)
adj irreparable

irrevocable (ee-rray-bhoa-*kah*-bhlay)
adj irrevocable

irritable (ee-rree-*tah*-bhlay) *adj*
irritable

irritante (ee-rree-*tahn*-tay) *adj*
irritating, annoying

irritar (ee-rree-*tahr*) *v* annoy, irritate

irrompible (ee-rroam-*pee*-bhlay) *adj*
unbreakable

irrupción (ee-rroop-*th^yoan*) *f* invasion,
raid

isla (*eez*-lah) *f* island

islandés (eez-lahn-*dayss*) *adj*

Icelandic; *m* Icelander

Islandia (eez-*lahn*-d^yah) *f* Iceland

Israel (eess-rah-*ayl*) *m* Israel

israelí (eess-rah-ay-*lee*) *adj* Israeli; *m*
Israeli

istmo (*eest*-moa) *m* isthmus

Italia (ee-*tah*-l^yah) *f* Italy

italiano (ee-tah-*l^yah*-noa) *adj* Italian;
m Italian

itinerario (ee-tee-nay-*rah*-r^yoa) *m*
itinerary

IVA (*ee*-bah) (= *impuesto sobre el valor
añadido*) *sales tax*, VAT (= value-
added tax)

izar (ee-*thahr*) *v* hoist

izquierda (eeth-*k^yayr*-dah) *f* left; **por
la ~** on the left

izquierdo (eeth-*k^yayr*-dhoa) *adj* left;
left-hand

J

jabón (khah-*bhoan*) *m* soap; **~ de
afeitar** shaving soap; **~ en polvo** soap
powder, washing powder

jade (*khah*-dhay) *m* jade

jadear (khah-dhay-*ahr*) *v* pant

jalar (khah-*lahr*) *vMe* *draw

jalea (khah-*lay*-ah) *f* jelly

jamás (khah-*mahss*) *adv* ever

jamón (khah-*moan*) *m* ham

Japón (khah-*poan*) *m* Japan

japonés (khah-poa-*nayss*) *adj*
Japanese; *m* Japanese

¡jaque! (*khah*-kay) check!

jarabe (khah-*rah*-bhay) *m* syrup

jardín (khahr-*dheen*) *m* garden; **~ de
infancia** kindergarten; **~ público**
public garden; **~ zoológico**
zoological gardens, zoo

jardinero (khahr-dhee-*nay*-roa) *m*, **-a**

f gardener

jarra (*khah*-rrah) *f* jar

jaula (*khou*-lah) *f* cage

jefe (*khay*-fay) *m* chief, manager, boss;
leader; chieftain; **~ de cocina** chef; **~
de Estado** head of state; **~ de
gobierno** premier

jengibre (khayng-*khee*-bhray) *m*
ginger

jerarquía (khay-rahr-*kee*-ah) *f*
hierarchy

jerez (khay-*rayth*) *m* sherry

jeringa (khay-*reeng*-gah) *f* syringe

jersey (khayr-*say*) *m* jersey, sweater;
jumper

jinete (khee-*nay*-tay) *m* horseman,
rider

jitomate (khee-toa-*mah*-tay) *mMe*
tomato

Jordania (khoar-*dhah*-n^yah) *f* Jordan

jordano (khoar-*dhah*-noa) *adj* Jordanian; *m* Jordanian

jornada (khoar-*nah*-dhah) *f* day trip; working day

joven (*khoa*-bhayn) *adj* young; *m* lad

jovial (khoa-*bh^yahl*) *adj* jovial; jolly

joya (*khoa*-^yah) *f* jewel, gem

joyería (khoa-^yay-*ree*-ah) *f* jewel(le)ry

joyero (khoa-^yay-roa) *m*, **-a** *f* jewel(l)er

jubilado (khoo-bhee-*lah*-dhoa) *adj* retired

judía (khoo-*dhee*-ah) *f* bean

judío (khoo-*dhee*-oa) *adj* Jewish; *m*, **-a** *f* Jew

juego (*khway*-goa) *m* game, play; set; ***hacer ~ con** match; **~ de bolos** bowling; **~ de damas** draughts, checkers *Am*; **~ de té** tea set; **~ electrónico** electronic game

juerga (*khwayr*-gah) *f colloquial* partying; **irse de ~** *colloquial* go out on the town, go out partying

jueves (*khway*-bhayss) *m* Thursday

juez (khwayth) *m/f* judge

jugada (khoo-*gah*-dhah) *f* move

jugador (khoo-gah-*dhoar*) *m* player

*jugar (khoo-*gahr*) *v* play

juguete (khoo-*gay*-tay) *m* toy

juguetería (khoo-gay-tay-*ree*-ah) *f* toy store

juicio (*khwee*-th^yoa) *m* sense; judgment

julio (*khoo*-l^yoa) July

junco (*khoong*-koa) *m* rush, reed

jungla (*khoong*-glah) *f* jungle

junio (*khoo*-n^yoa) June

junta (*khoon*-tah) *f* meeting, council

juntamente (khoon-tah-*mayn*-tay) *adv* jointly

juntar (khoon-*tahr*) *v* attach; collect; join; **juntarse** *v* gather

junto a (*khoon*-toa ah) beside; next to

juntos (*khoon*-toass) *adv* together

jurado (khoo-*rah*-dhoa) *m* jury

juramento (khoo-rah-*mayn*-toa) *m* vow, oath; **prestar ~** vow

jurar (khoo-*rahr*) *v* *swear

jurídico (khoo-*ree*-dhee-koa) *adj* legal

jurista (khoo-*reess*-tah) *m* lawyer

justamente (khooss-tah-*mayn*-tay) *adv* rightly; just

justicia (khooss-*tee*-th^yah) *f* justice

justificar (khooss-tee-fee-*kahr*) *v* justify

justo (*khooss*-toa) *adj* fair, just, righteous, right; correct, appropriate, proper

juvenil (khoo-bhay-*neel*) *adj* juvenile

juventud (khoo-bhayn-*toodh*) *f* youth

juzgar (khoodh-*gahr*) *v* judge

K

Kenya (*kay*-n^yah) *m* Kenya

kilogramo (kee-loa-*grah*-moa) *m* kilogram

kilometraje (kee-loa-may-*trah*-khay) *m* distance in kilometres, kilometers *Am*

kilómetro (kee-*loa*-may-troa) *m* kilometre, kilometer *Am*

L

la (lah) *pron* her

laberinto (lah-bhay-*reen*-toa) *m* maze, labyrinth

labio (*lah*-bh^yoa) *m* lip

labor (lah-*bhoar*) *f* labo(u)r

laboratorio (lah-bhoa-rah-*toa*-r^yoa) *m* laboratory; ~ **de lenguas** language laboratory

laca (*lah*-kah) *f* lacquer; ~ **para el cabello** hair-spray

ladera (lah-*dhay*-rah) *f* hillside

lado (*lah*-dhoa) *m* side; way; **al ~** next-door; **al otro ~** across; **al otro ~ de** across

ladrar (lah-*dhrahr*) *v* bark

ladrillo (lah-*dhree*-l^yoa) *m* brick

ladrón (lah-*dhroan*) *m*, **ladrona** *f* thief, robber; burglar

lago (*lah*-goa) *m* lake

lágrima (*lah*-gree-mah) *f* tear

laguna (lah-*goo*-nah) *f* lagoon

lamentable (lah-mayn-*tah*-bhlay) *adj* lamentable

lamentar (lah-mayn-*tahr*) *v* lament; grieve

lamer (lah-*mayr*) *v* lick

lámpara (*lahm*-pah-rah) *f* lamp; ~ **para lectura** reading lamp; ~ **sorda** hurricane lamp

lana (*lah*-nah) *f* wool; **de ~** wool(l)en

landa (*lahn*-dhah) *f* heath, moorland

langosta (lahng-*goass*-tah) *f* lobster

lanza (*lahn*-thah) *f* spear

lanzamiento (lahn-thah-*m^y*ayn-toa) *m* throw

lanzar (lahn-*thahr*) *v* *cast; launch

lápiz (*lah*-peeth) *m* pencil; ~ **labial** lipstick; ~ **para las cejas** eyebrow pencil

largo (*lahr*-goa) *adj* long; **a lo ~ de** along, past; **pasar de ~** pass by; *m* length

laringitis (lah-reeng-*khee*-teess) *f* laryngitis

lástima: ¡qué lástima! (kay *lahss*-tee-mah) what a pity!

lata (*lah*-tah) *f* tin, canister, can

lateralmente (lah-tay-rahl-*mayn*-tay) *adv* sideways

latín (lah-*teen*) *m* Latin

latinoamericano (lah-tee-noa-ah-may-ree-*kah*-noa) *adj* Latin American

latitud (lah-tee-*toodh*) *f* latitude

latón (lah-*toan*) *m* brass

lavable (lah-*bhah*-bhlay) *adj* washable

lavabos (lah-*bhah*-bhoass) *mpl* bathroom; ~ **para caballeros** men's room; ~ **para señoras** ladies' room

lavado (lah-*bhah*-dhoa) *m* washing

lavadora (lah-bhah-*dhoa*-rah) *f* washing machine

lavandería (lah-bhahn-day-*ree*-ah) *f* laundry; ~ **de autoservicio** launderette

lavar (lah-*bhahr*) *v* wash

laxante (lahk-*sahn*-tay) *m* laxative

le (lay) *pron* him; her

leal (lay-*ahl*) *adj* true, loyal

lección (layk-*th^y*oan) *f* lesson

lector (layk-toar) *m*, **-a** *f* reader

lectura (layk-*too*-rah) *f* reading

leche (*lay*-chay) *f* milk; **batido de ~** milk-shake

lechería (lay-chay-*ree*-ah) *f* dairy

lechero (lay-*chay*-roa) *m* milkman

lechoso (lay-*choa*-soa) *adj* milky

lechuga (lay-*choo*-gah) *f* lettuce

*leer (lay-*ayr*) *v* *read

legación (lay-gah-*th^y*oan) *f* legation

legal (lay-*gahl*) *adj* legal

legalización (lay-gah-lee-thah-*th^y*oan) *f* legalization

legible (lay-*khee*-bhlay) *adj* legible

legítimo (lay-*khee*-tee-moa) *adj* legitimate, legal

legumbre (lay-*goom*-bray) *f* vegetable

lejano (lay-*khah*-noa) *adj* remote, far, distant

lejos (*lay*-khoass) *adv* far

lema (*lay*-mah) *f* motto, slogan

lengua (*layng*-gwah) *f* tongue; language; **~ materna** native language, mother tongue

lenguado (layng-*gwah*-dhoa) *m* sole

lenguaje (layng-*gwah*-khay) *m* speech

lente (*layn*-tay) *m/f* lens; **~ de aumento** magnifying glass; **lentillas** *fpl* contact lenses

lento (*layn*-toa) *adj* slow; slack

león (lay-*oan*) *m* lion

lepra (*lay*-prah) *f* leprosy

lerdo (*layr*-dhoa) *adj* slow; clumsy; dull

les (layss) *pron* them

lesión (lay-s^y*oan*) *f* injury

letra (*lay*-trah) *f* letter

levadura (lay-bhah-*dhoo*-rah) *f* yeast

levantamiento (lay-bhahn-tah-m^y*ayn*-toa) *m* rise; rising

levantar (lay-bhahn-*tahr*) *v* lift; *bring up; **levantarse** *v* *rise, *get up

levante (lay-*bhan*-tay) *m* east

leve (*lay*-bhay) *adj* slight

ley (lay) *f* law

leyenda (lay-^y*ayn*-dah) *f* legend

liar (l^y*ahr*) *v* bundle; tie, tie up

libanés (lee-bhah-*nayss*) *adj* Lebanese; *m* Lebanese

Líbano (*lee*-bhah-noa) *m* Lebanon

liberación (lee-bhay-rah-th^y*oan*) *f* liberation; delivery

liberal (lee-bhay-*rahl*) *adj* liberal

liberalismo (lee-bhay-rah-*leez*-moa) *m* liberalism

Liberia (lee-*bhay*-r^yah) *f* Liberia

liberiano (lee-bhay-r^y*ah*-noa) *adj* Liberian; *m* Liberian

libertad (lee-bhayr-*tahdh*) *f* liberty, freedom

libra (*lee*-bhrah) *f* pound

libranza (lee-*bhrahn*-thah) *f* money order

librar (lee-*bhrahr*) *v* deliver; rescue

libre (*lee*-bhray) *adj* free

librería (lee-bhray-*ree*-ah) *f* bookstore

librero (lee-*bhray*-roa) *m*, **-a** *f* bookseller

libro (*lee*-bhroa) *m* book; **~ de bolsillo** paperback; **~ de cocina** cook(ery)-book; **~ de reclamaciones** complaints book; **~ de texto** textbook

licencia (lee-*thayn*-th^yah) *f* permission, licence, license *Am*; leave

lícito (*lee*-thee-toa) *adj* lawful

licor (lee-*koar*) *m* liquor; liqueur

líder (*lee*-dhayr) *m* leader

liebre (l^y*ay*-bhray) *f* hare

liga (*lee*-gah) *f* union, league

ligar (lee-*gahr*) *v* bind; tie; **~ con** *colloquial* pick up

ligero (lee-*khay*-roa) *adj* light; slight

lima (*lee*-mah) *f* file; lime; **~ para las uñas** nail file

limitar (lee-mee-*tahr*) *v* limit

límite (*lee*-mee-tay) *m* boundary, limit; **~ de velocidad** speed limit

limón (lee-*moan*) *m* lemon

limonada (lee-moa-*nah*-dhah) *f* lemonade

limpiaparabrisas (leem-p^yah-pah-rah-*bhree*-sahss) *m* windscreen wiper, windshield wiper *Am*

limpiar (leem-p^y*ahr*) *v* clean; **~ en seco** dry-clean

limpieza (leem-p^y*ay*-thah) *f* cleaning

limpio (*leem*-p^yoa) *adj* clean

lindo (*leen*-doa) *adj* pretty, lovely, nice

línea (*lee*-nay-ah) *f* line; **~ de navegación** shipping line; **~ de**

pesca fishing line; ~ **principal** main line

lino (*lee*-noa) *m* linen

linterna (leen-*tayr*-nah) *f* lantern; torch, flashlight

liquidación (lee-kee-dhah-*th*ʸoan) *f* clearance sale

líquido (*lee*-kee-dhoa) *adj* liquid

liso (*lee*-soa) *adj* smooth, plain, flat

lista (*leess*-tah) *f* list; ~ **de correos** poste restante; ~ **de espera** waiting list; ~ **de precios** price list

listín telefónico (leess-*teen* tay-lay-*foa*-nee-koa) telephone directory; telephone book *Am*

listo (*leess*-toa) *adj* bright; clever, smart; ready

litera (lee-*tay*-rah) *f* berth

literario (lee-tay-*rah*-rʸoa) *adj* literary

literatura (lee-tay-rah-*too*-rah) *f* literature

litoral (lee-toa-*rahl*) *m* seacoast

litro (*lee*-troa) *m* litre, liter *Am*

llaga (*l*ʸah-gah) *f* sore; wound

llama (*l*ʸah-mah) *f* flame

llamada (lʸah-*mah*-dhah) *f* call; ~ **local** local call; ~ **telefónica** telephone call

llamar (lʸah-*mahr*) *v* cry, call; **así llamado** so-called; ~ **por teléfono** phone; **llamarse** *v* *be called

llano (*l*ʸah-noa) *adj* flat; level, even, smooth; *m* plain

llanta (*l*ʸahn-tah) *f* rim; *fMe* tire

llave (*l*ʸah-bhay) *f* key; **ama de llaves** housekeeper; **guardar con** ~ lock up; ~ **de la casa** latchkey; ~ **inglesa** spanner, wrench *Am*

llegada (lʸay-*gah*-dhah) *f* arrival; coming

llegar (lʸay-*gahr*) *v* arrive; ~ **a** attain

llenar (lʸay-*nahr*) *v* fill; fill in; fill out *Am*; fill up

lleno (*l*ʸay-noa) *adj* full

llevar (lʸay-*bhahr*) *v* *take; *bear, carry; *wear; **llevarse** *v* *take away

llorar (lʸoa-*rahr*) *v* cry, *weep

*llover (lʸoa-*bhayr*) *v* rain

llovizna (lʸoa-*bheeth*-nah) *f* drizzle

lluvia (*l*ʸoo-bhʸah) *f* rain

lluvioso (lʸoo-*bh*ʸoa-soa) *adj* rainy

lo (loa) *pron* it; ~ **que** what

lobo (*loa*-bhoa) *m* wolf

local (loa-*kahl*) *adj* local

localidad (loa-kah-lee-*dhahdh*) *f* locality; seat

localizar (loa-kah-lee-*thahr*) *v* locate

loción (loa-*th*ʸoan) *f* lotion

loco (*loa*-koa) *adj* crazy; mad

locomotora (loa-koa-moa-*toa*-rah) *f* engine, locomotive

locuaz (loa-*kwahth*) *adj* talkative

locura (loa-*koo*-rah) *f* madness, lunacy

lodo (*loa*-dhoa) *m* mud

lodoso (loa-*dhoa*-soa) *adj* muddy

lógica (*loa*-khee-kah) *f* logic

lógico (*loa*-khee-koa) *adj* logical

lograr (loa-*grahr*) *v* achieve; secure

lomo (*loa*-moa) *m* back; loin; **a lomos de burro** on a donkey

lona (*loa*-nah) *f* canvas

longitud (loang-khee-*toodh*) *f* length; longitude; ~ **de onda** wavelength

lonja (*loan*-khah) *f* fish market; slice

loro (*loa*-roa) *m* parrot

lotería (loa-tay-*ree*-ah) *f* lottery

loza (*loa*-thah) *f* earthenware; pottery, faience, crockery

lubricación (loo-bhree-kah-*th*ʸoan) *f* lubrication

lubricar (loo-bhree-*kahr*) *v* lubricate

lucio (*loo*-thʸoa) *m* pike

*lucir (loo-*theer*) *v* *shine

lucha (*loo*-chah) *f* combat, fight; contest; struggle

luchar (loo-*chahr*) *v* struggle, *fight

luego (*lway*-goa) *adv* later; ¡**hasta**

luego! so long!

lugar (loo-gahr) m place; spot; **en ~ de** instead of; **~ de camping** camping site; **~ de descanso** holiday resort; **~ de nacimiento** place of birth; **~ de reunión** meeting place; ***tener ~** *take place

lujo (loo-khoa) m luxury

lujoso (loo-khoa-soa) adj luxurious

lumbago (loom-bah-goa) m lumbago

luminoso (loo-mee-noa-soa) adj luminous

luna (loo-nah) f moon; **~ de miel** honeymoon

lunático (loo-nah-tee-koa) adj insane, lunatic

lunes (loo-nayss) m Monday

lúpulo (loo-poo-loa) m hop

lustroso (looss-troa-soa) adj glossy

luto (loo-toa) m mourning

luz (looth) f light; **luces de freno** brake lights; **~ de estacionamiento** parking light; **~ de la luna** moonlight; **~ del día** daylight; **~ del sol** sunlight; **~ lateral** sidelight; **~ trasera** rear light

M

macizo (mah-thee-thoa) adj solid, massive

machacar (mah-chah-kahr) v mash

macho (mah-choa) adj male; masculine

madera (mah-dhay-rah) f wood; **de ~** wooden; **~ de construcción** timber

madero (mah-dhay-roa) m log

madrastra (mah-dhrahss-trah) f stepmother

madre (mah-dhray) f mother

madriguera (mah-dhree-gay-rah) f den

madrugada (mah-dhroo-gah-dhah) f daybreak

madrugar (mah-dhroo-gahr) v *rise early

madurez (mah-dhoo-rayth) f maturity

maduro (mah-dhoo-roa) adj mature, ripe

maestro (mah-ayss-troa) m, **-a** f master; schoolteacher, schoolmaster, teacher; **~ particular** tutor

magia (mah-khᶦah) f magic

mágico (mah-khee-koa) adj magic

magistrado (mah-kheess-trah-dhoa) m magistrate

magnético (mahg-nay-tee-koa) adj magnetic

magneto (mahg-nay-toa) m magneto

magnetófono (mahg-nay-toa-foa-noa) m tape recorder

magnífico (mahg-nee-fee-koa) adj splendid, gorgeous, magnificent, swell

magro (mah-groa) adj lean

magulladura (mah-goo-lᶦah-dhoo-rah) f bruise

magullar (mah-goo-lᶦahr) v bruise

majo (mah-khoa) adj colloquial nice; pretty

maíz (mah-eeth) m maize, corn Am; **~ en la mazorca** corn on the cob

majestad (mah-khayss-tahdh) f majesty

mal (mahl) m harm, evil; wrong; mischief

malaria (mah-lah-rᶦah) f malaria

Malasia (mah-lah-sᶦah) f Malaysia

malayo (mah-lah-ᶦoa) adj Malaysian;

m Malay

*maldecir (mahl-day-*theer*) *v* curse

maldición (mahl-dee-*th*ʸ*oan*) *f* curse

malentendido (mahl-ayn-tan-*dee*-doah) *m* misunderstanding

maleta (mah-*lay*-tah) *f* suitcase, bag

maletín (mah-lay-*teen*) *m* briefcase

malévolo (mah-*lay*-bhoa-loa) *adj* spiteful

malicia (mah-*lee*-thʸah) *f* mischief

malicioso (mah-lee-*th*ʸ*oa*-soa) *adj* malicious

maligno (mah-*leeg*-noa) *adj* malignant; ill

malo (*mah*-loa) *adj* bad; evil, ill

malva (*mahl*-bhah) *adj* mauve

malvado (mahl-*bhah*-dhoa) *adj* wicked, evil

malla (*mah*-lʸah) *f* mesh

mamífero (mah-*mee*-fay-roa) *m* mammal

mamut (mah-*moot*) *m* mammoth

manada (mah-*nah*-dhah) *f* herd

manantial (mah-nahn-t*ʸ*ahl) *m* spring

mancuernillas (mahn-kwayr-*nee*-lʸahss) *fplMe* cuff links *pl*

mancha (*mahn*-chah) *f* stain, spot, speck; blot

manchado (mahn-*chah*-dhoa) *adj* soiled

manchar (mahn-*chahr*) *v* stain

mandar (mahn-*dahr*) *v* command; *send; ~ **a buscar** *send for

mandarina (mahn-dah-*ree*-nah) *f* mandarin, tangerine

mandato (mahn-*dah*-toa) *m* mandate; order

mandíbula (mahn-*dee*-bhoo-lah) *f* jaw

mando (*mahn*-doa) *m* command

manejable (mah-nay-*khah*-bhlay) *adj* handy; manageable

manejar (mah-nay-*khahr*) *v* handle

manejo (mah-*nay*-khoa) *m* management

manera (mah-*nay*-rah) *f* way, manner; **de otra** ~ otherwise

manga (*mahng*-gah) *f* sleeve

mango (*mahng*-goa) *m* handle

manía (mah-*nee*-ah) *f* craze; mania

manicura (mah-nee-*koo*-rah) *f* manicure; ***hacer la** ~ manicure

manifestación (mah-nee-fayss-tah-*th*ʸ*oan*) *f* demonstration; ***hacer una** ~ demonstrate

*manifestar (mah-nee-fayss-*tahr*) *v* reveal, manifest, express

maniquí (mah-nee-*kee*) *m* model, mannequin

mano (*mah*-noa) *f* hand; **de segunda** ~ second-hand; **hecho a** ~ hand-made

mansión (mahn-s*ʸoan*) *f* mansion

manso (*mahn*-soa) *adj* tame

manta (*mahn*-tah) *f* blanket

mantel (mahn-*tayl*) *m* tablecloth

*mantener (mahn-tay-*nayr*) *v* maintain; support; service

mantenimiento (mahn-tay-nee-m*ʸ*ayn-toa) *m* maintenance; servicing

mantequilla (mahn-tay-*kee*-lʸah) *f* butter

manual (mah-*nwahl*) *adj* manual; *m* handbook; ~ **de conversación** phrase book

manuscrito (mah-nooss-*kree*-toa) *m* manuscript

manutención (mah-noo-tayn-*th*ʸ*oan*) *f* upkeep; maintenance; support

manzana (mahn-*thah*-nah) *f* apple; ~ **de casas** block *Am*

manzanilla (mahn-tha-*nee*-lʸah) *f* camomile tea

mañana (mah-*ñah*-nah) *f* morning; *adv* tomorrow; **esta** ~ this morning

mapa (*mah*-pah) *m* map; ~ **de carreteras** road map

maquillaje (mah-kee-*l*ʸ*ah*-khay) *m*

make-up

máquina (*mah*-kee-nah) *f* engine, machine; ~ **de billetes** ticket machine; ~ **de coser** sewing-machine; ~ **de escribir** typewriter; ~ **de lavar** washing machine; ~ **tragamonedas** slot machine

mar (mahr) *m* sea; **orilla del** ~ seaside, seashore

maravilla (mah-rah-*bhee*-lᵞah) *f* marvel

maravillarse (mah-rah-bhee-*lᵞahr*-say) *v* marvel

maravilloso (mah-rah-bhee-*lᵞoa*-soa) *adj* wonderful, marvel(l)ous, fine

marca (*mahr*-kah) *f* brand; mark; ~ **de fábrica** trademark

marcar (mahr-*kahr*) *v* mark; score

marco (*mahr*-koa) *m* frame

marcha (*mahr*-chah) *f* march; ***dar** ~ **atrás** reverse; ~ **atrás** reverse

marchar (mahr-*chahr*) *v* march

marea (mah-*ray*-ah) *f* tide ; ~ **alta** high tide; ~ **baja** low tide

mareado (mah-ray-*ah*-dhoa) *adj* dizzy, giddy; seasick

mareo (mah-*ray*-oa) *m* dizziness; giddiness; seasickness

marfil (mahr-*feel*) *m* ivory

margarina (mahr-gah-*ree*-nah) *f* margarine

margen (*mahr*-khayn) *m* margin

marido (mah-*ree*-dhoa) *m* husband

marina (mah-*ree*-nah) *f* navy; seascape

marinero (mah-ree-*nay*-roa) *m* sailor

marino (mah-*ree*-noa) *m* seaman; *adj* marine

mariposa (mah-ree-*poa*-sah) *f* butterfly

marisco (mah-*reess*-koa) *m*, **mariscos** *pl* seafood

marisma (mah-*reez*-mah) *f* swamp

marítimo (mah-*ree*-tee-moa) *adj* maritime

mármol (*mahr*-moal) *m* marble

marqués (mahr-*kayss*) *m* marquis

marrón (mah-rroan) *adj* brown

marroquí (mah-rroa-*kee*) *adj* Moroccan; *m* Moroccan

Marruecos (mah-*rway*-koass) *m* Morocco

martes (*mahr*-tayss) *m* Tuesday

martillo (mahr-*tee*-lᵞoa) *m* hammer

mártir (*mahr*-teer) *m* martyr

marzo (*mahr*-thoa) March

mas (mahss) *conj* but

más (mahss) *adv* more; plus; **algo** ~ some more; **el** ~ most; ~ **de** over

masa (*mah*-sah) *f* mass; crowd, lot; dough, batter

masaje (mah-*sah*-khay) *m* massage; ***dar** ~ massage; ~ **facial** face massage

masajista (mah-sah-*kheess*-tah) *m* masseur

máscara (*mahss*-kah-rah) *f* mask; ~ **facial** face pack

masculino (mahss-koo-*lee*-noa) *adj* masculine

masticar (mahss-tee-*kahr*) *v* chew

mástil (*mahss*-teel) *m* mast

matar (mah-*tahr*) *v* kill

mate (mah-tay) *adj* matt, dim, dull

matemáticas (mah-tay-*mah*-tee-kahss) *fpl* mathematics

matemático (mah-tay-*mah*-tee-koa) *adj* mathematical

materia (mah-*tay*-rᵞah) *f* matter; ~ **prima** raw material

material (mah-tay-*rᵞahl*) *adj* material, substantial; *m* material

matiz (mah-*teeth*) *m* nuance

matorral (mah-toa-*rrahl*) *m* scrub, bush

matrícula (mah-*tree*-koo-lah) *f* registration number

matrimonial (mah-tree-moa-*nᵞahl*) *adj* matrimonial

matrimonio (mah-tree-*moa*-nᵞoa) *m*

wedding, marriage; matrimony

matriz (mah-*treeth*) f uterus

máximo (*mahk*-see-moa) m maximum

mayo (*mah*-ʸoa) May

mayor (mah-ʸ*oar*) adj superior, major; bigger; main, eldest; m major;

mayores mpl ancestors; elders

mayoría (mah-ʸoa-*ree*-ah) f majority; bulk

mayorista (mah-ʸoa-*reess*-tah) m wholesale dealer

mayúscula (mah-ʸ*ooss*-koo-lah) f capital letter

mazo (*mah*-thoa) m mallet

me (may) pron me; myself

mecánico (may-kah-nee-koa) adj mechanical; m mechanic

mecanismo (may-kah-*neez*-moa) m mechanism, machinery

mecer (may-*thayr*) v rock; swing

mecha (*may*-chah) f fuse; wick

mechero (may-*chay*-roa) m cigarette lighter

medalla (may-*dhah*-lʸah) f medal

media (*may*-dhʸah) f stocking;
　medias elásticas support hose

mediador (may-dhʸah-*dhoar*) m mediator

medianamente (may-dhʸah-nah-*mayn*-tay) adv fairly

mediano (may-*dhʸah*-noa) adj medium

medianoche (may-dhʸah-*noa*-chay) f midnight

mediante (may-*dhʸahn*-tay) adv by means of

mediar (may-*dhʸahr*) v mediate

medicamento (may-dhee-kah-*mayn*-toa) m medicine, drug

medicina (may-dhee-*thee*-nah) f medicine

médico (*may*-dhee-koa) adj medical; m, **-a** f doctor, physician; **~ de**

cabecera general practitioner

medida (may-*dhee*-dhah) f measure;
　hecho a la ~ made to order, tailor-made

medidor (may-dhee-*dhoar*) m gauge

medieval (may-dhʸay-*bhahl*) adj medi(a)eval

medio (*may*-dhʸoa) adj half; medium; middle; m midst, middle; means; **en ~ de** amid; **~ ambiente** milieu, environment

mediocre (may-*dhʸoa*-kray) adj mediocre; below average

mediodía (may-dhʸoa-*dhee*-ah) m midday, noon

*medir (may-*dheer*) v measure

meditación (may-dhee-tah-thʸ*oan*) f meditation

meditar (may-dhee-*tahr*) v meditate

Mediterráneo (may-dhee-tay-*rrah*-nay-oa) Mediterranean

médula (*may*-dhoo-lah) f marrow

medusa (may-*dhoo*-sah) f jellyfish

mejicano (may-khee-*kah*-noa) adj Mexican; m Mexican

Méjico (*may*-khee-koa) m Mexico

mejilla (may-*khee*-lʸah) f cheek

mejillón (may-khee-lʸ*oan*) m mussel

mejor (may-*khoar*) adj better; superior

mejora (may-*khoa*-rah) f improvement

mejorar (may-khoa-*rahr*) v improve

melancolía (may-lahng-koa-*lee*-ah) f melancholy

melancólico (may-lahng-*koa*-lee-koa) adj sad

melocotón (may-loa-koa-*toan*) m peach

melodía (may-loa-*dhee*-ah) f melody

melodioso (may-loa-dhʸ*oa*-soa) adj melodious

melodrama (may-loa-*dhrah*-mah) m melodrama

melón (may-*loan*) *m* melon

memorable (may-moa-*rah*-bhlay) *adj* memorable

memoria (may-*moa*-r^yah) *f* memory; **de ~** by heart

menaje (may-*nah*-khay) *m* household

mención (mayn-*th^yoan*) *f* mention

mencionar (mayn-th^yoa-*nahr*) *v* mention

mendigar (mayn-dee-*gahr*) *v* beg

mendigo (mayn-*dee*-goa) *m*, **-a** *f* beggar

menor (may-*noar*) *adj* minor; junior

menos (*may*-noass) *adv* less; minus; but; **a ~ que** unless; **por lo ~** at least

menosprecio (may-noass-*pray*-th^yoa) *m* contempt; disdain

mensaje (mayn-*sah*-khay) *m* message

mensajero (mayn-sah-*khay*-roa) *m* messenger

menstruación (mayns-trwah-*th^yoan*) *f* menstruation

mensual (mayn-*swahl*) *adj* monthly

menta (*mayn*-tah) *f* mint; peppermint

mental (mayn-*tahl*) *adj* mental

mente (*mayn*-tay) *f* mind

*mentir (mayn-*teer*) *v* lie

mentira (mayn-*tee*-rah) *f* lie

menú (may-*noo*) *m* menu

menudo (may-*noo*-dhoa) *adj* minute, small, tiny; **a ~** often

mercado (mayr-*kah*-dhoa) *m* market; **~ negro** black market

mercancía (mayr-kahn-*thee*-ah) *f* merchandise

mercería (mayr-thay-*ree*-ah) *f* haberdashery; notions store *Am*

mercurio (mayr-*koo*-r^yoa) *m* mercury

*merecer (may-ray-*thayr*) *v* merit, deserve

meridional (may-ree-dh^yoa-*nahl*) *adj* southern, southerly

merienda (may-r^y*ayn*-dah) *f* snack; lunch

mérito (*may*-ree-toa) *m* merit

merluza (mayr-*loo*-thah) *f* whiting

mermelada (mayr-may-*lah*-dhah) *f* jam

mes (mayss) *m* month

mesa (*may*-sah) *f* table

mesera (may-*say*-rah) *fMe* waitress

mesero (may-*say*-roa) *mMe* waiter

meseta (may-*say*-tah) *f* plateau

meta (*may*-tah) *f* goal; finish

metal (may-*tahl*) *m* metal

metálico (may-*tah*-lee-koa) *adj* metal

meter (may-*tayr*) *v* *put

meticuloso (may-tee-koo-*loa*-soa) *adj* meticulous; precise

metódico (may-*toa*-dhee-koa) *adj* methodical

método (*may*-toa-dhoa) *m* method

metro (*may*-troa) *m* metre; underground; subway *Am*

mezcla (*mayth*-klah) *f* mixture

mezclar (mayth-*klahr*) *v* mix; **mezclarse en** interfere with

mezquino (mayth-*kee*-noa) *adj* narrow-minded, stingy; mean

mezquita (mayth-*kee*-tah) *f* mosque

mi (mee) *adj* my

micrófono (mee-*kroa*-foa-noa) *m* microphone

microscopio (mee-kroass-*koa*-p^yoa) *m* microscope

miedo (*m^yay*-dhoa) *m* fear, fright; ***tener ~** *be afraid

miel (m^yayl) *f* honey

miembro (*m^yaym*-broa) *m* limb; member

mientras (*m^yayn*-trahss) *conj* whilst, while

miércoles (*m^yayr*-koa-layss) *m* Wednesday

migaja (mee-*gah*-khah) *f* crumb

migraña (mee-*grah*-ñah) *f* migraine

mil (meel) *num* thousand

milagro (mee-*lah*-groa) *m* miracle;

wonder

milagroso (mee-lah-*groa*-soa) *adj*
miraculous

militar (mee-lee-*tahr*) *adj* military; *m*
soldier

milla (*mee*-lʸah) *f* mile

millaje (mee-lʸ*ah*-khay) *m* mileage

millón (mee-lʸ*oan*) *m* million

millonario (mee-lʸoa-*nah*-rʸoa) *m*, **-a** *f*
millionaire

mimar (mee-*mahr*) *v* *spoil

mina (*mee*-nah) *f* mine; pit; **~ de oro**
goldmine

mineral (mee-nay-*rahl*) *m* mineral;
ore

minería (mee-nay-*ree*-ah) *f* mining

minero (mee-*nay*-roa) *m* miner

miniatura (mee-nʸah-*too*-rah) *f*
miniature

mínimo (*mee*-nee-moa) *adj* least

mínimum (*mee*-nee-moom) *m*
minimum

ministerio (mee-neess-*tay*-rʸoa) *m*
ministry

ministro (mee-*neess*-troa) *m* minister

minoría (mee-noa-*ree*-ah) *f* minority

minorista (mee-noa-*reess*-tah) *m*/*f*
• retailer

minucioso (mee-noo-*thʸoa*-soa) *adj*
thorough

minusválido (mee-nooz-*bhah*-lee-
dhoa) *adj* disabled, handicapped

minuto (mee-*noo*-toa) *m* minute

mío (*mee*-oa) *pron* mine

miope (*mʸoa*-pay) *adj* short-sighted

mirada (mee-*rah*-dhah) *f* look; gaze

mirador (mee-rah-*dhoar*) *m*
viewpoint

mirar (mee-*rahr*) *v* look; watch, view,
look at; stare, gaze

mirlo (*meer*-loa) *m* blackbird

misa (*mee*-sah) *f* Mass

misceláneo (mee-thay-*lah*-nay-oa)
adj miscellaneous

miserable (mee-say-*rah*-bhlay) *adj*
unfortunate, stingy, vile

miseria (mee-*say*-rʸah) *f* poverty;
misery

misericordia (mee-say-ree-*koar*-
dʸah) *f* mercy

misericordioso (mee-say-ree-koar-
dʸoa-soa) *adj* merciful

misión (mee-*sʸoan*) *f* mission

mismo (*meez*-moa) *adj* same

misterio (meess-*tay*-rʸoa) *m* mystery

misterioso (meess-tay-*rʸoa*-soa) *adj*
mysterious; obscure

mitad (mee-*tahdh*) *f* half; **partir por la**
~ halve

mito (*mee*-toa) *m* myth

mixto (*meeks*-toa) *adj* mixed; joint

moción (moa-*thʸoan*) *f* motion

mochila (moa-*chee*-lah) *f* rucksack,
knapsack; backpack

moda (*moa*-dhah) *f* fashion; **a la ~**
fashionable

modales (moa-*dhah*-layss) *mpl*
manners *pl*

modelar (moa-dhay-*lahr*) *v* model

modelo (moa-*dhay*-loa) *m* model

moderado (moa-dhay-*rah*-dhoa) *adj*
moderate

moderno (moa-*dhayr*-noa) *adj*
modern

modestia (moa-dhayss-*tʸah*) *f*
modesty

modesto (moa-*dhayss*-toa) *adj*
modest

modificación (moa-dhee-fee-kah-
thʸoan) *f* change

modificar (moa-dhee-fee-*kahr*) *v*
change, modify

modismo (moa-*dheez*-moa) *m* idiom

modista (moa-*dheess*-tah) *f*
dressmaker

modo (*moa*-dhoa) *m* fashion, manner;
de cualquier ~ anyhow; **de ningún ~**
by no means; **de todos modos** any

way; at any rate; **en ~ alguno** at all; **~ de empleo** directions for use

moho (moa-oa) *m* mildew

mojado (moa-*khah*-dhoa) *adj* wet; moist, damp

mojigato (moa-khee-*gah*-toa) *adj* hypocritical

mojón (moa-*khoan*) *m* landmark

*****moler** (moa-*layr*) *v* *grind

molestar (moa-layss-*tahr*) *v* disturb, trouble, bother

molestia (moa-*layss*-t^{y}ah) *f* trouble, nuisance, bother

molesto (moa-*layss*-toa) *adj* troublesome, inconvenient

molinero (moa-lee-*nay*-roa) *m* miller

molino (moa-*lee*-noa) *m* mill; **~ de viento** windmill

momentáneo (moa-mayn-*tah*-nay-oa) *adj* momentary

momento (moa-*mayn*-toa) *m* moment

monarca (moa-*nahr*-kah) *m* monarch, ruler

monarquía (moa-nahr-*kee*-ah) *f* monarchy

monasterio (moa-nahss-*tay*-r^{y}oa) *m* monastery

moneda (moa-*nay*-dhah) *f* currency; coin; change; **~ extranjera** foreign currency

monedero (moa-nay-*dhay*-roa) *m* purse, wallet *Am*

monetario (moa-nay-*tah*-r^{y}oa) *adj* monetary; **unidad monetaria** monetary unit

monja (*moang*-khah) *f* nun

monje (*moang*-khay) *m* monk

mono (*moa*-noa) *m* monkey; overalls *pl*

monólogo (moa-*noa*-loa-goa) *m* monologue

monopolio (moa-noa-*poa*-l^{y}oa) *m* monopoly

monótono (moa-*noa*-toa-noa) *adj* monotonous

monstruo (*moans*-trwoa) *m* monster

montaña (moan-*tah*-ñah) *f* mountain

montañismo (moan-tah-*ñeez*-moa) *m* mountaineering

montañoso (moan-tah-*ñoa*-soa) *adj* mountainous

montar (moan-*tahr*) *v* mount, *get on; assemble; *ride

monte (*moan*-tay) *m* mount

montículo (moan-*tee*-koo-loa) *m* mound

montón (moan-*toan*) *m* heap, stack, pile

montuoso (moan-*twoa*-soa) *adj* hilly

monumento (moa-noo-*mayn*-toa) *m* monument; memorial

mora (*moa*-rah) *f* mulberry, blackberry

morado (moa-*rah*-dhoa) *adj* violet

moral (moa-*rahl*) *adj* moral; *f* moral; spirits

moralidad (moa-rah-lee-*dhahdh*) *f* morality

mordaza (moar-*dhah*-thah) *f* clamp

mordedura (moar-dhay-*dhoo*-rah) *f* bite

*****morder** (moar-*dhayr*) *v* *bite

morena (moa-*ray*-nah) *f* brunette

moreno (moa-*ray*-noa) *adj* dark brown

moretón (moa-ray-*toan*) *m* bruise

morfina (moar-*fee*-nah) *f* morphine, morphia

*****morir** (moa-*reer*) *v* die

moro (*moa*-roa) *m* Moor

mortal (moar-*tahl*) *adj* mortal; fatal

mosaico (moa-*sigh*-koa) *m* mosaic

mosca (*moass*-kah) *f* fly

mosquitero (moass-kee-*tay*-roa) *m* mosquito-net

mosquito (moass-*kee*-toa) *m* mosquito

mostaza (moass-*tah*-thah) *f* mustard

mostrador (moass-trah-*dhoar*) *m* counter

***mostrar** (moass-*trahr*) *v* display, *show

mote (*moa*-tay) *m* nickname

moteado (moa-tay-*ah*-dhoa) *adj* spotted

motel (moa-*tayl*) *m* motel

motín (moa-*teen*) *m* riot

motivo (moa-*tee*-bhoa) *m* motive; cause, occasion

motocicleta (moa-toa-thee-*klay*-tah) *f* motorcycle; motorbike *Am*

motoneta (moa-toa-*nay*-tah) *f* scooter

motor (moa-*toar*) *m* motor, engine; ~ de arranque starter motor

***mover** (moa-*bhayr*) *v* move; stir

movible (moa-*bhee*-bhlay) *adj* movable

móvil (*moa*-bheel) *adj* mobile

movimiento (moa-bhee-m^y^*ayn*-toa) *m* movement, motion

mozo (*moa*-thoa) *m* youth; porter

muchacha (moo-*chah*-chah) *f* girl; maid

muchacho (moo-*chah*-choa) *m* boy

muchedumbre (moo-chay-*dhoom*-bray) *f* crowd

mucho (*moo*-choa) *adv* much; far, very; *adj* much; con ~ by far; muchos *adj* many

mudanza (moo-*dhahn*-thah) *f* move

mudarse (moo-*dhahr*-say) *v* move; change

mudo (*moo*-dhoa) *adj* mute, dumb

muebles (*mway*-bhlayss) *mpl* furniture

muela (*mway*-lah) *f* molar; dolor de muelas toothache

muelle (*mway*-l^y^ay) *m* dock, wharf, quay; pier, jetty; spring

muerte (*mwayr*-tay) *f* death

muerto (*mwayr*-toa) *adj* dead

muestra (*mwayss*-trah) *f* sample

mugir (moo-*kheer*) *v* roar

mujer (moo-*khayr*) *f* woman; wife

mújol (*moo*-khoal) *m* mullet

muleta (moo-*lay*-tah) *f* crutch

mulo (*moo*-loa) *m* mule

multa (*mool*-tah) *f* fine; ticket

multiplicación (mool-tee-plee-kah-th^y^*oan*) *f* multiplication

multiplicar (mool-tee-plee-*kahr*) *v* multiply

multitud (mool-tee-*toodh*) *f* crowd

mundial (moon-d^y^*ahl*) *adj* world-wide, global

mundo (*moon*-doa) *m* world; todo el ~ everyone

municipal (moo-nee-thee-*pahl*) *adj* municipal

municipalidad (moo-nee-thee-pah-lee-*dhahdh*) *f* municipality

muñeca (moo-*ñay*-kah) *f* doll; wrist

muralla (moo-*rah*-l^y^ah) *f* wall

muro (*moo*-roa) *m* wall

músculo (*mooss*-koo-loa) *m* muscle

musculoso (mooss-koo-*loa*-soa) *adj* muscular

museo (moo-*say*-oa) *m* museum; ~ de figuras de cera waxworks *pl*

musgo (*mooz*-goa) *m* moss

música (*moo*-see-kah) *f* music

musical (moo-see-*kahl*) *adj* musical; comedia ~ musical comedy

músico (*moo*-see-koa) *m*, -a *f* musician

muslo (*mooz*-loa) *m* thigh

musulmán (moo-sool-*mahn*) *m* Muslim

mutuo (*moo*-twoa) *adj* mutual

muy (moo^ee^) *adv* very, quite

N

nácar (*nah*-kahr) *m* mother-of-pearl

*nacer (nah-*thayr*) *v* *be born

nacido (nah-*thee*-dhoa) *adj* born

nacimiento (nah-thee-*m^yayn*-toa) *m* birth; source; origin

nación (nah-th^yoa-*nal*) *f* nation

nacional (nah-th^yoa-*nahl*) *adj* national

nacionalidad (nah-th^yoa-nah-lee-*dhahdh*) *f* nationality

nacionalizar (nah-th^yoa-nah-lee-*thahr*) *v* nationalize

nada (*nah*-dhah) nothing; nil; **de ~** you're welcome

nadador (nah-dhah-*dhoar*) *m*, **-a** *f* swimmer

nadar (nah-*dhahr*) *v* *swim

nadie (*nah*-dh^yay) *pron* nobody, no one

naipe (*nigh*-pay) *m* playing card

nalga (*nahl*-gah) *m* buttock

naranja (nah-*rahng*-khah) *f* orange

narciso (nahr-*thee*-soa) *m* daffodil

narcosis (nahr-*koa*-seess) *f* narcosis

narcótico (nahr-*koa*-tee-koa) *m* narcotic

nariz (nah-*reeth*) *f* nose

narración (nah-rrah-*th^yoan*) *f* narration

nata (*nah*-tah) *f* cream

natación (nah-tah-*th^yoan*) *f* swimming

nativo (nah-*tee*-bhoa) *adj* native

natural (nah-too-*rahl*) *adj* natural; *m* nature

naturaleza (nah-too-rah-*lay*-thah) *f* nature

naturalmente (nah-too-rahl-*mayn*-tay) *adv* naturally

náusea (*nou*-say-ah) *f* nausea, sickness

navaja (nah-*bhah*-khah) *f* jack-knife; razor

naval (nah-*bhahl*) *adj* naval

nave (*nah*-bay) *f* ship; nave; **~ espacial** spacecraft

navegable (nah-bhay-*gah*-bhlay) *adj* navigable

navegación (nah-bhay-gah-*th^yoan*) *f* navigation

navegar (nah-bhay-*gahr*) *v* sail; navigate

Navidad (nah-bhee-*dhahdh*) *f* Christmas

nebuloso (nay-bhoo-*loa*-soa) *adj* cloudy; misty

necesario (nay-thay-*sah*-r^yoa) *adj* necessary; requisite

neceser (nay-thay-*sayr*) *m* toilet case

necesidad (nay-thay-see-*dhahdh*) *f* need, necessity; want; misery

necesitar (nay-thay-see-*tahr*) *v* need

necio (*nay*-th^yoa) *adj* foolish, silly

*negar (nay-*gahr*) *v* deny

negativa (nay-gah-*tee*-bhah) *f* refusal

negativo (nay-gah-*tee*-bhoa) *adj* negative; *m* negative

negligencia (nay-glee-*khayn*-th^yah) *f* negligence; neglect

negligente (nay-glee-*khayn*-tay) *adj* negligent, careless

negociación (nay-goa-th^yah-*th^yoan*) *f* negotiation

negociante (nay-goa-*th^yahn*-tay) *m/f* dealer

negociar (nay-goa-*th^yahr*) *v* negotiate

negocio (nay-*goa*-th^yoa) *m* business; ***hacer negocios con** *deal with; **hombre de negocios** businessman; **~ fotográfico** camera shop; **viaje de negocios** business trip

neón (nay-*oan*) *m* neon

nervio (*nayr*-bh^yoa) *m* nerve

nervioso (nayr-*bh^yoa*-soa) *adj*

nervous

neto (*nay*-toa) *adj* net

neumático (nay^{oo}-*mah*-tee-koa) *adj* pneumatic; *m* tyre, tire *Am*; ~ **de repuesto** spare tyre; ~ **desinflado** flat tyre

neumonía (nay^{oo}-moa-*nee*-ah) *f* pneumonia

neuralgia (nay^{oo}-*rahl*-kh^{y}ah) *f* neuralgia

neurosis (nay^{oo}-*roa*-seess) *f* neurosis

neutral (nay^{oo}-*trahl*) *adj* neutral

neutro (nay^{oo}-troa) *adj* neuter

*nevar (nay-*bhahr*) *v* snow

nevasca (nay-*bhahss*-kah) *f* snowstorm

nevoso (nay-*bhoa*-soa) *adj* snowy

ni ... ni (nee) neither ... nor

nicotina (nee-koa-*tee*-nah) *f* nicotine

nido (*nee*-dhoa) *m* nest

niebla (*n^{y}ay*-bhlah) *f* mist, fog; haze; **faro de ~** foglamp; ~ **tóxica** smog

nieta (*n^{y}ay*-tah) *f* granddaughter

nieto (*n^{y}ay*-toa) *m* grandson

nieve (*n^{y}ay*-bhay) *f* snow

Nigeria (nee-*khay*-r^{y}ah) *f* Nigeria

nigeriano (nee-khay-*r^{y}ah*-noa) *adj* Nigerian; *m* Nigerian

ninguno (neeng-*goo*-noa) *adj* no; *pron* none; ~ **de los dos** neither

niñera (nee-*ñay*-rah) *f* nanny

niño (*nee*-ñoa) *m* child; boy

níquel (*nee*-kayl) *m* nickel

nitrógeno (nee-*troa*-khay-noa) *m* nitrogen

nivel (nee-*bhayl*) *m* level; ~ **de vida** standard of living; **paso a ~** level crossing

nivelar (nee-bhay-*lahr*) *v* level

no (noa) not; no; **si ~** otherwise, else

noble (*noa*-bhlay) *adj* noble

nobleza (noa-*bhlay*-thah) *f* nobility

noción (noa-*th^{y}oan*) *f* notion; idea

nocturno (noak-*toor*-noa) *adj* nightly

noche (*noa*-chay) *f* night; **de ~** overnight, by night; **esta ~** tonight

Nochebuena (noa-chay-*bway*-nah) *f* Christmas Eve

Nochevieja (noa-chay-*b^{y}ay*-khah) *f* New Year's Eve

nogal (noa-*gahl*) *m* walnut

nombramiento (noam-brah-*m^{y}ayn*-toa) *m* appointment, nomination

nombrar (noam-*brahr*) *v* name, mention; appoint, nominate

nombre (*noam*-bray) *m* noun; name; denomination; **en ~ de** on behalf of, in the name of; ~ **de pila** Christian name, first name

nominación (noa-mee-nah-*th^{y}oan*) *f* nomination

nominal (noa-mee-*nahl*) *adj* nominal

nordeste (noar-*dhayss*-tay) *m* northeast

norma (*noar*-mah) *f* standard

normal (noar-*mahl*) *adj* normal; regular, standard

noroeste (noa-roa-*ayss*-tay) *m* northwest

norte (*noar*-tay) *m* north; **del ~** northerly; **polo ~** North Pole

norteño (noar-*tay*-ñoa) *adj* northern

Noruega (noa-*rway*-gah) *f* Norway

noruego (noa-*rway*-goa) *adj* Norwegian; *m* Norwegian

nos (noass) *pron* ourselves

nosotros (noa-*soa*-troass) *pron* we; us

nostalgia (noass-*tahl*-kh^{y}ah) *f* homesickness

nota (*noa*-tah) *f* ticket; note; mark

notable (noa-*tah*-bhlay) *adj* considerable; remarkable, striking, noticeable

notar (noa-*tahr*) *v* notice; note

notario (noa-*tah*-r^{y}oa) *m* notary

noticia (noa-*tee*-th^{y}ah) *f* news, notice; **noticias** *fpl* news

noticiario (noa-tee-*th^{y}ah*-r^{y}oa) *m*

news; newscast

notificar (noa-tee-fee-*kahr*) *v* notify

notorio (noa-*toa*-rʸoa) *adj* well-known

novedad (noa-bhay-*dhahdh*) *f* novelty

novela (noa-*bhay*-lah) *f* novel; ~ **policíaca** detective story; ~ **por entregas** serial

novelista (noa-bhay-*leess*-tah) *m/f* novelist

noveno (noa-*bhay*-noa) *num* ninth

noventa (noa-*bhayn*-tah) *num* ninety

novia (*noa*-bhʸah) *f* fiancée; bride

noviazgo (noa-*bhʸahth*-goa) *m* engagement

noviembre (noa-*bhʸaym*-bray) November

novillos: *****hacer** ~ (ah-*thayr* noa-bhee-lʸoass) play truant

novio (*noa*-bhʸoa) *m* fiancé; bridegroom

nube (*noo*-bhay) *f* cloud

nublado (noo-*bhlah*-dhoa) *adj* cloudy, overcast

nuca (*noo*-kah) *f* nape of the neck

nuclear (noo-klay-*ahr*) *adj* nuclear

núcleo (*noo*-klay-oa) *m* nucleus; heart, essence, core

nudillo (noo-*dhee*-lʸoa) *m* knuckle

nudo (*noo*-dhoa) *m* knot; lump; ~ **corredizo** loop

nuestro (*nwayss*-troa) *adj* our

Nueva Zelanda (*nway*-bhah thay-*lahn*-dah) New Zealand

nueve (*nway*-bhay) *num* nine

nuevo (*nway*-bhoa) *adj* new; **de** ~ again

nuez (nwayth) *f* nut; ~ **moscada** nutmeg

nulo (*noo*-loa) *adj* invalid, void

numeral (noo-may-*rahl*) *m* numeral

número (*noo*-may-roa) *m* number; digit; quantity; size; act

numeroso (noo-may-*roa*-soa) *adj* numerous

nunca (*noong*-kah) *adv* never

nutritivo (noo-tree-*tee*-bhoa) *adj* nutritious, nourishing

nylon (*nigh*-loan) *m* nylon

O

o (oa) *conj* or; **o ... o** either ... or

oasis (oa-*ah*-seess) *f* oasis

*****obedecer** (oa-bhay-dhay-*thayr*) *v* obey

obediencia (oa-bhay-*dhʸayn*-thʸah) *f* obedience

obediente (oa-bhay-*dhʸayn*-tay) *adj* obedient

obertura (oa-bhayr-*too*-rah) *f* overture

obesidad (oa-bhay-see-*dhahdh*) *f* obesity

obeso (oa-*bhay*-soa) *adj* obese, corpulent

obispo (oa-*bheess*-poa) *m* bishop

objeción (oabh-khay-*thʸoan*) *f* objection; *****hacer** ~ **a** mind

objetar (oabh-khay-*tahr*) *v* object

objetivo (oabh-khay-*tee*-bhoa) *adj* objective; *m* design, objective, target

objeto (oabh-*khay*-toa) *m* object; **objetos de valor** valuables *pl*; **objetos perdidos** lost and found

oblea (oa-*bhlay*-ah) *f* wafer

oblicuo (oa-*bhlee*-kwoa) *adj* slanting

obligar (oa-bhlee-*gahr*) *v* oblige; force

obligatorio (oa-bhlee-gah-*toa*-rʸoa) *adj* compulsory, obligatory

oblongo (oa-*bhloang*-goa) *adj* oblong

obra (*oa*-brahh) *f* work; ~ **de arte** work of art; ~ **de teatro** play; ~ **hecha a mano** handwork; ~ **maestra** masterpiece

obrar (oa-*bhrahr*) *v* work; perform

obrero (oa-*bhray*-roa) *m*, **-a** *f* worker; ~ **portuario** docker

obsceno (oabh-*thay*-noa) *adj* obscene

obscuridad (oabhs-koo-ree-*dhahdh*) *f* gloom; obscurity

obscuro (oabhs-*koo*-roa) *adj* dark, gloomy; obscure

observación (oabh-sayr-bhah-*th*^y*oan*) *f* observation; remark; ***hacer una ~** remark

observar (oabh-sayr-*bhahr*) *v* watch, observe, notice, note

observatorio (oabh-sayr-bhah-*toa*-r^yoa) *m* observatory

obsesión (oabh-say-*s*^y*oan*) *f* obsession

obstáculo (oabhs-*tah*-koo-loa) *m* obstacle

obstante: no ~ (noa oabhs-*tahn*-tay) nevertheless

obstinado (oabhs-tee-*nah*-dhoa) *adj* dogged, obstinate

*obstruir (oabhs-*trweer*) *v* block

*obtener (oabh-tay-*nayr*) *v* obtain

obtenible (oabh-tay-*nee*-bhlay) *adj* available

obtuso (oabh-*too*-soa) *adj* blunt

obvio (*oabh*-bh^yoa) *adj* apparent, obvious

oca (*oa*-kah) *f* goose

ocasión (oa-kah-*s*^y*oan*) *f* occasion; chance

ocasionalmente (oa-kah-s^yoa-nahl-*mayn*-tay) *adv* occasionally

ocaso (oa-*kah*-soa) *m* sunset

occidental (oak-thee-dhayn-*tahl*) *adj* westerly; western

occidente (oak-thee-*dhayn*-tay) *m* west

océano (oa-*thay*-ah-noa) *m* ocean; **Océano Pacífico** Pacific Ocean

ocio (*oa*-th^yoa) *m* leisure

ocioso (oa-*th*^y*oa*-soa) *adj* idle

octavo (oak-*tah*-bhoa) *num* eighth

octubre (oak-*too*-bhray) October

oculista (oa-koo-*leess*-tah) *m/f* oculist

ocultar (oa-kool-*tahr*) *v* *hide

ocupación (oa-koo-pah-*th*^y*oan*) *f* occupation; business

ocupante (oa-koo-*pahn*-tay) *m* occupant

ocupar (oa-koo-*pahr*) *v* occupy; *take up; **ocupado** *adj* engaged, busy; occupied; **ocuparse de** look after

ocurrencia (oa-koo-*rrayn*-th^yah) *f* idea

ocurrir (oa-koo-*rreer*) *v* occur

ochenta (oa-*chayn*-tah) *num* eighty

ocho (*oa*-choa) *num* eight

odiar (oa-*dh*^y*ahr*) *v* hate

odio (*oa*-dh^yoa) *m* hatred, hate

oeste (oa-*ayss*-tay) *m* west

ofender (oa-fayn-*dayr*) *v* offend; wound, *hurt

ofensa (oa-*fayn*-sah) *f* offence, offense *Am*

ofensivo (oa-fayn-*see*-bhoa) *adj* offensive; *m* offensive

oferta (oa-*fayr*-tah) *f* offer, supply

oficial (oa-fee-th^y*ahl*) *adj* official; *m* officer; ~ **de aduanas** Customs officer

oficina (oa-fee-*thee*-nah) *f* office; ~ **de cambio** exchange office; ~ **de colocación** employment exchange; ~ **de informaciones** information bureau; ~ **de objetos perdidos** lost property office

oficinista (oa-fee-thee-*neess*-tah) *m/f* clerk, office worker

oficio (oa-*fee*-th^yoa) *m* trade

*ofrecer (oa-fray-*thayr*) *v* offer

oído (oa-*ee*-dhoa) *m* hearing; **dolor de**

oídos earache

*oír (oa-*eer*) v *hear

ojal (oa-*khahl*) m buttonhole

ojeada (oa-khay-*ah*-dhah) f glimpse, glance; look

ojear (oa-khay-*ahr*) v glance

ojo (*oa*-khoa) m eye

ola (*oa*-lah) f wave

*oler (oa-*layr*) v *smell

olmo (*oal*-moa) m elm

olor (oa-*loar*) m smell, odo(u)r

olvidadizo (oal-bhee-dhah-*dhee*-thoa) adj forgetful

olvidar (oal-bhee-*dhahr*) v *forget

olla (*oa*-lʸah) f pot; kettle; ~ **a presión** pressure cooker

ombligo (oam-*blee*-goa) m navel

omitir (oa-mee-*teer*) v *leave out, omit; fail

omnipotente (oam-nee-poa-*tayn*-tay) adj omnipotent

once (*oan*-thay) num eleven

onceno (oan-*thay*-noa) num eleventh

onda (*oan*-dah) f wave

ondulación (oan-doo-lah-*thʸoan*) f wave; ~ **permanente** permanent wave

ondulado (oan-doo-*lah*-dhoa) adj wavy

ópalo (*oa*-pah-loa) m opal

opcional (oap-thʸoa-*nahl*) adj optional

ópera (*oa*-pay-rah) f opera

operación (oa-pay-rah-*thʸoan*) f operation, surgery

operar (oa-pay-*rahr*) v operate

opinar (oa-pee-*nahr*) v consider

opinión (oa-pee-*nʸoan*) f view, opinion

*oponerse (oa-poa-*nayr*-say) v oppose; ~ **a** object to

oportunidad (oa-poar-too-nee-*dhahdh*) f chance, opportunity

oportuno (oa-poar-*too*-noa) adj convenient; appropriate

oposición (oa-poa-see-*thʸoan*) f opposition

oprimir (oa-pree-*meer*) v oppress

óptico (*oap*-tee-koa) m, **-a** f optician

optimismo (oap-tee-*meez*-moa) m optimism

optimista (oap-tee-*meess*-tah) adj optimistic; m/f optimist

óptimo (*oap*-tee-moa) adj best; optimal

opuesto (oa-*pwayss*-toa) adj opposite; averse

oración (oa-rah-*thʸoan*) f prayer

oral (oa-*rahl*) adj oral

orar (oa-*rahr*) v pray

orden (*oar*-dhayn) f command; order; m method; **de primer** ~ first-rate; ~ **del día** agenda

ordenador (oar-dhay-nah-*dhoar*) m computer; ~ **personal** personal computer, PC; ~ **portátil** laptop

ordenar (oar-dhay-*nahr*) v arrange; order

ordinario (oar-dhee-*nah*-rʸoa) adj simple, ordinary; common, vulgar

oreja (oa-*ray*-khah) f ear

orfebre (oar-*fay*-bhray) m goldsmith

orgánico (oar-*gah*-nee-koa) adj organic

organismo (oar-gah-*neez*-moa) m organism

organización (oar-gah-nee-thah-*thʸoan*) f organization

organizar (oar-gah-nee-*thahr*) v organize; arrange

órgano (*oar*-gah-noa) m organ

orgullo (oar-*goo*-lʸoa) m pride

orgulloso (oar-goo-*lʸoa*-soa) adj proud

orientación (oa-rʸayn-tah-*thʸoan*) f orientation

oriental (oa-rʸayn-*tahl*) adj eastern; oriental

orientarse (oa-r^{y}ayn-*tahr*-say) *v* orient

oriente (oa-r^y*ayn*-tay) *m* Orient

origen (oa-*ree*-khayn) *m* origin

original (oa-ree-khee-*nahl*) *adj* original

originalmente (oa-ree-khee-nahl-*mayn*-tay) *adv* originally

originar (oa-ree-khee-*nahr*) *v* originate

orilla (oa-*ree*-l^{y}ah) *f* bank; shore

orina (oa-*ree*-nah) *f* urine

ornamental (oar-nah-mayn-*tahl*) *adj* ornamental

oro (*oa*-roa) *m* gold

orquesta (oar-*kayss*-tah) *f* orchestra; band

ortodoxo (oar-toa-*dhoak*-soa) *adj* orthodox

os (oass) *pron* you

osar (oa-*sahr*) *v* dare

oscilar (oa-thee-*lahr*) *v* *swing

oscuridad (oass-koo-ree-*dhahdh*) *f* dark

oscuro (oass-*koo*-roa) *adj* dark, dim, obscure

oso (*oa*-soa) *m* bear

ostra (*oass*-trah) *f* oyster

otoño (oa-*toa*-ñoa) *m* autumn; fall *Am*

otro (*oa*-troa) *adj* other, different; another; ~ **más** another

ovalado (oa-bhah-*lah*-dhoa) *adj* oval

oveja (oa-*bhay*-khah) *f* sheep

overol (oa-bhay-*roal*) *m*Me overalls *pl*

oxidado (oak-see-*dhah*-dhoa) *adj* rusty

oxígeno (oak-*see*-khay-noa) *m* oxygen

oyente (oa-^{y}*ayn*-tay) *m* auditor, listener

ozono (oa-*thoa*-noa) *m* ozone

P

pabellón (pah-bhay-l^y*oan*) *m* pavilion

*pacer (pah-*thayr*) *v* graze

paciencia (pah-th^y*ayn*-th^{y}ah) *f* patience

paciente (pah-th^y*ayn*-tay) *adj* patient; *m/f* patient

pacifismo (pah-thee-*feez*-moa) *m* pacifism

pacifista (pah-thee-*feess*-tah) *adj* pacifist; *m* pacifist

*padecer (pah-dhay-*thayr*) *v* suffer

padrastro (pah-*dhrahss*-troa) *m* stepfather

padre (*pah*-dhray) *m* father

padres (*pah*-dhrayss) *mpl* parents *pl*; ~ **adoptivos** foster-parents *pl*; ~ **políticos** parents-in-law *pl*

padrino (pah-*dhree*-noa) *m* godfather

paella (pah-*ay*-l^{y}ah) *f* paella

paga (*pah*-gah) *f* wages *pl*

pagano (pah-*gah*-noa) *adj* heathen, pagan; *m* heathen, pagan

pagar (pah-*gahr*) *v* *pay; **pagado por adelantado** prepaid; ~ **a plazos** *pay on account

página (*pah*-khee-nah) *f* page

pago (*pah*-goa) *m* payment; **primer ~** down payment

painel (pigh-*nayl*) *m* panel

país (pah-*eess*) *m* country, land; region; area; ~ **natal** native country

paisaje (pigh-*sah*-khay) *m* scenery, landscape

paisano (pigh-*sah*-noa) *m* civilian

Países Bajos (pah-ee-sayss-*bah*-khoass) *mpl* the Netherlands

paja (*pah*-khah) f straw

pájaro (*pah*-khah-roa) m bird

paje (*pah*-khay) m pageboy

pala (*pah*-lah) f spade, shovel

palabra (pah-*lah*-bhrah) f word

palacio (pah-*lah*-th^yoa) m palace

palanca (pah-*lahng*-kah) f lever; ~ **de cambios** gear lever

palangana (pah-lahng-*gah*-nah) f basin; washbasin

pálido (*pah*-lee-dhoa) adj pale; dull; light

palillo (pah-*lee*-l^yoa) m toothpick

palma (*pahl*-mah) f palm

palmera (pahl-*may*-rah) f palm tree; heart-shaped pastry

palo (*pah*-loa) m stick; ~ **de golf** golf club

paloma (pah-*loa*-mah) f pigeon

palpable (pahl-*pah*-bhlay) adj palpable

palpar (pahl-*pahr*) v *feel; touch

palpitación (pahl-pee-tah-*th^yoan*) f palpitation

pan (pahn) m bread, loaf; ~ **integral** wholemeal bread; ~ **tostado** toast

pana (*pah*-nah) f corduroy, velveteen

panadería (pah-nah-dhay-*ree*-ah) f bakery

panadero (pah-nah-*dhay*-roa) m baker

panecillo (pah-nay-*thee*-l^yoa) m roll

pánico (*pah*-nee-koa) m panic

pantalones (pahn-tah-*loa*-nayss) mpl trousers pl; slacks pl; pants plAm; ~ **cortos** shorts pl; ~ **de esquí** ski pants; ~ **de gimnasia** trunks, shorts

pantalla (pahn-*tah*-l^yah) f lampshade; screen

pantano (pahn-*tah*-noa) m marsh, bog

pantanoso (pahn-tah-*noa*-soa) adj marshy

pantorrilla (pahn-toa-*rree*-l^yah) f calf

panty media (*pahn*-tee *may*-dh^yah) f panty hose

pañal (pah-*ñahl*) m nappy; diaper Am

pañería (pah-ñay-*ree*-ah) f drapery

pañero (pah-*ñay*-roa) m draper

paño (*pah*-ñoa) m cloth

pañuelo (pah-*ñway*-loa) m handkerchief; ~ **de papel** tissue, Kleenex®

Papa (*pah*-pah) m pope

papa (*pah*-pah) fMe potato

papá (pah-*pah*) m dad

papel (pah-*payl*) m paper; role; **de ~** paper; ~ **de aluminio** foil; ~ **de envolver** wrapping paper; ~ **de escribir** writing-paper; ~ **de estaño** tinfoil; ~ **de lija** sandpaper; ~ **higiénico** toilet paper; ~ **para cartas** notepaper; ~ **pintado** wallpaper; ~ **(de) regalo** giftwrap

papelera (pah-pay-*lay*-rah) f wastepaper basket

papelería (pah-pay-lay-*ree*-ah) f stationery; stationer's

paperas (pah-*pay*-rahss) fpl mumps

paquete (pah-*kay*-tay) m packet, package, parcel; bundle

Paquistán (pah-keess-*tahn*) m Pakistan

paquistaní (pah-keess-tah-*nee*) adj Pakistani; m Pakistani

par (pahr) adj even (number); like; m pair

para (*pah*-rah) prep to, for; to, in order to; ~ **con** towards; ~ **qué?** what for?

parabrisas (pah-rah-*bhree*-sahss) m windscreen; windshield Am

parachoques (pah-rah-*choa*-kayss) m fender, bumper

parada (pah-*rah*-dhah) f parade; stop; ~ **de taxis** taxi rank; taxi stand Am

parado (pah-*rah*-dhoa) adjMe erect; standing; **los ~s** the unemployed

parador (pah-rah-*dhoar*) m inn; hotel

parafina (pah-rah-*fee*-nah) *f* paraffin

paraguas (pah-*rah*-gwahss) *m* umbrella

paraíso (pah-rah-*ee*-soa) *m* paradise

paralelo (pah-rah-*lay*-loa) *adj* parallel; *m* parallel

paralítico (pah-rah-*lee*-tee-koa) *adj* lame

paralizar (pah-rah-lee-*thahr*) *v* paralise

pararse (pah-*rahr*-say) *v* stop; pull up; *Me* stand up

parcela (pahr-*thay*-lah) *f* plot

parcial (pahr-*th^yahl*) *adj* partial

parecer (pah-ray-*thayr*) *m* view, opinion

*parecer (pah-ray-*thayr*) *v* appear, seem, look

parecido (pah-ray-*thee*-dhoa) *adj* alike; **bien ~** good-looking

pared (pah-*raydh*) *f* wall

pareja (pah-*ray*-khah) *f* couple; partner

pariente (pah-*r^yayn*-tay) *m* relative, relation

parking (*pahr*-keengh) *m* parking lot, car park

parlamentario (pahr-lah-mayn-*tah*-r^yoa) *adj* parliamentary

parlamento (pahr-lah-*mayn*-toa) *m* parliament

paro (*pah*-roa) *m* unemployment; **estar en ~** be unemployed; **~ cardíaco** cardiac arrest

párpado (*pahr*-pah-dhoa) *m* eyelid

parque (*pahr*-kay) *m* park; **~ de estacionamiento** car park; **~ de reserva zoológica** game reserve; **~ nacional** national park

parquímetro (pahr-*kee*-may-troa) *m* parking meter

párrafo (*pah*-rrah-foa) *m* paragraph

parrilla (pah-*ree*-l^yah) *f* grill; grill-room; **asar en ~** grill

parroquia (pah-*rroa*-k^yah) *f* parish

parsimonioso (pahr-see-moa-n^yoa-soa) *adj* economical

parte (*pahr*-tay) *f* part; share; **en alguna ~** somewhere; **en ninguna ~** nowhere; **en ~** partly; **otra ~** elsewhere; **~ posterior** rear; **~ superior** top, top side; **por otra ~** besides; **por todas partes** everywhere, throughout

participante (pahr-tee-thee-*pahn*-tay) *m/f* participant

participar (pahr-tee-thee-*pahr*) *v* participate

particular (pahr-tee-koo-*lahr*) *adj* private; particular; **en ~** specially, in particular

particularidad (pahr-tee-koo-lah-ree-*dhahdh*) *f* detail; peculiarity

partida (pahr-*tee*-dhah) *f* departure; certificate

partido (pahr-*tee*-dhoa) *m* side, party; match; **~ de fútbol** football match

partir (pahr-*teer*) *v* *leave, depart, pull out, *set out; **a ~ de** as from; from

parto (*pahr*-toa) *m* childbirth; delivery

pasa (*pah*-sah) *f* raisin; **~ de Corinto** currant

pasado (pah-*sah*-dhoa) *adj* past; *m* past

pasaje (pah-*sah*-khay) *m* passage

pasajero (pah-sah-*khay*-roa) *m* , **-a** *f* passenger

pasaporte (pah-sah-*poar*-tay) *m* passport

pasar (pah-*sahr*) *v* happen; *go through; pass; *spend; **~ por alto** overlook; **pasarse sin** spare

pasarela (pah-sah-*ray*-lah) *f* gangway; catwalk

pasatiempo (pah-sah-t^yaym-poa) *m* pastime

Pascua (*pahss*-kwah) Easter

paseante (pah-say-*ahn*-tay) *m* walker;

stroller

pasear (pah-say-*ahr*) *v* walk, stroll

paseo (pah-*say*-oa) *m* stroll; ride; promenade

pasillo (pah-*see*-lᵞoa) *m* corridor; aisle

pasión (pah-sᵞ*oan*) *f* passion

pasivo (pah-*see*-bhoa) *adj* passive

paso (*pah*-soa) *m* step, pace; move, gait; crossing; mountain pass; **de ~** casual; **~ a nivel** crossing; **prioridad de ~** right of way; **prohibido el ~** no entry

pasta (*pahss*-tah) *f* paste; **~ dentífrica** toothpaste

pastel (pahss-*tayl*) *m* cake

pastelería (pahss-tay-lay-*ree*-ah) *f* pastry, cake; pastry shop

pastilla (pahss-*tee*-lᵞah) *f* tablet

pastor (pahss-*toar*) *m* shepherd; clergyman, parson, rector

pata (*pah*-tah) *f* paw; leg

patada (pah-*tah*-dhah) *f* kick

patata (pah-*tah*-tah) *f* potato; **patatas fritas** chips, French fries *Am*

patear (pah-tay-*ahr*) *v* kick; stamp

patente (pah-*tayn*-tay) *f* patent

patillas (pah-*tee*-lᵞahss) *fpl* whiskers *pl*, sideburns *pl*

patín (pah-*teen*) *m* skate; scooter

patinaje (pah-tee-*nah*-khay) *m* skating

patinar (pah-tee-*nahr*) *v* skate; skid

pato (*pah*-toa) *m* duck

patria (*pah*-trᵞah) *f* native country, homeland

patriota (pah-trᵞ*oa*-tah) *m/f* patriot

patrón (pah-*troan*) *m* boss, master; employer; landlord

patrona (pah-*troa*-nah) *f* employer, landlady

patrulla (pah-*troo*-lᵞah) *f* patrol

pausa (*pou*-sah) *f* pause; ***hacer una ~** pause

pavimentar (pah-bhee-mayn-*tahr*) *v*

pave

pavimento (pah-bhee-*mayn*-toa) *m* pavement

pavo (*pah*-bhoa) *m* peacock; turkey

payaso (pah-ᵞ*ah*-soa) *m* clown

paz (pahth) *f* peace; quiet

peaje (pay-*ah*-khay) *m* toll

peatón (pay-ah-*toan*) *m* pedestrian; **prohibido para los peatones** no pedestrians

pecado (pay-*kah*-dhoa) *m* sin

peculiar (pay-koo-lᵏ*ahr*) *adj* peculiar

pecho (*pay*-choa) *m* chest; bosom

pechuga (pay-*choo*-gah) *f* breast; L.Am. *colloquial* nerve

pedal (pay-*dhahl*) *m* pedal

pedazo (pay-*dhah*-thoa) *m* piece; scrap

pedernal (pay-dhayr-*nahl*) *m* flint

pedicuro (pay-dhee-*koo*-roa) *m* chiropodist, pedicure

pedido (pay-*dhee*-dhoa) *m* order

*pedir (pay-*dheer*) *v* beg; order; charge

pegajoso (pay-gah-*khoa*-soa) *adj* sticky

pegar (pay-*gahr*) *v* smack, slap, *hit; *stick, paste; **pegarse** *v* *burn

peinado (pay-*nah*-dhoa) *m* hairdo

peinar (pay-*nahr*) *v* comb

peine (*pay*-nay) *m* comb

pelar (pay-*lahr*) *v* peel

peldaño (payl-*dah*-ñoa) *m* step

pelea (pay-*lay*-ah) *f* battle

peletero (pay-lay-*tay*-roa) *m* furrier

pelícano (pay-*lee*-kah-noa) *m* pelican

película (pay-*lee*-koo-lah) *f* film; **~ en colores** colo(u)r film

peligro (pay-*lee*-groa) *m* danger; peril, risk; distress

peligroso (pay-lee-*groa*-soa) *adj* dangerous; perilous

pelo (*pay*-loa) *m* hair; fur; **a ~** unprepared; **montar a ~** ride bareback

pelota (pay-*loa*-tah) f ball

peluca (pay-*loo*-kah) f wig

peluquero (pay-loo-*kay*-roa) m, **-a** f hairdresser

pelvis (*payl*-bheess) m pelvis

pellizcar (pay-lˡ*eeth*-kahr) v pinch

pena (*pay*-nah) f sorrow; pains; penalty; ~ **de muerte** death penalty

pendiente (payn-dˡ*ayn*-tay) adj slanting; m earring, pendant; f gradient, slope

penetrar (pay-nay-*trahr*) v penetrate

penicilina (pay-nee-thee-*lee*-nah) f penicillin

península (pay-*neen*-soo-lah) f peninsula

pensamiento (payn-sah-*mˡayn*-toa) m idea, thought

*pensar (payn-*sahr*) v *think; ~ **en** *think of

pensativo (payn-sah-*tee*-bhoa) adj thoughtful

pensión (payn-sˡ*oan*) f guesthouse, pension, boardinghouse; board; ~ **alimenticia** alimony; ~ **completa** full board, board and lodging

Pentecostés (payn-tay-koass-*tayss*) m Whitsun, Pentecost Am

peña (*pay*-ñah) f boulder

peón (pay-*oan*) m pawn; unskilled worker

peor (pay-*oar*) adj worse; adv worse

pepino (pay-*pee*-noa) m cucumber

pepita (pay-*pee*-tah) f pip

pequeño (pay-*kay*-ñoa) adj small, little; petty, minor

pera (*pay*-rah) f pear

perca (*payr*-kah) f perch, bass

percepción (payr-thayp-*thˡoan*) f perception

perceptible (payr-thayp-*tee*-bhlay) adj perceptible, noticeable

percibir (payr-thee-*bheer*) v perceive

percha (*payr*-chah) f hanger, coat-

hanger, peg; hat rack

*perder (payr-*dhayr*) v *lose; miss; waste

pérdida (*payr*-dhee-dhah) f loss

perdiz (payr-*dheeth*) f partridge

perdón (payr-*dhoan*) m pardon; grace; ¡**perdón!** sorry!

perdonar (payr-dhoa-*nahr*) v *forgive

perecedero (pay-ray-thay-*dhay*-roa) adj perishable

*perecer (pay-ray-*thayr*) v perish

peregrinación (pay-ray-gree-nah-*thˡoan*) f pilgrimage

peregrino (pay-ray-*gree*-noa) m pilgrim

perejil (pay-ray-*kheel*) m parsley

perezoso (pay-ray-*thoa*-soa) adj lazy

perfección (payr-fayk-*thˡoan*) f perfection

perfecto (payr-*fayk*-toa) adj perfect; faultless

perfil (payr-*feel*) m profile

perfume (payr-*foo*-may) m perfume; scent

perico (pay-*ree*-koa) m parakeet

periódico (pay-rˡ*oa*-dhee-koa) adj periodical; m periodical, paper; **vendedor de periódicos** newsagent

periodismo (pay-rˡ*oa*-*deez*-moa) m journalism

periodista (pay-rˡoa-*dheess*-tah) m/f journalist

período (pay-*ree*-oa-dhoa) m period, term

perito (pay-*ree*-toa) m expert, connoisseur

perjudicar (payr-khoo-dhee-*kahr*) v harm

perjudicial (payr-khoo-dhee-*thˡahl*) adj harmful, hurtful

perjuicio (payr-*khwee*-thˡoa) m harm, damage

perjurio (payr-*khoo*-rˡoa) m perjury

perla (*payr*-lah) f pearl

*permanecer (payr-mah-nay-*thayr*) v
remain

permanente (payr-mah-*nayn*-tay) adj
permanent; **planchado ~** permanent
press

permiso (payr-*mee*-soa) m
permission, authorization; permit,
licence, license Am; **~ de conducir**
driving licence; **~ de pesca** fishing
licence; **~ de residencia** residence
permit; **~ de trabajo** work permit;
labor permit Am

permitir (payr-mee-*teer*) v permit,
allow; enable; **permitirse** v afford

pero (*pay*-roa) conj yet, only, but

perpendicular (payr-payn-dee-koo-
lahr) adj perpendicular

perpetuo (payr-*pay*-twoa) adj
perpetual

perra (*pay*-rrah) f bitch

perrera (pay-*rray*-rah) f kennel

perro (*pay*-rroa) m dog; **~ lazarillo**
guide dog

persa (*payr*-sah) adj Persian; m
Persian

*perseguir (payr-say-*geer*) v pursue

perseverar (payr-say-bhay-*rahr*) v
*keep up

Persia (*payr*-s^y ah) f Persia

persiana (payr-s^y *ah*-nah) f shutter,
blind

persistir (payr-seess-*teer*) v insist

persona (payr-*soa*-nah) f person; **por
~** per person

personal (payr-soa-*nahl*) adj
personal, private; m personnel, staff

personalidad (payr-soa-nah-lee-
dhahdh) f personality

perspectiva (payrs-payk-*tee*-bhah) f
perspective; prospect

persuadir (payr-swah-dheer) v
persuade

*pertenecer (payr-tay-nay-*thayr*) v
belong

pertenencias (payr-tay-*nayn*-th^y ahss)
fpl belongings pl

pertinaz (payr-tee-*nahth*) adj
persistent

pesado (pay-*sah*-dhoa) adj heavy;
tedious

pesadumbre (pay-sah-*dhoom*-bray) f
grief

pesar (pay-*sahr*) v weigh; **a ~ de**
despite, in spite of

pesca (*payss*-kah) f fishing; fishing
industry

pescadería (payss-kah-dhay-*ree*-ah) f
fish shop

pescado (payss-*kah*-dhoa) m fish

pescador (payss-kah-*dhoar*) m
fisherman

pescar (payss-*kahr*) v fish; **~ con caña**
angle

pesebre (pay-*say*-bhray) m manger

pesimismo (pay-see-*meez*-moa) m
pessimism

pesimista (pay-see-*meess*-tah) adj
pessimistic; m/f pessimist

pésimo (*pay*-see-moa) adj worst;
terrible

peso (*pay*-soa) m weight; burden

pestaña (payss-*tah*-ñah) f eyelash

petaca (pay-*tah*-kah) f pouch; tobacco
pouch

pétalo (*pay*-tah-loa) m petal

petición (pay-tee-*th^y oan*) f petition

petirrojo (pay-tee-*rroa*-khoa) m robin

petróleo (pay-*troa*-lay-oa) m
petroleum, oil; **~ lampante** kerosene;
pozo de ~ oil well; **refinería de ~** oil
refinery

pez (payth) m fish

piadoso (p^y ah-*dhoa*-soa) adj pious

pianista (p^y ah-*neess*-tah) m pianist

piano (p^y *ah*-noa) m piano; **~ de cola**
grand piano

picadero (pee-kah-*dhay*-roa) m
riding school

picadura (pee-kah-*dhoo*-rah) *f* sting, bite; cigarette tobacco

picante (pee-*kahn*-tay) *adj* spicy, savo(u)ry

picar (pee-*kahr*) *v* itch; mince; *sting; nibble

pícaro (*pee*-kah-roa) *m* rascal

picazón (pee-kah-*thoan*) *f* itch

pico (*pee*-koa) *m* beak; peak; pick-axe

pie (p^yay) *m* foot; **a ~** on foot; walking; **de ~** upright; ***estar de ~** *stand; **~ de cabra** crowbar

piedad (p^yay-*dhahdh*) *f* pity; ***tener ~ de** pity

piedra (p^yay-dhrah) *f* stone; **de ~** stone; **~ miliar** milestone; **~ pómez** pumice stone; **~ preciosa** stone

piel (p^yayl) *f* skin; fur, hide; peel; **de ~** leather; **~ de cerdo** pigskin

pierna (p^yayr-nah) *f* leg

pieza (p^yay-thah) *f* part; **de dos piezas** two-piece; **~ de repuesto** spare part; **~ en un acto** one-act play

pijama (pee-*khah*-mah) *m* pyjamas *pl*

pilar (pee-*lahr*) *m* pillar

píldora (*peel*-doa-rah) *f* pill

pileta (pee-*lay*-tah) *f* sink

piloto (pee-*loa*-toa) *m* pilot

pillo (*pee*-l^yoa) *m* rascal

pimienta (pee-m^y*ayn*-tah) *f* pepper

pimiento (pee-m^y*ayn*-toa) *m* pepper

pincel (peen-*thayl*) *m* paint-brush

pinchado (peen-*chah*-dhoa) *adj* punctured

pinchar (peen-*chahr*) *v* puncture

pinchazo (peen-*chah*-thoa) *m* puncture

pingüino (peeng-*gwee*-noa) *m* penguin

pintar (peen-*tahr*) *v* paint

pintor (peen-*toar*) *m*, **-a** *f* painter

pintoresco (peen-toa-*rayss*-koa) *adj* picturesque, scenic

pintura (peen-*too*-rah) *f* paint;

painting; **~ al óleo** oil painting

pinzas (*peen*-thahss) *fpl* tweezers *pl*

pinzón (peen-*thoan*) *m* finch

piña (*pee*-ñah) *f* pineapple

pío (*pee*-oa) *adj* pious

piojo (p^y*oa*-khoa) *m* louse

pionero (p^yoa-*nay*-roa) *m* pioneer

pipa (*pee*-pah) *f* pipe

pirata (pee-*rah*-tah) *m* pirate

pisar (pee-*sahr*) *v* step on; walk on

piscina (pee-*thee*-nah) *f* swimming pool

piso (*pee*-soa) *m* stor(e)y, floor; flat; apartment *Am*; **~ bajo** ground floor

pista (*peess*-tah) *f* ring; track; lane; **~ de aterrizaje** runway; **~ de patinaje** skating rink; **~ para carreras** racecourse

pistola (peess-*toa*-lah) *f* pistol

pistón (peess-*toan*) *m* piston

pitar (pee-*tahr*) *v* whistle; beep, hoot; L.Am. smoke

pitillera (pee-tee-l^y*ay*-rah) *f* cigarette case

pizarra (pee-*thah*-rrah) *f* slate; blackboard

placa (*plah*-kah) *f* registration plate

placer (plah-*thayr*) *m* pleasure

***placer** (plah-*thayr*) *v* please

plaga (*plah*-gah) *f* plague

plan (plahn) *m* plan, project

plancha (*plahn*-chah) *f* iron; **no precisa ~** wash and wear, drip-dry

planchar (plahn-*chahr*) *v* iron; press

planeador (plah-nay-ah-*dhoar*) *m* glider

planear (plah-nay-*ahr*) *v* plan

planeta (plah-*nay*-tah) *m* planet

planetario (plah-nay-*tah*-r^yoa) *m* planetarium

plano (*plah*-noa) *adj* level, even, plane; *m* plan, map; **primer ~** foreground

planta (*plahn*-tah) *f* plant

plantación (plahn-tah-*th^yoan*) f
plantation

plantar (plahn-*tahr*) v plant

plantear (plahn-tay-*ahr*) v *put

plástico (*plahss*-tee-koa) m plastic; **de ~** plastic

plata (*plah*-tah) f silver; **de ~** silver; **~ labrada** silverware

plátano (*plah*-tah-noa) m banana

platero (plah-*tay*-roa) m silversmith

platija (plah-*tee*-khah) f plaice

platillo (plah-*tee*-l^yoa) m saucer

platino (plah-*tee*-noa) m platinum

plato (*plah*-toa) m dish, plate; course

playa (*plah*-^yah) f beach; **~ de veraneo** seaside resort; **~ para nudistas** nudist beach

plaza (*plah*-thah) f square; **~ de mercado** market-place; **~ de toros** bullring; **~ fuerte** stronghold

plazo (*plah*-thoa) m term; instal(l)ment; **compra a plazos** instal(l)ment plan

pleamar (play-ah-*mahr*) f high tide

plegable (play-*gah*-blay) adj collapsible, folding

***plegar** (play-*gahr*) v crease

pliegue (*pl^yay*-gay) m crease, fold

plomero (ploa-*may*-roa) m plumber

plomo (*ploa*-moa) m lead

pluma (*ploo*-mah) f feather; pen

plural (ploo-*rahl*) m plural

población (poa-bhlah-*th^yoan*) f population

pobre (*poa*-bhray) adj poor

pobreza (poa-*bhray*-thah) f poverty

poco (*poa*-koa) adj little; m bit; **dentro de ~** presently; **un ~** some; **pocos** adj few

poder (poa-*dhayr*) m power; authority

***poder** (poa-*dhayr*) v *be able to, *can; *might; *may

poderoso (poa-dhay-*roa*-soa) adj powerful

podrido (poa-*dhree*-dhoa) adj rotten

poema (poa-*ay*-mah) m poem; **~ épico** epic

poesía (poa-ay-*see*-ah) f poetry

poeta (poa-*ay*-tah) m poet

poético (poa-*ay*-tee-koa) adj poetic

polaco (poa-*lah*-koa) adj Polish; m Pole

polea (poa-*lay*-ah) f pulley

policía (poa-lee-*thee*-ah) f police pl

polilla (poa-*lee*-l^yah) f moth

polio (*poa*-l^yoa) f polio

poliomielitis (poa-l^yoa-m^yay-*lee*-tees) f polio

política (poa-*lee*-tee-kah) f policy; politics

político (poa-*lee*-tee-koa) adj political; m politician

póliza (*poa*-lee-thah) f policy

Polonia (poa-*loa*-n^yah) f Poland

polución (poa-loo-*th^yoan*) f pollution

polvera (poal-*bhay*-rah) f powder compact

polvo (*poal*-bhoa) m dust; powder; grit; **~ facial** face powder; **~ para los dientes** toothpowder; **~ para los pies** foot powder

pólvora (*poal*-bhoa-rah) f gunpowder

polvoriento (poal-bhoa-r^y*ayn*-toa) adj dusty

pollero (poa-*l^yay*-roa) m poulterer

pollo (*poa*-l^yoa) m chicken

pomelo (poa-*may*-loa) m grapefruit

pómulo (*poa*-moo-loa) m cheekbone

ponderado (poan-day-*rah*-dhoa) adj cautious; steady

***poner** (poa-*nayr*) v place, *lay, *put, *set; ***ponerse** v *put on

pony (*poa*-nee) m pony

popular (poa-poo-*lahr*) adj popular; vulgar; **canción ~** folk song; **danza ~** folk dance

populoso (poa-poo-*loa*-soa) adj populous

por (poar) *prep* by; for; via; times

porcelana (poar-thay-*lah*-nah) *f* china, porcelain

porcentaje (poar-thayn-*tah*-khay) *m* percentage

porción (poar-*th*ʸoan) *f* portion, helping

porque (*poar*-kay) *conj* because, for, as; **por qué?** why?

porra (*poa*-rrah) *f* club

portabagajes (poar-tah-bah-*khah*-gayss) *m* luggage rack

portador (poar-tah-*dhoar*) *m* carrier

portaequipajes (poar-tah-ay-kee-*pah*-khayss) *m* boot; trunk *Am*

portafolio (poar-tah-*foa*-lʸoa) *m* attaché case, briefcase

portátil (poar-*tah*-teel) *adj* portable

portero (poar-*tay*-roa) *m* doorman, door-keeper, porter; goalkeeper

portilla (poar-*tee*-lʸah) *f* porthole

portón (poar-*toan*) *m* gate

Portugal (poar-too-*gahl*) *m* Portugal

portugués (poar-too-*gayss*) *adj* Portuguese; *m* Portuguese

porvenir (poar-bhay-*neer*) *m* future

posada (poa-*sah*-dhah) *f* inn

posadero (poa-sah-*dhay*-roa) *m* innkeeper

*poseer (poa-say-*ayr*) *v* own, possess

posesión (poa-say-*s*ʸoan) *f* possession

posibilidad (poa-see-bhee-lee-*dhahdh*) *f* possibility

posible (poa-*see*-bhlay) *adj* possible

posición (poa-see-*th*ʸoan) *f* position

positiva (poa-see-*tee*-bhah) *f* positive, print

positivo (poa-see-*tee*-bhoa) *adj* positive

postal ilustrada (poass-*tahl* ee-looss-*trah*-dhah) picture postcard

poste (*poass*-tay) *m* post, pole; **~ de farol** lamppost; **~ de indicador** signpost

posterior (poass-tay-rʸoar) *adj* subsequent

postizo (poass-*tee*-thoa) *adj* false, artificial; *m* hairpiece

postre (*poass*-tray) *m* dessert

potable (poa-*tah*-bhlay) *adj* drinkable

potencia (poa-*tayn*-thʸah) *f* capacity; power

pozo (*poa*-thoa) *m* well; **~ de petróleo** oil well

práctica (*prahk*-tee-kah) *f* practice

practicar (prahk-tee-*kahr*) *v* practise

práctico (*prahk*-tee-koa) *adj* practical; skilled; *m* pilot

prado (*prah*-dhoa) *m* meadow, pasture

precario (pray-*kah*-rʸoa) *adj* critical, precarious

precaución (pray-kou-*th*ʸoan) *f* precaution

precedente (pray-thay-*dhayn*-tay) *adj* previous, preceding, last

preceder (pray-thay-*dhayr*) *v* precede

precio (*pray*-thʸoa) *m* price; charge, cost, rate; **~ de compra** purchase price; **~ del billete** fare

precioso (pray-*th*ʸoa-soa) *adj* precious; lovely

precipicio (pray-thee-*pee*-thʸoa) *m* precipice

precipitación (pray-thee-pee-tah-*th*ʸoan) *f* precipitation

precipitarse (pray-thee-pee-*tahr*-say) *v* rush; crash; **precipitado** *adj* rash

preciso (pray-*thee*-soa) *adj* precise; very

predecesor (pray-dhay-thay-*soar*) *m* predecessor

*predecir (pray-dhay-*theer*) *v* predict

predicar (pray-dhee-*kahr*) *v* preach

preferencia (pray-fay-*rayn*-thʸah) *f* preference

preferible (pray-fay-*ree*-bhlay) *adj* preferable

*preferir (pray-fay-*reer*) *v* prefer;
  preferido *adj* favo(u)rite
prefijo (pray-*fee*-khoa) *m* prefix
pregunta (pray-*goon*-tah) *f* question;
  query, inquiry
preguntar (pray-goon-*tahr*) *v* ask;
  enquire; **preguntarse** *v* wonder
prejuicio (pray-*khwee*-th^yoa) *m*
  prejudice
preliminar (pray-lee-mee-*nahr*) *adj*
  preliminary
prematuro (pray-mah-*too*-roa) *adj*
  premature
premio (*pray*-m^yoa) *m* award, prize; ~
  de consolación consolation prize
prender (prayn-*dayr*) *v* attach
prensa (*prayn*-sah) *f* press;
  conferencia de ~ press conference
preocupación (pray-oa-koo-pah-
  th^yoan) *f* concern, anxiety, worry;
  trouble
preocupado (pray-oa-koo-*pah*-dhoa)
  adj concerned, anxious
preocuparse de (pray-oa-koo-*pahr*-
  say) care about; see to
preparación (pray-pah-rah-*th^yoan*) *f*
  preparation
preparado (pray-pah-*rah*-dhoa) *adj*
  prepared, ready
preparar (pray-pah-*rahr*) *v* prepare;
  cook
preposición (pray-poa-see-*th^yoan*) *f*
  preposition
presa (*pray*-sah) *f* dam
prescindir (pray-theen-*deer*) *v* omit;
  disregard; **prescindiendo de** apart
  from
prescribir (prayss-kree-*bheer*) *v*
  prescribe
prescripción (prayss-kreep-*th^yoan*) *f*
  prescription
presencia (pray-*sayn*-th^yah) *f*
  presence
presenciar (pray-sayn-*th^yahr*) *v*
  witness
presentación (pray-sayn-tah-*th^yoan*) *f*
  introduction
presentar (pray-sayn-*tahr*) *v*
  introduce, present; offer;
  presentarse *v* report
presente (pray-*sayn*-tay) *adj* present;
  m present
preservativo (pray-sayr-bhah-*tee*-
  bhoa) *m* condom
preservar (pray-sayr-*bhahr*) *v*
  preserve
presidente (pray-see-*dhayn*-tay) *m*
  president, chairman
presidir (pray-see-*dheer*) *v* preside at
presión (pray-s^yoan) *f* pressure; ~
  atmosférica atmospheric pressure; ~
  del aceite oil pressure; ~ **del
  neumático** tyre pressure, tire
  pressure *Am*
preso (*pray*-soa) *m* prisoner; **coger ~**
  capture
préstamo (*prayss*-tah-moa) *m* loan
prestar (prayss-*tahr*) *v* *lend; ~
  atención a attend to, *pay attention
  to; **tomar prestado** borrow
prestigio (prayss-*tee*-kh^yoa) *m*
  prestige
presumible (pray-soo-*mee*-bhlay) *adj*
  presumable
presumido (pray-soo-*mee*-dhoa) *adj*
  presumptuous
presumir (pray-soo-*meer*) *v* assume;
  boast
presuntuoso (pray-soon-*twoa*-soa)
  adj conceited; presumptuous
presupuesto (pray-soo-*pwayss*-toa)
  m budget
pretender (pray-tayn-*dayr*) *v* claim
pretensión (pray-tayn-s^yoan) *f* claim
pretexto (pray-*tayks*-toa) *m* pretext,
  pretence, pretense *Am*
*prevenir (pray-bhay-*neer*) *v*
  anticipate, prevent

preventivo (pray-bhayn-*tee*-bhoa) *adj* preventive

*prever (pray-*bhayr*) *v* anticipate

previo (*pray*-bh^yoa) *adj* previous

previsión (pray-bhee-s^yoan) *f* outlook, forecast

prima (*pree*-mah) *f* cousin; premium

primario (pree-*mah*-r^yoa) *adj* primary

primavera (pree-mah-*bhay*-rah) *f* springtime, spring

primero (pree-*may*-roa) *num* first; *adj* foremost; primary

primitivo (pree-mee-*tee*-bhoa) *adj* primitive

primo (*pree*-moa) *m* cousin

primordial (pree-moar-*dh*^y*ahl*) *adj* primary

princesa (preen-*thay*-sah) *f* princess

principal (preen-thee-*pahl*) *adj* principal; chief, main, cardinal; *m* principal

principalmente (preen-thee-pahl-*mayn*-tay) *adv* mainly

príncipe (*preen*-thee-pay) *m* prince

principiante (preen-thee-p^y*ahn*-tay) *m* beginner, novice

principio (preen-*thee*-p^yoa) *m* principle; **al ~** at first

prioridad (pr^yoa-ree-*dhahdh*) *f* priority

prisa (*pree*-sah) *f* haste, speed, hurry; ***dar ~** *speed; ***darse ~** hurry; **de ~** in a hurry

prisión (pree-s^yoan) *f* prison

prisionero (pree-s^yoa-*nay*-roa) *m* prisoner; **~ de guerra** prisoner of war

prismáticos (preez-mah-tee-koass) *mpl* binoculars *pl*

privado (pree-*bhah*-dhoa) *adj* private

privar de (pree-*bhahr*) deprive of

privilegio (pree-bhee-*lay*-kh^yoa) *m* privilege

probable (proa-*bhah*-bhlay) *adj* probable; likely

probablemente (proa-bhah-bhlay-*mayn*-tay) *adv* probably

probador (proa-bhah-*dhoar*) *m* fitting room

*probar (proa-*bhahr*) *v* attempt; test; taste; ***probarse** *v* try on

problema (proa-*bhlay*-mah) *m* problem, question

procedencia (proa-thay-*dhayn*-th^yah) *f* origin

proceder (proa-thay-*dhayr*) *v* proceed

procedimiento (proa-thay-dhee-m^y*ayn*-toa) *m* procedure; process

procesión (proa-thay-s^yoan) *f* procession

proceso (proa-*thay*-soa) *m* process, trial, lawsuit

proclamar (proa-klah-*mahr*) *v* proclaim

procurador (proa-koo-rah-*dhoar*) *m* solicitor

procurar (proa-koo-*rahr*) *v* furnish

pródigo (*proa*-dhee-goa) *adj* lavish

producción (proa-dhook-th^yoan) *f* production, output; **~ en serie** mass production

*producir (proa-dhoo-*theer*) *v* produce

producto (proa-*dhook*-toa) *m* product, produce

productor (proa-dhook-*toar*) *m* producer

profano (proa-*fah*-noa) *m* layman

profesar (proa-fay-*sahr*) *v* confess

profesión (proa-fay-s^yoan) *f* profession

profesional (proa-fay-s^yoa-*nahl*) *adj* professional

profesor (proa-fay-*soar*) *m*, **-a** *f* teacher; professor

profesora (proa-fay-*soa*-rah) *f* teacher

profeta (proa-*fay*-tah) *m* prophet

profundidad (proa-foon-dee-*dhahdh*) *f* depth

profundo (proa-*foon*-doa) *adj* low;
profound

programa (proa-*grah*-mah) *m*
programme

progresista (proa-gray-*seess*-tah) *adj*
progressive

progresivo (proa-gray-*see*-bhoa) *adj*
progressive

progreso (proa-*gray*-soa) *m* progress

prohibición (proa-ee-bhee-*th*ᵞ*oan*) *f*
prohibition

prohibido (proa-ee-*bhee*-dhoa) *adj*
prohibited

prohibir (proa-ee-*bheer*) *v* prohibit,
*forbid

prolongación (proa-loang-gah-
*th*ᵞ*oan*) *f* prolongation

prolongar (proa-loang-*gahr*) *v* extend

promedio (proa-*may*-dh*ᵞ*oa) *adj*
average; *m* average, mean; **en ~** on
the average

promesa (proa-*may*-sah) *f* promise

prometer (proa-may-*tayr*) *v* promise

prometido (proa-may-*tee*-dhoa) *adj*
engaged

promoción (proa-moa-*th*ᵞ*oan*) *f*
promotion

***promover** (proa-moa-*bhayr*) *v*
promote; advance

pronombre (proa-*noam*-bray) *m*
pronoun

pronosticar (proa-noass-tee-*kahr*) *v*
forecast

pronto (*proan*-toa) *adj* prompt; *adv*
soon, shortly; **tan ~ como** as soon as

pronunciación (proa-noon-th*ᵞ*ah-
*th*ᵞ*oan*) *f* pronunciation

pronunciar (proa-noon-*th*ᵞ*ahr*) *v*
pronounce

propaganda (proa-pah-*gahn*-dah) *f*
propaganda

propicio (proa-*pee*-th*ᵞ*oa) *adj*
favo(u)rable; well-disposed

propiedad (proa-p*ᵞ*ay-*dhahdh*) *f*
property; estate

propietario (proa-p*ᵞ*ay-*tah*-r*ᵞ*oa) *m*, **-a**
f owner, proprietor; landlord

propina (proa-*pee*-nah) *f* gratuity, tip

propio (*proa*-p*ᵞ*oa) *adj* own

***proponer** (proa-poa-*nayr*) *v* propose

proporción (proa-poar-*th*ᵞ*oan*) *f*
proportion

proporcional (proa-poar-th*ᵞ*oa-*nahl*)
adj proportional

proporcionar (proa-poar-th*ᵞ*oa-*nahr*)
v adjust; procure

propósito (proa-*poa*-see-toa) *m*
purpose; **a ~** by the way

propuesta (proa-*pwayss*-tah) *f*
proposition, proposal

prórroga (*proa*-rroa-gah) *f* extension

prosa (*proa*-sah) *f* prose

***proseguir** (proa-say-*geer*) *v* proceed,
continue, carry on

prospecto (proass-*payk*-toa) *m*
prospectus

prosperidad (proass-pay-ree-*dhahdh*)
f prosperity

próspero (*proass*-pay-roa) *adj*
prosperous

prostituta (proass-tee-*too*-tah) *f*
prostitute

protección (proa-tayk-*th*ᵞ*oan*) *f*
protection

proteger (proa-tay-*khayr*) *v* protect

proteína (proa-tay-*ee*-nah) *f* protein

protesta (proa-*tayss*-tah) *f* protest

protestante (proa-tayss-*tahn*-tay) *adj*
Protestant

protestar (proa-tayss-*tahr*) *v* protest

provechoso (proa-bhay-*choa*-soa)
adj profitable

***proveer** (proa-bhay-*ayr*) *v* provide; **~
de** furnish with

proverbio (proa-*bhayr*-bh*ᵞ*oa) *m*
proverb

provincia (proa-*bheen*-th*ᵞ*ah) *f*
province

provincial (proa-bheen-*th*ʸ*ahl*) *adj* provincial

provisional (proa-bhee-sʸoa-*nahl*) *adj* provisional, temporary

provisiones (proa-bhee-sʸoa-nayss) *fpl* provisions *pl*

provocar (proa-bhoa-*kahr*) *v* cause

próximamente (*proak*-see-mah-mayn-tay) *adv* shortly

próximo (*proak*-see-moa) *adj* next

proyectar (proa-ʸayk-*tahr*) *v* project

proyecto (proa-ʸ*ayk*-toa) *m* project, scheme

proyector (proa-ʸayk-*toar*) *m* spotlight

prudente (proo-*dhayn*-tay) *adj* cautious, wary; sensible; wise

prueba (*prway*-bhah) *f* experiment, trial, test; proof, token, evidence; **a ~** on approval

psicoanalista (see-koa-ah-nah-*leess*-tah) *m* analyst, psychoanalyst

psicología (see-koa-loa-*khee*-ah) *f* psychology

psicológico (see-koa-*loa*-khee-koa) *adj* psychological

psicólogo (see-*koa*-loa-goa) *m* psychologist

psiquiatra (see-*k*ʸ*ah*-trah) *m* psychiatrist

psíquico (*see*-kee-koa) *adj* psychic

publicación (poo-bhlee-kah-*th*ʸ*oan*) *f* publication

publicar (poo-bhlee-*kahr*) *v* publish

publicidad (poo-bhlee-thee-*dhahdh*) *f* advertising, publicity

público (*poo*-bhlee-koa) *adj* public; *m* public

pueblo (*pway*-bhloa) *m* nation, people; village

puente (*pwayn*-tay) *m* bridge; **~ colgante** suspension bridge; **~ levadizo** drawbridge; **~ superior** main deck

puerta (*pwayr*-tah) *f* door; **~ corrediza** sliding door; **~ giratoria** revolving door

puerto (*pwayr*-toa) *m* harbo(u)r, port; **~ de mar** seaport

pues (pwayss) *conj* since; *adv* well then

puesta (*pwayss*-tah) *f* bet

puesto (loo-*gahr*) *m* spot; job, post, position; stand, stall, booth; **~ de gasolina** service station; gas station *Am*; **~ de libros** bookstand

puesto que (*pwayss*-toa kay) because, since

pulcro (*pool*-kroa) *adj* neat, tidy; clean

pulgar (pool-*gahr*) *m* thumb

pulir (poo-*leer*) *v* polish

pulmón (pool-*moan*) *m* lung

pulóver (poo-*loa*-bhayr) *m* pullover

púlpito (*pool*-pee-toa) *m* pulpit

pulpo (*pool*-poa) *m* octopus

pulsera (pool-*say*-rah) *f* bracelet, bangle

pulso (*pool*-soa) *m* pulse

pulverizador (pool-bhay-ree-thah-*dhoar*) *m* atomizer

punta (*poon*-tah) *f* tip, point

puntiagudo (poon-tʸah-*goo*-dhoa) *adj* pointed

puntilla (poon-*tee*-lʸah) *f* lace edging; nib

punto (*poon*-toa) *m* point; item, issue; period, full stop; stitch; **géneros de ~** hosiery; ***hacer ~** *knit; **~ de congelación** freezing-point; **~ de partida** starting-point; **~ de vista** point of view; **~ y coma** semi-colon

puntual (poon-*twahl*) *adj* punctual

punzada (poon-*thah*-dhah) *f* stitch

punzar (poon-*thahr*) *v* pierce, prick

puñado (poo-*ñah*-dhoa) *m* handful

puñetazo (poo-ñay-*tah*-thoa) *m* punch; ***dar puñetazos** punch

puño (*poo*-ñoa) *m* fist; cuff
pupitre (poo-*pee*-tray) *m* school desk
puro (*poo*-roa) *adj* pure; clean, neat, sheer; *m* cigar

purpúreo (poor-*poo*-ray-oa) *adj* purple
pus (pooss) *f* pus
puta (*poo*-tah) *f vulgar* whore

Q

que (kay) *pron* who, which, that; *conj* that; as, than
qué (kay) *pron* what; *adv* how
quebradizo (kay-bhrah-*dhee*-thoa) *adj* crumbly; brittle, frail
quebrantar (kay-bhrahn-*tahr*) *v* *break
*quebrar (kay-*bhrahr*) *v* crack, *break, *burst
quedar (kay-*dhahr*) *v* remain, stay; ~ **con uno** make a date with; **quedarse** *v* remain, stay; ~ **con** hold on to
queja (*kay*-khah) *f* complaint
quejarse (kay-*khahr*-say) *v* complain
quemadura (kay-mah-*dhoo*-rah) *f* burn; ~ **del sol** sunburn
quemar (kay-*mahr*) *v* *burn
*querer (kay-*rayr*) *v* *will, want; like, *be fond of
querida (kay-*ree*-dhah) *f* sweetheart; mistress
querido (kay-*ree*-dhoa) *adj* beloved, dear; precious; *m* darling
queso (*kay*-soa) *m* cheese
quien (kʸayn) *pron* who; **a ~** whom

quienquiera (kʸayng-kʸay-rah) *pron* whoever
quieto (kʸay-toa) *adj* still, quiet; ***estarse ~** *keep quiet
quilate (kee-*lah*-tay) *m* carat
quilla (*kee*-lʸah) *f* keel
química (*kee*-mee-kah) *f* chemistry
químico (*kee*-mee-koa) *adj* chemical
quincalla (keeng-*kah*-lʸah) *f* small hardware
quince (*keen*-thay) *num* fifteen
quincena (keen-*thay*-nah) *f* fortnight
quinceno (keen-*thay*-noa) *num* fifteenth
quinta (*keen*-tah) *f* country house
quinto[1] (*keen*-toa) *num* fifth
quinto[2] (*keen*-toa) *m* conscript
quiosco (kʸoass-koa) *m* kiosk; ~ **de periódicos** newsstand
quitamanchas (kee-tah-*mahn*-chahss) *m* cleaning fluid, stain remover
quitar (kee-*tahr*) *v* *take away
quitasol (kee-tah-*soal*) *m* sunshade
quizás (kee-*thahss*) *adv* maybe, perhaps

R

rábano (*rah*-bhah-noa) *m* radish; ~ **picante** horseradish

rabia (*rah*-bhʸah) *f* rage; rabies
rabiar (rah-*bhʸahr*) *v* rage

rabioso (rah-*bh*ᵞ*oa*-soa) *adj* mad
racial (rah-*th*ᵞ*ahl*) *adj* racial
ración (rah-*th*ᵞ*oan*) *f* ration
radiador (rah-dhᵞah-*dhoar*) *m* radiator
radical (rah-dhee-*kahl*) *adj* radical
radio (*rah*-dhᵞoa) *m* radius; spoke; *f* radio
radiografía (rah-dhᵞoa-grah-*fee*-ah) *f* X-ray
radiografiar (rah-dhᵞoa-grah-*fᵞahr*) *v* X-ray
raedura (rah-ay-*dhoo*-rah) *f* scratch; ***hacer raeduras** scratch
ráfaga (*rah*-fah-gah) *f* gust, blow
raíz (rah-*eeth*) *f* root
rallar (rah-*lᵞahr*) *v* grate
rama (*rah*-mah) *f* branch, bough
ramita (rah-*mee*-tah) *f* twig
ramo (*rah*-moa) *m* bouquet
rampa (*rahm*-pah) *f* ramp
rana (*rah*-nah) *f* frog
rancio (*rahn*-thᵞoa) *adj* rancid
rancho (*rahn*-choa) *mMe* farmhouse
rango (*rahng*-goa) *m* rank
ranura (rah-*noo*-rah) *f* slot
rápidamente (*rah*-pee-dah-mayn-tay) *adv* soon
rapidez (*rah*-pee-dhayth) *f* speed
rápido (*rah*-pee-dhoa) *adj* fast, rapid, quick; **rápidos de río** rapids *pl*
raptar (rahp-*tahr*) *v* kidnap
raqueta (rah-*kay*-tah) *f* rackuet
raro (*rah*-roa) *adj* uncommon, rare; strange, odd; **raras veces** rarely
rascacielos (rahss-kah-*th*ᵞ*ay*-loass) *m* skyscraper
rascar (rahss-*kahr*) *v* scratch
rasgar (rahz-*gahr*) *v* rip; tear up
rasgo (*rahz*-goa) *m* trait; feature; **~ característico** characteristic
rasgón (rahz-*goan*) *m* tear
rasguño (rahz-*goo*-ñoa) *m* scratch
raso (*rah*-soa) *adj* bare; *m* satin

raspar (rahss-*pahr*) *v* scrape
rastrear (rahss-tray-*ahr*) *v* trace
rastrillo (rahss-*tree*-lᵞoa) *m* rake
rastro (*rahss*-troa) *m* trail
rasurarse (rah-soo-*rahr*-say) *v* shave
rata (*rah*-tah) *f* rat
rato (*rah*-toa) *m* while
ratón (rah-*toan*) *m* mouse
raya (*rah*-ᵞah) *f* line, stripe; crease; parting
rayado (rah-ᵞ*ah*-dhoa) *adj* striped
rayador (rah-ᵞah-*dhoar*) *m* grater
rayo (*rah*-ᵞoa) *m* beam, ray
rayón (rah-ᵞ*oan*) *m* rayon
raza (*rah*-thah) *f* race; breed
razón (rah-*thoan*) *f* wits *pl*, sense, reason; **no *tener ~** *be wrong; ***tener ~** *be right
razonable (rah-thoa-*nah*-bhlay) *adj* reasonable
razonar (rah-thoa-*nahr*) *v* reason
reacción (ray-ahk-*th*ᵞ*oan*) *f* reaction
reaccionar (ray-ahk-thᵞoa-*nahr*) *v* react
real (ray-*ahl*) *adj* factual, true, substantial; royal
realidad (ray-ah-lee-*dhahdh*) *f* reality; **en ~** actually, as a matter of fact
realizable (ray-ah-lee-*thah*-bhlay) *adj* feasible, realizable
realización (ray-ah-lee-thah-*th*ᵞ*oan*) *f* achievement
realizar (ray-ah-lee-*thahr*) *v* realize; attain; carry out
rebaja (ray-*bhah*-khah) *f* reduction, rebate; **rebajas** *fpl* sales
rebajar (ray-bhah-*khahr*) *v* lower, reduce
rebaño (ray-*bhah*-ñoa) *m* flock
rebelde (ray-*bhayl*-day) *m* rebel
rebelión (ray-bhay-*lᵞoan*) *f* revolt, rebellion
recado (ray-*kah*-dhoa) *m* errand
recambio (ray-*kahm*-bᵞoa) *m* spare

part; refill

recepción (ray-thayp-th^yoan) *f* reception

recepcionista (ray-thayp-th^yoa-*neess*-tah) *m/f* receptionist

receptáculo (ray-thayp-tah-koo-loa) *m* container

receptor (ray-thayp-*toar*) *m* receiver

receta (ray-*thay*-tah) *f* recipe

recibir (ray-thee-*bheer*) *v* receive

recibo (ray-*thee*-bhoa) *m* voucher, receipt; **oficina de ~** reception office

reciclable (ray-thee-*clah*-bhlay) *adj* recyclable

reciclar (ray-thee-*clahr*) *v* recycle

recién (ray-th^y*ayn*) *adv* recently

reciente (ray-th^y*ayn*-tay) *adj* recent

recientemente (ray-th^yayn-tay-*mayn*-tay) *adv* lately, recently

recíproco (ray-*thee*-proa-koa) *adj* mutual

recital (ray-thee-*tahl*) *m* recital

reclamar (ray-klah-*mahr*) *v* claim

recluta (ray-*kloo*-tah) *m* recruit

recoger (ray-koa-*khayr*) *v* pick up, pick; collect, gather; *overtake

recogida (ray-koa-*khee*-dhah) *f* collection

recomendación (ray-koa-mayn-dah-th^y*oan*) *f* recommendation

***recomendar** (ray-koa-mayn-*dahr*) *v* recommend

***recomenzar** (ray-koa-mayn-*thahr*) *v* recommence

recompensa (ray-koam-*payn*-sah) *f* prize, reward

recompensar (ray-koam-payn-*sahr*) *v* reward

reconciliación (ray-koan-thee-l^yah-th^y*oan*) *f* reconciliation

***reconocer** (ray-koa-noa-*thayr*) *v* recognize; admit, confess, acknowledge; realize

reconocimiento (ray-koa-noa-thee-m^yayn-toa) *m* recognition; medical check-up

récord (*ray*-koardh) *m* record

***recordar** (ray-koar-*dhahr*) *v* remind; *think of

recorrer (ray-koa-*rrayr*) *v* cross; go through

recorrido (ray-koa-*rreeh*-doa) *m* route; round

recortar (ray-koar-*tahr*) *v* trim

recreación (ray-kray-ah-th^y*oan*) *f* recreation

recreo (ray-*kray*-oa) *m* recreation; **patio de ~** playground

recriar (ray-kr^y*ahr*) *v* *breed

rectangular (rayk-tahng-goo-*lahr*) *adj* rectangular

rectángulo (rayk-*tahng*-goo-loa) *m* oblong, rectangle

rectificación (rayk-tee-fee-kah-th^y*oan*) *f* correction

recto (*rayk*-toa) *adj* straight; direct; upright

rector (rayk-*toar*) *m* rector

rectoría (rayk-toa-*ree*-ah) *f* rectory

recuerdo (ray-*kwayr*-dhoa) *m* remembrance, memory; souvenir; **~s** regards

recuperación (ray-koo-pay-rah-th^y*oan*) *f* recovery

recuperar (ray-koo-pay-*rahr*) *v* recover

rechazar (ray-chah-*thahr*) *v* reject, turn down

red (raydh) *f* net; network; **~ de carreteras** road system; **~ de pescar** fishing net

redacción (ray-dhahk-th^y*oan*) *f* wording; editorial staff

redactar (ray-dhahk-*tahr*) *v* *write up; *draw up; edit

redactor (ray-dhahk-*toar*) *m* editor

redecilla (ray-dhay-*thee*-l^yah) *f* hair net

redimir (ray-dhee-*meer*) v redeem

rédito (*ray*-dhee-toa) m revenue, income, interest

redondeado (ray-dhoan-day-*ah*-dhoa) adj rounded

redondo (ray-*dhoan*-doa) adj round

reducción (ray-dhook-th^y*oan*) f reduction, rebate

*reducir (ray-dhoo-*theer*) v *cut, decrease, reduce

reembolsar (ray-aym-boal-*sahr*) v reimburse

reemplazar (ray-aym-plah-*thahr*) v replace

reemprender (ray-aym-prayn-*dayr*) v resume

reexpedir (ray-ayks-pay-*dheer*) v forward

referencia (ray-fay-*rayn*-th^{y}ah) f reference; **punto de ~** landmark

*referir (ray-fay-*reer*) v refer; narrate

refinería (ray-fee-nay-*ree*-ah) f refinery

reflector (ray-flayk-*toar*) m reflector; searchlight

reflejar (ray-flay-*khahr*) v reflect

reflejo (ray-*flay*-khoa) m reflection

reflexionar (ray-flayk-s^{y}oa-*nahr*) v *think

Reforma (ray-*foar*-mah) f reformation

refractario (ray-frahk-*tah*-r^{y}oa) adj fireproof

refrenar (ray-fray-*nahr*) v curb

refrescar (ray-frayss-*kahr*) v refresh

refresco (ray-*frayss*-koa) m refreshment

refrigerador (ray-free-khay-rah-*dhoar*) m fridge, refrigerator

refugio (ray-*foo*-kh^{y}oa) m cover, shelter

refugiado (ray-foo-kh^{y}ah-doa) m, **-a** f refugee

refunfuñar (ray-foon-foo-*ñahr*) v grumble

regalar (ray-gah-*lahr*) v present

regaliz (ray-gah-*leeth*) m liquorice

regalo (ray-*gah*-loa) m present, gift

regata (ray-*gah*-tah) f regatta

regatear (ray-gah-tay-*ahr*) v bargain

régimen (*ray*-khee-mayn) m (pl regímenes) régime; government, rule; diet

regimiento (ray-khee-m^y*ayn*-toa) m regiment

región (ray-kh^y*oan*) f region; zone, country, area

regional (ray-kh^{y}oa-*nahl*) adj regional

*regir (ray-*kheer*) v govern, rule

registrar (ray-kheess-*trahr*) v book, record

registro (ray-*kheess*-troa) m record

regla (*ray*-glah) f rule; regulation; ruler; **en ~** in order; **por ~ general** as a rule

reglamento (ray-glah-*mayn*-toa) m regulation

regocijo (ray-goa-*thee*-khoa) m joy; rejoicing

regordete (ray-goar-*dhay*-tay) adj plump

regresar (ray-gray-*sahr*) v *go back, *get back

regreso (ray-*gray*-soa) m return; **viaje de ~** return journey; **vuelo de ~** return flight

regulación (ray-goo-lah-th^y*oan*) f regulation

regular (ray-goo-*lahr*) v regulate; adj regular

rehabilitación (ray-ah-bhee-lee-tah-th^y*oan*) f rehabilitation

rehén (ray-*ayn*) m hostage

rehusar (ray^{oo}-*sahr*) v refuse; reject

reina (*ray*-nah) f queen

reinado (ray-*nah*-dhoa) m reign

reino (*ray*-noa) m kingdom

reintegrar (rayn-tay-*grahr*) v *repay, refund

reintegro (rayn-*tay*-groa) *m* repayment, refund

*reír (ray-*eer*) *v* laugh

reivindicación (ray-bheen-dee-kah-*th*^y*oan*) *f* claim

reivindicar (ray-bheen-dee-*kahr*) *v* claim

reja (*ray*-khah) *f* grate; fence, gate

rejilla (ray-*khee*-l^yah) *f* luggage rack

relación (ray-lah-*th*^y*oan*) *f* connection, relation(ship); reference; report

relacionar (ray-lah-th^yoa-*nahr*) *v* relate

relajación (ray-lah-khah-*th*^y*oan*) *f* relaxation

relajado (ray-lah-*khah*-dhoa) *adj* relaxed; easygoing

relámpago (ray-*lahm*-pah-goa) *m* lightning; flash

relatar (ray-lah-*tahr*) *v* report

relativo (ray-lah-*tee*-bhoa) *adj* comparative, relative; ~ **a** regarding

relato (ray-*lah*-toa) *m* report; narrative

relevar (ray-lay-*bhahr*) *v* relieve

relieve (ray-l^y*ay*-bhay) *m* relief

religión (ray-lee-*kh*^y*oan*) *f* religion

religioso (ray-lee-*kh*^y*oa*-soa) *adj* religious

reliquia (ray-lee-kyah) *f* relic

reloj (ray-*loakh*) *m* clock; watch; ~ **de pulsera** wristwatch

relojero (ray-loa-*khay*-roa) *m*, **-a** *f* watchmaker

reluciente (ray-loo-*th*^y*ayn*-tay) *adj* bright

*relucir (ray-loo-*theer*) *v* *shine

rellenado (ray-l^yay-*nah*-doa) *adj* stuffed

relleno (ray-l^y*ay*-noa) *m* stuffing; filling

remanente (ray-mah-*nayn*-tay) *m* remnant

remar (ray-*mahr*) *v* row

remedio (ray-*may*-dh^yoa) *m* remedy

*remendar (ray-mayn-*dahr*) *v* mend; patch

remesa (ray-*may*-sah) *f* remittance

remitente (ray-mee-*tayn*-tay) *m/f* sender

remitir (ray-mee-*teer*) *v* remit; ~ **a** refer to

remo (*ray*-moa) *m* paddle, oar

remoción (ray-moa-*th*^y*oan*) *f* removal

remojar (ray-moa-*khahr*) *v* soak

remolacha (ray-moa-*lah*-chah) *f* beetroot, beet

remolcador (ray-moal-kah-*dhoar*) *m* tug

remolcar (ray-moal-*kahr*) *v* tug, tow

remolque (ray-*moal*-kay) *m* trailer

remoto (ray-*moa*-toa) *adj* remote, far-away, far-off

*remover (ray-moa-*bhayr*) *v* remove

remuneración (ray-moo-nay-rah-*th*^y*oan*) *f* remuneration

remunerar (ray-moo-nay-*rahr*) *v* remunerate

Renacimiento (ray-nah-thee-*m*^y*ayn*-toa) *m* Renaissance

rendición (rayn-dee-*th*^y*oan*) *f* surrender

*rendir (rayn-*deer*) *v* *pay; ~ **homenaje** hono(u)r; ***rendirse** *v* surrender

renglón (rayng-*gloan*) *m* line

reno (*ray*-noa) *m* reindeer

renombre (ray-*noam*-bray) *m* reputation

*renovar (ray-noa-*bhahr*) *v* renew

renta (*rayn*-tah) *f* revenue

rentable (rayn-*tah*-bhlay) *adj* paying

renunciar (ray-noon-*th*^y*ahr*) *v* *give up

*reñir (ray-*ñeer*) *v* dispute, quarrel

reparación (ray-pah-rah-*th*^y*oan*) *f* reparation; repair

reparar (ray-pah-*rahr*) *v* repair, mend

repartir (ray-pahr-*teer*) v divide, *deal, share out

reparto (ray-*pahr*-toa) m delivery; **camioneta de ~** pick-up van

repelente (ray-pay-*layn*-tay) adj repellent, revolting

repentinamente (ray-payn-tee-nah-*mayn*-tay) adv suddenly

repertorio (ray-payr-*toa*-rʸoa) m repertory

repetición (ray-pay-tee-*thʸoan*) f repetition

repetidamente (ray-pay-tee-dhah-*mayn*-tay) adv again and again

*repetir (ray-pay-*teer*) v repeat

repleto (ray-*play*-toa) adj crowded

reportero (ray-poar-*tay*-roa) m, **-a** f reporter

reposado (ray-poa-*sah*-dhoa) adj restful

reposo (ray-*poa*-soa) m rest

reprender (ray-prayn-*dayr*) v reprimand, scold

representación (ray-pray-sayn-tah-*thʸoan*) f representation; show, performance

representante (ray-pray-sayn-*tahn*-tay) m agent

representar (ray-pray-sayn-*tahr*) v represent

representativo (ray-pray-sayn-tah-tee-bhoa) adj representative

reprimir (ray-pree-*meer*) v suppress

*reprobar (ray-proa-*bhahr*) v reject

reprochar (ray-proa-*chahr*) v reproach

reproche (ray-*proa*-chay) m reproach, blame

reproducción (ray-proa-dhook-*thʸoan*) f reproduction

*reproducir (ray-proa-dhoo-*theer*) v reproduce

reptil (rayp-*teel*) m reptile

república (ray-*poo*-bhlee-kah) f republic

republicano (ray-poo-bhlee-*kah*-noa) adj republican

repuesto (ray-*pwayss*-toa) m store; refill

repugnancia (ray-poog-*nahn*-thʸah) f dislike

repugnante (ray-poog-*nahn*-tay) adj repellent, disgusting, revolting

repulsivo (ray-pool-*see*-bhoa) adj repulsive

reputación (ray-poo-tah-*thʸoan*) f reputation, fame

requerimiento (ray-kay-ree-*mʸayn*-toa) m requirement

*requerir (ray-kay-*reer*) v require, demand

resaca (ray-*sah*-kah) f undercurrent; hangover

resbaladizo (rayz-bhah-lah-*dhee*-thoa) adj slippery

resbalar (rayz-bhah-*lahr*) v slip, glide

rescatar (rayss-kah-*tahr*) v rescue

rescate (rayss-*kah*-tay) m rescue; ransom

*resentirse por (ray-sayn-*teer*-say) resent

reseña (ray-*say*-ñah) f review

reserva (ray-*sayr*-bhah) f qualification; reserve; booking; **de ~** spare

reservación (ray-sayr-bhah-*thʸoan*) f reservation, booking

reservar (ray-sayr-*bhahr*) v engage; reserve, book

resfriado (rayss-*frʸah*-dhoa) m cold

resfriarse (rayss-*frʸahr*-say) v catch a cold

residencia (ray-see-*dhayn*-thʸah) f residence

residente (ray-see-*dhayn*-tay) adj resident; m/f resident

residir (ray-see-*dheer*) v reside

residuo (ray-*see*-dhwoa) m remnant

resignación (ray-seeg-nah-*th^{y}oan*) *f* resignation

resignar (ray-seeg-*nahr*) *v* resign

resina (ray-*see*-nah) *f* resin

resistencia (ray-seess-*tayn*-th^{y}ah) *f* resistance

resistir (ray-seess-*teer*) *v* resist

resolución (ray-soa-loo-*th^{y}oan*) *f* resolution

*resolver (ray-soal-*bhayr*) *v* solve

*resonar (ray-soa-*nahr*) *v* sound

respectivo (rayss-payk-*tee*-bhoa) *adj* respective

respecto a (rayss-*payk*-toa ah) about, regarding

respetable (rayss-pay-*tah*-bhlay) *adj* respectable

respetar (rayss-pay-*tahr*) *v* respect

respeto (rayss-*pay*-toa) *m* respect, esteem, regard

respetuoso (rayss-pay-*twoa*-soa) *adj* respectful

respiración (rayss-pee-rah-*th^{y}oan*) *f* respiration, breathing

respirar (rayss-pee-*rahr*) *v* breathe

*resplandecer (rayss-plahn-day-*thayr*) *v* *shine

resplandor (rayss-plahn-*doar*) *m* glare

responder (rayss-poan-*dayr*) *v* reply, answer

responsabilidad (rayss-poan-sah-bhee-lee-*dhahdh*) *f* responsibility; liability

responsable (rayss-poan-*sah*-bhlay) *adj* responsible; liable

respuesta (rayss-*pwayss*-tah) *f* reply, answer

*restablecerse (rayss-tah-bhlay-*thayr*-say) *v* recover

restablecimiento (rayss-tah-bhlay-thee-*m^{y}ayn*-toa) *m* recovery

restante (rayss-*tahn*-tay) *adj* remaining

restar (rayss-*tahr*) *v* subtract

restaurante (rayss-tou-*rahn*-tay) *m* restaurant; **~ de autoservicio** self-service restaurant

resto (*rayss*-toa) *m* rest; remnant, remainder

restricción (rayss-treek-*th^{y}oan*) *f* restriction; qualification

resuelto (ray-*swayl*-toa) *adj* resolute, determined

resultado (ray-sool-*tah*-dhoa) *m* result; issue, outcome, effect

resultar (ray-sool-*tahr*) *v* result; prove

resumen (ray-*soo*-mayn) *m* résumé, survey, summary

retardar (ray-tahr-*dhahr*) *v* delay

*retener (ray-tay-*nayr*) *v* *hold

retina (ray-*tee*-nah) *f* retina

retirar (ray-tee-*rahr*) *v* *withdraw

reto (*ray*-toa) *m* challenge

retrasado (ray-trah-*sah*-dhoa) *adj* late

retraso (ray-*trah*-soa) *m* delay

retrato (ray-*trah*-toa) *m* portrait

retrete (ray-*tray*-tay) *m* toilet

retroceso (ray-troa-*thay*-soa) *m* recession; retreat

retumbo (ray-*toom*-boa) *m* boom; reverberation; rumble

reumatismo (ray^{oo}-mah-*teez*-moa) *m* rheumatism

reunión (ray^{oo}-*n^{y}oan*) *f* meeting, assembly, rally

reunir (ray^{oo}-*neer*) *v* join, assemble; reunite

revelación (ray-bhay-lah-*th^{y}oan*) *f* revelation

revelar (ray-bhay-*lahr*) *v* reveal; *give away; develop

revendedor (ray-bhayn-day-*dhoar*) *m*, **-a** *f* retailer

*reventar (ray-bhayn-*tahr*) *v* crack, *burst

reventón (ray-bhayn-*toan*) *m* blow-out

reverencia (ray-bhay-*rayn*-th\(^y\)ah) *f* respect

reverso (ray-*bhayr*-soa) *m* reverse

revés (ray-*bhayss*) *m* reverse; **al ~ the** other way round; upside-down; inside out

revisar (ray-bhee-*sahr*) *v* revise, overhaul

revisión (ray-bhee-s\(^y\)*oan*) *f* revision

revisor (ray-bhee-*soar*) *m* ticket collector

revista (ray-*bheess*-tah) *f* journal; review, magazine; revue; **~ mensual** monthly magazine

revocar (ray-bhoa-*kahr*) *v* revoke; recall

revolución (ray-bhoa-loo-th\(^y\)*oan*) *f* revolution

revolucionar (ray-bhoa-loo-th\(^y\)oa-*nahr*) *v* rebel

revolucionario (ray-bhoa-loo-th\(^y\)oa-nah-r\(^y\)oa) *adj* revolutionary

***revolver** (ray-bhoal-*bhayr*) *v* stir

revólver (ray-*bhoal*-bhayr) *m* revolver, gun

revuelta (ray-*bhwayl*-tah) *f* revolt

rey (ray) *m* king

rezar (ray-*thahr*) *v* pray

ribera (ree-*bhay*-rah) *f* riverside, river bank, shore

rico (*ree*-koa) *adj* rich; wealthy; nice, enjoyable, tasty

ridiculizar (ree-dhee-koo-lee-*thahr*) *v* ridicule

ridículo (ree-*dhee*-koo-loa) *adj* ridiculous, ludicrous

riesgo (r\(^y\)*ayz*-goa) *m* hazard, chance, risk

rima (*ree*-mah) *f* rhyme

rímel (*ree*-mayl) *m* mascara

rincón (reeng-*koan*) *m* angle

rinoceronte (ree-noa-thay-*roan*-tay) *m* rhinoceros

riña (*ree*-ñah) *f* dispute

riñón (ree-*ñoan*) *m* kidney

río (*ree*-oa) *m* river; **~ abajo** downstream; **~ arriba** upstream

riqueza (ree-*kay*-thah) *f* riches *pl*, wealth

risa (*ree*-sah) *f* laughter, laugh

ritmo (*reet*-moa) *m* rhythm; pace

rival (ree-*bhahl*) *m/f* rival

rivalidad (ree-bhah-lee-*dhahdh*) *f* rivalry

rivalizar (ree-bhah-lee-*thahr*) *v* rival

rizadores (ree-thah-*dhoa*-rayss) *mpl* hair rollers

rizar (ree-*thahr*) *v* curl

rizo (*ree*-thoa) *m* curl

robar (roa-*bhahr*) *v* rob; burgle

roble (*roa*-bhlay) *m* oak

robo (*roa*-bhoa) *m* robbery, theft

robusto (roa-*bhooss*-toa) *adj* solid, robust

roca (*roa*-kah) *f* rock

rocío (roa-*thee*-oa) *m* dew

rocoso (roa-*koa*-soa) *adj* rocky

rodaballo (roa-dhah-*bhah*-l\(^y\)oa) *m* brill

***rodar** (roa-*dhahr*) *v* roll

rodear (roa-dhay-*ahr*) *v* circle, surround; by-pass

rodilla (roa-*dhee*-l\(^y\)ah) *f* knee

***rogar** (roa-*gahr*) *v* ask

rojo (*roa*-khoa) *adj* red

rollo (*roa*-l\(^y\)oa) *m* roll

romano (roa-*mah*-noa) *adj* Roman

romántico (roa-*mahn*-tee-koa) *adj* romantic

rompecabezas (roam-pay-kah-*bhay*-thahss) *m* puzzle; jigsaw puzzle

romper (roam-*payr*) *v* *break

roncar (roang-*kahr*) *v* snore

ronco (*roang*-koa) *adj* hoarse

ropa (*roa*-pah) *f* clothes *pl*; **~ blanca** linen; **~ de cama** bedding; **~ interior** underwear; **~ interior de mujer** lingerie; **~ sucia** washing, laundry

rosa (*roa*-sah) *f* rose; *adj* rose
rosado (roa-*sah*-dhoa) *adj* pink
rosario (roa-*sah*-r^yoa) *m* beads *pl*, rosary
rostro (*roas*-troa) *m* face
rota (*roa*-tah) *f* rattan
roto (*roa*-toa) *adj* broken
rótula (*roa*-too-lah) *f* kneecap
rotular (roa-too-*lahr*) *v* label
rótulo (*roa*-too-loa) *m* label
rozadura (roa-thah-*dhoo*-rah) *f* graze
rubí (roo-*bhee*) *m* ruby
rubia (*roo*-bh^yah) *f* blonde
rubio (*roo*-bh^yoa) *adj* fair, blond
ruborizarse (roo-bhoa-ree-*thahr*-say) blush
rueda (*rway*-dhah) *f* wheel; ring; **patinaje de ruedas** roller-skating; ~ **de repuesto** spare wheel
ruego (*rway*-goa) *m* request
rugido (roo-*khee*-dhoa) *m* roar
rugir (roo-*kheer*) *v* roar
ruibarbo (rwee-*bhahr*-bhoa) *m* rhubarb
ruido (*rwee*-dhoa) *m* noise
ruidoso (rwee-*dhoa*-soa) *adj* noisy
ruina (*rwee*-nah) *f* ruins; ruin, destruction
ruinoso (rwee-*noa*-soa) *adj* dilapidated
ruiseñor (rwee-say-*ñoar*) *m* nightingale
ruleta (roo-*lay*-tah) *f* roulette
rulo (*roo*-loa) *m* curler
Rumania (roo-*mah*-n^yah) *f* Rumania
rumano (roo-*mah*-noa) *adj* Rumanian; *m* Rumanian
rumbo (*room*-boa) *m* course
rumor (roo-*moar*) *m* rumo(u)r
rural (roo-*rahl*) *adj* rural
Rusia (*roo*-s^yah) *f* Russia
ruso (*roo*-soa) *adj* Russian; *m* Russian
rústico (*roos*-tee-koa) *adj* rustic
ruta (*roo*-tah) *f* route; ~ **principal** thoroughfare
rutina (roo-*tee*-nah) *f* routine

S

sábado (*sah*-bhah-dhoa) *m* Saturday
sábana (*sah*-bhah-nah) *f* sheet
***saber** (sah-*bhayr*) *v* *know; *be able to; **a** ~ namely; ~ **a** taste
sabiduría (sah-bhee-dhoo-*ree*-ah) *f* wisdom
sabio (*sah*-bh^yoa) *adj* wise
sabor (sah-*bhoar*) *m* flavo(u)r
sabroso (sah-*bhroa*-soa) *adj* savo(u)ry, tasty
sacacorchos (sah-kah-*koar*-choass) *mpl* corkscrew
sacapuntas (sah-kah-*poon*-tahss) *m* pencil sharpener
sacar (sah-*kahr*) *v* *take out; *draw; ~
brillo brush
sacerdote (sah-thayr-*dhoa*-tay) *m* priest
saco (*sah*-koa) *m* sack; *mMe* jacket; ~ **de compras** shopping bag; ~ **de dormir** sleeping bag
sacrificar (sah-kree-fee-*kahr*) *v* sacrifice
sacrificio (sah-kree-*fee*-th^yoa) *m* sacrifice
sacrilegio (sah-kree-*lay*-kh^yoa) *m* sacrilege
sacudir (sah-koo-*dheer*) *v* *shake
sagrado (sah-*grah*-dhoa) *adj* sacred
sal (sahl) *f* salt; **sales de baño** bath

salts

sala (*sah*-lah) *f* hall; lounge; ~ de **conciertos** concert hall; ~ **de espera** waiting room; ~ **de estar** sitting room, living room; ~ **de lectura** reading room; ~ **para fumar** smoking room

salado (sah-*lah*-dhoa) *adj* salty

salario (sah-*lah*-r^yoa) *m* pay

salchicha (sahl-*chee*-chah) *f* sausage

saldo (*sahl*-doa) *m* balance

salero (sah-*lay*-roa) *m* salt cellar, salt shaker *Am*

salida (sah-*lee*-dhah) *f* issue, exit, way out; ~ **de emergencia** emergency exit

*****salir** (sah-*leer*) *v* *go out; appear

saliva (sah-*lee*-bhah) *f* spit

salmón (sahl-*moan*) *m* salmon

salón (sah-*loan*) *m* salon, lounge, drawing-room; ~ **de baile** ballroom; ~ **de belleza** beauty parlo(u)r; ~ **de demostraciones** showroom; ~ **de té** tea-shop

salpicar (sahl-pee-*kahr*) *v* splash; splatter; sprinkle

salsa (*sahl*-sah) *f* sauce; gravy

saltamontes (sahl-tah-*moan*-tayss) *m* grasshopper

saltar (sahl-*tahr*) *v* jump, *leap; skip; hop

salto (*sahl*-toa) *m* jump, leap, hop

salud (sah-*loodh*) *f* health

saludable (sah-loo-*dhah*-bhlay) *adj* wholesome

saludar (sah-loo-*dhahr*) *v* greet; salute

saludo (sah-*loo*-dhoa) *m* greeting

salvador (sahl-bhah-*dhoar*) *m* savio(u)r

salvaje (sahl-*bhah*-khay) *adj* wild, savage; fierce; desert

salvar (sahl-*bhahr*) *v* save

sanatorio (sah-nah-*toa*-r^yoa) *m* sanatorium

sandalia (sahn-*dah*-l^yah) *f* sandal

sandía (sahn-*dee*-ah) *f* watermelon

sangrar (sahng-*grahr*) *v* *bleed

sangre (*sahng*-gray) *f* blood

sangriento (sahng-gr^y*ayn*-toa) *adj* bloody

sanitario (sah-nee-*tah*-r^yoa) *adj* sanitary

sano (*sah*-noa) *adj* healthy, well

santo (*sahn*-toa) *adj* holy; *m* saint; ~ **y seña** password

santuario (sahn-*twah*-r^yoa) *m* shrine

sapo (*sah*-poa) *m* toad

sarampión (sah-rahm-p^y*oan*) *m* measles

sardina (sahr-*dhee*-nah) *f* sardine

sartén (sahr-*tayn*) *f* frying pan

sastre (*sahss*-tray) *m* tailor

satélite (sah-*tay*-lee-tay) *m* satellite

satisfacción (sah-teess-fahk-*th^yoan*) *f* satisfaction

*****satisfacer** (sah-teess-fah-*thayr*) *v* satisfy; **satisfecho** satisfied

saudí (sou-*dhee*) *adj* Saudi Arabian

sauna (*sou*-nah) *f* sauna

sazonar (sah-thoa-*nahr*) *v* season, flavo(u)r

se (say) *pron* himself; herself; yourselves; themselves

secadora (say-kah-*dhoa*-rah) *f* dryer

secar (say-*kahr*) *v* dry

sección (sayk-*th^yoan*) *f* section; agency

seco (*say*-koa) *adj* dry

secretario (say-kray-*tah*-r^yoa) *m*, **-a** *f* secretary

secreto (say-*kray*-toa) *adj* secret; *m* secret

sector (sayk-*toar*) *m* sector

secuencia (say-*kwayn*-th^yah) *f* shot

secuestrador (say-kwayss-trah-*dhoar*) *m* hijacker

secundario (say-koon-*dah*-r^yoa) *adj* secondary; minor

sed (saydh) f thirst

seda (say-dhah) f silk

sede (say-dhay) f seat; headquarters

sediento (say-dh^{y}ayn-toa) adj thirsty

***seducir** (say-dhoo-theer) v seduce

en seguida (ayn say-gee-dhah) straight away, at once, presently

***seguir** (say-geer) v follow; ~ **el paso** *keep up with; **todo seguido** straight on, straight ahead

según (say-goon) prep according to

segundo (say-goon-doa) num second; m second

seguramente (say-goo-rah-mayn-tay) adv surely

seguridad (say-goo-ree-dhahdh) f security, safety; **cinturón de ~** safety belt

seguro (say-goo-roa) adj safe; sure; m insurance; **póliza de ~** insurance policy; ~ **de viaje** travel insurance; ~ **de vida** life insurance

seis (sayss) num six

selección (say-layk-th^{y}oan) f selection; choice

seleccionado (say-layk-th^{y}oa-nah-dhoa) adj select

seleccionar (say-layk-th^{y}oa-nahr) v select

selecto (say-layk-toa) adj select

selva (sayl-bhah) f jungle, forest

selvoso (sayl-bhoa-soa) adj wooded

sellar (say-l^{y}ahr) v stamp; seal

sello (say-l^{y}oa) m stamp; seal

semáforo (say-mah-foa-roa) m traffic light

semana (say-mah-nah) f week; **fin de ~** weekend

semanal (say-mah-nahl) adj weekly

***sembrar** (saym-brahr) v *sow

semejante (say-may-khahn-tay) adj like

semejanza (say-may-khahn-thah) f resemblance, similarity

semi- (say-mee) semi-

semicírculo (say-mee-theer-koo-loa) m semicircle

semilla (say-mee-l^{y}ah) f seed

senado (say-nah-dhoa) m senate

senador (say-nah-dhoar) m senator

sencillo (sayn-thee-l^{y}oa) adj plain

senda (sayn-dah) f footpath

sendero (sayn-day-roa) m trail

senil (say-neel) adj senile

seno (say-noa) m bosom; breast

sensación (sayn-sah-th^{y}oan) f sensation; feeling

sensacional (sayn-sah-th^{y}oa-nahl) adj sensational

sensato (sayn-sah-toa) adj sensible; down-to-earth

sensibilidad (sayn-see-bhee-lee-dhahdh) f sensibility

sensible (sayn-see-bhlay) adj sensitive; noticeable; sentient

sensitivo (sayn-see-tee-bhoa) adj sensitive

***sentarse** (sayn-tahr-say) v *sit down; ***estar sentado** *sit; ***sentar bien** *become

sentencia (sayn-tayn-th^{y}ah) f sentence, verdict

sentenciar (sayn-tayn-th^{y}ahr) v sentence

sentido (sayn-tee-dhoa) m sense; reason; ~ **del honor** sense of hono(u)r; **sin ~** meaningless

sentimental (sayn-tee-mayn-tahl) adj sentimental

sentimiento (sayn-tee-m^{y}ayn-toa) m sentiment

***sentir** (sayn-teer) v *feel, sense; regret

seña (say-ñah) f sign; **señas personales** description

señal (say-ñahl) f signal, sign, indication; m token, tick; ***hacer señales** signal; wave; ~ **de alarma** distress signal

señalar (say-ñah-*lahr*) *v* tick off, indicate

señor (say-*ñoar*) *m* mister; sir

señora (say-*ñoa*-rah) *f* lady; madam

señorita (say-ñoa-*ree*-tah) *f* young lady; miss

separación (say-pah-rah-th^y*oan*) *f* division

separadamente (say-pah-rah-dhah-*mayn*-tay) *adv* apart

separado (say-pah-*rah*-dhoa) *adj* separate; **por ~** apart, separately

separar (say-pah-*rahr*) *v* separate, part; divide; detach

sepia (say-p^{y}ah) *f* cuttlefish

septentrional (sayp-tayn-tr^{y}oa-*nahl*) *adj* north

septicemia (sayp-tee-*thay*-m^{y}ah) *f* blood-poisoning

séptico (*sayp*-tee-koa) *adj* septic

septiembre (sayp-t^y*aym*-bray) September

séptimo (*sayp*-tee-moa) *num* seventh

sepulcro (say-*pool*-kroa) *m* sepulchre, sepulcher *Am*

sepultura (say-pool-*too*-rah) *f* grave

sequía (say-*kee*-ah) *f* drought

ser (sayr) *m* being, creature; **~ humano** human being

***ser** (sayr) *v* *be

sereno (say-*ray*-noa) *adj* serene

serie (say-r^{y}ay) *f* series; sequence

seriedad (say-r^{y}ay-*dhahdh*) *f* seriousness, gravity

serio (say-r^{y}oa) *adj* serious

sermón (sayr-*moan*) *m* sermon

serpiente (sayr- p^y*ayn*-tay) *f* snake; **~ de cascabel** rattlesnake

serrín (say-*rreen*) *m* sawdust

servicial (sayr-bhee-th^y*ahl*) *adj* helpful

servicio (sayr-bhee-th^{y}oa) *m* service; service charge; **~ de habitación** room service; **~ de mesa** dinner service; **~ postal** postal service

servilleta (sayr-bhee-l^y*ay*-tah) *f* napkin, serviette; **~ de papel** paper napkin

***servir** (sayr-*bheer*) *v* serve; attend on, wait on; *be of use

sesenta (say-*sayn*-tah) *num* sixty

sesión (say-s^y*oan*) *f* session

seta (say-tah) *f* mushroom

setenta (say-*tayn*-tah) *num* seventy

seto (say-toa) *m* hedge

severo (say-*bhay*-roa) *adj* harsh, strict, severe

sexo (*sayk*-soa) *m* sex

sexto (*sayks*-toa) *num* sixth

sexual (sayk-*swahl*) *adj* sexual

sexualidad (sayk-swah-lee-*dhahdh*) *f* sexuality; sex

si (see) *conj* if; in case; whether; **si … o** whether … or; **~ bien** though

sí (see) yes

siamés (s^{y}ah-*mayss*) *adj* Siamese; *m* Siamese

SIDA (*see*-dhah) *m* AIDS

siempre (s^y*aym*-pray) *adv* ever, always

sien (s^{y}ayn) *f* temple

sierra (s^y*ay*-rrah) *f* saw

siesta (s^y*ayss*-tah) *f* nap

siete (s^y*ay*-tay) *num* seven

siglo (*see*-gloa) *m* century

significado (seeg-nee-fee-*kah*-dhoa) *m* meaning

significar (seeg-nee-fee-*kahr*) *v* *mean

significativo (seeg-nee-fee-kah-*tee*-bhoa) *adj* significant

signo (*seeg*-noa) *m* sign; **~ de interrogación** question mark

siguiente (see-g^y*ayn*-tay) *adj* following

sílaba (*see*-lah-bhah) *f* syllable

silbar (seel-*bhahr*) *v* whistle

silbato (seel-*bhah*-toa) *m* whistle

silenciador (see-layn-th^{y}ah-*dhoar*) *m*

silencer

silencio (see-*layn*-thʸoa) *m* quiet, silence

silencioso (see-layn-*thʸoa*-soa) *adj* silent

silla (see-lʸah) *f* chair; **~ de montar** saddle; **de ruedas** wheelchair

sillón (see-lʸoan) *m* armchair

simbólico (seem-*boa*-lee-koa) *adj* symbolic

símbolo (*seem*-boa-loa) *m* symbol

similar (see-mee-*lahr*) *adj* similar

simpatía (seem-pah-*tee*-ah) *f* sympathy

simpático (seem-*pah*-tee-koa) *adj* nice, pleasant; obliging

simple (*seem*-play) *adj* simple

simular (see-moo-*lahr*) *v* simulate

simultáneo (see-mool-*tah*-nay-oa) *adj* simultaneous

sin (seen) *prep* without

sinagoga (see-nah-*goa*-gah) *f* synagogue

sincero (seen-*thay*-roa) *adj* sincere; open, honest

sindicato (seen-dee-*kah*-toa) *m* trade-union

sinfonía (seen-foa-*nee*-ah) *f* symphony

singular (seeng-goo-*lahr*) *adj* singular, queer; *m* singular

siniestro (see-nʸayss-troa) *adj* ominous, sinister

sino (*see*-noa) *conj* but

sinónimo (see-*noa*-nee-moa) *m* synonym

sintético (seen-*tay*-tee-koa) *adj* synthetic

síntoma (*seen*-toa-mah) *m* symptom

sintonizar (seen-toa-nee-*thahr*) *v* tune in

siquiera (see-kʸay-rah) *adv* at least; *conj* even though

sirena (see-*ray*-nah) *f* siren; mermaid

Siria (*see*-rʸah) *f* Syria

sirio (*see*-rʸoa) *adj* Syrian; *m* Syrian

sirviente (seer-bhʸayn-tay) *m* domestic

sistema (seess-*tay*-mah) *m* system; **~ decimal** decimal system; **~ de lubricación** lubrication system; **~ de refrigeración** cooling system

sistemático (seess-tay-*mah*-tee-koa) *adj* systematic

sitio (*see*-tʸoa) *m* site; seat, room; siege

situación (see-twah-thʸoan) *f* situation

situado (see-*twah*-dhoa) *adj* situated

situar (see-*twahr*) *v* locate

slogan (*sloa*-gahn) *m* slogan

smoking (*smoa*-keeng) *m* dinner jacket; tuxedo *Am*

soberano (soa-bhay-*rah*-noa) *m* sovereign

soberbio (soa-*bhayr*-bhʸoa) *adj* superb

sobornar (soa-bhoar-*nahr*) *v* bribe

soborno (soa-*bhoar*-noa) *m* bribery

sobra (*soa*-bhrah) *f* surplus

sobrar (soa-*bhrahr*) *v* *be left over; *be in plenty

sobre (*soa*-bhray) *prep* on, upon; *m* envelope

sobrecubierta (soa-bhray-koo-bhʸayr-tah) *f* jacket (of book)

sobreexcitado (soa-bhray-ayk-thee-*tah*-dhoa) *adj* overexcited

sobrepeso (soa-bhray-*pay*-soa) *m* overweight

sobretasa (soa-bhray-*tah*-sah) *f* surcharge

sobrevivir (soa-bhray-bhee-*bheer*) *v* survive

sobrina (soa-*bhree*-nah) *f* niece

sobrino (soa-*bhree*-noa) *m* nephew

sobrio (*soa*-bhrʸoa) *adj* sober

social (soa-thʸahl) *adj* social

socialismo (soa-thʸah-*leez*-moa) *m*

socialism

socialista (soa-th^yah-*leess*-tah) *adj* socialist; *m* socialist

sociedad (soa-th^yay-*dhahdh*) *f* community, society; company

socio (*soa*-th^yoa) *m*, **-a** *f* associate; partner

socorro (soa-*koa*-rroa) *m* aid; **puesto de ~** first aid post

soda (*soa*-dhah) *f* soda water

sofá (soa-*fah*) *m* sofa

sofocante (soa-foa-*kahn*-tay) *adj* stuffy

sofocarse (soa-foa-*kahr*-say) *v* choke

soga (*soa*-gah) *f* rope

sol (soal) *m* sun; **tomar el ~** sunbathe

solamente (soa-lah-*mayn*-tay) *adv* merely, only

solapa (soa-*lah*-pah) *f* lapel

soldado (soal-*dah*-dhoa) *m* soldier

soldadura (soal-dah-*dhoo*-rah) *f* joint

soleado (soa-lay-*ah*-dhoa) *adj* sunny

soledad (soa-lay-*dhahdh*) *f* solitude

solemne (soa-*laym*-nay) *adj* solemn

***soler** (soa-*layr*) *v* would

solicitar (soa-lee-thee-*tahr*) *v* request; **~ un puesto** apply

solicitud (soa-lee-thee-*toodh*) *f* application

sólido (*soa*-lee-dhoa) *adj* solid, firm; *m* solid

solitario (soa-lee-*tah*-r^yoa) *adj* lonely

solo (*soa*-loa) *adj* alone, lonely, single

sólo (*soa*-loa) *adv* only; solely; just

solomillo (soa-loa-*mee*-l^yoa) *m* sirloin

***soltar** (soal-*tahr*) *v* loosen

soltero (soal-*tay*-roa) *adj* single, unmarried

solterón (soal-tay-*roan*) *m* confirmed bachelor

solterona (soal-tay-*roa*-nah) *f* spinster

soluble (soa-*loo*-bhlay) *adj* soluble

solución (soa-loo-th^yoan) *f* solution

sombra (*soam*-brah) *f* shade; shadow; **~ para los ojos** eye shadow

sombreado (soam-bray-*ah*-dhoa) *adj* shady

sombrerera (soam-bray-*ray*-rah) *f* milliner

sombrero (soam-*bray*-roa) *m* hat

sombrío (soam-*bree*-oa) *adj* sombre, somber *Am*; gloomy

someter (soa-may-*tayr*) *v* subject; **someterse** *v* submit

somnífero (soam-*nee*-fay-roa) *m* sleeping pill

***sonar** (soa-*nahr*) *v* sound; *ring

sonido (soa-*nee*-dhoa) *m* sound

sonreír (soan-ray-*eer*) *v* smile

sonrisa (soan-*ree*-sah) *f* smile

***soñar** (soa-*ñahr*) *v* *dream

soñoliento (soa-ñoa-l^yayn-toa) *adj* sleepy

sopa (*soa*-pah) *f* soup

soplar (soa-*plahr*) *v* *blow

soportar (soa-poar-*tahr*) *v* *bear, endure, sustain; support

sóquet (*soa*-kayt) *mMe* socket

sorbo (*soar*-bhoa) *m* sip

sórdido (*soar*-dhee-dhoa) *adj* filthy

sordo (*soar*-dhoa) *adj* deaf

sorprender (soar-prayn-*dayr*) *v* surprise; *catch

sorpresa (soar-*pray*-sah) *f* surprise; astonishment

sorteo (soar-*tay*-oa) *m* draw

soso (*soa*-soa) *adj* dull, boring; tasteless

sospecha (soass-*pay*-chah) *f* suspicion

sospechar (soass-pay-*chahr*) *v* suspect

sospechoso (soass-pay-*choa*-soa) *adj* suspicious; **persona sospechosa** suspect

sostén (soass-*tayn*) *m* brassière, bra; support

*sostener (soass-tay-*nayr*) v support, *hold up

sota (*soa*-tah) f knave

sótano (*soa*-tah-noa) m basement; cellar

soto (*soa*-toa) m grove

stárter (*stahr*-tayr) m choke

su (soo) adj his; her; their

suahili (swah-*ee*-lee) m Swahili

suave (*swah*-bhay) adj mild, mellow; gentle

subacuático (soo-bhah-*kwah*-tee-koa) adj underwater

subalterno (soo-bhahl-*tayr*-noa) adj subordinate

subasta (soo-*bhahss*-tah) f auction

súbdito (*soobh*-dhee-toa) m subject

subestimar (soo-bhayss-tee-*mahr*) v underestimate

subida (soo-*bhee*-dhah) f climb, rise, ascent

subir (soo-*bheer*) v *rise, ascend; *get on

súbito (*soo*-bhee-toa) adj sudden

sublevación (soo-bhlay-bhah-*th*y*oan*) f rebellion

sublevarse (soo-bhlay-*bhahr*-say) v revolt

subordinado (soo-bhoar-dhee-*nah*-dhoa) adj subordinate

subrayar (soobh-rah-y*ahr*) v underline

subsidio (soobh-*see*-dhyoa) m subsidy

substancia (soobhs-*tahn*-thyah) f substance

substantivo (soobh-stahn-*tee*-bhoa) m noun

*substituir (soobhs-tee-*tweer*) v replace

subterráneo (soobh-tay-*rrah*-nay-oa) adj underground

subtítulo (soobh-*tee*-too-loa) m subtitle

suburbano (soo-bhoor-*bhah*-noa) adj

suburban; m commuter

suburbio (soo-*bhoor*-bhyoa) m suburb

subvención (soobh-bhayn-*th*y*oan*) f grant

suceder (soo-thay-*dhayr*) v happen, occur; succeed

sucesión (soo-thay-*s*y*oan*) f sequence

suceso (soo-*thay*-soa) m event

suciedad (soo-thyay-*dhahdh*) f dirt; filth

sucio (*soo*-thyoa) adj dirty; unclean, foul

sucursal (soo-koor-*sahl*) f branch

sudar (soo-*dhahr*) v perspire, sweat

sudeste (soo-*dhayss*-tay) m south-east

sudoeste (soo-dhoa-*ayss*-tay) m south-west

sudor (soo-*dhoar*) m perspiration, sweat

Suecia (*sway*-thyah) f Sweden

sueco (*sway*-koa) adj Swedish; m Swede

suegra (*sway*-grah) f mother-in-law

suegro (*sway*-groa) m father-in-law

suela (*sway*-lah) f sole

sueldo (*swayl*-doa) m salary, pay; **aumento de ~** rise; raise Am

suelo (*sway*-loa) m soil, earth; floor

suelto (*swayl*-toa) adj loose; free; detached

sueño (*sway*-ñoa) m sleep; dream

suero (*sway*-roa) m serum

suerte (*swayr*-tay) f luck; fortune, lot; chance; **mala ~** bad luck

suéter (*sway*-tayr) m sweater

suficiente (soo-fee-thy*ayn*-tay) adj enough, sufficient; ***ser ~** *do

sufragio (soo-*frah*-khyoa) m suffrage

sufrimiento (soo-free-my*ayn*-toa) m affliction, sorrow, suffering

sufrir (soo-*freer*) v suffer

*sugerir (soo-khay-*reer*) v suggest

sugestión (soo-khayss-*t^yoan*) *f* suggestion

suicidio (swee-*thee*-dh^yoa) *m* suicide

Suiza (*swee*-thah) *f* Switzerland

suizo (*swee*-thoa) *adj* Swiss; *m* Swiss

sujetador (soo-khay-tah-*dhoar*) *m* fastener; clip; bra

sujeto (soo-*khay*-toa) *m* subject; theme

sujeto a (soo-*khay*-toa ah) liable to, subject to

suma (*soo*-mah) *f* amount, sum

sumar (soo-*mahr*) *v* add; amount to

sumario (soo-*mah*-r^yoa) *m* summary

suministrar (soo-mee-neess-*trahr*) *v* furnish, supply

suministro (soo-mee-*neess*-troa) *m* supply

sumo (*soo*-moa) *adj* supreme; **a lo ~** at most

superar (soo-pay-*rahr*) *v* exceed, *outdo

superficial (soo-payr-fee-*th^yahl*) *adj* superficial

superficie (soo-payr-*fee*-th^yay) *f* surface; area

superfluo (soo-*payr*-flwoa) *adj* superfluous, redundant

superior (soo-pay-*r^yoar*) *adj* superior, upper; top

superlativo (soo-payr-lah-*tee*-bhoa) *adj* superlative; *m* superlative

supermercado (soo-payr-mayr-*kah*-dhoa) *m* supermarket

superstición (soo-payrs-tee-*th^yoan*) *f* superstition

supervisar (soo-payr-bhee-*sahr*) *v* supervise

supervisión (soo-payr-bhee-*s^yoan*) *f* supervision

supervisor (soo-payr-bhee-*soar*) *m*, **-a** *f* supervisor

supervivencia (soo-payr-bhee-*bhayn*-th^yah) *f* survival

suplemento (soo-play-*mayn*-toa) *m* supplement

suplicar (soo-plee-*kahr*) *v* beg

***suponer** (soo-poa-*nayr*) *v* assume, suppose

supositorio (soo-poa-see-*toa*-r^yoa) *m* suppository

supremo (soo-*pray*-moa) *adj* supreme

suprimir (soo-pree-*meer*) *v* discontinue

por supuesto (poar soo-*pwayss*-toa) naturally, of course

sur (soor) *m* south; **polo ~** South Pole

surco (*soor*-koa) *m* groove

surgir (soor-*kheer*) *v* *arise

surtido (soor-*tee*-dhoa) *m* assortment

suscribir (sooss-kree-*bheer*) *v* sign

suscripción (sooss-kreep-*th^yoan*) *f* subscription

suspender (sooss-payn-*dayr*) *v* suspend; ***ser suspendido** fail

suspensión (sooss-payn-*s^yoan*) *f* suspension

suspicacia (sooss-pee-*kah*-th^yah) *f* suspicion

suspicaz (sooss-pee-*kahth*) *adj* suspicious

sustancia (sooss-*tahn*-th^yah) *f* substance

sustancial (sooss-tahn-*th^yahl*) *adj* substantial

sustento (sooss-*tayn*-toa) *m* livelihood

***sustituir** (sooss-tee-*tweer*) *v* substitute

sustituto (sooss-tee-*too*-toa) *m*, **-a** *f* deputy, substitute

susto (*sooss*-toa) *m* scare

susurrar (soo-soo-*rrahr*) *v* whisper

susurro (soo-*soo*-rroa) *m* whisper

sutil (soo-*teel*) *adj* subtle; fine; delicate

sutura (soo-*too*-rah) *f* stitch; ***hacer una ~** sew up

suyo (*soo*-^yoa) *pron* his

T

tabaco (tah-*bhah*-koa) *m* tobacco; ~ **de pipa** pipe tobacco

taberna (tah-*bhayr*-nah) *f* public house, pub; tavern; **moza de ~** barmaid

tabla (*tah*-bhlah) *f* board; chart, table; ~ **de conversión** conversion chart; ~ **para surf** surfboard

tablero (tah-*bhlay*-roa) *m* board; ~ **de ajedrez** chessboard; ~ **de damas** draughtboard, checkerboard *AmAm*; ~ **de instrumentos** dashboard

tablón (tah-*bhloan*) *m* plank

tabú (tah-*bhoo*) *m* taboo

taburete (tah-bhoo-*ray*-tay) *m* stool

tacón (tah-*koan*) *m* heel

táctica (*tahk*-tee-kah) *f* tactics *pl*

tacto (*tahk*-toa) *m* touch; tact

tailandés (tigh-lahn-*dayss*) *adj* Thai; *m* Thai

Tailandia (tigh-*lahn*-d^y ah) *f* Thailand

tajada (tah-*khah*-dhah) *f* slice

tajar (tah-*khahr*) *v* chop

tal (tahl) *adj* such; **con ~ que** provided that; ~ **como** such as

taladrar (tah-lah-*dhrahr*) drill, bore

taladro (tah-*lah*-dhroa) *m* drill

talco (*tahl*-koa) *m* talc powder

talento (tah-*layn*-toa) *m* gift, talent

talentoso (tah-layn-*toa*-soa) *adj* gifted, talented

talismán (tah-leez-*mahn*) *m* lucky charm

talón (tah-*loan*) *m* heel; counterfoil, stub

talonario (tah-loa-*nah*-r^y oa) *m* chequebook; checkbook *Am*

talla (*tah*-l^y ah) *f* carving

tallar (tah-*l^y ahr*) *v* carve

taller (tah-*l^y ayr*) *m* workshop

tallo (*tah*-l^y oa) *m* stem

tamaño (tah-*mah*-ñoa) *m* size; ~ **extraordinario** outsize

también (tahm-*b^y ayn*) *adv* too, also, as well; **así ~** likewise

tambor (tahm-*boar*) *m* drum; ~ **del freno** brake drum

tamiz (tah-*meeth*) *m* sieve

tamizar (tah-mee-*thahr*) *v* sift, sieve

tampoco (tahm-*poa*-koa) *adv* not … either

tampón (tahm-*poan*) *m* tampon

tan (tahn) *adv* so, such

tangible (tahng-*khee*-bhlay) *adj* tangible

tanque (*tahng*-kay) *m* tank

tanteo (tahn-*tay*-oa) *m* score

tanto (*tahn*-toa) *adv* as much; as; **por lo ~** therefore; **por ~** so; **tanto … como** both … and

tapa (*tah*-pah) *f* lid, top, cover; appetizer

tapizar (tah-pee-*thahr*) *v* upholster

tapón (tah-*poan*) *m* stopper, cork

taquigrafía (tah-kee-grah-*fee*-ah) *f* shorthand

taquilla (tah-*kee*-l^y ah) *f* box office

tararear (tah-rah-ray-*ahr*) *v* hum

tardanza (tahr-*dhahn*-thah) *f* delay

tardar (tahr-*dhar*) *v* take a long time; **a más ~** at the latest; **¡no tardes!** don't be late; **¿cuánto se tarda …?** how long does it take to …?

tarde (*tahr*-dhay) *f* afternoon; evening

tardío (tahr-*dhee*-oa) *adj* late

tarea (tah-*ray*-ah) *f* duty, task; job

tarifa (tah-*ree*-fah) *f* rate; ~ **nocturna** night rate

tarjeta (tahr-*khay*-tah) *f* card; ~ **de crédito** credit card; charge plate *Am*; ~ **de temporada** season ticket; ~ **de visita** visiting-card; ~ **postal** postcard, card; ~ **postal ilustrada**

picture postcard; ~ **telefónica** phone card; ~ **verde** green card

tarta (*tahr*-tah) *f* cake

taxi (*tahk*-see) *m* cab, taxi

taxímetro (tahk-*see*-may-troa) *m* taximeter

taxista (tahk-*seess*-tah) *m*/*f* cab driver, taxi driver

taza (*tah*-thah) *f* cup; mug; ~ **de café** cup of coffee; ~ **de té** cup of tea

tazón (tah-*thoan*) *m* bowl, basin

te (tay) *pron* yourself

té (tay) *m* tea

teatro (tay-*ah*-troa) *m* drama; theatre; ~ **de la ópera** opera house; ~ **de variedades** music hall, variety theatre (theater *Am*); ~ **guiñol** puppet show

tebeo (tay-*bhay*-oa) *m* comics *pl*

técnica (*tayk*-nee-kah) *f* technique

técnico (*tayk*-nee-koa) *adj* technical; *m* technician

tecnología (tayk-noa-loa-*khee*-ah) *f* technology

techo (*tay*-choa) *m* roof; ~ **de paja** thatched roof

tecla (*tay*-klah) *f* key

teja (*tay*-khah) *f* tile

tejado (tay-*khah*-doa) *m* roof

tejedor (tay-khay-*dhoar*) *m*, **-a** *f* weaver

tejer (tay-*khayr*) *v* *weave

tejido (tay-*khee*-dhoa) *m* fabric, tissue, material

tele (*tay*-lay) *f* TV

tela (*tay*-lah) *f* cloth; ~ **para toallas** towel(l)ing

telaraña (tay-lah-*rah*-ñah) *f* spider's web

telefax (tay-lay-*fahks*) *m* fax; **mandar un** ~ send a fax

telefonear (tay-lay-foa-nay-*ahr*) *v* phone; call up *Am*

telefonista (tay-lay-foa-*neess*-tah) *f*

telephonist, telephone operator

teléfono (tay-*lay*-foa-noa) *m* phone, telephone; **llamar por** ~ ring up

telegrafiar (tay-lay-grah-*f*y*ahr*) *v* telegraph

teleobjetivo (tay-lay-oabh-khay-*tee*-bhoa) *m* telephoto lens

telepatía (tay-lay-pah-*tee*-ah) *f* telepathy

telesilla (tay-lay-*see*-l*y*ah) *m* ski lift

televisión (tay-lay-bhee-s*y*oan) *f* television; ~ **por cable** cable television; ~ **por satélite** satellite television

televisor (tay-lay-bhee-*soar*) *m* television set

télex (*tay*-layks) *m* telex

telón (tay-*loan*) *m* stage curtain

tema (*tay*-mah) *m* theme

***temblar** (taym-*bhlahr*) *v* tremble, shiver

temer (tay-*mayr*) *v* fear, dread

temor (tay-*moar*) *m* fear, dread

temperamento (taym-pay-rah-*mayn*-toa) *m* temperament

temperatura (taym-pay-rah-*too*-rah) *f* temperature; ~ **ambiente** room temperature

tempestad (taym-payss-*tahdh*) *f* tempest

tempestuoso (taym-payss-*twoa*-soa) *adj* stormy

templo (*taym*-ploa) *m* temple

temporada (taym-poa-*rah*-dhah) *f* season; **alta** ~ high season; ~ **baja** low season

temporal (taym-poa-*rahl*) *adj* temporary

temprano (taym-*prah*-noa) *adj* early

tenazas (tay-*nah*-thahss) *f* tongs *pl*, pincers *pl*

tendencia (tayn-*dayn*-th*y*ah) *f* tendency

***tender** (tayn-*dayr*): ~ **a** tend;

*tenderse *v* *lie down

tendero (tayn-*day*-roa) *m*, **-a** *f* shopkeeper; tradesman

tendón (tayn-*doan*) *m* sinew, tendon

tenedor (tay-nay-*dhoar*) *m* fork

*tener (tay-*nayr*) *v* *have; *keep; *hold; **~ que** *must; *ought to, *should, *shall; *be obliged to; **tenga usted** here you are

teniente (tay-n'*ayn*-tay) *m* lieutenant

tenis (*tay*-neess) *m* tennis; **~ de mesa** ping-pong, table tennis

tensión (tayn-s'*oan*) *f* strain, pressure, tension; **~ arterial** blood pressure

tenso (*tayn*-soa) *adj* tense

tentación (tayn-tah-th'*oan*) *f* temptation

*tentar (tayn-*tahr*) *v* tempt

tentativa (tayn-tah-*tee*-bhah) *f* attempt, try

tentempié (tayn-taym-p'*ay*) *m* snack

*teñir (tay-*ñeer*) *v* dye

teología (tay-oa-loa-*khee*-ah) *f* theology

teoría (tay-oa-*ree*-ah) *f* theory

teórico (tay-*oa*-ree-koa) *adj* theoretical

terapia (tay-*rah*-p'ah) *f* therapy

tercero (tayr-*thay*-roa) *num* third

terciopelo (tayr-th'oa-*pay*-loa) *m* velvet

terminación (tayr-mee-nah-th'*oan*) *f* finish

terminar (tayr-mee-*nahr*) *v* end, finish; accomplish; **terminarse** *v* expire, end

término (*tayr*-mee-noa) *m* term; issue

termo (*tayr*-moa) *m* vacuum flask, thermos flask

termómetro (tayr-*moa*-may-troa) *m* thermometer

termostato (tayr-moass-*tah*-toa) *m* thermostat

ternero (tayr-*nay*-roa) *m* calf

ternura (tayr-*noo*-rah) *f* tenderness

terraplén (tay-rrah-*playn*) *m* embankment

terraza (tay-*rrah*-thah) *f* terrace

terremoto (tay-rray-*moa*-toa) *m* earthquake

terreno (tay-*rray*-noa) *m* terrain; field, grounds

terrible (tay-*rree*-bhlay) *adj* frightful; awful, horrible, terrible, dreadful

territorio (tay-rree-*toa*-r'oa) *m* territory

terrón (tay-*rroan*) *m* lump

terror (tay-*rroar*) *m* terror; terrorism

terrorismo (tay-rroa-*reez*-moa) *m* terrorism

terrorista (tay-rroa-*reess*-tah) *m/f* terrorist

tesis (*tay*-seess) *f* thesis

Tesorería (tay-soa-ray-*ree*-ah) *f* treasury

tesorero (tay-soa-*ray*-roa) *m* treasurer

tesoro (tay-*soa*-roa) *m* treasure

testamento (tayss-tah-*mayn*-toa) *m* will

testarudo (tayss-tah-*roo*-dhoa) *adj* pig-headed, stubborn

testigo (tayss-*tee*-goa) *m* witness; **~ de vista** eyewitness

testimoniar (tayss-tee-moa-n'*ahr*) *v* testify

testimonio (tayss-tee-*moa*-n'oa) *m* testimony

tetera (tay-*tay*-rah) *f* teapot

textil (tayks-*teel*) *m* textile

texto (*tayks*-toa) *m* text

textura (tayks-*too*-rah) *f* texture

tez (tayth) *f* complexion

ti (tee) *pron* you

tía (*tee*-ah) *f* aunt

tibio (*tee*-bh'oa) *adj* tepid, lukewarm

tiburón (tee-bhoo-*roan*) *m* shark

tiempo (t'*aym*-poa) *m* time; weather; period; tense; tempo; **a ~** in time; **~**

libre spare time

tienda (*t'ayn*-dah) *f* shop; tent

tierno (*t'ayr*-noa) *adj* gentle, tender

tierra (*t'ay*-rrah) *f* earth; ground, soil; land; **en ~** ashore; **~ baja** lowlands *pl*; **~ firme** mainland

tieso (*t'ay*-soa) *adj* stiff

tifus (*tee*-fooss) *m* typhoid

tigre (*tee*-gray) *m* tiger

tijeras (tee-*khay*-rahss) *fpl* scissors *pl*; **~ para las uñas** nail scissors *pl*

tilo (*tee*-loa) *m* limetree, lime

timbre (*teem*-bray) *m* tone; bell; doorbell; *mMe* postage stamp

timidez (tee-mee-*dhayth*) *f* timidity, shyness

tímido (*tee*-mee-dhoa) *adj* timid, embarrassed, shy

timón (tee-*moan*) *m* helm, rudder

timonel (tee-moa-*nayl*) *m* steersman

timonero (tee-moa-*nay*-roa) *m* helmsman

tímpano (*teem*-pah-noa) *m* ear-drum

tinta (*teen*-tah) *f* ink

tinto (*teen*-toa) *adj:* vino ~ red wine

tintorería (teen-toa-ray-*ree*-ah) *f* dry-cleaner's

tintura (teen-*too*-rah) *f* dye

tío (*tee*-oa) *m* uncle

tiovivo (tee-oa-*bee*-boa) *m* carousel, merry-go-round

típico (*tee*-pee-koa) *adj* typical, characteristic

tipo (*tee*-poa) *m* type; fellow, guy

tirada (tee-*rah*-dhah) *f* issue

tirano (tee-*rah*-noa) *m*, **-a** *f* tyrant

tirantes (tee-*rahn*-tayss) *mpl* braces *pl*; suspenders *plAm*

tirar (tee-*rahr*) *v* pull; *hit; *shoot

tirita (tee-*ree*-tah) *f* Bandaid®, plaster

tiritar (tee-ree-*tahr*) *v* shiver

tiro (*tee*-roa) *m* shot; throw

tirón (tee-*roan*) *m* jerk, tug; pull

titular (tee-too-*lahr*) *m* headline

título (*tee*-too-loa) *m* heading, title; degree

toalla (toa-*ah*-l'ah) *f* towel; **~ de baño** bath towel

tobera (toa-*bhay*-rah) *f* nozzle

tobillo (toa-*bhee*-l'oa) *m* ankle

tobogán (toa-bhoa-*gahn*) *m* slide

tocadiscos (toa-kah-*deess*-koass) *m* record player

tocador (toa-kah-*dhoar*) *m* dressing table; powder room; **artículos de ~** toiletries

tocante a (toa-*kahn*-tay ah) regarding

tocar (toa-*kahr*) *v* touch; *hit; play; **no ~** *keep off

tocino (toa-*thee*-noa) *m* bacon

todavía (toa-dhah-*bhee*-ah) *adv* still, however

todo (*toa*-dhoa) *adj* all; entire; *pron* everything; **sobre ~** most of all, essentially, especially; **todos** *pron* everybody

toldo (*toal*-doa) *m* awning

tolerable (toa-lay-*rah*-bhlay) *adj* tolerable

tomar (toa-*mahr*) *v* *catch; *take; **~ el pelo** tease

tomate (toa-*mah*-tay) *m* tomato

tomillo (toa-*mee*-l'oa) *m* thyme

tomo (*toa*-moa) *m* volume

tonada (toa-*nah*-dhah) *f* tune

tonel (toa-*nayl*) *m* barrel, cask

tonelada (toa-nay-*lah*-dhah) *f* ton

tónico (*toa*-nee-koa) *m* tonic; **~ para el cabello** hair tonic

tono (*toa*-noa) *m* tone; note; shade

tontería (toan-tay-*ree*-ah) *f* nonsense, rubbish; ***decir tonterías** talk rubbish

tonto (*toan*-toa) *adj* foolish; *m* fool

topetar (toa-pay-*tahr*) *v* bump

topetón (toa-pay-*toan*) *m* bump

toque (*toa*-kay) *m* touch

torcedura (toar-thay-*dhoo*-rah) *f*

sprain

*torcer (toar-*thayr*) *v* twist; ***torcerse** *v* sprain

tordo (*toar*-dhoa) *m* thrush

torero (toa-*ray*-roa) *m* bullfighter

tormenta (toar-*mayn*-tah) *f* storm

tormento (toar-*mayn*-toa) *m* torment

tormentoso (toar-mayn-*toa*-soa) *adj* stormy

tornar (toar-*nahr*) *v* give back; transform

torneo (toar-*nay*-oa) *m* tournament

tornillo (toar-*nee*-l^yoa) *m* screw

torno (*toar*-noa): **en ~** about, around; **en ~ de** round, around

toro (*toa*-roa) *m* bull

toronja (toa-*roan*-khah) *f*Me grapefruit

torpe (*toar*-pay) *adj* clumsy, awkward

torre (*toa*-rray) *f* tower

torsión (toar-s^y*oan*) *f* twist

tortilla (toar-*tee*-l^yah) *f* omelette; *Me* corn flatcake

tortuga (toar-*too*-gah) *f* turtle

tortuoso (toar-*twoa*-soa) *adj* winding

tortura (toar-*too*-rah) *f* torture

torturar (toar-too-*rahr*) *v* torture

tos (toass) *f* cough

toser (toa-*sayr*) *v* cough

tostado (toass-*tah*-dhoa) *adj* toasted; tanned

tostar (toas-*tahr*) *v* toast; roast; tan; **tostarse** (toas-*tahr*-say) tan, get brown

total (toa-*tahl*) *adj* total; overall, utter; *m* total; whole; **en ~** altogether

totalitario (toa-tah-lee-*tah*-r^yoa) *adj* totalitarian

totalmente (toa-tahl-*mayn*-tay) *adv* completely, altogether, wholly

tóxico (*toak*-see-koa) *adj* toxic

trabajar (trah-bah-*khahr*) *v* work; work at; work on

trabajo (trah-*bhah*-khoa) *m* work,

labo(u)r; difficulty; **~ manual** handicraft

tractor (trahk-*toar*) *m* tractor

tradición (trah-dhee-th^y*oan*) *f* tradition

tradicional (trah-dhee-th^yoa-*nahl*) *adj* traditional

traducción (trah-dhook-th^y*oan*) *f* translation

*traducir (trah-dhoo-*theer*) *v* translate

traductor (trah-dhook-*toar*) *m*, **-a** *f* translator

*traer (trah-*ayr*) *v* *bring

tragar (trah-*gahr*) *v* swallow

tragedia (trah-*khay*-dh^yah) *f* drama, tragedy

trágico (*trah*-khee-koa) *adj* tragic

trago (*trah*-goa) *m* mouthful; *colloquial* drink; **de un ~** in one gulp; **pasar un mal ~** have a hard time

traición (trigh-th^y*oan*) *f* treason

traicionar (trigh-th^yoa-*nahr*) *v* betray

traidor (trigh-*dhoar*) *m* traitor

traje (*trah*-khay) *m* suit; gown; robe; **~ de baño** bathing suit; **~ de etiqueta** evening dress; **~ del país** national dress; **~ de malla** tights *pl*; **~ pantalón** pant suit

trama (*trah*-mah) *f* plot

trampa (*trahm*-pah) *f* trap; hatch

tranquilidad (trahng-kee-lee-*dhahdh*) *f* calmness; tranquillity

tranquilizar (trahng-kee-lee-*thahr*) *v* reassure; calm

tranquilo (trahng-*kee*-loa) *adj* tranquil, quiet, calm; peaceful

transacción (trahn-sahk-th^y*oan*) *f* transaction, deal; **volumen de transacciones** turnover

transatlántico (trahn-saht-*lahn*-tee-koa) *adj* transatlantic

transbordador (trahnz-bhoar-dhah-*dhoar*) *m* ferry-boat; **~ de trenes** train ferry

transcurrir (trahns-koo-*rreer*) *v* pass

transeúnte (trahn-say-*oon*-tay) *m* passer-by

*transferir (trahns-fay-*reer*) *v* transfer

transformador (trahns-foar-mah-*dhoar*) *m* transformer

transformar (trahns-foar-*mahr*) *v* transform

transgredir (trahnz-gray-*deer*) *v* transgress

transición (trahn-see-th*y*oan) *f* transition

tránsito (*trahn*-see-toa) *m* traffic

transmisión (trahnz-mee-s*y*oan) *f* transmission, broadcast

transmitir (trahnz-mee-*teer*) *v* transmit

transparente (trahns-pah-*rayn*-tay) *adj* transparent

transpiración (trahns-pee-rah-th*y*oan) *f* perspiration

transpirar (trahns-pee-*rahr*) *v* perspire

transportar (trahns-poar-*tahr*) *v* transport; ship

transporte (trahns-*poar*-tay) *m* transportation, transport

tranvía (trahm-*bee*-ah) *m* tram; streetcar *Am*

trapo (*trah*-poa) *m* rag; ~ **de cocina** tea cloth, kitchen towel *Am*

tras (trahss) *prep* behind

trasbordo: *hacer ~ (ah-*thayr* trahz-*bhoar*-dhoa) change, transfer

trasero (trah-*say*-roa) *m* bottom, buttocks, rump; *adj* back, rear

trasladar (trahz-lah-*dhahr*) *v* move

traslúcido (trahz-*loo*-thee-dhoa) *adj* sheer

trastornado (trahss-toar-*nah*-dhoa) *adj* upset

trastornar (trahss-toar-*nahr*) *v* upset

trastos (*trahss*-toass) *mpl* junk

tratado (trah-*tah*-dhoa) *m* essay; treaty

tratamiento (trah-tah-*m*y*ayn*-toa) *m* treatment; ~ **de belleza** beauty treatment

tratar (trah-*tahr*) *v* handle, treat; ~ **con** *deal with

trato (*trah*-toa) *m* relationship; treatment; manner ~**s** dealings

través: a ~ de (ah trah-*bhayss day*) across, through

travesía (trah-bhay-*see*-ah) *f* crossing, passage

travieso (trah-bh*y*ay-soa) *adj* naughty, bad; mischievous

trazar (trah-*thahr*) *v* sketch

trébol (*tray*-bhoal) *m* clover, shamrock

trece (*tray*-thay) *num* thirteen

treceno (tray-*thay*-noa) *num* thirteenth

trecho (*tray*-choa) *m* stretch

treinta (*trayn*-tah) *num* thirty

treintavo (trayn-*tah*-bhoa) *num* thirtieth

tremendo (tray-*mayn*-doa) *adj* awful, terrible; tremendous, terrific

trementina (tray-mayn-*tee*-nah) *f* turpentine

tren (trayn) *m* train; ~ **de cercanías** local train; ~ **de mercancías** goods train; ~ **de pasajeros** passenger train; ~ **directo** through train; ~ **expreso** express train; ~ **nocturno** night train

trenza (*trayn*-thah) *f* braid

trepar (tray-*pahr*) *v* climb

tres (trayss) *num* three

triangular (tr*y*ahng-goo-*lahr*) *adj* triangular

triángulo (tr*y*ahng-goo-loa) *m* triangle

tribu (*tree*-bhoo) *m* tribe

tribuna (tree-*bhoo*-nah) *f* stand

tribunal (tree-bhoo-*nahl*) *m* court, law

court

trigal (tree-*gahl*) *m* cornfield

trigo (*tree*-goa) *m* grain, corn; wheat

trimestral (tree-mayss-*trahl*) *adj* quarterly

trimestre (tree-*mayss*-tray) *m* quarter

trinchar (treen-*chahr*) *v* carve

trineo (tree-*nay*-oa) *m* sleigh, sledge, sled *Am*

triste (*treess*-tay) *adj* sad

tristeza (treess-*tay*-thah) *f* sorrow, sadness

triturar (tree-too-*rahr*) *v* *grind

triunfante (tr^yoon-*fahn*-tay) *adj* triumphant

triunfar (tr^yoon-*fahr*) *v* triumph

triunfo (tr^yoon-foa) *m* triumph

*trocar (troa-*kahr*) *v* swap

trompeta (troam-*pay*-tah) *f* trumpet

tronada (troa-*nah*-dhah) *f* thunderstorm

*tronar (troa-*nahr*) *v* thunder

tronco (*troang*-koa) *m* trunk

trono (*troanoa*) *m* throne

tropas (*troa*-pahss) *fpl* troops *pl*

*tropezarse (troa-pay-*thahr*-say) *v* stumble

tropical (troa-pee-*kahl*) *adj* tropical

trópicos (*troa*-pee-koass) *mpl* tropics *pl*

trozo (*troa*-thoa) *m* chunk, morsel, bit; fragment, passage

truco (*troo*-koa) *m* trick

trucha (*troo*-chah) *f* trout

trueno (*trway*-noa) *m* thunder

tu (too) *adj* your

tú (too) *pron* you

tuberculosis (too-bhayr-koo-*loa*-seess) *f* tuberculosis

tubo (*too*-bhoa) *m* tube

tuerca (*twayr*-kah) *f* nut

tulipán (too-lee-*pahn*) *m* tulip

tumba (*toom*-bah) *f* tomb

tumbona (toom-*boa*-nah) *f* (sun) lounger

tumor (too-*moar*) *m* growth, tumo(u)r

tunecino (too-nay-*thee*-noa) *adj* Tunisian; *m* Tunisian

túnel (*too*-nayl) *m* tunnel

Túnez (*too*-nayth) *m* Tunisia

túnica (*too*-nee-kah) *f* tunic, robe

turbar (toor-*bhahr*) *v* disturb; upset

turbina (toor-*bhee*-nah) *f* turbine

turco (*toor*-koa) *adj* Turkish; *m* Turk

turismo (too-*reez*-moa) *m* tourism

turista (too-*reess*-tah) *m/f* tourist; **oficina para turistas** tourist office

turno (*toor*-noa) *m* turn; shift

Turquía (toor-*kee*-ah) *f* Turkey

turrón (too-*rroan*) *m* nougat

tutela (too-*tay*-lah) *f* custody

tutor (too-*toar*) *m* tutor; guardian

tuyos (*too*-^yoass) *adj* your

U

ubicación (oo-bhee-kah-*th^yoan*) *f* situation, location

UE (oo-ay) *f* EU

úlcera (*ool*-thay-rah) *f* ulcer, sore; ~ **gástrica** gastric ulcer

ulterior (ool-tay-*r^yoar*) *adj* further;

subsequent

últimamente (*ool*-tee-mah-mayn-tay) *adv* lately; finally

último (*ool*-tee-moa) *adj* ultimate; last; latest

ultramar (ool-trah-*mahr*) *adv* overseas

ultravioleta (ool-trah-bh^{y}oa-*lay*-tah) *adj* ultraviolet

umbral (oom-*brahl*) *m* threshold

un (oon) *art* a

unánime (oo-*nah*-nee-may) *adj* unanimous

ungüento (oong-*gwayn*-toa) *m* ointment, salve

únicamente (*oo*-nee-kah-mayn-tay) *adv* exclusively

único (*oo*-nee-koa) *adj* unique, sole

unidad (oo-nee-*dhahdh*) *f* unity; unit

unido (oo-*nee*-dhoa) *adj* joint

uniforme (oo-nee-*foar*-may) *adj* uniform; *m* uniform

unilateral (oo-nee-lah-tay-*rahl*) *adj* one-sided

unión (oo-*n^{y}oan*) *f* union

Unión Europea (oo-*n^{y}oan* ay^{oo}-roa-*pay*-ah) European Union

unir (oo-*neer*) *v* unite; combine; **unirse a** join

universal (oo-nee-bhayr-*sahl*) *adj* universal

universidad (oo-nee-bhayr-see-*dhahdh*) *f* university

universo (oo-nee-*bhayr*-soa) *m* universe

uno (*oo*-noa) *num* one; *pron* one;

unos *adj* some; *pron* some

untar (oon-*tahr*) *v* rub, spread

uña (*oo*-ñah) *f* nail

urbano (oor-*bhah*-noa) *adj* urban

urgencia (oor-*khayn*-th^{y}ah) *f* urgency; emergency; **botiquín de ~** first-aid kit

urgente (oor-*khayn*-tay) *adj* pressing, urgent

urraca (oo-*rrah*-kah) *f* magpie

Uruguay (oo-roo-*gwigh*) *m* Uruguay

uruguayo (oo-roo-*gwah*-^{y}oa) *adj* Uruguayan; *m* Uruguayan

usar (oo-*sahr*) *v* use

uso (*oo*-soa) *m* use, usage

usted (ooss-*taydh*) *pron* you; **a ~** you; **de ~** your

usual (oo-*swahl*) *adj* common, customary, usual

usuario (oo-swah-r^{y}oa) *m* user

utensilio (oo-tayn-*see*-l^{y}oa) *m* utensil

útil (*oo*-teel) *adj* useful

utilidad (oo-tee-lee-*dhahdh*) *f* utility, use

utilizable (oo-tee-lee-*thah*-bhlay) *adj* usable

utilizar (oo-tee-lee-*thahr*) *v* utilize

uva (*oo*-bhah) *f* grape; **uvas** *fpl* grapes *pl*

V

vaca (*bah*-kah) *f* cow

vacaciones (bah-kah-th^{y}oa-nayss) *fpl* holiday, vacation; **de ~** on holiday

vacante (bah-*kahn*-tay) *adj* vacant; *f* vacancy

vaciar (bah-th^y*ahr*) *v* empty; vacate

vacilante (bah-thee-lahn-tay) *adj* unsteady, shaky

vacilar (bah-thee-*lahr*) *v* hesitate; falter

vacío (bah-*thee*-oa) *adj* empty; *m* vacuum

vacunación (bah-koo-nah-th^{y}oan) *f* vaccination

vacunar (bah-koo-*nahr*) *v* vaccinate, inoculate

vadear (bah-dhay-*ahr*) *v* wade

vado (*bah*-dhoa) *m* ford

vagabundear (bah-gah-bhoon-day-*ahr*) *v* tramp, roam

vagabundo (bah-gah-*bhoon*-doa) *m* tramp

vagar (bah-*gahr*) *v* wander

vago (*bah*-goa) *adj* vague; faint, dim; idle

vagón (bah-*goan*) *m* wag(g)on, carriage; coach

vainilla (bigh-*nee*-l'ah) *f* vanilla

vale (bah-*lay*) *m* voucher; coupon; receipt

*valer (bah-*layr*) *v* *be worth; ~ **la pena** *be worthwhile

valiente (bah-*l'ayn*-tay) *adj* courageous, brave; bold

valija (bah-*lee*-khah) *f* case; valise

valioso (bah-*l'oa*-soa) *adj* valuable

valor (bah-*loar*) *m* worth, value; courage; **bolsa de valores** stock exchange; **sin** ~ worthless

vals (bahls) *m* waltz

valuar (bah-*lwahr*) *v* value; appreciate

válvula (*bahl*-bhoo-lah) *f* valve

valle (*bah*-l'ay) *m* valley

vanidoso (bah-nee-*dhoa*-soa) *adj* vain

vano (*bah*-noa) *adj* idle, vain; **en** ~ in vain

vapor (bah-*poar*) *m* steam, vapo(u)r; steamer; ~ **de línea** liner

vaporizador (bah-poa-ree-thah-*dhoar*) *m* atomizer

vaqueros (bah-*kay*-roass) *mpl* jeans *pl*

variable (bah-r'ah-bhlay) *adj* variable

variación (bah-r'ah-th'oan) *f* variation

variado (bah-r'ah-dhoa) *adj* varied

variar (bah-r'ahr) *v* vary

varice (*bah*-ree-thay) *f* varicose vein

varicela (bah-ree-*thay*-lah) *f* chickenpox

variedad (bah-r'ay-*dhahdh*) *f* variety;

espectáculo de variedades variety show

varios (*bah*-r'oass) *adj* various, several

vaselina (bah-say-*lee*-nah) *f* vaseline

vasija (bah-*see*-khah) *f* receptacle

vaso (*bah*-soa) *m* glass; mug; tumbler; vase; ~ **sanguíneo** blood vessel

vasto (*bahss*-toa) *adj* wide, vast; extensive

vatio (*bah*-t'oa) *m* watt

Vd. *pron* (usted)

vecindad (bay-theen-*dahdh*) *f* neighbo(u)rhood, vicinity

vecindario (bay-theen-*dah*-r'oa) *m* community

vecino (bay-*thee*-noa) *adj* neighbo(u)ring; *m*, **-a** *f* neighbo(u)r

vegetación (bay-khay-tah-*th'oan*) *f* vegetation

vegetariano (bay-khay-tah-*r'ah*-noa) *m*, **-a** *f* vegetarian

vehículo (bay-*ee*-koo-loa) *m* vehicle

veinte (*bayn*-tay) *num* twenty

vejez (bay-*khayth*) *f* old age

vejiga (bay-*khee*-gah) *f* bladder

vela (*bay*-lah) *f* sail; **deporte de** ~ yachting

velo (*bay*-loa) *m* veil

velocidad (bay-loa-thee-*dhahdh*) *f* speed; rate; gear; **límite de** ~ speed limit; ~ **de cruce** cruising speed

velocímetro (bay-loa-*thee*-may-troa) *m* speedometer

veloz (bay-*loath*) *adj* swift

vena (*bay*-nah) *f* vein

vencedor (bayn-thay-*dhoar*) *m* winner

vencer (bayn-*thayr*) *v* *overcome, conquer; *win

vencimiento (bayn-thee-*m'ayn*-toa) *m* expiry

vendaje (bayn-*dah*-khay) *m* bandage

vendar (bayn-*dahr*) *v* bandage

vendedor (bayn-day-*dhoar*) *m*
salesman

vendedora (bayn-day-*dhoa*-rah) *f*
salesgirl

vender (bayn-*dayr*) *v* *sell; **~ al
detalle** retail

vendible (bayn-*dee*-bhlay) *adj*
saleable

vendimia (bayn-*dee*-m^yah) *f* vintage

veneno (bay-*nay*-noa) *m* poison

venenoso (bay-nay-*noa*-soa) *adj*
poisonous

venerable (bay-nay-*rah*-bhlay) *adj*
venerable

venerar (bay-nay-*rahr*) *v* worship

venezolano (bay-nay-thoa-*lah*-noa)
adj Venezuelan; *m* Venezuelan

Venezuela (bay-nay-*thway*-lah) *f*
Venezuela

venganza (bayng-*gahn*-thah) *f*
revenge

venidero (bay-nee-*dhay*-roa) *adj*
upcoming; future

*venir (bay-*neer*) *v* *come

venta (*bayn*-tah) *f* sale; **de ~** for sale; **~
al por mayor** wholesale

ventaja (bayn-*tah*-khah) *f* benefit,
advantage; profit; lead

ventajoso (bayn-tah-*khoa*-soa) *adj*
advantageous; profitable

ventana (bayn-*tah*-nah) *f* window; **~
de la nariz** nostril

ventanilla (bayn-tah-nee-l^yah) *f*
window; porthole

ventarrón (bayn-tah-*rroan*) *m* gale

ventilación (bayn-tee-lah-*th^yoan*) *f*
ventilation

ventilador (bayn-tee-lah-*dhoar*) *m*
fan, ventilator

ventilar (bayn-tee-*lahr*) *v* ventilate

ventisca (bhayn-*teess*-kah) *f* blizzard

ventoso (bayn-*toa*-soa) *adj* windy

*ver (bayr) *v* *see, notice

veranda (bay-*rahn*-dah) *f* veranda

verano (bay-*rah*-noa) *m* summer;
pleno ~ midsummer

verbal (bayr-*bhahl*) *adj* verbal

verbena (bayr-*bay*-nah) *f* party

verbo (*bayr*-bhoa) *m* verb

verdad (bayr-*dhahdh*) *f* truth

verdaderamente (bayr-dhah-dhay-
rah-*mayn*-tay) *adv* really

verdadero (bayr-dhah-*dhay*-roa) *adj*
true; real, very; actual

verde (*bayr*-dhay) *adj* green

verdulero (bayr-dhoo-*lay*-roa) *m*
greengrocer

veredicto (bay-ray-*dheek*-toa) *m*
verdict

vergel (bayr-gayl) *m* orchard

vergüenza (bayr-*gwayn*-thah) *f*
shame; **¡qué vergüenza!** shame!

verídico (bay-*ree*-dhee-koa) *adj*
truthful

verificar (bay-ree-fee-*kahr*) *v* check,
verify

verosímil (bay-roa-*see*-meel) *adj*
credible

versión (bayr-*s^yoan*) *f* version

verso (*bayr*-soa) *m* verse

*verter (bayr-*tayr*) *v* pour; *spill

vertical (bayr-tee-*kahl*) *adj* vertical

vestíbulo (bayss-*tee*-bhoo-loa) *m* hall,
lobby; foyer

vestido (bayss-*tee*-dhoa) *m* dress;
garment; **vestidos** *mpl* clothes *pl*

*vestir (bayss-*teer*) *v* dress; ***vestirse** *v*
dress

vestuario (bayss-*twah*-r^yoa) *m*
wardrobe; dressing room

veterinario (bay-tay-ree-*nah*-r^yoa) *m*,
-a *f* veterinary surgeon

vez (bayth) *f* time; **alguna ~** some
time; **a veces** sometimes; **de ~ en
cuando** occasionally, now and then;
otra ~ again, once more; **pocas
veces** seldom; **una ~** once

vía (*bee*-ah) *f* way; track; **~ del tren**

railroad *Am*; ~ **navegable** waterway

viaducto (b^yah-*dhook*-toa) *m* viaduct

viajar (b^yah-*khahr*) *v* travel

viaje (b^yah-khay) *m* journey; trip, voyage

viajero (b^yah-*khay*-roa) *m*, **-a** *f* travel(l)er

vibración (bee-bhrah-*th^yoan*) *f* vibration

vibrar (bee-*bhrahr*) *v* tremble, vibrate

vicario (bee-*kah*-r^yoa) *m* vicar

vicepresidente (bee-thay-pray-see-*dhayn*-tay) *m* vice-president

vicio (*bee*-th^yoa) *m* vice; **pasarlo de ~** *colloquial* have a great time

vicioso (bee-*th^yoa*-soa) *adj* vicious

víctima (*beek*-tee-mah) *f* casualty, victim

victoria (beek-*toa*-r^yah) *f* victory

vida (*bee*-dhah) *f* life; lifetime; **en ~** alive; **~ privada** privacy

videocámara (bee-dhay-oa-*kah*-mah-rah) *f* video camera

videocasete (bee-dhay-oa-kah-*say*-tay) *m* video cassette

videograbadora (bee-dhay-oa-grah-bhah-*dhoa*-rah) *f* video recorder

vidrio (*bee*-dhr^yoa) *m* glass; **de ~** glass; **~ de color** stained glass

viejo (b^yay-khoa) *adj* old; ancient, aged; stale

viento (b^y*ayn*-toa) *m* wind

vientre (b^y*ayn*-tray) *m* belly

viernes (b^y*ayr*-nayss) *m* Friday

vigente (bee-*khayn*-tay) *adj* in force

vigésimo (bee-*khay*-see-moa) *num* twentieth

vigilar (bee-khee-*lahr*) *v* watch, patrol

villa (*bee*-l^yah) *f* villa

villano (bee-*l^yah*-noa) *adj* villainous, base

vinagre (bee-*nah*-gray) *m* vinegar

vino (*bee*-noa) *m* wine

viña (*bee*-ñah) *f* vineyard

violación (b^yoa-lah-*th^yoan*) *f* violation

violar (b^yoa-*lahr*) *v* violate; rape; force

violencia (b^yoa-*layn*-th^yah) *f* violence

violento (b^yoa-*layn*-toa) *adj* violent; fierce, severe

violeta (b^yoa-*lay*-tah) *f* violet

violín (b^yoa-*leen*) *m* violin

virgen (*beer*-khayn) *f* virgin

virtud (beer-*toodh*) *f* virtue

visado (bee-*sah*-dhoa) *m* visa

visar (bee-*sahr*) *v* endorse

visibilidad (bee-see-bhee-lee-*dhahdh*) *f* visibility

visible (bee-*see*-bhlay) *adj* visible

visión (bee-s^y*oan*) *f* vision

visita (bee-*see*-tah) *f* visit, call

visitante (bee-see-*tahn*-tay) *m/f* visitor

visitar (bee-see-*tahr*) *v* visit, call on

vislumbrar (beez-loom-*brahr*) *v* glimpse

vislumbre (beez-*loom*-bray) *m* glimpse

visón (bee-*soan*) *m* mink

visor (bee-*soar*) *m* viewfinder

vista (*beess*-tah) *f* sight; view; **punto de ~** point of view

vistoso (beess-*toa*-soa) *adj* colo(u)rful; showy

vital (bee-*tahl*) *adj* vital

vitamina (bee-tah-*mee*-nah) *f* vitamin

vitrina (bee-*tree*-nah) *f* showcase

viuda (b^y*oo*-dhah) *f* widow

viudo (b^y*oo*-dhoa) *m* widower

vivaz (bee-*bhahth*) *adj* lively

vivero (bee-*bhay*-roa) *m* tree nursery; hatchery

vivienda (bee-bh^y*ayn*-dah) *f* accommodation; dwelling

vivir (bee-*bheer*) *v* live; experience

vivo (*bee*-bhoa) *adj* alive, live; brisk, vivid, lively

vocabulario (boa-kah-bhoo-*lah*-r^yoa) *m* vocabulary

vocación (boa-kah-*th*ʸ*oan*) *f* vocation

vocal (boa-*kahl*) *f* vowel; *adj* vocal

vocalista (boa-kah-*leess*-tah) *m* vocalist

volante (boa-*lahn*-tay) *m* steering-wheel

***volar** (boa-*lahr*) *v* *fly

volatería (boa-lah-tay-*ree*-ah) *f* fowls

volcán (boal-*kahn*) *m* volcano

voleibol (boa-lay-*boal*) *m* volleyball

voltaje (boal-*tah*-khay) *m* voltage

voltio (*boal*-tʸoa) *m* volt

volumen (boa-*loo*-mayn) *m* volume

voluminoso (boa-loo-mee-*noa*-soa) *adj* bulky; big

voluntad (boa-loon-*tahdh*) *f* will; **buena ~** goodwill

voluntario (boa-loon-*tah*-rʸoa) *adj* voluntary; *m* volunteer

***volver** (boal-*bhayr*) *v* return, turn back; turn over, turn, turn round; **~ a casa** *go home; ***volverse** *v* turn round

vomitar (boa-mee-*tahr*) *v* vomit

vosotros (boa-*soa*-troass) *pron* you

votación (boa-tah-*th*ʸ*oan*) *f* vote

votar (boa-*tahr*) *v* vote

voto (*boa*-toa) *m* vote; vow

voz (boath) *f* voice; cry; **en ~ alta** aloud

vuelo (*bway*-loa) *m* flight; **~ charter** charter flight; **~ nocturno** night flight

vuelta (*bwayl*-tah) *f* return journey, way back; tour; turning, turn; round; reverse; **ida y ~** round trip *Am*

vuestro (*bwayss*-troa) *adj* your

vulgar (bool-*gahr*) *adj* vulgar

vulnerable (bool-nay-*rah*-bhlay) *adj* vulnerable

Y

y (ee) *conj* and

ya (ʸah) *adv* already; **~ no** no longer; **~ que** as

***yacer** (ʸah-*thayr*) *v* *lie

yacimiento (ʸah-thee-*m*ʸ*ayn*-toa) *m* deposit

yate (ʸah-tay) *m* yacht

yegua (ʸay-gwah) *f* mare

yema (ʸay-mah) *f* yolk

yerno (ʸayr-noa) *m* son-in-law

yeso (ʸay-soa) *m* plaster

yo (ʸoa) *pron* I

yodo (ʸoa-dhoa) *m* iodine

yugo (ʸoo-goa) *m* yoke

yogur (ʸoa-*goor*) *m* yog(h)urt

Z

zafiro (thah-*fee*-roa) *m* sapphire

zanahoria (thah-nah-*oa*-rʸah) *f* carrot

zanja (*thahng*-khah) *f* ditch

zapatería (thah-pah-tay-*ree*-ah) *f* shoe shop

zapatero (thah-pah-*tay*-roa) *m* shoemaker

zapatilla (thah-pah-*tee*-lʸah) *f* slipper

zapato (thah-*pah*-toa) *m* shoe;
  zapatos de gimnasia *pl* plimsolls;
  sneakers *Am*; **zapatos de tenis**
  tennis shoes
zodíaco (thoa-*dhee*-ah-koa) *m* zodiac
zona (*thoa*-nah) *f* zone; area; ~
  industrial industrial area
zoología (thoa-oa-loa-*khee*-ah) *f*

zoology
zorro (*thoa*-rroa) *m* fox
zueco (*thway*-koa) *m* wooden shoe
zumo (*thoo*-moa) *m* juice; squash
zurcir (thoor-*theer*) *v* darn
zurdo (*thoor*-dhoa) *adj* left-handed
zurra (*thoo*-rrah) *f* spanking

Menu Reader

Food

a caballo steak topped with two eggs

acedera sorrel

aceite oil

aceituna olive

achicoria endive (US chicory)

(al) adobo marinated

aguacate avocado (pear)

ahumado smoked

ajiaceite garlic mayonnaise

ajiaco bogotano chicken soup with potatoes

(al) ajillo cooked in garlic and oil

ajo garlic

al, a la in the style of, with

albahaca basil

albaricoque apricot

albóndiga spiced meat- or fishball

alcachofa artichoke

alcaparra caper

aliñado seasoned

alioli garlic mayonnaise

almeja clam, cockle

almejas a la marinera cooked in hot, pimento sauce

almendra almond

~ **garrapiñada** sugared almond

almíbar syrup

almuerzo lunch

alubia bean

anchoa anchovy

anguila eel

angula baby eel

anticucho beef heart grilled on a skewer with green peppers

apio celery

a punto medium (done)

arenque herring

~ **en escabeche** marinated, pickled herring

arepa flapjack made of maize (corn)

arroz rice

~ **blanco** boiled, steamed

~ **escarlata** with tomatoes and prawns

~ **a la española** with chicken liver, pork, tomatoes, fish stock

~ **con leche** rice pudding

~ **con pollo** chicken and rice

~**primavera** with spring vegetables

~ **a la valenciana** with vegetables, chicken, shellfish (and sometimes eel)

asado roast

~ **antiguo a la venezolana mechado** roast beef stuffed with capers

asturias a strong, fermented cheese with a sharp flavour

atún tunny (US tuna)

avellana hazelnut

azafrán saffron

azúcar sugar

bacalao cod

~ **a la vizcaína** with green peppers, potatoes, tomato sauce

barbo barbel (fish)

batata sweet potato, yam

becada woodcock

berberecho cockle

berenjena aubergine (US eggplant)

berraza parsnip

berro cress

berza cabbage

besugo sea bream

bien hecho well-done

biftec, bistec beef steak

bizcocho sponge cake, sponge finger (US ladyfinger)

~ **borracho** cake steeped in rum (or wine) and syrup

bizcotela glazed biscuit (US cookie)
blando soft
bocadillo 1) sandwich 2) sweet (Colombia)
bollito, bollo roll, bun
bonito a kind of tunny (US tuna)
boquerón 1) anchovy 2) whitebait
(en) brocheta (on a) skewer
budín blancmange, custard
buey ox
buñuelo 1) doughnut 2) fritter with ham, mussels and prawns (sometimes flavoured with brandy)
burgos a popular soft, creamy cheese named after the Spanish province of its origin
burrito Mexican tortilla wrap with cheese or meat filling
butifarra spiced sausage
caballa fish of the mackerel family
cabeza de ternera calf's head
cabra goat
cabrales blue-veined goat's-milk cheese
cabrito kid
cacahuete peanut
cachelos diced potatoes boiled with cabbage, paprika, garlic, bacon, chorizo sausage
calabacín vegetable marrow, courgette (US zucchini)
calabaza pumpkin
calamar squid
calamares a la romana squids fried in batter
caldereta de cabrito kid stew (often cooked in red wine)
caldillo de congrio conger-eel soup with tomatoes and potatoes
caldo consommé
~ **gallego** meat and vegetable broth
callos tripe (often served in pimento sauce)
~ **a la madrileña** in piquant sauce

with chorizo sausage and tomatoes
camarón shrimp
canela cinnamon
cangrejo de mar crab
cangrejo de río crayfish
cantarela chanterelle mushroom
caracol snail
carbonada criolla baked pumpkin stuffed with diced beef
carne meat
~ **asada al horno** roast meat
~ **molida** minced beef
~ **a la parrilla** charcoal-grilled steak
~ **picada** minced beef
carnero mutton
carpa carp
casero home made
castaña chestnut
castañola sea perch
(a la) catalana with onions, parsley, tomatoes and herbs
caza game
(a la) cazadora with mushrooms, spring onions, herbs in wine
cazuela de cordero lamb stew with vegetables
cebolla onion
cebolleta chive
cebrero blue-veined cheese of creamy texture with a pale, yellow rind; sharp taste
cena dinner, supper
centolla spider-crab, served cold
cerdo pork
cereza cherry
ceviche fish marinated in lemon and lime juice
cigala Dublin Bay prawn
cincho a hard cheese made from sheep's milk
ciruela plum
~ **pasa** prune
cocido 1) cooked, boiled 2) stew of beef with ham, fowl, chick peas,

potatoes and vegetables (the broth is eaten first)

cochifrito de cordero highly seasoned stew of lamb or kid

cochinillo roasted suckling pig

codorniz quail

col cabbage

~ **de Bruselas** brussels sprout

coliflor cauliflower

comida meal

compota stewed fruit

conejo rabbit

confitura jam

congrio conger eel

consomé al jerez chicken broth with sherry

copa nuria egg-yolk and egg-white, whipped and served with jam

corazón de alcachofa artichoke heart

corazonada heart stewed in sauce

cordero lamb

~ **recental** spring lamb

cortadillo small pancake with lemon

corzo deer

costilla chop

crema 1) cream or mousse

~ **batida** whipped cream

~ **española** dessert of milk, eggs, fruit jelly

~ **nieve** frothy egg-yolk, sugar, rum (or wine)

crema 2) soup

criadillas (de toro) glands (of bull)

(a la) criolla with green peppers, spices and tomatoes

croqueta croquette, fish or meat dumpling

crudo raw

cubierto cover charge

cuenta bill (US check)

curanto dish consisting of seafood, vegetables and suck(l)ing pig, all cooked in an earthen well, lined with charcoal

chabacano apricot

chalote shallot

champiñón mushroom

chancho adobado pork braised with sweet potatoes, orange and lemon juice

chanfaina goat's liver and kidney stew, served in a thick sauce

chanquete whitebait

chile chili pepper

chiles en nogada green peppers stuffed with whipped cream and nut sauce

chimichurri hot parsley sauce

chipirón small squid

chopa a kind of sea bream

chorizo pork sausage, highly seasoned with garlic and paprika

chuleta cutlet

chupe de mariscos scallops served with a creamy sauce and gratinéed with cheese

churro sugared tubular fritter

damasco variety of apricot

dátil date

desayuno breakfast

dorada gilt-head

dulce sweet

~ **de naranja** marmalade

durazno peach

embuchado stuffed with meat

embutido spicy sausage

empanada pie or tart with meat or fish filling

~ **de horno** dough filled with minced meat, similar to ravioli

empanadilla small patty stuffed with seasoned meat or fish

empanado breaded

emperador swordfish

encurtido pickle

enchilada a maizeflour (US cornmeal) pancake (tortilla) stuffed and usually served with vegetable garnish and sauce

~ roja sausage-filled maizeflour pancake dipped into a red sweet-pepper sauce

~ verde maizeflour pancake stuffed with meat or fowl and braised in a green-tomato sauce

endibia chicory (US endive)

eneldo dill

ensalada salad

~ común green

~ de frutas fruit salad

~ (a la) primavera spring

~ valenciana with green peppers, lettuce and oranges

ensaladilla rusa diced cold vegetables with mayonnaise

entremés appetizer, hors-d'oeuvre

erizo de mar sea urchin

(en) escabeche marinated, pickled

~ de gallina chicken marinated in vinegar

escarcho red gurnard (fish)

escarola endive (US chicory)

espalda shoulder

(a la) española with tomatoes

espárrago asparagus

especia spice

especialidad de la casa chef's speciality

espinaca spinach

esqueixada mixed fish salad

(al) estilo de in the style of

estofado stew(ed)

estragón tarragon

fabada (asturiana) stew of pork, beans, bacon and sausage

faisán pheasant

fajitas spiced pork slices served with condiments, guacamole and tortillas

fiambres cold meat (US cold cuts)

fideo thin noodle

filete steak

~ de lomo fillet steak (US tenderloin)

~ de res beef steak

~ de lenguado empanado breaded fillet of sole

(a la) flamenca with onions, peas, green peppers, tomatoes and spiced sausage

flan caramel mould, custard

frambuesa raspberry

(a la) francesa sautéed in butter

fresa strawberry

~ de bosque wild

fresco fresh, chilled

fresón large strawberry

fricandó veal bird, thin slice of meat rolled in bacon and braised

frijol bean

frijoles refritos fried mashed beans

frío cold

frito 1) fried 2) fry

~ de patata deep-fried potato croquette

fritura fry

~ mixta meat, fish or vegetables deep-fried in batter

fruta fruit

~ escarchada crystallized (US candied) fruit

galleta salted or sweet biscuit (US cracker or cookie)

~ de nata cream biscuit (US sandwich cookie)

gallina hen

~ de Guinea guinea fowl

gallo cockerel

gamba shrimp

~ grande prawn

gambas shrimp

~ al ajillo shrimp in garlic sauce

~ con mayonesa shrimp cocktail

ganso goose

garbanzo chick pea

gazpacho seasoned broth made of

raw onions, garlic, tomatoes, cucumber and green pepper; served chilled

(a la) gitanilla with garlic

gordo fatty, rich (of food)

granada pomegranate

grande large

(al) gratín gratinéed

gratinado gratinéed

grelo turnip greens

grosella currant

~ espinosa gooseberry

~ negra blackcurrant

~ roja redcurrant

guacamole a purée of avocado and spices used as a dip, in a salad, for a tortilla filling or as a garnish

guarnición garnish, trimming

guayaba guava (fruit)

guinda sour cherry

guindilla chili pepper

guisado stew(ed)

guisante green pea

haba broad bean

habichuela verde French bean (US green bean)

hamburguesa hamburger

hayaca central maizeflour (US cornmeal) pancake, usually with a minced-meat filling

helado ice-cream, ice

hervido 1) boiled 2) stew of beef and vegetables (Latin America)

hielo ice

hierba herb

hierbas finas finely chopped mixture of herbs

hígado liver

higo fig

hinojo fennel

hongo mushroom

(al) horno baked

hortaliza greens

hueso bone

huevo egg

~ cocido boiled

~ duro hard-boiled

~ escalfado poached

~ a la española stuffed with tomatoes and served with cheese sauce

~ a la flamenca baked with asparagus, peas, peppers, onions, tomatoes and sausage

~ frito fried

~ al nido egg-yolk placed into small, soft roll, fried, then covered with egg-white

~ pasado por agua soft-boiled

~ revuelto scrambled

~ con tocino bacon and egg

humita boiled maize (US corn) with tomatoes, green peppers, onions and cheese

(a la) inglesa 1) underdone (of meat) 2) boiled 3) served with boiled vegetables

jabalí wild boar

jalea jelly

jamón ham

~ cocido boiled (often referred to as jamón de York)

~ en dulce boiled and served cold

~ gallego smoked and cut thinly

~ serrano cured and cut thinly

(a la) jardinera with carrots, peas and other vegetables

jengibre ginger

(al) jerez braised in sherry

judía bean

~ verde French bean (US green bean)

jugo gravy, meat juice

en su ~ in its own juice

juliana with shredded vegetables

jurel variety of mackerel

lacón shoulder of pork

~ curado salted pork

lamprea lamprey
langosta spiny lobster
langostino Norway lobster, Dublin Bay prawn
laurel bay leaf
leche frita sweet fried custard squares
lechón suck(l)ing pig
lechuga lettuce
legumbre vegetable
lengua tongue
lenguado sole, flounder
~ **frito** fried fillet of sole on bed of vegetables
lenteja lentil
liebre hare
~ **estofada** jugged hare
lima 1) lime 2) sweet lime (Latin America)
limón lemon
lista de platos menu
lista de vinos wine list
lobarro a variety of bass
lombarda red cabbage
lomo loin
longaniza long, highly seasoned sausage
lonja slice of meat
lubina bass
macarrones macaroni
(a la) madrileña with chorizo sausage, tomatoes and paprika
magras al estilo de Aragón cured ham in tomato sauce
maíz maize (US corn)
(a la) mallorquina usually refers to highly seasoned fish and shellfish
manchego hard cheese from La Mancha, made from sheep's milk, white or golden-yellow in colour
maní peanut
mantecado 1) small butter cake 2) custard ice-cream
mantequilla butter
manzana apple

~ **en dulce** in honey
(a la) marinera usually with mussels, onions, tomatoes, herbs and wine
marisco seafood
matambre rolled beef stuffed with vegetables
mayonesa mayonnaise
mazapán marzipan, almond paste
mejillón mussel
mejorana marjoram
melaza treacle, molasses
melocotón peach
membrillo quince
menestra boiled green vegetable soup
~ **de pollo** chicken and vegetable soup
menta mint
menú menu
~ **del día** set menu
~ **turístico** tourist menu
menudillos giblets
merengue meringue
merienda snack
merluza hake
mermelada jam
mezclado mixed
miel honey
(a la) milanesa with cheese, generally baked
minuta menu
mixto mixed
mole poblano chicken served with a sauce of chili peppers, spices and chocolate
molusco mollusc (snail, mussel, clam)
molleja sweetbread
mora mulberry
morcilla black pudding (US blood sausage)
morilla morel mushroom
moros y cristianos rice and black beans with diced ham, garlic, green peppers and herbs
mostaza mustard

mújol mullet
nabo turnip
naranja orange
nata cream
  ~ batida whipped cream
natillas custard
  ~ al limón lemon cream
níspola medlar (fruit)
nopalito young cactus leaf served with salad dressing
nuez nut
  ~ moscada nutmeg
olla stew
  ~ gitana vegetable stew
  ~ podrida stew made of vegetables, meat, fowl and ham
ostra oyster
oveja ewe
pabellón criollo beef in tomato sauce garnished with beans, rice and bananas
paella consists basically of saffron rice with assorted seafood and sometimes meat
  ~ alicantina with green peppers, onions, tomatoes, artichokes and fish
  ~ catalana with sausages, pork, squid, tomatoes, red sweet peppers and peas
  ~ marinera with fish, shellfish and meat
  ~ (a la) valenciana with chicken, shrimps, peas, tomatoes, mussels and garlic
palmito palm heart
palta avocado (pear)
pan bread
panecillo roll
papa potato
papas a la huancaína with cheese and green peppers
(a la) parrilla grilled
parrillada mixta mixed grill
pasado done, cooked

bien ~ well-done
poco ~ underdone (US rare)
pastas noodles, macaroni, spaghetti
pastel cake, pie
  ~ de choclo maize with minced beef, chicken, raisins and olives
pastelillo small tart
pata trotter (US foot)
patatas potatoes
  ~ bravas in a spicy tomato sauce
  ~ fritas fried; usually chips (US french fries)
  ~ (a la) leonesa with onions
  ~ nuevas new
pato duck, duckling
pavo turkey
pechuga breast (of fowl)
pepinillo gherkin (US pickle)
pepino cucumber
(en) pepitoria stewed with onions, green peppers and tomatoes
pera pear
perca perch
percebe barnacle (shellfish)
perdiz partridge
  ~ en escabeche cooked in oil with vinegar, onions, parsley, carrots and green pepper; served cold
  ~ estofada stewed and served with a white-wine sauce
perejil parsley
perifollo chervil
perilla a firm, bland cheese
pescadilla whiting
pescado fish
pez espada swordfish
picadillo minced meat, hash
picado minced
picante sharp, spicy, highly seasoned
picatoste deep-fried slice of bread
pichoncillo young pigeon (US squab)
pierna leg
pimentón chili pepper
pimienta pepper

pimiento sweet pepper

~ **morrón** red (sweet) pepper

pincho moruno grilled meat (often kidneys) on a skewer, sometimes served with spicy sauces

pintada guinea fowl

piña pineapple

pisto diced and sautéed vegetables: mainly aubergines, green peppers and tomatoes; served cold

(a la) plancha grilled on a girdle

plátano banana

plato plate, dish, portion

~ **típico de la región** regional speciality

pollito spring chicken

pollo chicken

~ **pibil** simmered in fruit juice and spices

polvorón hazelnut biscuit (US cookie)

pomelo grapefruit

porción portion

porotos granados shelled beans served with pumpkin and maize (US corn)

postre dessert, sweet

potaje vegetable soup

puchero stew

puerro leek

pulpo octopus

punta de espárrago asparagus tip

punto de nieve dessert of whipped cream with beaten egg-whites

puré de patatas mashed potatoes

queso cheese

quisquilla shrimp

rábano radish

~ **picante** horse-radish

raja slice or portion

rallado grated

rape angler fish

ravioles ravioli

raya skate, ray

rebanada slice

rebozado breaded or fried in batter

recargo extra charge

rehogada sautéed

relleno stuffed

remolacha beetroot

repollo cabbage

requesón a fresh-curd cheese

riñón kidney

róbalo haddock

rodaballo turbot, flounder

(a la) romana dipped in batter and fried

romero rosemary

roncal cheese made from sheep's milk; close grained and hard in texture with a few small holes; piquant flavour

ropa vieja cooked, left-over meat and vegetables, covered with tomatoes and green peppers

rosbif roast beef

rosquilla doughnut

rubio red mullet

ruibarbo rhubarb

sal salt

salado salted, salty

salchicha small pork sausage for frying

salchichón salami

salmón salmon

salmonete red mullet

salsa sauce

~ **blanca** white

~ **española** brown sauce with herbs, spices and wine

~ **mayordoma** butter and parsley

~ **picante** hot pepper

~ **romana** bacon or ham, egg, cream (sometimes flavoured with nutmeg)

~ **tártara** tartar

~ **verde** parsley

salsifí salsify

salteado sauté(ed)

salvia sage

san simón a firm, bland cheese resembling perilla; shiny yellow rind

sandía watermelon

sardina sardine, pilchard

sémola semolina

sencillo plain

sepia cuttlefish

servicio service

~ **(no) incluido** (not) included

sesos brains

seta mushroom

sobrasada pork sausage from Mallorca

solomillo fillet steak (US tenderloin)

sopa soup

~ **(de) cola de buey** oxtail

~ **sevillana** a highly spiced fish soup

suave soft

suflé soufflé

suizo bun

surtido assorted

taco wheat or maizeflour (US cornmeal) shell usually with a meat filling and garnished with chile sauce

tajada slice

tallarín noodle

tamal a pastry dough of coarsely ground maizeflour with meat or fruit filling, steamed in maizehusks (US corn husks)

tapa appetizer, snack

tarta cake, tart

~ **helada** ice-cream tart

ternera veal

tocino bacon

~ **de cielo** 1) caramel mould 2) custard-filled cake

tomate tomato

tomillo thyme

tordo thrush

toronja variety of grapefruit

torrijas bread dipped in a milk-egg mixture and fried

tortilla 1) potato omelet 2) a type of pancake made with maizeflour (US cornmeal)

~ **de chorizo** with pieces of a spicy sausage

~ **a la española** with onions, potatoes and seasoning

~ **a la francesa** plain

~ **gallega** potatoes with ham, red sweet peppers and peas

~ **a la jardinera** with mixed, diced vegetables

~ **al ron** rum

tortita waffle

tortuga turtle

tostada toast

tripas tripe

trucha trout

~ **frita a la asturiana** floured and fried in butter, garnished with lemon

trufa truffle

turrón nougat

ulloa a soft cheese from Galicia, rather like a mature camembert

uva grape

~ **pasa** raisin

vaca salada corned beef

vainilla vanilla

(a la) valenciana with rice, tomatoes and garlic

variado varied, assorted

varios sundries

venado venison

venera scallop, coquille St. Jacques

verdura greens

vieira scallop

villalón a cheese from sheep's milk

vinagre vinegar

vinagreta a piquant vinegar dressing (vinaigrette) to accompany salads

(a la) ~ marinated in oil and vinegar or lemon juice with mixed herbs

(a la) vizcaína with green peppers, tomatoes, garlic and paprika

yema egg-yolk
yemas a dessert of whipped egg-yolks and sugar
zanahoria carrot
zarzamora blackberry
zarzuela savoury stew of assorted fish and shellfish
~ de mariscos seafood stew
~ de pescado selection of fish served with a highly seasoned sauce
~ de verduras vegetable stew

Drinks

abocado sherry made from a blend of sweet and dry wines
agua water
aguardiente spirits
Alicante this region to the south of Valencia produces a large quantity of red table wine and some good rosé, particularly from Yecla
Amontillado medium-dry sherry, light amber in colour, with a nutty flavour
Andalucía a drink of dry sherry and orange juice
Angélica a Basque herb liqueur similar to yellow Chartreuse
anís aniseed liqueur
Anís del Mono a Calatonian aniseed liqueur
anís seco aniseed brandy
anisado an aniseed-based soft drink which may be slightly alcoholic
batido milk shake
bebida drink
Bobadilla Gran Reserva a wine-distilled brandy
botella bottle
media ~ half bottle
café coffee
~ cortado small cup of espresso coffee with a dash of milk or cream
~ descafeinado coffeine-free
~ exprés espresso
~ granizado iced (white)

~ con leche white (US with milk)
~ negro/solo black
Calisay a quinine-flavoured liqueur
Carlos I a wine-distilled brandy
Cataluña Catalonia; this region southwest of Barcelona is known for its xampañ, bearing little resemblance to the famed French sparkling wine
Cazalla an aniseed liqueur
cerveza beer
~ de barril draught (US draft)
~ dorada light
~ negra dark
cola de mono a blend of coffee, milk, rum and pisco
coñac 1) French Cognac 2) term applied to any Spanish wine-distilled brandy
Cordoníu a brand-name of Catalonian sparkling wine locally referred to as xampañ (champagne)
cosecha harvest; indicates the vintage of wine
crema de cacao cocoa liqueur, crème de cacao
Cuarenta y Tres an egg liqueur
Cuba libre rum and Coke
champán, champaña 1) French Champagne 2) term applied to any Spanish sparkling wine
chicha de manzana apple brandy

Chinchón an aniseed liqueur

chocolate chocolate drink

~ **con leche** hot chocolate with milk

Dulce dessert wine

Fino dry sherry wine, very pale and straw-coloured

Fundador a wine-distilled brandy

Galicia this Atlantic coastal region has good table wines

gaseosa fizzy (US carbonated) water

ginebra gin

gran vino term found on Chilean wine labels to indicate a wine of exceptional quality

granadina pomegranate syrup mixed with wine or brandy

horchata de almendra (or **de chufa**) drink made from ground almonds (or Jerusalem artichoke)

Jerez 1) sherry 2) the Spanish region near the Portuguese border, internationally renowned for its Jerez

jugo fruit juice

leche milk

limonada lemonade, lemon squash

Málaga 1) dessert wine 2) the region in the south of Spain, is particularly noted for its dessert wine

Manzanilla dry sherry, very pale and straw-coloured

margarita tequila with lime juice

Montilla a dessert wine from near Cordoba, often drunk as an aperitif

Moscatel fruity dessert wine

naranjada orangeade

Oloroso sweet, dark sherry, drunk as dessert wine, resembles brown cream sherry

Oporto port (wine)

pisco grape brandy

ponche crema eggnog liquor

Priorato the region south of Barcelona produces good quality red

and white wine but also a dessert wine, usually called Priorato but renamed Tarragona when it is exported

refresco a soft drink

reservado term found on Chilean wine labels to indicate a wine of exceptional quality

Rioja the northern region near the French border is considered to produce Spain's best wines- especially red; some of the finest Rioja wines resemble good Bordeaux wines

ron rum

sangría a mixture of red wine, ice, orange, lemon, brandy and sugar

sangrita tequila with tomato, orange and lime juices

sidra cider

sol y sombra a blend of wine-distilled brandy and aniseed liqueur

sorbete (iced) fruit drink

té tea

tequila brandy made from agave (US aloe)

tinto 1) red wine 2) black coffee with sugar (Colombia)

Tío Pepe a brand-name sherry

Triple Seco an orange liqueur

Valdepeñas the region south of Madrid is an important wine- producing area

vermú vermouth

Veterano Osborne a wine-distilled brandy

vino wine

~ **blanco** white

~ **clarete** rosé

~ **común** table wine

~ **dulce** dessert

~ **espumoso** sparkling

~ **de mesa** table wine

~ **del país** local wine

~ **rosado** rosé
~ **seco** dry
~ **suave** sweet
~ **tinto** red

xampañ Catalonian sparkling wine
Yerba mate South American holly tea
zumo juice

Mini-Grammar

Articles

Nouns in Spanish are either masculine or feminine. Articles agree in gender and number with the noun.

1. Definite article (the):

	singular		plural
	el tren	the train	**los trenes**
masc.			
fem.	**la casa**	the house	**las casas**

2. Indefinite article (a/an):

masc.	**un lápiz**	a pencil	**unos lápices**
fem.	**una carta**	a letter	**unas cartas**

Nouns

1. Most nouns which end in **o** are masculine. Those ending in **a** are generally feminine.
2. Normally, nouns which end in a vowel add **s** to form the plural; nouns ending in a consonant add **es.**
3. To show possession, use the preposition **de** (of).

el fin de la fiesta	the end of the party
el principio del* mes	the beginning of the month
las maletas de los viajeros	the travellers' suitcases
los ojos de las niñas	the girls' eyes
la habitación de Roberto	Robert's room

Adjectives

1. Adjectives agree with the noun in gender and number. If the masculine form ends in **o** the feminine ends in **a.** As a rule, the adjective comes after the noun.

el niño pequeño	the small boy
la niña pequeña	the small girl

If the masculine form ends in **e** or with a consonant, the feminine keeps in general the same form.

el muro/la casa grande	the big wall/house
el mar/la flor azul	the blue sea/flower

2. Most adjectives form their plurals in the same way as nouns.

---

* (**del** is the contraction of **de** + **el**)

un coche inglés	an English car
dos coches ingleses	two English cars

3. Possessive adjectives: They agree with the thing possessed, not with the possessor.

	sing.	plur.
my	**mi**	**mis**
your (fam.)	**tu**	**tus**
your (polite form)	**su**	**sus**
his/her/its	**su**	**sus**
our	**nuestro(a)**	**nuestros(as)**
your	**vuestro(a)**	**vuestros(as)**
their	**su**	**sus**

su hijo	*his* or *her* son
su habitación	*his* or *her* or *their* room
sus maletas	*his* or *her* or *their* suitcases

4. Comparative and superlative: These are formed by adding **más** (more) or **menos** (less) and **lo más** or **lo menos**, respectively, before the adjective.

alto	high	**más alto**	lo más alto

Adverbs

These are generally formed by adding **-mente** to the feminine form of the adjective (if it differs from the masculine); otherwise to the masculine.

cierto(a)	sure	**fácil**	easy
ciertamente	surely	**fácilmente**	easily

Possessive pronouns

	sing.	plur.
mine	**mío(a)**	**míos(as)**
yours (fam. sing.)	**tuyo(a)**	**tuyos(as)**
yours (polite form)	**suyo(a)**	**suyos(as)**
his/hers/its	**suyo(a)**	**suyos(as)**
ours	**nuestro(a)**	**nuestros(as)**
yours (fam. pl.)	**vuestro(a)**	**vuestros(as)**
theirs	**suyo(a)**	**suyos(as)**

Demonstrative pronouns

	masc.	fem.	neut.
this	**éste**	**ésta**	**esto**
these	**éstos**	**éstas**	**estos**
that	**ése/aquél**	**ésa/aquélla**	**eso/aquello**
those	**ésos/aquéllos**	**ésas/aquéllas**	**esos/aquellos**

The above masculine and feminine forms are also used as demonstrative adjectives, but accents are dropped. The two forms for "that" designate difference in place; **ése** means "that one", **aquél** "that one over there".

Esos libros no me gustan.	I don't like those books.
Eso no me gusta.	I don't like that.

Personal pronouns

	subject	direct object	indirect object
I	**yo**	**me**	**me**
you	**tú**	**te**	**te**
you	**usted**	**lo**	**le**
he	**él**	**lo**	**le**
she	**ella**	**la**	**le**
it	**él/ella**	**lo/la**	**le**
we	**nosotros(as)**	**nos**	**nos**
you	**vosotros(as)**	**os**	**os**
	ustedes	**los**	**les**
they	**ellos(as)**	**los**	**les**

Subject pronouns are generally omitted, except in the polite form (**usted, ustedes**) which corresponds to "you". **Tú** (sing.) and **vosotros** (plur.) are used when talking to relatives, close friends and children and between young people; **usted** and the plural **ustedes** (often abbreviated to **Vd./Vds.**) are used in all other cases.

Negatives

Negatives are formed by placing **no** before the verb.

Es nuevo.	It's new.	**No es nuevo.**	It's not new.

Questions

In Spanish, questions are often formed by changing the intonation of your voice. Very often, the personal pronoun is left out, both in affirmative sentences and in questions.

Hablo español.   I speak Spanish.
¿Habla español?   Do you speak Spanish?

Note the double question mark used in Spanish.
The same is true of exclamation marks.

¡Qué tarde se hace!   How late it's getting!

Verbs

Below are some examples of Spanish verbs in the three regular conjugations, grouped by families according to their infinitive endings, *-ar*, *-er* and *-ir*. Verbs which do not follow the conjugations below are considered irregular (see irregular verb list). Note that there are some verbs which follow the regular conjugation of the category they belong to, but present some minor changes in spelling. Examples: *tocar, toque; cargar, cargue.* The personal pronoun is not generally expressed, since the verb endings clearly indicate the person.

		1st conj.	2nd conj.	3rd conj.
		am ar	**tem er**	**viv ir**
Infinitive		(*to love*)	(*to fear*)	(*to live*)
Present	(yo)	am **o**	tem **o**	viv **o**
	(tú)	am **as**	tem **es**	viv **es**
	(él)	am **a**	tem **e**	viv **e**
	(nosotros)	am **amos**	tem **emos**	viv **imos**
	(vosotros)	am **áis**	tem **éis**	viv **ís**
	(ellos)	am **an**	tem **en**	viv **en**
Imperfect	(yo)	am **aba**	tem **ía**	viv **ía**
	(tú)	am **abas**	tem **ías**	viv **ías**
	(él)	am **aba**	tem **ía**	viv **ía**
	(nosotros)	am **ábamos**	tem **íamos**	viv **íamos**
	(vosotros)	am **abais**	tem **íais**	viv **íais**
	(ellos)	am **aban**	tem **ían**	viv **ían**
Past. def.	(yo)	am **é**	tem **í**	viv **í**
	(tú)	am **aste**	tem **iste**	viv **iste**
	(él)	am **ó**	tem **ió**	viv **ió**
	(nosotros)	am **amos**	tem **imos**	viv **imos**
	(vosotros)	am **asteis**	tem **isteis**	viv **isteis**
	(ellos)	am **aron**	tem **ieron**	viv **ieron**
Future	(yo)	am **aré**	tem **eré**	viv **iré**
	(tú)	am **arás**	tem **erás**	viv **irás**
	(él)	am **ará**	tem **erá**	viv **irá**
	(nosotros)	am **aremos**	tem **eremos**	viv **iremos**
	(vosotros)	am **aréis**	tem **eréis**	viv **iréis**
	(ellos)	am **arán**	tem **erán**	viv **irán**
Conditional	(yo)	am **aría**	tem **ería**	viv **iría**
	(tú)	am **arías**	tem **erías**	viv **irías**
	(él)	am **aría**	tem **ería**	viv **iría**
	(nosotros)	am **aríamos**	tem **eríamos**	viv **iríamos**
	(vosotros)	am **aríais**	tem **eríais**	viv **iríais**
	(ellos)	am **arían**	tem **erían**	viv **irían**

Subj. Pres.	(yo)	am **e**	tem **a**	viv **a**
	(tú)	am **es**	tem **as**	viv **as**
	(él)	am **e**	tem **a**	viv **a**
	(nosotros)	am **emos**	tem **amos**	viv **amos**
	(vosotros)	am **éis**	tem **áis**	viv **áis**
	(ellos)	am **en**	tem **an**	viv **an**
Pres. Part./Gerund		am **ando**	tem **iendo**	viv **iendo**
Past. Part.		am **ado**	tem **ido**	viv **ido**

Auxiliary verbs

The verb **to have** is translated either by *haber* or by *tener*. *Haber* is the auxiliary (e.g. he has gone) and *tener* (see list of irregular verbs) is a transitive verb, which conveys the idea of possession (e.g. she has a house).

The verb **to be** is translated either by *ser* or *estar*. *Ser* is used as an auxiliary verb to form the passive (e.g. they are understood) and to express an intrinsic quality of a fundamental characteristic (e.g. man is mortal). *Estar* (see list of irregular verbs) expresses a state or an attitude, whether lasting or not, of a thing or a person (e.g. she is hungry).

	haber (*to have*)		**ser** (*to be*)	
	Present	*Imperfect*	*Present*	*Imperfect*
(yo)	he	había	soy	era
(tú)	has	habías	eres	eras
(él)	ha	había	es	era
(nosotros)	hemos	habíamos	somos	éramos
(vosotros)	habéis	habíais	sois	erais
(ellos)	han	habían	son	eran
	Future	*Conditional*	*Future*	*Conditional*
(yo)	habré	habría	seré	sería
(tú)	habrás	habrías	serás	serías
(él)	habrá	habría	será	sería
(nosotros)	habremos	habríamos	seremos	seríamos
(vosotros)	habréis	habríais	seréis	seríais
(ellos)	habrán	habrían	serán	serían
	Present subjunctive	*Present perfect*	*Present subjunctive*	*Present perfect*
(yo)	haya	he habido	sea	he sido
(tú)	hayas	has habido	seas	has sido
(él)	haya	ha habido	sea	ha sido
(nosotros)	hayamos	hemos habido	seamos	hemos sido
(vosotros)	hayáis	habéis habido	seáis	habéis sido
(ellos)	hayan	han habido	sean	han sido

	Present participle habiendo	Past participle habido	Present participle siendo	Past participle sido

Irregular verbs

Below is a list of the verbs and tenses commonly used in spoken Spanish. In the listing, a) stands for the present tense, b) for the imperfect, c) for the past def., d) for the future, e) for the present participle and f) for the past participle. The only forms given below are the irregular ones commonly used. There can be other irregular forms, but they are considered rare. In tenses other than present, all persons can be regularly formed from the first person. Unless otherwise indicated, verbs with prefixes (*ad-*, *ante-*, *com-*, *con-*, *de-*, *des-*, *dis-*, *en-*, *ex-*, *im-*, *pos-*, *pre-*, *pro-*, *re-*, *sobre-*, *sub-*, *tras-*, etc.) are conjugated like the stem verb.

abstenerse *refrain*	→tener
acertar *guess*	→cerrar
acontecer *happen*	→agradecer
acordar *agree; decide*	→contar
acostarse *lie down*	→contar
acrecentar *increase;* *advance*	→cerrar
adormecer *put to sleep*	→agradecer
adquirir *acquire*	a) adquiero, adquieres, adquiere, adquirimos, adquirís, adquieren; b) adquiría; c) adquirí; d) adquiriré; e) adquiriendo; f) adquirido
advertir *notice*	→sentir
agradecer *thank*	a) agradezco, agradeces, agradece, agradecemos, agradecéis, agradecen; b) agradecía; c) agradecí; d) agradeceré; e) agradeciendo; f) agradecido
alentar *encourage*	→cerrar
almorzar *have lunch*	→contar
amanecer *dawn*	→agradecer

andar	a) ando, andas, anda, andamos, andáis, andan; b) andaba; c)
walk	anduve; d) andaré; e) andando; f) andado
anochecer	→agradecer
begin to get dark	
apetecer	→agradecer
want	
apostar	→contar
bet	
apretar	→cerrar
tighten, squeeze	
arrendar	→cerrar
let, lease, rent	
arrepentirse	→sentir
repent, regret	
ascender	→perder
climb, reach	
atenerse	→tener
obey; rely on	
atravesar	→cerrar
cross, pierce	
atribuir	→instruir
attribute	
aventar	→cerrar
fan, air	
avergonzar	→contar
put to shame,	
embarrass	
bendecir	→decir
bless	
caber	a) quepo, cabes, cabe, cabemos, cabéis, caben; b) cabía; c)
contain; fit	cupe; d) cabré; e) cabiendo; f) cabido
caer	a) caigo, caes, cae, caemos, caéis, caen; b) caía; c) caí; d) caeré;
fall	e) cayendo; f) caído
calentar	→cerrar
heat	
carecer	→agradecer
lack	
cegar	→cerrar
blind	
cerrar	a) cierro, cierras, cierra, cerramos, cerráis, cierran; b) cerraba;
close	c) cerré; d) cerraré; e) cerrando; f) cerrado
cocer	a) cuezo, cueces, cuece, cocemos, cocéis, cuecen; b) cocía; c)
boil	cocí; d) coceré; e) cociendo; f) cocido

colar	→contar
strain; filter	
colgar	→contar
hang	
comenzar	→cerrar
begin	
competir	→pedir
compete	
concebir	→pedir
conceive	
concernir	→sentir
concern	
concluir	→instruir
conclude, finish	
concordar	→contar
agree, reconcile	
conducir	→traducir
drive	
conferir	→sentir
confer	
confesar	→cerrar
confess	
conocer	a) conozco, conoces, conoce, conocemos, conocéis, conocen;
know	b) conocía; c) conocí; d) conoceré; e) conociendo; f) conocido
consolar	→contar
console, comfort	
constituir	→instruir
constitute, be	
construir	→instruir
build, erect	
contar	a) cuento, cuentas, cuenta, contamos, contáis, cuentan; b)
count,	contaba; c) conté; d) contaré; e) contando; f) contado
bear in mind	
contribuir	→instruir
contribute	
convertir	→sentir
convert	
corregir	→pedir
correct	
costar	→contar
cost	
crecer	→agradecer
grow, rise	

dar a) doy, das, da, damos, dais, dan; b) daba; c) di; d) daré; e)
give dando; f) dado

decir a) digo, dices, dice, decimos, decís, dicen; b) decía; c) dije; d)
say diré e) diciendo; f) dicho

deducir →traducir
deduce

defender →perder
defend

derretir →pedir
melt

descender →perder
descend, *let*
down

descollar →contar
be outstanding

desconcertar →cerrar
damage; upset

despertar →cerrar
awaken, revive

desterrar →cerrar
banish

destituir →instruir
deprive, dismiss

destruir →instruir
destroy

desvanecer →agradecer
make disappear,
take out

diferir →sentir
defer

digerir →sentir
digest

diluir →instruir
dilute

discernir →sentir
discern

disminuir →instruir
diminish

disolver →morder
dissolve

distribuir →instruir
distribute

divertir
  entertain,
  distract
	→sentir

doler *hurt*	→morder
dormir *sleep*	a) duermo, duermes, duerme, dormimos, dormís duermen; b) dormía; c) dormí; d) dormiré; e) durmiendo; f) dormido
elegir *elect, choose*	→pedir
embestir *assault*	→pedir
empezar *begin, start*	→cerrar
enaltecer *exalt, praise*	→agradecer
enardecer *excite; inflame*	→agradecer
encender *light, ignite*	→perder
encomendar *entrust*	→cerrar
encontrar *find*	→contar

engrandecer
  enlarge,
  exaggerate
	→agradecer

enloquecer *madden*	→agradecer
enmendar *emend, correct*	→cerrar
enmudecer *silence*	→agradecer
enorgullecer *fill with pride*	→agradecer
enriquecer *enrich*	→agradecer
ensangrentar *stain with blood*	→cerrar
ensoberbecer *make proud*	→agradecer
ensordecer *deafen*	→agradecer
enternecer *soften; affect*	→agradecer

enterrar	→cerrar
bury	
entristecer	→agradecer
sadden	
envejecer	→agradecer
age	
errar	→cerrar
miss; wander	
escarmentar	→cerrar
chastise, punish	
escarnecer	→agradecer
scoff	
establecer	→agradecer
establish	
estar	a) estoy, estás, está, estamos, estáis, están; b) estaba; c) estuve;
be	d) estaré; e) estando; f) estado
estremecer	→agradecer
shake	
excluir	→instruir
exclude	
fallecer	→agradecer
die	
favorecer	→agradecer
favour	
florecer	→agradecer
blossom	
fluir	→instruir
flow	
fortalecer	→agradecer
strengthen	
forzar	→contar
compel, force	
fregar	→cerrar
wash up; scrub	
freír	→reír
fry	
gemir	→pedir
groan	
gobernar	→cerrar
govern	
gruñir	a) gruño, gruñes, gruñe, gruñimos, gruñís, gruñen; b) gruñía;
grunt	c) gruñí; d) gruñiré; e) gruñiendo; f) gruñido
haber	a) he, has, ha, hemos, habéis, han; b) había; c) hube; d) habré;
have	e) habiendo; f) habido

hacer	a) hago, haces, hace, hacemos, hacéis, hacen; b) hacía; c) hice;
make	d) haré; e) haciendo; f) hecho
heder	→perder
stink	
helar	→cerrar
freeze	
hender	→perder
crack	
herir	→sentir
injure	
hervir	→sentir
boil	
huir	→instruir
escape	
humedecer	→agradecer
humidify	
incluir	→instruir
include	
inducir	→traducir
induce	
ingerir	→sentir
swallow;	
consume	
instituir	→instruir
institute	
instruir	a) instruyo, instruyes, instruye, instruimos, instruís, instruyen;
instruct	b) instruía; c) instruí; d) instruiré; e) instruyendo; f) instruido
introducir	→traducir
introduce	
invertir	→sentir
invest	
ir	a) voy, vas, va, vamos, vais, van; b) iba; c) fui; d) iré; e) yendo; f)
go	ido
jugar	a) juego, juegas, juega, jugamos, jugáis, juegan; b) jugaba; c)
play	jugué; d) jugaré; e) jugando; f) jugado
lucir	a) luzco, luces, luce, lucimos, lucís, lucen; b) lucía; c) lucí; d)
shine	luciré; e) luciendo; f) lucido
llover	a) llueve; b) llovía; c) llovió; d) lloverá; e) lloviendo; f) llovido
rain	
manifestar	→cerrar
manifest	
mantener	→tener
maintain	

medir	→pedir
measure	
mentir	→sentir
tell a lie	
merecer	→agradecer
deserve	
merendar	→cerrar
have tea, snack	
moler	→morder
grind	
morder	a) muerdo, muerdes, muerde, mordemos, mordéis, muerden;
bite	b) mordía; c) mordí; d) morderé; e) mordiendo; f) mordido
morir	→dormir
die	
mostrar	→contar
show	
mover	→morder
move	
nacer	a) nazco, naces, nace, nacemos, nacéis, nacen; b) nacía; c) nací;
be born	d) naceré; e) naciendo; f) nacido
negar	→cerrar
deny	
nevar	a) nieva; b) nevaba; c) nevó; d) nevará; e) nevando; f) nevado
snow	
obedecer	→agradecer
obey	
obscurecer	→agradecer
darken	
obstruir	→instruir
obstruct	
obtener	→tener
obtain	
ofrecer	→agradecer
offer	
oír	a) oigo, oyes, oye, oímos, oís, oyen; b) oía; c) oí; d) oiré; e)
hear, listen	oyendo; f) oído
oler	→morder
smell	
pacer	→nacer
graze	
padecer	→agradecer
suffer	
parecer	→agradecer
seem	

pedir	a) pido, pides, pide, pedimos, pedís, piden; b) pedía; c) pedí; d)
ask for, request	pediré; e) pidiendo; f) pedido
pensar	→cerrar
think	
perder	a) pierdo, pierdes, pierde, perdemos, perdéis, pierden; b)
lose	perdía; c) perdí; d) perderé; e) perdiendo; f) perdido
perecer	→agradecer
perish	
permanecer	→agradecer
stay	
pertenecer	→agradecer
belong to	
pervertir	→sentir
pervert	
placer	a) plazco, places, place, placemos, placéis, placen; b) placía; c)
please	plací; d) placeré; e) placiendo; f) placido
plegar	→cerrar
fold	
poblar	→contar
populate	
poder	a) puedo, puedes, puede, podemos, podéis, pueden; b) podía;
can, be able	c) pude; d) podré; e) pudiendo; f) podido
poner	a) pongo, pones, pone, ponemos, ponéis, ponen; b) ponía; c)
put	puse; d) pondré; e) poniendo; f) puesto
preferir	→sentir
prefer	
probar	→contar
try	
producir	→traducir
produce	
proferir	→sentir
utter	
quebrar	→cerrar
break	
querer	a) quiero, quieres, quiere, queremos, queréis, quieren; b)
want, wish	quería; c) quise; d) querré; e) queriendo; f) querido
recomendar	→cerrar
recommend	
recordar	→contar
remember	
reducir	→traducir
reduce	
referir	→sentir
refer, relate	

regar   →cerrar
water

regir   →pedir
govern

reír   a) río, ríes, ríe, reímos, reís, ríen; b) reía; c) reí; d) reiré; e)
laugh   riendo; f) reído

remendar   →cerrar
mend

rendir   →pedir
produce;
overcome

renovar   →contar
renew

reñir   →teñir
scold; quarrel

repetir   →pedir
repeat

requerir   →sentir
request

resolver   →morder
resolve

resplandecer   →agradecer
shine

restituir   →instruir
restore, return

retribuir   →instruir
pay; reward

reventar   →cerrar
burst

robustecer   →agradecer
strengthen

rodar   →contar
drive; roll

rogar   →contar
beg, plead

saber   a) sé, sabes, sabe, sabemos, sabéis, saben; b) sabía; c) supe; d)
know   sabré; e) sabiendo; f) sabido

salir   a) salgo, sales, sale, salimos, salís, salen; b) salía; c) salí; d)
go out   saldré; e) saliendo; f) salido

satisfacer   →hacer
satisfy

seducir   →traducir
seduce

seguir *follow*	→pedir
sembrar *sow*	→cerrar
sentar *sit, seat*	→cerrar
sentir *feel*	a) siento, sientes, siente, sentimos, sentís, sienten; b) sentía; c) sentí; d) sentiré; e) sintiendo; f) sentido
ser *be*	a) soy, eres, es, somos, sois, son; b) era c) fui; d) seré; e) siendo; f) sido
servir *serve*	→pedir
soldar *solder; join*	→contar
soler *be used to*	a) suelo, sueles, suele, solemos, soléis, suelen; b) solía; c) solí; e) soliendo; f) solido
soltar *release; loosen*	→contar
sonar *ring, sound*	→contar
soñar *dream*	→contar
sugerir *suggest*	→sentir
sustituir *substitute*	→instruir
temblar *tremble*	→cerrar
tender *stretch, extend*	→perder
tener *have (got)*	a) tengo, tienes, tiene, tenemos, tenéis, tienen; b) tenía; c) tuve; d) tendré; e) teniendo; f) tenido
tentar *touch; try*	→cerrar
teñir *dye*	a) tiño, tiñes, tiñe, teñimos, teñís, tiñen; b) teñía; c) teñí; d) teñiré; e) tiñiendo; f) teñido
torcer *twist*	→cocer
tostar *roast*	→contar
traducir *translate*	a) traduzco, traduces, traduce, traducimos, traducís, traducen; b) traducía; c) traduje; d) traduciré; e) traduciendo; f) traducido

traer *bring*	a) traigo, traes, trae, traemos, traéis, traen; b) traía; c) traje; d) traeré; e) trayendo; f) traído
transferir *transfer*	→sentir
trocar *(ex)change*	→contar
tronar *thunder*	a) trueno, truenas, truena, tronamos, tronáis, truenan; b) tronaba; c) troné; d) tronaré; e) tronando; f) tronado
tropezar *stumble*	→cerrar
valer *protect; be worth*	a) valgo, vales, vale, valemos, valéis, valen; b) valía; c) valí; d) valdré; e) valiendo; f) valido
venir *come*	a) vengo, vienes, viene, venimos, venís, vienen; b) venía; c) vine; d) vendré; e) viniendo; f) venido
ver *see*	a) veo, ves, ve, vemos, veis, ven; b) veía; c) vi; d) veré; e) viendo; f) visto
verter *pour; spill*	→perder
vestir *dress*	→pedir
volar *fly*	→contar
volcar *tip over*	→contar
volver *(re)turn*	→morder
yacer *lie, rest*	→nacer
zambullir *plunge*	a) zambullo, zambulles, zambulle, zambullimos, zambullís, zambullen; b) zambullía; c) zambullí; d) zambulliré; e) zambullendo; f) zambullido

Spanish Abbreviations

a.C.	*antes de Cristo*	B.C.
A.C.	*año de Cristo*	A.D.
admón.	*administración*	administration
A.L.A.L.C.	*Asociación Latino-Americana de Libre Comercio*	Latin American Free Trade Association
apdo.	*apartado de correos*	P.O. Box
Av./Avda.	*Avenida*	avenue
Barna.	*Barcelona*	Barcelona
C/	*Calle*	street, road
c/c.	*cuenta corriente*	current account
Cía.	*Compañía*	company
cta.	*cuenta*	account; bill
cte.	*corriente*	inst., of this month
CV.	*caballos de vapor*	horsepower
D.	*Don*	courtesy title for gentlemen only used together with the Christian name
D.ª	*Doña*	courtesy title for ladies, only used together with the Christian name
dcha.	*derecha*	right (direction)
D.N.I.	*Documento Nacional de Identidad*	identity card
d. v.	*días de visita*	open days
EE.UU.	*Estados Unidos*	USA
Exc.ª	*Excelencia*	Your Excellency
f.c.	*ferrocarril*	railway
G.C.	*Guardia Civil*	Spanish police force
gral.	*general*	general
h.	*hora*	hour
hab.	*habitantes*	inhabitants, population
hnos.	*hermanos*	brothers (in firms)
íd.	*ídem*	ditto
igla.	*iglesia*	church
izq./izqda.	*izquierda*	left (direction)
lic.	*licenciado*	licentiate; lawyer
M.I.T.	*Ministerio de Información y Turismo*	Spanish Ministry of Information and Tourism
Mons.	*Monseñor*	Roman Catholic title (approx. Your Grace)
N.ª S.ª	*Nuestra Señora*	Our Lady, Virgin Mary

n.°/núm.	*número*	number
O.E.A.	*Organización de Estados Americanos*	Organization of American States
P.	*Padre*	Father (ecclesiastical title)
pág.	*página*	page
P.D.	*posdata*	P.S.
p. ej.	*por ejemplo*	e.g.
P.P.	*porte pagado*	postage paid
P.V.P.	*precio de venta al público*	retail price
R.A.C.E.	*Real Automóvil Club de España*	Royal Automobile Association of Spain
R.A.E.	*Real Academia Española*	Royal Academy of the Spanish Language
R.C.	*Real Club...*	Royal... Association
RENFE	*Red Nacional de los Ferrocarriles Españoles*	Spanish National Railways
R.M.	*Reverenda Madre*	Mother Superior, abbess
R.P.	*Reverendo Padre*	Reverend Father (title for Catholic priests and abbots)
Rte.	*Remite, Remitente*	sender (of a letter)
RTVE	*Radio Televisión Española*	Spanish Radio and Television Corporation
S./Sto./Sta.	*San/Santo/Santa*	saint
S.A.	*Sociedad Anónima*	Ltd., Inc.
S.A.R.	*Su Alteza Real*	His/Her Royal Highness
s.a.s.s.	*su atento y seguro servidor*	approx. Yours faithfully
S.E.	*Su Excelencia*	His Excellency
sgte.	*siguiente*	following
S.M.	*Su Majestad*	His/Her Majesty
Sr.	*Señor*	Mr.
Sra.	*Señora*	Mrs.
S.R.C.	*se ruega contestación*	please reply
Sres./Srs.	*Señores*	Sirs, Gentlemen
Srta.	*Señorita*	Miss
S.S.	*Su Santidad*	His Holiness
Ud./Vd.	*Usted*	you (singular)
Uds./Vds.	*Ustedes*	you (plural)
Vda.	*viuda*	widow
v.g./v.gr.	*verbigracia*	e.g.

Numerals

Cardinal numbers

0	cero
1	uno
2	dos
3	tres
4	cuatro
5	cinco
6	seis
7	siete
8	ocho
9	nueve
10	diez
11	once
12	doce
13	trece
14	catorce
15	quince
16	dieciséis
17	diecisiete
18	dieciocho
19	diecinueve
20	veinte
21	veintiuno
30	treinta
31	treinta y uno
40	cuarenta
50	cincuenta
60	sesenta
70	setenta
80	ochenta
90	noventa
100	ciento (cien)
101	ciento uno
230	doscientos treinta
500	quinientos
700	setecientos
900	novecientos
1.000	mil
100.000	cien mil
1.000.000	un millón

Ordinal numbers

1.º	primero
2.º	segundo
3.º	tercero
4.º	cuarto
5.º	quinto
6.º	sexto
7.º	séptimo
8.º	octavo
9.º	noveno (nono)
10.º	décimo
11.º	undécimo
12.º	duodécimo
13.º	decimotercero
14.º	decimocuarto
15.º	decimoquinto
16.º	decimosexto
17.º	decimoséptimo
18.º	decimoctavo
19.º	decimonoveno
20.º	vigésimo
21.º	vigésimo primero
22.º	vigésimo segundo
30.º	trigésimo
40.º	cuadragésimo
50.º	quincuagésimo
60.º	sexagésimo
70.º	septuagésimo
80.º	octogésimo
90.º	nonagésimo
100.º	centésimo
230.º	ducentésimo trigésimo
300.º	tricentésimo
400.º	cuadringentésimo
500.º	quingentésimo
600.º	sexcentésimo
700.º	septingentésimo
800.º	octingentésimo
900.º	noningentésimo
1.000.º	milésimo

Time

Although official time in Spain is based on the 24-hour clock, the 12-hour system is used in conversation.

In some Latin American countries you can specify *a.m.* or *p.m.* as in English, but it is far more common to add *de la mañana*, *de la tarde* or *de la noche* as in Spain.

Thus:

las ocho de la mañana	8 a.m.
la una de la tarde	1 p.m.
las ocho de la noche	8 p.m.

Days of the Week

domingo	Sunday	*jueves*	Thursday
lunes	Monday	*viernes*	Friday
martes	Tuesday	*sábado*	Saturday
miércoles	Wednesday		

Some Basic Phrases   Algunas expresiones útiles

Please.	Por favor.
Thank you very much.	Muchas gracias.
Don't mention it.	No hay de qué.
Good morning.	Buenos días.
Good afternoon.	Buenas tardes.
Good evening.	Buenas noches.
Good night.	Buenas noches (despedida).
Good-bye.	Adiós.
See you later.	Hasta luego.
Where is/Where are…?	¿Dónde está/Dónde están…?
What do you call this?	¿Cómo se llama esto?
What does that mean?	¿Qué quiere decir eso?
Do you speak English?	¿Habla usted inglés?
Do you speak German?	¿Habla usted alemán?
Do you speak French?	¿Habla usted francés?
Do you speak Spanish?	¿Habla usted español?
Do you speak Italian?	¿Habla usted italiano?
Could you speak more slowly, please?	¿Puede usted hablar más despacio, por favor?
I don't understand.	No comprendo.
Can I have…?	¿Puede darme…?
Can you show me…?	¿Puede usted enseñarme…?
Can you tell me…?	¿Puede usted decirme…?
Can you help me, please?	¿Puede usted ayudarme, por favor?
I'd like…	Quisiera…
We'd like…	Quisiéramos…
Please give me…	Por favor, déme…
Please bring me…	Por favor, tráigame…
I'm hungry.	Tengo hambre.
I'm thirsty.	Tengo sed.
I'm lost.	Me he perdido.
Hurry up!	¡Dése prisa!
There is/There are…	Hay…
There isn't/There aren't…	No hay…

Arrival   Llegada

Your passport, please.	Su pasaporte, por favor.
Have you anything to declare?	¿Tiene usted algo que declarar?
No, nothing at all.	No, nada en absoluto.
Can you help me with my luggage, please?	¿Puede usted ayudarme con mi equipaje, por favor?

Where's the bus to the centre of town, please?	¿Dónde está el autobús que va al centro, por favor?
This way, please.	Por aquí, por favor.
Where can I get a taxi?	¿Dónde puedo tomar un taxi?
What's the fare to…?	¿Cuánto es la tarifa a…?
Take me to this address, please.	Lléveme a esta dirección, por favor.
I'm in a hurry.	Tengo mucha prisa.

Hotel

Hotel

My name is…	Me llamo…
Have you a reservation?	¿Ha hecho usted una reserva?
I'd like a room with a bath.	Quisiera una habitación con baño.
What's the price per night?	¿Cuánto cuesta por noche?
May I see the room?	¿Puedo ver la habitación?
What's my room number, please?	¿Cuál es el número de mi habitación, por favor?
There's no hot water.	No hay agua caliente.
May I see the manager, please?	¿Puedo ver al director, por favor?
Did anyone telephone me?	¿Me ha llamado alguien?
Is there any mail for me?	¿Hay correo para mí?
May I have my bill (check), please?	¿Puede darme la cuenta, por favor?

Eating out

Restaurante

Do you have a fixed-price menu?	¿Tiene usted un menú de precio fijo?
May I see the menu?	¿Puedo ver la carta?
May we have an ashtray, please?	¿Nos puede traer un cenicero, por favor?
Where's the toilet, please?	¿Dónde están los servicios, por favor?
I'd like an hors d'œuvre (starter).	Quisiera entremeses.
Have you any soup?	¿Tiene usted sopa?
I'd like some fish.	Quisiera pescado.
What kind of fish do you have?	¿Qué clases de pescado tiene usted?
I'd like a steak.	Quisiera un bistec.
What vegetables have you got?	¿Qué verduras tiene usted?
Nothing more, thanks.	Nada más, gracias.
What would you like to drink?	¿Qué le gustaría beber?
I'll have a beer, please.	Tomaré una cerveza, por favor.
I'd like a bottle of wine.	Quisiera una botella de vino.
May I have the bill (check), please?	¿Podría darme la cuenta, por favor?
Is service included?	¿Está incluido el servicio?
Thank you, that was a very good meal.	Gracias. Ha sido una comida muy buena.

Travelling

Where's the railway station, please?	¿Dónde está la estación de ferrocarril, por favor?
Where's the ticket office, please?	¿Dónde está la taquilla, por favor?
I'd like a ticket to...	Quisiera un billete para...
First or second class?	¿Primera o segunda clase?
First class, please.	Primera clase, por favor.
Single or return (one way or roundtrip)?	¿Ida, o ida y vuelta?
Do I have to change trains?	¿Tengo que transbordar?
What platform does the train for ... leave from?	¿De qué andén sale el tren para...?
Where's the nearest underground (subway) station?	¿Dónde está la próxima estación de Metro?
Where's the bus station, please?	¿Dónde está la estación de autobuses, pot favor?
When's the first bus to...?	¿Cuándo sale el primer autobús para...?
Please let me off at the next stop.	Por favor, deténgase en la próxima parada.

Viajes

Relaxing

What's on at the cinema (movies)?	¿Qué dan en el cine?
What time does the film begin?	¿A qué hora empieza la película?
Are there any tickets for tonight?	¿Quedan entradas para esta noche?
Where can we go dancing?	¿Dónde se puede ir a bailar?

Diversiones

Meeting people

How do you do.	Buenos días Señora/Señorita/Señor.
How are you?	¿Cómo está usted?
Very well, thank you. And you?	Muy bien, gracias. ¿Y usted?
May I introduce...?	¿Me permite presentarle a...?
My name is...	Me llamo...
I'm very pleased to meet you.	Tanto gusto (en conocerle).
How long have you been here?	¿Cuánto tiempo lleva usted aquí?
It was nice meeting you.	Ha sido un placer conocerle.
Do you mind if I smoke?	¿Le molesta si fumo?
Do you have a light, please?	¿Tiene usted fuego, por favor?
May I get you a drink?	¿Me permite invitarle a una bebida (una copa)?
May I invite you for dinner tonight?	¿Me permite invitarle a cenar esta noche?
Where shall we meet?	¿Dónde quedamos citados?

Presentaciones — Citas

Shops, stores and services

Where's the nearest bank, please?
Where can I cash some travellers' cheques?
Can you give me some small change, please?
Where's the nearest chemist's (pharmacy)?
How do I get there?
Is it within walking distance?
Can you help me, please?
How much is this? And that?
It's not quite what I want.
I like it.
Can you recommend something for sunburn?
I'd like a haircut, please.
I'd like a manicure, please.

Street directions

Can you show me on the map where I am?
You are on the wrong road.
Go/Walk straight ahead.
It's on the left/on the right.

Emergencies

Call a doctor quickly.
Call an ambulance.
Please call the police.

Comercios y servicios

Dónde está el banco más cercano, por favor?
¿Dónde puedo cambiar unos cheques de viaje?
¿Puede usted darme algún dinero suelto, por favor?
¿Dónde está la farmacia más cercana?
¿Cómo podría ir hasta allí?
¿Se puede ir andando?
¿Puede usted atenderme, por favor?
¿Cuánto cuesta éste? ¿Y ése?
No es exactamente lo que quiero.
Me gusta.
¿Podría recomendarme algo para las quemaduras del sol?
Quisiera cortarme el pelo, por favor.
Quisiera una manicura, por favor.

Direcciones

¿Puede enseñarme en el mapa dónde estoy?
Está usted equivocado de camino.
Siga todo derecho.
Está a la izquierda/a la derecha.

Urgencias

Llame a un médico rápidamente.
Llame a una ambulancia.
Llame a la policía, por favor.

Inglés-Español

English-Spanish

Introducción

Este diccionario ha sido concebido para resolver de la mejor manera posible sus problemas prácticos de lenguaje. Se han suprimido las informaciones lingüísticas innecesarias. Los vocablos se suceden en un estricto orden alfabético, sin tener en cuenta si la palabra es simple o compuesta, o si se trata de una expresión formada por dos o más términos separados. Como única excepción, algunas expresiones idiomáticas están colocadas en orden alfabético, considerando para ello la palabra más característica. Cuando un término principal va seguido de otras palabras, expresiones o locuciones, éstas se hallan anotadas también en orden alfabético.

Cada palabra va seguida de una transcripción fonética (véase la guía de pronunciación). Después de la transcripción fonética se encuentra una indicación de la parte de la oración a que pertenece el vocablo. Cuando una palabra puede desempeñar distintos oficios en la oración, las diferentes traducciones se dan una a continuación de la otra, precedidas de la indicación correspondiente.

Se indica el plural de los nombres cuando son irregulares y en algunos otros casos dudosos.

Cuando haya que repetir una palabra para formar el plural irregular o en las series de palabras se usa la tilde (~) para representar el vocablo principal.

En los plurales irregulares de las palabras compuestas sólo se escribe la parte que cambia, mientras que la parte invariable se representa por un guión (-).

Un asterisco (*) colocado antes de un verbo indica que dicho verbo es irregular. Para más detalles puede consultar la lista de los verbos irregulares.

Las palabras de este diccionario están escritas en su forma inglesa. La forma y significado americanos están señalados como tales (véase la lista de abreviaturas empleadas en el texto).

Abreviaturas

adj	adjetivo	*n*	nombre
adv	adverbio		(sustantivo)
Am	inglés americano	*nAm*	nombre
art	artículo		(inglés americano)
conj	conjunción	*num*	numeral
f	femenino	*p*	tiempo pasado
fMe	femenino (mexicano)	*pl*	plural
fpl	femenino plural	*plAm*	plural (inglés americano)
fplMe	femenino plural	*pp*	participio pasado
	(mexicano)	*pr*	tiempo presente
L.Am.	América Latina		
m	masculino	*pref*	prefijo
Me	mexicano	*prep*	preposición
mMe	masculino (mexicano)	*pron*	pronombre
mpl	masculino plural	*v*	verbo
mplMe	masculino plural	*vAm*	verbo (inglés americano)
	(mexicano)	*vMe*	verbo (mexicano)

Guía de pronunciación

Cada vocablo principal de esta parte del diccionario va acompañado de una transcripción fonética destinada a indicar la pronunciación. Esta representación fonética debe leerse como si se tratara del idioma español hablado en Castilla. A continuación figuran tan solo las letras y los símbolos ambiguos o particularmente difíciles de comprender.

Cada sílaba está separada por un guión y la que lleva el acento está impresa en letra *bastardilla*.

Por supuesto, los sonidos de dos lenguas rara vez coinciden exactamente, pero siguiendo con atención nuestras explicaciones, el lector de habla española llegará a pronunciar las palabras extranjeras de manera que pueda ser comprendido. A fin de facilitar su tarea, algunas veces nuestras transcripciones simplifican ligeramente el sistema fonético del idioma, sin dejar por ello de reflejar las diferencias de sonido esenciales.

Consonantes

b	como en **b**ueno
dd	como en **d**ía
ð	como **d** en rui**d**o
ʤ	como la **ll** argentina, precedida por una **d**
gh	como **g** en **g**ato
h	sonido que es una espiración suave
ng	como **n** en bla**n**co
r	ponga la lengua en la misma posición que para pronunciar ʒ (véase más abajo), luego abra ligeramente la boca y baje la lengua
s	sonido siempre suave y sonoro como en mi**s**mo
ʃ	como **ch** en mu**ch**o, pero sin la **t** inicial que compone el sonido
v	más o menos como en la**v**a; sonido que se obtiene colocando los dientes incisivos superiores sobre el labio inferior y expulsando suavemente el aire
ʒ	como la **ll** argentina

Vocales y diptongos

æ   sonido que combina el de la **a** en c**a**so con el de la **e** en sab**e**r

ê   como **e** en sab**e**r

o   como **o** en p**o**r

ö   vocal neutral; sonido parecido al de la **a** española, pero con los labios extendidos

1) Las vocales largas están impresas a doble.

2) Las letras situadas más arriba que las otras (por ej.: **"i, uö**) deben pronunciarse con menor intensidad y rápidamente.

3) Algunas palabras inglesas toman del francés las vocales nasales, que están indicadas con un símbolo de vocal mas **ng** (por ej.: **ang**). Este signo **ng** *no* se debe pronunciar y sólo sirve para indicar la nasalidad de la vocal precedente. Las vocales nasales se pronuncian con la boca y la nariz simultáneamente.

Pronunciación americana

Nuestra transcripción representa la pronunciación de Gran Bretaña. Aunque existen notables variaciones regionales en la lengua americana, ésta presenta en general algunas diferencias importantes respecto al inglés de Gran Bretaña.

He aquí algunos ejemplos:

1) La **r,** delante de una consonante o al final de una palabra, siempre se pronuncia, lo cual es contrario a la costumbre inglesa.

2) En muchas palabras (por ej.: *ask*, *castle*, *laugh*, etc.) la **aa** se transforma en **ææ.**

3) El sonido inglés **o** se pronuncia **a** o también **oo.**

4) En palabras como *duty*, *tune*, *new*, etc., el sonido **y** se omite a menudo antes de **uu.**

5) Por último, el acento tónico de algunas palabras puede variar considerablemente.

A

a (ei, ö) *art* (an) un *art*

abbey (æ-bi) *n* abadía *f*

abbreviation (ö-brii-vi-*ei*-ʃön) *n*
abreviatura *f*

ability (ö-*bi*-lö-ti) *n* habilidad *f*

able (*ei*-böl) *adj* capaz; hábil; ***be ~ to**
*ser capaz de; *saber, *poder

aboard (ö-*bood*) *adv* a bordo

abolish (ö-*bo*-liʃ) *v* abolir

abortion (ö-*boo*-ʃön) *n* aborto *m*

about (ö-*baut*) *prep* acerca de;
respecto a; alrededor de; *adv* hacia,
aproximadamente; en torno

above (ö-*bav*) *prep* encima de; *adv*
encima

abroad (ö-*brood*) *adv* en el extranjero

abscess (æb-ssêss) *n* absceso *m*

absence (æb-ssönss) *n* ausencia *f*

absent (æb-ssönt) *adj* ausente

absolutely (æb-ssö-luut-li) *adv*
absolutamente

abstain from (öb-*sstein*) *abstenerse
de

abstract (æb-ssträkt) *adj* abstracto

absurd (öb-*ssööd*) *adj* absurdo

abundance (ö-*ban*-dönss) *n*
abundancia *f*

abundant (ö-*ban*-dönt) *adj* abundante

abuse (ö-*byuuss*) *n* abuso *m*

abyss (ö-*biss*) *n* abismo *m*

academy (ö-*kæ*-dö-mi) *n* academia *f*

accelerate (ök-ssê-lö-reit) *v* acelerar

accelerator (ök-ssê-lö-rei-tö) *n*
acelerador *m*

accent (æk-ssönt) *n* acento *m*

accept (ök-*ssêpt*) *v* aceptar

access (æk-ssêss) *n* acceso *m*

accessible (ök-ssê-ssö-böl) *adj*
accesible

accessories (ök-ssê-ssö-ris) *pl*
accesorios *mpl*

accident (æk-ssi-dönt) *n* accidente *m*

accidental (æk-ssi-*dên*-töl) *adj*
accidental

accommodate (ö-*ko*-mö-deit) *v*
acomodar

accommodation (ö-ko-mö-*dei*-ʃön) *n*
acomodación *f*, alojamiento *m*

accompany (ö-*kam*-pö-ni) *v*
acompañar

accomplish (ö-*kam*-pliʃ) *v* terminar;
cumplir

accordance: in ~ with (in ö-*koo*-
dönss ⁿi) con arreglo a; conforme a

according to (ö-*koo*-ding tuu) según

account (ö-*kaunt*) *n* cuenta *f*;
factura *f*; relato *m*; **~ for** explicar; **on ~ of** a
causa de

accountable (ö-*kaun*-tö-böl) *adj*
explicable; responsable

accurate (æ-kyu-röt) *adj* exacto;
preciso; acertado

accuse (ö-*kyuus*) *v* acusar

accused (ö-*kyuusd*) *n* acusado *m*, -a *f*

accustom (ö-*ka*-sstöm) *v*
acostumbrar; **accustomed**
acostumbrado

ache (eik) *v* *doler; *n* dolor *m*

achieve (ö-*chiiv*) *v* alcanzar; lograr

achievement (ö-*chiiv*-mönt) *n*
realización *f*

acid (æ-ssid) *n* ácido *m*

acknowledge (ök-*no*-lidʒ) *v*
*reconocer; admitir; confirmar

acne (æk-ni) *n* acné *m*

acorn (*ei*-koon) *n* bellota *f*

acquaintance (ö-kⁿ*ein*-tönss) *n*
conocido *m*

acquire (ö-kⁿ*ai*ᵒ) *v* *adquirir

acquisition (æ-kⁿi-si-ʃön) *n*
adquisición *f*

acquittal (ö-kⁿ*i*-töl) *n* absolución *f*

across (ö-*kross*) *prep* a través de; al
otro lado de; *adv* al otro lado

act (ækt) *n* acto *m*; hecho *m*; *v* actuar, *hacer; comportarse

action (æk-ʃön) *n* acción *f*

active (æk-tiv) *adj* activo; vivaz

activity (æk-*ti*-vö-ti) *n* actividad *f*

actor (æk-tö) *n* actor *m*

actress (æk-triss) *n* actriz *f*

actual (æk-chu-öl) *adj* verdadero

actually (æk-chu-ö-li) *adv* en realidad

acute (ö-*kyuut*) *adj* agudo

adapt (ö-*dæpt*) *v* adaptar

adaptor (ö-*dæpt*-tö) *n* adaptador *m*

add (æd) *v* sumar, adicionar; añadir

addition (ö-*di*-ʃön) *n* adición *f*

additional (ö-*di*-ʃö-nöl) *adj* adicional; accesorio

address (ö-*drèss*) *n* dirección *f*; senas *fpl*; *v* destinar; dirigirse a

addressee (æ-drê-*ssii*) *n* destinatario *m*, -a *f*

adequate (æ-di-k^uöt) *adj* adecuado; conveniente

adjective (æ-dʒik-tiv) *n* adjetivo *m*

adjourn (ö-dʒöön) *v* aplazar

adjust (ö-dʒasst) *v* ajustar

administer (öd-*mi*-ni-sstö) *v* administrar

administration (öd-mi-ni-*sstrei*-ʃön) *n* administración *f*; gestión *f*

administrative (öd-*mi*-ni-sströ-tiv) *adj* gerencial; administrativo; ~ **law** derecho administrativo

admiration (æd-mö-*rei*-ʃön) *n* admiración *f*

admire (öd-*mai*^ö) *v* admirar

admission (öd-*mi*-ʃön) *n* entrada *f*; admisión *f*

admit (öd-*mit*) *v* admitir; *reconocer

admittance (öd-*mi*-tönss) *n* admisión *f*; **no** ~ prohibida la entrada

adopt (ö-*dopt*) *v* adoptar

adorable (ö-*doo*-rö-böl) *adj* adorable

adult (æ-dalt) *n* adulto *m*; *adj* adulto

advance (öd-*vaans*) *n* adelanto *m*;

anticipo *m*; *v* avanzar; anticipar; **in** ~ por adelantado

advanced (öd-*vaansst*) *adj* avanzado

advantage (öd-*vaan*-tidʒ) *n* ventaja *f*

advantageous (æd-vön-*tei*-dʒöss) *adj* ventajoso

adventure (öd-*vên*-chö) *n* aventura *f*

adverb (æd-vööb) *n* adverbio *m*

advertise (æd-vöö-tais) *v* anunciar; anunciarse, poner un anuncio

advertisement (öd-*vöö*-tiss-mönt) *n* anuncio *m*

advertising (æd-vö-tai-sing) *n* publicidad *f*

advice (öd-*vaiss*) *n* consejo *m*

advise (öd-*vais*) *v* aconsejar

advocate (æd-vö-köt) *n* abogado *m*

aerial (ê^ö-ri-öl) *n* antena *f*

aeroplane (ê^ö-rö-plein) *n* avión *m*

affair (ö-*fê*^ö) *n* asunto *m*; amorío *m*

affect (ö-*fêkt*) *v* afectar

affected (ö-*fêk*-tid) *adj* afectado

affection (ö-*fêk*-ʃön) *n* afección *f*; cariño *m*

affectionate (ö-*fêk*-ʃö-nit) *adj* cariñoso

affiliated (ö-*fi*-li-ei-tid) *adj* afiliado

affirmative (ö-*föö*-mö-tiv) *adj* afirmativo

afford (ö-*food*) *v* permitirse

afraid (ö-*freid*) *adj* angustioso, asustado; ***be** ~ *tener miedo

Africa (æ-fri-kö) *África f*

African (æ-fri-kön) *adj* africano

after (*aaf*-tö) *prep* después de; detrás de; tras; *conj* después de que

afternoon (aaf-tö-*nuun*) *n* tarde *f*

afterwards (*aaf*-tö-^uöds) *adv* después, más tarde

again (ö-*ghên*) *adv* otra vez; de nuevo; ~ **and again** repetidamente

against (ö-*ghênsst*) *prep* contra

age (eidʒ) *n* edad *f*; vejez *f*; época *f*; **of** ~ mayor de edad; **under** ~ menor de edad

aged (*ei*-dʒid) *adj* viejo; anciano

agency (*ei*-dʒön-ssi) *n* agencia *f*; sección *f*

agenda (ö-*dʒên*-dö) *n* orden del día

agent (*ei*-dʒönt) *n* agente *m*, representante *m*

aggressive (ö-*ghrê*-ssiv) *adj* agresivo

ago (ö-*ghou*) *adv* hace; **long ~** hace mucho tiempo

agree (ö-*ghrii*) *v* *convenir, *concordar; *consentir; *acordar

agreeable (ö-*ghrii*-ö-böl) *adj* agradable

agreement (ö-*ghrii*-mönt) *n* contrato *m*; acuerdo *m*; conformidad *f*

agriculture (*æ*-ghri-kal-chö) *n* agricultura *f*

ahead (ö-*hêd*) *adv* adelante; **~ of** delante de; *go ~ continuar; **straight ~** todo seguido

aid (eid) *n* socorro *m*; *v* asistir, ayudar

AIDS (eids) *n* SIDA *m*

aim (eim) *n* fin *m*; **~ at** apuntar; aspirar a

air (ê°) *n* aire *m*; *v* airear

air conditioning (ê°-kön-di-*ʃö*-ning) *n* aire acondicionado; **air conditioned** *adj* climatizado

aircraft (ê°-kraaft) *n* (pl ~) avión *m*

airfield (ê°-fiild) *n* campo de aviación

airline (ê°-lain) *n* aerolínea *f*

airmail (ê°-meil) *n* correo aéreo

airplane (ê°-plein) *nAm* avión *m*

airport (ê°-poot) *n* aeropuerto *m*

airsickness (ê°-ssik-nöss) *n* mal de las alturas; mareo *m*

airtight (ê°-tait) *adj* hermético

airy (ê°-ri) *adj* espacioso; ventiloso; ligero

aisle (ail) *n* nave lateral; pasillo *m*

alarm (ö-*laam*) *n* alarma *f*; *v* alarmar; **~ clock** despertador *m*

album (*æl*-böm) *n* álbum *m*

alcohol (*æl*-kö-hol) *n* alcohol *m*

alcoholic (æl-kö-*ho*-lik) *adj* alcohólico

ale (eil) *n* cerveza *f*

algebra (*æl*-dʒi-brö) *n* álgebra *f*

Algeria (æl-*dʒi*°-ri-ö) Argelia *f*

Algerian (æl-*dʒi*°-ri-ön) *adj* argelino

alien (*ei*-li-ön) *n* extranjero *m*, -a *f*; *adj* extranjero

alike (ö-*laik*) *adj* igual, parecido; *adv* igualmente

alive (ö-*laiv*) *adj* en vida, vivo

all (ool) *adj* todo; *adv* del todo; **~ day** todo el día; **~ in** con todo; **~ right!** ¡está bien!; **at ~** en modo alguno; siquiera

allergy (*æ*-lö-dʒi) *n* alergia *f*

alley (*æ*-li) *n* callejón *m*

alliance (ö-*lai*-önss) *n* alianza *f*

allow (ö-*lau*) *v* permitir, autorizar; **~ to** autorizar a; *be allowed *estar autorizado

allowance (ö-*lau*-önss) *n* asignación *f*

all-round (ool-*raund*) *adj* polifacético

almond (aa-mönd) *n* almendra *f*

almost (*ool*-mousst) *adv* casi; cerca de

alone (ö-*loun*) *adv* sólo

along (ö-*long*) *prep* a lo largo de

aloud (ö-*laud*) *adv* en voz alta

alphabet (*æl*-fö-bêt) *n* abecedario *m*

already (ool-*rê*-di) *adv* ya

also (*ool*-ssou) *adv* también; asimismo

altar (*ool*-tö) *n* altar *m*

alter (*ool*-tö) *v* cambiar, alterar

alteration (ool-tö-*rei*-ʃön) *n* cambio *m*, alteración *f*

alternate (ool-*töö*-nöt) *adj* alternativo

alternative (ool-*töö*-nö-tiv) *n* alternativa *f*

although (ool-*ðou*) *conj* aunque

altitude (*æl*-ti-tyuud) *n* altitud *f*

alto (*æl*-tou) *n* (pl ~s) contralto *m*

altogether (ool-tö-*ghê*-ðö) *adv* en total

always (*ool-*ᵘeis) *adv* siempre

am (æm) *v* (pr be)

amaze (ö-*meis*) *v* extrañar, asombrar

amazement (ö-*meis*-mönt) *n* asombro *m*

amazing (ö-*mei*-sing) *adj* asombroso; alucinante

ambassador (æm-*bæ*-ssö-dö) *n* embajador *m*

amber (*æm*-bö) *n* ámbar *m*

ambiguous (æm-*bi*-ghyu-öss) *adj* ambiguo; equívoco

ambition (æm-bi-*ʃön*) *n* ambición *f*

ambitious (æm-bi-*ʃöss*) *adj* ambicioso

ambulance (*æm*-byu-lönss) *n* ambulancia *f*

ambush (*æm*-buʃ) *n* emboscada *f*

America (ö-*mê*-ri-kö) América *f*

American (ö-*mê*-ri-kön) *adj* americano

amethyst (*æ*-mi-zisst) *n* amatista *f*

amid (ö-*mid*) *prep* entre; en medio de

ammonia (ö-*mou*-ni-ö) *n* amoníaco *m*

amnesty (*æm*-ni-ssti) *n* amnistía *f*

among (ö-*mang*) *prep* entre; ~ **other things** entre otras cosas

amount (ö-*maunt*) *n* cantidad *f*; suma *f*; ~ **to** sumar

amuse (ö-*myuus*) *v* *divertir, *entretener

amusement (ö-*myuus*-mönt) *n* distracción *f*, entretenimiento *m*

amusing (ö-*myuu*-sing) *adj* divertido

an(a)emia (ö-*nii*-mi-ö) *n* anemia *f*

an(a)esthesia (æ-niss-*zii*-si-ö) *n* anestesia *f*

analyse (*æ*-nö-lais) *v* analizar

analysis (ö-*næ*-lö-ssiss) *n* (pl -ses) análisis *f*

analyst (*æ*-nö-lisst) *n* analista *m*; psicoanalista *m*

anarchy (*æ*-nö-ki) *n* anarquía *f*

anatomy (ö-*næ*-tö-mi) *n* anatomía *f*

ancestor (*æn*-ssê-sstö) *n* antepasado

m, -a *f*

anchor (*æng*-kö) *n* ancla *f*

anchovy (*æn*-chö-vi) *n* anchoa *f*

ancient (*ein*-ʃönt) *adj* viejo, antiguo; anticuado

and (ænd, önd) *conj* y

angel (*ein*-dʒöl) *n* ángel *m*

anger (*æng*-ghö) *n* cólera *f*, enojo *m*; furia *f*; *v* enojar

angle (*æng*-ghöl) *v* pescar con caña; *n* ángulo *m*

angry (*æng*-ghri) *adj* enfadado, enojado

animal (*æ*-ni-möl) *n* animal *m*

ankle (*æng*-köl) *n* tobillo *m*

annex¹ (*æ*-nêkss) *n* anexo *m*

annex² (ö-*nêkss*) *v* anexar

anniversary (æ-ni-*vöö*-ssö-ri) *n* aniversario *m*

announce (ö-*naunss*) *v* anunciar; informar; proclamar

announcement (ö-*naunss*-mönt) *n* anuncio *m*; informe *m*; proclama *f*

annoy (ö-*noi*) *v* irritar, fastidiar; molestar

annoyance (ö-*noi*-önss) *n* molestia *f*; fastidio *m*

annoying (ö-*noi*-ing) *adj* molesto; fastidioso

annual (*æ*-nyu-öl) *adj* anual; *n* anuario *m*

annum: per ~ (pör *æ*-nöm) al año

anonymous (ö-*no*-ni-möss) *adj* anónimo

another (ö-*na*-ðö) *adj* otro más; otro

answer (*aan*-ssö) *v* responder a; *n* respuesta *f*

ant (ænt) *n* hormiga *f*

antibiotic (æn-ti-bai-*o*-tik) *n* antibiótico *m*

anticipate (æn-*ti*-ssi-peit) *v* *prever; *prevenir

antifreeze (*æn*-ti-friis) *n* anticongelante *m*

antipathy (æn-*ti*-pö-zi) *n* antipatía *f*

antique (æn-*tiik*) *adj* antiguo; *n* antigüedad *f*; ~ **dealer** anticuario *m*

antiquity (æn-*ti*-kᵘö-ti) *n* Antigüedad *f*; **antiquities** *pl* antigüedades *fpl*

anxiety (æng-*sai*-ö-ti) *n* ansiedad *f*; preocupación *f*

anxious (*ængk*-ʃöss) *adj* ansioso; preocupado

any (ê-ni) *adj* alguno, alguna

anybody (ê-ni-bo-di) *pron* cualquiera

anyhow (ê-ni-hau) *adv* de cualquier modo

anyone (ê-ni-ᵘan) *pron* cualquiera

anything (ê-ni-zing) *pron* cualquier cosa

anyway (ê-ni-ᵘei) *adv* en todo caso

anywhere (ê-ni-ᵘê͂ö) *adv* en donde sea; dondequiera

apart (ö-*paat*) *adv* por separado, separadamente; ~ **from** aparte de

apartment (ö-*paat*-mönt) *nAm* apartamento *m*; piso *m*; ~ **house** *Am* casa de pisos

aperitif (ö-pê-rö-tiv) *n* aperitivo *m*

apologize (ö-*po*-lö-dʒais) *v* disculparse

apology (ö-*po*-lö-dʒi) *n* excusa *f*, disculpa *f*

apparatus (æ-pö-*rei*-töss) *n* aparato *m*

apparent (ö-*pæ*-rönt) *adj* aparente; obvio

apparently (ö-*pæ*-rönt-li) *adv* por lo visto; evidentemente

appeal (ö-*piil*) *n* apelación *f*

appear (ö-*pi*ᵒ) *v* *parecer; *salir; *aparecer

appearance (ö-*pi*ᵒ-rönss) *n* apariencia *f*; aspecto *m*; entrada *f*

appendicitis (ö-pên-di-*ssai*-tiss) *n* apendicitis *f*

appendix (ö-*pên*-dikss) *n* (pl -dices, -dixes) apéndice *m*

appetite (*æ*-pö-tait) *n* apetito *m*

appetizer (*æ*-pö-tai-sö) *n* tapa *f*; aperitivo *m*

appetizing (*æ*-pö-tai-sing) *adj* apetitoso

applaud (ö-*plood*) *v* aplaudir

applause (ö-*ploos*) *n* aplauso *m*

apple (*æ*-pöl) *n* manzana *f*

appliance (ö-*plai*-önss) *n* aparato *m*

application (æ-pli-*kei*-ʃön) *n* aplicación *f*; demanda *f*; solicitud *f*

apply (ö-*plai*) *v* aplicar; solicitar un puesto; aplicarse a

appoint (ö-*point*) *v* designar, nombrar

appointment (ö-*point*-mönt) *n* cita *f*; nombramiento *m*

appreciate (ö-*prii*-ʃi-eit) *v* valuar; apreciar

appreciation (ö-prii-ʃi-*ei*-ʃön) *n* aprecio *m*

apprentice (ö-*prên*-tis) aprendiz *m*, -a *f*

approach (ö-*prouch*) *v* acercarse; *n* enfoque *m*; acceso *m*

appropriate (ö-*prou*-pri-öt) *adj* justo, apropiado, adecuado

approval (ö-*pruu*-völ) *n* aprobación *f*; consentimiento *m*, acuerdo *m*; **on** ~ a prueba

approve (ö-*pruuv*) *v* *aprobar; ~ **of** *estar de acuerdo con

approximate (ö-*prok*-ssi-möt) *adj* aproximado

approximately (ö-*prok*-ssi-möt-li) *adv* aproximadamente

apricot (*ei*-pri-kot) *n* albaricoque *m*; chabacano *mMe*

April (*ei*-pröl) abril *m*

apron (*ei*-prön) *n* delantal *m*

Arab (*æ*-röb) *adj* árabe

arbitrary (*aa*-bi-trö-ri) *adj* arbitrario

arcade (aa-*keid*) *n* pórtico *m*, arcada *f*

arch (aach) *n* arco *m*; bóveda *f*

arch(a)eologist (aa-ki-o-lö-dʒisst) *n* arqueólogo *m*, -a *f*

arch(a)eology (aa-ki-*o*-lö-dӡi) *n* arqueología *f*

archbishop (aach-*bi*-ʃöp) *n* arzobispo *m*

arched (aacht) *adj* arqueado

architect (*aa*-ki-têkt) *n* arquitecto *m*

architecture (*aa*-ki-têk-chö) *n* arquitectura *f*

archives (*aa*-kaivs) *pl* archivo *m*

are (aa) *v* (pr be)

area (*e*ᵒ-ri-ö) *n* región *f*; zona *f*; superficie *f*; ~ **code** indicativo *m*

Argentina (aa-dӡön-*tii*-nö) Argentina *f*

Argentinian (aa-dӡön-*ti*-ni-ön) *adj* argentino

argue (*aa*-ghyuu) *v* argumentar, discutir; disputar; razonar

argument (*aa*-ghyu-mönt) *n* argumento *m*; discusión *f*; disputa *f*

*arise (ö-*rais*) *v* surgir

arm (aam) *n* brazo *m*; arma *f*; *v* armar

armchair (*aam*-chêᵒ) *n* butaca *f*, sillón *m*

armed (aamd) *adj* armado; ~ **forces** fuerzas armadas

armour (*aa*-mö) *n* armadura *f*

army (*aa*-mi) *n* ejército *m*

aroma (ö-*rou*-mö) *n* aroma *m*

around (ö-*raund*) *prep* alrededor de, en torno de; *adv* en torno; **all** ~ por todas partes

arrange (ö-*reind*ӡ) *v* clasificar, ordenar; organizar

arrangement (ö-*reind*ӡ-mönt) *n* arreglo *m*; orden *m*; acuerdo *m*

arrest (ö-*rêsst*) *v* arrestar; *n* arresto *m*

arrival (ö-*rai*-völ) *n* llegada *f*

arrive (ö-*raiv*) *v* llegar

arrow (*æ*-rou) *n* flecha *f*

art (aat) *n* arte *m/f*; habilidad *f*; ~ **collection** colección de arte; ~ **exhibition** exposición de arte; ~ **gallery** galería de arte; ~ **history**

historia del arte; **arts and crafts** artes industriales; ~ **school** academia de bellas artes

artery (*aa*-tö-ri) *n* arteria *f*

artichoke (*aa*-ti-chouk) *n* alcachofa *f*

article (*aa*-ti-köl) *n* artículo *m*

artificial (aa-ti-*fi*-ʃöl) *adj* artificial

artist (*aa*-tisst) *n* artista *m/f*

artistic (aa-*ti*-sstik) *adj* artístico

as (æs) *conj* como; tanto; que; ya que, porque; ~ **from** a partir de; ~ **if** como si

asbestos (æs-*bê*-sstoss) *n* asbesto *m*

ascend (ö-*ssênd*) *v* subir; escalar

ascent (ö-*ssênt*) *n* subida *f*

ascertain (æ-ssö-*tein*) *v* *comprobar; asegurarse de

ash (æʃ) *n* ceniza *f*

ashamed (ö-*ʃeimd*) *adj* avergonzado; ***be** ~ *avergonzarse

ashore (ö-*ʃoo*) *adv* en tierra

ashtray (*æʃ*-trei) *n* cenicero *m*

Asia (*ei*-ʃö) Asia *f*

Asian (*ei*-ʃön) *adj* asiático

aside (ö-*ssaid*) *adv* aparte

ask (aassk) *v* preguntar; *rogar; invitar

asleep (ö-*ssliip*) *adj* dormido

asparagus (ö-*sspæ*-rö-ghöss) *n* espárrago *m*

aspect (*æ*-sspêkt) *n* aspecto *m*

asphalt (*æss*-fælt) *n* asfalto *m*

aspire (ö-*sspai*ᵒ) *v* aspirar

aspirin (*æ*-sspö-rin) *n* aspirina *f*

assassination (ö-ssæ-ssi-*nei*-ʃön) *n* asesinato *m*

assault (ö-*ssoolt*) *v* atacar; violar

assemble (ö-*ssêm*-böl) *v* reunir; montar

assembly (ö-*ssêm*-bli) *n* reunión *f*, asamblea *f*

assignment (ö-*ssain*-mönt) *n* encargo *m*

assign to (ö-*ssain*) asignar a; *atribuir a

assist (ö-*ssisst*) v asistir

assistance (ö-*ssi*-sstönss) n auxilio m; apoyo m, asistencia f

assistant (ö-*ssi*-sstönt) n asistente m

associate[1] (ö-*ssou*-ʃi-öt) n compañero m, -a f; colega m/f; aliado m, -a f; socio m, -a f

associate[2] (ö-*ssou*-ʃi-eit) v asociar; ~ **with** frecuentar

association (ö-ssou-ssi-*ei*-ʃön) n asociación f

assort (ö-*ssoot*) v clasificar

assortment (ö-*ssoot*-mönt) n surtido m

assume (ö-*ssyuum*) v *suponer, presumir

assure (ö-ʃu^ö) v asegurar

asthma (*æss*-mö) n asma f

astonish (ö-*ssto*-niʃ) v asombrar

astonishing (ö-*ssto*-ni-ʃing) adj asombroso

astonishment (ö-*ssto*-niʃ-mönt) n asombro m; sorpresa f

astronaut (*æss*-tro-noot) astronauta m/f

astronomy (ö-*sstro*-nö-mi) n astronomía f

asylum (ö-*ssai*-löm) n asilo m

at (æt) prep en, a; hacia

ate (êt) v (p eat)

atheist (*ei*-zi-isst) n ateo m

athlete (*æz*-liit) n atleta m

athletics (æz-*lê*-tikss) pl atletismo m

Atlantic (öt-*læn*-tik) Atlántico m

atmosphere (*æt*-möss-fi^ö) n atmósfera f; esfera f, ambiente m

atom (*æ*-töm) n átomo m

atomic (ö-*to*-mik) adj atómico

atomizer (*æ*-tö-mai-sö) n vaporizador m; aerosol m, pulverizador m

attach (ö-*tæch*) v prender; fijar; juntar; **attached to** encariñado con

attack (ö-*tæk*) v atacar; n ataque m

attain (ö-*tein*) v llegar a

attainable (ö-*tei*-nö-böl) adj alcanzable

attempt (ö-*têmpt*) v intentar; *probar; n tentativa f

attend (ö-*tênd*) v asistir a; ~ **on** *servir; ~ **to** cuidar de, *atender a; prestar atención a

attendance (ö-*tên*-dönss) n asistencia f; presencia f

attendant (ö-*tên*-dönt) n asistente m; acompañante m

attention (ö-*tên*-ʃön) n atención f; *pay ~ prestar atención

attentive (ö-*tên*-tiv) adj atento

attic (*æ*-tik) n buhardilla f

attitude (*æ*-ti-tyuud) n actitud f

attorney (ö-*töö*-ni) n abogado m

attract (ö-*trækt*) v *atraer

attraction (ö-*træk*-ʃön) n atracción f

attractive (ö-*træk*-tiv) adj atractivo

auction (*ook*-ʃön) n subasta f

audible (*oo*-di-böl) adj audible

audience (*oo*-di-önss) n auditorio m

auditor (*oo*-di-tö) n auditor m, -a f

auditorium (oo-di-*too*-ri-öm) n aula f

August (*oo*-ghösst) agosto

aunt (aant) n tía f

Australia (o-*sstrei*-li-ö) Australia f

Australian (o-*sstrei*-li-ön) adj australiano

Austria (o-*sstri*-ö) Austria f

Austrian (o-*sstri*-ön) adj austríaco

authentic (oo-*zên*-tik) adj auténtico

author (*oo*-zö) n autor m

authoritarian (oo-zo-ri-*tê^ö*-ri-ön) adj autoritario

authority (oo-*zo*-rö-ti) n autoridad f; poder m

authorization (oo-zö-rai-*sei*-ʃön) n autorización f; permiso m

authorize (*oo*-zö-rais) v autorizar; **be authorized to** estar autorizado para

automatic (oo-tö-*mæ*-tik) adj automático; ~ **teller** cajero

automático
automobile (*oo*-tö-mö-biil) *n*
  automóvil *m*; ~ **club** automóvil club
autonomous (*oo-to-n*i-möss) *adj*
  autónomo
autopsy (*oo*-to-pssi) *n* autopsia *f*
autumn (*oo*-töm) *n* otoño *m*
available (ö-*vei*-lö-böl) *adj* adquirible,
  obtenible, disponible
avalanche (*æ*-vö-laanʃ) *n* avalancha *f*
avenue (*æ*-vö-nyuu) *n* avenida *f*
average (*æ*-vö-ridʒ) *adj* medio;
  mediano; *n* promedio *m*; **on the** ~ por
  término medio
averse (ö-*vööss*) *adj* opuesto,
  contrario

aversion (ö-*vöö*-ʃön) *n* aversión *f*
avert (ö-*vööt*) *v* desviar
avoid (ö-*void*) *v* evitar
await (ö-*u eit*) *v* esperar
awake (ö-*u eik*) *adj* despierto
*awake (ö-*u eik*) *v* *despertar
award (ö-*u ood*) *n* premio *m*; *v*
  conceder
aware (ö-*u eᶿ*) *adj* consciente
away (ö-*u ei*) *adv* fuera; ***go** ~ *irse
awful (*oo*-föl) *adj* terrible, tremendo
awkward (*oo*-kⁿöd) *adj* embarazoso;
  torpe
awning (*oo*-ning) *n* toldo *m*
axe (*æ*kss) *n* hacha *f*
axle (*æ*k-ssöl) *n* eje *m*

B

baby (*bei*-bi) *n* bebé *m*; ~ **carriage**
  Am cochecillo *m*
babysitter (*bei*-bi-ssi-tö) *n* babysitter
  m
bachelor (*bæ*-chö-lö) *n* soltero *m*
back (bæk) *n* espalda *f*; *adv* atrás; ***go**
  ~ regresar
backache (*bæ*-keik) *n* dolor de
  espalda
backbone (*bæk*-boun) *n* espina dorsal
background (*bæk*-ghraund) *n* fondo
  m; antecedentes *mpl*
backwards (*bæk*-ⁿöds) *adv* hacia atrás
bacon (*bei*-kön) *n* tocino *m*
bacterium (bæk-*tii*-ri-öm) *n* (pl -ria)
  bacteria *f*
bad (bæd) *adj* malo; grave; travieso
bag (bægh) *n* bolsa *f*; bolso *m*, cartera
  f; maleta *f*
baggage (*bæ*-ghidʒ) *n* equipaje *m*; ~
  check *nAm* consigna *f*; **hand** ~ *Am*
  equipaje de mano

bail (beil) *n* fianza *f*
bait (beit) *n* cebo *m*
bake (beik) *v* cocer al horno
baker (*bei*-kö) *n* panadero *m*
bakery (*bei*-kö-ri) *n* panadería *f*
balance (*bæ*-lönss) *n* equilibrio *m*;
  balance *m*; saldo *m*
balcony (*bæl*-kö-ni) *n* balcón *m*
bald (boold) *adj* calvo
ball (bool) *n* pelota *f*; baile *m*
ballet (*bæ*-lei) *n* ballet *m*
balloon (bö-*luun*) *n* globo *m*
ballpoint pen (*bool*-point-pên) *n*
  bolígrafo *m*
ballroom (*bool*-ruum) *n* salón de baile
bamboo (bæm-*buu*) *n* (pl ~s) bambú
  m
banana (bö-*naa*-nö) *n* plátano *m*
band (bænd) *n* orquesta *f*; banda *f*
bandage (*bæn*-didʒ) *n* vendaje *m*
bandit (*bæn*-dit) *n* bandido *m*
bangle (*bæng*-ghöl) *n* pulsera *f*

bank (bængk) *n* orilla *f*; banco *m*; *v*
depositar; **~ account** cuenta
bancaria; **~ rate** descuento bancario

banknote (bængk-nout) *n* billete de
banco

bankrupt (bængk-rapt) *adj* en quiebra

banner (bæ-nö) *n* bandera *f*;
estandarte *m*

banquet (bæng-k^{u}it) *n* banquete *m*

baptism (bæp-ti-söm) *n* bautismo *m*,
bautizo *m*

baptize (bæp-*tais*) *v* bautizar

bar (baa) *n* bar *m*; barra *f*; barrote *m*

barbecue (baa-bi-kyuu) *n* barbacoa *f*;
v cocinar en la barbacoa

barbed wire (baarbd-^{u}ai^ö) alambre *f*
de espino

barber (baa-bö) *n* barbero *m*;
peluquero *m*

bare (bê^ö) *adj* desnudo; raso

barely (bê^ö-li) *adv* apenas

bargain (baa-ghin) *n* ganga *f*; *v*
regatear

baritone (bæ-ri-toun) *n* barítono *m*

bark (baak) *n* corteza *f*; *v* ladrar

barley (baa-li) *n* cebada *f*

barman (baa-mön) *n* (pl -men)
barman *m*

barn (baan) *n* granero *m*

barometer (bö-*ro*-mi-tö) *n* barómetro
m

baroque (bö-*rok*) *adj* barroco

barracks (bæ-rökss) *pl* cuartel *m*

barrel (bæ-röl) *n* tonel *m*, barril *m*

barrier (bæ-ri-ö) *n* barrera *f*

barrister (bæ-ri-sstö) *n* abogado *m*

bartender (baa-tên-dö) *n* barman *m*

base (beiss) *n* base *f*; fundamento *m*; *v*
basar

baseball (beiss-bool) *n* béisbol *m*

basement (beiss-mönt) *n* sótano *m*

basic (bei-ssik) *adj* fundamental; **the
basics** *npl* lo básico, los
fundamentos; **get down to basics**
centrarse en lo esencial

basilica (bö-si-li-kö) *n* basílica *f*

basin (bei-ssön) *n* tazón *m*, palangana
f

basis (bei-ssiss) *n* (pl bases)
fundamento *m*, base *f*

basket (baa-sskit) *n* cesta *f*

bass[1] (beiss) *n* bajo *m*

bass[2] (bæss) *n* (pl ~) perca *f*

bastard (baa-sstöd) *n* bastardo *m*

batch (bæch) *n* carga *f*

bath (baaz) *n* baño *m*; **~ salts** sales de
baño; **~ towel** toalla de baño

bathe (beið) *v* bañarse

bathing cap (bei-ðing-kæp) *n* gorro
de baño

bathing suit (bei-ðing-ssuut) *n* traje
de baño

bathing trunks (bei-ðing-trangkss) *n*
bañador *m*

bathrobe (baaz-roub) *n* bata de baño

bathroom (baaz-ruum) *n* cuarto de
baño; lavabos *mpl*; baño *mMe*

batter (bæ-tö) *n* masa *f*

battery (bæ-tö-ri) *n* batería *f*;
acumulador *m*

battle (bæ-töl) *n* batalla *f*; pelea *f*,
combate *m*; *v* combatir

bay (bei) *n* bahía *f*; *v* aullar

***be** (bii) *v* *estar, *ser

beach (biich) *n* playa *f*; **nudist ~** playa
para nudistas

bead (biid) *n* cuenta *f*; **beads** *pl* collar
m; rosario *m*

beak (biik) *n* pico *m*

beam (biim) *n* rayo *m*; viga *f*

bean (biin) *n* judía *f*; ejote *mMe*

bear (bê^ö) *n* oso *m*

***bear** (bê^ö) *v* llevar; aguantar; soportar

beard (bi^{ö}d) *n* barba *f*

bearer (bê^ö-rö) *n* portador *m*

beast (biisst) *n* animal *m*; **~ of prey**
animal de presa

***beat** (biit) *v* batir, golpear

beautiful (*byuu*-ti-föl) *adj* hermoso

beauty (*byuu*-ti) *n* belleza *f*; ~ **parlo(u)r** salón de belleza; ~ **salon** salón de belleza; ~ **treatment** tratamiento de belleza

beaver (*bii*-vö) *n* castor *m*

because (bi-*kos*) *conj* porque; puesto que; ~ **of** a causa de

***become** (bi-*kam*) *v* *hacerse; *sentar bien

bed (bêd) *n* cama *f*; ~ **and board** pensión completa; ~ **and breakfast** cama y desayuno

bedding (*bê*-ding) *n* ropa de cama

bedroom (*bêd*-ruum) *n* dormitorio *m*

bee (bii) *n* abeja *f*

beech (bii-ch) *n* haya *f*

beef (biif) *n* carne de vaca; **beefburger** hamburguesa *f*

beehive (*bii*-haiv) *n* colmena *f*

been (biin) *v* (pp be)

beer (bi⁰) *n* cerveza *f*

beet (biit) *n* remolacha *f*

beetle (*bii*-töl) *n* escarabajo *m*

beetroot (*biit*-ruut) *n* remolacha *f*

before (bi-*foo*) *prep* antes de; delante de; *conj* antes de que; *adv* antes

beg (bêgh) *v* mendigar; suplicar; *pedir

beggar (*bê*-ghö) *n* mendigo *m*, -a *f*

***begin** (bi-*ghin*) *v* *empezar; *comenzar

beginner (bi-*ghi*-nö) *n* principiante *m*

beginning (bi-*ghi*-ning) *n* comienzo *m*

behalf (bi-*haaf*): **on** ~ **of** en nombre de; a favor de; **on my/his** ~ en nombre mío/suyo

behave (bi-*heiv*) *v* comportarse

behavio(u)r (bi-*hei*-vyö) *n* conducta *f*

behind (bi-*haind*) *prep* detrás de; *adv* detrás

beige (beiჳ) *adj* beige

being (*bii*-ing) *n* ser *m*

Belgian (*bêl*-dჳön) *adj* belga

Belgium (*bêl*-dჳöm) Bélgica *f*

belief (bi-*liif*) *n* creencia *f*

believe (bi-*liiv*) *v* *creer

bell (bêl) *n* campana *f*; timbre *m*

bellboy (*bêl*-boi) *n* botones *mpl*

belly (*bê*-li) *n* vientre *m*; panza *f*

belong (bi-*long*) *v* *pertenecer

belongings (bi-*long*-ings) *pl* pertenencias *fpl*

beloved (bi-*lavd*) *adj* querido

below (bi-*lou*) *prep* debajo de; bajo; *adv* debajo

belt (bêlt) *n* cinturón *m*

bench (bênch) *n* banco *m*

bend (bênd) *n* comba *f*, curva *f*

***bend** (bênd) *v* doblar; ~ **down** bajarse

beneath (bi-*niiz*) *prep* debajo de; *adv* debajo

benefit (*bê*-ni-fit) *n* beneficio *m*; ventaja *f*; *v* aprovechar

bent (bênt) *adj* (pp bend) doblado; torcido

beret (*bê*-rei) *n* boina *f*

berry (*bê*-ri) *n* baya *f*

beside (bi-*ssaid*) *prep* junto a

besides (bi-*ssaids*) *adv* además; por otra parte; *prep* además de

best (bêsst) *adj* óptimo

bet (bêt) *n* apuesta *f*

***bet** (bêt) *v* *apostar

betray (bi-*trei*) *v* traicionar

better (*bê*-tö) *adj* mejor

between (bi-*t"iin*) *prep* entre

beverage (*bê*-vö-ridჳ) *n* bebida *f*

beware (bi-*"e⁰*) *v* precaverse, guardarse

bewitch (bi-*"ich*) *v* hechizar, encantar

beyond (bi-*yond*) *prep* más allá de; además de; *adv* más allá

bible (*bai*-böl) *n* biblia *f*

bicycle (*bai*-ssi-köl) *n* bicicleta *f*; biciclo *m*

bid (bid) *n* puja *f*; intento *m*

*bid (bid) *v* pujar

big (bigh) *adj* grande; voluminoso; gordo; importante

bike (baik) *n colloquial* bici *f*; moto *f*; *v* ir en bici

bile (bail) *n* bilis *f*

bilingual (bai-*ling*-gh^uöl) *adj* bilingüe

bill (bil) *n* cuenta *f*; factura *f*; billete *mAm*; *v* facturar

billiards (*bil*-yöds) *pl* billar *m*

billion (*bil*-yön) mil millones *mpl*, millardo *m*

*bind (baind) *v* atar

binding (*bain*-ding) *n* atadura *f*

binoculars (bi-*no*-kyö-lös) *pl* prismáticos *mpl*; gemelos *mpl*

biology (bai-*o*-lö-dʒi) *n* biología *f*

birch (bööch) *n* abedul *m*

bird (bööd) *n* pájaro *m*

Biro (*bai*-rou) *n* bolígrafo *m*

birth (bööz) *n* nacimiento *m*

birthday (*bööz*-dei) *n* cumpleaños *m*

biscuit (*biss*-kit) *n* galleta *f*; bollo *mAm*

bishop (*bi*-ʃöp) *n* obispo *m*

bit (bit) *n* trozo *m*; poco *m*

bitch (bich) *n* perra *f*

bite (bait) *n* bocado *m*; mordedura *f*; picadura *f*

*bite (bait) *v* *morder

bitter (*bi*-tö) *adj* amargo

black (blæk) *adj* negro; ~ **market** mercado negro

blackberry (*blæk*-bö-ri) *n* mora *f*

blackbird (*blæk*-bööd) *n* mirlo *m*

blackboard (*blæk*-bood) *n* pizarra *f*

blackcurrant (blæk-*ka*-rönt) *n* grosella negra

blackmail (*blæk*-meil) *n* chantaje *m*; *v* *hacer chantaje

blacksmith (*blæk*-ssmiz) *n* herrero *m*

bladder (*blæ*-dö) *n* vejiga *f*

blade (bleid) *n* hoja *f*; ~ **of grass** brizna de hierba

blame (bleim) *n* culpa *f*; reproche *m*; *v* echar la culpa, culpar

blank (blængk) *adj* blanco

blanket (*blæng*-kit) *n* manta *f*

blast (blaasst) *n* explosión *f*

blazer (*blei*-sö) *n* chaqueta de sport, chaqueta ligera

bleach (bliich) *v* blanquear

bleak (bliik) *adj* desolador

*bleed (bliid) *v* sangrar

bless (blêss) *v* *bendecir

blessing (*blê*-ssing) *n* bendición *f*

blind (blaind) *n* persiana *f*; *adj* ciego; *v* *cegar

blinker (*bling*-kö) *nAm* indicador *m*

blister (*bli*-sstö) *n* ampolla *f*

blizzard (*bli*-söd) *n* ventisca *f*

block (blok) *v* *obstruir, bloquear; *n* bloque *m*; ~ **of flats** casa de pisos

blond (blond) *adj* rubio

blonde (blond) *n* rubia *f*

blood (blad) *n* sangre *f*; ~ **poisoning** septicemia *f*; ~ **pressure** tensión arterial; ~ **vessel** vaso sanguíneo

bloody (*bla*-di) *adj* ensangrentado; sangriento; *colloquial* maldito, puñetero; **bloody ~!** ¡ostras!

blossom (*bla*-söm) *n* flores *fpl*; *v* florecer

blot (blot) *n* borrón *m*; mancha *f*; **blotting paper** papel secante

blouse (blaus) *n* blusa *f*

blow (blou) *n* golpe *m*; ráfaga *f*

*blow (blou) *v* soplar; ~ **up** volar; hinchar; ampliar; explotar

blowout (*blou*-aut) *n* reventón *m*

blue (bluu) *adj* azul; deprimido

blunt (blant) *adj* desafilado; directo, abrupto

blush (blaʃ) *v* ruborizarse; *n* rubor *m*, sonrojo *m*

board (bood) *n* tabla *f*; tablero *m*; pensión *f*; consejo *m*; ~ **and lodging**

pensión completa
boarder (*boo-*dö) *n* huésped *m*
boardinghouse (*boo-*ding-hauss) *n* pensión *f*
boarding school (*boo-*ding-sskuul) *n* internado *m*
boast (bousst) *v* presumir
boat (bout) *n* barco *m*, barca *f*
body (*bo-*di) *n* cuerpo *m*
bodyguard (*bo-*di-ghaad) *n* guardaespaldas *m/f*
bog (bogh) *n* pantano *m*
boil (boil) *v* *hervir; *n* forúnculo *m*
bold (bould) *adj* audaz; impertinente, atrevido
Bolivia (bö-*li-*vi-ö) Bolivia *f*
Bolivian (bö-*li-*vi-ön) *adj* boliviano
bolt (boult) *n* cerrojo *m*; perno *m*
bomb (bom) *n* bomba *f*; *v* bombardear
bond (bond) *n* vínculo *m*; obligación *f*
bone (boun) *n* hueso *m*; espina *f*; *v* deshuesar
bonnet (*bo-*nit) *n* capó *m*
book (buk) *n* libro *m*; *v* reservar; inscribir, registrar
booking (*bu-*king) *n* reservación *f*, reserva *f*
bookmaker (*buk-*mei-kö) *n* corredor *m* de apuestas
bookseller (*buk-*ssê-lö) *n* librero *m*, -a *f*
bookstand (*buk-*sstænd) *n* puesto de libros
bookstore (*buk-*sstoo) *n* librería *f*
boot (buut) *n* bota *f*; portaequipajes *m*
booth (buuð) *n* puesto *m*; cabina *f*
booze (buus) *n* *colloquial* bebida *f*, priva *f*
border (*boo-*dö) *n* frontera *f*, borde *m*
bore¹ (boo) *v* aburrir; taladrar; *n* pelmazo *m*
bore² (boo) *v* (p bear)
boring (*boo-*ring) *adj* aburrido
born (boon) *adj* nacido

borrow (*bo-*rou) *v* tomar prestado
bosom (*bu-*söm) *n* pecho *m*; seno *m*
boss (boss) *n* jefe *m*, patrón *m*
botany (*bo-*tö-ni) *n* botánica *f*
both (bouz) *adj* ambos; **both ... and** tanto ... como
bother (*bo-*ðö) *v* fastidiar, molestar; *esforzarse; *n* molestia *f*
bottle (*bo-*töl) *n* botella *f*; **~ opener** destapador de botellas; **hot-water ~** calorífero *m*
bottleneck (*bo-*töl-nêk) *n* atasco de tráfico; atascadero *m*
bottom (*bo-*töm) *n* fondo *m*; trasero *m*; *adj* inferior
bought (boot) *v* (p, pp buy)
boulder (*boul-*dö) *n* pedrón *m*
bound (baund) *n* límite *m*; ***be ~ to** deber de; **~ for** camino de
boundary (*baun-*dö-ri) *n* límite *m*; frontera *f*
bouquet (bu-*kei*) *n* ramo *m*
bourgeois (buᵒ-ʒ'aa) *adj* burgués
boutique (bu-*tiik*) *n* boutique *f*
bow¹ (bau) *v* inclinar
bow² (bou) *n* arco *m*; **~ tie** corbata de lazo, corbatín *m*
bowels (bauᵒls) *pl* intestinos *mpl*
bowl (boul) *n* tazón *m*
bowling (*bou-*ling) *n* bowling *m*, juego de bolos; **~ alley** bolera *f*
box¹ (bokss) *v* boxear; **boxing match** partido de boxeo
box² (bokss) *n* caja *f*
box office (*bokss-*o-fiss) *n* taquilla *f*
boy (boi) *n* muchacho *m*; chico *m*, mozo *m*; sirviente *m*; **~ scout** explorador *m*
boyfriend (*boi-*frênd) novio *m*
bra (braa) *n* sujetador *m*, sostén *m*
bracelet (*breiss-*lit) *n* pulsera *f*
braces (*brei-*ssis) *pl* tirantes *mpl*
brain (brein) *n* cerebro *m*; **~s** inteligencia *f*

brainwave (*brein*-ᵘeiv) *n* inspiración *f*

brake (breik) *n* freno *m*; ~ **drum** tambor del freno; ~ **lights** luces de freno

branch (braanch) *n* rama *f*; sucursal *f*

brand (brænd) *n* marca *f*

brand-new (brænd-*nyuu*) *adj* novísimo

brass (braass) *n* latón *m*; cobre *m*, cobre amarillo; ~ **band** *n* charanga *f*

brave (breiv) *adj* valiente

Brazil (brö-*sil*) Brasil *m*

Brazilian (brö-*sil*-yön) *adj* brasileño

breach (briich) *n* brecha *f*

bread (brêd) *n* pan *m*; **wholemeal** ~ pan integral

breadth (brêdz) *n* ancho *m*

break (breik) *n* fractura *f*; descanso *m*

***break** (breik) *v* *quebrar, quebrantar; ~ **down** averiarse; romperse; detallar, desglosar

breakdown (*breik*-daun) *n* avería *f*, colapso *m*; descompostura *fMe*

breakfast (*brêk*-fösst) *n* desayuno *m*

breast (brêsst) *n* seno *m*

breaststroke (*brêsst*-sstrouk) *n* braza *f*

breath (brêz) *n* aliento *m*; respiración *f*

breathe (briið) *v* respirar

breathing (*brii*-ðing) *n* respiración *f*

breed (briid) *n* raza *f*; especie *f*

***breed** (briid) *v* recriar

breeze (briis) *n* brisa *f*

brew (bruu) *v* fabricar cerveza

brewery (*bruu*-ö-ri) *n* cervecería *f*

bribe (braib) *v* sobornar

bribery (*brai*-bö-ri) *n* soborno *m*

brick (brik) *n* ladrillo *m*

bricklayer (*brik*-leiᵒ) *n* albañil *m*

bride (braid) *n* novia *f*

bridegroom (*braid*-ghruum) *n* novio *m*

bridge (bridȝ) *n* puente *m*; bridge *m*

brief (briif) *adj* breve

briefcase (*briif*-keiss) *n* portafolio *m*; maletín *m*

briefs (briifss) *pl* bragas *f*, calzoncillos *mpl*

bright (brait) *adj* claro; reluciente; listo

brill (bril) *n* rodaballo *m*

brilliant (*bril*-yönt) *adj* brillante

brim (brim) *n* borde *m*

***bring** (bring) *v* *traer; ~ **back** *devolver; ~ **up** educar; *introducir, levantar

brisk (brissk) *adj* enérgico, rápido

Britain (*bri*-tön) Inglaterra *f*

British (*bri*-tiʃ) *adj* británico

Briton (*bri*-tön) *n* británico *m*; inglés *m*

broad (brood) *adj* ancho; amplio; general

***broadcast** (*brood*-kaasst) *n* transmisión *f*

***broadcast** (*brood*-kaasst) *v* emitir

brochure (*brou*-ʃuᵒ) *n* folleto *m*

broke[1] (brouk) *v* (p break)

broke[2] (brouk) *adj* arruinado

broken (*brou*-kön) *adj* (pp break) estropeado, roto

broker (*brou*-kö) *n* corredor *m*, bolsista *m*

bronchitis (brong-*kai*-tiss) *n* bronquitis *f*

bronze (brons) *n* bronce *m*; *adj* de bronce

brooch (brouch) *n* broche *m*

brook (bruk) *n* arroyo *m*

broom (bruum) *n* escoba *f*

brothel (*bro*-zöl) *n* burdel *m*

brother (*bra*-ðö) *n* hermano *m*

brother-in-law (*bra*-ðö-rin-loo) *n* (pl brothers-) cuñado *m*

brought (broot) *v* (p, pp bring)

brown (braun) *adj* marrón

bruise (bruus) *n* moretón *m*,

magulladura f; v magullar

brunette (bruu-nêt) n morena f

brush (braʃ) n cepillo m; brocha f; v sacar brillo, cepillar

brutal (bruu-töl) adj brutal

bubble (ba-böl) n burbuja f

buck (bak) n colloquial dólar m

bucket (ba-kit) n balde m

buckle (ba-köl) n hebilla f

bud (bad) n capullo m

buddy (ba-di) colloquial amigo m, -a f, colega m/f, L.Am. compadre m/f

budget (ba-dʒit) n presupuesto m

buffet (bu-fei) n buffet m

bug (bagh) n chinche f; escarabajo m; nAm insecto m

***build** (bild) v *construir

building (bil-ding) n edificio m

bulb (balb) n bulbo m; **light ~** bombilla f; foco mMe

Bulgaria (bal-ghêº-ri-ö) Bulgaria f

Bulgarian (bal-ghêº-ri-ön) adj búlgaro

bulk (balk) n bulto m; mayoría f

bulky (bal-ki) adj voluminoso

bull (bul) n toro m

bullet (bu-lit) n bala f

bulletin (bu-li-tin) boletín m

bullfight (bul-fait) n corrida de toros

bullring (bul-ring) n plaza de toros

bump (bamp) v topetar; chocar; darse contra; *dar golpes; n golpe m, topetón m

bumper (bam-pö) n parachoques m

bumpy (bam-pi) adj lleno de baches

bun (ban) n bollo m

bunch (banch) n ramo m; grupo m

bundle (ban-döl) n paquete m; v atar, liar

bunk (bangk) n camastro m

buoy (boi) n boya f

burden (böö-dön) n peso m; carga f

bureau (byuº-rou) n (pl ~x, ~s) escritorio m; nAm cómoda f

bureaucracy (byuº-ro-krö-ssi) n burocracia f

burglar (böö-ghlö) n ladrón m, ladrona f

burgle (böö-ghöl) v robar

burial (bê-ri-öl) n entierro m

burn (böön) n quemadura f

***burn** (böön) v quemar; pegarse

***burst** (böösst) v *reventar; *quebrar

bury (bê-ri) v *enterrar

bus (bass) n autobús m

bush (buʃ) n matorral m

business (bis-nöss) n negocios mpl, comercio m; empresa f, negocio m; ocupación f; asunto m; ~ **hours** horas hábiles, horas de oficina; ~ **trip** viaje de negocios; **on ~** por asuntos de negocio

business-like (bis-niss-laik) adj práctico; serio

businessman (bis-nöss-mön) n (pl -men) hombre de negocios

bust (basst) n busto m

bustle (ba-ssöl) n bullicio m

busy (bi-si) adj ocupado; concurrido, atareado

but (bat) conj mas; pero; prep menos

butcher (bu-chö) n carnicero m

butter (ba-tö) n mantequilla f

butterfly (ba-tö-flai) n mariposa f; ~ **stroke** braza de mariposa

buttock (ba-tök) n nalga f

button (ba-tön) n botón m; v abrochar

buttonhole (ba-tön-houl) n ojal m

buzz (bas) n zumbido m; v zumbar; llamar por el interfono

***buy** (bai) v comprar; *adquirir

buyer (bai-ö) n comprador m, -a f

by (bai) prep por; con; cerca de

by-pass (bai-paass) n desviación f; v evitar; pasar por alto

C

cab (kæb) *n* taxi *m*; ~ **driver** taxista *m/f*

cabaret (kæ-bö-rei) *n* cabaret *m*

cabbage (kæ-bidʒ) *n* col *m*

cabin (kæ-bin) *n* cabina *f*; cabaña *f*

cabinet (kæ-bi-nöt) *n* gabinete *m*

cable (kei-böl) *n* cable *m*

café (kæ-fei) *n* cafetería *f*, café *m*

cafeteria (kæ-fö-ti°-ri-ö) *n* cafetería *f*

caffeine (kæ-fiin) *n* cafeína *f*

cage (keidʒ) *n* jaula *f*

cake (keik) *n* pastel *m*; pastelería *f*, tarta *f*, dulces; **sponge** ~ bizcocho *m*

calamity (kö-læ-mö-ti) *n* calamidad *f*; desastre *m*, catástrofe *f*

calcium (kæl-ssi-öm) *n* calcio *m*

calculate (kæl-kyu-leit) *v* calcular

calculation (kæl-kyu-lei-ʃön) *n* cálculo *m*

calculator (kæl-kyu-lei-tö) *n* calculadora *f*

calendar (kæ-lön-dö) *n* calendario *m*

calf (kaaf) *n* (pl calves) ternero *m*; pantorrilla *f*; ~ **skin** becerro *m*

call (kool) *v* llamar; *n* llamada *f*; visita *f*; *be called llamarse; ~ names insultar; ~ off cancelar; ~ on visitar; ~ up Am telefonear; ; **long-distance** ~ conferencia interurbana

calm (kaam) *adj* tranquilo; ~ **down** calmar

calorie (kæ-lö-ri) *n* caloría *f*

Calvinism (kæl-vi-ni-söm) *n* calvinismo *m*

came (keim) *v* (p come)

camel (kæ-möl) *n* camello *m*

cameo (kæ-mi-ou) *n* (pl ~s) camafeo *m*

camera (kæ-mö-rö) *n* cámara fotográfica; cámara *f*; ~ **shop** negocio fotográfico

camp (kæmp) *n* campamento *m*; *v* acampar; ~ **bed** catre de campaña, cama de tijera

campaign (kæm-pein) *n* campaña *f*

camper (kæm-pö) *n* acampador *m*

camping (kæm-ping) *n* camping *m*; ~ **site** camping *m*, lugar de camping

can (kæn) *n* lata *f*; bote *m*; ~ **opener** abrelatas *m*

***can** (kæn) *v* *poder

Canada (kæ-nö-dö) Canadá *m*

Canadian (kö-nei-di-ön) *adj* canadiense

canal (kö-næl) *n* canal *m*

canary (kö-nê°-ri) *n* canario *m*

cancel (kæn-ssöl) *v* cancelar; anular

cancellation (kæn-ssö-lei-ʃön) *n* cancelación *f*

cancer (kæn-ssö) *n* cáncer *m*

candidate (kæn-di-döt) *n* candidato *m*, interesado *m*

candle (kæn-döl) *n* vela *f*; candela *f*

candy (kæn-di) *nAm* bombón *m*; dulces, golosinas

cane (kein) *n* caña *f*; bastón *m*

canister (kæ-ni-sstö) *n* caja metálica, lata *f*

canoe (kö-nuu) *n* canoa *f*

canteen (kæn-tiin) *n* cantina *f*

canvas (kæn-vöss) *n* lona *f*

cap (kæp) *n* gorra *f*, gorro *m*

capable (kei-pö-böl) *adj* capaz

capacity (kö-pæ-ssö-ti) *n* capacidad *f*; potencia *f*; competencia *f*

cape (keip) *n* capa *f*; cabo *m*

capital (kæ-pi-töl) *n* capital *f*; capital *m*; *adj* importante, capital; ~ **letter** mayúscula *f*

capitalism (kæ-pi-tö-li-söm) *n* capitalismo *m*

capitulation (kö-pi-tyu-lei-ʃön) *n* capitulación *f*

capsule (kæp-ssyuul) *n* cápsula *f*

captain (kæp-tin) *n* capitán *m*;

comandante *m*

capture (*kæp*-chö) *v* coger preso, capturar; conquistar; *n* captura *f*; conquista *f*

car (kaa) *n* coche *m*; carro *mMe*; ~ **hire** alquiler de coches; ~ **park** parque de estacionamiento; aparcamiento *m*

caramel (*kæ*-rö-möl) *n* caramelo *m*

carat (*kæ*-röt) *n* quilate *m*

caravan (*kæ*-rö-væn) *n* caravana *f*; remolque *m*

carburet(t)or (kaa-byu-*rê*-tö) *n* carburador *m*

card (kaad) *n* tarjeta *f*; tarjeta postal

cardboard (*kaad*-bood) *n* cartón *m*; *adj* de cartón

cardigan (*kaa*-di-ghön) *n* chaqueta *f* de punto

cardinal (*kaa*-di-nöl) *n* cardenal *m*; *adj* cardinal, principal

care (kê⁰) *n* cuidado *m*; ~ **about** preocuparse de; ~ **for** gustar; *take ~ of** cuidar de

career (kö-*ri⁰*) *n* carrera *f*

carefree (*kê⁰*-frii) *adj* despreocupado

careful (*kê⁰*-föl) *adj* cuidadoso; escrupuloso

careless (*kê⁰*-löss) *adj* descuidado; indiferente; negligente

caretaker (*kê⁰*-tei-kö) *n* guardián *m*

cargo (*kaa*-ghou) *n* (pl ~es) carga *f*

carnival (*kaa*-ni-völ) *n* carnaval *m*

carp (kaap) *n* (pl ~) carpa *f*

carpenter (*kaa*-pin-tö) *n* carpintero *m*

carpet (*kaa*-pit) *n* alfombra *f*

carriage (*kæ*-ridʒ) *n* vagón *m*; coche *m*, carruaje *m*; **baby ~** *Am* cochecillo de niño

carriageway (*kæ*-ridʒ-ᵘei) *n* calzada *f*

carrot (*kæ*-röt) *n* zanahoria *f*

carry (*kæ*-ri) *v* llevar; *conducir; ~ **on** continuar; *proseguir; ~ **out** realizar

carrycot (*kæ*-ri-kot) *n* cuna de viaje

cart (kaat) *n* carro *m*

carton (*kaa*-tön) *n* caja de cartón; cartón *m*

cartoon (kaa-*tuun*) *n* dibujos animados

cartridge (*kaa*-tridʒ) *n* cartucho *m*

carve (kaav) *v* trinchar; entallar, tallar

carving (*kaa*-ving) *n* talla *f*

case (keiss) *n* caso *m*; causa *f*; valija *f*; estuche *m*; funda *f*; **attaché ~** portafolio *m*; **in ~ of** en caso de; **just in ~** por si acaso

cash (kæʃ) *n* dinero contante, efectivo *m*; *v* cobrar; *hacer efectivo; ~ **dispenser** cajero automático

cashier (kæ-*ʃi⁰*) *n* cajero *m*; cajera *f*

cashmere (*kæʃ*-mi⁰) *n* cachemira *f*

casino (kö-*ssii*-nou) *n* casino *m*

cask (kaassk) *n* barril *m*, tonel *m*

cassette (kö-*sset*) *n* cinta *f*, casete *f*

cast (kaasst) *n* echada *f*; molde *m*; reparto *m*

***cast** (kaasst) *v* lanzar; **cast iron** hierro fundido

castle (*kaa*-ssöl) *n* castillo *m*

casual (*kæ*-ʒu-öl) *adj* informal; de paso, por casualidad

casualty (*kæ*-ʒu-öl-ti) *n* víctima *f*

cat (kæt) *n* gato *m*

catacomb (*kæ*-tö-koum) *n* catacumba *f*

catalogue (*kæ*-tö-logh) *n* catálogo *m*

catarrh (kö-*taa*) *n* catarro *m*

catastrophe (kö-*tæ*-sströ-fi) *n* catástrofe *f*

***catch** (kætʃ) *v* coger; sorprender

category (*kæ*-ti-ghö-ri) *n* categoría *f*

cathedral (kö-*zii*-dröl) *n* catedral *f*

catholic (*kæ*-ʒö-lik) *adj* católico

cattle (*kæ*-töl) *pl* ganado *m*

caught (koot) *v* (p, pp catch)

cauliflower (*ko*-li-flau⁰) *n* coliflor *f*

cause (koos) *v* causar; provocar; *n* causa *f*; motivo *m*; ~ **to** *hacer

causeway (*koos*-ᵘei) *n* calzada *f*

caution (*koo*-ʃön) *n* cautela *f*; *v*
*advertir

cautious (*koo*-ʃöss) *adj* cauteloso,
cauto

cave (keiv) *n* cueva *f*; grieta *f*

cavern (*kæ*-vön) *n* caverna *f*

caviar (*kæ*-vi-aa) *n* caviar *m*

cavity (*kæ*-vö-ti) *n* cavidad *f*

cease (ssiiss) *v* cesar

cease-fire *n* (*ssiiss*- faiö) alto *m* el
fuego

ceiling (*ssii*-ling) *n* techo *m*, cielo raso
m

celebrate (*ssê*-li-breit) *v* celebrar

celebration (ssê-li-*brei*-ʃön) *n*
celebración *f*

celebrity (ssi-*lê*-brö-ti) *n* celebridad *f*

celery (*ssê*-lö-ri) *n* apio *m*

cell (ssêl) *n* celda *f*; célula *f*

cellar (*ssê*-lö) *n* sótano *m*

cement (ssi-*mênt*) *n* cemento *m*

cemetery (*ssê*-mi-tri) *n* cementerio *m*

censorship (*ssên*-ssö-ʃip) *n* censura *f*

center (*ssên*-tö) *n* centro *m*

centigrade (*ssên*-ti-ghreid) *adj*
centígrado

centimetre (*ssên*-ti-mii-tö) *n*
centímetro *m*

central (*ssên*-tröl) *adj* central; ~
heating calefacción central; ~
station estación central

centralize (*ssên*-trö-lais) *v* centralizar

centre (*ssên*-tö) *n* centro *m*

century (*ssên*-chö-ri) *n* siglo *m*

ceramics (ssi-*ræ*-mikss) *pl* cerámica *f*

ceremony (*ssê*-rö-mö-ni) *n* ceremonia
f

certain (*ssöö*-tön) *adj* cierto; **certainly**
adv ciertamente, por cierto;
certainly not! ¡por supuesto que no!

certificate (ssö-*ti*-fi-köt) *n* certificado
m; certificación *f*, acta *f*, diploma *m*

chain (chein) *n* cadena *f*

chair (chêö) *n* silla *f*

chairman (*chê*ö-mön) *n* (pl -men)
presidente *m*

chalet (ʃæ-lei) *n* chalet *m*

chalk (chook) *n* creta *f*

challenge (*chæ*-löndʒ) *v* desafiar; *n*
reto *m*, desafío *m*

chamber (*cheim*-bö) *n* cámara *f*;
recámara *f*

champagne (ʃæm-*pein*) *n* champán *m*

champion (*chæm*-pyön) *n* campeón
m, campeona *f*; abanderado *m*, -a *f*

chance (chaanss) *n* azar *m*; casualidad
f, ocasión *f*; riesgo *m*; suerte *f*;
oportunidad *f*; **by** ~ por casualidad

change (cheindʒ) *v* modificar,
cambiar; mudarse; *hacer trasbordo;
n modificación *f*, cambio *m*; moneda
f

channel (*chæ*-nöl) *n* canal *m*; **English
Channel** Canal de la Mancha

chaos (*kei*-oss) *n* caos *m*

chaotic (kei-*o*-tik) *adj* caótico

chap (chæp) *n* tipo *m*, chico *m*, tío *m*

chapel (*chæ*-pöl) *n* capilla *f*

chaplain (*chæ*-plin) *n* capellán *m*

character (*kæ*-rök-tö) *n* carácter *m*

characteristic (kæ-rök-tö-*ri*-sstik) *adj*
típico, característico; *n* característica
f; rasgo característico

characterize (*kæ*-rök-tö-rais) *v*
caracterizar

charcoal (*chaa*-koul) *n* carbón de leña

charge (chaadʒ) *v* *pedir; cargar;
acusar; *n* precio *m*; carga *f*; acusación
f; **free of** ~ gratuito; **in** ~ **of**
encargado de; ***take** ~ **of** encargarse
de

charity (*chæ*-rö-ti) *n* caridad *f*

charm (chaam) *n* encanto *m*; amuleto
m

charming (*chaa*-ming) *adj* encantador

chart (chaat) *n* tabla *f*; gráfico *m*; carta
marina; **conversion** ~ tabla de
conversión

chase (cheiss) v cazar; expulsar, ahuyentar; perseguir; n caza f

chasm (kæ-söm) n grieta f

chassis (ʃæ-ssi) n (pl ∼) chasis m

chaste (cheisst) adj casto

chat (chæt) v charlar; n charla f

chatterbox (chæ-tö-bokss) n charlador(a) m/f; parlanchín(ina) m/f

chauffeur (ʃou-fö) n chófer m

cheap (chiip) adj barato; económico

cheat (chiit) v engañar; estafar

check (chêk) v controlar, verificar; n escaque m; nAm cuenta f; cheque m; **check!** ¡jaque!; ∼ **in** inscribirse; ∼ **out** *despedirse

checkbook (chêk-buk) nAm talonario m

checkerboard (chê-kö-bood) nAm tablero de damas

checkroom (chêk-ruum) nAm guardarropa m

checkup (chê-kap) n reconocimiento m

cheek (chiik) n mejilla f

cheekbone (chiik-boun) n pómulo m

cheer (chiᵒ) v aclamar; alentar; ∼ **up** alegrar

cheerful (chiᵒ-föl) adj alegre

cheese (chiis) n queso m

chef (ʃêf) n jefe de cocina

chemical (kê-mi-köl) adj químico

chemist (kê-misst) n farmacéutico m; **chemist's** farmacia f; droguería f

chemistry (kê-mi-sstri) n química f

cheque (chêk) n cheque m

chequebook (chêk-buk) n talonario m

chequered (chê-köd) adj a cuadros, cuadriculado

cherry (chê-ri) n cereza f

chess (chêss) n ajedrez m

chest (chêsst) n pecho m; arca f; cofre m; ∼ **of drawers** cómoda f

chestnut (chêss-nat) n castaña f

chew (chuu) v masticar

chewing gum (chuu-ing-gham) n goma de mascar, chicle m

chic (ʃik) adj elegante

chicken (chi-kin) n pollo m

chickenpox (chi-kin-pokss) n varicela f

chief (chiif) n jefe m; adj principal

chiefly (chiif-li) adv sobre todo

chieftain (chiif-tön) n cacique m

child (chaild) n (pl children) niño m, niña f

childbirth (chaild-bööz) n parto m

childhood (chaild-hud) n infancia f

Chile (chi-li) Chile m

Chilean (chi-li-ön) adj chileno m

chill (chil) n escalofrío m

chilly (chi-li) adj fresco

chimes (chaims) pl carillón m

chimney (chim-ni) n chimenea f

chin (chin) n barbilla f

China (chai-nö) China f

china (chai-nö) n porcelana f

Chinese (chai-niis) adj chino

chip (chip) n astilla f; ficha f; v cortar, astillar; **chips** patatas fritas

chisel (chi-söl) n cincel m

chives (chaivs) pl cebollino m

chlorine (kloo-riin) n cloro m

chocolate (cho-klöt) n chocolate m

choice (choiss) n elección f; selección f

choir (kᵘaiᵒ) n coro m

choke (chouk) v sofocarse; estrangular; n starter m

***choose** (chuus) v escoger

chop (chop) n chuleta f; v tajar

Christ (kraisst) Cristo

christen (kri-ssön) v bautizar

christening (kri-ssö-ning) n bautizo m

Christian (kriss-chön) adj cristiano; ∼ **name** nombre de pila

Christmas (kriss-möss) Navidad f

chromium (*krou*-mi-öm) *n* cromo *m*

chronic (*kro*-nik) *adj* crónico

chronological (kro-nö-*lo*-dʒi-köl) *adj* cronológico

chuckle (*cha*-köl) *v* *reírse entre dientes

chunk (changk) *n* trozo *m*; pedazo *m*

church (chööch) *n* iglesia *f*

churchyard (*chööch*-yaad) *n* cementerio *m*

cigar (ssi-*ghaa*) *n* puro *m*; cigarro *m*; ~ **shop** estanco *m*

cigarette (ssi-ghö-*rêt*) *n* cigarrillo *m*; ~ **lighter** encendedor *m*; ~ **tobacco** picadura *f*

cinema (*ssi*-nö-mö) *n* cinematógrafo *m*

cinnamon (*ssi*-nö-mön) *n* canela *f*

circle (*ssöö*-köl) *n* círculo *m*; balcón *m*; *v* rodear, circundar

circulation (ssöö-kyu-*lei*-ʃön) *n* circulación *f*; circulación de la sangre

circumstance (*ssöö*-köm-sstænss) *n* circunstancia *f*

circus (*ssöö*-köss) *n* circo *m*

citizen (*ssi*-ti-sön) *n* ciudadano *m*, -a *f*

citizenship (*ssi*-ti-sön-ʃip) *n* ciudadanía *f*

city (*ssi*-ti) *n* ciudad *f*

civic (*ssi*-vik) *adj* cívico

civil (*ssi*-völ) *adj* civil; cortés; ~ **law** derecho civil; ~ **servant** funcionario *m*

civilian (ssi-*vil*-yön) *adj* civil; *n* paisano *m*

civilization (ssi-vö-lai-*sei*-ʃön) *n* civilización *f*

civilized (*ssi*-vö-laisd) *adj* civilizado

claim (kleim) *v* reivindicar, reclamar; afirmar; *n* reivindicación *f*, pretensión *f*

clamp (klæmp) *n* mordaza *f*; grapa *f*

clap (klæp) *v* aplaudir

clarify (*klæ*-ri-fai) *v* aclarar, clarificar

class (klaass) *n* clase *f*

classical (*klæ*-ssi-köl) *adj* clásico

classify (*klæ*-ssi-fai) *v* clasificar

classmate (*klaass*-meit) *n* compañero *m*, -a *f* de clase

classroom (*klaass*-ruum) *n* clase *f*

clause (kloos) *n* cláusula *f*

claw (kloo) *n* garra *f*

clay (klei) *n* arcilla *f*

clean (kliin) *adj* puro, limpio; *v* limpiar

cleaning (*klii*-ning) *n* limpieza *f*; ~ **fluid** quitamanchas *m*

clear (kli⁰) *adj* claro; *v* limpiar

clearing (*kli⁰*-ring) *n* claro *m*

cleft (klêft) *n* grieta *f*

clergyman (*klöö*-dʒi-mön) *n* (pl -men) pastor *m*; clérigo *m*

clerk (klaak) *n* oficinista *m/f*; dependiente *m*, -a *f*

clever (*klê*-vö) *adj* inteligente; astuto, listo

click (klik) *n* clic *m*; *v* hacer clic

client (*klai*-önt) *n* cliente *m*

cliff (klif) *n* acantilado *m*, farallón *m*

climate (*klai*-mit) *n* clima *m*

climb (klaim) *v* trepar; *n* subida *f*

*cling (kling) *v* adherirse; pegarse al cuerpo

clinic (*kli*-nik) *n* clínica *f*

cloak (klouk) *n* capa *f*; manto *m*

cloakroom (*klouk*-ruum) *n* guardarropa *m*

clock (klok) *n* reloj *m*; **at ... o'clock** a las ...

cloister (*kloi*-sstö) *n* claustro *m*

close[1] (klous) *v* *cerrar

close[2] (klouss) *adj* cercano

closet (*klo*-sit) *n* armario *m*; ropero *m*

cloth (kloz) *n* tela *f*; paño *m*

clothes (klouðs) *pl* ropa *f*, vestidos *mpl*

clothing (*klou*-ðing) *n* ropa *f*

cloud (klaud) *n* nube *f*

cloudy (*klau*-di) *adj* cubierto, nublado

clover (*klou*-vö) *n* trébol *m*
clown (klaun) *n* payaso *m*
club (klab) *n* club *m*; círculo *m*,
asociación *f*; porra *f*, garrote *m*
clumsy (*klam*-si) *adj* torpe
clutch (klach) *n* embrague *m*; apretón
m
coach (kouch) *n* autobús *m*; vagón *m*;
carroza *f*; entrenador *m*, -a *f*
coal (koul) *n* carbón *m*
coarse (kooss) *adj* burdo; grosero
coast (kousst) *n* costa *f*
coat (kout) *n* sobretodo *m*, abrigo *m*
coathanger (*kout*-hæng-ö) *n* percha *f*
cocaine (kou-*kein*) *n* cocaína *f*
cock (kok) *n* gallo *m*
cocktail (*kok*-teil) *n* cóctel *m*
coconut (*kou*-kö-nat) *n* coco *m*
cod (kod) *n* (pl ~) bacalao *m*
code (koud) *n* código *m*
coffee (*ko*-fi) *n* café *m*; ~ **shop** *n* café
m
cognac (*ko*-nyæk) *n* coñac *m*
coherence (kou-*hiᵒ*-rönss) *n*
coherencia *f*
coin (koin) *n* moneda *f*
coincide (kou-in-*ssaid*) *v* coincidir
cold (kould) *adj* frío; *n* frío *m*;
resfriado *m*; **catch a ~** resfriarse
collaborate (kö-*læ*-bö-reit) *v*
colaborar
collapse (kö-*læpss*) *v* desplomarse,
derrumbarse
collar (*ko*-lö) *n* collar *m*; cuello *m*; ~
stud botón del cuello
collarbone (*ko*-lö-boun) *n* clavícula *f*
colleague (*ko*-liigh) *n* colega *m/f*
collect (kö-*lêkt*) *v* juntar; recoger;
coleccionar; *hacer una colecta
collection (kö-*lêk*-ʃön) *n* colección *f*;
recogida *f*
collective (kö-*lêk*-tiv) *adj* colectivo
collector (kö-*lêk*-tö) *n* coleccionista
m; colector *m*

college (*ko*-lidʒ) *n* colegio *m*;
universidad *f*
collide (kö-*laid*) *v* chocar
collision (kö-*li*-ʒön) *n* colisión *f*
Colombia (kö-*lom*-bi-ö) Colombia *f*
Colombian (kö-*lom*-bi-ön) *adj*
colombiano
colonel (*köö*-nöl) *n* coronel *m*
colony (*ko*-lö-ni) *n* colonia *f*
colo(u)r (*ka*-lö) *n* color *m*; *v* colorear;
~ **film** película en colores
colo(u)r-blind (*ka*-lö-blaind) *adj*
daltoniano
colo(u)red (*ka*-löd) *adj* de color
colo(u)rful (*ka*-lö-föl) *adj* colorado,
lleno de color
column (*ko*-löm) *n* columna *f*
coma (*kou*-mö) *n* coma *m*
comb (koum) *v* peinar; *n* peine *m*
combat (*kom*-bæt) *n* lucha *f*, combate
m; *v* combatir
combination (kom-bi-*nei*-ʃön) *n*
combinación *f*
combine (köm-*bain*) *v* combinar; unir
*come (kam) *v* *venir; ~ **across**
*encontrar; hallar
comedian (kö-*mii*-di-ön) *n* humorista
m/f; cómico *m*, -a *f*
comedy (*ko*-mö-di) *n* comedia *f*;
musical ~ comedia musical
comfort (*kam*-föt) *n* comodidad *f*,
confort *m*; consuelo *m*; *v* *consolar
comfortable (*kam*-fö-tö-böl) *adj*
confortable
comic (*ko*-mik) *adj* cómico
comics (*ko*-mikss) *pl* tebeo *m*
coming (*ka*-ming) *n* llegada *f*
comma (*ko*-mö) *n* coma *f*
command (kö-*maand*) *v* mandar; *n*
orden *f*
commander (kö-*maan*-dö) *n*
comandante *m*
commemoration (kö-mê-mö-*rei*-ʃön)
n conmemoración *f*

commence (kö-*mênss*) v *comenzar

comment (*ko*-mênt) n comentario m; v comentar

commerce (*ko*-mööss) n comercio m

commercial (kö-*möö*-ʃöl) adj comercial; n anuncio publicitario; ~ **law** derecho comercial

commission (kö-*mi*-ʃön) n comisión f

commit (kö-*mit*) v confiar, entregar; cometer

committee (kö-*mi*-ti) n comisión f, comité m

common (*ko*-mön) adj común; usual; ordinario

commune (*ko*-myuun) n comuna f

communicate (kö-*myuu*-ni-keit) v comunicar

communication (kö-myuu-ni-*kei*-ʃön) n comunicación f

communiqué (kö-*myuu*-ni-kei) n comunicado m

communism (*ko*-myu-ni-söm) n comunismo m

community (kö-*myuu*-nö-ti) n sociedad f, vecindario m

commuter (kö-*myuu*-tö) n viajero m, -a f (al trabajo)

compact (*kom*-pækt) adj compacto

compact disc (*kom*-pækt dissk) n disco compacto m; ~ **player** reproductor de discos compactos

companion (köm-*pæ*-nyön) n compañero m, -a f

company (*kam*-pö-ni) n compañía f; sociedad f

comparative (köm-*pæ*-rö-tiv) adj relativo

compare (köm-*pê*ᵒ) v comparar

comparison (köm-*pæ*-ri-ssön) n comparación f

compartment (köm-*paat*-mönt) n compartimento m

compass (*kam*-pöss) n brújula f

compel (köm-*pêl*) v compeler

compensate (*kom*-pön-sseit) v compensar

compensation (kom-pön-*ssei*-ʃön) n compensación f; indemnización f

compete (köm-*piit*) v *competir

competition (kom-pö-*ti*-ʃön) n concurso m; competencia f

competitor (köm-*pê*-ti-tör) n competidor m

compile (köm-*pail*) v compilar

complain (köm-*plein*) v quejarse

complaint (köm-*pleint*) n queja f

complete (köm-*pliit*) adj completo; v completar

completely (köm-*pliit*-li) adv enteramente, totalmente, completamente

complex (*kom*-plêkss) n complejo m; adj complejo

complexion (köm-*plêk*-ʃön) n tez f

complicated (*kom*-pli-kei-tid) adj complicado

compliment (*kom*-pli-mönt) n cumplido m; piropo m; v cumplimentar

compose (köm-*pous*) v *componer

composer (köm-*pou*-sö) n compositor m, -a f

composition (kom-pö-*si*-ʃön) n composición f

comprehensive (kom-pri-*hên*-ssiv) adj extenso

comprise (köm-*prais*) v comprender

compromise (*kom*-prö-mais) n compromiso m

compulsory (köm-*pal*-ssö-ri) adj obligatorio

computer (köm-*pyu*-tö) n ordenador m

comrade (*kom*-reid) n camarada m

conceal (kön-*ssiil*) v disimular; ocultar

conceited (kön-*ssii*-tid) adj presuntuoso

conceive (kön-*ssiiv*) v *concebir, *entender; imaginar

concentrate (*kon*-ssön-treit) v concentrarse

concentration (kon-ssön-*trei*-ʃön) n concentración f

concern (kön-*ssöön*) v *concernir, atañer; n preocupación f; asunto m; empresa f, consorcio m

concerned (kön-*ssöönd*) adj preocupado; interesado

concerning (kön-*ssöö*-ning) prep en lo que se refiere a: acerca de

concert (*kon*-ssöt) n concierto m; ~ **hall** sala de conciertos

concession (kön-*ssê*-ʃön) n concesión f

concierge (koñg-ssi-*ê⁰*ʒ) n conserje m

concise (kön-*ssaiss*) adj conciso

conclusion (köng-*kluu*-ʒön) n conclusión f

concrete (*kong*-kriit) adj concreto; n hormigón m

concurrence (köng-*ka*-rönss) n conformidad f

concussion (köng-*ka*-ʃön) n conmoción cerebral

condemn (kön-*dêm*) v condenar

condition (kön-*di*-ʃön) n condición f; estado m; circunstancia f

conditional (kön-*di*-ʃö-nöl) adj condicional

conditioner (kön-*di*-ʃö-nö) n suavizante de cabello m

condom (*kon*-dom) n preservativo m

conduct (*kon*-dakt) n conducta f

conductor (kön-*dak*-tö) n director m, -a f de orquesta; revisor m, -a f; conductor m

conference (*kon*-fö-rönss) n conferencia f

confess (kön-*fêss*) v *reconocer; *confesarse; profesar

confession (kön-*fê*-ʃön) n confesión f

confidence (*kon*-fi-dönss) n confianza f

confident (*kon*-fi-dönt) adj lleno de confianza; seguro

confidential (kon-fi-*dên*-ʃöl) adj confidencial

confirm (kön-*fööm*) v confirmar

confirmation (kon-fö-*mei*-ʃön) n confirmación f

confiscate (*kon*-fi-sskeit) v embargar, confiscar

conflict (*kon*-flikt) n conflicto m

confuse (kön-*fyuus*) v confundir; **confused** adj confuso

confusion (kön-*fyuu*-ʒön) n confusión f

congratulate (köng-*ghræ*-chu-leit) v felicitar

congratulation (köng-ghræ-chu-*lei*-ʃön) n felicitación f

congregation (köng-ghri-*ghei*-ʃön) n comunidad f, congregación f

congress (*kong*-ghrêss) n congreso m

connect (kö-*nêkt*) v conectar

connection (kö-*nêk*-ʃön) n relación f; conexión f; enlace m

connoisseur (ko-nö-*ssöö*) n perito m

connotation (ko-nö-*tei*-ʃön) n connotación f

conquer (*kong*-kö) v conquistar; vencer

conqueror (*kong*-kö-rö) n conquistador m

conquest (*kong*-kⁿêsst) n conquista f

conscience (*kon*-ʃönss) n conciencia f

conscious (*kon*-ʃöss) adj consciente

consciousness (*kon*-ʃöss-nöss) n conciencia f

conscript (*kon*-sskript) n quinto m

consent (kön-*ssênt*) v *consentir; n consentimiento m

consequence (*kon*-ssi-kⁿönss) n consecuencia f

consequently (*kon*-ssi-k^uönt-li) *adv*
por consiguiente

conservative (kön-*ssöö*-vö-tiv) *adj*
conservador

consider (kön-*ssi*-dö) *v* considerar;
opinar

considerable (kön-*ssi*-dö-rö-böl) *adj*
considerable; importante, notable

considerate (kön-*ssi*-dö-röt) *adj*
considerado; respetuoso

consideration (kön-ssi-dö-*rei*-ʃön) *n*
consideración *f*; atención *f*

considering (kön-*ssi*-dö-ring) *prep*
considerando

consignment (kön-*ssain*-mönt) *n*
envío *m*

consist of (kön-*ssisst*) constar de

conspire (kön-*sspai*^ö) *v* conspirar

constant (*kon*-sstönt) *adj* constante

constipation (kon-ssti-*pei*-ʃön) *n*
estreñimiento *m*

constituency (kön-*ssti*-chu-ön-ssi) *n*
distrito electoral

constitution (kon-ssti-*tyuu*-ʃön) *n*
constitución *f*

construct (kön-*sstrakt*) *v* *construir;
edificar

construction (kön-*sstrak*-ʃön) *n*
construcción *f*; edificio *m*

consul (*kon*-ssöl) *n* cónsul *m*

consulate (*kon*-ssyu-löt) *n* consulado
m

consult (kön-*ssalt*) *v* consultar

consultation (kon-ssöl-*tei*-ʃön) *n*
consulta *f*; ~ **hours** *n* horas de
consulta

consume (kön-*ssyuum*) *v* consumir

consumer (kön-*ssyuu*-mö) *n*
consumidor *m*, -a *f*

contact (*kon*-tækt) *n* contacto *m*; *v*
*ponerse en contacto con; ~ **lenses**
lentillas *fpl*

contagious (kön-*tei*-dʒöss) *adj*
contagioso

contain (kön-*tein*) *v* *contener;
comprender

container (kön-*tei*-nö) *n* recipiente *m*;
contenedor *m*

contemporary (kön-*têm*-pö-rö-ri) *adj*
contemporáneo; de entonces; *n*
contemporáneo *m*

contempt (kön-*têmpt*) *n* desprecio *m*,
menosprecio *m*

content (kön-*tênt*) *adj* contento

contents (*kon*-têntss) *pl* contenido *m*

contest (*kon*-têsst) *n* lucha *f*; concurso
m

continent (*kon*-ti-nönt) *n* continente
m

continental (kon-ti-*nên*-töl) *adj*
continental

continual (kön-*ti*-nyu-öl) *adj* continuo

continue (kön-*ti*-nyuu) *v* continuar;
*proseguir, durar

continuous (kön-*ti*-nyu-öss) *adj*
continuo, ininterrumpido

contour (*kon*-tu^ö) *n* contorno *m*

contraceptive (kon-trö-*ssêp*-tiv) *n*
anticonceptivo *m*

contract[1] (*kon*-trækt) *n* contrato *m*

contract[2] (kön-*trækt*) *v* atrapar

contractor (kön-*træk*-tö) *n* contratista
m/f; **building** ~ constructora *f*

contradict (kon-trö-*dikt*) *v*
*contradecir

contradictory (kon-trö-*dik*-tö-ri) *adj*
contradictorio

contrary (*kon*-trö-ri) *n* contrario *m*;
adj contrario; **on the** ~ al contrario

contrast (*kon*-traasst) *n* contraste *m*;
diferencia *f*

contribution (kon-tri-*byuu*-ʃön) *n*
contribución *f*

control (kön-*troul*) *n* control *m*; *v*
controlar

controversial (kon-trö-*vöö*-ʃöl) *adj*
controvertido, controvertible

convenience (kön-*vii*-nyönss) *n*

comodidad f

convenient (kön-*vii*-nyönt) *adj* cómodo; adecuado, conveniente

convent (*kon*-vönt) *n* convento *m*

conversation (kon-vö-*ssei*-ʃön) *n* conversación f

convert (kön-*vööt*) *v* *convertir

convict[1] (kön-*vikt*) *v* condenar

convict[2] (*kon*-vikt) *n* condenado *m*

conviction (kön-*vik*-ʃön) *n* convencimiento *m*; condena f

convince (kön-*vinss*) *v* convencer

convulsion (kön-*val*-ʃön) *n* convulsión f

cook (kuk) *n* cocinero *m*; *v* cocinar; guisar, preparar comidas

cooker (*ku*-kö) *n* cocina f; **gas ~** cocina de gas

cook(ery) book (*ku*-kö-ri-buk) *n* libro de cocina

cookie (*ku*-ki) *nAm* galleta f

cool (kuul) *adj* fresco

cooperation (kou-o-pö-*rei*-ʃön) *n* cooperación f; colaboración f

cooperative (kou-o-pö-rö-tiv) *adj* cooperativo; cooperador; *n* cooperativa f

coordinate (kou-*oo*-di-neit) *v* coordinar

coordination (kou-oo-di-*nei*-ʃön) *n* coordinación f

cope (koup) *v* arreglárselas; **~ with** poder con

copper (*ko*-pö) *n* cobre *m*

copy (*ko*-pi) *n* copia f; ejemplar *m*; *v* copiar; imitar; **carbon ~** copia f

coral (*ko*-röl) *n* coral *m*

cord (kood) *n* cuerda f; cordón *m*

cordial (*koo*-di-öl) *adj* cordial

corduroy (*koo*-dö-roi) *n* pana f

core (koo) *n* núcleo *m*; corazón *m*

cork (kook) *n* corcho *m*; tapón *m*

corkscrew (*kook*-sskruu) *n* sacacorchos *mpl*

corn (koon) *n* grano *m*; cereales *mpl*, trigo *m*; maíz *m*; callo *m*; **~ on the cob** maíz en la mazorca

corner (*koo*-nö) *n* esquina f

cornfield (*koon*-fiild) *n* trigal *m*

corpse (koopss) *n* cadáver *m*

corpulent (*koo*-pyu-lönt) *adj* corpulento; grueso

correct (kö-*rêkt*) *adj* correcto, justo; *v* *corregir

correction (kö-*rêk*-ʃön) *n* corrección f; rectificación f

correctness (kö-*rêkt*-nöss) *n* exactitud f

correspond (ko-ri-*sspond*) *v* corresponderse; corresponder

correspondence (ko-ri-*sspon*-dönss) *n* correspondencia f

correspondent (ko-ri-*sspon*-dönt) *n* corresponsal *m/f*

corridor (*ko*-ri-doo) *n* pasillo *m*

corrupt (kö-*rapt*) *adj* corrupto; *v* corromper

corruption (kö-*rap*-ʃön) *n* corrupción f

corset (*koo*-ssit) *n* corsé *m*

cosmetics (kos-*mê*-tikss) *pl* productos cosméticos, cosméticos *mpl*

cost (kosst) *n* coste *m*; precio *m*

*cost (kosst) *v* *costar

cosy (*kou*-si) *adj* acogedor; confortable

cot (kot) *nAm* catre *m*

cottage (*ko*-tidʒ) *n* casita de campo

cotton (*ko*-tön) *n* algodón *m*; de algodón

cotton wool (*ko*-tön-ᵘul) *n* algodón *m*

couch (kauch) *n* diván *m*

cough (kof) *n* tos f; *v* toser

could (kud) *v* (p can)

council (*kaun*-ssöl) *n* consejo *m*

councillor (*kaun*-ssö-lö) *n* consejal *m*, -a f

counsel (*kaun*-ssöl) *n* consejo *m*

counsellor (*kaun*-ssö-lö) *n* consejero *m*

count (kaunt) *v* *contar; adicionar; *incluir; considerar; *n* conde *m*

counter (*kaun*-tö) *n* mostrador *m*; barra *f*

counterfeit (*kaun*-tö-fiit) *v* falsificar

counterfoil (*kaun*-tö-foil) *n* talón *m*

countess (*kaun*-tiss) *n* condesa *f*

country (*kan*-tri) *n* país *m*; campo *m*; región *f*; ~ **estate** finca *f*; ~ **house** quinta *f*

countryman (*kan*-tri-mön) *n* (pl -men) compatriota *m*

countryside (*kan*-tri-ssaid) *n* campo *m*

county (*kaun*-ti) *n* condado *m*

couple (*ka*-pöl) *n* pareja *f*; par *m*

coupon (*kuu*-pon) *n* cupón *m*

courage (*ka*-ridȝ) *n* valor *m*

courageous (kö-*rei*-dȝöss) *adj* valiente

course (kooss) *n* rumbo *m*; plato *m*; curso *m*; **intensive** ~ curso intensivo; **of** ~ por supuesto

court (koot) *n* tribunal *m*; corte *f*

courteous (*köö*-ti-öss) *adj* cortés

cousin (*ka*-sön) *n* prima *f*, primo *m*

cover (*ka*-vö) *v* cubrir; *n* refugio *m*; tapa *f*; cubierta *f*; ~ **charge** precio del cubierto

cow (kau) *n* vaca *f*

coward (*kau*-öd) *n* cobarde *m*

cowardly (*kau*-öd-li) *adj* cobarde

cozy (*kou*-si) *adj* acogedor; confortable

crab (kræb) *n* cangrejo *m*

crack (kræk) *n* crujido *m*; hendidura *f*; *v* crujir; *quebrar, *reventar

cradle (*krei*-döl) *n* cuna *f*

cramp (kræmp) *n* calambre *m*

crane (krein) *n* grúa *f*

crash (kræʃ) *n* choque *m*; *v* chocar;

precipitarse; ~ **barrier** barrera de protección

crate (kreit) *n* caja *f*

crater (*krei*-tö) *n* cráter *m*

crawl (krool) *v* arrastrarse; *n* crawl *m*

craze (kreis) *n* manía *f*

crazy (*krei*-si) *adj* loco

creak (kriik) *v* crujir

cream (kriim) *n* crema *f*; nata *f*; *adj* de color crema

creamy (*krii*-mi) *adj* cremoso

crease (kriiss) *v* *plegar; *n* raya *f*; pliegue *m*

create (kri-*eit*) *v* crear

creative (kri-*ei*-tiv) *adj* creativo

creature (*krii*-chö) *n* criatura *f*; ser *m*

credible (*krê*-di-böl) *adj* creíble; verosímil

credit (*krê*-dit) *n* crédito *m*; *v* acreditar; ~ **card** tarjeta de crédito

creditor (*krê*-di-tö) *n* acreedor *m*

credulous (*krê*-dyu-löss) *adj* crédulo

creek (kriik) *n* ensenada *f*

***creep** (kriip) *v* gatear; arrastrarse

creepy (*krii*-pi) *adj* lúgubre, espeluznante

cremate (kri-*meit*) *v* incinerar

cremation (kri-*mei*-ʃön) *n* incineración *f*

crew (kruu) *n* equipo *m*; tripulación *f*

cricket (*kri*-kit) *n* grillo *m*

crime (kraim) *n* crimen *m*

criminal (*kri*-mi-nöl) *n* delincuente *m*, criminal *m*; *adj* criminal; ~ **law** derecho penal

criminality (kri-mi-*næ*-lö-ti) *n* criminalidad *f*

crimson (*krim*-sön) *adj* carmesí

crippled (*kri*-pöld) *adj* lisiado; incapacitado; minusválido

crisis (*krai*-ssiss) *n* (pl crises) crisis *f*

crisp (krissp) *adj* crujiente, quebradizo

critic (*kri*-tik) *n* crítico *m*, -a *f*

critical (*kri*-ti-köl) *adj* crítico; precario

criticism (*kri*-ti-ssi-söm) *n* crítica *f*

criticize (*kri*-ti-ssais) *v* criticar

crochet (*krou*-ʃei) *v* *hacer ganchillo

crockery (*krou*-kö-ri) *n* cerámica *f*, loza *f*

crocodile (*kro*-kö-dail) *n* cocodrilo *m*

crooked (*kru*-kid) *adj* torcido, curvo; deshonesto

crop (krop) *n* cosecha *f*

cross (kross) *v* *atravesar; *adj* enojado, enfadado; *n* cruz *f*

cross-eyed (*kross*-aid) *adj* bizco

crossing (*kro*-ssing) *n* travesía *f*; encrucijada *f*; paso *m*; paso a nivel

crossroads (*kross*-rouds) *n* encrucijada *f*

crosswalk (*kross*-ᵘook) *nAm* cruce para peatones

crow (krou) *n* corneja *f*

crowbar (*krou*-baa) *n* pie de cabra

crowd (kraud) *n* masa *f*, muchedumbre *f*

crowded (*krau*-did) *adj* animado; repleto; concurrido

crown (kraun) *n* corona *f*; *v* coronar

crucifix (*kruu*-ssi-fikss) *n* crucifijo *m*

crucifixion (kruu-ssi-*fik*-ʃön) *n* crucifixión *f*

crucify (*kruu*-ssi-fai) *v* crucificar

cruel (kruᵘl) *adj* cruel

cruise (kruus) *n* crucero *m*

crumb (kram) *n* migaja *f*

crusade (kruu-*sseid*) *n* cruzada *f*

crust (krasst) *n* corteza *f*

crutch (krach) *n* muleta *f*

cry (krai) *v* llorar; gritar; llamar; *n* grito *m*

crystal (*kri*-sstöl) *n* cristal *m*; *adj* de cristal

Cuba (*kyuu*-bö) Cuba *f*

Cuban (*kyuu*-bön) *adj* cubano

cube (kyuub) *n* cubo *m*

cuckoo (*ku*-kuu) *n* cuclillo *m*

cucumber (*kyuu*-köm-bö) *n* pepino *m*

cuddle (*ka*-döl) *v* acariciar

cuff links (*kaf*-lingkss) *pl* gemelos *mpl*; mancuernillas *fplMe*

cul-de-sac (*kal*-dö-ssæk) *n* callejón sin salida

cultivate (*kal*-ti-veit) *v* cultivar

culture (*kal*-chö) *n* cultura *f*

cultured (*kal*-chöd) *adj* culto

cunning (*ka*-ning) *adj* astuto

cup (kap) *n* taza *f*; copa *f*

cupboard (*ka*-böd) *n* armario *m*

curb (kööb) *n* bordillo *m*; *v* refrenar

cure (kyuᵒ) *v* curar; *n* cura *f*; curación *f*

curiosity (kyuᵒ-ri-*o*-ssö-ti) *n* curiosidad *f*

curious (*kyu*ᵒ-ri-öss) *adj* curioso

curl (kööl) *v* rizar; *n* rizo *m*

curler (*köö*-lö) *n* rulo *m*

curly (*köö*-li) *adj* crespo; chino *adjMe*

currant (*ka*-rönt) *n* pasa de Corinto; grosella *f*

currency (*ka*-rön-ssi) *n* moneda *f*; **foreign ~** moneda extranjera

current (*ka*-rönt) *n* corriente *f*; *adj* corriente; **alternating ~** corriente alterna; **direct ~** corriente continua

curry (*ka*-ri) *n* curry *m*

curse (kööss) *v* *maldecir; *n* maldición *f*

curtain (*köö*-tön) *n* cortina *f*; telón *m*

curve (kööv) *n* curva *f*

curved (köövd) *adj* curvado, encorvado

cushion (*ku*-ʃön) *n* almohadón *m*; cojín *m*

custody (*ka*-sstö-di) *n* detención *f*; custodia *f*; tutela *f*

custom (*ka*-sstöm) *n* costumbre *f*

customary (*ka*-sstö-mö-ri) *adj* usual, corriente, acostumbrado

customer (*ka*-sstö-mö) *n* cliente *m*

Customs (*ka*-sstöms) *pl* aduana *f*; **~ duty** impuesto *m*; **~ officer** oficial de

aduanas
cut (kat) *n* incisión *f*; cortadura *f*
*cut (kat) *v* cortar; *reducir; ~ **off**
  cortar
cutlery (*kat*-lö-ri) *n* cubiertos *mpl*
cutlet (*kat*-löt) *n* chuleta *f*
cycle (*ssai*-köl) *n* biciclo *m*; bicicleta *f*;

ciclo *m*
cyclist (*ssai*-klisst) *n* ciclista *m*
cylinder (*ssi*-lin-dö) *n* cilindro *m*; ~
  head culata del cilindro
Cyprus (*ssai*-prös) Chipre *f*
cystitis (ssi-*sstai*-tiss) *n* cistitis *f*
Czech (chêk) *adj* checo

D

dad (däd) *n* papá *m*
daffodil (*dä*-fö-dil) *n* narciso *m*
daily (*dei*-li) *adj* diario; *n* diario *m*
dairy (*dêᵒ*-ri) *n* lechería *f*
dam (däm) *n* presa *f*; dique *m*
damage (*dä*-midʒ) *n* perjuicio *m*; *v*
  dañar
damn (däm) *colloquial adj* maldito;
  damn! ¡mecachis!; *v* condenar;
  damn it! ¡maldita sea!
damp (dämp) *adj* húmedo; mojado; *n*
  humedad *f*; *v* *humedecer
dance (daanss) *v* bailar; *n* baile *m*
dandelion (*dän*-di-lai-ön) *n* diente de
  león
dandruff (*dän*-dröf) *n* caspa *f*
Dane (dein) *n* danés *m*
danger (*dein*-dʒö) *n* peligro *m*
dangerous (*dein*-dʒö-röss) *adj*
  peligroso
Danish (*dei*-niʃ) *adj* danés
dare (dêᵒ) *v* atreverse, osar; desafiar
daring (*dêᵒ*-ring) *adj* atrevido
dark (daak) *adj* oscuro, obscuro; *n*
  oscuridad *f*
darling (*daa*-ling) *n* amor *m*, querido
  m, -a *f*
darn (daan) *v* zurcir
dash (däʃ) *v* correr; *n* guión *m*
dashboard (*däʃ*-bood) *n* tablero de
  instrumentos

data (*dei*-tö) *pl* datos *m*
date[1] (deit) *n* fecha *f*; cita *f*; *v* datar;
  out of ~ anticuado
date[2] (deit) *n* dátil *m*
daughter (*doo*-tö) *n* hija *f*; **daughter-
  in-law** (pl daughters-in-law) nuera *f*
dawn (doon) *n* alba *f*; aurora *f*
day (dei) *n* día *m*; **by** ~ de día; ~ **trip**
  jornada *f*; **per** ~ a diario; **the** ~ **before
  yesterday** anteayer
daybreak (*dei*-breik) *n* amanecer *m*
daylight (*dei*-lait) *n* luz del día
dead (dêd) *adj* muerto; difunto
deaf (dêf) *adj* sordo
deal (diil) *n* transacción *f*
*deal (diil) *v* repartir; ~ **with** *v* tratar
  con; *hacer negocios con
dealer (*dii*-lö) *n* negociante *m*/*f*;
  comerciante *m*/*f*; traficante *m*/*f*
dear (diᵒ) *adj* querido; caro; amado
death (dêʒ) *n* muerte *f*; ~ **penalty** pena
  de muerte
debate (di-*beit*) *n* debate *m*
debit (*dê*-bit) *n* debe *m*
debt (dêt) *n* deuda *f*
decaffeinated (dii-*kä*-fi-nei-tid) *adj*
  descafeinado
deceit (di-*ssiit*) *n* engaño *m*
deceive (di-*ssiiv*) *v* engañar
December (di-*ssêm*-bö) diciembre *m*
decency (*dii*-ssön-ssi) *n* decencia *f*

decent (*dii*-ssönt) *adj* decente

decide (di-*ssaid*) *v* decidir

decision (di-*ssi*-ʒön) *n* decisión *f*

deck (dêk) *n* cubierta *f*; ~ **cabin** camarote en cubierta; ~ **chair** silla de tijera

declaration (dê-klö-*rei*-ʃön) *n* declaración *f*

declare (di-*klēᵒ*) *v* declarar; indicar

decorate (*dê*-kö-reit) *v* pintar; empapelar; decorar; condecorar

decoration (dê-kö-*rei*-ʃön) *n* decoración *f*

decrease (dii-*kriiss*) *v* *reducir; *disminuir; *n* disminución *f*

dedicate (*dê*-di-keit) *v* dedicar

deduce (di-*dyuuss*) *v* *deducir

deduct (di-*dakt*) *v* *deducir

deed (diid) *n* acción *f*, acto *m*

deep (diip) *adj* hondo

deep-freeze (diip-*friis*) *n* congelador *m*

deer (diⁱᵒ) *n* (pl ~) ciervo *m*

defeat (di-*fiit*) *v* derrotar; *n* derrota *f*

defective (di-*fêk*-tiv) *adj* defectuoso

defence (di-*fênss*) *n* defensa *f*

defend (di-*fênd*) *v* *defender

deficiency (di-*fi*-ʃön-ssi) *n* deficiencia *f*

deficit (*dê*-fi-ssit) *n* déficit *m*

define (di-*fain*) *v* definir, determinar

definite (*dê*-fi-nit) *adj* determinado; definido

definition (dê-fi-*ni*-ʃön) *n* definición *f*

deformed (di-*foomd*) *adj* deforme

degree (di-*ghrii*) *n* grado *m*; título *m*

delay (di-*lei*) *v* retardar; *diferir; *n* retraso *m*, tardanza *f*; dilación *f*

delegate (*dê*-li-ghöt) *n* delegado *m*

delegation (dê-li-*ghei*-ʃön) *n* delegación *f*

deliberate¹ (di-*li*-bö-reit) *v* discutir, deliberar

deliberate² (di-*li*-bö-röt) *adj* deliberado

deliberation (di-li-bö-*rei*-ʃön) *n* deliberación *f*

delicacy (*dê*-li-kö-ssi) *n* golosina *f*; delicadeza *f*; **delicacies** *n* gollerías *fpl*

delicate (*dê*-li-köt) *adj* delicado; fino

delicatessen (dê-li-kö-*tê*-ssön) tienda de comestibles finos; tienda de ultramarinos

delicious (di-*li*-ʃöss) *adj* exquisito, delicioso

delight (di-*lait*) *n* delicia *f*, deleite *m*; *v* encantar

delighted (di-*lai*-töd) *adj* encantado; **I'd be ~ to come** me encantaría venir

delightful (di-*lait*-föl) *adj* delicioso, deleitoso

deliver (di-*li*-vö) *v* entregar; librar

delivery (di-*li*-vö-ri) *n* entrega *f*, reparto *m*; parto *m*; liberación *f*; ~ **van** furgoneta *f*

demand (di-*maand*) *v* *requerir, exigir; *n* exigencia *f*; demanda *f*

democracy (di-*mo*-krö-ssi) *n* democracia *f*

democratic (dê-mö-*kræ*-tik) *adj* democrático

demolish (di-*mo*-liʃ) *v* *demoler

demolition (dê-mö-*li*-ʃön) *n* demolición *f*

demonstrate (*dê*-mön-sstreit) *v* *demostrar; *hacer una manifestación

demonstration (dê-mön-*sstrei*-ʃön) *n* manifestación *f*; demostración *f*

den (dên) *n* madriguera *f*

Denmark (*dên*-maak) Dinamarca *f*

denomination (di-no-mi-*nei*-ʃön) *n* denominación *f*

dense (dênss) *adj* denso

dent (dênt) *n* abolladura *f*

dentist (*dên*-tisst) *n* dentista *m*

denture (*dên*-chö) *n* dentadura

postiza

deny (di-*nai*) v *negar; *denegar

deodorant (dii-*ou*-dö-rönt) n
desodorante m

depart (di-*paat*) v partir; irse;
marcharse; *fallecer

department (di-*paat*-mönt) n
departamento m; ~ **store** grandes
almacenes

departure (di-*paa*-chö) n despedida f,
partida f

dependant (di-*pên*-dönt) adj
dependiente

depend on (di-*pênd*) depender de;
that depends depende

deposit (di-*po*-sit) n depósito m;
fianza f; capa f, yacimiento m; v
ingresar

depository (di-*po*-si-tö-ri) n almacén
m

depot (*dê*-pou) n deposito m; nAm
estación f

depress (di-*prêss*) v deprimir

depression (di-*prê*-ʃön) n desánimo
m; depresión f

deprive of (di-*praiv*) privar de

depth (dêpz) n profundidad f

deputy (*dê*-pyu-ti) n segundo m, -a f;
sustituto m, -a f

descend (di-*ssênd*) v *descender

descendant (di-*ssên*-dönt) n
descendiente m/f

descent (di-*ssênt*) n bajada f

describe (di-*sskraib*) v describir

description (di-*sskrip*-ʃön) n
descripción f

desert[1] (*dê*-söt) n desierto m; adj
yermo, desierto

desert[2] (di-*sö't*) v desertar; dejar

deserve (di-*sööv*) v *merecer

design (di-*sain*) v diseñar; n diseño m;
objetivo m

designate (*dê*-sigh-neit) v designar

desirable (di-*sai*ᵒ-rö-böl) adj deseable

desire (di-*sai*ᵒ) n deseo m; ganas fpl; v
anhelar, desear

desk (dêssk) n escritorio m; pupitre m

despair (di-*sspê*ᵒ) n desesperación f; v
*estar desesperado

despatch (di-*sspæch*) v despachar

desperate (*dê*-sspö-röt) adj
desesperado

despise (di-*sspais*) v despreciar

despite (di-*sspait*) prep a pesar de

dessert (di-*sööt*) n postre m

destination (dê-ssti-*nei*-ʃön) n destino
m

destine (*dê*-sstin) v destinar

destiny (*dê*-ssti-ni) n destino m

destroy (di-*sstroi*) v *destruir

destruction (di-*sstrak*-ʃön) n
destrucción f; ruina f

detach (di-*tæch*) v separar

detail (*dii*-teil) n particularidad f,
detalle m

detailed (*dii*-teild) adj detallado

detect (di-*têkt*) v descubrir

detective (di-*têk*-tiv) n detective m/f; ~
story novela policíaca

detergent (di-*töö*-dʒönt) n detergente
m

determine (di-*töö*-min) v determinar

determined (di-*töö*-mind) adj
resuelto

detest (di-*têsst*) v detestar

detour (*dii*-tuᵒ) n desvío m

devaluation (dii-væl-yu-*ei*-ʃön) n
desvalorización f

devalue (dii-*væl*-yuu) v desvalorizar

develop (di-*vê*-löp) v desarrollar;
revelar

development (di-*vê*-löp-mönt) n
desarrollo m

deviate (*dii*-vi-eit) v desviarse

devil (*dê*-völ) n diablo m

devise (di-*vais*) v idear; proyectar

devote (di-*vout*) v dedicar

dew (dyuu) n rocío m

diabetes (dai-ö-*bii*-tiis) *n* diabetes *f*
diabetic (dai-ö-*bê*-tik) *n* diabético *m*, -a *f*
diagnose (dai-ögh-*nous*) *v* diagnosticar; *comprobar
diagnosis (dai-ögh-*nou*-ssiss) *n* (pl -ses) diagnosis *m*
diagonal (dai-æ-ghö-nöl) *n* diagonal *f*; *adj* diagonal
diagram (*dai*-ö-ghræm) *n* esquema *m*; gráfico *m*
dial (*dai*-öl) *n* esfera *f*; cuadrante *m*; disco *m*; *v* marcar
dialect (*dai*-ö-lêkt) *n* dialecto *m*
diamond (*dai*-ö-mönd) *n* diamante *m*
diaper (*dai*-ö-pö) *nAm* pañal *m*
diaphragm (*dai*-ö-fræm) *n* membrana *f*
diarrh(o)ea (dai-ö-*ri*-ö) *n* diarrea *f*
diary (*dai*-ö-ri) *n* agenda *f*; diario *m*
dictaphone (*dik*-tö-foun) *n* dictáfono *m*
dictate (dik-*teit*) *v* dictar
dictation (dik-*tei*-jön) *n* dictado *m*
dictator (dik-*tei*-tö) *n* dictador *m*
dictionary (*dik*-jö-nö-ri) *n* diccionario *m*
did (did) *v* (p do)
die (dai) *v* *morir
diesel (*dii*-söl) *n* diesel *m*
diet (*dai*-öt) *n* régimen *m*
differ (*di*-fö) *v* *diferir
difference (*di*-fö-rönss) *n* diferencia *f*; distinción *f*
different (*di*-fö-rönt) *adj* diferente; otro
difficult (*di*-fi-költ) *adj* difícil; fastidioso
difficulty (*di*-fi-köl-ti) *n* dificultad *f*; trabajo *m*
***dig** (digh) *v* cavar
digest (di-*dʒêsst*) *v* *digerir
digestible (di-*dʒê*-sstö-böl) *adj* digerible

digestion (di-*dʒêss*-chön) *n* digestión *f*
digit (*di*-dʒit) *n* número *m*
digital (*di*-dʒi-töl) *adj* digital
dignified (*digh*-ni-faid) *adj* distinguido
dignity (*digh*-ni-ti) dignidad *f*
dilapidated (di-*læ*-pi-dei-tid) *adj* ruinoso
diligence (*di*-li-dʒönss) *n* diligencia *f*
diligent (*di*-li-dʒönt) *adj* diligente
dilute (dai-*lyuut*) *v* *diluir
dim (dim) *adj* deslucido, mate; oscuro, vago, difuso
dine (dain) *v* cenar
dinghy (*ding*-ghi) *n* chinchorro *m*
dining car (*dai*-ning-kaa) *n* coche comedor
dining room (*dai*-ning-ruum) *n* comedor *m*
dinner (*di*-nö) *n* comida principal; cena *f*
dinner jacket (*di*-nö-dʒæ-kit) *n* smoking *m*
dinner service (*di*-nö-ssöö-viss) *n* servicio de mesa
diphtheria (dif-*zi*ᵒ-ri-ö) *n* difteria *f*
diploma (di-*plou*-mö) *n* diploma *m*
diplomat (*di*-plö-mæt) *n* diplomático *m*
direct (di-*rêkt*) *adj* directo; *v* dirigir; administrar
direction (di-*rêk*-ʃön) *n* dirección *f*; instrucción *f*; dirección de escena; administración *f*; **directions for use** modo de empleo
directive (di-*rêk*-tiv) *n* directriz *f*
director (di-*rêk*-tö) *n* director *m*, -a *f*; director de escena
directory (di-*rêk*-tö-ri) *n* directorio *m*; guía *f* telefónica
dirt (dööt) *n* suciedad *f*
dirty (*döö*-ti) *adj* sucio
disabled (di-*ssei*-böld) *adj*

minusválido, inválido

disadvantage (di-ssöd-*vaan*-tidʒ) *n* desventaja *f*

disagree (di-ssö-*ghrii*) *v* no *estar de acuerdo, *disentir

disagreeable (di-ssö-*ghrii*-ö-böl) *adj* desagradable

disappear (di-ssö-*piᵒ*) *v* *desaparecer

disappoint (di-ssö-*point*) *v* decepcionar

disappointment (di-ssö-*point*-mönt) *n* desengaño *m*

disapprove (di-ssö-*pruuv*) *v* *desaprobar

disaster (di-*saa*-sstö) *n* desastre *m*; catástrofe *f*, calamidad *f*

disastrous (di-*saa*-sströss) *adj* desastroso

disc (dissk) *n* disco *m*; **slipped ~** hernia intervertebral

discard (di-*sskaad*) *v* desechar

discharge (diss-*chaadʒ*) *v* descargar; **~ of** dispensar de

discipline (*di*-ssi-plin) *n* disciplina *f*

discolo(u)r (di-*sska*-lö) *v* *desteñirse; **discolo(u)red** descolorido

disconnect (di-sskö-*nêkt*) *v* desconectar

discontented (di-sskön-*tên*-tid) *adj* descontento

discontinue (di-sskön-*ti*-nyuu) *v* suprimir, cesar

discount (*di*-sskaunt) *n* descuento *m*

discourage (diss-*ka*-ridʒ) *v* disuadir (**from** de); desanimar, desalentar

discover (di-*sska*-vö) *v* descubrir

discovery (di-*sska*-vö-ri) *n* descubrimiento *m*

discuss (di-*sskass*) *v* discutir; debatir

discussion (di-*sska*-ʃön) *n* discusión *f*; conversación *f*, debate *m*

disease (di-*siis*) *n* enfermedad *f*

disembark (di-ssim-*baak*) *v* desembarcar

disgrace (diss-*ghreiss*) *n* deshonor *m*

disguise (diss-*ghais*) *v* disfrazarse; *n* disfraz *m*

disgust (diss-*ghasst*) *n* asco *m*, repugnancia *f*; *v* dar asco, repugnar

disgusting (diss-*gha*-ssting) *adj* repugnante, asqueroso

dish (diʃ) *n* plato *m*; fuente *f*; guiso *m*

dishonest (di-*sso*-nisst) *adj* tramposo; fraudulento

dishwasher (*diʃ*-ᵘo-ʃö) lavaplatos *m/f*; lavavajillas *m*, lavaplatos *m*

disinfect (di-ssin-*fêkt*) *v* desinfectar

disinfectant (di-ssin-*fêk*-tönt) *n* desinfectante *m*

dislike (di-*sslaik*) *v* detestar, no gustar; *n* repugnancia *f*, aversión *f*, antipatía *f*

dislocated (*di*-sslö-kei-tid) *adj* dislocado

dismiss (diss-*miss*) *v* *despedir

disorder (di-*ssoo*-dö) *n* desorden *m*

dispatch (di-*sspæch*) *v* enviar, despachar

display (di-*ssplei*) *v* exhibir; *mostrar; *n* exposición *f*

displease (di-*sspliis*) *v* disgustar, desagradar

disposable (di-*sspou*-sö-böl) *adj* desechable

disposal (di-*sspou*-söl) *n* disposición *f*

dispose of (di-*sspous*) *disponer de

dispute (di-*sspyuut*) *n* disputa *f*; riña *f*, contienda *f*; *v* *reñir, disputar

dissatisfied (di-*ssæ*-tiss-faid) *adj* insatisfecho

dissolve (di-*solv*) *v* *disolver

dissuade from (di-*ssᵘeid*) disuadir

distance (*di*-sstönss) *n* distancia *f*; **~ in kilometres** (**kilometers** *Am*) kilometraje *m*

distant (*di*-sstönt) *adj* lejano

distinct (di-*sstingkt*) *adj* claro; distinto

distinction (di-*sstingk*-ʃön) *n*

distinción f, diferencia f

distinguish (di-*ssting*-gh^uiʃ) v
distinguir

distinguished (di-*ssting*-gh^uiʃt) adj
distinguido

distress (di-*sstréss*) n peligro m; ~
signal señal de alarma

distribute (di-*sstri*-byuut) v *distribuir

distributor (di-*sstri*-byu-tö) n
distribuidor m

district (*di*-sstrikt) n distrito m;
comarca f; barrio m

disturb (di-*sstööb*) v estorbar,
molestar

disturbance (di-*sstöö*-bönss) n
disturbio m; confusión f

ditch (dich) n zanja f, cuneta f

dive (daiv) v bucear

diversion (dai-*vöö*-ʃön) n desvío m;
diversión f

divide (di-*vaid*) v dividir; repartir;
separar

divine (di-*vain*) adj divino

division (di-*vi*-ʒön) n división f;
separación f; departamento m

divorce (di-*vooss*) n divorcio m; v
divorciar

dizziness (*di*-si-nöss) n vértigo m

dizzy (*di*-si) adj mareado

***do** (duu) v *hacer; *ser suficiente

dock (dok) n dock m; muelle m; v
atracar

docker (*do*-kö) n obrero portuario

doctor (*dok*-tö) n médico m; doctor m

document (*do*-kyu-mönt) n
documento m

dog (dogh) n perro m

dogged (*do*-ghid) adj obstinado;
tenaz

doll (dol) n muñeca f

dollar (*do*-lö) n dólar m

dome (doum) n cúpula f

domestic (dö-*mê*-sstik) adj
doméstico; interior; n sirviente m

domicile (*do*-mi-ssail) n domicilio m

domination (do-mi-*nei*-ʃön) n
dominación f

dominion (dö-*mi*-nyön) n dominio m

donate (dou-*neit*) v donar

donation (dou-*nei*-ʃön) n donación f

done (dan) v (pp do)

donkey (*dong*-ki) n burro m

donor (*dou*-nö) n donante m

door (doo) n puerta f; **revolving ~**
puerta giratoria; **sliding ~** puerta
corrediza

doorbell (*doo*-bêl) n timbre m

doorman (*doo*-mön) n (pl -men)
portero m

dormitory (*doo*-mi-tri) n dormitorio
m (colectivo)

dose (douss) n dosis f

dot (dot) n punto m

double (da-böl) adj doble

doubt (daut) v dudar; n duda f;
without ~ sin duda

doubtful (*daut*-föl) adj dudoso;
inseguro

dough (dou) n masa f

down¹ (daun) adv abajo; hacia abajo;
adj abatido; prep a lo largo de, debajo
de; ~ **payment** primer pago

down² (daun) n flojel m

downpour (*daun*-poo) n aguacero m

downstairs (daun-*sstê*^os) adv abajo

downstream (daun-*sstriim*) adv río
abajo

down-to-earth (daun-tu-*ööz*) adj
sensato

downwards (*daun*-^uöds) adv hacia
abajo

dozen (*da*-sön) n (pl ~, ~s) docena f

draft (draaft) n giro m; Am corriente
de aire

drag (drægh) v arrastrar

dragon (*dræ*-ghön) n dragón m

drain (drein) v desecar; drenar; n
desagüe m

drama (*draa*-mö) *n* drama *m*; tragedia *f*; teatro *m*

dramatic (drö-*mæ*-tik) *adj* dramático

drank (drængk) *v* (p drink)

drapery (*drei*-pö-ri) *n* pañería *f*

draught (draaft) *n* corriente de aire; **draughts** juego de damas

draw (droo) *n* sorteo *m*

***draw** (droo) *v* dibujar; arrastrar; sacar; jalar *vMe*; **~ up** redactar

drawbridge (*droo*-bridʒ) *n* puente levadizo

drawer (*droo*-ö) *n* cajón *m*; **drawers** calzoncillos *mpl*

drawing (*droo*-ing) *n* dibujo *m*; **~ pin** (*droo*-ing-pin) *n* chinche *f*

dread (drêd) *v* temer; *n* temor *m*

dreadful (*drêd*-föl) *adj* terrible, espantoso

dream (driim) *n* sueño *m*

***dream** (driim) *v* *soñar

dress (drêss) *v* *vestir; *vestirse; vendar; *n* vestido *m*

dressing gown (*drê*-ssing-ghaun) *n* bata *f*

dressing room (*drê*-ssing-ruum) *n* vestuario *m*

dressing table (*drê*-ssing-tei-böl) *n* tocador *m*

dressmaker (*drêss*-mei-kö) *n* modista *f*

drill (dril) *v* taladrar; entrenar; *n* taladro *m*

drink (dringk) *n* aperitivo *m*, bebida *f*

***drink** (dringk) *v* beber

drinking water (*dring*-king-ᵘoo-tö) *n* agua potable

drip-dry (drip-*drai*) *adj* no precisa plancha

drive (draiv) *n* calzada *f*; paseo en coche

***drive** (draiv) *v* *conducir

driver (*drai*-vö) *n* conductor *m*; **driver's license** *Am*, **driving**

licence carné *m* de conducir

drizzle (*dri*-söl) *n* llovizna *f*

drop (drop) *v* dejar caer; *n* gota *f*

drought (draut) *n* sequía *f*

drown (draun) *v* ahogar; ***be drowned** ahogarse

drug (dragh) *n* droga *f*; estupefaciente *m*; medicamento *m*

drugstore (*dragh*-sstoo) *nAm* droguería *f*, farmacia *f*; almacén *m*

drum (dram) *n* tambor *m*

drunk (drangk) *adj* (pp drink) borracho

dry (drai) *adj* seco; *v* secar

dry-clean (drai-*kliin*) *v* limpiar en seco

dry cleaner's (drai-*klii*-nös) *n* tintorería *f*

dryer (*drai*-ö) *n* secadora *f*

duchess (da-chiss) *n* duquesa *f*

duck (dak) *n* pato *m*

due (dyuu) *adj* adeudado; debido

dues (dyuus) *pl* derechos *mpl*

dug (dagh) *v* (p, pp dig)

duke (dyuuk) *n* duque *m*

dull (dal) *adj* aburrido; pálido, mate; embotado

dumb (dam) *adj* tomto; atontado, estúpido; mudo

dune (dyuun) *n* duna *f*

dung (dang) *n* estiércol *m*

dunghill (*dang*-hil) *n* estercolero *m*

duration (dyu-*rei*-ʃön) *n* duración *f*

during (*dyu*ᵒ-ring) *prep* durante

dusk (dassk) *n* crepúsculo *m*

dust (dasst) *n* polvo *m*

dustbin (*dasst*-bin) *n* cubo de la basura

dusty (*da*-ssti) *adj* polvoriento

Dutch (dach) *adj* holandés

Dutchman (*dach*-mön) *n* (pl -men) holandés *m*

duty (*dyuu*-ti) *n* deber *m*; tarea *f*; arancel *m*; **Customs ~** impuesto de aduana

duty-free (dyuu-ti-*frii*) *adj* exento de impuestos

dwarf (d^uoof) *n* enano *m*

dye (dai) *v* *teñir; *n* tintura *f*

dynamo (*dai*-nö-mou) *n* (pl ～s) dínamo *f*

E

each (iich) *adj* cada; ～ **other** el uno al otro

eager (*ii*-ghö) *adj* ansioso, impaciente

eagle (*ii*-ghöl) *n* águila *m*

ear (i^ö) *n* oreja *f*

earache (*i^ö*-reik) *n* dolor de oídos

eardrum (*i^ö*-dram) *n* tímpano *m*

earl (ööl) *n* conde *m*

early (*öö*-li) *adj* temprano

earn (öön) *v* ganar

earnest (*öö*-nisst) *adj* serio, formal

earnings (*öö*-nings) *pl* ingresos *mpl*, ganancias *fpl*

earring (*i^ö*-ring) *n* pendiente *m*

earth (ööz) *n* tierra *f*; suelo *m*

earthquake (*ööz*-k^ueik) *n* terremoto *m*

ease (iis) *n* desenvoltura *f*, facilidad *f*; bienestar *m*

east (iisst) *n* este *m*

Easter (*ii*-sstö) Pascua

easterly (*ii*-sstö-li) *adj* oriental

eastern (*ii*-sstön) *adj* oriental

easy (*ii*-si) *adj* fácil; cómodo; ～ **chair** butaca *f*

easy-going (*ii*-si-ghou-ing) *adj* relajado; despreocupado

*eat (iit) *v* comer; cenar

eavesdrop (*iivs*-drop) *v* escuchar a escondidas

ebony (*ê*-bö-ni) *n* ébano *m*

eccentric (ik-*ssên*-trik) *adj* excéntrico

echo (*ê*-kou) *n* (pl ～es) eco *m*

eclipse (i-*klipss*) *n* eclipse *m*

economic (ii-kö-*no*-mik) *adj* económico

economical (ii-kö-*no*-mi-köl) *adj* rentable; económico

economist (i-*ko*-nö-misst) *n* economista *m*

economize (i-*ko*-nö-mais) *v* economizar

economy (i-*ko*-nö-mi) *n* economía *f*

ecstasy (*êk*-sstö-si) *n* éxtasis *m*

Ecuador (*ê*-k^uö-doo) Ecuador *m*

Ecuadorian (ê-k^uö-*doo*-ri-ön) *n* ecuatoriano *m*

eczema (*êk*-ssi-mö) *n* eczema *m*

edge (êdʒ) *n* borde *m*; filo *m*

edible (*ê*-di-böl) *adj* comestible

edit (*ê*-dit) *v* corregir; editar; dirigir; montar

edition (i-*di*-ʃön) *n* edición *f*; **morning** ～ edición de mañana

editor (*ê*-di-tö) *n* redactor *m*

educate (*ê*-dʒu-keit) *v* formar, educar

education (ê-dʒu-*kei*-ʃön) *n* educación *f*

eel (iil) *n* anguila *f*

effect (i-*fêkt*) *n* resultado *m*, efecto *m*; *v* efectuar; **in** ～ en realidad

effective (i-*fêk*-tiv) *adj* eficaz

efficient (i-*fi*-ʃönt) *adj* eficiente

effort (*ê*-föt) *n* esfuerzo *m*

egg (êgh) *n* huevo *m*; ～ **yolk** yema de huevo

eggcup (*êgh*-kap) *n* huevera *f*

eggplant (*êgh*-plaant) *n* berenjena *f*

egoistic (ê-ghou-*i*-sstik) *adj* egoísta

Egypt (*ii*-dʒipt) Egipto *m*

Egyptian (i-*dʒip*-ʃön) *adj* egipcio
eiderdown (*ai*-dö-daun) *n* edredón *m*
eight (eit) *num* ocho
eighteen (ei-*tiin*) *num* dieciocho
eighteenth (ei-*tiinz*) *num* decimoctavo
eighth (eitz) *num* octavo
eighty (*ei*-ti) *num* ochenta
either (*ai*-öö) *pron* cualquiera de los dos; **either ... or** o ... o, bien ... bien
elaborate (i-*læ*-bö-reit) *v* elaborar
elastic (i-*læ*-sstik) *adj* elástico; flexible; ~ **band** cinta de goma
elasticity (ê-læ-*ssti*-ssö-ti) *n* elasticidad *f*
elbow (*êl*-bou) *n* codo *m*
elder (*êl*-dö) *adj* mayor
elderly (*êl*-dö-li) *adj* anciano
eldest (*êl*-disst) *adj* mayor
elect (i-*lêkt*) *v* *elegir
election (i-*lêk*-ʃön) *n* elección *f*
electric (i-*lêk*-trik) *adj* eléctrico; ~ **razor** afeitadora eléctrica
electrician (i-lêk-*tri*-ʃön) *n* electricista *m/f*
electricity (i-lêk-*tri*-ssö-ti) *n* electricidad *f*
electronic (i-lêk-*tro*-nik) *adj* electrónico; ~ **game** juego electrónico
elegance (ê-li-ghönss) *n* elegancia *f*
elegant (ê-li-ghönt) *adj* elegante
element (ê-li-mönt) *n* elemento *m*
elephant (ê-li-fönt) *n* elefante *m*
elevator (ê-li-vei-tö) *n Am* ascensor *m*; elevador *m Me*
eleven (i-*lê*-vön) *num* once
eleventh (i-*lê*-vönz) *num* onceno
elf (êlf) *n* (pl elves) duende *m*
eliminate (i-*li*-mi-neit) *v* eliminar
elm (êlm) *n* olmo *m*
else (êlss) *adv* más; otro; diferente
elsewhere (êl-ss"ê^ö) *adv* otra parte
elucidate (i-*luu*-ssi-deit) *v* elucidar

e-mail (*ii*-meil) *n* correo *m* electrónico; *v* mandar un correo electrónico a
emancipation (i-mæn-ssi-*pei*-ʃön) *n* emancipación *f*
embankment (im-*bængk*-mönt) *n* terraplén *m*
embargo (êm-*baa*-ghou) *n* (pl ~es) embargo *m*
embark (im-*baak*) *v* embarcar
embarkation (êm-baa-*kei*-ʃön) *n* embarcación *f*
embarrass (im-*bæ*-röss) *v* turbar; *desconcertar; estorbar; **embarrassed** tímido; **embarrassment** embarazo *m*, apuro *m*
embassy (*êm*-bö-ssi) *n* embajada *f*
emblem (*êm*-blöm) *n* emblema *m*
embrace (im-*breiss*) *v* abrazar; *n* abrazo *m*
embroider (im-*broi*-dö) *v* bordar
embroidery (im-*broi*-dö-ri) *n* bordado *m*
emerald (ê-*mö*-röld) *n* esmeralda *f*
emergency (i-*möö*-dʒön-ssi) *n* caso de urgencia, urgencia *f*; emergencia *f*; ~ **exit** salida de emergencia
emigrant (ê-mi-ghrönt) *n* emigrante *m*
emigrate (ê-mi-ghreit) *v* emigrar
emigration (ê-mi-*ghrei*-ʃön) *n* emigración *f*
emotion (i-*mou*-ʃön) *n* emoción *f*
emotional (i-*mou*-ʃö-nöl) *adj* sentimental; emotivo
emperor (*êm*-pö-rö) *n* emperador *m*
emphasize (*êm*-fö-ssais) *v* enfatizar, acentuar
empire (*êm*-pai^ö) *n* imperio *m*
employ (im-*ploi*) *v* emplear
employee (êm-ploi-*ii*) *n* empleado *m*, -a *f*
employer (im-*ploi*-ö) *n* jefe *m*; patrón *m*; empresario *m*, -a *f*

employment (im-*ploi*-mönt) *n* empleo *m*; **~ exchange** oficina de colocación

empress (*êm*-priss) *n* emperatriz *f*

empty (*êmp*-ti) *adj* vacío; *v* vaciar

enable (i-*nei*-böl) *v* permitir

enamel (i-*næ*-möl) *n* esmalte *m*

enamelled (i-*næ*-möld) *adj* esmaltado

enchanting (in-*chaan*-ting) *adj* espléndido, encantador

encircle (in-*ssöö*-köl) *v* *circuir, cercar; *encerrar

enclose (ing-*klous*) *v* *incluir

enclosure (ing-*klou*-зö) *n* anexo *m*

encounter (ing-*kaun*-tö) *v* *encontrarse con; *n* encuentro *m*

encourage (ing-*ka*-ridз) *v* *alentar

encyclop(a)edia (ên-ssai-klö-*pii*-di-ö) *n* enciclopedia *f*

end (ênd) *n* fin *m*, extremo *m*; final *m*; *v* terminar, acabar; terminarse

ending (*ên*-ding) *n* conclusión *f*

endless (*ênd*-löss) *adj* infinito

endorse (in-*dooss*) *v* visar, endosar

endure (in-*dyu*ᵒ) *v* soportar

enemy (*ê*-nö-mi) *n* enemigo *m*, -a *f*

energetic (ê-nö-*dзe*-tik) *adj* enérgico

energy (*ê*-nö-dзi) *n* energía *f*; fuerza *f*

engage (ing-*gheidз*) *v* emplear; reservar; comprometerse; **engaged** prometido; ocupado

engagement (ing-*gheidз*-mönt) *n* noviazgo *m*; compromiso *m*; **~ ring** anillo de esponsales, anillo de compromiso

engine (*ên*-dзin) *n* máquina *f*, motor *m*; locomotora *f*

engineer (ên-dзi-*ni*ᵒ) *n* ingeniero *m*

England (*ing*-ghlönd) Inglaterra *f*

English (*ing*-ghli∫) *adj* inglés

Englishman (*ing*-ghli∫-mön) *n* (pl -men) inglés *m*

Englishwoman (*ing*-ghli∫-ᵘu-mön) (pl -women) inglesa *f*

engrave (ing-*ghreiv*) *v* grabar

engraver (ing-*ghrei*-vö) *n* grabador *m*

engraving (ing-*ghrei*-ving) *n* estampa *f*; grabado *m*

enigma (i-*nigh*-mö) *n* enigma *m*

enjoy (in-*dзoi*) *v* disfrutar, gozar

enjoyable (in-*dзoi*-ö-böl) *adj* agradable, grato, deleitable

enjoyment (in-*dзoi*-mönt) *n* disfrute *m*; goce *m*

enlarge (in-*laadз*) *v* ampliar; aumentar; extender

enlargement (in-*laadз*-mönt) *n* ampliación *f*

enormous (i-*noo*-möss) *adj* gigantesco, enorme

enough (i-*naf*) *adv* bastante; *adj* suficiente

enquire (ing-*k*ᵘ*ai*ᵒ) *v* preguntar; investigar

enquiry (ing-*k*ᵘ*ai*ᵒ-ri) *n* información *f*; investigación *f*; encuesta *f*

enter (*ên*-tö) *v* entrar; ingresar

enterprise (*ên*-tö-prais) *n* empresa *f*

entertain (ên-tö-*tein*) *v* *divertir, *entretener; hospedar

entertainer (ên-tö-*tei*-nö) *n* artista *m*

entertaining (ên-tö-*tei*-ning) *adj* divertido, entretenido

entertainment (ên-tö-*tein*-mönt) *n* diversión *f*, entretenimiento *m*

enthusiasm (in-*zyuu*-si-æ-söm) *n* entusiasmo *m*

enthusiastic (in-zyuu-si-æ-sstik) *adj* entusiasta

entire (in-*tai*ᵒ) *adj* todo, entero

entirely (in-*tai*ᵒ-li) *adv* enteramente

entrance (*ên*-trönss) *n* entrada *f*; acceso *m*; **~ fee** entrada *f*

entry (*ên*-tri) *n* entrada *f*, ingreso *m*; anotación *f*; **no ~** prohibido el paso

envelop (in-*vö*-loup) *v* cubrir

envelope (*ên*-vö-loup) *n* sobre *m*

envious (*ên*-vi-öss) *adj* envidioso, celoso

environment (in-*vai*ö-rön-mönt) *n* medio ambiente; alrededores *mpl*

envoy (*ên*-voi) *n* enviado *m*

envy (*ên*-vi) *n* envidia *f*; *v* envidiar

epic (*ê*-pik) *n* poema épico; *adj* épico

epidemic (ê-pi-*dê*-mik) *n* epidemia *f*

epilepsy (*ê*-pi-lêp-ssi) *n* epilepsia *f*

epilogue (*ê*-pi-logh) *n* epílogo *m*

episode (*ê*-pi-ssoud) *n* episodio *m*

equal (*ii*-kᵘöl) *adj* igual; *v* igualar

equality (i-*kᵘo*-lö-ti) *n* igualdad *f*

equalize (*ii*-kᵘö-lais) *v* igualar

equally (*ii*-kᵘö-li) *adv* igualmente

equator (i-*kᵘei*-tö) *n* ecuador *m*

equip (i-*kᵘip*) *v* equipar

equipment (i-*kᵘip*-mönt) *n* equipo *m*

equivalent (i-*kᵘi*-vö-lönt) *adj* equivalente

eraser (i-*rei*-sö) *n* goma de borrar

erect (i-*rêkt*) *v* erigir; *adj* erguido, recto; parado *adjMe*

err (öö) *v* *errar

errand (*ê*-rönd) *n* recado *m*

error (*ê*-rö) *n* falta *f*, error *m*

escalator (*ê*-sskö-lei-tö) *n* escalera móvil

escape (i-*sskeip*) *v* escaparse; *huir, escapar; *n* evasión *f*

escort¹ (*ê*-sskoot) *n* escolta *f*

escort² (i-*sskoot*) *v* escoltar

especially (i-*sspê*-ʃö-li) *adv* sobre todo, especialmente

essay (*ê*-ssei) *n* ensayo *m*; tratado *m*, composición *f*

essence (*ê*-ssönss) *n* esencia *f*; núcleo *m*

essential (i-*ssên*-ʃöl) *adj* indispensable; esencial

essentially (i-*ssên*-ʃö-li) *adv* sobre todo

establish (i-*sstæ*-bliʃ) *v* *establecer; *comprobar

estate (i-*ssteit*) *n* propiedad *f*; finca *f*; bienes *mpl*

esteem (i-*sstiim*) *n* respeto *m*, estima *f*; *v* estimar

estimate¹ (*ê*-ssti-meit) *v* evaluar, estimar

estimate² (*ê*-ssti-möt) *n* estimación *f*

estuary (*êss*-chu-ö-ri) *n* estuario *m*

etcetera (êt-*ssê*-tö-rö) etcétera

etching (*ê*-ching) *n* aguafuerte *f*

eternal (i-*töö*-nöl) *adj* eterno

eternity (i-*töö*-nö-ti) *n* eternidad *f*

ether (*ii*-zö) *n* éter *m*

Ethiopia (i-zi-*ou*-pi-ö) Etiopía *f*

Ethiopian (i-zi-*ou*-pi-ön) *adj* etíope

EU (ii-*yu*) (= **European Union**) UE *f* (=Unión Europea)

Europe (*yu*ö-röp) Europa *f*

European (yu*ö*-rö-*pii*-ön) *adj* europeo

European Union (yu*ö*-rö-pii-ön *yuu*-nyön) Unión Europea

evacuate (i-*væ*-kyu-eit) *v* evacuar

evade (i-*veid*) *v* evadir

evaluate (i-*væl*-yu-eit) *v* evaluar

evaporate (i-*væ*-pö-reit) *v* evaporar

even (*ii*-vön) *adj* llano, plano, igual; constante; par; *adv* aun

evening (*iiv*-ning) *n* tarde *f*; ~ **dress** traje de etiqueta

event (i-*vênt*) *n* acontecimiento *m*; caso *m*

eventual (i-*vên*-chu-öl) *adj* eventual; final; **eventually** *adv* finalmente

ever (*ê*-vö) *adv* jamás; siempre; alguna vez

every (*êv*-ri) *adj* cada; todo; todos los

everybody (*êv*-ri-bo-di) *pron* todos

everyday (*êv*-ri-dei) *adj* cotidiano

everyone (*êv*-ri-ᵘan) *pron* cada uno, todo el mundo

everything (*êv*-ri-zing) *pron* todo

everywhere (*êv*-ri-ᵘêᵒ) *adv* por todas partes

evidence (*ê*-vi-dönss) *n* prueba *f*

evident (*ê*-vi-dönt) *adj* evidente

evil (*ii*-völ) *n* mal *m*; *adj* malo,

malvado

evolution (ii-vö-*luu*-ʃön) *n* evolución *f*

exact (igh-*sækt*) *adj* exacto

exactly (igh-*sækt*-li) *adv* exactamente

exaggerate (igh-*sæ*-dʒö-reit) *v* exagerar

exam (igh-*sæm*) examen *m*; **take an ~** hacer un examen; **pass/fail an ~** aprobar/ suspender un examen

examination (igh-sæ-mi-*nei*-ʃön) *n* examen *m*; interrogatorio *m*

examine (igh-*sæ*-min) *v* examinar

example (igh-*saam*-pöl) *n* ejemplo *m*; **for ~** por ejemplo

excavation (êkss-kö-*vei*-ʃön) *n* excavación *f*

exceed (ik-*ssiid*) *v* exceder; superar

excel (ik-*ssêl*) *v* distinguirse

excellent (*êk*-ssö-lönt) *adj* excelente

except (ik-*ssêpt*) *prep* excepto

exception (ik-*ssêp*-ʃön) *n* excepción *f*

exceptional (ik-*ssêp*-ʃö-nöl) *adj* extraordinario, excepcional

excerpt (*êk*-ssööpt) *n* extracto *m*

excess (ik-*ssêss*) *n* exceso *m*

excessive (ik-*ssê*-ssiv) *adj* excesivo

exchange (ikss-*cheind*ʒ) *v* intercambiar, cambiar; *n* cambio *m*; bolsa *f*; **~ office** oficina de cambio; **~ rate** cambio *m*

excite (ik-*ssait*) *v* excitar; **excited** *adj* emocionado, excitado; **get excited about** emocionarse con, excitarse con

excitement (ik-*ssait*-mönt) *n* agitación *f*, excitación *f*

exciting (ik-*ssai*-ting) *adj* excitante

exclaim (ik-*sskleim*) *v* exclamar

exclamation (êk-ssklö-*mei*-ʃön) *n* exclamación *f*

exclude (ik-*sskluud*) *v* *excluir

exclusive (ik-*sskluu*-ssiv) *adj* exclusivo

exclusively (ik-*sskluu*-ssiv-li) *adv* exclusivamente, únicamente

excursion (ik-*ssköö*-ʃön) *n* excursión *f*

excuse¹ (ik-*sskyuuss*) *n* excusa *f*

excuse² (ik-*sskyuus*) *v* excusar, disculpar

execute (*êk*-ssi-kyuut) *v* ejecutar

execution (êk-ssi-*kyuu*-ʃön) *n* ejecución *f*

executioner (êk-ssi-*kyuu*-ʃö-nö) *n* verdugo *m*

executive (igh-*sê*-kyu-tiv) *adj* ejecutivo; *n* poder ejecutivo; ejecutivo *m*, -a *f*

exempt (igh-ʒêmpt) *v* dispensar, eximir; *adj* exento

exemption (igh-*sêmp*-ʃön) *n* exención *f*

exercise (*êk*-ssö-ssais) *n* ejercicio *m*; *v* ejercitar; ejercer

exhale (êkss-*heil*) *v* exhalar

exhaust (igh-*soosst*) *n* tubo de escape, escape *m*; *v* extenuar; **~ gases** gases de escape

exhibit (igh-*si*-bit) *v* *exponer; exhibir

exhibition (êk-ssi-*bi*-ʃön) *n* exposición *f*

exile (*êk*-ssail) *n* exilio *m*; exiliado *m*

exist (igh-*sisst*) *v* existir

existence (igh-*si*-sstönss) *n* existencia *f*

exit (*êk*-ssit) *n* salida *f*

exotic (igh-*so*-tik) *adj* exótico

expand (ik-*sspænd*) *v* *extender; *desplegar

expansion (ik-*sspæn*-ʃön) expansión *f*; dilatación *f*

expect (ik-*sspêkt*) *v* aguardar, esperar

expectation (êk-sspêk-*tei*-ʃön) *n* esperanza *f*; expectativa *f*

expedition (êk-ssppö-*di*-ʃön) *n* expedición *f*

expel (ik-*sspêl*) *v* expulsar

expenditure (ik-*sspên*-di-chö) *n* gasto *m*

expense (ik-*sspênss*) *n* gasto *m*

expensive (ik-*sspên*-ssiv) *adj* caro; costoso

experience (ik-*sspi*ᵒ-ri-önss) *n* experiencia *f*; *v* experimentar, vivir; **experienced** experimentado

experiment (ik-*sspê*-ri-mönt) *n* prueba *f*, experimento *m*; *v* experimentar

expert (*êk*-sspööt) *n* perito *m*, experto *m*; *adj* competente

expire (ik-*sspai*ᵒ) *v* expirar, terminarse; espirar; **expired** caducado

explain (ik-*ssplein*) *v* explicar

explanation (êk-ssplö-*nei*-∫ön) *n* aclaración *f*, explicación *f*

explicit (ik-*sspli*-ssit) *adj* expreso, explícito

explode (ik-*ssploud*) *v* estallar

exploit (ik-*ssploit*) *v* abusar de, explotar

explore (ik-*ssploo*) *v* explorar

explosion (ik-*ssplou*-ჳön) *n* explosión *f*

explosive (ik-*ssplou*-ssiv) *adj* explosivo; *n* explosivo *m*

export¹ (ik-*sspoot*) *v* exportar

export² (*êk*-sspoot) *n* exportación *f*

exportation (êk-sspoo-*tei*-∫ön) *n* exportación *f*

exports (*êk*-sspootss) *pl* exportación *f*

expose (ik-*sspous*) *v* exponer

exposition (êk-sspö-*si*-∫ön) *n* exposición *f*

exposure (ik-*sspou*-ჳö) *n* exposición *f*; ~ **meter** exposímetro *m*

express (ik-*ssprêss*) *v* expresar; *adj* expreso; explícito; ~ **train** tren expreso

expression (ik-*ssprê*-∫ön) *n* expresión *f*

exquisite (ik-*ssk*ᵘ*i*-sit) *adj* exquisito

extend (ik-*sstênd*) *v* prolongar; ampliar; conceder

extension (ik-*sstên*-∫ön) *n* prórroga *f*; ampliación *f*; extensión *f*; ~ **cord** cordón de extensión

extensive (ik-*sstên*-ssiv) *adj* extenso; amplio

extent (ik-*sstênt*) *n* alcance *m*; dimensión *f*

exterior (êk-*sstî*ᵒ-ri-ö) *adj* exterior; *n* exterior *m*

external (êk-*sstöö*-nöl) *adj* exterior

extinguish (ik-*ssting*-ghᵘi∫) *v* extinguir, apagar

extort (ik-*sstoot*) *v* extorsionar

extortion (ik-*sstoo*-∫ön) *n* extorsión *f*

extra (*êk*-sströ) *adj* extra

extract¹ (ik-*sstrækt*) *v* *extraer

extract² (*êk*-sstrækt) *n* fragmento *m*

extradite (*êk*-sströ-dait) *v* entregar

extraordinary (ik-*sstroo*-dön-ri) *adj* extraordinario

extravagant (ik-*sstræ*-vö-ghönt) *adj* exagerado, extravagante

extreme (ik-*sstriim*) *adj* extremo; *n* extremo *m*

exuberant (igh-*syuu*-bö-rönt) *adj* exuberante

eye (ai) *n* ojo *m*; ~ **shadow** sombra para los ojos

eyebrow (*ai*-brau) *n* ceja *f*; ~ **pencil** lápiz para las cejas

eyelash (*ai*-læ∫) *n* pestaña *f*

eyelid (*ai*-lid) *n* párpado *m*

eyewitness (*ai*-ᵘit-nöss) *n* testigo de vista

F

fable (*fei*-böl) *n* fábula *f*

fabric (*fæ*-brik) *n* tejido *m*; estructura *f*

façade (fö-*ssaad*) *n* fachada *f*

face (feiss) *n* cara *f*; rostro *m*; *v* enfrentarse con; **~ cream** crema facial; **~ down** boca abajo; **~ massage** masaje facial; **~ pack** máscara facial; **~ powder** polvo facial

facing (*fei*-ssing) enfrente de; frente a

facilities (fö-*ssi*-lö-tiis) *npl* instalaciones *fpl*

fact (fækt) *n* hecho *m*; **in ~** efectivamente; en realidad

factor (*fæk*-tö) *n* factor *m*

factory (*fæk*-tö-ri) *n* fábrica *f*

factual (*fæk*-chu-öl) *adj* real

faculty (*fæ*-köl-ti) *n* facultad *f*; don *m*, aptitud *f*

fade (feid) *v* *desteñirse; descolorarse

fail (feil) *v* fallar; faltar; omitir; *ser suspendido; **without ~** sin falta

failure (*feil*-yö) *n* fracaso *m*; fiasco *m*

faint (feint) *v* desmayarse; *adj* débil, vago

fair (fê⁰) *n* feria *f*; *adj* justo; rubio; claro

fairly (*fê⁰*-li) *adv* bastante

fairy (*fê⁰*-ri) *n* hada *f*

fairytale (*fê⁰*-ri-teil) *n* cuento de hadas

faith (feiz) *n* fe *f*; confianza *f*

faithful (*feiz*-ful) *adj* fiel; leal

fake (feik) *n* falsificación *f*

fall (fool) *n* caída *f*; *nAm* otoño *m*

*fall (fool) *v* *caer

false (foolss) *adj* falso; inexacto; **~ teeth** dentadura postiza

falter (*fool*-tö) *v* vacilar; balbucear

fame (feim) *n* fama *f*; reputación *f*

familiar (fö-*mil*-yö) *adj* familiar

family (*fæ*-mö-li) *n* familia *f*; **~ name** apellido *m*

famous (*fei*-möss) *adj* famoso

fan (fæn) *n* ventilador *m*; abanico *m*; admirador *m*, -a *f*, seguidor *m*, -a *f*; **~ belt** correa del ventilador

fanatical (fö-*næ*-ti-köl) *adj* fanático

fancy (*fæn*-ssi) *v* gustar, antojarse; imaginarse; *n* capricho *m*; gusto *m*

fantastic (fæn-*tæ*-sstik) *adj* fantástico

fantasy (*fæn*-tö-si) *n* fantasía *f*

far (faa) *adj* lejano; *adv* lejos; **by ~** con mucho; **so ~** hasta ahora

far-away (faa-rö-⁰ei) *adj* remoto

fare (fê⁰) *n* gastos de viaje, precio del billete; comida *f*

farm (faam) *n* granja *f*; cortijo *m*;

farmer (*faa*-mö) *n* granjero *m*, -a *f*, agricultor *m*, -a *f*

farmhouse (*faam*-hauss) *n* cortijo *m*; rancho *mMe*

far-off (*faa*-rof) *adj* a lo lejos

farther (*faa*-ðö) *adv* más lejos; **~ away** más allá, más lejos

fascinate (*fæ*-ssi-neit) *v* fascinar

fascism (*fæ*-ʃi-söm) *n* fascismo *m*

fascist (*fæ*-ʃisst) *adj* fascista

fashion (*fæ*-ʃön) *n* moda *f*; modo *m*; uso *m*

fashionable (*fæ*-ʃö-nö-böl) *adj* de moda

fast (faasst) *adj* rápido; firme; *n* ayuno *m*

fasten (*faa*-ssön) *v* atar; *cerrar

fastener (*faa*-ssö-nö) *n* cierre *m*

fat (fæt) *adj* graso, gordo; *n* grasa *f*

fatal (*fei*-töl) *adj* fatal, mortal

fate (feit) *n* destino *m*

father (*faa*-ðö) *n* padre *m*

father-in-law (*faa*-ðö-rin-loo) *n* (pl fathers-) suegro *m*

fatty (*fæ*-ti) *adj* grasiento

faucet (*foo*-ssit) *nAm* grifo *m*

fault (foolt) *n* culpa *f*; imperfección *f*,

defecto *m*

faultless (*foolt*-löss) *adj* impecable; perfecto

faulty (*fool*-ti) *adj* defectuoso

favo(u)r (*fei*-vö) *n* favor *m*; *v* *favorecer

favo(u)rable (*fei*-vö-rö-böl) *adj* favorable

favo(u)rite (*fei*-vö-rit) *n* favorito *m*, -a *f*; *adj* preferido

fax (fakss) *n* telefax *m*; **send a ~** mandar un telefax

fear (fiᵉ) *n* temor *m*, miedo *m*; *v* temer

feasible (*fii*-sö-böl) *adj* realizable

feast (fiisst) *n* fiesta *f*

feat (fiit) *n* hazaña *f*

feather (*fê*-ðö) *n* pluma *f*

feature (*fii*-chö) *n* característica *f*; rasgo *m*

February (*fê*-bru-ö-ri) febrero

federal (*fê*-dö-röl) *adj* federal

federation (fê-dö-*rei*-ʃön) *n* federación *f*

fee (fii) *n* honorarios *mpl*

feeble (*fii*-böl) *adj* débil; enfermizo

*feed (fiid) *v* alimentar; **fed up with** harto de

*feel (fiil) *v* *sentir; palpar; **~ like** antojarse; tener ganas de

feeling (*fii*-ling) *n* sensación *f*; sentimiento *m*; tacto *m*

feet (fiit) *n* (pl foot)

fell (fêl) *v* (p fall)

fellow (*fê*-lou) *n* tipo *m*; **~ countryman** compatriota *m/f*

felt[1] (fêlt) *n* fieltro *m*

felt[2] (fêlt) *v* (p, pp feel)

female (*fii*-meil) *adj* femenino

feminine (*fê*-mi-nin) *adj* femenino

fence (fênss) *n* cerca *f*; reja *f*; *v* esgrimir

ferment (föö-*mênt*) *v* fermentar

ferry-boat (*fê*-ri-bout) *n* transbordador *m*

fertile (*föö*-tail) *adj* fértil

festival (*fê*-ssti-völ) *n* festival *m*

festive (*fê*-sstiv) *adj* festivo

fetch (fêch) *v* *ir por; *ir a buscar

feudal (*fyuu*-döl) *adj* feudal

fever (*fii*-vö) *n* fiebre *f*

feverish (*fii*-vö-riʃ) *adj* febril

few (fyuu) *adj* pocos

fiancé (fi-*ang*-ssei) *n* novio *m*

fiancée (fi-*ang*-ssei) *n* novia *f*

fibre (*fai*-bö) *n* fibra *f*

fiction (*fik*-ʃön) *n* ficción *f*

field (fiild) *n* campo *m*; terreno *m*; **~ glasses** gemelos de campaña

fierce (fiᵉss) *adj* fiero; salvaje, violento

fifteen (fif-*tiin*) *num* quince

fifteenth (fif-*tiinz*) *num* quinceno

fifth (fifz) *num* quinto

fifty (*fif*-ti) *num* cincuenta

fig (figh) *n* higo *m*

fight (fait) *n* combate *m*, lucha *f*

*fight (fait) *v* combatir, luchar

figure (*fi*-ghö) *n* estatura *f*, figura *f*; cifra *f*

file (fail) *n* lima *f*; expediente *m*; cola *f*

fill (fil) *v* llenar; **~ in** completar, llenar; **filling station** estación de servicio; **~ out** *Am* completar, llenar; **~ up** llenar

filling (*fi*-ling) *n* empaste *m*; relleno *m*

film (film) *n* película *f*; *v* filmar

filter (*fil*-tö) *n* filtro *m*

filthy (*fil*-zi) *adj* sucio; sórdido, inmundo

final (*fai*-nöl) *adj* final; **finally** *adv* finalmente, por último; por fin

finance (fai-*nænss*) *v* financiar

finances (fai-*næn*-ssis) *pl* finanzas *fpl*

financial (fai-*næn*-ʃöl) *adj* financiero

finch (finch) *n* pinzón *m*

*find (faind) *v* *encontrar

fine (fain) *n* multa *f*; *adj* fino; bello; excelente, maravilloso; **~ arts** bellas artes

finger (*fing*-ghö) *n* dedo *m*; **little ~**

dedo meñique

fingerprint (*fing*-ghö-print) *n*
impresión digital

finish (*fi*-niʃ) *v* terminar; *n*
terminación *f*; meta *f*; **finished**
acabado

Finland (*fin*-lönd) Finlandia *f*

Finn (fin) *n* finlandés *m*

Finnish (*fi*-niʃ) *adj* finlandés

fire (faiö) *n* fuego *m*; incendio *m*; *v*
disparar; *despedir; **~ alarm** alarma
de incendio; **~ brigade,** *Am* **~**
department bomberos *mpl*; **~**
escape escala de incendios; **~**
extinguisher extintor *m*

fireplace (*faiö*-pleiss) *n* chimenea *f*

fireproof (*faiö*-pruuf) *adj*
incombustible; refractario

firm (fööm) *adj* firme; sólido; *n* firma *f*

first (föösst) *num* primero; **at ~** antes;
al principio; **~ name** nombre de pila

first aid (föösst-*eid*) *n* primeros
auxilios; **~ kit** botiquín de urgencia; **~**
post puesto de socorro

first-class (föösst-*klaass*) *adj* de
primera calidad

first-rate (föösst-*reit*) *adj* de primer
orden, de primera clase

fir tree (*föö*-trii) *n* abeto *m*

fish¹ (fiʃ) *n* (pl ~, ~es) pez *m*; **~ shop**
pescadería *f*

fish² (fiʃ) *v* pescar; **fishing gear** avíos
de pesca; **fishing fly** mosca artificial;
fishing hook anzuelo *m*; **fishing**
licence permiso de pesca; **fishing**
line línea de pesca; **fishing net** red
de pescar; **fishing rod** caña de
pescar; **fishing tackle** aparejo de
pesca

fishbone (*fiʃ*-boun) *n* espina *f*

fisherman (*fi*-ʃö-mön) *n* (pl -men)
pescador *m*

fist (fisst) *n* puño *m*

fit (fit) *adj* apropiado; *n* ataque *m*; *v*

*convenir; **fitting room** probador *m*

five (faiv) *num* cinco

fix (fikss) *v* arreglar

fixed (fiksst) *adj* fijo

fizz (fis) *n* efervescencia *f*

flag (flægh) *n* bandera *f*

flame (fleim) *n* llama *f*

flamingo (flö-*ming*-ghou) *n* (pl ~s,
~es) flamenco *m*

flannel (*flæ*-nöl) *n* franela *f*

flash (flæʃ) *n* relámpago *m*

flash bulb (*flæʃ*-balb) *n* bombilla de
flash

flashlight (*flæʃ*-lait) *n* linterna *f*

flask (flaassk) *n* frasco *m*; **thermos ~**
termo *m*

flat (flæt) *adj* llano; liso; *n* piso *m*; **~ tire**
Am, **~ tyre** neumático desinflado

flavo(u)r (*flei*-vö) *n* sabor *m*; gusto *m*;
v sazonar

***flee** (flii) *v* escapar, huir

fleet (fliit) *n* flota *f*

flesh (flêʃ) *n* carne *f*

flew (fluu) *v* (p fly)

flex (flêkss) *n* cordón flexible; *v*
doblar, flexionar

flexible (*flêk*-ssi-böl) *adj* flexible

flight (flait) *n* vuelo *m*; **charter ~** vuelo
charter

flint (flint) *n* pedernal *m*

float (flout) *v* flotar; *n* flotador *m*

flock (flok) *n* rebaño *m*

flood (flad) *n* inundación *f*; riada *f*

floor (floo) *n* suelo *m*; piso *m*; **~ show**
espectáculo de variedades

florist (*flo*-risst) *n* florista *m/f*

flour (flauö) *n* harina *f*

flow (flou) *v* correr, *fluir

flower (flauö) *n* flor *f*; **~ shop**
floristería *f*

flowerbed (*flauö*-bêd) *n* arriate *m*

flown (floun) *v* (pp fly)

flu (fluu) *n* gripe *f*

fluent (*fluu*-önt) *adj* corriente;

elocuente

fluid (*fluu*-id) *adj* fluido; *n* fluido *m*

flute (fluut) *n* flauta *f*

fly (flai) *n* mosca *f*; bragueta *f*

***fly** (flai) *v* *volar

foam (foum) *n* espuma *f*; *v* espumar; ~ **rubber** goma espumada

focus (*fou*-köss) *n* foco *m*

fog (fogh) *n* niebla *f*

foggy (*fo*-ghi) *adj* brumoso

foglamp (*fogh*-læmp) *n* faro de niebla

fold (fould) *v* doblar; *n* pliegue *m*

folk (fouk) *n* gente *f*; ~ **dance** danza popular; ~ **song** canción popular

folklore (*fouk*-loo) *n* folklore *m*

follow (*fo*-lou) *v* *seguir; **following** *adj* siguiente

fond: *be ~ **of** (bii fond ov) *querer

food (fuud) *n* comida *f*; alimento *m*; ~ **poisoning** intoxicación alimentaria

foodstuffs (*fuud*-sstafss) *pl* comestibles

fool (fuul) *n* idiota *m*, tonto *m*; *v* engañar

foolish (*fuu*-liʃ) *adj* necio, tonto; absurdo

foot (fut) *n* (pl feet) pie *m*; **on** ~ a pie; ~ **brake** freno de pie

football (*fut*-bool) *n* fútbol *m*; ~ **match** partido de fútbol

footbridge (*fut*-bridʒ) *n* puente *m* peatonal

footpath (*fut*-paaz) *n* senda *f*

footwear (*fut*-ᵘêᵒ) *n* calzado *m*

for (foo, fö) *prep* para; durante; a causa de, por; *conj* porque

***forbid** (fö-*bid*) *v* prohibir

force (fooss) *v* obligar, *forzar; *n* fuerza *f*; **by** ~ forzosamente; **driving** ~ fuerza motriz

forecast (*foo*-kaasst) *n* pronóstico *m*; previsión *f*; *v* pronosticar; predecir

foreground (*foo*-ghraund) *n* primer plano

forehead (fo-rêd) *n* frente *f*

foreign (*fo*-rin) *adj* extranjero; extraño

foreigner (*fo*-ri-nö) *n* extranjero *m*; forastero *m*

foreman (*foo*-mön) *n* (pl -men) capataz *m*

foremost (*foo*-mousst) *adj* primero; principal

forest (*fo*-risst) *n* selva *f*, bosque *m*

forester (*fo*-ri-sstö) *n* guardabosques *m*

forever (fö-rê-vö) *adv* siempre; constantemente

forge (foodʒ) *v* falsificar

***forget** (fö-*ghêt*) *v* olvidar

forgetful (fö-*ghêt*-föl) *adj* olvidadizo

***forgive** (fö-*ghiv*) *v* perdonar

fork (fook) *n* tenedor *m*; bifurcación *f*; *v* bifurcarse

form (foom) *n* forma *f*; formulario *m*; clase *f*; *v* formar

formal (*foo*-möl) *adj* formal

formality (foo-*mæ*-lö-ti) *n* formalidad *f*

former (*foo*-mö) *adj* antiguo; anterior; **formerly** antes

formula (*foo*-myu-lö) *n* (pl ~e, ~s) fórmula *f*

fortnight (*foot*-nait) *n* quincena *f*

fortress (*foo*-triss) *n* fortaleza *f*

fortunate (*foo*-chö-nöt) *adj* afortunado; **fortunately** *adv* afortunadamente

fortune (*foo*-chuun) *n* fortuna *f*; suerte *f*

forty (*foo*-ti) *num* cuarenta

forward (*foo*-ᵘöd) *adv* hacia adelante, adelante; *v* reexpedir

foster parents (*fo*-sstö-pêᵒ-röntss) *pl* padres adoptivos

fought (foot) *v* (p, pp fight)

foul (faul) *adj* sucio; vil; obsceno; *n* falta *f*

found[1] (faund) *v* (p, pp find)

found² (faund) *v* fundar

foundation (faun-*dei*-ʃön) *n* fundación *f*; ~ **cream** crema de base

fountain (*faun*-tin) *n* fuente *f*

fountain pen (*faun*-tin-pên) *n* estilográfica *f*

four (foo) *num* cuatro

fourteen (foo-*tiin*) *num* catorce

fourteenth (foo-*tiinz*) *num* catorceno

fourth (fooz) *num* cuarto

fowl (faul) *n* (pl ~s, ~) ave *f* de corral

fox (fokss) *n* zorro *m*

foyer (*foi*-ei) *n* vestíbulo *m*

fraction (fræk-ʃön) *n* fracción *f*

fracture (*fræk*-chö) *v* fracturar; *n* fractura *f*

fragile (*fræ*-dʒail) *adj* frágil

fragment (*frægh*-mönt) *n* fragmento *m*; trozo *m*

frame (freim) *n* marco *m*; armadura *f*

France (fraanss) Francia *f*

franchise (*fræn*-chais) *n* derecho electoral

fraternity (frö-*töö*-nö-ti) *n* fraternidad *f*

fraud (frood) *n* fraude *m*

fray (frei) *v* deshilacharse

free (frii) *adj* libre; gratuito; ~ **of charge** gratis; ~ **ticket** billete gratuito

freedom (*frii*-döm) *n* libertad *f*

*freeze (friis) *v* *helar; congelar

freezer (*frii*-sör) congelador *m*

freezing (*frii*-sing) *adj* helado

freezing point (*frii*-sing-point) *n* punto de congelación

freight (freit) *n* carga *f*, cargo *m*

French (frênch) *adj* francés

Frenchman (*frênch*-mön) *n* (pl -men) francés *m*

Frenchwoman (*frênch*-ᵘu-mön) *n* (pl -women) francesa *f*

frequency (*frii*-kᵘön-ssi) *n* frecuencia *f*

frequent (*frii*-kᵘönt) *adj* frecuente

fresh (frêʃ) *adj* fresco; ~**water** *adj* de agua dulce

friction (*frik*-ʃön) *n* fricción *f*

Friday (*frai*-di) viernes *m*

fridge (fridʒ) *n* frigorífico *m*, refrigerador *m*

friend (frênd) *n* amigo *m*; amiga *f*

friendly (*frênd*-li) *adj* amable; amistoso

friendship (*frênd*-ʃip) *n* amistad *f*

fright (frait) *n* miedo *m*, espanto *m*

frighten (*frai*-tön) *v* espantar

frightened (*frai*-tönd) *adj* espantado; ***be ~** asustarse

frightful (*frait*-föl) *adj* terrible; espantoso

fringe (frindʒ) *n* fleco *m*; franja *f*

frock (frok) *n* vestido *m*

frog (frogh) *n* rana *f*

from (from) *prep* desde; de; a partir de

front (frant) *n* frente *m*; **in ~ of** delante de

frontier (*fran*-tiᵒ) *n* frontera *f*

frost (frosst) *n* escarcha *f*

froth (froz) *n* espuma *f*

frozen (*frou*-sön) *adj* congelado; ~ **food** alimento congelado

fruit (fruut) *n* fruta *f*; fruto *m*

fry (frai) *v* *freír

frying pan (*frai*-ing-pæn) *n* sartén *f*

fuck (fak) *v vulgar* follar con; *L.Am.* coger; **fuck!** ¡joder!

fuel (*fyuu*-öl) *n* combustible *m*; ~ **pump** *Am* bomba de gasolina

full (ful) *adj* lleno; ~ **board** pensión completa; ~ **stop** punto *m*; ~ **up** completo

fun (fan) *n* diversión *f*

function (*fangk*-ʃön) *n* función *f*

fund (fand) *n* fondos *mpl*

fundamental (fan-dö-*mên*-töl) *adj* fundamental

funeral (*fyuu*-nö-röl) *n* funerales *mpl*

funnel (*fa*-nöl) *n* embudo *m*

funny (*fa*-ni) *adj* gracioso, cómico; extraño

fur (föö) *n* piel *f*; ~ **coat** abrigo de pieles

furious (*fyuᵒ*-ri-öss) *adj* furioso

furnace (*föö*-niss) *n* horno *m*

furnish (*föö*-niʃ) *v* suministrar, procurar; instalar, amueblar; ~ **with** *proveer de

furniture (*föö*-ni-chö) *n* muebles *mpl*

furrier (*fa*-ri-ö) *n* peletero *m*

further (*föö*-ðö) *adj* más lejos; adicional

furthermore (*föö*-ðö-moo) *adv* además

furthest (*föö*-ðisst) *adj* el más alejado

fuse (fyuus) *n* fusible *m*; mecha *f*

fuss (fass) *n* agitación *f*; lío *m*; ostentación *f*, bulla *f*; **make a** ~ armar un lío

future (*fyuu*-chö) *n* porvenir *m*; futuro *m*; *adj* futuro

G

gable (*ghei*-böl) *n* faldón *m*

gadget (*ghæ*-dʒit) *n* aparato *m*

gain (ghein) *v* ganar; *n* ganancia *f*

gale (gheil) *n* ventarrón *m*

gall (ghool) *n* bilis *f*; ~ **bladder** vesícula biliar

gallery (*ghæ*-lö-ri) *n* galería *f*

gallon (*ghæ*-lön) galón *m* (en EE.UU. 3,785 litros, en GB 4,546)

gallop (*ghæ*-löp) *n* galope *m*

gallows (*ghæ*-lous) *pl* horca *f*

gallstone (*ghool*-sstoun) *n* cálculo biliar

game (gheim) *n* juego *m*; caza *f*; ~ **reserve** parque de reserva zoológica

gang (ghæng) *n* banda *f*; pandilla *f*

gangway (*ghæng*-ᵘei) *n* pasarela *f*; pasillo *m*

gap (ghæp) *n* hueco *m*

garage (*ghæ*-raaʒ) *n* garaje *m*; *v* dejar en garaje

garbage (*ghaa*-bidʒ) *n* basura *f*

garden (*ghaa*-dön) *n* jardín *m*; **public** ~ jardín público; **zoological gardens** jardín zoológico

gardener (*ghaa*-dö-nö) *n* jardinero *m*, -a *f*

gargle (*ghaa*-ghöl) *v* *hacer gárgaras

garlic (*ghaa*-lik) *n* ajo *m*

gas (ghæss) *n* gas *m*; *nAm* gasolina *f*; ~ **cooker** cocina de gas; ~ **station** *Am* puesto de gasolina; ~ **stove** estufa de gas; ~ **tank** *Am* depósito de gasolina

gasoline (*ghæ*-ssö-liin) *nAm* gasolina *f*

gastric (*ghæ*-sstrik) *adj* gástrico; ~ **ulcer** úlcera gástrica

gasworks (*ghæss*-ᵘöökss) *n* fábrica de gas

gate (gheit) *n* portón *m*; verja *f*; puerta *f*

gather (*ghæ*-ðö) *v* coleccionar; juntarse; recoger

gauge (gheidʒ) *n* medida *f*; calibre *m*; *v* medir; calibrar

gave (gheiv) *v* (p give)

gay (ghei) *adj* alegre; gaitero; homosexual

gaze (gheis) *v* mirar

gazetteer (ghæ-sö-tiᵒ) *n* diccionario geográfico

gear (ghiᵒ) *n* prendas *fpl*; aparejo *m*;

engranaje *m*; **change** ~ cambiar de marcha; ~ **lever**, ~ **shift** palanca de cambios

gearbox (*ghiᵒ*-bokss) *n* caja de velocidades

geese (giis) *n* (pl goose)

gem (dʒêm) *n* joya *f*, gema *f*; alhaja *f*

gender (*dʒên*-dö) *n* género *m*

general (*dʒê*-nö-röl) *adj* general; *n* general *m*; ~ **practitioner** médico de cabecera; **in** ~ en general

generate (*dʒê*-nö-reit) *v* generar

generation (dʒê-nö-*rei*-ʃön) *n* generación *f*

generator (*dʒê*-nö-rei-tör) *n* generador *m*

generosity (dʒê-nö-*ro*-ssö-ti) *n* generosidad *f*

generous (*dʒê*-nö-röss) *adj* generoso

genital (*dʒê*-ni-töl) *adj* genital

genius (*dʒiī*-ni-öss) *n* genio *m*

gentle (*dʒên*-töl) *adj* gentil; tierno, suave; prudente

gentleman (*dʒên*-töl-mön) *n* (pl -men) caballero *m*

genuine (*dʒê*-nyu-in) *adj* genuino

geography (dʒi-*o*-ghrö-fi) *n* geografía *f*

geology (dʒi-*o*-lö-dʒi) *n* geología *f*

geometry (dʒi-*o*-mö-tri) *n* geometría *f*

germ (dʒööm) *n* germen *m*

German (*dʒöö*-mön) *adj* alemán

Germany (*dʒöö*-mö-ni) Alemania *f*

gesticulate (dʒi-*ssti*-kyu-leit) *v* gesticular

*get (ghêt) *v* *conseguir; *ir a buscar; *hacerse; ~ **back** regresar; ~ **off** apearse; ~ **on** subir, montar; adelantar; ~ **up** levantarse

ghost (ghousst) *n* fantasma *m*; espíritu *m*

giant (*dʒai*-önt) *n* gigante *m*

giddiness (*ghi*-di-nöss) *n* mareo *m*

giddy (*ghi*-di) *adj* mareado

gift (ghift) *n* regalo *m*; talento *m*

gifted (*ghif*-tid) *adj* talentoso

gigantic (dʒai-*ghæn*-tik) *adj* gigantesco

giggle (*ghi*-ghöl) *v* *soltar risitas

gill (ghil) *n* branquia *f*

gilt (ghilt) *adj* dorado

ginger (*dʒin*-dʒö) *n* jengibre *m*

girdle (*ghöö*-döl) *n* faja *f*

girl (ghööl) *n* muchacha *f*; ~ **guide** exploradora *f*

girlfriend (*ghööl*-frênd) *n* novia *f*; amiga *f*

*give (ghiv) *v* *dar; entregar; ~ **away** revelar; ~ **in** ceder; ~ **up** renunciar

glacier (*ghlæ*-ssi-ö) *n* glaciar *m*

glad (ghlæd) *adj* alegre, contento; **gladly** con mucho gusto, gustosamente

gladness (*ghlæd*-nöss) *n* alegría *f*

glamorous (*ghlæ*-mö-röss) *adj* encantador

glamour (*ghlæ*-mö) *n* encanto *m*

glance (ghlaanss) *n* ojeada *f*; *v* ojear

gland (ghlænd) *n* glándula *f*

glare (ghlêᵒ) *n* relumbrón *m*; mirada *f* feroz

glaring (*ghlêᵒ*-ring) *adj* deslumbrador

glass (ghlaass) *n* vaso *m*; vidrio *m*; de vidrio; **glasses** anteojos *mpl*, gafas *fpl*; **magnifying** ~ lente de aumento

glaze (ghleis) *v* esmaltar

glide (ghlaid) *v* resbalar

glider (*ghlai*-dö) *n* planeador *m*

glimpse (ghlimpss) *n* vislumbre *m*; ojeada *f*; *v* vislumbrar

global (*ghlou*-böl) *adj* mundial; global

globe (ghloub) *n* globo *m*

gloom (ghluum) *n* oscuridad *f*; lobreguez *f*

gloomy (*ghluu*-mi) *adj* sombrío; tenebroso

glorious (*ghloo*-ri-öss) *adj* glorioso

glory (*ghloo*-ri) *n* gloria *f*; honor *m*,

elogio *m*

gloss (ghloss) *n* brillo *m*

glossy (*ghlo*-ssi) *adj* lustroso; satinado

glove (ghlav) *n* guante *m*

glow (ghlou) *v* brillar; *n* brillo *m*

glue (ghluu) *n* cola *f*; goma *f*

*go (ghou) *v* *ir; caminar; *hacerse; ~ **ahead** continuar; ~ **away** *irse; ~ **back** regresar; ~ **home** *volver a casa; ~ **in** entrar; ~ **on** continuar; ~ **out** *salir; ~ **through** pasar

goal (ghoul) *n* meta *f*; gol *m*

goalkeeper (*ghoul*-kii-pö) *n* portero *m*

goat (ghout) *n* cabrón *m*, cabra *f*

god (ghod) *n* dios *m*

goddess (*gho*-diss) *n* diosa *f*

godfather (*ghod*-faa-ðö) *n* padrino *m*

goggles (*gho*-ghöls) *pl* gafas *fpl* submarinas

gold (ghould) *n* oro *m*; ~ **leaf** hojas de oro

golden (*ghoul*-dön) *adj* dorado

goldmine (*ghould*-main) *n* mina de oro

goldsmith (*ghould*-ssmiz) *n* orfebre *m*

golf (gholf) *n* golf *m*; ~ **course**, ~ **links** campo de golf

golfclub (*gholf*-klab) *n* palo de golf

gondola (*ghon*-dö-lö) *n* góndola *f*

gone (ghon) *adv* (pp go) ido

good (ghud) *adj* bueno

goodbye! (ghud-*bai*) ¡adiós!

good-humo(u)red (ghud-*hyuu*-möd) *adj* de buen humor

good-looking (ghud-*lu*-king) *adj* bien parecido; guapo

good-natured (ghud-*nei*-chöd) *adj* bondadoso

goods (ghuds) *pl* mercancías *fpl*, bienes *mpl*; ~ **train** tren de mercancías

good-tempered (ghud-*têm*-pöd) *adj*

de buen humor

goodwill (ghud-*u̇il*) *n* buena voluntad

goose (ghuuss) *n* (pl geese) oca *f*; ~ **bumps** *Am*, ~ **flesh** carne de gallina

gooseberry (*ghus*-bö-ri) *n* grosella espinosa

gorge (ghoodȝ) *n* cañón *m*

gorgeous (*ghoo*-dȝöss) *adj* magnífico

gospel (*ghoo*-sspöl) *n* evangelio *m*

gossip (*gho*-ssip) *n* chisme *m*; *v* *contar chismes

got (ghot) *v* (p, pp get)

Gothic (*gho*-zik) *adj* gótico

gourmet (*ghuᵒ*-mei) *n* gastrónomo *m*, -a *f*

gout (ghaut) *n* gota *f*

govern (*gha*-vön) *v* *regir

governess (*gha*-vö-niss) *n* aya *f*

government (*gha*-vön-mönt) *n* régimen *m*, gobierno *m*

governor (*gha*-vö-nö) *n* gobernador *m*

gown (ghaun) *n* traje largo (de mujer) *m*

grace (ghreiss) *n* gracia *f*; perdón *m*

graceful (*ghreiss*-föl) *adj* gracioso

grade (ghreid) *n* grado *m*; *v* graduar

gradient (*ghrei*-di-önt) *n* pendiente *f*

gradual (*ghræ*-dȝu-öl) *adj* gradual; **gradually** *adv* paulatinamente

graduate (*ghræ*-dȝu-eit) *v* graduarse

grain (ghrein) *n* grano *m*, trigo *m*

gram (ghræm) *n* gramo *m*

grammar (*ghræ*-mö) *n* gramática *f*

grammatical (ghrö-*mæ*-ti-köl) *adj* gramatical

grand (ghrænd) *adj* imponente

grandchild nieto *m*, -a *f*

granddad (*ghræn*-dæd) *n* abuelito *m*

granddaughter (*ghræn*-doo-tö) *n* nieta *f*

grandfather (*ghræn*-faa-ðö) *n* abuelo *m*

grandmother (*ghræn*-ma-ðö) *n*

abuela f

grandparents (*ghræn*-pê⁰-röntss) *pl* abuelos *mpl*

grandson (*ghræn*-ssan) *n* nieto *m*

granite (*ghræ*-nit) *n* granito *m*

grant (ghraant) *v* conceder; *n* subvención *f*, beca *f*

grape (ghreip) uva *f*

grapefruit (*ghreip*-fruut) *n* pomelo *m*; toronja *fMe*

grapes (ghreipss) *pl* uvas *fpl*

graph (ghræf) *n* gráfico *m*

graphic (*ghræ*-fik) *adj* gráfico

grasp (ghraassp) *v* agarrar; *n* agarre *m*

grass (ghraass) *n* césped *m*

grasshopper (*ghraass*-ho-pö) *n* saltamontes *m*

grate (ghreit) *n* reja *f*; *v* rallar

grateful (*ghreit*-föl) *adj* agradecido

grater (*ghrei*-tö) *n* rayador *m*

gratis (*ghræ*-tiss) *adj* gratuito

gratitude (*ghræ*-ti-tyuud) *n* gratitud *f*

gratuity (ghrö-*tyuu*-ö-ti) *n* propina *f*

grave (ghreiv) *n* sepultura *f*; *adj* grave

gravel (*ghræ*-völ) *n* grava *f*

gravestone (*ghreiv*-sstoun) *n* lápida *f*

graveyard (*ghreiv*-yaad) *n* cementerio *m*

gravity (*ghræ*-vö-ti) *n* gravedad *f*; seriedad *f*

gravy (*ghrei*-vi) *n* salsa *f*

graze (ghreis) *v* *pacer; *n* rozadura *f*

grease (ghriiss) *n* grasa *f*; *v* engrasar

greasy (*ghrii*-ssi) *adj* grasiento, grasoso

great (ghreit) *adj* grande; **Great Britain** Gran Bretaña

Greece (ghriiss) Grecia *f*

greed (ghriid) *n* codicia *f*

greedy (*ghrii*-di) *adj* codicioso; glotón

Greek (ghriik) *adj* griego

green (ghriin) *adj* verde; ~ **card** tarjeta verde

greengrocer (*ghriin*-ghrou-ssö) *n*

verdulero *m*

greenhouse (*ghriin*-hauss) *n* invernadero *m*, invernáculo *m*

greens (ghriins) *pl* legumbres *fpl*

greet (ghriit) *v* saludar

greeting (*ghrii*-ting) *n* saludo *m*

grey (ghrei) *adj* gris

greyhound (*ghrei*-haund) *n* galgo *m*

grief (ghriif) *n* pesadumbre *f*; aflicción *f*, dolor *m*

grieve (ghriiv) *v* *estar afligido

grill (ghril) *n* parrilla *f*; *v* asar en parrilla

grillroom (*ghril*-ruum) *n* parrilla *f*

grim (ghrim) *adj* severo; desolador; lúgubre

grin (ghrin) *v* *sonreír; *n* sonrisa sardónica

*grind (ghraind) *v* *moler; triturar

grip (ghrip) *v* *asir; *n* agarradero *m*, agarre *m*; *nAm* maletín *m*

grit (ghrit) *n* arena *f*; cascajo *m*; valor *m*

groan (ghroun) *v* *gemir

grocer (*ghrou*-ssö) *n* abacero *m*; abarrotero *mMe*; **grocer's** abacería *f*; abarrotería *fMe*

groceries (*ghrou*-ssö-ris) *pl* comestibles *mpl*

groin (ghroin) *n* ingle *f*

groom (ghruum) *n* novio *m*; mozo *m* de cuadra; *v* almohazar; preparar; **well groomed** bien arreglado

groove (ghruuv) *n* surco *m*

gross¹ (ghrouss) *n* (*pl* ~) gruesa *f*

gross² (ghrouss) *adj* grosero; bruto

grotto (*ghro*-tou) *n* (*pl* ~es, ~s) gruta *f*

ground¹ (ghraund) *n* fondo *m*, tierra *f*; ~ **floor** piso bajo; **grounds** terreno *m*

ground² (ghraund) *v* (p, pp grind)

group (ghruup) *n* grupo *m*

grouse (ghrauss) *n* (*pl* ~) gallo de bosque

grove (ghrouv) *n* soto *m*

*grow (ghrou) *v* *crecer; cultivar; *hacerse

growl (ghraul) *v* *gruñir

grown-up (*ghroun*-ap) *adj* adulto; *n* adulto *m*, -a *f*

growth (ghrouz) *n* crecimiento *m*; desarrollo *m*; tumor *m*

grudge (ghradʒ) *n* rencor *m*

grumble (*ghram*-böl) *v* refunfuñar

guarantee (ghæ-rön-*tii*) *n* garantía *f*; *v* garantizar

guard (ghaad) *n* guardia *f*; *v* guardar

guardian (*ghaa*-di-ön) *n* tutor *m/f*; guardián *m*

guess (ghêss) *v* adivinar; *creer, conjeturar; *n* conjetura *f*

guest (ghêsst) *n* huésped *m*, invitado *m*; ~ room habitación para huéspedes

guesthouse (*ghêsst*-hauss) *n* pensión *f*

guide (ghaid) *n* guía *m*; *v* guiar

guidebook (*ghaid*-buk) *n* guía *f*

guide dog (*ghaid*-dogh) *n* perro lazarillo

guilt (ghilt) *n* culpa *f*

guilty (*ghil*-ti) *adj* culpable

guinea pig (*ghi*-ni-pigh) *n* conejillo de Indias

guitar (ghi-*taa*) *n* guitarra *f*

gulf (ghalf) *n* golfo *m*

gull (ghal) *n* gaviota *f*

gum (gham) *n* encía *f*; goma *f*; cola *f*

gun (ghan) *n* fusil *m*, revólver *m*; cañón *m*

gunpowder (*ghan*-pau-dö) *n* pólvora *f*

gust (ghasst) *n* ráfaga *f*

gusty (*gha*-ssti) *adj* borrascoso

gut (ghat) *n* intestino *m*; guts coraje *m*

gutter (*gha*-tö) *n* cuneta *f*

guy (ghai) *n* tipo *m*

gym (dʒim) gimnasio *m*

gymnasium (dʒim-*nei*-si-öm) *n* (pl ~s, -sia) gimnasio *m*

gymnast (*dʒim*-næsst) *n* gimnasta *m*

gymnastics (dʒim-*næ*-sstikss) *pl* gimnasia *f*

gyn(a)ecologist (ghai-nö-*ko*-lö-dʒisst) *n* ginecólogo *m*, -a *f*

H

habit (*hæ*-bit) *n* hábito *m*

habitable (*hæ*-bi-tö-böl) *adj* habitable

habitual (hö-*bi*-chu-öl) *adj* habitual

had (hæd) *v* (p, pp have)

haddock (*hæ*-dök) *n* (pl ~) bacalao *m*

h(a)emorrhage (*hê*-mö-ridʒ) *n* hemorragia *f*

h(a)emorrhoids (*hê*-mö-roids) *pl* hemorroides *fpl*

hail (heil) *n* granizo *m*

hair (hêᵒ) *n* cabello *m*; ~ cream brillantina *f*; ~ gel gel fijador de cabello; ~ piece postizo *m*; ~ rollers

rizadores *mpl*; ~ tonic tónico para el cabello

hairbrush (*hêᵒ*-braʃ) *n* cepillo para el cabello

haircut (*hêᵒ*-kat) *n* corte de pelo

hairdo (*hêᵒ*-duu) *n* peinado *m*

hairdresser (*hêᵒ*-drê-ssö) *n* peluquero *m*, -a *f*

hairdrier, hairdryer (*hêᵒ*-drai-ö) *n* secador para el pelo

hairgrip (*hêᵒ*-ghrip) *n* horquilla *f*

hair net (*hêᵒ*-nêt) *n* redecilla *f*

hairpin (*hêᵒ*-pin) *n* horquilla *f*

hair spray (*hê⁰-*sprei) *n* laca para el cabello

hairy (*hê⁰-*ri) *adj* cabelludo

half¹ (haaf) *adj* medio

half² (haaf) *n* (pl halves) mitad *f*

half time (haaf-*taim*) *n* descanso *m*

halfway (haaf-*ᵘei*) *adv* a mitad de camino

halibut (*hæ-*li-böt) *n* (pl ∼) halibut *m*

hall (hool) *n* vestíbulo *m*; sala *f*

halt (hoolt) *v* pararse

halve (haav) *v* partir por la mitad

ham (hæm) *n* jamón *m*

hamlet (*hæm-*löt) *n* aldea *f*

hammer (*hæ-*mö) *n* martillo *m*

hammock (*hæ-*mök) *n* hamaca *f*

hamper (*hæm-*pö) *n* cesto *m*

hand (hænd) *n* mano *f*; *v* alargar; ∼ **cream** crema para las manos

handbag (*hænd-*bægh) *n* bolso *m*

handbook (*hænd-*buk) *n* manual *m*

handbrake (*hænd-*breik) *n* freno de mano

handcuffs (*hænd-*kafss) *pl* esposas *fpl*

handful (*hænd-*ful) *n* puñado *m*

handicap (*hæn-*di-kæp) *n* desventaja *f*

handicapped (*hæn-*di-kæpt) *n* minusválido *m*

handicraft (*hæn-*di-kraaft) *n* trabajo manual; artesanía *f*

handkerchief (*hæng-*kö-chif) *n* pañuelo *m*

handle (*hæn-*döl) *n* mango *m*; *v* manejar; tratar

hand-made (*hænd-*meid) *adj* hecho a mano

handshake (*hænd-*ʃeik) *n* apretón de manos

handsome (*hæn-*ssöm) *adj* guapo

handwork (*hænd-*ᵘöök) *n* obra hecha a mano

handwriting (*hænd-*rai-ting) *n* escritura *f*

handy (*hæn-*di) *adj* manejable

***hang** (hæng) *v* *colgar

hanger (*hæng-*ö) *n* percha *f*

hangover (*hæng-*ou-vö) *n* resaca *f*

happen (*hæ-*pön) *v* suceder, pasar

happening (*hæ-*pö-ning) *n* acontecimiento *m*

happiness (*hæ-*pi-nöss) *n* felicidad *f*

happy (*hæ-*pi) *adj* contento, feliz

harbo(u)r (*haa-*bö) *n* puerto *m*

hard (haad) *adj* duro; difícil; ∼ **disk** disco *m* duro; **hardly** apenas

hardware (*haad-*ᵘê⁰) *n* quincalla *f*; hardware *m*; ∼ **store** ferretería *f*

hare (hê⁰) *n* liebre *f*

harm (haam) *n* perjuicio *m*; mal *m*, daño *m*; *v* perjudicar

harmful (*haam-*föl) *adj* perjudicial, dañoso

harmless (*haam-*löss) *adj* inocuo; inofensivo

harmony (*haa-*mö-ni) *n* armonía *f*

harp (haap) *n* arpa *f*

harpsichord (*haap-*ssi-kood) *n* clavicémbalo *m*

harsh (haaʃ) *adj* áspero; severo; cruel

harvest (*haa-*visst) *n* cosecha *f*

has (hæs) *v* (pr have)

haste (heisst) *n* prisa *f*

hasten (*hei-*ssön) *v* apresurarse

hasty (*hei-*ssti) *adj* apresurado

hat (hæt) *n* sombrero *m*; ∼ **rack** percha *f*

hatch (hæch) *n* trampa *f*

hate (heit) *v* detestar; odiar; *n* odio *m*

hatred (*hei-*trid) *n* odio *m*

haughty (*hoo-*ti) *adj* altivo

haul (hool) *v* arrastrar; transportar

***have** (hæv) *v* *haber, *tener, *hacer; ∼ **to** deber

hawk (hook) *n* halcón *m*

hay (hei) *n* heno *m*; ∼ **fever** fiebre del heno

hazard (*hæ-*söd) *n* riesgo *m*

haze (heis) *n* calina *f*; niebla *f*

hazelnut (*hei*-söl-nat) *n* avellana *f*

hazy (*hei*-si) *adj* calinoso; brumoso

he (hii) *pron* él

head (hêd) *n* cabeza *f*; *v* dirigir; ~ **of state** jefe de Estado; ~ **teacher** director *m*, -a *f* de escuela; ~ **waiter** jefe de camareros

headache (*hê*-deik) *n* dolor de cabeza

heading (*hê*-ding) *n* título *m*

headlamp (*hêd*-læmp) *n* fanal *m*

headland (*hêd*-lönd) *n* promontorio *m*

headlight (*hêd*-lait) *n* faro *m*

headline (*hêd*-lain) *n* titular *m*

headmaster (hêd-*maa*-sstö) *n* director de escuela

headmistress (hêd-*mi*-sströss) *n* directora de escuela

headquarters (hêd-kʷoo-tös) *pl* cuartel general

headstrong (*hêd*-sstrong) *adj* cabezudo

heal (hiil) *v* curar

health (hêlz) *n* salud *f*; ~ **center** *Am*, ~ **centre** dispensario *m*; ~ **certificate** certificado de salud

healthy (*hêl*-zi) *adj* sano

heap (hiip) *n* montón *m*

***hear** (hiⁱ) *v* *oír

hearing (*hiⁱ*-ring) *n* oído *m*

heart (haat) *n* corazón *m*; núcleo *m*; **by ~** de memoria; ~ **attack** ataque cardíaco

heartburn (*haat*-böön) *n* acidez *f*

hearth (haaz) *n* fogón *m*

heartless (*haat*-löss) *adj* insensible; cruel

hearty (*haa*-ti) *adj* cordial

heat (hiit) *n* calor *m*; *v* *calentar; **heating pad** almohada eléctrica

heater (*hii*-tö) *n* calefactor *m*; **immersion ~** calentador de inmersión

heath (hiiz) *n* brezal *m*

heathen (*hii*-ðön) *n* pagano *m*

heather (*hê*-ðö) *n* brezo *m*

heating (*hii*-ting) *n* calefacción *f*

heaven (*hê*-vön) *n* cielo *m*

heavy (*hê*-vi) *adj* pesado

Hebrew (*hii*-bruu) *n* hebreo *m*

hedge (hêdʒ) *n* seto *m*

hedgehog (*hêdʒ*-hogh) *n* erizo *m*

heel (hiil) *n* talón *m*; tacón *m*

height (hait) *n* altura *f*; colmo *m*, apogeo *m*

heir (êr) *n* heredero *m*

heiress (*ê*-ris) *n* heredera *f*

helicopter (*hê*-li-kop-tö) helicóptero *m*

hell (hêl) *n* infierno *m*

hello (hê-*lou*) hola; ¿sí?, ¿diga?, *Am* ¿alo?; **say ~ to** saludar a

helm (hêlm) *n* timón *m*

helmet (*hêl*-mit) *n* casco *m*

helmsman (*hêlms*-mön) *n* timonero *m*

help (hêlp) *v* ayudar; *n* ayuda *f*

helper (*hêl*-pö) *n* ayudante *m/f*

helpful (*hêlp*-föl) *adj* útil; atento

helping (*hêl*-ping) *n* porción *f*

hemp (hêmp) *n* cáñamo *m*

hen (hên) *n* gallina *f*

her (höö) *pron* la, le; *adj* su

herb (hööb) *n* hierba *f*

herd (hööd) *n* manada *f*; rebaño *m*

here (hiⁱ) *adv* acá; ~ **you are** tenga usted

hereditary (hi-*rê*-di-to-ri) *adj* hereditario

hernia (*höö*-ni-ö) *n* hernia *f*

hero (*hiⁱ*-rou) *n* (pl ~es) héroe *m*

heron (*hê*-rön) *n* garza *f*

herring (*hê*-ring) *n* (pl ~, ~s) arenque *m*

herself (höö-*ssêlf*) *pron* se; ella misma

hesitate (*hê*-si-teit) *v* vacilar

heterosexual (hê-tö-rö-*ssêk*-ʃu-öl) *adj* heterosexual

hiccup (*hi*-kap) *n* hipo *m*
hide (haid) *n* piel *f*; cuero *m*
*hide (haid) *v* esconder
hideous (*hi*-di-öss) *adj* horrible
hierarchy (*hai*⁰-raa-ki) *n* jerarquía *f*
high (hai) *adj* alto
highway (*hai*-ᵘei) *n* carretera *f*; *nAm* autopista *f*
hijack (*hai*-dʒæk) *v* secuestrar
hijacker (*hai*-dʒæ-kö) *n* secuestrador *m*
hike (haik) *v* caminar; ir de excursión a pie
hill (hil) *n* colina *f*
hillside (*hil*-ssaid) *n* ladera *f*
hilltop (*hil*-top) *n* cima *f*
hilly (*hi*-li) *adj* montuoso
him (him) *pron* le
himself (him-*ssêlf*) *pron* se; él mismo
hinder (*hin*-dö) *v* *impedir
hinge (hindʒ) *n* bisagra *f*
hint (hint) *n* pista *f*; consejo *m*; indirecta *f*; rastro *m*
hip (hip) *n* cadera *f*
hire (hai⁰) *v* alquilar; **for ~** de alquiler; **~ purchase** compra a plazos
his (his) *adj* su
historic (hi-*ssto*-rik) *adj* histórico
historical (hi-*ssto*-ri-köl) *adj* histórico
history (*hi*-sstö-ri) *n* historia *f*
hit (hit) *n* golpe *m*; éxito *m*
*hit (hit) *v* pegar; tocar, *acertar
hitchhike (*hich*-haik) *v* *hacer autostop
hitchhiker (*hich*-hai-kö) *n* autoestopista *m/f*
hoarse (hooss) *adj* ronco
hobby (*ho*-bi) *n* afición *f*
hobbyhorse (*ho*-bi-hooss) *n* comidilla *f*
hockey (*ho*-ki) *n* hockey *m*
hoist (hoisst) *v* izar
hold (hould) *n* presa *f*; dominio *m*; bodega *f*

*hold (hould) *v* *tener; *retener; **~ on** agarrarse; **~ up** *sostener
hold-up (*houl*-dap) *n* atraco *m*
hole (houl) *n* bache *m*, agujero *m*; hoyo *m*
holiday (*ho*-lö-di) *n* vacaciones *fpl*; **~ camp** colonia veraniega; **~ resort** lugar de descanso; **on ~** de vacaciones
Holland (*ho*-lönd) Holanda *f*
hollow (*ho*-lou) *adj* hueco; vacío
holy (*hou*-li) *adj* santo
homage (*ho*-midʒ) *n* homenaje *m*
home (houm) *n* casa *f*; hospicio *m*; *adv* en casa, a casa; **at ~** en casa; **~land** *n* patria *f*
home-made (houm-*meid*) *adj* casero
homesickness (*houm*-ssik-nöss) *n* nostalgia *f*
homework (*houm*-ᵁöök) *deberes mpl*
homosexual (hou-mö-*ssêk*-ʃu-öl) *adj* homosexual
honest (*o*-nisst) *adj* honesto; sincero
honesty (*o*-ni-ssti) *n* honradez *f*
honey (*ha*-ni) *n* miel *f*
honeymoon (*ha*-ni-muun) *n* luna de miel
honk (hongk) *vAm* tocar la bocina
hono(u)r (*o*-nö) *n* honor *m*; *v* honrar, *rendir homenaje
hono(u)rable (*o*-nö-rö-böl) *adj* honorable; honesto
hood (hud) *n* capucha *f*; *nAm* capó *m*
hoof (huuf) *n* casco *m*; pezuña *f*
hook (huk) *n* gancho *m*
hoot (huut) *v* tocar la bocina
hooter (*huu*-tö) *n* bocina *f*
hoover (*huu*-vö) *v* pasar el aspirador
hop¹ (hop) *v* brincar; *n* salto *m*
hop² (hop) *n* lúpulo *m*
hope (houp) *n* esperanza *f*; *v* esperar
hopeful (*houp*-föl) *adj* esperanzado
hopeless (*houp*-löss) *adj* desesperado
horizon (hö-*rai*-sön) *n* horizonte *m*

horizontal (ho-ri-*son*-töl) *adj* horizontal

horn (hoon) *n* cuerno *m*; bocina *f*

horrible (*ho*-ri-böl) *adj* horrible; terrible, atroz

horror (*ho*-rö) *n* espanto *m*, horror *m*

hors d'œuvre (oo-*döövr*) *n* entremeses *mpl*

horse (hooss) *n* caballo *m*

horseman (*hooss*-mön) *n* (pl -men) jinete *m*

horsepower (*hooss*-pau⁶) *n* caballo de vapor

horserace (*hooss*-reiss) *n* carrera de caballos

horseradish (*hooss*-ræ-diʃ) *n* rábano picante

horseshoe (*hooss*-ʃuu) *n* herradura *f*

horticulture (*hoo*-ti-kal-chö) *n* horticultura *f*

hospitable (*ho*-sspi-tö-böl) *adj* hospitalario

hospital (*ho*-sspi-töl) *n* hospital *m*

hospitality (ho-sspi-*tæ*-lö-ti) *n* hospitalidad *f*

host (housst) *n* anfitrión *m*

hostage (*ho*-sstidʒ) *n* rehén *m*

hostel (*ho*-sstöl) *n* hospedería *f*

hostess (*hou*-sstiss) *n* azafata *f*

hostile (*ho*-sstail) *adj* hostil

hot (hot) *adj* caliente

hotel (hou-*têl*) *n* hotel *m*

hot-tempered (hot-*têm*-pöd) *adj* colérico

hour (au⁶) *n* hora *f*

hourly (*au⁶*-li) *adj* a cada hora

house (hauss) *n* casa *f*; vivienda *f*; inmueble *m*; ~ **agent** corredor de casas; ~ **block** *Am* manzana de casas; ~ **public** ~ taberna *f*

houseboat (*hauss*-bout) *n* casa flotante

household (*hauss*-hould) *n* menaje *m*

housekeeper (*hauss*-kii-pö) *n* ama de llaves

housekeeping (*hauss*-kii-ping) *n* gobierno de la casa

housemaid (*hauss*-meid) *n* criada *f*

housewife (*hauss*-ᵘaif) *n* ama de casa

housework (*hauss*-ᵘöök) *n* faenas domésticas

how (hau) *adv* cómo; qué; ~ **many** cuánto; ~ **much** cuánto

however (hau-ê-vö) *conj* todavía, sin embargo

hug (hagh) *v* abrazar; *n* abrazo *m*

huge (hyuudʒ) *adj* enorme; vasto, inmenso

hum (ham) *v* tararear

human (*hyuu*-mön) *adj* humano; ~ **being** ser humano

humanity (hyu-*mæ*-nö-ti) *n* humanidad *f*

humble (*ham*-böl) *adj* humilde

humid (*hyuu*-mid) *adj* húmedo

humidity (hyu-*mi*-dö-ti) *n* humedad *f*

humorous (*hyuu*-mö-röss) *adj* chistoso, gracioso, humorístico

humo(u)r (*hyuu*-mö) *n* humor *m*

hundred (*han*-dröd) *n* ciento

Hungarian (hang-*ghê⁶*-ri-ön) *adj* húngaro

Hungary (*hang*-ghö-ri) Hungría *m*

hunger (*hang*-ghö) *n* hambre *f*

hungry (*hang*-ghri) *adj* hambriento

hunt (hant) *v* cazar; *n* caza *f*; ~ **for** buscar

hunter (*han*-tö) *n* cazador *m*, -a *f*

hurricane (*ha*-ri-kön) *n* huracán *m*; ~ **lamp** lámpara sorda

hurry (*ha*-ri) *v* *darse prisa, apresurarse; *n* prisa *f*; **in a** ~ de prisa

*****hurt** (hööt) *v* *hacer daño, dañar; ofender

hurtful (*hööt*-föl) *adj* perjudicial

husband (*has*-bönd) *n* esposo *m*, marido *m*

hut (hat) *n* cabaña *f*

hydrogen (*hai*-drö-dʒön) *n* hidrógeno *m*

hygiene (*hai*-dʒiin) *n* higiene *f*

hygienic (hai-*dʒii*-nik) *adj* higiénico

hymn (him) *n* himno *m*

hyphen (*hai*-fön) *n* guión *m*

hypocrisy (hi-*po*-krö-ssi) *n* hipocresía *f*

hypocrite (*hi*-pö-krit) *n* hipócrita *m*

hypocritical (hi-pö-*kri*-ti-köl) *adj* hipócrita, mojigato

hysterical (hi-*sstê*-ri-köl) *adj* histérico

I

I (ai) *pron* yo

ice (aiss) *n* hielo *m*; ~ **bag** bolsa de hielo; ~ **cream** helado *m*

Iceland (*aiss*-lönd) Islandia *f*

Icelander (*aiss*-lön-dö) *n* islandés *m*

Icelandic (aiss-*læn*-dik) *adj* islandés

icon (*ai*-kon) *n* icono *m*

idea (ai-*di*ᵒ) *n* idea *f*; pensamiento *m*; noción *f*, concepto *m*

ideal (ai-*di*ᵒl) *adj* ideal; *n* ideal *m*

identical (ai-*dên*-ti-köl) *adj* idéntico

identification (ai-dên-ti-fi-*kei*-ʃön) *n* identificación *f*

identify (ai-*dên*-ti-fai) *v* identificar

identity (ai-*dên*-ti-ti) *n* identidad *f*; ~ **card** carnet de identidad

idiom (*i*-di-öm) *n* lenguaje *m*; modismo *m*

idiomatic (i-di-ö-*mæ*-tik) *adj* idiomático

idiot (*i*-di-öt) *n* idiota *m*

idiotic (i-di-o-tik) *adj* idiota

idle (*ai*-döl) *adj* ocioso; vago; vano

idol (*ai*-döl) *n* ídolo *m*

if (if) *conj* si

ignition (igh-*ni*-ʃön) *n* encendido *m*; ~ **coil** bobina del encendido

ignorant (*igh*-nö-rönt) *adj* ignorante

ignore (igh-*noo*) *v* ignorar

ill (il) *adj* enfermo; malo; maligno

illegal (i-*lii*-ghöl) *adj* ilegal

illegible (i-*lê*-dʒö-böl) *adj* ilegible

illiterate (i-*li*-tö-röt) *n* analfabeto *m*

illness (*il*-nöss) *n* enfermedad *f*

illuminate (i-*luu*-mi-neit) *v* iluminar

illumination (i-luu-mi-*nei*-ʃön) *n* iluminación *f*

illusion (i-*luu*-ʒön) *n* ilusión *f*

illustrate (*i*-lö-sstreit) *v* ilustrar

illustration (i-lö-*sstrei*-ʃön) *n* ilustración *f*

image (*i*-midʒ) *n* imagen *f*

imaginary (i-*mæ*-dʒi-nö-ri) *adj* imaginario

imagination (i-mæ-dʒi-*nei*-ʃön) *n* imaginación *f*

imagine (i-*mæ*-dʒin) *v* imaginarse; figurarse

imitate (*i*-mi-teit) *v* imitar

imitation (i-mi-*tei*-ʃön) *n* imitación *f*

immediate (i-*mii*-dyöt) *adj* inmediato

immediately (i-*mii*-dyöt-li) *adv* inmediatamente, de inmediato

immense (i-*mênss*) *adj* inmenso, enorme

immigrant (*i*-mi-ghrönt) *n* inmigrante *m*

immigrate (*i*-mi-ghreit) *v* inmigrar

immigration (i-mi-*ghrei*-ʃön) *n* inmigración *f*

immodest (i-*mo*-disst) *adj* inmodesto

immunity (i-*myuu*-nö-ti) *n* inmunidad *f*

immunize (*i*-myu-nais) *v* inmunizar

impartial (im-*paa*-ʃöl) *adj* imparcial

impassable (im-*paa*-ssö-böl) *adj* intransitable

impatient (im-*pei*-ʃönt) *adj* impaciente

impede (im-*piid*) *v* *impedir

impediment (im-*pê*-di-mönt) *n* impedimento *m*

imperfect (im-*pöö*-fikt) *adj* imperfecto

imperial (im-*pi⁰*-ri-öl) *adj* imperial

impersonal (im-*pöö*-ssö-nöl) *adj* impersonal

impertinence (im-*pöö*-ti-nönss) *n* impertinencia *f*

impertinent (im-*pöö*-ti-nönt) *adj* grosero, descarado, impertinente

implement¹ (*im*-pli-mönt) *n* instrumento *m*; herramienta *f*

implement² (*im*-pli-mênt) *v* efectuar

implicate (*im*-pli-keit) *v* implicar

imply (im-*plai*) *v* implicar, suponer

impolite (im-pö-*lait*) *adj* descortés

import¹ (im-*poot*) *v* importar

import² (*im*-poot) *n* importación *f*; ∼ **duty** impuestos de importación

importance (im-*poo*-tönss) *n* importancia *f*

important (im-*poo*-tönt) *adj* importante

importer (im-*poo*-tö) *n* importador *m*

imposing (im-*pou*-sing) *adj* imponente

impossible (im-*po*-ssö-böl) *adj* imposible

impotence (*im*-pö-tönss) *n* impotencia *f*

impotent (*im*-pö-tönt) *adj* impotente

impress (im-*prêss*) *v* impresionar

impression (im-*prê*-ʃön) *n* impresión *f*

impressive (im-*prê*-ssiv) *adj* impresionante

imprison (im-*pri*-sön) *v* encarcelar

imprisonment (im-*pri*-sön-mönt) *n* encarcelamiento *m*

improbable (im-*pro*-bö-böl) *adj* improbable

improper (im-*pro*-pö) *adj* impropio

improve (im-*pruuv*) *v* mejorar

improvement (im-*pruuv*-mönt) *n* mejora *f*

improvise (*im*-prö-vais) *v* improvisar

impudent (*im*-pyu-dönt) *adj* impudente

impulse (*im*-palss) *n* impulso *m*; estímulo *m*

impulsive (im-*pal*-ssiv) *adj* impulsivo

in (in) *prep* en; dentro de; *adv* adentro

inaccessible (i-næk-*ssê*-ssö-böl) *adj* inaccesible

inaccurate (i-*næ*-kyu-röt) *adj* inexacto

inadequate (i-*næ*-di-kʰöt) *adj* inadecuado

incapable (ing-*kei*-pö-böl) *adj* incapaz

incense (*in*-ssênss) *n* incienso *m*

inch (inch) *n* pulgada *f*

incident (*in*-ssi-dönt) *n* incidente *m*

incidental (in-ssi-*dên*-töl) *adj* imprevisto

incite (in-*ssait*) *v* incitar

inclination (ing-kli-*nei*-ʃön) *n* inclinación *f*

incline (ing-*klain*) *n* inclinación *f*

inclined (ing-*klaind*) *adj* dispuesto, inclinado; *be ∼ to *v* inclinarse

include (ing-*kluud*) *v* *incluir

inclusive (ing-*kluu*-ssiv) *adj* incluso

income (*ing*-köm) *n* ingresos *mpl*; ∼ **tax** impuesto sobre los ingresos

incompetent (ing-*kom*-pö-tönt) *adj* incompetente

incomplete (in-köm-*pliit*) *adj* incompleto

inconceivable (ing-kön-*ssii*-vö-böl) *adj* inconcebible

inconspicuous (ing-kön-*sspi*-kyuöss) *adj* discreto

inconvenience (ing-kön-*vii*-nyönss) *n* incomodidad *f*, inconveniencia *f*

inconvenient (ing-kön-*vii*-nyönt) *adj* inoportuno; molesto

incorrect (ing-kö-*rêkt*) *adj* inexacto, incorrecto

increase[1] (ing-*kriiss*) *v* aumentar; incrementar; *acrecentarse

increase[2] (*ing*-kriiss) *n* aumento *m*

incredible (ing-*krê*-dö-böl) *adj* increíble

incurable (ing-*kyu*[o]-rö-böl) *adj* incurable

indecent (in-*dii*-ssönt) *adj* indecente

indeed (in-*diid*) *adv* en efecto

indefinite (in-*dê*-fi-nit) *adj* indefinido

indemnity (in-*dêm*-nö-ti) *n* indemnización *f*

independence (in-di-*pên*-dönss) *n* independencia *f*

independent (in-di-*pên*-dönt) *adj* independiente; autónomo

index (*in*-dêkss) *n* índice *m*; ~ **finger** índice *m*

India (*in*-di-ö) India *f*

Indian (*in*-di-ön) *adj* indio; *n* indio *m*

indicate (*in*-di-keit) *v* señalar, indicar

indication (in-di-*kei*-ʃön) *n* señal *f*, indicación *f*

indicator (*in*-di-kei-tö) *n* indicador *m*

indifferent (in-*di*-fö-rönt) *adj* indiferente

indigestion (in-di-*dʒêss*-chön) *n* indigestión *f*

indignation (in-digh-*nei*-ʃön) *n* indignación *f*

indirect (in-di-*rêkt*) *adj* indirecto

individual (in-di-*vi*-dʒu-öl) *adj* aparte, individual; *n* individuo *m*

Indonesia (in-dö-*nii*-si-ö) Indonesia *f*

Indonesian (in-dö-*nii*-si-ön) *adj* indonesio

indoor (*in*-doo) *adj* interior

indoors (in-*doos*) *adv* en casa

indulge (in-*daldʒ*) *v* consentir a

industrial (in-*da*-sstri-öl) *adj* industrial; ~ **area** zona industrial

industrious (in-*da*-sstri-öss) *adj* aplicado

industry (*in*-dö-sstri) *n* industria *f*

inedible (i-*nê*-di-böl) *adj* incomible

inefficient (i-ni-*fi*-ʃönt) *adj* ineficiente

inevitable (i-*nê*-vi-tö-böl) *adj* inevitable

inexpensive (i-nik-*sspên*-ssiv) *adj* barato

inexperienced (i-nik-*sspi*[o]-ri-önsst) *adj* inexperto

infant (*in*-fönt) *n* criatura *f*

infantry (*in*-fön-tri) *n* infantería *f*

infect (in-*fêkt*) *v* infectar

infection (in-*fêk*-ʃön) *n* infección *f*

infectious (in-*fêk*-ʃöss) *adj* contagioso

infer (in-*föö*) *v* *deducir

inferior (in-*fi*[o]-ri-ö) *adj* inferior

infinite (*in*-fi-nöt) *adj* infinito

infinitive (in-*fi*-ni-tiv) *n* infinitivo *m*

inflammable (in-*flæ*-mö-böl) *adj* inflamable

inflammation (in-flö-*mei*-ʃön) *n* inflamación *f*

inflatable (in-*flei*-tö-böl) *adj* inflable

inflate (in-*fleit*) *v* hinchar

inflation (in-*flei*-ʃön) *n* inflación *f*

inflict (in-*flikt*) *v* infligir

influence (*in*-flu-önss) *n* influencia *f*; *v* *influir

influential (in-flu-*ên*-ʃöl) *adj* influyente

influenza (in-flu-*ên*-sö) *n* gripe *f*

inform (in-*foom*) *v* informar; comunicar

informal (in-*foo*-möl) *adj* informal

information (in-fö-*mei*-ʃön) *n* información *f*; informes *mpl*, comunicado *m*; ~ **bureau** oficina de informaciones

infra-red (in-frö-*rêd*) *adj* infrarrojo

infrequent (in-*frii*-kᵘönt) *adj* infrecuente

ingredient (ing-*ghrii*-di-önt) *n* ingrediente *m*

inhabit (in-*hæ*-bit) *v* habitar

inhabitable (in-*hæ*-bi-tö-böl) *adj* habitable

inhabitant (in-*hæ*-bi-tönt) *n* habitante *m*

inhale (in-*heil*) *v* inhalar

inherit (in-*hê*-rit) *v* heredar

inheritance (in-*hê*-ri-tönss) *n* herencia *f*

inhibit (in-*hi*-bit) *v* impedir; inhibir, cohibir

initial (i-*ni*-ʃöl) *adj* inicial; *n* inicial *f*; *v* rubricar

initiate (i-*ni*-ʃyeit) *v* iniciar

initiative (i-*ni*-ʃö-tiv) *n* iniciativa *f*

inject (in-*dʒêkt*) *v* inyectar

injection (in-*dʒêk*-ʃön) *n* inyección *f*

injure (*in*-dʒö) *v* *herir; ofender

injury (*in*-dʒö-ri) *n* herida *f*; lesión *f*

injustice (in-*dʒa*-sstiss) *n* injusticia *f*

ink (ingk) *n* tinta *f*

inlet (*in*-lêt) *n* ensenada *f*

inn (in) *n* posada *f*; parador *m*

inner (*i*-nö) *adj* interior; ~ **tube** cámara de aire

innocence (*i*-nö-ssönss) *n* inocencia *f*

innocent (*i*-nö-ssönt) *adj* inocente

inoculate (i-*no*-kyu-leit) *v* vacunar

inoculation (i-no-kyu-*lei*-ʃön) *n* inoculación *f*

inquire (ing-kᵘ*ai*ᵒ) *v* informarse, *pedir informes

inquiry (ing-kᵘ*ai*ᵒ-ri) *n* pregunta *f*, indagación *f*; encuesta *f*; ~ **office** oficina de informaciones

inquisitive (ing-kᵘ*i*-sö-tiv) *adj* curioso

insane (in-*ssein*) *adj* loco

inscription (in-*sskrip*-ʃön) *n* inscripción *f*

insect (*in*-ssêkt) *n* insecto *m*; ~ **repellent** insectífugo *m*

insecticide (in-*ssêk*-ti-ssaid) *n* insecticida *m*

insensitive (in-*ssên*-ssö-tiv) *adj* insensible

insert (in-*ssööt*) *v* insertar

inside (in-*ssaid*) *n* interior *m*; *adj* interior; *adv* adentro; dentro; *prep* en, dentro de; ~ **out** al revés; **insides** entrañas *fpl*

insight (*in*-ssait) *n* entendimiento *m*; perspicacia *f*

insignificant (in-ssigh-ni-fi-könt) *adj* insignificante; irrelevante; baladí

insist (in-*ssisst*) *v* insistir; persistir

insolence (*in*-ssö-lönss) *n* insolencia *f*

insolent (*in*-ssö-lönt) *adj* insolente

insomnia (in-*ssom*-ni-ö) *n* insomnio *m*

inspect (in-*sspêkt*) *v* inspeccionar

inspection (in-*sspêk*-ʃön) *n* inspección *f*; control *m*

inspector (in-*sspêk*-tö) *n* inspector *m*, -a *f*; revisor *m*, -a *f*

inspire (in-*sspai*ᵒ) *v* inspirar

install (in-*sstool*) *v* instalar

installation (in-sstö-*lei*-ʃön) *n* instalación *f*

instal(l)ment (in-*sstool*-mönt) *n* plazo *m*; ~ **plan** compra a plazos

instance (*in*-sstönss) *n* ejemplo *m*; caso *m*; **for** ~ por ejemplo

instant (*in*-sstönt) *n* instante *m*

instantly (*in*-sstönt-li) *adv* instantáneamente, inmediatamente, al instante

instead of (in-*sstêd* ov) en lugar de; en vez de

instinct (*in*-sstingkt) *n* instinto *m*

institute (*in*-ssti-tyuut) *n* instituto *m*; institución *f*; *v* *instituir

institution (in-ssti-*tyuu*-ʃön) *n* instituto *m*, institución *f*

instruct (in-*sstrakt*) *v* *instruir
instruction (in-*sstrak*-ʃön) *n* instrucción *f*
instructive (in-*sstrak*-tiv) *adj* instructivo
instructor (in-*sstrak*-tö) *n* instructor *m*, -a *f*
instrument (*in*-sstru-mönt) *n* instrumento *m*; **musical ~** instrumento músico
insufficient (in-ssö-*fi*-ʃönt) *adj* insuficiente
insulate (*in*-ssyu-leit) *v* aislar
insulation (in-ssyu-*lei*-ʃön) *n* aislamiento *m*
insulator (*in*-ssyu-lei-tö) *n* aislador *m*
insult[1] (in-*ssalt*) *v* insultar
insult[2] (*in*-ssalt) *n* insulto *m*
insurance (in-ʃu⁰-rönss) *n* seguro *m*; **~ policy** póliza de seguro
insure (in-ʃu⁰) *v* asegurar
intact (in-*tækt*) *adj* intacto
integrate (*in*-ti-greit) *v* integrar
intellect (*in*-tö-lêkt) *n* intelecto *m*
intellectual (in-tö-*lêk*-chu-öl) *adj* intelectual
intelligence (in-*tê*-li-dʒönss) *n* inteligencia *f*
intelligent (in-*tê*-li-dʒönt) *adj* inteligente
intend (in-*tênd*) *v* intentar, *tener la intención de
intense (in-*tênss*) *adj* intenso
intensify (in-*tên*-si-fai) *v* intensificar; intensificarse
intention (in-*tên*-ʃön) *n* intención *f*
intentional (in-*tên*-ʃö-nöl) *adj* intencional
intercourse (*in*-tö-kooss) *n* trato *m*; comercio *m*; coito *m*
interest (*in*-trösst) *n* interés *m*; rédito *m*; *v* interesar; **interested** *adj* interesado
interesting (*in*-trö-ssting) *adj* interesante

interfere (in-tö-*fi*⁰) *v* interferir; **~ with** mezclarse en
interference (in-tö-*fi*⁰-rönss) *n* interferencia *f*
interim (*in*-tö-rim) *n* ínterin *m*
interior (in-*ti*⁰-ri-ö) *n* interior *m*
interlude (*in*-tö-luud) *n* intermedio *m*
intermediary (in-tö-*mii*-dyö-ri) *n* intermediario *m*
intermission (in-tö-*mi*-ʃön) *n* entreacto *m*
internal (in-*töö*-nöl) *adj* interno
international (in-tö-*næ*-ʃö-nöl) *adj* internacional
Internet (in-*töö*-nöl) Internet *f*; **on the Internet** en Internet
interpret (in-*töö*-prit) *v* interpretar
interpreter (in-*töö*-pri-tö) *n* intérprete *m*
interrogate (in-*tê*-rö-gheit) *v* interrogar
interrogation (in-tê-rö-*ghei*-ʃön) *n* interrogatorio *m*
interrogative (in-tö-*ro*-ghö-tiv) *adj* interrogativo
interrupt (in-tö-*rapt*) *v* interrumpir
interruption (in-tö-*rap*-ʃön) *n* interrupción *f*
intersection (in-tö-*ssêk*-ʃön) *n* intersección *f*
interval (*in*-tö-völ) *n* intervalo *m*
intervene (in-tö-*viin*) *v* *intervenir
interview (*in*-tö-vyuu) *n* entrevista *f*
intestine (in-*tê*-sstin) *n* intestino *m*
intimate (*in*-ti-möt) *adj* íntimo
into (*in*-tu) *prep* dentro de
intolerable (in-*to*-lö-rö-böl) *adj* insoportable; inaguantable
intoxicated (in-*tok*-ssi-kei-tid) *adj* borracho
intrigue (in-*trüigh*) *n* intriga *f*
introduce (in-trö-*dyuuss*) *v* presentar; *introducir

introduction (in-trö-*dak*-ʃön) *n* presentación *f*; introducción *f*

invade (in-*veid*) *v* invadir

invalid[1] (*in*-vö-liid) *n* inválido *m*; *adj* inválido

invalid[2] (in-*væ*-lid) *adj* nulo

invasion (in-*vei*-ʒön) *n* irrupción *f*, invasión *f*

invent (in-*vênt*) *v* inventar

invention (in-*vên*-ʃön) *n* invención *f*

inventive (in-*vên*-tiv) *adj* inventivo

inventor (in-*vên*-tö) *n* inventor *m*

inventory (*in*-vön-tri) *n* inventario *m*

invert (in-*vööt*) *v* *invertir

invest (in-*vêsst*) *v* *invertir

investigate (in-*vê*-ssti-gheit) *v* investigar

investigation (in-vê-ssti-*ghei*-ʃön) *n* investigación *f*

investment (in-*vêsst*-mönt) *n* inversión *f*

investor (in-*vê*-sstö) *n* inversionista *m*

invisible (in-*vi*-sö-böl) *adj* invisible

invitation (in-vi-*tei*-ʃön) *n* invitación *f*

invite (in-*vait*) *v* invitar, convidar

invoice (*in*-voiss) *n* factura *f*

involve (in-*volv*) *v* *envolver; implicar

involved implicado; complicado

inwards (*in*-ᵘöds) *adv* hacia adentro

iodine (*ai*-ö-diin) *n* yodo *m*

Iran (i-*raan*) Irán *m*

Iranian (i-*rei*-ni-ön) *adj* iraní

Iraq (i-*raak*) Irak *m*

Iraqi (i-*raa*-ki) *adj* iraquí

Ireland (*ai*ᵒ-lönd) Irlanda *f*

Irish (*ai*ᵒ-riʃ) *adj* irlandés

Irishman (*ai*ᵒ-riʃ-mön) *n* (pl -men) irlandés *m*

iron (*ai*-ön) *n* hierro *m*; plancha *f*; de hierro; *v* planchar

ironical (ai-*ro*-ni-köl) *adj* irónico

irony (*ai*ᵒ-ni) *n* ironía *f*

irregular (i-*rê*-ghyu-lö) *adj* irregular

irreparable (i-*rê*-pö-rö-böl) *adj* irreparable

irrevocable (i-*rê*-vö-kö-böl) *adj* irrevocable

irritable (*i*-ri-tö-böl) *adj* irritable

irritate (*i*-ri-teit) *v* irritar

is (is) *v* (pr be)

island (*ai*-lönd) *n* isla *f*

isolate (*ai*-ssö-leit) *v* aislar

isolation (ai-ssö-*lei*-ʃön) *n* aislamiento *m*

Israel (*is*-reil) Israel *m*

Israeli (is-*rei*-li) *adj* israelí

issue (*i*-ʃuu) *v* *distribuir; *n* emisión *f*, tirada *f*, edición *f*; cuestión *f*, punto *m*; consecuencia *f*, resultado *m*, conclusión *f*, término *m*; salida *f*

it (it) *pron* lo; **its** *adj* su

itself (it-*ssêlf*) *pron* se; **by ~** aislado, solo

Italian (i-*tæl*-yön) *adj* italiano

Italy (*i*-tö-li) Italia *f*

itch (ich) *n* picazón *f*; prurito *m*; *v* picar

item (*ai*-töm) *n* ítem *m*; punto *m*

itinerary (ai-*ti*-nö-rö-ri) *n* itinerario *m*

ivory (*ai*-vö-ri) *n* marfil *m*

ivy (*ai*-vi) *n* hiedra *f*

J

jack (dʒæk) *n* gato *m*

jacket (dʒæ-kit) *n* americana *f*, chaqueta *f*; sobrecubierta *f*; saco *m* Me

jade (dʒeid) *n* jade *m*

jail (dʒeil) *n* cárcel *f*

jam (dʒæm) *n* mermelada *f*; congestión *f*

janitor (dʒæ-ni-tö) *n* conserje *m*

January (dʒæ-nyu-ö-ri) enero

Japan (dʒö-*pæn*) Japón *m*

Japanese (dʒæ-pö-*niis*) *adj* japonés

jar (dʒaa) *n* jarra *f*

jaundice (dʒoon-diss) *n* ictericia *f*

jaw (dʒoo) *n* mandíbula *f*

jealous (dʒê-löss) *adj* celoso

jealousy (dʒê-lö-ssi) *n* celos *m*

jeans (dʒiins) *pl* vaqueros *mpl*

jelly (dʒê-li) *n* jalea *f*

jellyfish (dʒê-li-fiʃ) *n* medusa *f*

jersey (dʒöö-si) *n* jersey *m*

jet (dʒêt) *n* chorro *m*; avión a reacción

jetty (dʒê-ti) *n* muelle *m*

Jew (dʒuu) *n* judío *m*, -a *f*

jewel (dʒuu-öl) *n* joya *f*

jewel(l)er (dʒuu-ö-lö) *n* joyero *m*, -a *f*

jewellery, *Am* **jewelry** (dʒuu-öl-ri) *n* joyería *f*

Jewish (dʒuu-iʃ) *adj* judío

job (dʒob) *n* tarea *f*; puesto *m*, empleo *m*

jobless (dʒob-löss) *adj* desempleado, *Span* parado

jockey (dʒo-ki) *n* jockey *m*

join (dʒoin) *v* juntar; unirse a, asociarse a; ensamblar, reunir

joint (dʒoint) *n* articulación *f*; soldadura *f*; *adj* unido, en común

jointly (dʒoint-li) *adv* juntamente

joke (dʒouk) *n* broma *f*

jolly (dʒo-li) *adj* jovial

Jordan (dʒoo-dön) Jordania *f*

Jordanian (dʒoo-*dei*-ni-ön) *adj* jordano

journal (dʒöö-nöl) *n* diario *m*; periódico *m*; revista *f*

journalism (dʒöö-nö-li-söm) *n* periodismo *m*

journalist (dʒöö-nö-lisst) *n* periodista *m/f*

journey (dʒöö-ni) *n* viaje *m*

joy (dʒoi) *n* alegría *f*, júbilo *m*

joyful (dʒoi-föl) *adj* alegre, jubiloso

jubilee (dʒuu-bi-lii) *n* aniversario *m*

judge (dʒadʒ) *n* juez *m/f*; *v* juzgar

judgment (dʒadʒ-mönt) *n* juicio *m*

jug (dʒagh) *n* cántaro *m*

juggernaut (dʒagh-ö-noot) *n* camión grande *m*

juice (dʒuuss) *n* zumo *m*; jugo *m*

juicy (dʒuu-ssi) *adj* zumoso; jugoso

July (dʒu-*lai*) julio

jump (dʒamp) *v* saltar; *n* salto *m*

jumper (dʒam-pö) *n* jersey *m*; *Am* vestido sin mangas

junction (dʒangk-ʃön) *n* encrucijada *f*; empalme *m*

June (dʒuun) junio

jungle (dʒang-ghöl) *n* selva *f*, jungla *f*

junior (dʒuu-nyö) *adj* menor; ~ **school** escuela primaria

junk (dʒangk) *n* cachivache *m*

jury (dʒu⁰-ri) *n* jurado *m*

just (dʒasst) *adj* justo; recto; merecido; *adv* apenas; exactamente; solamente

justice (dʒa-sstiss) *n* derecho *m*; justicia *f*

justify (dʒass-ti-fai) *v* justificar

juvenile (dʒuu-vö-nail) *adj* juvenil

K

kangaroo (kæng-ghö-*ruu*) n canguro m

keel (kiil) n quilla f

keen (kiin) adj entusiasta; agudo

***keep** (kiip) v *tener; guardar; continuar; ~ **away from** *mantenerse alejado de; ~ **off** no tocar; ~ **on** continuar; ~ **quiet** *estarse quieto; ~ **up** perseverar; ~ **up with** *seguir el paso

kennel (kê-nöl) n perrera f; perrera m

Kenya (kê-nyö) Kenya m

kerosene (kê-rö-ssiin) n petróleo lampante

kettle (kê-töl) n olla f

key (kii) n llave f

keyboard (kii-bood) teclado m

keyhole (kii-houl) n ojo de la cerradura

khaki (kaa-ki) n caqui m

kick (kik) v patear; n patada f

kickoff (ki-kof) n saque inicial

kid (kid) n niño m, chico m; cabritilla f; v bromearse

kidney (kid-ni) n riñón m

kill (kil) v matar

kilogram (ki-lö-ghræm) n kilogramo m

kilometer Am, **kilometre** (ki-lö-mii-tö) n kilómetro m

kind (kaind) adj amable, bondadoso; bueno; n género m

kindergarten (kin-dö-ghaa-tön) n escuela de párvulos, jardín de infancia

king (king) n rey m

kingdom (king-döm) n reino m

kiosk (kii-ossk) n quiosco m

kiss (kiss) n beso m; v besar

kit (kit) n avíos mpl

kitchen (ki-chin) n cocina f; ~ **garden** huerto m; ~ **towel** Am paño de cocina

Kleenex® (klii-nêkss) n pañuelo de papel

knapsack (næp-ssæk) n mochila f

knave (neiv) n sota f

knee (nii) n rodilla f

kneecap (nii-kæp) n rótula f

***kneel** (niil) v arrodillarse

knew (nyuu) v (p know)

knife (naif) n (pl knives) cuchillo m

knight (nait) n caballero m

***knit** (nit) v *hacer punto

knob (nob) n botón m; bulto m

knock (nok) v golpear; llamar (a la puerta); n golpe m; llamada f (a la puerta); ~ **against** chocar contra; ~ **down** derribar

knot (not) n nudo m; v anudar

***know** (nou) v *saber, *conocer

knowledge (no-lidჳ) n conocimiento m

knuckle (na-köl) n nudillo m

L

label (lei-böl) n rótulo m; etiqueta f; v rotular

laboratory (lö-bo-rö-tö-ri) n laboratorio m

labo(u)r (lei-bö) n trabajo m, labor f; dolores mpl; v ajetrearse, bregar; **labor permit** Am permiso de trabajo

labo(u)rer (lei-bö-rö) n obrero m

labo(u)r-saving (*lei*-bö-ssei-ving) *adj* economizador de trabajo

labyrinth (*læ*-bö-rinz) *n* laberinto *m*

lace (leiss) *n* encaje *m*, puntilla *f*; cordón *m*

lack (læk) *n* falta *f*; *v* *carecer

lacquer (*læ*-kö) *n* laca *f*

lad (læd) *n* joven *m*, muchacho *m*

ladder (*læ*-dö) *n* escalera de mano

lady (*lei*-di) *n* señora *f*; **ladies' room** lavabos para señoras

lagoon (lö-*ghuun*) *n* laguna *f*

lake (leik) *n* lago *m*

lamb (læm) *n* cordero *m*

lame (leim) *adj* cojo

lamentable (*læ*-mön-tö-böl) *adj* lamentable

lamp (læmp) *n* lámpara *f*

lamppost (*læmp*-pousst) *n* poste de farol

lampshade (*læmp*-ʃeid) *n* pantalla *f*

land (lænd) *n* país *m*, tierra *f*; *v* aterrizar; desembarcar

landlady (*lænd*-lei-di) *n* proprietaria *m*, dueña *f*, patrona *f*

landlord (*lænd*-lood) *n* propietario *m*, dueño *m*; patrón *m*

landmark (*lænd*-maak) *n* punto de referencia; mojón *m*

landscape (*lænd*-sskeip) *n* paisaje *m*

lane (lein) *n* callejón *m*; pista *f*

language (*læng*-gh^{u}idʒ) *n* lengua *f*; **~ laboratory** laboratorio de lenguas

lantern (*læn*-tön) *n* linterna *f*

lap (læp) *n* regazo *m*; falta *f*; *v* traslapar(se)

lapel (lö-*pêl*) *n* solapa *f*

larder (*laa*-dö) *n* despensa *f*

large (laadʒ) *adj* grande; espacioso; **largely** *adv* en gran parte, principalmente

lark (laak) *n* alondra *f*

laryngitis (læ-rin-dʒai-tiss) *n* laringitis *f*

last (laasst) *adj* último; precedente; *v* durar; **at ~** al fin; al final

lasting (*laa*-ssting) *adj* duradero

latchkey (*læch*-kii) *n* llave de la casa

late (leit) *adj* tardío; retrasado

lately (*leit*-li) *adv* últimamente, recientemente

lather (*laa*-ðö) *n* espuma *f*

Latin America (*læ*-tin ö-*mê*-ri-kö) América Latina

Latin-American (*læ*-tin-ö-*mê*-ri-kön) *adj* latinoamericano

latitude (*læ*-ti-tyuud) *n* latitud *f*

laugh (laaf) *v* *reír; *n* risa *f*; carcajada *f*

laughter (*laaf*-tö) *n* risa *f*; risas *fpl*

launch (loonch) *v* lanzar; *n* buque a motor

launching (*loon*-ching) *n* botadura *f*

launderette (loon-dö-*rêt*) *n* lavandería de autoservicio

laundry (*loon*-dri) *n* lavandería *f*; ropa sucia

lavatory (*læ*-vö-tö-ri) *n* lavabo *m*; aseos *mpl*

lavish (*læ*-viʃ) *adj* pródigo; profuso

law (loo) *n* ley *f*; derecho *m*; **~ court** tribunal *m*

lawful (*loo*-föl) *adj* lícito

lawn (loon) *n* césped *m*

lawsuit (*loo*-ssuut) *n* proceso *m*, causa *f*

lawyer (*loo*-yö) *n* abogado *m*; jurista *m*

laxative (*læk*-ssö-tiv) *n* laxante *m*

***lay** (lei) *v* colocar, *poner; **~ bricks** mampostear

layer (lei^ö) *n* capa *f*

layman (*lei*-mön) *n* lego *m*; profano *m*

lazy (*lei*-si) *adj* perezoso

lead[1] (liid) *n* ventaja *f*; dirección *f*; traílla *f*

lead[2] (lêd) *n* plomo *m*

***lead** (liid) *v* *conducir

leader (*lii*-dö) *n* jefe *m*, líder *m*

leadership (*lii*-dö-ʃip) *n* dirección *f*
leading (*lii*-ding) *adj* dominante, principal
leaf (liif) *n* (pl leaves) hoja *f*
league (liigh) *n* liga *f*
leak (liik) *v* gotear; *n* goteo *m*
leaky (*lii*-ki) *adj* agujerado
lean (liin) *adj* magro
*lean (liin) *v* apoyarse
leap (liip) *n* salto *m*
*leap (liip) *v* saltar
leap year (*liip*-yiˆ) *n* año bisiesto
*learn (löön) *v* aprender
learner (*löö*-nö) *n* principiante *m*
lease (liiss) *n* contrato de arrendamiento; arrendamiento *m*; *v* *arrendar, alquilar
leash (liiʃ) *n* correa *f*
least (liisst) *adj* mínimo, menos; **at ~** por lo menos
leather (*lê*-ðö) *n* cuero *m*
leave (liiv) *n* licencia *f*; permiso *m*
*leave (liiv) *v* partir, dejar; salir de; **~ out** omitir
Lebanese (lê-bö-*niis*) *adj* libanés
Lebanon (*lê*-bö-nön) Líbano *m*
lecture (*lêk*-chö) *n* curso *m*, conferencia *f*
left[1] (lêft) *adj* izquierdo
left[2] (lêft) *v* (p, pp leave)
left-hand (*lêft*-hænd) *adj* izquierdo, de izquierda
left-handed (lêft-*hæn*-did) *adj* zurdo
leg (lêgh) *n* pata *f*, pierna *f*
legacy (*lê*-ghö-ssi) *n* herencia *f*
legal (*lii*-ghöl) *adj* legítimo, legal; jurídico
legalization (lii-ghö-lai-*sei*-ʃön) *n* legalización *f*
legation (li-*ghei*-ʃön) *n* legación *f*
legible (*lê*-dʒi-böl) *adj* legible
legitimate (li-*dʒi*-ti-möt) *adj* legítimo
leisure (*lê*-ʒö) *n* ocio *m*; tiempo *m* libre

lemon (*lê*-mön) *n* limón *m*
lemonade (lê-mö-*neid*) *n* limonada *f*
*lend (lênd) *v* prestar
length (lêngz) *n* longitud *f*
lengthen (*lêng*-zön) *v* alargar
lengthways (*lêngz*-ˆeis) *adv* longitudinalmente
lens (lêns) *n* lente *m*/*f*; **telephoto ~** teleobjetivo *m*; **zoom ~** lente de foco regulable
leprosy (*lê*-prö-ssi) *n* lepra *f*
less (lêss) *adv* menos
lessen (*lê*-ssön) *v* *disminuir
lesson (*lê*-ssön) *n* lección *f*
*let (lêt) *v* dejar; permitir; alquilar; **~ down** decepcionar
letter (*lê*-tö) *n* carta *f*; letra *f*; **~ of credit** carta de crédito; **~ of recommendation** carta de recomendación; **~ opener** *Am* abrecartas *m*
letterbox (*lê*-tö-bokss) *n* buzón *m*
lettuce (*lê*-tiss) *n* lechuga *f*
level (*lê*-völ) *adj* igual; plano, llano; *n* nivel *m*; *v* igualar, nivelar; **~ crossing** paso a nivel
lever (*lii*-vö) *n* palanca *f*
Levis (*lii*-vais) *pl* jeans *mpl*
liability (lai-ö-*bi*-lö-ti) *n* responsabilidad *f*
liable (*lai*-ö-böl) *adj* responsable; **~ to** sujeto a
liar (lair) *n* mentiroso *m*, -a *f*
liberal (*li*-bö-röl) *adj* liberal; generoso, dadivoso
liberation (li-bö-*rei*-ʃön) *n* liberación *f*
Liberia (lai-*bi*ˆ-ri-ö) Liberia *f*
Liberian (lai-*bi*ˆ-ri-ön) *adj* liberiano
liberty (*li*-bö-ti) *n* libertad *f*
library (*lai*-brö-ri) *n* biblioteca *f*
licence (*lai*-ssönss) *n* licencia *f*; permiso *m*; **driving ~** permiso de conducir
license (*lai*-ssönss) *v* autorizar; *nAm*

licencia f; permiso m; ~ **number** (número de) matrícula; ~ **plate** (placa de) matrícula

lick (lik) v lamer

lid (lid) n tapa f

lie (lai) v *mentir; n mentira f

***lie** (lai) v *yacer; ~ **down** *tenderse

life (laif) n (pl lives) vida f; ~ **insurance** seguro de vida

lifebelt (laif-bêlt) n chaleco salvavidas

lifetime (laif-taim) n vida f

lift (lift) v levantar; n ascensor m; elevador mMe

light (lait) n luz f; adj ligero; pálido; ~ **bulb** bombilla f

***light** (lait) v *encender

lighter (lai-tö) n encendedor m

lighthouse (lait-hauss) n faro m

lighting (lai-ting) n alumbrado m

lightning (lait-ning) n relámpago m

like (laik) v *querer; gustar; adj semejante; conj como

likely (lai-kli) adj probable

like-minded (laik-main-did) adj unánime

likewise (laik-ᵘais) adv así también, asimismo

lily (li-li) n azucena f

limb (lim) n miembro m

lime (laim) n cal f; tilo m; lima f

limetree (laim-trii) n tilo m

limit (li-mit) n límite m; v limitar

limp (limp) v cojear; adj inerte

line (lain) n renglón m; raya f; cordón m; línea f; cola f

linen (li-nin) n lino m; ropa blanca

liner (lai-nö) n vapor de línea

lingerie (lon͞g-ȝö-rii) n ropa interior de mujer

lining (lai-ning) n forro m

link (lingk) v enlazar; n enlace m; eslabón m

lion (lai-ön) n león m

lip (lip) n labio m

lipstick (lip-sstik) n lápiz labial

liqueur (li-kyuᵒ) n licor m

liquid (li-kᵘid) adj líquido; n líquido m

liquor (li-kö) n bebidas alcohólicas; ~ **store** Am almacén de licores

liquorice (li-kö-riss) n regaliz m

list (lisst) n lista f; v inscribir

listen (li-ssön) v escuchar

listener (liss-nö) n oyente m

literary (li-trö-ri) adj literario

literature (li-trö-chö) n literatura f

liter Am, **litre** (lii-tö) n litro m

litter (li-tö) n desperdicio m; trastos mpl; lechigada f

little (li-töl) adj pequeño; poco

live[1] (liv) v vivir

live[2] (laiv) adj vivo

livelihood (laiv-li-hud) n sustento m

lively (laiv-li) adj animado

liver (li-vö) n hígado m

living (li-ving) adj vivo; n vida f; **standard of ~** estándar m de vida; ~ **room** n sala de estar

lizard (li-zörd) lagarto m

load (loud) n carga f; fardo m; v cargar

loaf (louf) n (pl loaves) barra f (de pan)

loan (loun) n préstamo m

lobby (lo-bi) n vestíbulo m

lobster (lob-sstö) n langosta f

local (lou-köl) adj local; ~ **call** llamada local; ~ **train** tren de cercanías

locality (lou-kæ-lö-ti) n localidad f

locate (lou-keit) v localizar

location (lou-kei-ʃön) n colocación f; localidad f

lock (lok) v *cerrar con llave; n cerradura f; esclusa f; ~ **up** guardar con llave

locker (lo-kö) n taquilla f

locomotive (lou-kö-mou-tiv) n locomotora f

lodge (lodȝ) v alojar; n apeadero de caza; posada f

lodger (*lo*-dʒö) *n* huésped *m*

lodgings (*lo*-dʒings) *pl* alojamiento *m*

log (logh) *n* madero *m*; tronco *m*

logic (*lo*-dʒik) *n* lógica *f*

logical (*lo*-dʒi-köl) *adj* lógico

lonely (*loun*-li) *adj* solitario; aislado

long (long) *adj* largo; **~ for** anhelar; **no longer** ya no

longing (*long*-ing) *n* anhelo *m*

longitude (*lon*-dʒi-tyuud) *n* longitud *f*

look (luk) *v* mirar; *parecer, *tener aires de; *n* ojeada *f*, mirada *f*; aspecto *m*; **~ after** ocuparse de, cuidar de; **~ at** mirar; **~ for** buscar; **~ out** prestar atención, *tener cuidado; **~ up** buscar

looking-glass (*lu*-king-ghlaass) *n* espejo *m*

loop (luup) *n* lazo *m*; presilla *f*

loose (luuss) *adj* suelto

loosen (*luu*-ssön) *v* *soltar

lord (lood) *n* lord *m*; señor *m*

lorry (*lo*-ri) *n* camión *m*

*lose (luus) *v* *perder

loser (*luu*-sö) *n* perdedor *m*, -a *f*; fracasado *m*, -a *f*

loss (loss) *n* pérdida *f*

lost (losst) *adj* perdido; desaparecido; **~ and found** objetos perdidos; **~ property office** oficina de objetos perdidos

lot (lot) *n* lote *m*; suerte *f*, destino *m*; masa *f*, cantidad *f*; parcela *f*; **a ~** mucho(s)

lotion (*lou*-ʃön) *n* loción *f*; **aftershave ~** loción para después de afeitarse

lottery (*lo*-tö-ri) *n* lotería *f*

loud (laud) *adj* alto; ruidoso; fuerte

loudspeaker (laud-*sspü*-kö) *n* altavoz *m*

lounge (laundʒ) *n* salón *m*

louse (lauss) *n* (pl lice) piojo *m*

love (lav) *v* amar; *n* amor *m*; **in ~** enamorado

lovely (*lav*-li) *adj* encantador; bonito

lover (*la*-vö) *n* amante *m/f*

love story (*lav*-sstoo-ri) *n* historia de amor

low (lou) *adj* bajo; profundo; deprimido; **~ tide** bajamar *f*

lower (*lou*-ö) *v* bajar; rebajar; arriar; *adj* inferior

lowlands (*lou*-lönds) *pl* tierra baja

loyal (*loi*-öl) *adj* leal

lubricate (*luu*-bri-keit) *v* lubrificar, lubricar

lubrication (luu-bri-*kei*-ʃön) *n* lubricación *f*; **~ oil** aceite lubricante; **~ system** sistema de lubricación

luck (lak) *n* éxito *m*, suerte *f*; azar *m*

lucky (*la*-ki) *adj* afortunado; dichoso; **~ charm** talismán *m*

ludicrous (*luu*-di-kröss) *adj* ridículo, grotesco

luggage (*la*-ghidʒ) *n* equipaje *m*; **hand ~** equipaje de mano; **left ~ office** consigna *f*; **~ rack** portabagajes *m*, rejilla *f*; **~ van** furgón de equipajes

lukewarm (*luuk*-ᵘoom) *adj* tibio

lumbago (lam-*bei*-ghou) *n* lumbago *m*

luminous (*luu*-mi-nöss) *adj* luminoso

lump (lamp) *n* nudo *m*, grumo *m*, terrón *m*; chichón *m*; **~ of sugar** terrón de azúcar; **~ sum** suma global

lumpy (*lam*-pi) *adj* apelmazado; deforme; desproporcionado

lunacy (*luu*-nö-ssi) *n* locura *f*

lunatic (*luu*-nö-tik) *adj* lunático; *n* alienado *m*

lunch (lanch) *n* almuerzo *m*

luncheon (*lan*-chön) *n* almuerzo *m*

lung (lang) *n* pulmón *m*

lust (lasst) *n* lujuria *f*; concupiscencia *f*

luxurious (lagh-ʒuᵒ-ri-öss) *adj* lujoso

luxury (*lak*-ʃö-ri) *n* lujo *m*

M

machine (mö-ʃiin) n aparato m, máquina f

machinery (mö-ʃii-nö-ri) n maquinaria f; mecanismo m

mackerel (mæ-kröl) n (pl ~) escombro m

mackintosh (mæ-kin-toʃ) n impermeable m

mad (mæd) adj loco; rabioso; furioso

madam (mæ-döm) n señora f

madness (mæd-nöss) n locura f

magazine (mæ-ghö-siin) n revista f

magic (mæ-dʒik) n magia f; adj mágico

magician (mö-dʒi-ʃön) n mago m, prestidigitador m

magistrate (mæ-dʒi-sstreit) n magistrado m

magnetic (mægh-nê-tik) adj magnético

magneto (mægh-nii-tou) n (pl ~s) magneto m

magnificent (mægh-ni-fi-ssönt) adj magnífico; grandioso, espléndido

magnify (mægh-ni-fai) v aumentar; magnificar

magpie (mægh-pai) n urraca f

maid (meid) n criada f; sirvienta f

maiden name (mei-dön neim) apellido de soltera

mail (meil) n correo m; v enviar por correo

mailbox (meil-bokss) nAm buzón m

main (mein) adj principal; mayor; ~ deck puente superior; ~ line línea principal; ~ road camino principal; ~ street calle mayor

mainland (mein-lönd) n tierra firme

mainly (mein-li) adv principalmente

mains (meins) pl conducción principal

maintain (mein-tein) v *mantener

maintenance (mein-tö-nönss) n mantenimiento m

maize (meis) n maíz m

major (mei-dʒö) adj grande; mayor; n mayor m

majority (mö-dʒo-rö-ti) n mayoría f

***make** (meik) v *hacer; ganar; *conseguir; ~ do with arreglarse con; ~ good compensar; ~ up redactar

make-up (mei-kap) n maquillaje m

malaria (mö-lê⁰-ri-ö) n malaria f

Malay (mö-lei) n malayo m

Malaysia (mö-lei-si-ö) Malasia f

Malaysian (mö-lei-si-ön) adj malayo

male (meil) adj macho

malicious (mö-li-ʃöss) adj malicioso

malignant (mö-ligh-nönt) adj maligno

mallet (mæ-lit) n mazo m

malnutrition (mæl-nyu-tri-ʃön) n desnutrición f

mammal (mæ-möl) n mamífero m

mammoth (mæ-möz) n mamut m

man (mæn) n (pl men) hombre m; men's room lavabos para caballeros

manage (mæ-nidʒ) v administrar; *tener éxito

manageable (mæ-ni-dʒö-böl) adj manejable

management (mæ-nidʒ-mönt) n manejo m; gestión f

manager (mæ-ni-dʒö) n jefe m, director m, -a f

mandarin (mæn-dö-rin) n mandarina f

mandate (mæn-deit) n mandato m

manger (mein-dʒö) n pesebre m

manicure (mæ-ni-kyu⁰) n manicura f; v *hacer la manicura

manipulate (mæ-ni-pyö-leit) v person, bones manipular

mankind (mæn-kaind) n humanidad f

mannequin (mæ-nö-kin) n maniquí m

manner (mæ-nö) n modo m, manera f;

manners *pl* modales *mpl*

manor house (*mæ*-nö-hauss) *n* casa señorial

mansion (*mæn*-ʃön) *n* mansión *f*

manual (*mæ*-nyu-öl) *adj* manual

manufacture (mæ-nyu-*fæk*-chö) *v* fabricar

manufacturer (mæ-nyu-*fæk*-chö-rö) *n* fabricante *m*

manure (mö-*nyu*ᵉ) *n* estiércol *m*, abono *m*

manuscript (*mæ*-nyu-sskript) *n* manuscrito *m*

many (*mê*-ni) *adj* muchos

map (mæp) *n* carta *f*; mapa *m*; plano *m*

maple (*mei*-pöl) *n* arce *m*

marble (*maa*-böl) *n* mármol *m*; canica *f*

March (maach) marzo

march (maach) *v* marchar; *n* marcha *f*

mare (mêᵉ) *n* yegua *f*

margarine (maa-dʒö-*riin*) *n* margarina *f*

margin (*maa*-dʒin) *n* margen *m*

marine (mæ-*riin*) *adj* marino; *m* marine *m/f*

maritime (*mæ*-ri-taim) *adj* marítimo

mark (maak) *v* marcar; caracterizar; *n* marca *f*; nota *f*; blanco *m*

market (*maa*-kit) *n* mercado *m*

marketplace (*maa*-kit-pleiss) *n* plaza de mercado

marmalade (*maa*-mö-leid) *n* confitura *f*

marriage (*mæ*-ridʒ) *n* matrimonio *m*

marrow (*mæ*-rou) *n* médula *f*

marry (*mæ*-ri) *v* casarse; **married** *adj* casado; **married couple** cónyuges *mpl*

marsh (maaʃ) *n* pantano *m*

martyr (*maa*-tö) *n* mártir *m*

marvel (*maa*-völ) *n* maravilla *f*; *v* maravillarse

marvellous (*maa*-vö-löss) *adj* maravilloso

mascara (mæ-*sskaa*-rö) *n* rímel *m*

masculine (*mæ*-sskyu-lin) *adj* masculino

mash (mæʃ) *v* machacar

mask (maassk) *n* máscara *f*

Mass (mæss) *n* misa *f*

mass (mæss) *n* masa *f*; ~ **production** producción en serie

massage (*mæ*-ssaaʒ) *n* masaje *m*; *v* *dar masaje

masseur (mæ-*ssöö*) *n* masajista *m*

massive (*mæ*-ssiv) *adj* macizo

mast (maasst) *n* mástil *m*

master (*maa*-sstö) *n* maestro *m*; patrón *m*; profesor *m*; *v* dominar

masterpiece (*maa*-sstö-piiss) *n* obra maestra

mat (mæt) *n* estera *f*; *adj* mate, apagado

match (mæch) *n* cerilla *f*; partido *m*; cerillo *mMe*; *v* *hacer juego con

matchbox (*mæch*-bokss) *n* caja de cerillas

material (mö-*ti*ᵉ-ri-öl) *n* material *m*; tejido *m*; *adj* material

mathematical (mæ-zö-*mæ*-ti-köl) *adj* matemático

mathematics (mæ-zö-*mæ*-tikss) *n* matemáticas *fpl*

matrimony (*mæ*-tri-mö-ni) *n* matrimonio *m*

matter (*mæ*-tö) *n* materia *f*; asunto *m*, cuestión *f*; *v* *tener importancia; **as a** ~ **of fact** efectivamente, en realidad

matter-of-fact (mæ-tö-röv-*fækt*) *adj* desapasionado; práctico

mattress (*mæ*-tröss) *n* colchón *m*

mature (mö-*tyu*ᵉ) *adj* maduro

maturity (mö-*tyu*ᵉ-rö-ti) *n* madurez *f*

mauve (mouv) *adj* malva

May (mei) mayo

***may** (mei) *v* *poder

maybe (*mei*-bii) *adv* quizás

mayor (mê⁰) *n* alcalde *m*

maze (meis) *n* laberinto *m*

me (mii) *pron* me

meadow (mê-dou) *n* prado *m*

meal (miil) *n* comida *f*

mean (miin) *adj* mezquino; *n* promedio *m*

***mean** (miin) *v* significar; *querer decir

meaning (mii-ning) *n* significado *m*

meaningless (mii-ning-löss) *adj* sin sentido

means (miins) *n* medio *m*; **by no ~** en ningún caso, de ningún modo

meantime: in the ~ (in ðö miin-taim) entretanto

meanwhile (miin-ᵘail) *adv* entretanto

measles (mii-söls) *n* sarampión *m*

measure (mê-ʒö) *v* *medir; *n* medida *f*

meat (miit) *n* carne *m*

mechanic (mi-kæ-nik) *n* mecánico *m*

mechanical (mi-kæ-ni-köl) *adj* mecánico

mechanism (mê-kö-ni-söm) *n* mecanismo *m*

medal (mê-döl) *n* medalla *f*

media (mii-diö) *npl*: **the ~** los medios de comunicación

mediaeval (mê-di-ii-völ) *adj* medieval

mediate (mii-di-eit) *v* mediar

mediator (mii-di-ei-tö) *n* mediador *m*

medical (mê-di-köl) *adj* médico

medicine (mêd-ssin) *n* medicamento *m*; medicina *f*

meditate (mê-di-teit) *v* meditar

Mediterranean (mê-di-tö-rei-ni-ön) Mediterráneo

medium (mii-di-öm) *adj* mediano, medio

***meet** (miit) *v* *encontrarse con

meeting (mii-ting) *n* asamblea *f*, reunión *f*; encuentro *m*

meeting place (mii-ting-pleiss) *n* lugar de reunión

melancholy (mê-löng-kö-li) *n* melancolía *f*

mellow (mê-lou) *adj* suave

melodrama (mê-lö-draa-mö) *n* melodrama *m*

melody (mê-lö-di) *n* melodía *f*

melon (mê-lön) *n* melón *m*

melt (mêlt) *v* fundir

member (mêm-bö) *n* miembro *m*; **Member of Parliament** diputado *m*

membership (mêm-bö-ʃip) *n* afiliación *f*

memo (mê-mou) *n* (pl ~s) apunte *m*

memorable (mê-mö-rö-böl) *adj* memorable

memorial (mö-moo-ri-öl) *n* monumento *m*

memorize (mê-mö-rais) *v* aprenderse de memoria

memory (mê-mö-ri) *n* memoria *f*; recuerdo *m*

mend (mênd) *v* reparar, *remendar

menstruation (mên-sstru-ei-ʃön) *n* menstruación *f*

mental (mên-töl) *adj* mental

mention (mên-ʃön) *v* nombrar, mencionar; *n* mención *f*

menu (mê-nyuu) *n* menú *m*

merchandise (möö-chön-dais) *n* mercancía *f*

merchant (möö-chönt) *n* comerciante *m*

merciful (möö-ssi-föl) *adj* misericordioso

mercury (möö-kyu-ri) *n* mercurio *m*

mercy (möö-ssi) *n* misericordia *f*, clemencia *f*

mere (mi⁰) *adj* puro; mero

merely (mi⁰-li) *adv* solamente

merge (möödʒ) *v* juntarse, unirse; fusionarse

merger (möö-dʒö) *n* fusión *f*

merit (mê-rit) *v* *merecer; *n* mérito *m*

merry (*mê*-ri) *adj* alegre; feliz

merry-go-round (*mê*-ri-ghou-raund) *n* tiovivo *m*, caballitos *mpl*

mesh (mêʃ) *n* malla *f*

mess (mêss) *n* desorden *m*; confusión *f*; ~ **up** estropear

message (*mê*-ssidʒ) *n* mensaje *m*

messenger (*mê*-ssin-dʒö) *n* mensajero *m*

metal (*mê*-töl) *n* metal *m*; metálico

meter (*mii*-tö) *n* contador *m*; *nAm* metro *m*

method (*mê*-zöd) *n* método *m*; orden *m*

methodical (mö-*zo*-di-köl) *adj* metódico

metre (*mii*-tö) *n* metro *m*

Mexican (*mêk*-ssi-kön) *adj* mejicano; *n* mejicano *m*

Mexico (*mêk*-ssi-kou) Méjico *m*

mice (mais) *n* (pl mouse)

microphone (*mai*-krö-foun) *n* micrófono *m*

midday (*mid*-dei) *n* mediodía *m*

middle (*mi*-döl) *n* medio *m*; *adj* medio; **Middle Ages** Edad Media; ~ **class** clase media; **middle-class** *adj* de la clase media

midnight (*mid*-nait) *n* medianoche *f*

midst (midsst) *n* medio *m*

midsummer (*mid*-ssa-mö) *n* pleno verano

midwife (*mid*-ᵘaif) *n* (pl -wives) comadrona *f*

might (mait) *n* fuerza *f*; poder *m*

***might** (mait) *v* *poder

mighty (*mai*-ti) *adj* fuerte; poderoso

migraine (*mi*-ghrein) *n* migraña *f*; jaqueca *f*

mild (maild) *adj* suave; templado; manso

mildew (*mil*-dyu) *n* moho *m*

mile (mail) *n* milla *f*

mileage (*mai*-lidʒ) *n* millaje *m*

milepost (*mail*-pousst) *n* cipo *m*

milestone (*mail*-sstoun) *n* piedra miliar

milieu (*mii*-lyöö) *n* ambiente *m*; mundo circundante

military (*mi*-li-tö-ri) *adj* militar; ~ **force** fuerzas armadas

milk (milk) *n* leche *f*

milkman (*milk*-mön) *n* (pl -men) lechero *m*

milkshake (*milk*-ʃeik) *n* batido de leche

milky (*mil*-ki) *adj* lechoso

mill (mil) *n* molino *m*; fábrica *f*

miller (*mi*-lö) *n* molinero *m*

million (*mil*-yön) *n* millón *m*

millionaire (mil-yö-*nêᵒ*) *n* millonario *m*, -a *f*

mince (minss) *v* picar

mind (maind) *n* mente *f*; *v* *hacer objeción a; fijarse en, *tener cuidado con

mine (main) *n* mina *f*

miner (*mai*-nö) *n* minero *m*

mineral (*mi*-nö-röl) *n* mineral *m*; ~ **water** agua mineral

mingle (*ming*-göl) *v* of sounds, smells mezclarse; at party alternar

miniature (*min*-yö-chö) *n* miniatura *f*

minimum (*mi*-ni-möm) *n* mínimum *m*

mining (*mai*-ning) *n* minería *f*

minister (*mi*-ni-sstö) *n* ministro *m*; clérigo *m*; **Prime Minister** Presidente de Consejo de ministros

ministry (*mi*-ni-sstri) *n* ministerio *m*

mink (mingk) *n* visón *m*

minor (*mai*-nö) *adj* pequeño, escaso, menor; secundario; *n* menor de edad

minority (mai-*no*-rö-ti) *n* minoría *f*

mint (mint) *n* menta *f*

minus (*mai*-nöss) *prep* menos

minute¹ (*mi*-nit) *n* minuto *m*; **minutes** actas

minute² (mai-*nyuut*) *adj* menudo

miracle (*mi*-rö-köl) *n* milagro *m*

miraculous (mi-*ræ*-kyu-löss) *adj* milagroso

mirror (*mi*-rö) *n* espejo *m*

misbehave (miss-bi-*heiv*) *v* portarse mal

miscarriage (miss-*kæ*-ridʒ) *n* aborto *m*

miscellaneous (mi-ssö-*lei*-ni-öss) *adj* misceláneo

mischief (*miss*-chif) *n* diabluras *fpl*; mal *m*, daño *m*, malicia *f*

mischievous (*miss*-chi-vöss) *adj* travieso

miserable (*mi*-sö-rö-böl) *adj* desdichado; triste; abatido

misery (*mi*-sö-ri) *n* tristeza *f*; necesidad *f*

misfortune (miss-*foo*-chên) *n* desgracia *f*; contratiempo *m*, infortunio *m*

mishap (*miss*-hæp) contratiempo *m*

*mislay (miss-*lei*) *v* extraviar

misplaced (miss-*pleisst*) *adj* inoportuno; fuera de lugar

mispronounce (miss-prö-*naunss*) *v* pronunciar mal

miss[1] (miss) señorita *f*

miss[2] (miss) *v* *perder; echar de menos

missing (*mi*-ssing) *adj* que falta; **~ person** desaparecido *m*

mist (misst) *n* niebla *f*

mistake (mi-*ssteik*) *n* error *m*, equivocación *f*

*mistake (mi-*ssteik*) *v* confundir

mistaken (mi-*sstei*-kön) *adj* equivocado; ***be ~** equivocarse

mister (*mi*-sstö) señor *m*

mistress (*mi*-sströss) *n* señora *f*; dueña *f*; querida *f*

mistrust (miss-*trasst*) *v* desconfiar de

misty (*mi*-ssti) *adj* nebuloso

*misunderstand (mi-ssan-dö-*sstænd*) *v* comprender mal

misunderstanding (mi-ssan-dö-*sstæn*-ding) *n* equivocación *f*

misuse (miss-*yuuss*) *n* abuso *m*

mittens (*mi*-töns) *pl* guantes *mpl*

mix (mikss) *v* mezclar; **~ with** alternar con

mixed (miksst) *adj* mezclado

mixer (*mik*-ssö) *n* batidora *f*

mixture (*mikss*-chö) *n* mezcla *f*

moan (moun) *v* *gemir

moat (mout) *n* foso *m*

mobile (*mou*-bail) *adj* móvil; **~ phone** teléfono *m* móvil

mock (mok) *v* burlarse de

mockery (mo-kö-ri) *n* burla *f*

model (*mo*-döl) *n* modelo *m/f*; patrón *m*; *v* modelar

modem (*mou*-dêm) *n* módem *m*

moderate (*mo*-dö-röt) *adj* moderado

modern (*mo*-dön) *adj* moderno

modest (*mo*-disst) *adj* modesto

modesty (*mo*-di-ssti) *n* modestia *f*

modify (*mo*-di-fai) *v* modificar

moist (moisst) *adj* húmedo

moisten (*moi*-ssön) *v* *humedecer

moisture (*moiss*-chö) *n* humedad *f*; **moisturizing cream** crema hidratante

molar (*mou*-lö) *n* muela *f*

moment (*mou*-mönt) *n* momento *m*

momentary (*mou*-mön-tö-ri) *adj* momentáneo

monarch (*mo*-nök) *n* monarca *m*

monarchy (*mo*-nö-ki) *n* monarquía *f*

monastery (*mo*-nö-sstri) *n* monasterio *m*

Monday (*man*-di) lunes *m*

monetary (*ma*-ni-tö-ri) *adj* monetario; **~ unit** unidad monetaria

money (*ma*-ni) *n* dinero *m*; **~ exchange** oficina de cambio; **~ order** giro *m* postal

monk (mangk) *n* monje *m*

monkey (*mang*-ki) *n* mono *m*

monologue (*mo*-no-logh) *n* monólogo *m*

monopoly (mö-*no*-pö-li) *n* monopolio *m*

monotonous (mö-*no*-tö-nöss) *adj* monótono

month (manz) *n* mes *m*

monthly (*manz*-li) *adj* mensual; ~ **magazine** revista mensual

monument (*mo*-nyu-mönt) *n* monumento *m*

mood (muud) *n* humor *m*; disposición *f*

moon (muun) *n* luna *f*

moonlight (*muun*-lait) *n* luz de la luna

moor (mu°) *n* brezal *m*, turbera *f*

moose (muuss) *n* (pl ~, ~s) alce *m*

moped (*mou*-pêd) *n* bicimotor *m*

moral (*mo*-röl) *n* moraleja *f*; *adj* moral; virtuoso; **morals** moralidad *f*; ética *f*

morality (mö-*ræ*-lö-ti) *n* moralidad *f*

more (moo) *adj* más; **once** ~ otra vez

moreover (moo-*rou*-vö) *adv* además

morning (*moo*-ning) *n* mañana *f*; ~ **paper** diario matutino

Moroccan (mö-*ro*-kön) *adj* marroquí

Morocco (mö-*ro*-kou) Marruecos *m*

morphia (*moo*-fi-ö) *n* morfina *f*

morphine (*moo*-fiin) *n* morfina *f*

morsel (*moo*-ssöl) *n* trozo *m*; bocado *m*

mortal (*moo*-töl) *adj* fatal, mortal

mortgage (*moo*-ghidȝ) *n* hipoteca *f*

mosaic (mö-*sei*-ik) *n* mosaico *m*

mosque (mossk) *n* mezquita *f*

mosquito (mö-*sskii*-tou) *n* (pl ~es) mosquito *m*; ~ **net** mosquitero *m*

moss (moss) *n* musgo *m*

most (mousst) *adj* el más; **at** ~ a lo sumo, como máximo; ~ **of all** sobre todo

mostly (*mousst*-li) *adv* generalmente

motel (mou-*têl*) *n* motel *m*

moth (moz) *n* polilla *f*

mother (*ma*-ðö) *n* madre *f*; ~ **tongue** lengua materna

mother-in-law (*ma*-ðö-rin-loo) *n* (pl mothers-) suegra *f*

mother of pearl (ma-ðö-röv-*pööl*) *n* nácar *m*

motion (*mou*-ʃön) *n* movimiento *m*; moción *f*

motivate (*mou*-ti-veit) *v* motivar

motive (*mou*-tiv) *n* motivo *m*

motor (*mou*-tö) *n* motor *m*; *v* *ir en coche; **starter** ~ motor de arranque

motorbike (*mou*-tö-baik) *nAm* motocicleta *f*

motorboat (*mou*-tö-bout) *n* bote a motor

motorcar (*mou*-tö-kaa) *n* automóvil *m*

motorcycle (*mou*-tö-ssai-köl) *n* motocicleta *f*

motoring (*mou*-tö-ring) *n* automovilismo *m*

motorist (*mou*-tö-risst) *n* automovilista *m*

motorway (mou-tö-^{u}ei) *n* autopista *f*

motto (*mo*-tou) *n* (pl ~es, ~s) lema *m*

mo(u)ldy (*moul*-di) *adj* enmohecido

mound (maund) *n* montículo *m*

mount (maunt) *v* montar; *n* monte *m*

mountain (*maun*-tin) *n* montaña *f*; ~ **pass** paso *m*; ~ **range** cordillera *f*

mountaineering (maun-ti-ni^ö-ring) *n* montañismo *m*

mountainous (*maun*-ti-nöss) *adj* montañoso

mourning (*moo*-ning) *n* luto *m*

mouse (mauss) *n* (pl mice) ratón *m*

moustache (mö-*sstaaʃ*) *n* bigote *m*

mouth (mauz) *n* boca *f*; hocico *m*; desembocadura *f*

mouthwash (*mauz*-^{u}oʃ) *n* enjuague bucal

movable (*muu*-vö-böl) *adj* movible

move (muuv) *v* *mover; trasladar; mudarse; *conmover; *n* jugada *f*, paso *m*; mudanza *f*

movement (*muuv*-mönt) *n* movimiento *m*

movie (*muu*-vi) *n* película *f*; **the ~s** el cine

much (mach) *adj* mucho; **as ~** tanto

muck (mak) *n* suciedad *f*

mud (mad) *n* lodo *m*

muddle (*ma*-döl) *n* dédalo *m*, embrollo *m*; *v* embrollar

muddy (*ma*-di) *adj* lodoso

mug (magh) *n* vaso *m*, taza *f*

mule (myuul) *n* mulo *m*; mula *f*

multiplication (mal-ti-pli-*kei*-ʃön) *n* multiplicación *f*

multiply (*mal*-ti-plai) *v* multiplicar

mumps (mampss) *n* paperas *fpl*

municipal (myuu-*ni*-ssi-pöl) *adj* municipal

municipality (myuu-ni-ssi-*pæ*-lö-ti) *n* municipalidad *f*

murder (*möö*-dö) *n* asesinato *m*; *v* asesinar

murderer (*möö*-dö-rö) *n* asesino *m*, -a *f*

muscle (*ma*-ssöl) *n* músculo *m*

muscular (*ma*-sskyu-lö) *adj* musculoso

museum (myuu-*sii*-öm) *n* museo *m*

mushroom (*maʃ*-ruum) *n* seta *f*; hongo *m*

music (*myuu*-sik) *n* música *f*; **~ academy** conservatorio *m*; **~ hall** teatro de variedades

musical (*myuu*-si-köl) *adj* musical; comedia musical

musician (myuu-*si*-ʃön) *n* músico *m*, -a *f*

mussel (*ma*-ssöl) *n* mejillón *m*

*must (masst) *v* *tener que

mustard (*ma*-sstöd) *n* mostaza *f*

mute (myuut) *adj* mudo

mutiny (*myuu*-ti-ni) *n* amotinamiento *m*

mutton (*ma*-tön) *n* carnero *m*

mutual (*myuu*-chu-öl) *adj* mutuo, recíproco

my (mai) *adj* mi

myself (mai-*ssêlf*) *pron* me; yo mismo

mysterious (mi-*ssti*ᵒ-ri-öss) *adj* misterioso

mystery (*mi*-sstö-ri) *n* enigma *m*, misterio *m*

myth (miz) *n* mito *m*

N

nail (neil) *n* uña *f*; clavo *m*

nailbrush (*neil*-braʃ) *n* cepillo para las uñas

nail file (*neil*-fail) *n* lima para las uñas

nail polish (*neil*-po-liʃ) *n* laca de uñas

nail scissors (*neil*-ssi-sös) *pl* tijeras para las uñas

naïve (naa-*iiv*) *adj* ingenuo

naked (*nei*-kid) *adj* desnudo

name (neim) *n* nombre *m*; *v* nombrar; **in the ~ of** en nombre de

namely (*neim*-li) *adv* a saber

nap (næp) *n* siesta *f*

napkin (*næp*-kin) *n* servilleta *f*

nappy (*næ*-pi) *n* pañal *m*

narcosis (naa-*kou*-ssiss) *n* (pl -ses) narcosis *f*

narcotic (naa-*ko*-tik) *n* narcótico *m*

narration (nö-*rei*-ʃön) *n* narración *f*

narrow (*næ*-rou) *adj* angosto, estrecho

narrow-minded (*næ*-rou-*main*-did) *adj* intolerante

nasty (*naa*-ssti) *adj* antipático, desagradable; repulsivo; sucio

nation (*nei*-ʃön) *n* nación *f*; pueblo *m*

national (*næ*-ʃö-nöl) *adj* nacional; del Estado; ~ **anthem** himno nacional; ~ **dress** traje del país; ~ **park** parque nacional

nationality (næ-ʃö-*næ*-lö-ti) *n* nacionalidad *f*

nationalize (*næ*-ʃö-nö-lais) *v* nacionalizar

native (*nei*-tiv) *n* nativo *m*, -a *f*; indígena *m*; *adj* nativo; ~ **country** patria *f*, país natal; ~ **language** lengua materna

natural (*næ*-chö-röl) *adj* natural; innato

naturally (*næ*-chö-rö-li) *adv* naturalmente, por supuesto

nature (*nei*-chö) *n* naturaleza *f*; natural *m*

naughty (*noo*-ti) *adj* travieso

nausea (*noo*-ssi-ö) *n* náusea *f*

naval (*nei*-völ) *adj* naval

navel (*nei*-völ) *n* ombligo *m*

navigable (*næ*-vi-ghö-böl) *adj* navegable

navigate (*næ*-vi-gheit) *v* navegar

navigation (næ-vi-*ghei*-ʃön) *n* navegación *f*

navy (*nei*-vi) *n* marina *f*

near (niö) *prep* cerca de; *adj* cercano

nearby (*niö*-bai) *adj* cercano; próximo

nearly (*niö*-li) *adv* casi, de cerca; por poco

neat (niit) *adj* pulcro; bien arreglado; puro

necessary (*nê*-ssö-ssö-ri) *adj* necesario

necessity (nö-*ssê*-ssö-ti) *n* necesidad *f*

neck (nêk) *n* cuello *m*; **nape of the** ~ nuca *f*

necklace (*nêk*-löss)*n* collar *m*

necktie (*nêk*-tai) *n* corbata *f*

need (niid) *v* deber, necesitar; *n* necesidad *f*; ~ **to** deber

needle (*nii*-döl) *n* aguja *f*

needlework (*nii*-döl-ᵘöök) *n* labor de aguja

negative (*nê*-ghö-tiv) *adj* negativo; *n* negativo *m*

neglect (ni-*ghlêkt*) *v* descuidar; no cumplir; olvidar; *n* negligencia *f*; abandono *m*

neglectful (ni-*ghlêkt*-föl) *adj* negligente

negligee (*nê*-ghli-ʒei) *n* bata suelta

negotiate (ni-*ghou*-ʃi-eit) *v* negociar

negotiation (ni-ghou-ʃi-*ei*-ʃön) *n* negociación *f*

neighbo(u)r (*nei*-bö) *n* vecino *m*, -a *f*

neighbo(u)rhood (*nei*-bö-hud) *n* vecindad *f*

neighbo(u)ring (*nei*-bö-bring) *adj* contiguo, vecino

neither (*nai*-ðö) *pron* ninguno de los dos; **neither ... nor** ni ... ni

neon (*nii*-on) *n* neón *m*

nephew (*nê*-fyuu) *n* sobrino *m*

nerve (nööv) *n* nervio *m*; valor *m*; descaro *m*

nervous (*nöö*-vöss) *adj* nervioso

nest (nêsst) *n* nido *m*

net (nêt) *n* red *f*; *adj* neto

Netherlands (*nê*-ðö-lönds): **the ~** Países Bajos *mpl*

network (*nêt*-ᵘöök) *n* red *f*

neuralgia (nyuᵒ-*ræl*-dʒö) *n* neuralgia *f*

neurosis (nyuᵒ-*rou*-ssiss) *n* neurosis *f*

neuter (*nyuu*-tö) *adj* neutro

neutral (*nyuu*-tröl) *adj* neutral

never (*nê*-vö) *adv* nunca

nevertheless (nê-vö-ðö-*lêss*) *adv* no obstante

new (nyuu) *adj* nuevo; **New Year** año nuevo

news (nyuus) *n* noticiario *m*, noticia *f*; noticias *fpl*

newsagent (*nyuu*-sei-dʒönt) *n* vendedor de periódicos

newspaper (*nyuus*-pei-pö) *n* diario *m*; periódico *m*

newsreel (*nyuus*-riil) *n* noticiario *m*

newsstand (*nyuus*-sstænd) *n* quiosco de periódicos

New Zealand (nyuu *sii*-lönd) Nueva Zelanda

next (nêksst) *adj* próximo; siguiente; ~ **to** junto a

next-door (nêksst-*doo*) *adv* al lado

nice (naiss) *adj* agradable, bonito, ameno; rico; simpático

nickel (*ni*-köl) *n* níquel *m*

nickname (*nik*-neim) *n* mote *m*

nicotine (*ni*-kö-tiin) *n* nicotina *f*

niece (niiss) *n* sobrina *f*

Nigeria (nai-dʒiˀ-ri-ö) Nigeria *f*

Nigerian (nai-dʒiˀ-ri-ön) *adj* nigeriano

night (nait) *n* noche *f*; **by** ~ de noche; ~ **cream** crema de noche; ~ **flight** vuelo nocturno; ~ **rate** tarifa nocturna; ~ **train** tren nocturno

nightclub (*nait*-klab) *n* cabaret *m*

nightdress (*nait*-drêss) *n* camisón *m*

nightingale (*nai*-ting-gheil) *n* ruiseñor *m*

nightly (*nait*-li) *adj* nocturno

nightmare (*nait*-mær) pesadilla *f*

nil (nil) nada

nine (nain) *num* nueve

nineteen (nain-*tiin*) *num* diecinueve

nineteenth (nain-*tiinz*) *num* decimonono

ninety (*nain*-ti) *num* noventa

ninth (nainz) *num* noveno

nitrogen (*nai*-trö-dʒön) *n* nitrógeno *m*

no (nou) no; *adj* ninguno; ~ **one** nadie

nobility (nou-*bi*-lö-ti) *n* nobleza *f*

noble (*nou*-böl) *adj* noble

nobody (*nou*-bo-di) *pron* nadie

nod (nod) *n* cabeceo *m*; *v* cabecear

noise (nois) *n* ruido *m*; alboroto *m*

noisy (*noi*-si) *adj* ruidoso

nominal (*no*-mi-nöl) *adj* nominal

nominate (*no*-mi-neit) *v* nombrar

nomination (no-mi-*nei*-ʃön) *n* nominación *f*; nombramiento *m*

none (nan) *pron* ninguno

nonsense (*non*-ssönss) *n* tontería *f*

noon (nuun) *n* mediodía *m*

nor (noor) *conj* ni; **nor do I** yo tampoco, ni yo

normal (*noo*-möl) *adj* normal

north (nooz) *n* norte *m*; *adj* septentrional; **North Pole** polo norte

north-east (nooz-*iisst*) *n* nordeste *m*

northerly (*noo*-ðö-li) *adj* del norte

northern (*noo*-ðön) *adj* norteño

north-west (nooz-ᵘêsst) *n* noroeste *m*

Norway (*noo*-ᵘei)Noruega *f*

Norwegian (noo-ᵘii-dʒön) *adj* noruego

nose (nous) *n* nariz *f*

nosebleed (*nous*-bliid) *n* hemorragia nasal

nostril (*no*-sstril) *n* ventana de la nariz

nosy (*nou*-si) *adj colloquial* entrometido

not (not) *adv* no

notary (*nou*-tö-ri) *n* notario *m*

note (nout) *n* apunte *m*, esquela *f*; nota *f*; tono *m*; *v* notar; observar, *comprobar

notebook (*nout*-buk) *n* libreta de apuntes; cuaderno *m*; ordenador portátil, *L.Am.* computadora portátil

noted (*nou*-tid) *adj* afamado, conocido

notepaper (*nout*-pei-pö) *n* papel de escribir, papel para cartas

nothing (*na*-zing) *n* nada *f*, nada

notice (*nou*-tiss) *v* observar, notar,

*advertir; *ver; n aviso m, noticia f; atención f

noticeable (*nou*-ti-ssö-böl) adj perceptible; notable

notify (*nou*-ti-fai) v notificar

notion (*nou*-ʃön) n noción f; opinión f

notorious (nou-*too*-ri-öss) adj de mala fama

nougat (*nuu*-ghaa) n turrón m

nought (noot) n cero m

noun (naun) n nombre m, substantivo m

nourishing (*na*-ri-ʃing) adj nutritivo

novel (*no*-völ) n novela f

novelist (*no*-vö-lisst) n novelista m/f

November (nou-*vêm*-bö) noviembre

now (nau) adv ahora; actualmente; ~ **and then** de vez en cuando

nowadays (*nau*-ö-deis) adv hoy en día

nowhere (*nou*-ᵘê̂ᵒ) adv en ninguna parte

nozzle (*no*-söl) n tobera f

nuance (nyuu-*aᵑgss*) n matiz m

nuclear (*nyuu*-kli-ö) adj nuclear; ~

energy energía nuclear

nucleus (*nyuu*-kli-öss) n núcleo m

nude (nyuud) adj desnudo; n desnudo m

nuisance (*nyuu*-ssönss) n molestia f

numb (nam) adj entumecido; aterido

number (*nam*-bö) n número m; cifra f; cantidad f

numeral (*nyuu*-mö-röl) n numeral m

numerous (*nyuu*-mö-röss) adj numeroso

nun (nan) n monja f

nunnery (*na*-nö-ri) n convento m

nurse (nööss)n enfermero m, -a f; niñera f; v *atender a; amamantar

nursery (*nöö*-ssö-ri) n cuarto de niños; guardería f; vivero m

nut (nat) n nuez f; tuerca f

nutcrackers (*nat*-kræ-kös) pl cascanueces m

nutmeg (*nat*-mêgh) n nuez moscada

nutritious (nyuu-*tri*-ʃöss) adj nutritivo

nutshell (*nat*-ʃêl) n cáscara de nuez

nylon (*nai*-lon) n nilón m

O

oak (ouk) n roble m

oar (oo) n remo m

oasis (ou-*ei*-ssiss) n (pl oases) oasis f

oath (ouz) n juramento m

oats (outss) pl avena f

obedience (ö-*bii*-di-önss) n obediencia f

obedient (ö-*bii*-di-önt) adj obediente

obesity (ö-*bii*-ssi-ti) n obesidad f

obey (ö-*bei*) v *obedecer

object[1] (*ob*-dʒikt) n objeto m

object[2] (öb-*dʒêkt*) v objetar; ~ **to** *oponerse a

objection (öb-dʒêk-ʃön)n objeción f

objective (öb-*dʒêk*-tiv) adj objetivo; n objetivo m

obligatory (ö-*bli*-ghö-tö-ri) adj obligatorio

oblige (ö-*blaidʒ*) v obligar; *be **obliged to** *estar obligado a; *tener que

obliging (ö-*blai*-dʒing) adj atento; servicial

oblong (*ob*-long) adj oblongo; n rectángulo m

obscene (öb-*ssiin*) adj obsceno

obscure (öb-*sskyuᵒ*) adj oscuro, misterioso, oscuro

observation (ob-sö-*vei*-ʃön) *n*
observación *f*

observatory (öb-*söö*-vö-tri) *n*
observatorio *m*

observe (öb-*sööv*) *v* observar

obsession (öb-*ssê*-ʃön) *n* obsesión *f*

obstacle (*ob*-sstö-köl) *n* obstáculo *m*

obstinate (*ob*-ssti-nöt) *adj* obstinado;
pertinaz

obtain (öb-*tein*) *v* *conseguir,
*obtener

obtainable (öb-*tei*-nö-böl) *adj*
adquirible

obvious (*ob*-vi-öss) *adj* obvio

occasion (ö-*kei*-ʒön) *n* ocasión *f*;
motivo *m*

occasionally (ö-*kei*-ʒö-nö-li) *adv* de
vez en cuando, ocasionalmente

occupant (*o*-kyu-pönt) *n* ocupante *m*

occupation (o-kyu-*pei*-ʃön) *n*
ocupación *f*; empleo *m*; profesión *f*

occupy (*o*-kyu-pai) *v* ocupar

occur (ö-*köö*) *v* suceder, ocurrir,
*acontecer

occurrence (ö-*ka*-rönss) *n*
acontecimiento *m*

ocean (*ou*-ʃön)*n* océano *m*

October (ok-*tou*-bö) octubre

octopus (*ok*-tö-pöss) *n* pulpo *m*

oculist (*o*-kyu-lisst) *n* oculista *m*/*f*

odd(od) *adj* raro; impar

odo(u)r (*ou*-dö) *n* olor *m*

of (ov, öv) *prep* de

off (of) *adv* fuera; *prep* de

offence (ö-*fênss*) *n* falta *f*; ofensa *f*,
escándalo *m*

offend (ö-*fênd*) *v* ofender; transgredir

offense (ö-*fênss*) *n*Am falta *f*; ofensa *f*,
escándalo *m*

offensive (ö-*fên*-ssiv) *adj* ofensivo;
insultante; *n* ofensivo *m*

offer (*o*-fö) *v* *ofrecer; presentar; *n*
oferta *f*

office (*o*-fiss) *n* oficina *f*; despacho *m*;

cargo *m*; ~ **hours** horas de oficina

officer (*o*-fi-ssö) *n* oficial *m*

official (ö-*fi*-ʃöl) *adj* oficial

off-licence (*of*-lai-ssönss) *n* almacén
de licores

often (*o*-fön) *adv* a menudo,
frecuentemente

oil (oil) *n* aceite *m*; petróleo *m*; **fuel** ~
combustible líquido; ~ **filter** filtro del
aceite; ~ **painting** pintura al óleo; ~
pressure presión del aceite; ~
refinery refinería de petróleo; ~ **well**
pozo de petróleo

oily (*oi*-li) *adj* aceitoso

ointment (*oint*-mönt) *n* ungüento *m*

okay! (ou-*kei*) ¡de acuerdo!

old (ould) *adj* viejo; ~ **age** vejez *f*

old-fashioned (ould-*fæ*-ʃönd) *adj*
anticuado; pasado de moda

olive (*o*-liv) *n* aceituna *f*; ~ **oil** aceite de
oliva

omelette (*om*-löt) *n* tortilla *f*

ominous (*o*-mi-nöss) *adj* siniestro; de
mal agüero

omit (ö-*mit*) *v* omitir

omnipotent (om-*ni*-pö-tönt) *adj*
omnipotente

on (on) *prep* sobre; encima de; acerca
de

once (ᵘanss) *adv* una vez; antes; **at** ~
en seguida; ~ **more** otra vez

oncoming (*on*-ka-ming) *adj* venidero;
que viene

one (ᵘan) *num* uno; *pron* uno

oneself (ᵘan-*ssêlf*) *pron* uno mismo

onion (*a*-nyön) *n* cebolla *f*

only (*oun*-li) *adj* solo; *adv* sólo,
solamente; *conj* pero

onwards (*on*-ᵘöds) *adv* adelante

onyx (*o*-nikss) *n* ónix *m*

opal (*ou*-pöl) *n* ópalo *m*

open (*ou*-pön) *v* abrir; *adj* abierto;
sincero

opening (*ou*-pö-ning) *n* abertura *f*

opera (*o*-pö-rö) *n* ópera *f*; **~ house** teatro de la ópera

operate (*o*-pö-reit) *v* operar, funcionar

operation (o-pö-*rei*-ʃön) *n* funcionamiento *m*; operación *f*

operator (o-pö-rei-tö) *n* operador *m*, -a *f*; operario *m*, -a *f*

operetta (o-pö-*rê*-tö) *n* opereta *f*; zarzuela *f*

opinion (ö-*pi*-nyön) *n* parecer *m*, opinión *f*

opponent (ö-*pou*-nönt) *n* contrincante *m/f*; adversario *m*, -a *f*

opportunity (o-pö-*tyuu*-nö-ti) *n* oportunidad *f*

oppose (ö-*pous*) *v* *oponerse

opposite (*o*-pö-sit) *prep* enfrente de; *adj* contrario, opuesto

opposition (o-pö-*si*-ʃön)*n* oposición *f*

oppress (ö-*prêss*)*v* oprimir

optician (o-*ti*-ʃön) *n* óptico *m*, -a *f*

optimism (*op*-ti-mi-söm) *n* optimismo *m*

optimist (*op*-ti-misst) *n* optimista *m/f*

optimistic (op-ti-*mi*-sstik) *adj* optimista

optional (*op*-ʃö-nöl) *adj* opcional

or (oo) *conj* o

oral (*oo*-röl) *adj* oral

orange (*o*-rindʒ) *n* naranja *f*; *adj* de color naranja

orbit (*oo*-bit) *n* órbita *f*; *v* girar alrededor de; **send into ~** poner en órbita

orchard (*oo*-chöd) *n* vergel *m*

orchestra (*oo*-ki-sströ) *n* orquesta *f*; **~ seat** *Am* butaca *f*

order (*oo*-dö) *v* ordenar; *pedir; *n* orden *m*; orden *f*, mandato *m*; pedido *m*; **in ~** en regla; **in ~ to** para; **made to ~** hecho a la medida; **out of ~** averiado; **postal ~** giro postal

order form (*oo*-dö-foom) *n* hoja de pedido

ordinary (*oo*-dön-ri) *adj* común, ordinario

ore (oo) *n* mineral *m*

organ (*oo*-ghön) *n* órgano *m*

organic (oo-*ghæ*-nik) *adj* orgánico

organization (oo-ghö-nai-*sei*-ʃön) *n* organización *f*

organize (*oo*-ghö-nais) *v* organizar

Orient (*oo*-ri-önt) *n* oriente *m*

oriental (oo-ri-*ên*-töl) *adj* oriental

orientate (*oo*-ri-ön-teit) *v* orientarse

origin (*o*-ri-dʒin) *n* origen *m*; descendencia *f*, procedencia *f*

original (ö-*ri*-dʒi-nöl) *adj* auténtico, original

originally (ö-*ri*-dʒi-nö-li) *adv* originalmente

orlon (*oo*-lon) *n* orlón *m*

ornament (*oo*-nö-mönt) *n* adorno *m*

ornamental (oo-nö-*mên*-töl) *adj* ornamental

orphan (*oo*-fön) *n* huérfano *m*

orthodox (*oo*-zö-dokss) *adj* ortodoxo

ostrich (*o*-sstrich) *n* avestruz *m*

other (*a*-ðö) *adj* otro

otherwise (*a*-ðö-ᵘais) *conj* si no; *adv* de otra manera

*ought to (oot) *v/aux* *tener que; **he/they ~ know** debe/deben saberlo; **you ~ have done it** deberías haberlo hecho

ounce (auns) onza *f*

our (au⁰) *adj* nuestro

ours (au⁰s) *pron* el nuestro, la nuestra; **a friend of ~** un amigo nuestro

ourselves (au⁰-*ssêlvs*)*pron* nos; nosotros mismos

out (aut) *adv* fuera; afuera; de fuera; apagado; al descubierto; **~ of** fuera de

outbreak (*aut*-breik) *n* explosión *f*

outburst (*aut*-böösst) *n* arrebato *m*, arranque *m*

outcome (*aut*-kam) *n* resultado *m*

*outdo (aut-*duu*) *v* superar

outdoors (aut-*doos*) *adv* afuera; al aire libre

outer (*au*-tö) *adj* exterior, externo

outfit (*aut*-fit) *n* equipo *m*; conjunto *m*

outing (*au*-ting) excursión *f*

outline (*aut*-lain) *n* contorno *m*; *v* bosquejar

outlook (*aut*-luk) *n* previsión *f*; punto de vista; perspectiva *f*

output (*aut*-put) *n* producción *f*

outside (aut-*ssaid*) *adv* afuera; *prep* fuera de; *n* exterior *m*

outsize (*aut*-ssais) *n* tamaño extra grande

outskirts (*aut*-ssköötss) *pl* afueras *fpl*

outstanding (aut-*sstæn*-ding) *adj* eminente, destacado; pendiente

outward (*aut*-ᵘöd) *adj* externo

outwards (*aut*-ᵘöds) *adv* hacia afuera

oval (*ou*-völ) *adj* ovalado

oven (*a*-vön) *n* horno *m*; **microwave ~** horno de microonda

over (*ou*-vö) *prep* sobre; encima de; durante; por; *adv* encima; **~ here** acá; **~ there** allá; **to be ~** estar terminado

overall (*ou*-vö-rool) *adj* por lo general; en conjunto

overalls (*ou*-vö-rools) *pl* mono *m*; overol *mMe*

overcast (*ou*-vö-kaasst) *adj* anublado

overcoat (*ou*-vö-kout) *n* abrigo *m*

*overcome (ou-vö-*kam*) *v* vencer

*overdo (ou-vö-*duu*) *v* exagerar; recocer, cocinar demasiado; **you're overdoing things** te estás excediendo

overdue (ou-vö-*dyuu*) *adj* retrasado

overdraft (*ou*-vö-draaft) *n* descubierto *m*

*overdraw (ou-vö-*droo*) *v* dejar al descubierto

overgrown (ou-vö-*ghroun*) *adj* cubierto de verdor

overhaul (ou-vö-*hool*) *v* revisar

overhead (ou-vö-*hêd*) *adv* en alto, de arriba; *n* gastos generales

overlook (ou-vö-*luk*) *v* pasar por alto

overnight (ou-vö-*nait*) *adv* de noche

overseas (ou-vö-*ssiis*) *adj* ultramar

oversight (*ou*-vö-ssait) *n* descuido *m*

*oversleep (ou-vö-*ssliip*) *v* quedarse dormido

overstrung (ou-vö-*sstrang*) *adj* sobreexcitado; muy tenso

*overtake (ou-vö-*teik*) *v* alcanzar; adelantar; **no overtaking** prohibido adelantar

over-tired (ou-vö-*taiᵒd*) *adj* agobiado; muy fatigado

overture (*ou*-vö-chö) *n* obertura *f*

overweight (*ou*-vö-ᵘeit) *n* sobrepeso *m*

overwhelm (ou-vö-ᵘ*êlm*) *v* *desconcertar, subyugar; abrumar

overwork (ou-vö-ᵘ*öök*) *v* trabajar demasiado

owe (ou) *v* deber; **owing to** a causa de, debido a

owl (aul) *n* buho *m*

own (oun) *v* *poseer; *adj* propio

owner (*ou*-nö) *n* propietario *m*, -a *f*

ox (okss) *n* (pl oxen) buey *m*

oxygen (*ok*-ssi-dʒön)*n* oxígeno *m*

oyster (*oi*-sstö) *n* ostra *f*

ozone (*ou*-soun) *n* ozono *m*

P

pace (peiss) *n* paso *m*; ritmo *m*

Pacific Ocean (pö-*ssi*-fik *ou*-jön) Océano Pacífico

pacifism (*pæ*-ssi-fi-söm) *n* pacifismo *m*

pacifist (*pæ*-ssi-fisst) *n* pacifista *m*

pack (pæk) *v* embalar; **~ up** empaquetar

package (*pæ*-kidʒ) *n* paquete *m*

packet (*pæ*-kit) *n* paquete *m* pequeño

packing (*pæ*-king) *n* embalaje *m*

pact (pækt) *n* pacto *m*

pad (pæd) *n* almohadilla *f*; bloc *m*

paddle (*pæ*-döl) *n* remo *m*

padlock (*pæd*-lok) *n* candado *m*

pagan (*pei*-ghön) *adj* pagano; *n* pagano *m*

page (peidʒ) *n* página *f*

pageboy (*peidʒ*-boi) *n* paje *m*

pail (peil) *n* balde *m*

pain (pein) *n* dolor *m*; **pains** pena *f*

painful (*pein*-föl) *adj* doloroso

painkiller (*pein*-ki-lö) *n* analgésico *m*

painless (*pein*-löss) *adj* sin dolor

paint (peint) *n* pintura *f*; *v* pintar

paintbox (*peint*-bokss) *n* caja de colores

paintbrush (*peint*-braʃ) *n* pincel *m*

painter (*pein*-tö) *n* pintor *m*, -a *f*

painting (*pein*-ting) *n* pintura *f*

pair (pê°) *n* par *m*

Pakistan (paa-ki-*sstaan*) Paquistán *m*

Pakistani (paa-ki-*sstaa*-ni) *adj* paquistaní

pal (pæl) *n colloquial* amigo *m*, -a *f*; colega *m/f*

palace (*pæ*-löss) *n* palacio *m*

pale (peil) *adj* pálido

palm (paam) *n* palma *f*

palpable (*pæl*-pö-böl) *adj* palpable

palpitation (pæl-pi-*tei*-ʃön) *n* palpitación *f*

pan (pæn) *n* cazuela *f*; **frying ~** sartén *f*

pancake (*pæn*-keik) *n* crepe *m*, *L.Am.* panqueque *m*

pane (pein) *n* cristal *m*

panel (*pæ*-nöl) *n* panel *m*, entrepaño *m*; tablero *m*

panel(l)ing (*pæ*-nö-ling) *n* enmaderado *m*

panic (*pæ*-nik) *n* pánico *m*

pant (pænt) *v* jadear

panties (*pæn*-tis) *pl* braga *f*

pants (pæntss) *pl* calzoncillos *mpl*; *plAm* pantalones *mpl*

pant suit (*pænt*-ssuut) *n* traje pantalón

panty hose (*pæn*-ti-hous) *n* media panty

paper (*pei*-pö) *n* papel *m*; periódico *m*; de papel; **carbon ~** papel carbón; **~ bag** bolsa de papel; **~ knife** abrecartas *m*; **~ napkin** servilleta de papel; **typing ~** papel para mecanografiar; **wrapping ~** papel de envolver

paperback (*pei*-pö-bæk) *n* libro de bolsillo

parade (pö-*reid*) *n* parada *f*, desfile *m*

paradise (*pæ*-rö-dais) *n* paraíso *m*

paraffin (*pæ*-rö-fin) *n* parafina *f*

paragraph (*pæ*-rö-ghraaf)*n* párrafo *m*

parakeet (*pæ*-rö-kiit) *n* perico *m*

parallel (*pæ*-rö-lêl) *adj* paralelo; *n* paralelo *m*

paralyse *Am*, **paralyze** (*pæ*-rö-lais) *v* paralizar

parcel (*paa*-ssöl) *n* paquete *m*

pardon (*paa*-dön)*n* perdón *m*; indulto *m*

parent (*pê°*-rönt) *n* padre *m*; madre *f*; **parents** *pl* padres *mpl*

parents-in-law (*pê°*-röntss-in-loo) *pl* padres políticos

parish (*pæ*-riʃ) *n* parroquia *f*

park (paak) *n* parque *m*; *v* estacionar

parking (*paa*-king) *n* aparcamiento *m*; **no ~** prohibido estacionarse; **~ fee** derechos de estacionamiento; **~ light** luz de estacionamiento; **~ lot** *Am* estacionamiento *m*; **~ meter** parquímetro *m*; **~ zone** zona de aparcamiento

parliament (*paa*-lö-mönt) *n* parlamento *m*

parliamentary (paa-lö-*mên*-tö-ri) *adj* parlamentario

parrot (*pæ*-röt) *n* loro *m*; papagayo *m*

parsley (*paa*-ssli) *n* perejil *m*

parson (*paa*-ssön) *n* pastor *m*

parsonage (*paa*-ssö-nidʒ) *n* curato *m*

part (paat) *n* parte *f*; pieza *f*; *v* separar; **spare ~** recambio *m*

partial (*paa*-ʃöl) *adj* parcial

participant (paa-*ti*-ssi-pönt) *n* participante *m/f*

participate (paa-*ti*-ssi-peit) *v* participar

particular (pö-*ti*-kyu-lö) *adj* especial, particular; exigente; **in ~** en particular

parting (*paa*-ting) *n* despedida *f*; raya *f*

partition (paa-*ti*-ʃön) *n* tabique *m*

partly (*paat*-li) *adv* en parte

partner (*paat*-nö) *n* pareja *f*; socio *m*, -a *f*; compañero *m*, -a *f*

partridge (*paa*-tridʒ) *n* perdiz *f*

party (*paa*-ti) *n* partido *m*; guateque *m*, fiesta *f*; grupo *m*

pass (paass) *v* transcurrir, pasar; *aprobar; **~ by** pasar de largo; **~ through** *atravesar

passage (*pæ*-ssidʒ) *n* pasaje *m*; travesía *f*; trozo *m*

passenger (*pæ*-ssön-dʒö) *n* pasajero *m*, -a *f*; **~ train** tren de pasajeros

passer-by (paa-ssö-*bai*) *n* transeúnte *m*

passion (*pæ*-ʃön) *n* pasión *f*; cólera *f*

passionate (*pæ*-ʃö-nöt) *adj* apasionado

passive (*pæ*-ssiv) *adj* pasivo

passport (*paass*-poot) *n* pasaporte *m*; **~ control** inspección de pasaportes; **~ photograph** fotografía de pasaporte

password (*paass*-ᵘööd) *n* santo y seña; contraseña de acceso

past (paasst) *n* pasado *m*; *adj* pasado; transcurrido; *prep* a lo largo de, más allá de

paste (peisst) *n* pasta *f*; *v* pegar

pastime (*paass*-taim) *n* pasatiempo *m*

pastry (*pei*-sstri) *n* pasteles *mpl*; **~ shop** pastelería *f*

pasture (*paass*-chö) *n* prado *m*

pasty (*pei*-ssti) *adj* pálido

patch (pæch) *v* *remendar

patent (*pei*-tönt) *n* patente *f*

path (paaz) *n* senda *f*; sendero *m*

patience (*pei*-ʃönss) *n* paciencia *f*

patient (*pei*-ʃönt) *adj* paciente; *n* paciente *m/f*

patriot (*pei*-tri-öt) *n* patriota *m/f*

patrol (pö-*troul*) *n* patrulla *f*; *v* patrullar; vigilar

pattern (*pæ*-tön) *n* modelo *m*; dibujo *m*; patrón *m*

pause (poos) *n* pausa *f*; *v* *hacer una pausa

pave (peiv) *v* pavimentar

pavement (*peiv*-mönt) *n* acera *f*; pavimento *m*

pavilion (pö-*vil*-yön) *n* pabellón *m*

paw (poo) *n* pata *f*

pawn (poon) *v* empeñar; *n* peón *m*

pawnbroker (*poon*-brou-kö) *n* prestamista *m*

pay (pei) *n* salario *m*, sueldo *m*

*pay (pei) *v* pagar; *rendir; **~ attention to** prestar atención a; **~ desk** caja *f*; **~ off** amortizar; **~ on account** pagar a plazos; **~ phone** teléfono público; **paying** rentable

payee (pei-*ii*) n favorecido m, -a f

payment (*pei*-mönt) n pago m

PC (pii-*ssii*)n PC m, ordenador m personal, computadora f personal; adj políticamente correcto

pea (pii)n guisante m

peace (piiss) n paz f

peaceful (*piiss*-föl) adj tranquilo

peach (piich) n melocotón m

peacock (*pii*-kok) n pavo m

peak (piik)n pico m; cumbre f; ~ **hours** horas punta; ~ **season** apogeo de la temporada

peanut (*pii*-nat)n cacahuete m; cacahuate mMe

pear (pê⁰) n pera f

pearl (pööl) n perla f

peasant (*pê*-sönt) n campesino m

pebble (*pê*-böl) n guijarro m

peculiar (pi-*kyuul*-yö) adj extraño; especial, peculiar

peculiarity (pi-kyuu-li-æ-rö-ti) n particularidad f

pedal (*pê*-döl) n pedal m

pedestrian (pi-*dê*-sstri-ön) n peatón m; **no pedestrians** prohibido para los peatones; ~ **crossing** cruce para peatones

peel (piil) v pelar; n piel f

peep (piip) v espiar

peg (pêgh) n percha f

pelican (*pê*-li-kön)n pelícano m

pelvis (*pêl*-viss) n pelvis m

pen (pên) n pluma f

penalty (*pê*-nöl-ti) n pena f; castigo m; ~ **kick** penalty m

pencil (*pên*-ssöl) n lápiz m; ~ **sharpener** sacapuntas m

pendant (*pên*-dönt) n pendiente m

penetrate (*pê*-ni-treit) v penetrar

penguin (*pêng*-ghᵘin) n pingüino m

penicillin (pê-ni-*ssi*-lin) n penicilina f

peninsula (pö-*nin*-ssyu-lö) n península f

penknife (*pên*-naif) n (pl -knives) cortaplumas m

penny (*pê*-ni) n penique m

pension¹ (*pang*-ssi-ong) n pensión f

pension² (*pên*-ʃön)n pensión f

people (*pii*-pöl) pl gente f; n pueblo m

pepper (*pê*-pö) n pimienta f

peppermint (*pê*-pö-mint) n menta f

per (pö) prep por; **per** ~ al año, por año

perceive (pö-*ssiiv*) v percibir

percent (pö-*ssênt*) n por ciento

percentage (pö-*ssên*-tidʒ) n porcentaje m

perceptible (pö-*ssêp*-ti-böl) adj perceptible

perception (pö-*ssêp*-ʃön) n percepción f

perch (pööch) (pl ~) perca f

percolator (*pöö*-kö-lei-tö) n cafetera filtradora

perfect (*pöö*-fikt) adj perfecto

perfection (pö-*fêk*-ʃön) n perfección f

perform (pö-*foom*) v ejecutar, desempeñar

performance (pö-*foo*-mönss) n representación f

perfume (*pöö*-fyuum) n perfume m

perhaps (pö-*hæpss*) adv quizás

peril (*pê*-ril) n peligro m; riesgo m

perilous (*pê*-ri-löss) adj peligroso

period (*pi⁰*-ri-öd) n época f, período m; punto m

periodical (pi⁰-ri-*o*-di-köl) n periódico m; adj periódico

perish (*pê*-riʃ) v *perecer

perishable (*pê*-ri-ʃö-böl) adj perecedero

perjury (*pöö*-dʒö-ri) n perjurio m

perm (pööm) n permanente f; v hacer la permanente; **she had her hair permed** se hizo la permanente

permanent (*pöö*-mö-nönt) adj duradero, permanente; estable, fijo;

~ **press** planchado permanente; ~ **wave** ondulación permanente

permission (pö-*mi*-ʃön) *n* permiso *m*, autorización *f*; licencia *f*

permit[1] (pö-*mit*) *v* permitir

permit[2] (*pöö*-mit) *n* permiso *m*

peroxide (pö-*rok*-ssaid) *n* peróxido *m*

perpendicular (pöö-pön-*di*-kyu-lö) *adj* perpendicular

Persian (*pöö*-ʃön) *adj* persa

person (*pöö*-ssön) *n* persona *f*; **per ~** por persona

personal (*pöö*-ssö-nöl) *adj* personal

personality (pöö-ssö-*næ*-lö-ti) *n* personalidad *f*

personnel (pöö-ssö-*nêl*) *n* personal *m*

perspective (pö-*sspêk*-tiv) *n* perspectiva *f*

perspiration (pöö-sspö-*rei*-ʃön) *n* transpiración *f*, sudor *m*

perspire (pö-*sspai*[o]) *v* transpirar, sudar

persuade (pö-ss[u]*eid*) *v* persuadir; convencer

persuasion (pö-ss[u]*ei*-ʒön) *n* convicción *f*

pessimism (*pê*-ssi-mi-söm) *n* pesimismo *m*

pessimist (*pê*-ssi-misst) *n* pesimista *m/f*

pessimistic (pê-ssi-*mi*-sstik) *adj* pesimista

pet (pêt) *n* animal doméstico; cariño *m*; favorito

petal (*pê*-töl) *n* pétalo *m*

petition (pi-*ti*-ʃön) *n* petición *f*

petrol (*pê*-tröl) *n* gasolina *f*; **unleaded ~** gasolina sin plomo; ~ **pump** bomba de gasolina; ~ **station** puesto de gasolina; ~ **tank** depósito de gasolina

petroleum (pi-*trou*-li-öm) *n* petróleo *m*

petty (*pê*-ti) *adj* pequeño, fútil, insignificante; ~ **cash** calderilla *f*

pewit (*pii*-[u]it) *n* avefría *f*

pewter (*pyuu*-tö) *n* estaño *m*

phantom (*fæn*-töm) *n* fantasma *m*

pharmacy (*faa*-mö-ssi) *n* farmacia *f*; droguería *f*

pheasant (*fê*-sönt) *n* faisán *m*

Philippine (*fi*-li-pain) *adj* filipino

Philippines (*fi*-li-piins) *pl* Filipinas *fpl*

philosopher (fi-*lo*-ssö-fö) *n* filósofo *m*, -a *f*

philosophy (fi-*lo*-ssö-fi) *n* filosofía *f*

phone (foun) *n* teléfono *m*; *v* llamar por teléfono, telefonear; ~ **card** tarjeta *f* telefónica

phonetic (fö-*nê*-tik) *adj* fonético

photo (*fou*-tou) *n* (pl ~s) foto *f*

photocopy (*fou*-tö-ko-pi) *n* fotocopia *f*; *v* fotocopiar

photograph (*fou*-tö-ghraaf) *n* fotografía *f*; *v* fotografiar

photographer (fö-*to*-ghrö-fö) *n* fotógrafo *m*

photography (fö-*to*-ghrö-fi) *n* fotografía *f*

phrase (freis) *n* frase *f*; ~ **book** manual de conversación

physical (*fi*-si-köl) *adj* físico

physician (fi-*si*-ʃön) *n* médico *m*, -a *f*

physicist (*fi*-si-ssisst) *n* físico *m*

physics (*fi*-sikss) *n* física *f*

physiology (fi-si-*o*-lö-dʒi) *n* fisiología *f*

pianist (*pii*-ö-nisst) *n* pianista *m*

piano (pi-*æ*-nou) *n* piano *m*; **grand ~** piano de cola

pie (pai) *n* pastel *m*

pick (pik) *v* recoger; escoger; *n* elección *f*; ~ **up** recoger; *ir a buscar; **pick-up van** camioneta de reparto

pickles (*pi*-köls) *pl* encurtidos *mpl*

picnic (*pik*-nik) *n* picnic *m*; merienda en el campo; *v* *hacer un día de campo

picture (*pik*-chö) *n* cuadro *m*;

ilustración f, grabado m; imagen f; ~ **postcard** tarjeta postal ilustrada

picturesque (pik-chö-*rêssk*) *adj* pintoresco

piece (piiss) *n* fragmento m, pedazo m

pier (pi⁰) *n* muelle m

pierce (pi⁰ss) *v* punzar

pig (pigh) *n* cerdo m

pigeon (*pi*-dʒön) *n* paloma f

pig-headed (pigh-*hê*-did) *adj* testarudo

piglet (*pigh*-löt) *n* cochinillo m

pigskin (*pigh*-sskin) *n* piel de cerdo

pike (paik)(pl ~) lucio m

pile (pail) *n* montón m; *v* amontonar; **piles** *pl* hemorroides *fpl*

pilgrim (*pil*-ghrim) *n* peregrino m

pilgrimage (*pil*-ghri-midʒ) *n* peregrinación f

pill (pil) *n* píldora f

pillar (*pi*-lö) *n* columna f, pilar m

pillarbox (*pi*-lö-bokss) *n* buzón m

pillow (*pi*-lou) *n* almohadón m, almohada f

pillowcase (*pi*-lou-keiss) *n* funda de almohada

pilot (*pai*-löt) *n* piloto m; práctico m

pimple (*pim*-pöl) *n* grano m

pin (pin) *n* alfiler m; *v* sujetar; prender; enclavijar; **bobby ~** *Am* horquilla f

pincers (*pin*-ssös) *pl* tenazas *fpl*

pinch (pinch) *v* pellizcar; *n* pellizco m; aprieto m

pineapple (*pai*-næ-pöl) *n* piña f

ping-pong (*ping*-pong) *n* tenis de mesa

pink (pingk) *adj* rosado

pint (paint) *n* pinta f, (medida equivalente a 0,473 litros en Estados Unidos o a 0,568 litros en Gran Bretaña)

pioneer (pai-ö-ni⁰) *n* pionero m

pious (*pai*-öss) *adj* pío

pip (pip) *n* pepita f

pipe (paip) *n* pipa f; conducto m; ~ **cleaner** limpiapipas m; ~ **tobacco** tabaco de pipa

pipeline (*paip*-lain) *n* oleoducto m; gasoducto m; **in the ~** en trámite

pirate (*pai⁰*-röt) *n* pirata m

pistol (*pi*-sstöl) *n* pistola f

piston (*pi*-sstön) *n* pistón m; ~ **ring** aro de émbolo

pit (pit) *n* hoyo m; mina f

pitcher (*pi*-chö) *n* cántaro m

pity (*pi*-ti) *n* piedad f; *v* *tener piedad de, compadecerse de; **what a pity!** ¡qué lástima!

placard (*plæ*-kaad) *n* cartel m

place (pleiss) *n* lugar m; *v* *poner, colocar; ~ **of birth** lugar de nacimiento; *take ~ *tener lugar

plague (pleigh) *n* plaga f

plaice (pleiss) (pl ~) platija f

plain (plein) *adj* claro; corriente, sencillo; *n* llano m

plan (plæn) *n* plan m; plano m; *v* planear

plane (plein) *adj* plano; *n* avión m; ~ **crash** accidente aéreo

planet (*plæ*-nit) *n* planeta m

planetarium (plæ-ni-*tê⁰*-ri-öm) *n* planetario m

plank (plængk) *n* tablón m

plant (plaant) *n* planta f; instalación f; *v* plantar

plantation (plæn-*tei*-ʃön) *n* plantación f

plaster (*plaa*-sstö) *n* estuco m, yeso m; esparadrapo m

plastic (*plæ*-sstik) *adj* de plástico; *n* plástico m; ~ **bag** bolsa f de plástico

plate (pleit) *n* plato m; chapa f

plateau (*plæ*-tou) *n* (pl ~x, ~s) meseta f

platform (*plæt*-foom) *n* andén m; ~ **ticket** billete de andén

platinum (*plæ*-ti-nöm) *n* platino m

play (plei) *v* *jugar; tocar; *n* juego *m*; obra de teatro; **one-act** ~ pieza en un acto; ~ **truant** *hacer novillos

player (plei^{ö}) *n* jugador *m*

playground (*plei*-ghraund) *n* patio de recreo

playing card (*plei*-ing-kaad) *n* naipe *m*

playwright (*plei*-rait) *n* dramaturgo *m*

plea (plii) *n* argumento *m*; súplica *f*; defensa *f*

plead (pliid) *v* suplicar; defender

pleasant (plê-sönt) *adj* agradable, simpático

please (pliis) por favor; *v* *placer; **pleased** contento; **pleasing** agradable

pleasure (plê-ʒö) *n* placer *m*, diversión *f*

plentiful (plên-ti-föl) *adj* abundante

plenty (plên-ti) *n* abundancia *f*; ~ **of** muchos; bastante

pliers (plai^{ö}s) *pl* alicates *mpl*

plimsolls (*plim*-ssöls) *pl* zapatos de gimnasia

plot (plot) *n* complot *m*; trama *f*; parcela *f*

plough (plau) *n* arado *m*; *v* arar

plucky (*pla*-ki) *adj* valiente; animoso

plug (plagh) *n* enchufe *m*; ~ **in** enchufar

plum (plam) *n* ciruela *f*

plumber (*pla*-mö) *n* fontanero *m*

plump (plamp) *adj* regordete

plural (plu^{ö}-röl) *n* plural *m*

plus (plass) *prep* más

pneumatic (nyuu-*mæ*-tik) *adj* neumático

pneumonia (nyuu-*mou*-ni-ö) *n* neumonía *f*

poach (pouch) *v* cazar en vedado

pocket (*po*-kit) *n* bolsillo *m*

pocketknife (*po*-kit-naif) *n* (pl -knives) navaja *f*

poem (*pou*-im) *n* poema *m*

poet (*pou*-it) *n* poeta *m*

poetry (*pou*-i-tri) *n* poesía *f*

point (point) *n* punto *m*; punta *f*; *v* señalar con el dedo; ~ **of view** punto de vista; ~ **out** apuntar

pointed (*poin*-tid) *adj* puntiagudo

poison (*poi*-sön) *n* veneno *m*; *v* envenenar

poisonous (*poi*-sö-nöss) *adj* venenoso

Poland (*pou*-lönd) Polonia *f*

Pole (poul) *n* polaco *m*

pole (poul) *n* palo *m*; polo *m*; pértiga *f*

police (pö-*liiss*) *pl* policía *f*; ~ **station** comisaría *f*

policeman (pö-*liiss*-mön) *n* (pl -men) agente de policía, guardia *m*

policy (*po*-li-ssi) *n* política *f*; póliza *f*

polio (*pou*-li-ou) *n* polio *f*, poliomielitis *f*

Polish (*pou*-liʃ) *adj* polaco

polish (*po*-liʃ) *v* pulir

polite (pö-*lait*) *adj* cortés

political (pö-*li*-ti-köl) *adj* político

politician (po-li-*ti*-ʃön) *n* político *m*

politics (*po*-li-tikss) *n* política *f*

poll (poul) *n* encuesta *f*, sondeo *m*; *v* sondear; **the polls** las elecciones; **go to the polls** acudir a las urnas

pollute (pö-*luut*) *v* contaminar

pollution (pö-*luu*-ʃön) *n* contaminación *f*, polución *f*

pond (pond) *n* estanque *m*

pony (*pou*-ni) *n* caballito *m*; jaca *f*; poni *m*

pool[1] (puul) *n* piscina *f*, *L.Am.* pileta *f*, *Me* alberca *f*; charco *m*

pool[2] (puul) *n* fondo común; *v* juntar

poor (pu^{ö}) *adj* pobre; mediocre

pope (poup) *n* Papa *m*

pop music (pop *myuu*-sik) música pop

poppy (*po*-pi) *n* amapola *f*;

adormidera f

popular (*po*-pyu-lö) *adj* popular

population (po-pyu-*lei*-ʃön) *n* población f

populous (*po*-pyu-löss) *adj* populoso

porcelain (*poo*-ssö-lin) *n* porcelana f

porcupine (*poo*-kyu-pain) *n* puerco espín

pork (pook) *n* carne de cerdo

port (poot) *n* puerto m; babor m

portable (*poo*-tö-böl) *adj* portátil

porter (*poo*-tö) *n* mozo m; portero m

porthole (*poot*-houl) *n* portilla f

portion (*poo*-ʃön) *n* porción f

portrait (*poo*-trit) *n* retrato m

Portugal (*poo*-tyu-ghöl) Portugal m

Portuguese (poo-tyu-*ghiis*) *adj* portugués

posh (poʃ) *adj colloquial* elegante; pijo

position (pö-*si*-ʃön) *n* posición f; actitud f; puesto m

positive (*po*-sö-tiv) *adj* positivo; *n* positiva f

possess (pö-*sêss*) *v* *poseer; **possessed** *adj* poseído

possession (pö-*sê*-ʃön) *n* posesión f; **possessions** bienes *mpl*

possibility (po-ssö-*bi*-lö-ti) *n* posibilidad f

possible (*po*-ssö-böl) *adj* posible; eventual

post (pousst) *n* poste m; puesto m; correo m; *v* echar al correo; ~ **office** (oficina de) correos

postage (*pou*-sstidʒ) *n* franqueo m; ~ **paid** franco; ~ **stamp** sello de correos; timbre *mMe*

postcard (*pousst*-kaad) *n* tarjeta postal

poster (*pou*-sstö) *n* cartel m

poste restante (pousst rê-*sstaⁿgt*) lista de correos

postman (*pousst*-mön) *n* (pl -men)

cartero m

post-paid (pousst-*peid*) *adj* franco

postpone (pö-*sspoun*) *v* aplazar

pot (pot) *n* olla f; maceta f

potato (pö-*tei*-tou) *n* (pl ~es) patata f; papa fMe

pottery (*po*-tö-ri) *n* cerámica f; loza f

pouch (pauch) *n* bolsa f; morral m

poulterer (*poul*-tö-rö) *n* pollero m

poultry (*poul*-tri) *n* aves de corral

pound (paund) *n* libra f

pour (poo) *v* *verter

poverty (*po*-vö-ti) *n* pobreza f

powder (*pau*-dö) *n* polvo m; *v* emplvarse; ~ **compact** polvera f; **talc** ~ talco m

power (pauᵒ) *n* fuerza f, energía f; poder m; potencia f; ~ **station** central eléctrica

powered by impulsado por

powerful (*pauᵒ*-föl) *adj* poderoso; fuerte

powerless (*pauᵒ*-löss) *adj* impotente

practical (*præk*-ti-köl) *adj* práctico

practically (*præk*-ti-kli) *adv* prácticamente

practice (*præk*-tiss) *n* práctica f

practise (*præk*-tiss) *v* practicar; ensayarse

praise (preis) *v* alabar; *n* elogio m

pram (præm) *n* cochecillo de niño

prawn (proon) *n* gamba f

pray (prei) *v* orar

prayer (prêᵒ) *n* oración f

preach (priich) *v* predicar

precarious (pri-*kêᵒ*-ri-öss) *adj* precario

precaution (pri-*koo*-ʃön) *n* precaución f

precede (pri-*ssiid*) *v* preceder

preceding (pri-*ssii*-ding) *adj* precedente

precious (*prê*-ʃöss) *adj* precioso; querido

precipice (*prê*-ssi-piss) *n* precipicio *m*

precipitation (pri-ssi-pi-*tei*-ʃön) *n* precipitación *f*

precise (pri-*ssaiss*) *adj* preciso, exacto; meticuloso

predecessor (*prii*-di-ssê-ssö) *n* predecesor *m*

predict (pri-*dikt*) *v* *predecir

prefer (pri-*föö*) *v* *preferir

preferable (*prê*-fö-rö-böl) *adj* preferible

preference (*prê*-fö-rönss) *n* preferencia *f*

prefix (*prii*-fikss) *n* prefijo *m*

pregnant (*prêgh*-nönt) *adj* encinta, embarazada

prejudice (*prê*-dʒö-diss) *n* prejuicio *m*

preliminary (pri-*li*-mi-nö-ri) *adj* preliminar

premature (*prê*-mö-chuᵒ) *adj* prematuro

premier (*prêm*-iᵒ) *n* jefe de gobierno

premises (*prê*-mi-ssis) *pl* finca *f*

premium (*prii*-mi-öm) *n* prima *f*

prepaid (prii-*peid*) *adj* pagado por adelantado

preparation (prê-pö-*rei*-ʃön) *n* preparación *f*

prepare (pri-*pêᵒ*) *v* preparar

preposition (prê-pö-*si*-ʃön) *n* preposición *f*

prescribe (pri-*sskraib*) *v* prescribir

prescription (pri-*sskrip*-ʃön) *n* prescripción *f*

presence (*prê*-sönss) *n* presencia *f*

present[1] (*prê*-sönt) *n* regalo *m*, presente *m*; *adj* actual; presente

present[2] (pri-*sênt*) *v* presentar

presently (*prê*-sönt-li) *adv* en seguida, dentro de poco

preservation (prê-sö-*vei*-ʃön) *n* conservación *f*

preserve (pri-*sööv*) *v* preservar; conservar

president (*prê*-si-dönt) *n* presidente *m*

press (prêss) *n* prensa *f*; *v* empujar, *apretar; planchar; ~ **agency** agencia de prensa; ~ **conference** conferencia de prensa

pressing (*prê*-ssing) *adj* urgente

pressure (*prê*-ʃö) *n* presión *f*; tensión *f*; **atmospheric** ~ presión atmosférica

prestige (prê-*sstiiʒ*) *n* prestigio *m*

presumable (pri-*syuu*-mö-böl) *adj* presumible

presume (pri-*syuum*) *v* suponer

presumptuous (pri-*samp*-ʃöss) *adj* presuntuoso; presumido

pretence (pri-*tênss*) *n* pretexto *m*

pretend (pri-*tênd*) *v* fingir

pretext (*prii*-têksst) *n* pretexto *m*

pretty (*pri*-ti) *adj* bonito; *adv* bastante

prevent (pri-*vênt*) *v* *impedir; *prevenir

preventive (pri-*vên*-tiv) *adj* preventivo

preview (*prii*-vyuu) *n* preestreno *m*; *v* hacer la presentación previa de

previous (*prii*-vi-öss) *adj* precedente, anterior, previo

pre-war (prii-ᵘ*oo*) *adj* de la preguerra

price (praiss) *n* precio *m*; *v* fijar el precio

priceless (*praiss*-löss) *adj* inapreciable

price list (*praiss*-lisst) *n* lista de precios

prick (prik) *v* pinchar

pride (praid) *n* orgullo *m*

priest (priisst) *n* cura *m*

primary (*prai*-mö-ri) *adj* primario; primero, primordial; elemental

prince (prinss) *n* príncipe *m*

princess (prin-*ssêss*) *n* princesa *f*

principal (*prin*-ssö-pöl) *adj* principal; *n* principal *m*/*f*; director *m*, -a *f*

principle (*prin*-ssö-pöl) *n* principio *m*

print (print) v *imprimir; n positiva f; grabado m; **printed matter** impreso m

printer (prin-tö) n impresor m; impresora f; imprenta f

printout (print-aut) n copia f impresa

prior (prai°) adj anterior

priority (prai-o-rö-ti) n prioridad f

prison (pri-sön) n prisión f

prisoner (pri-sö-nö) n preso m, prisionero m; ~ **of war** prisionero de guerra

privacy (prai-vö-ssi) n intimidad f, vida privada

private (prai-vit) adj particular, privado; personal

privilege (pri-vi-lidʒ) n privilegio m

prize (prais) n premio m; recompensa f

probable (pro-bö-böl) adj probable

probably (pro-bö-bli) adv probablemente

problem (pro-blöm) n problema m

procedure (prö-ssii-dʒö) n procedimiento m

proceed (prö-ssiid) v *proseguir; proceder

process (prou-ssêss) n procedimiento m, proceso m

procession (prö-ssê-ʃön) n procesión f, comitiva f

proclaim (prö-kleim) v proclamar

produce¹ (prö-dyuuss) v *producir

produce² (prod-yuuss) n producto m

producer (prö-dyuu-ssö) n productor m

product (pro-dakt) n producto m

production (prö-dak-ʃön) n producción f

profession (prö-fê-ʃön) n profesión f

professional (prö-fê-ʃö-nöl) adj profesional

professor (prö-fê-ssö) n profesor m, -a f

profit (pro-fit) n beneficio m, ganancia

f; ventaja f; v aprovechar

profitable (pro-fi-tö-böl) adj provechoso

profound (prö-faund) adj profundo

program(me) (prou-ghræm) n programa m

progress¹ (prou-ghrêss) n progreso m

progress² (prö-ghrêss) v progresar

progressive (prö-ghrê-ssiv) adj progresista; progresivo

prohibit (prö-hi-bit) v prohibir

prohibition (prou-i-bi-ʃön) n prohibición f

prohibitive (prö-hi-bi-tiv) adj exorbitante

project (pro-dʒêkt) n plan m, proyecto m

promenade (pro-mö-naad) n paseo m

promise (pro-miss) n promesa f; v prometer

promote (prö-mout) v *promover

promotion (prö-mou-ʃön) n promoción f

prompt (prompt) adj inmediato, pronto

pronoun (prou-naun) n pronombre m

pronounce (prö-naunss) v pronunciar

pronunciation (prö-nan-ssi-ei-ʃön) n pronunciación f

proof (pruuf) n prueba f

propaganda (pro-pö-ghæn-dö) n propaganda f

propel (prö-pêl) v propulsar

propeller (prö-pê-lö) n hélice f

proper (pro-pö) adj justo; debido, conveniente, apropiado

property (pro-pö-ti) n propiedad f; bienes mpl; cualidad f

prophet (pro-fit) n profeta m

proportion (prö-poo-ʃön) n proporción f

proportional (prö-poo-ʃö-nöl) adj proporcional

proposal (prö-pou-söl) n propuesta f

propose (prö-*pous*) v *proponer

proposition (pro-pö-*si*-ʃön) n
propuesta f

proprietor (prö-*prai*-ö-tö) n
propietario m, -a f

prospect (*pro*-sspêkt) n perspectiva f

prospectus (prö-*sspêk*-töss) n
prospecto m

prosperity (pro-*sspê*-rö-ti) n
prosperidad f

prosperous (*pro*-sspö-röss) adj
próspero

prostitute (*pro*-ssti-tyuut) n prostituta
f

protect (prö-*têkt*) v proteger

protection (prö-*têk*-ʃön) n protección
f

protein (*prou*-tiin) n proteína f

protest[1] (*prou*-têsst) n protesta f

protest[2] (prö-*têsst*) v protestar

Protestant (*pro*-ti-sstönt) adj
protestante

proud (praud) adj orgulloso

prove (pruuv) v *demostrar,
*comprobar; resultar

proverb (*pro*-vööb) n proverbio m

provide (prö-*vaid*) v *proveer;
provided that con tal que

province (*pro*-vinss) n provincia f

provincial (prö-*vin*-ʃöl) adj provincial

provisional (prö-*vi*-ʒö-nöl) adj
provisional

provisions (prö-*vi*-ʒöns) pl
provisiones fpl

prune (pruun) n ciruela pasa

psychiatrist (ssai-*kai*-ö-trisst) n
psiquiatra m

psychic (*ssai*-kik) adj psíquico

psychoanalyst (ssai-kou-*æ*-nö-lisst) n
psicoanalista m

psychological (ssai-ko-*lo*-dʒi-köl) adj
psicológico

psychologist (ssai-*ko*-lö-dʒisst) n
psicólogo m

psychology (ssai-*ko*-lö-dʒi) n
psicología f

pub (pab) n bar m; taberna f

public (*pa*-blik) adj público; general; n
público m; ~ **garden** jardín público; ~
house taberna f

publication (pa-bli-*kei*-ʃön) n
publicación f

publicity (pa-*bli*-ssö-ti) n publicidad f

publish (*pa*-bliʃ) v publicar

publisher (*pa*-bli-ʃö) n editor m, -a f

puddle (*pa*-döl) n charco m

pull (pul) v tirar; ~ **out** arrancar; ~ **up**
pararse

pulley (*pu*-li) n (pl ~s) polea f

Pullman (*pul*-mön) n coche Pullman

pullover (*pu*-lou-vö) n jersey m;
pulóver m

pulpit (*pul*-pit) n púlpito m

pulse (palss) n pulso m

pump (pamp) n bomba f; v bombear

pun (pan) n juego m de palabras

punch (panch) v *dar puñetazos; n
puñetazo m

punctual (*pangk*-chu-öl) adj puntual

puncture (*pangk*-chö) n pinchazo m

punctured (*pangk*-chöd) adj
pinchado

punish (*pa*-niʃ) v castigar

punishment (*pa*-niʃ-mönt) n castigo
m

pupil[1] (*pyuu*-pöl) n alumno m, -a f

pupil[2] (*pyuu*-pöl) n pupila f

puppet show (*pa*-pit-ʃou) n teatro de
títeres

purchase (*pöö*-chöss) v comprar; n
compra f; ~ **price** precio de compra; ~
tax impuesto sobre la venta

purchaser (*pöö*-chö-ssö) n
comprador m, -a f

pure (pyu⁰) adj casto, puro

purple (*pöö*-pöl) adj purpúreo,
morado

purpose (*pöö*-pöss) n propósito m, fin

m, intención *f*; **on ~** intencionado
purse (pööss) *n* bolsa *f*, monedero *m*
pursue (pö-*ssyuu*) *v* *perseguir
pus (pass) *n* pus *f*
push (puʃ) *n* empujón *m*; *v* empujar
push button (puʃ-ba-tön) *n* pulsador *m*
***put** (put) *v* colocar, *poner; meter;

plantear; **~ away** guardar; **~ off** aplazar; **~ on** *ponerse; **~ out** apagar
puzzle (*pa*-söl) *n* rompecabezas *m*; enigma *m*; *v* confundir; **jigsaw ~** rompecabezas *m*
puzzling (*pas*-ling) *adj* incomprensible; misterioso
pyjamas (pö-dʒaa-mös) *pl* pijama *m*

Q

quadrangle (kᵘod-*ræng*-göl) *n* cuadrángulo *m*; patio *m*
quail (kᵘeil) *n* (pl ~, ~s) codorniz *f*
quaint (kᵘeint) *adj* curioso; anticuado
qualification (kᵘo-li-fi-*kei*-ʃön) *n* aptitud *f*; reserva *f*, restricción *f*
qualified (*kᵘo*-li-faid) *adj* calificado; competente
qualify (*kᵘo*-li-fai) *v* *ser capaz de, *ser apto para
quality (*kᵘo*-lö-ti) *n* calidad *f*; característica *f*
quantity (*kᵘon*-tö-ti) *n* cantidad *f*; número *m*
quarantine (*kᵘo*-rön-tiin) *n* cuarentena *f*
quarrel (*kᵘo*-röl) *v* disputar, *reñir; *n* disputa *f*
quarry (*kᵘo*-ri) *n* cantera *f*; presa *f*
quarter (*kᵘoo*-tö) *n* cuarto *m*; trimestre *m*; barrio *m*; **~ of an hour** cuarto de hora
quarterly (*kᵘoo*-tö-li) *adj* trimestral
quay (kii) *n* muelle *m*

queen (kᵘiin) *n* reina *f*
queer (kᵘiö̈) *adj* singular, extraño
query (*kᵘiö̈*-ri) *n* pregunta *f*; *v* indagar; *poner en duda
question (*kᵘêss*-chön) *n* pregunta *f*; cuestión *f*, problema *m*; *v* interrogar; *poner en duda; **~ mark** signo de interrogación
queue (kyuu) *n* cola *f*; *v* *hacer cola
quick (kᵘik) *adj* rápido; ágil
quick-tempered (kᵘik-*têm*-pöd) *adj* irascible; irritable
quiet (*kᵘai*-öt) *adj* quieto, tranquilo; *n* silencio *m*, paz *f*
quilt (kᵘilt) *n* edredón *m*
quit (kᵘit) *v* cesar; dejar; abandonar
quite (kᵘait) *adv* enteramente, completamente; bastante; muy
quiz (kᵘis) *n* (pl ~zes) concurso *m*
quota (*kᵘou*-tö) *n* cuota *f*
quotation (kᵘou-*tei*-ʃön) *n* cita *f*; **~ marks** comillas *fpl*
quote (kᵘout) *v* citar

R

rabbit (*ræ*-bit) *n* conejo *m*

rabies (*rei*-bis) *n* rabia *f*

race (reiss) *n* carrera *f*; raza *f*

racecourse (*reiss*-kooss) *n* pista para carreras, hipódromo *m*

racehorse (*reiss*-hooss) *n* caballo de carrera

racetrack (*reiss*-træk) *n* pista para carreras

racial (*rei*-ʃöl) *adj* racial

racket (*ræ*-kit) *n* raqueta *f*; alboroto *m*

radiator (*rei*-di-ei-tö) *n* radiador *m*

radical (*ræ*-di-köl) *adj* radical

radio (*rei*-di-ou) *n* radio *f*

radish (*ræ*-diʃ) *n* rábano *m*

radius (*rei*-di-öss) *n* (pl radii) radio *m*

raft (raaft) *n* balsa *f*

rag (rægh) *n* trapo *m*

rage (reidʒ) *n* furor *m*, rabia *f*; *v* rabiar

raid (reid) *n* irrupción *f*

rail (reil) *n* barandilla *f*, barrera *f*

railing (*rei*-ling) *n* barandilla *f*

railroad (*reil*-roud) *nAm* vía del tren, ferrocarril *m*

railway (*reil*-ᵘei) *n* ferrocarril *m*

rain (rein) *n* lluvia *f*; *v* *llover

rainbow (*rein*-bou) *n* arco iris

raincoat (*rein*-kout) *n* impermeable *m*

rainproof (*rein*-pruuf) *adj* impermeable

rainy (*rei*-ni) *adj* lluvioso

raise (reis) *v* alzar; aumentar; educar, cultivar, criar; recaudar; *nAm* aumento de sueldo

raisin (*rei*-sön) *n* pasa *f*

rake (reik) *n* rastrillo *m*

rally (*ræ*-li) *n* reunión *f*

ramp (ræmp) *n* rampa *f*

ramshackle (*ræm*-ʃæ-köl) *adj* destartalado

rancid (*ræn*-ssid) *adj* rancio

rang (ræng) *v* (p ring)

range (reindʒ) *n* extensión *f*; alcance *m*; **mountain ~** sierra cordillera; **~ finder** telémetro *m*

rank (rængk) *n* rango *m*; fila *f*

ransom (*ræn*-ssöm) *n* rescate *m*

rape (reip) *v* violar

rapid (*ræ*-pid) *adj* rápido

rapids (*ræ*-pids) *pl* rápidos de río

rare (rê⁶) *adj* raro

rarely (*rê⁶*-li) *adv* raras veces

rascal (*raa*-ssköl) *n* pícaro *m*, pillo *m*

rash (ræʃ) *n* erupción *f*; *adj* precipitado, imprudente

raspberry (*raas*-bö-ri) *n* frambuesa *f*

rat (ræt) *n* rata *f*

rate (reit) *n* precio *m*, tarifa *f*; velocidad *f*; **at any ~** de todos modos, en todo caso; **~ of exchange** cambio *m*

rather (*raa*-ðö) *adv* bastante; más bien, algo

ration (*ræ*-ʃön) *n* ración *f*

rattan (ræ-*tæn*) *n* rota *f*

raven (*rei*-vön) *n* cuervo *m*

raw (roo) *adj* crudo; **~ material** materia prima

ray (rei) *n* rayo *m*

rayon (*rei*-on) *n* rayón *m*

razor (*rei*-sö) *n* máquina de afeitar; **~ blade** hoja de afeitar

reach (riich) *v* alcanzar; *n* alcance *m*

react (ri-*ækt*) *v* reaccionar

reaction (ri-*æk*-ʃön) *n* reacción *f*

*read (riid) *v* *leer

reader (*rii*-dö) *n* lector *m*, -a *f*

reading (*rii*-ding) *n* lectura *f*; **~ lamp** lámpara para lectura; **~ room** sala de lectura

ready (*rê*-di) *adj* preparado, listo

ready-made (rê-di-*meid*) *adj* confeccionado; hecho

real (ri⁶l) *adj* verdadero

reality (ri-*æ*-lö-ti) *n* realidad *f*

realizable (*ri*⁰-lai-sö-böl) *adj* realizable

realize (*ri*⁰-lais) *v* *reconocer; realizar

really (*ri*⁰-li) *adv* verdaderamente, en realidad; de veras

rear (ri⁰) *n* parte posterior; *v* criar

rear light (ri⁰-*lait*) *n* luz trasera

reason (rii-sön) *n* causa *f*, razón *f*; sentido *m*; *v* razonar

reasonable (rii-sö-nö-böl) *adj* razonable

reassure (rii-ö-*ʃu*⁰) *v* tranquilizar

rebate (rii-beit) *n* reducción *f*, rebaja *f*

rebellion (ri-*bél*-yön) *n* sublevación *f*, rebelión *f*

recall (ri-*kool*) *v* *acordarse; llamar; revocar

receipt (ri-*ssiit*) *n* recibo *m*

receive (ri-*ssiiv*) *v* recibir

receiver (ri-*ssii*-vö) *n* receptor *m*

recent (*rii*-ssönt) *adj* reciente

recently (*rii*-ssönt-li) *adv* recientemente

reception (ri-*ssép*-ʃön) *n* recepción *f*; acogida *f*; **~ desk** recepción

receptionist (ri-*ssép*-ʃö-nisst) *n* recepcionista *m/f*

recession (ri-*ssé*-ʃön) *n* retroceso *m*; recesión *f*

recipe (*ré*-ssi-pi) *n* receta *f*

recital (ri-*ssai*-töl) *n* recital *m*

reckon (*ré*-kön) *v* calcular; considerar; *creer

recognition (ré-kögh-*ni*-ʃön) *n* reconocimiento *m*

recognize (*ré*-kögh-nais) *v* *reconocer

recollect (ré-kö-*lékt*) *v* *acordarse

recommence (rii-kö-*ménss*) *v* *recomenzar

recommend (ré-kö-*ménd*) *v* *recomendar; aconsejar

recommendation (ré-kö-mên-*dei*-ʃön) *n* recomendación *f*

reconciliation (rê-kön-ssi-li-*ei*-ʃön) *n* reconciliación *f*

record¹ (*rê*-kood) *n* disco *m*; récord *m*; registro *m*; partida *f*; **~ player** tocadiscos *m*

record² (ri-*kood*) *v* registrar; grabar

recorder (ri-*koo*-dö) *n* registrador *m*; flauta *f* dulce

recording (ri-*koo*-ding) *n* grabación *f*

recover (ri-*ka*-vö) *v* recuperar; *restablecerse, curarse

recovery (ri-*ka*-vö-ri) *n* curación *f*, restablecimiento *m*

recreation (rê-kri-*ei*-ʃön) *n* recreación *f*, recreo *m*; **~ center** *Am*, **~ centre** centro de recreo; **~ ground** terreno de recreo público

recruit (ri-*kruut*) *n* recluta *m/f*

rectangle (*rêk*-tæng-ghöl) *n* rectángulo *m*

rectangular (rêk-*tæng*-ghyu-lö) *adj* rectangular

rector (*rêk*-tö) *n* pastor *m*, rector *m*

rectory (*rêk*-tö-ri) *n* rectoría *f*

rectum (*rêk*-töm) *n* intestino recto

recyclable (ri-*ssai*-klö-böl) *adj* reciclable

recycle (ri-*ssai*-köl) *v* reciclar

red (rêd) *adj* rojo

redeem (ri-*diim*) *v* redimir

reduce (ri-*dyuuss*) *v* *reducir, *disminuir, rebajar

reduction (ri-*dak*-ʃön) *n* rebaja *f*, reducción *f*

redundant (ri-*dan*-dönt) *adj* superfluo

reed (riid) *n* junquillo *m*

reef (riif) *n* arrecife *m*

refer (ri-*föö*) *v*: **~ to** remitir a

reference (*réf*-rönss) *n* referencia *f*; relación *f*; **with ~ to** con respecto a

referee (rê-fö-*rii*) árbitro *m*, -a *f*; persona que pueda dar referencias

refill (*rii*-fil) *n* repuesto *m*; recambio *m*

refinery (ri-*fai*-nö-ri) *n* refinería *f*

reflect (ri-*flĕkt*) v reflejar

reflection (ri-*flĕk*-ʃön) n reflejo m; imagen reflejada

refresh (ri-*frĕʃ*) v refrescar

refreshment (ri-*frĕʃ*-mönt) n refresco m

refrigerator (ri-*fri*-dʒö-rei-tö) n refrigerador m

refugee (rê-fyuu-ʒii) n refugiado m, -a f

refund[1] (ri-*fand*) v reintegrar

refund[2] (*rii*-fand) n reintegro m

refusal (ri-*fyuu*-söl) n negativa f

refuse[1] (ri-*fyuus*) v rehusar

refuse[2] (*rê*-fyuuss) n desecho m

regard (ri-*ghaad*) v considerar; n respeto m; **with ~ to** en cuanto a

regarding (ri-*ghaa*-ding) prep relativo a, tocante a; respecto a

regatta (ri-*ghæ*-tö) n regata f

régime (rei-ʒiim) n régimen m

region (*rii*-dʒön) n región f; comarca f

regional (*rii*-dʒö-nöl) adj regional

register (*rê*-dʒi-sstö) v inscribirse; certificar; **registered letter** carta certificada

registration (rê-dʒi-*sstrei*-ʃön) n inscripción f; **~ form** formulario de matriculación; **~ number** matrícula f; **~ plate** placa f

regret (ri-*ghrêt*) v *sentir; n arrepentimiento m

regular (*rê*-ghyu-lö) adj regular; corriente, normal

regulate (*rê*-ghyu-leit) v regular

regulation (rê-ghyu-*lei*-ʃön) n reglamento m, regulación f; regla f

rehabilitation (rii-hö-bi-li-*tei*-ʃön) n rehabilitación f

rehearsal (ri-*höö*-ssöl) n ensayo m

rehearse (ri-*hööss*) v ensayar

reign (rein) n reinado m; v *gobernar

reimburse (rii-im-*bööss*) v reembolsar

reindeer (*rein*-diö) n (pl ~) reno m

reject (ri-*dʒêkt*) v rehusar, rechazar; *reprobar

relate (ri-*leit*) v *contar

related (ri-*lei*-tid) adj emparentado

relation (ri-*lei*-ʃön) n relación f; pariente m; **relationship** relación f

relative (*rê*-lö-tiv) n pariente m; adj relativo

relax (ri-*lækss*) v descansar

relaxation (ri-læk-*ssei*-ʃön) n relajación f

reliable (ri-*lai*-ö-böl) adj fiable, fidedigno

relic (*rê*-lik) n reliquia f

relief (ri-*liif*) n alivio m; ayuda f; relieve m

relieve (ri-*liiv*) v aliviar

religion (ri-*li*-dʒön) n religión f

religious (ri-*li*-dʒöss) adj religioso

rely on (ri-*lai*) *contar con

remain (ri-*mein*) v quedarse; quedar; sobrar

remainder (ri-*mein*-dö) n resto m

remaining (ri-*mei*-ning) adj demás, restante

remark (ri-*maak*) n observación f; v *hacer una observación

remarkable (ri-*maa*-kö-böl) adj notable

remedy (*rê*-mö-di) n remedio m

remember (ri-*mêm*-bö) v *acordarse

remembrance (ri-*mêm*-brönss) n recuerdo m

remind (ri-*maind*) v *recordar

remit (ri-*mit*) v remitir

remittance (ri-*mi*-tönss) n remesa f

remnant (*rêm*-nönt) n resto m, residuo m, remanente m

remote (ri-*mout*) adj remoto, lejano

removal (ri-*muu*-völ) n remoción f

remove (ri-*muuv*) v *remover

remunerate (ri-*myuu*-nö-reit) v remunerar

remuneration (ri-myuu-nö-*rei*-ʃön) *n*
remuneración *f*

renew (ri-*nyuu*) *v* *renovar; alargar

rent (rênt) *v* alquilar; *n* alquiler *m*

repair (ri-*pêⁱ*) *v* arreglar, reparar; *n*
reparación *f*

reparation (rê-pö-*rei*-ʃön) *n*
reparación *f*

***repay** (ri-*pei*) *v* reintegrar

repayment (ri-*pei*-mönt) *n* reintegro
m

repeat (ri-*piit*) *v* *repetir

repellent (ri-*pê*-lönt) *adj* repugnante,
repelente

repentance (ri-*pên*-tönss) *n*
arrepentimiento *m*

repertory (*rê*-pö-tö-ri) *n* repertorio *m*

repetition (rê-pö-*ti*-ʃön) *n* repetición *f*

replace (ri-*pleiss*) *v* reemplazar

reply (ri-*plai*) *v* responder; *n* respuesta
f; **in ~** en contestación

report (ri-*poot*) *v* relatar; informar;
presentarse; *n* relato *m*, informe *m*

reporter (ri-*poo*-tö) *n* reportero *m*, -a *f*

represent (rê-pri-*sênt*) *v* representar

representation (rê-pri-sên-*tei*-ʃön) *n*
representación *f*

representative (rê-pri-*sên*-tö-tiv) *adj*
representativo

reprimand (*rê*-pri-maand) *v*
reprender

reproach (ri-*prouch*) *n* reproche *m*; *v*
reprochar

reproduce (rii-prö-*dyuuss*) *v*
*reproducir

reproduction (rii-prö-*dak*-ʃön) *n*
reproducción *f*

reptile (*rêp*-tail) *n* reptil *m*

republic (ri-*pa*-blik) *n* república *f*

republican (ri-*pa*-bli-kön) *adj*
republicano

repulsive (ri-*pal*-ssiv) *adj* repulsivo

reputation (rê-pyu-*tei*-ʃön) *n*
reputación *f*; renombre *m*

request (ri-*kᵘêsst*) *n* ruego *m*;
demanda *f*; *v* solicitar; pedir

require (ri-*kᵘaiᵒ*) *v* *requerir

requirement (ri-*kᵘaiᵒ*-mönt) *n*
requerimiento *m*

requisite (*rê*-kᵘi-sit) *adj* necesario

rescue (*rê*-sskyuu) *v* rescatar; *n*
rescate *m*

research (ri-*ssööch*) *n* investigación *f*

resemblance (ri-*sêm*-blönss) *n*
semejanza *f*

resemble (ri-*sêm*-böl) *v* asemejarse

resent (ri-*sênt*) *v* *resentirse por

reservation (rê-sö-*vei*-ʃön) *n*
reservación *f*

reserve (ri-*sööv*) *v* reservar; *n* reserva
f

reserved (ri-*söövd*) *adj* reservado

reservoir (*rê*-sö-vᵘaa) *n* embalse *m*

reside (ri-*said*) *v* residir

residence (*rê*-si-dönss) *n* residencia *f*;
~ permit permiso de residencia

resident (*rê*-si-dönt) *n* residente *m/f*;
adj residente; interno

resign (ri-*sain*) *v* resignar

resignation (rê-sigh-*nei*-ʃön) *n*
resignación *f*

resin (*rê*-sin) *n* resina *f*

resist (ri-*sisst*) *v* resistir

resistance (ri-*si*-sstönss) *n* resistencia
f

resolute (*rê*-sö-luut) *adj* resuelto,
decidido

respect (ri-*sspêkt*) *n* respeto *m*;
estimación *f*, reverencia *f*; *v* respetar

respectable (ri-*sspêk*-tö-böl) *adj*
respetable

respectful (ri-*sspêkt*-föl) *adj*
respetuoso

respective (ri-*sspêk*-tiv) *adj*
respectivo

respiration (rê-sspö-*rei*-ʃön) *n*
respiración *f*

respite (*rê*-sspait) *n* respiro *m*

responsibility (ri-sspon-ssö-*bi*-lö-ti) *n*
responsabilidad *f*

responsible (ri-*sspon*-ssö-böl) *adj*
responsable

rest (rêsst) *n* descanso *m*; resto *m*; *v*
*hacer reposo, descansar; ~ **home**
residencia de ancianos; ~ **room** aseo,
servicios

restaurant (rê-sstö-roñg) *n*
restaurante *m*

restful (*rêsst*-föl) *adj* reposado

restless (*rêsst*-löss) *adj* inquieto

restrain (ri-*sstrein*) *v* *contener,
*impedir

restriction (ri-*sstrik*-ʃön) *n* restricción
f

result (ri-*salt*) *n* resultado *m*;
consecuencia *f*; *v* resultar

resume (ri-*syuum*) *v* reemprender

résumé (*rê*-syu-mei) *n* resumen *m*;
Am currículum vitae

retail (*rii*-teil) *v* vender al detalle; ~
trade comercio al por menor

retailer (*rii*-tei-lö) *n* comerciante al
por menor, minorista *m/f*;
revendedor *m*, -a *f*

retina (*rê*-ti-nö) *n* retina *f*

retire (ri-*tai*⁰) *v* jubilarse; retirar;
retired jubilado; **retirement**
jubilación *f*

return (ri-*töön*) *v* *volver; *n* regreso *m*;
vuelta *f*; devolución *f*; ~ **flight** vuelo
de regreso; ~ **ticket** billete de ida y
vuelta

reunite (rii-yuu-*nait*) *v* reunir

reveal (ri-*viil*) *v* *manifestar, revelar

revelation (rê-vö-*lei*-ʃön) *n* revelación
f

revenge (ri-*vênd*ʒ) *n* venganza *f*

revenue (*rê*-vö-nyuu) *n* ingresos *mpl*,
renta *f*

reverse (ri-*vööss*) *n* contrario *m*;
reverso *m*; marcha atrás; revés *m*; *adj*
inverso; *v* *dar marcha atrás

review (ri-*vyuu*) *n* reseña *f*; revista *f*

revise (ri-*vais*) *v* revisar

revision (ri-*vi*-ʒön) *n* revisión *f*

revival (ri-*vai*-völ) *n* recuperación *f*

revolt (ri-*voult*) *v* sublevarse; *n*
rebelión *f*, revuelta *f*

revolting (ri-*voul*-ting) *adj*
repugnante, chocante, repelente

revolution (rê-vö-*luu*-ʃön) *n*
revolución *f*

revolutionary (rê-vö-*luu*-ʃö-nö-ri) *adj*
revolucionario

revolver (ri-*vol*-vö) *n* revólver *m*

revue (ri-*vyuu*) *n* revista *f*

reward (ri-ᵘ*ood*) *n* recompensa *f*; *v*
recompensar

rheumatism (*ruu*-mö-ti-söm) *n*
reumatismo *m*

rhinoceros (rai-*no*-ssö-röss) *n* (pl ~,
~es) rinoceronte *m*

rhubarb (*ruu*-baab) *n* ruibarbo *m*

rhyme (raim) *n* rima *f*

rhythm (*ri*-ðöm) *n* ritmo *m*

rib (rib) *n* costilla *f*

ribbon (*ri*-bön) *n* cinta *f*

rice (raiss) *n* arroz *m*

rich (rich) *adj* rico

riches (*ri*-chis) *pl* riqueza *f*

rid (rid) : **get** ~ **of** deshacerse de

riddle (*ri*-döl) *n* adivinanza *f*

ride (raid) *n* paseo *m*

***ride** (raid) *v* *ir en coche; montar

rider (*rai*-dö) *n* jinete *m*

ridge (ridʒ) *n* cresta *f*; lomo *m*

ridicule (*ri*-di-kyuul) *v* ridiculizar

ridiculous (ri-*di*-kyu-löss) *adj* ridículo

riding (*rai*-ding) *n* equitación *f*; ~
school picadero *m*; escuela de
equitación

rifle (*rai*-föl) *v* rifle *m*

right (rait) *n* derecho *m*; *adj* correcto;
derecho; justo; **all right!** ¡de
acuerdo!; ***be** ~ *tener razón; ~ **now**
ahora mismo; ~ **of way** prioridad de

paso

righteous (*rai*-chöss) *adj* justo; recto; honrado

right-hand (*rait*-hænd) *adj* derecho

rightly (*rait*-li) *adv* justamente

rim (rim) *n* llanta *f*; borde *m*

ring (ring) *n* anillo *m*; círculo *m*; pista *f*

*ring (ring) *v* *sonar; ~ **up** llamar por teléfono

rinse (rinss) *v* enjuagar; *n* enjuague *m*

riot (*rai*-öt) *n* motín *m*

rip (rip) *v* rasgar

ripe (raip) *adj* maduro

rise (rais) *n* aumento de sueldo, aumento *m*; levantamiento *m*; subida *f*; nacimiento *m*

*rise (rais) *v* levantarse; subir

rising (*rai*-sing) *n* levantamiento *m*

risk (rissk) *n* riesgo *m*; peligro *m*; *v* arriesgar

risky (*ri*-sski) *adj* arriesgado

rival (*rai*-völ) *n* rival *m/f*; competidor *m*, -a *f*; *v* rivalizar

rivalry (*rai*-völ-ri) *n* rivalidad *f*; competencia *f*

river (*ri*-vö) *n* río *m*; ~ **bank** ribera *f*

riverside (*ri*-vö-ssaid) *n* ribera *f*

roach (rouch) *n* (pl ~) escarcho *m*

road (roud) *n* calle *f*, camino *m*; ~ **fork** *n* bifurcación *f*; ~ **map** mapa de carreteras; ~ **system** red de carreteras; ~ **up** cerrado por obras

roadhouse (*roud*-hauss) *n* albergue *m* de carretera

roadside (*roud*-ssaid) *n* borde del camino

roam (roum) *v* vagar; recorrer

roar (roo) *v* mugir, rugir; *n* rugido *m*, retumbo *m*

roast (rousst) *v* asar, asar en parrilla

rob (rob) *v* robar

robber (*ro*-bö) *n* ladrón *m*

robbery (*ro*-bö-ri) *n* robo *m*

robe (roub) *n* manto *m*, túnica *f*

robin (*ro*-bin) *n* petirrojo *m*

robust (rou-*basst*) *adj* robusto

rock (rok) *n* roca *f*; *v* mecer

rocket (*ro*-kit) *n* cohete *m*

rocky (*ro*-ki) *adj* rocoso

rod (rod) *n* barra *f*

roe (rou) *n* huevos de los peces, hueva *f*

role (roul) *n* papel *m*

roll (roul) *v* *rodar; *n* rollo *m*; panecillo *m*

roller-skating (*rou*-lö-sskei-ting) *n* patinaje de ruedas

Roman Catholic (*rou*-mön *kæ*-zö-lik) católico

romance (rö-*mænss*) *n* amorío *m*

romantic (rö-*mæn*-tik) *adj* romántico

roof (ruuf) *n* techo *m*; **thatched** ~ techo de paja

room (ruum) *n* habitación *f*; espacio *m*, sitio *m*; ~ **and board** pensión completa; ~ **service** servicio de habitación; ~ **temperature** temperatura ambiente

roomy (*ruu*-mi) *adj* espacioso

root (ruut) *n* raíz *f*

rope (roup) *n* soga *f*

rosary (*rou*-sö-ri) *n* rosario *m*

rose (rous) *n* rosa *f*; *adj* rosa

rotten (*ro*-tön) *adj* podrido

rouge (ruuз) *n* colorete *m*

rough (raf) *adj* áspero

roulette (ruu-*lêt*) *n* ruleta *f*

round (raund) *adj* redondo; *prep* alrededor de, en torno de; *n* vuelta *f*; ~ **trip** *Am* ida y vuelta

roundabout (*raun*-dö-baut) *n* glorieta *f*

rounded (*raun*-did) *adj* redondeado

route (ruut) *n* ruta *f*

routine (ruu-*tiin*) *n* rutina *f*

row[1] (rou) *n* fila *f*; *v* remar

row[2] (rau) *n* bronca *f*

rowdy (*rau*-di) *adj* alborotador

row(ing) boat (*rou*-ing-bout) *n* bote *m*
royal (*roi*-öl) *adj* real
rub (rab) *v* frotar
rubber (*ra*-bö) *n* caucho *m*; goma de borrar; hule *mMe*; **~ band** elástico *m*
rubbish (*ra*-biʃ) *n* basura *f*; habladuría *f*, tontería *f*; **talk ~** *decir tonterías
rubbish bin (*ra*-biʃ-bin) *n* cubo de la basura
ruby (*ruu*-bi) *n* rubí *m*
rucksack (*rak*-ssæk) *n* mochila *f*
rudder (*ra*-dö) *n* timón *m*
rude (ruud) *adj* grosero
rug (ragh) *n* alfombrilla *f*
ruin (*ruu*-in) *v* arruinar; *n* ruina *f*
rule (ruul) *n* regla *f*; régimen *m*, gobierno *m*, dominio *m*; *v* *gobernar, *regir; **as a ~** generalmente, por regla general
ruler (*ruu*-lö) *n* monarca *m*, gobernante *m*; regla *f*

Rumania (ruu-*mei*-ni-ö) Rumania *f*
Rumanian (ruu-*mei*-ni-ön) *adj* rumano
rumo(u)r (*ruu*-mö) *n* rumor *m*
***run** (ran) *v* correr; dirigir; funcionar; fluir; **~ into** *encontrarse con
runaway (*ra*-nö-ᵘei) *n* fugitivo *m*
rung (ran) *v* (pp ring)
runner (*ra*-nö) *n* corredor *m*, -a *f*
runway (*ran*-ᵘei) *n* pista de despegue; pista de aterrizaje
rural (*ruᵒ*-röl) *adj* rural
ruse (ruus) *n* astucia *f*
rush (raʃ) *v* precipitarse; ir de prisa; *n* junco *m*; **~ hour** hora punta
Russia (*ra*-ʃö) Rusia *f*
Russian (*ra*-ʃön) *adj* ruso
rust (rasst) *n* herrumbre *f*
rustic (*ra*-sstik) *adj* rústico
rusty (*ra*-ssti) *adj* oxidado

S

sack (ssæk) *n* saco *m*
sacred (*ssei*-krid) *adj* sagrado
sacrifice (*ssæ*-kri-faiss) *n* sacrificio *m*; *v* sacrificar
sacrilege (*ssæ*-kri-lidʒ) *n* sacrilegio *m*
sad (ssæd) *adj* triste; afligido, melancólico
saddle (*ssæ*-döl) *n* silla *f* de montar
sadness (*ssæd*-nöss) *n* tristeza *f*
safe (sseif) *adj* seguro; ileso; *n* caja fuerte
safety (*sseif*-ti) *n* seguridad *f*; **~ belt** cinturón de seguridad; **~ pin** imperdible *m*
sail (sseil) *v* navegar; *n* vela *f*
sail(ing) boat (*ssei*-ling-bout) *n* velero *m*

sailor (*ssei*-lö) *n* marinero *m*
saint (sseint) *n* santo *m*
salad (*ssæ*-löd) *n* ensalada *f*; **~ dressing** aderezo para ensalada
salary (*ssæ*-lö-ri) *n* sueldo *m*
sale (sseil) *n* venta *f*; **clearance ~** liquidación *f*; **for ~** de venta; **sales** rebajas *fpl*
saleable (*ssei*-lö-böl) *adj* vendible
salesgirl (*sseils*-ghööl) *n* vendedora *f*
salesman (*sseils*-mön) *n* (pl -men) vendedor *m*
salmon (*ssæ*-mön) *n* (pl **~**) salmón *m*
salon (*ssæ*-lon͞g) *n* salón *m*
saloon (ssö-*luun*) *n* bar *m*; cantina *fMe*
salt (ssoolt) *n* sal *f*; **~ cellar,** *Am* **~**

shaker salero *m*

salty (*ssool*-ti) *adj* salado

salute (ssö-*luut*) *v* saludar

salve (ssaav) *n* ungüento *m*

same (sseim) *adj* mismo; idéntico

sample (*ssaam*-pöl) *n* muestra *f*

sanatorium (ssæ-nö-*too*-ri-öm) *n* (pl ~s, -ria) sanatorio *m*

sand (ssænd) *n* arena *f*

sandal (*ssæn*-döl) *n* sandalia *f*

sandpaper (*ssænd*-pei-pö) *n* papel de lija

sandwich (*ssæn*-ᵘidȝ) *n* bocadillo *m*; sandwich *m*

sandy (*ssæn*-di) *adj* arenoso

sanitary (ssæ-ni-tö-ri) *adj* sanitario; ~ **napkin** *Am*, ~ **towel** paño higiénico, compresa

sapphire (*ssæ*-faiᵒ) *n* zafiro *m*

sardine (ssaa-*diin*) *n* sardina *f*

satchel (*ssæ*-chöl) *n* cartapacio *m*; bolso *m*

satellite (*ssæ*-tö-lait) *n* satélite *m*

satin (*ssæ*-tin) *n* raso *m*

satisfaction (ssæ-tiss-*fæk*-ʃön) *n* satisfacción *f*

satisfactory (ssæ-tiss-*fæk*-tö-ri) *adj* satisfactorio; suficiente

satisfy (*ssæ*-tiss-fai) *v* *satisfacer

Saturday (*ssæ*-tö-di) sábado *m*

sauce (ssooss) *n* salsa *f*

saucepan (*ssooss*-pön) *n* cacerola *f*

saucer (*ssoo*-ssö) *n* platillo *m*

Saudi Arabia (ssau-di-ö-*rei*-bi-ö) Arabia Saudí

Saudi Arabian (ssau-di-ö-*rei*-bi-ön) *adj* saudí

sauna (*ssoo*-nö) *n* sauna *f*

sausage (*sso*-ssidȝ) *n* salchicha *f*

savage (*ssæ*-vidȝ) *adj* salvaje

save (sseiv) *v* salvar; ahorrar

savings (*ssei*-vings) *pl* ahorros *mpl*; ~ **bank** caja de ahorros

savio(u)r (*ssei*-vyö) *n* salvador *m*

savo(u)ry (*ssei*-vö-ri) *adj* sabroso; picante

saw¹ (ssoo) *v* (p see)

saw² (ssoo) *n* sierra *f*

sawdust (*ssoo*-dasst) *n* serrín *m*

sawmill (*ssoo*-mil) *n* serrería de maderas

***say** (ssei) *v* *decir

scaffolding (*sskæ*-föl-ding) *n* andamio *m*

scale (sskeil) *n* escala *f*; escala musical; escama *f*; **scales** *pl* balanza *f*, báscula *f*

scandal (*sskæn*-döl) *n* escándalo *m*

Scandinavia (sskæn-di-*nei*-vi-ö) Escandinavia *f*

Scandinavian (sskæn-di-*nei*-vi-ön) *adj* escandinavo

scapegoat (*sskeip*-ghout) *n* cabeza de turco

scar (sskaa) *n* cicatriz *f*

scarce (sskêᵒss) *adj* escaso

scarcely (*sskêᵒ*-ssli) *adv* apenas

scarcity (*sskêᵒ*-ssö-ti) *n* escasez *f*

scare (sskêᵒ) *v* asustar; *n* susto *m*

scarf (sskaaf) *n* (pl ~s, scarves) bufanda *f*

scarlet (*sskaa*-löt) *adj* escarlata

scary (*sskêᵒ*-ri) *adj* alarmante; asustadizo

scatter (*sskæ*-tö) *v* esparcir

scene (ssiin) *n* escena *f*

scenery (*ssii*-nö-ri) *n* paisaje *m*

scenic (*ssii*-nik) *adj* pintoresco

scent (ssênt) *n* perfume *m*; olor *m*

schedule (ʃé-dyuul) *n* horario *m*

scheme (sskiim) *n* esquema *m*; proyecto *m*

scholar (*ssko*-lö) *n* erudito *m*, -a *f*; alumno *m*, -a *f*

scholarship (*ssko*-lö-ʃip) *n* beca *f*

school (sskuul) *n* escuela *f*

schoolboy (*sskuul*-boi) *n* alumno *m*; colegial *m*

schoolgirl (*sskuul*-ghööl) n alumna f; colegiala f

schoolmaster (*sskuul*-maa-sstö) n maestro m

schoolteacher (*sskuul*-tii-chö) n maestro m, -a f

science (*ssai*-önss) n ciencia f

scientific (ssai-ön-*ti*-fik) adj científico

scientist (*ssai*-ön-tisst) n científico m, -a f

scissors (*ssi*-sös) pl tijeras fpl

scold (sskould) v reprender; regañar

scooter (*sskuu*-tö) n motoneta f; patín m

score (sskoo) n tanteo m; partitura f; v marcar un gol; tantear

scorn (sskoon) n escarnio m, desprecio m; v despreciar

Scot (sskot) n escocés m

Scotch (sskoch) adj escocés; **scotch tape** cinta adhesiva

Scotland (*sskot*-lönd) Escocia f

Scotsman (*sskots*-mön) escocés m

Scotswoman (*sskots*-ᵘu-mön) escocesa f

Scottish (*sskot*-tiʃ) adj escocés

scout (sskaut) n explorador m

scrap (sskræp) n pedazo m

scrapbook (*sskræp*-buk) n álbum m

scrape (sskreip) v raspar

scratch (sskræch) v *hacer raeduras, rascar; n raedura f, rasguño m

scream (sskriim) v gritar, chillar; n grito m, chillido m

screen (sskriin) n pantalla f

screw (sskruu) n tornillo m; v atornillar

screwdriver (*sskruu*-drai-vö) n destornillador m

scrub (sskrab) v *fregar; n matorral m

sculptor (*sskalp*-tö) n escultor m, -a f

sculpture (*sskalp*-chö) n escultura f

sea (ssii) n mar m; ~ **urchin** erizo de mar; ~ **water** agua de mar

seabird (*ssii*-bööd) n ave marina

seacoast (*ssii*-kousst) n litoral m

seafood (*ssii*-fuud) n marisco(s) m(pl)

seagull (*ssii*-ghal) n gaviota f

seal (ssiil) n sello m; foca f

seam (ssiim) n costura f

seaman (*ssii*-mön) n (pl -men) marino m

seamless (*ssiim*-löss) adj sin costura

seaport (*ssii*-poot) n puerto de mar

search (ssööch) v buscar; cachear; n búsqueda f

searchlight (*ssööch*-lait) n reflector m

seascape (*ssii*-sskeip) n marina f

seashell (*ssii*-ʃêl) n concha f

seashore (*ssii*-ʃoo) n orilla del mar

seasick (*ssii*-ssik) adj mareado

seasickness (*ssii*-ssik-nöss) n mareo m

seaside (*ssii*-ssaid) n orilla del mar; ~ **resort** playa de veraneo

season (*ssii*-sön) n temporada f, estación f; **high ~** temporada alta; **low ~** temporada baja; **off ~** fuera de temporada

season ticket (*ssii*-sön-ti-kit) n tarjeta de temporada

seat (ssiit) n asiento m; sitio m, localidad f; sede f; ~ **belt** cinturón de seguridad

second (*ssê*-könd) num segundo; n segundo m; instante m

secondary (*ssê*-kön-dö-ri) adj secundario; ~ **school** escuela secundaria

second-hand (ssê-könd-*hænd*) adj de segunda mano

secret (*ssii*-kröt) n secreto m; adj secreto

secretary (*ssê*-krö-tri) n secretaria f; secretario m

section (*ssêk*-ʃön) n sección f; división f, departamento m

secure (ssi-*kyuᵒ*) adj seguro; firme; v

asegurar; conseguir

security (ssi-*kyu*ᵒ-rö-ti) *n* seguridad *f*; fianza *f*

sedative (*ssê*-dö-tiv) *n* calmante *m*

seduce (ssi-*dyuuss*) *v* *seducir

*see (ssii) *v* *ver; comprender, *darse cuenta; **~ to** *atender a

seed (ssiid) *n* semilla *f*

*seek (ssiik) *v* buscar

seem (ssiim) *v* *parecer

seen (ssiin) *v* (pp see)

seesaw (*ssii*-ssoo) *n* columpio *m*

seize (ssiis) *v* agarrar; prender

seldom (*ssêl*-döm) *adv* pocas veces, rara vez

select (ssi-*lêkt*) *v* seleccionar, *elegir; *adj* seleccionado, selecto

selection (ssi-*lêk*-ʃön) *n* elección *f*, selección *f*

self (ssêlf) (pl selves) ego *m*; **my other ~** mi otro yo

self-centered *Am*, **self-centred** (ssêlf-*ssên*-töd) *adj* egocéntrico

self-employed (ssêl-fim-*ploid*) *adj* que trabaja por cuenta propia

self-evident (ssêl-*fê*-vi-dönt) *adj* evidente por sí mismo

self-government (ssêlf-*gha*-vö-mönt) *n* autonomía *f*

selfish (*ssêl*-fiʃ) *adj* egoísta

selfishness (*ssêl*-fiʃ-nöss) *n* egoísmo *m*

self-service (ssêlf-*ssöö*-viss) *n* autoservicio *m*

*sell (ssêl) *v* vender

semblance (*ssêm*-blönss) *n* apariencia *f*

semi- (*ssê*-mi) semi-

semicircle (*ssê*-mi-ssöö-köl) *n* semicírculo *m*

semicolon (ssê-mi-*kou*-lön) *n* punto y coma

senate (*ssê*-nöt) *n* senado *m*

senator (*ssê*-nö-tö) *n* senador *m*

*send (ssênd) *v* enviar, mandar; **~ back** *devolver; **~ for** mandar a buscar; **~ off** despachar

sender (*ssên*-dö) *n* remitente *m*/*f*

senile (*ssii*-nail) *adj* senil

senior (*ssiin*-yö) *adj* mayor; superior; **~ citizen** persona de la tercera edad

sensation (ssên-*ssei*-ʃön) *n* sensación *f*

sensational (ssên-*ssei*-ʃö-nöl) *adj* sensacional

sense (ssênss) *n* sentido *m*; juicio *m*, razón *f*; *v* *sentir; **~ of humo(u)r** sentido del humor

senseless (*ssênss*-löss) *adj* insensato; sin sentido

sensible (*ssên*-ssö-böl) *adj* sensato; razonable; práctico

sensitive (*ssên*-ssi-tiv) *adj* sensible

sentence (*ssên*-tönss) *n* frase *f*; sentencia *f*; *v* sentenciar

sentimental (ssên-ti-*mên*-töl) *adj* sentimental

separate¹ (*ssê*-pö-reit) *v* separar

separate² (*ssê*-pö-röt) *adj* separado

separately (*ssê*-pö-röt-li) *adv* por separado

September (ssêp-*têm*-bö) septiembre

septic (*ssêp*-tik) *adj* séptico; ***become ~** infectarse

sequel (*ssii*-kᵘöl) *n* continuación *f*

sequence (*ssii*-kᵘönss) *n* sucesión *f*; serie *f*

serene (ssö-*riin*) *adj* sereno; claro

serial (*ssi*ᵒ-ri-öl) *n* novela por entregas

series (*ssi*ᵒ-riis) *m* (pl **~**) serie *f*

serious (*ssi*ᵒ-ri-öss) *adj* serio

seriousness (*ssi*ᵒ-ri-öss-nöss) *n* seriedad *f*

sermon (*ssöö*-mön) *n* sermón *m*

serum (*ssi*ᵒ-röm) *n* suero *m*

servant (*ssöö*-vönt) *n* criado *m*

serve (ssööv) *v* *servir

service (*ssöö*-viss) *n* servicio *m*; **~**

charge servicio *m*; **~ station** puesto de gasolina

serviette (ssöö-vi-*êt*) *n* servilleta *f*

session (*ssê*-ʃön) *n* sesión *f*

set (ssêt) *n* juego *m*, grupo *m*

*set (ssêt) *v* *poner; colocar; montar; fijar; **~ menu** cubierto a precio fijo; **~ out** partir; **~ up** establecer

setting (*ssê*-ting) *n* escena *f*; **~ lotion** fijador *m*

settle (*ssê*-töl) *v* arreglar; **~ down** arraigarse

settlement (*ssê*-töl-mönt) *n* acuerdo *m*, arreglo *m*, convenio *m*

seven (*ssê*-vön) *num* siete

seventeen (ssê-vön-*tiin*) *num* diecisiete

seventeenth (ssê-vön-*tiinz*) *num* decimoséptimo

seventh (*ssê*-vönz) *num* séptimo

seventy (*ssê*-vön-ti) *num* setenta

several (*ssê*-vö-röl) *adj* varios

severe (ssi-*vi*⁰) *adj* severo; grave; duro

sew (ssou) *v* coser; **~ up** *hacer una sutura

sewer (*ssuu*-ö) *n* desagüe *m*

sewing machine (*ssou*-ing-mö-ʃiin) *n* máquina de coser

sex (ssêkss) *n* sexo *m*; sexualidad *f*

sexual (*ssêk*-ʃu-öl) *adj* sexual

sexuality (ssêk-ʃu-æ-lö-ti) *n* sexualidad *f*

shade (ʃeid) *n* sombra *f*; tono *m*

shadow (*ʃæ*-dou) *n* sombra *f*

shady (*ʃei*-di) *adj* sombreado

*shake (ʃeik) *v* sacudir

shaky (*ʃei*-ki) *adj* vacilante

*shall (ʃæl) *v* *tener que

shallow (*ʃæ*-lou) *adj* poco profundo; superficial

shame (ʃeim) *n* vergüenza *f*; deshonra *f*; **shame!** ¡qué vergüenza!

shampoo (ʃæm-*puu*) *n* champú *m*

shamrock (*ʃæm*-rok) *n* trébol *m*

shape (ʃeip) *n* forma *f*; *v* formar

share (ʃê⁰) *v* compartir; *n* parte *f*; acción *f*

shark (ʃaak) *n* tiburón *m*

sharp (ʃaap) *adj* afilado

sharpen (*ʃaa*-pön) *v* afilar

shave (ʃeiv) *v* rasurarse, afeitarse

shaver (*ʃei*-vö) *n* máquina de afeitar

shaving brush (*ʃei*-ving-braʃ) *n* brocha de afeitar

shaving cream (*ʃei*-ving-kriim) *n* crema de afeitar

shaving soap (*ʃei*-ving-ssoup) *n* jabón de afeitar

shawl (ʃool) *n* chal *m*

she (ʃii) *pron* ella

shed (ʃêd) *n* cobertizo *m*

*shed (ʃêd) *v* derramar; esparcir

sheep (ʃiip) *n* (pl ~) oveja *f*

sheer (ʃi⁰) *adj* absoluto, puro; fino, traslúcido

sheet (ʃiit) *n* sábana *f*; hoja *f*; chapa *f*

shelf (ʃêlf) *n* (pl shelves) estante *m*

shell (ʃêl) *n* concha *f*; cáscara *f*

shellfish (*ʃêl*-fiʃ) *n* marisco *m*

shelter (*ʃêl*-tö) *n* refugio *m*; *v* abrigar

shepherd (*ʃê*-pöd) *n* pastor *m*

shift (ʃift) *n* turno *m*

*shine (ʃain) *v* *relucir; brillar, *resplandecer

ship (ʃip) *n* buque *m*; *v* transportar; **shipping line** línea de navegación

shipowner (*ʃi*-pou-nö) *n* armador *m*

shipyard (*ʃip*-yaad) *n* astillero *m*

shirt (ʃööt) *n* camisa *f*

shiver (*ʃi*-vö) *v* *temblar, tiritar; *n* escalofrío *m*

shock (ʃok) *n* choque *m*; *v* chocar; **~ absorber** amortiguador *m*

shocking (*ʃo*-king) *adj* chocante

shoe (ʃuu) *n* zapato *m*; **gym shoes** zapatos de gimnasia; **~ polish** betún *m*; grasa *fMe*; **~ shop** zapatería *f*

shoelace (*ʃuu*-leiss) *n* cordón *m*

shoemaker (ʃuu-mei-kö) n zapatero m

shook (ʃuk) v (p shake)

*shoot (ʃuut) v tirar

shop (ʃop) n tienda f; v *ir de compras; ~ **assistant** dependiente m, -a

shopping (ʃo-ping) compra f; **do one's** ~ hacer la compra; ~ **bag** saco de compras; ~ **centre**, ~ **mall** centro comercial

shopkeeper (ʃop-kii-pö) n tendero m, -a f

shopwindow (ʃop-ᵘin-dou) n escaparate m

shore (ʃoo) n ribera f, orilla f

short (ʃoot) adj corto; bajo; ~ **circuit** cortocircuito m

shortage (ʃoo-tidʒ) n carencia f, escasez f

shorten (ʃoo-tön) v acortar

shorthand (ʃoot-hænd) n taquigrafía f

shortly (ʃoot-li) adv pronto, próximamente

shorts (ʃootss) pl pantalones cortos, pantalones de gimnasia; plAm calzoncillos mpl

short-sighted (ʃoot-ssai-tid) adj miope

shot (ʃot) n disparo m; inyección f; secuencia f

*should (ʃud) v *tener que

shoulder (ʃoul-dö) n hombro m

shout (ʃaut) v gritar; n grito m

shovel (ʃa-völ) n pala f

show (ʃou) n representación f, espectáculo m; exposición f

*show (ʃou) v *mostrar; enseñar; *demostrar

showcase (ʃou-keiss) n vitrina f

shower (ʃauᵒ) n ducha f; aguacero m

showroom (ʃou-ruum) n sala de exposición; salón de demostraciones

shriek (ʃriik) v chillar; n chillido m

shrimp (ʃrimp) n camarón m

shrine (ʃrain) n santuario m

*shrink (ʃringk) v encogerse

shrinkproof (ʃringk-pruuf) adj no encoge

shrub (ʃrab) n arbusto m

shudder (ʃa-dö) n estremecimiento m

shuffle (ʃa-föl) v barajar

*shut (ʃat) v *cerrar; ~ **in** *encerrar

shutter (ʃa-tö) n persiana f

shy (ʃai) adj esquivo, tímido

shyness (ʃai-nöss) n timidez f

Siamese (ssai-ö-miis) adj siamés

sick (ssik) adj enfermo; que tiene náuseas

sickness (ssik-nöss) n enfermedad f; náusea f

side (ssaid) n lado m; partido m; **one-sided** adj unilateral

sideburns (ssaid-bööns) pl patillas fpl

sidelight (ssaid-lait) n luz lateral

side street (ssaid-sstriit) n calle lateral

sidewalk (ssaid-ᵘook) nAm acera f

sideways (ssaid-ᵘeis) adv lateralmente

siege (ssiidʒ) n sitio m

sieve (ssiv) n tamiz m; v tamizar

sift (ssift) v tamizar

sight (ssait) n vista f; aspecto m; curiosidad f

sightseeing (ssait-sii-ying) n: **go** ~ hacer turismo

sign (ssain) n signo m, señal f; gesto m, seña f; v suscribir, firmar

signal (ssigh-nöl) n señal f; v *hacer señales

signature (ssigh-nö-chö) n firma f

significant (ssigh-ni-fi-könt) adj significativo

signpost (ssain-pousst) n poste de indicador

silence (ssai-lönss) n silencio m; v acallar

silencer (ssai-lön-ssö) n silenciador m

silent (*ssai*-lönt) *adj* callado; *be ~
callarse

silk (ssilk) *n* seda *f*

silly (*ssi*-li) *adj* necio, bobo

silver (*ssil*-vö) *n* plata *f*; de plata

silversmith (*ssil*-vö-ssmiz) *n* platero
m

silverware (*ssil*-vö-ʰêᵒ) *n* plata
labrada

similar (*ssi*-mi-lö) *adj* similar

similarity (ssi-mi-*læ*-rö-ti) *n*
semejanza *f*

simple (*ssim*-pöl) *adj* ingenuo, simple;
ordinario

simply (*ssim*-pli) *adv* simplemente

simulate (*ssi*-myu-leit) *v* simular

simultaneous (ssi-möl-*tei*-ni-öss) *adj*
simultáneo

sin (ssin) *n* pecado *m*

since (ssinss) *prep* desde; *adv* desde
entonces; *conj* desde que; puesto que

sincere (ssin-*ssiᵒ*) *adj* sincero; **Yours
sincerely** atentamente

sinew (*ssi*-nyuu) *n* tendón *m*

***sing** (ssing) *v* cantar

singer (*ssing*-ö) *n* cantante *m/f*

single (*ssing*-ghöl) *adj* solo; soltero

singular (*ssing*-ghyu-lö) *n* singular *m*;
adj singular

sinister (*ssi*-ni-sstö) *adj* siniestro

sink (ssingk) *n* fregadero *m*

***sink** (ssingk) *v* hundirse; disminuir

sip (ssip) *n* sorbo *m*

sir (ssöö) señor *m*

siren (*ssaiᵒ*-rön) *n* sirena *f*

sister (*ssi*-sstö) *n* hermana *f*

sister-in-law (*ssi*-sstö-rin-loo) *n* (pl
sisters-) cuñada *f*

***sit** (ssit) *v* *estar sentado; ~ **down**
*sentarse

site (ssait) *n* sitio *m*

sitting room (*ssi*-ting-ruum) *n* sala de
estar

situated (*ssi*-chu-ei-tid) *adj* situado

situation (ssi-chu-*ei*-ʃön) *n* situación *f*;
ubicación *f*

six (ssiks) *num* seis

sixteen (ssiks-*tiin*) *num* dieciséis

sixteenth (ssikss-*tiinz*) *num*
decimosexto

sixth (ssikssz) *num* sexto

sixty (*ssikss*-ti) *num* sesenta

size (ssais) *n* tamaño *m*, número *m*;
dimensión *f*; formato *m*

skate (sskeit) *v* patinar; *n* patín *m*

skating (*sskei*-ting) *n* patinaje *m*

skating rink (*sskei*-ting-ringk) *n* pista
de patinaje

skeleton (*sskê*-li-tön) *n* esqueleto *m*

sketch (sskêch) *n* dibujo *m*, bosquejo
m; *v* dibujar, bosquejar

ski¹ (sskii) *v* esquiar

ski² (sskii) *n* (pl ~, ~s) esquí *m*; ~ **boots**
botas de esquí; ~ **pants** pantalones
de esquí; ~ **sticks** bastones de esquí

skid (sskid) *v* patinar

skier (*sskii*-ö) *n* esquiador *m*

skiing (*sskii*-ing) *n* esquí *m*

ski jump (*sskii*-dӡamp) *n* salto de
esquí

skil(l)ful (*sskil*-föl) *adj* hábil, diestro

ski lift (*sskii*-lift) *n* telesilla *m*

skill (sskil) *n* habilidad *f*

skilled (sskild) *adj* hábil;
especializado

skin (sskin) *n* piel *f*; cutis *m*; cáscara *f*;
~ **cream** crema para la piel

skip (sskip) *v* saltar; brincar

skirt (sskööt) *n* falda *f*

skull (sskal) *n* cráneo *m*; calavera *f*

sky (sskai) *n* cielo *m*

skyscraper (*sskai*-sskrei-pö) *n*
rascacielos *m*

slack (sslæk) *adj* flojo

slacks (sslækss) *pl* pantalones *mpl*

slam (sslæm) *v* *dar un portazo

slander (*sslaan*-dö) *n* calumnia *f*

slang (sslaang) argot *m*, jerga *f*

slant (sslaant) v inclinarse

slanting (sslaan-ting) adj oblicuo, pendiente, inclinado

slap (sslæp) v pegar; abofetear; n bofetada f

slate (ssleit) n pizarra f

slave (ssleiv) n esclavo m

sledge (sslêdʒ) Am sled n trineo m

sleep (ssliip) n sueño m

*sleep (ssliip) v *dormir

sleeping bag (sslii-ping-bægh) n saco de dormir

sleeping car (sslii-ping-kaa) n coche cama

sleeping pill (sslii-ping-pil) n somnífero m

sleepless (ssliip-löss) adj desvelado

sleepy (sslii-pi) adj soñoliento

sleeve (ssliiv) n manga f; funda f

sleigh (sslei) n trineo m

slender (sslên-dö) adj esbelto; delgado

slice (sslaiss) n tajada f

slide (sslaid) n desliz m; tobogán m; diapositiva f

*slide (sslaid) v deslizarse

slight (sslait) adj ligero; leve

slim (sslim) adj esbelto; v adelgazar

slip (sslip) v deslizarse, resbalar; n desliz m; combinación f; fondo mMe

slipper (ssli-pö) n zapatilla f

slippery (ssli-pö-ri) adj resbaladizo

slogan (sslou-ghön) n lema m, slogan m

slope (ssloup) n pendiente f; v inclinarse

sloping (sslou-ping) adj inclinado

sloppy (sslo-pi) adj chapucero

slot (sslot) n ranura f; ~ **machine** máquina tragamonedas

slovenly (ssla-vön-li) adj descuidado

slow (sslou) adj lerdo, lento; ~ **down** desacelerar, *ir más despacio; frenar

sluice (ssluuss) n compuerta f

slum (sslam) n barrio bajo

slump (sslamp) n baja f

slush (sslaʃ) n aguanieve f

sly (sslai) adj astuto

smack (ssmæk) v pegar (con la mano); n palmada f

small (ssmool) adj pequeño; menudo

smallpox (ssmool-pokss) n viruelas fpl

smart (ssmaat) adj inteligente, listo; elegante

smash (ssmæʃ) n estruendo m; choque m; smash m, mate m; v acer pedazos, acer añicos; romperse

smell (ssmêl) n olor m; olfato m

*smell (ssmêl) v *oler

smelly (ssmê-li) adj que huele mal

smile (ssmail) v sonreír; n sonrisa f

smith (ssmiz) n herrero m

smog (ssmog) n niebla f tóxica

smoke (ssmouk) v fumar; n humo m; **no smoking** prohibido fumar

smoker (ssmou-kö) n fumador m; compartimento para fumadores

smoking compartment (ssmou-king-köm-paat-mönt) n compartimento para fumadores

smooth (ssmuuð) adj llano, liso; suave

smuggle (ssma-ghöl) v contrabandear

snack (ssnæk) n tentempié m; ~ **bar** cafetería f

snail (ssneil) n caracol m

snake (ssneik) n culebra f

snapshot (ssnæp-ʃot) n instantánea f

sneakers (ssnii-kös) plAm zapatos de gimnasia

sneeze (ssniis) v estornudar

sniper (ssnai-pö) n francotirador m

snooty (ssnuu-ti) adj arrogante

snore (ssnoo) v roncar

snorkel (ssnoo-köl) n esnórquel m

snout (ssnaut) n hocico m

snow (ssnou) n nieve f; v *nevar

snowstorm (ssnou-sstoom) n nevasca

f

snowy (*ssnou*-i) *adj* nevoso; cubierto de nieve

so (ssou) *conj* por tanto; *adv* así; a tal grado, tan; **and ~ on** etcétera; **~ far** hasta ahora; **~ that** así que, a fin de

soak (ssouk) *v* empapar, remojar

soap (ssoup) *n* jabón *m*; **~ powder** jabón en polvo

sober (*ssou*-bö) *adj* sobrio; ponderado

so-called (ssou-*koold*) *adj* así llamado; supuesto

soccer (*sso*-kö) *n* fútbol *m*; **~ team** equipo *m*

social (*ssou*-ʃöl) *adj* social

socialism (*ssou*-ʃö-li-söm) *n* socialismo *m*

socialist (*ssou*-ʃö-lisst) *adj* socialista; *n* socialista *m*

society (ssö-*ssai*-ö-ti) *n* sociedad *f*; asociación *f*; compañía *f*

sock (ssok) *n* calcetín *m*

socket (*sso*-kit) *n* casquillo *m*; sóquet *mMe*

soda water (*ssou*-dö-ᵘoo-tö) *n* gaseosa *f*

sofa (*ssou*-fö) *n* sofá *m*

soft (ssoft) *adj* blando; **~ drink** bebida no alcohólica

soften (*sso*-fön) *v* ablandar

software (*ssoft*-ᵘêᵒ) software *m*

soil (ssoil) *n* suelo *m*; tierra *f*; *v* ensuciar

soiled (ssoild) *adj* manchado

sold (ssould) *v* (p, pp sell); **~ out** agotado

soldier (*ssoul*-dʒö) *n* militar *m*, soldado *m*

sole[1] (ssoul) *adj* único

sole[2] (ssoul) *n* suela *f*; lenguado *m*

solely (*ssoul*-li) *adv* exclusivamente

solemn (*sso*-löm) *adj* solemne

solicitor (ssö-*li*-ssi-tö) *n* procurador *m*, -a *f*, abogado *m*, -a *f*

solid (*sso*-lid) *adj* robusto, sólido; macizo; *n* sólido *m*

soluble (*sso*-lyu-böl) *adj* soluble

solution (ssö-*luu*-ʃön) *n* solución *f*

solve (ssolv) *v* *resolver

somber *Am*, **sombre** (*ssom*-bö) *adj* sombrío

some (ssam) *adj* algunos, unos; *pron* algunos, unos; un poco; **~ day** uno u otro día; **~ more** algo más; **~ time** alguna vez

somebody (*ssam*-bö-di) *pron* alguien

somehow (*ssam*-hau) *adv* de un modo u otro

someone (*ssam*-ᵘan) *pron* alguien

something (*ssam*-zing) *pron* algo

sometimes (*ssam*-taims) *adv* a veces

somewhat (*ssam*-ᵘot) *adv* algo

somewhere (*ssam*-ᵘêᵒ) *adv* en alguna parte

son (ssan) *n* hijo *m*

song (ssong) *n* canción *f*

son-in-law (*ssa*-nin-loo) *n* (pl sons-) yerno *m*

soon (ssuun) *adv* rápidamente, pronto, en breve; **as ~ as** tan pronto como

sooner (*ssuu*-nö) *adv* más bien

sore (ssoo) *adj* doloroso; *n* llaga *f*; úlcera *f*; **~ throat** dolor de garganta

sorrow (*sso*-rou) *n* tristeza *f*, sufrimiento *m*, pena *f*

sorry (*sso*-ri) *adj* apenado; **sorry!** ¡dispense usted!, ¡disculpe!, ¡perdón!

sort (ssoot) *v* clasificar, *disponer; *n* clase *f*; **all sorts of** toda clase de

soul (ssoul) *n* alma *f*

sound (ssaund) *n* sonido *m*; *v* *sonar, *resonar; *adj* bueno

soundproof (*ssaund*-pruuf) *adj* insonorizado

soup (ssuup) *n* sopa *f*

sour (ssauᵒ) *adj* agrio

source (ssooss) *n* fuente *f*

south (ssauz) *n* sur *m*; **South Pole** polo sur

South Africa (ssauz æ-fri-kö) África del Sur

southeast (ssauz-*iisst*) *n* sudeste *m*

southerly (ssa-ðö-li) *adj* meridional

southern (ssa-ðön) *adj* meridional

southwest (ssauz-*ꞷêsst*) *n* sudoeste *m*

souvenir (ssuu-vö-ni⁰) *n* recuerdo *m*

sovereign (ssov-rin) *n* soberano *m*

*****sow** (ssou) *v* *sembrar

soy (ssoi) *n* soja *f*

spa (sspaa) *n* balneario *m*

space (sspeiss) *n* espacio *m*; distancia *f*; *v* espaciar; **~ shuttle** transbordador espacial

spacious (sspei-ʃöss) *adj* espacioso

spade (sspeid) *n* azada *f*, pala *f*

Spain (sspein) España *f*

Spaniard (sspæ-nyöd) *n* español *m*, -a *f*

Spanish (sspæ-niʃ) *adj* español

spanking (sspæng-king) *n* zurra *f*

spanner (sspæ-nö) *n* llave inglesa

spare (sspê⁰) *adj* de reserva, disponible; *v* pasarse sin; **~ part** pieza de repuesto; **~ room** cuarto para huéspedes; **~ time** tiempo libre; **~ tire** *Am*, **~ tyre** neumático de repuesto; **~ wheel** rueda de repuesto

sparing (sspê⁰-ing) *adj* escaso; económico

spark (sspaak) *n* chispa *f*

spark(ing) plug (sspaa-king-plagh) *n* bujía *f*

sparkling (sspaa-kling) *adj* centelleante; espumante

sparrow (sspæ-rou) *n* gorrión *m*

*****speak** (sspiik) *v* hablar

spear (sspi⁰) *n* lanza *f*

special (sspê-ʃöl) *adj* especial; **~ delivery** por expreso

specialist (sspê-ʃö-lisst) *n* especialista *m/f*

speciality (sspê-ʃi-æ-lö-ti) *n* especialidad *f*

specialize (sspê-ʃö-lais) *v* especializarse

specially (sspê-ʃö-li) *adv* en particular

species (sspii-ʃiis) *n* (pl **~**) especie *f*

specific (sspö-*ssi*-fik) *adj* específico

specimen (sspê-ssi-mön) *n* espécimen *m*; muestra *f*

speck (sspêk) *n* mancha *f*

spectacle (sspêk-tö-köl) *n* espectáculo *m*; **spectacles** anteojos *mpl*, gafas *fpl*

spectator (sspêk-*tei*-tö) *n* espectador *m*

speculate (sspê-kyu-leit) *v* especular

speech (sspiich) *n* habla *f*; discurso *m*; lenguaje *m*

speechless (sspiich-löss) *adj* atónito

speed (sspiid) *n* velocidad *f*; rapidez *f*, prisa *f*; **cruising ~** velocidad de cruce; **~ limit** límite de velocidad

*****speed** (sspiid) *v* *dar prisa; correr demasiado

speeding (sspii-ding) *n* exceso de velocidad

speedometer (sspii-*do*-mi-tö) *n* velocímetro *m*

spell (sspêl) *n* encanto *m*

*****spell** (sspêl) *v* deletrear

spelling (sspê-ling) *n* deletreo *m*

*****spend** (sspênd) *v* gastar; pasar

sphere (ssfi⁰) *n* esfera *f*

spice (sspaiss) *n* especia *f*

spiced (sspaisst) *adj* condimentado

spicy (sspai-ssi) *adj* picante

spider (sspai-dö) *n* araña *f*; **spider's web** telaraña *f*

*****spill** (sspil) *v* *verter

*****spin** (sspin) *v* hilar; *hacer girar

spinach (sspi-nidʒ) *n* espinacas *fpl*

spine (sspain) *n* espinazo *m*

spinster (sspin-sstö) *n* solterona *f*

spire (sspai⁰) *n* aguja *f*

spirit (*sspi*-rit) *n* espíritu *m*; ánimo *m*; humor *m*; **spirits** bebidas espirituosas; moral *f*; ~ **stove** calentador de alcohol

spiritual (*sspi*-ri-chu-öl) *adj* espiritual

spit (sspit) *n* esputo *m*, saliva *f*; espetón *m*

***spit** (sspit) *v* escupir

spit: in ~ of (in sspait ov) a pesar de

spiteful (*sspait*-föl) *adj* malévolo

splash (ssplæʃ) *v* salpicar

splendid (*ssplên*-did) *adj* magnífico, espléndido

splendo(u)r (*ssplên*-dö) *n* esplendor *m*

splint (ssplint) *n* tablilla *f*

splinter (*ssplin*-tö) *n* astilla *f*

***split** (ssplit) *v* *hender

***spoil** (sspoil) *v* echar a perder; mimar

spoke[1] (sspouk) *v* (p speak)

spoke[2] (sspouk) *n* radio *m*

sponge (sspandʒ) *n* esponja *f*

spook (sspuuk) *n* fantasma *m*

spool (sspuul) *n* bobina *f*

spoon (sspuun) *n* cuchara *f*

spoonful (*sspuun*-ful) *n* cucharada *f*

sport (sspoot) *n* deporte *m*

sports car (*sspootss*-kaa) *n* coche de carreras

sports jacket (*sspootss*-dʒæ-kit) *n* chaqueta de deporte

sportsman (*sspootss*-mön) *n* (pl -men) deportista *m*

sportswoman (*sspootss*-ᵘu-mön) *n* (pl -women) deportista *f*

sportswear (*sspootss*-ᵘêᵒ) *n* conjunto de deporte

spot (sspot) *n* mancha *f*; lugar *m*, puesto *m*

spotless (*sspot*-löss) *adj* inmaculado

spotlight (*sspot*-lait) *n* foco *m*, proyector *m*

spotted (*sspo*-tid) *adj* moteado; manchado

spout (sspaut) *n* chorro *m*; pico *m*; conducto *m*

sprain (ssprein) *v* *torcerse; *n* torcedura *f*

spray (ssprei) *n* rociada *f*; spray *m*; aerosol *m*; *v* rociar; echar spray (a)

***spread** (ssprêd) *v* *extender

spring (sspring) *n* primavera *f*; muelle *m*; manantial *m*

springtime (*sspring*-taim) *n* primavera *f*

sprouts (ssprautss) *pl* col de Bruselas

spy (sspai) *n* espía *m*

squadron (*ssk*ᵘo-drön) *n* escuadrilla *f*

square (sskᵘêᵒ) *adj* cuadrado; *n* cuadrado *m*; plaza *f*

squash (sskᵘoʃ) *n* zumo *m*; *Am* calabacín

squeeze (sskᵘiis) *n* apretón *m*; *v* apretar; exprimir

squirrel (*ssk*ᵘi-röl) *n* ardilla *f*

squirt (sskᵘööt) *n* chorretada *f*

stable (*sstei*-böl) *adj* estable; *n* establo *m*

stack (sstæk) *n* montón *m*

stadium (*sstei*-di-öm) *n* estadio *m*

staff (sstaaf) *n* personal *m*; palo *m*; vara *f*

stage (ssteidʒ) *n* escenario *m*; fase *f*; etapa *f*

stain (sstein) *v* manchar; *n* mancha *f*; **stained glass** vidrio de color; ~ **remover** quitamanchas *m*

stainless (*sstein*-löss) *adj* inmaculado; ~ **steel** acero inoxidable

staircase (*sstêᵒ*-keiss) *n* escalera *f*

stairs (sstêᵒs) *pl* escalera *f*

stale (ssteil) *adj* viejo, viciado, rancio

stall (sstool) *n* puesto *m*; butaca *f*

stamp (sstæmp) *n* sello *m*; *v* sellar; patear; *n* estampilla *fMe*; ~ **machine** máquina expendedora de sellos

stand (sstænd) *n* puesto *m*; tribuna *f*

***stand** (sstænd) *v* *estar de pie

standard (*sstæn*-död) *n* norma *f*; normal; ~ **of living** nivel de vida

stanza (*sstæn*-sö) *n* estrofa *f*

staple (*sstei*-pöl) *n* grapa *f*

star (sstaa) *n* estrella *f*

starboard (*sstaa*-böd) *n* estribor *m*

stare (sstê°) *v* mirar fijamente

starling (*sstaa*-ling) *n* estornino *m*

start (sstaat) *v* *empezar; *n* comienzo *m*

starting point (*sstaa*-ting-point) *n* punto de partida

state (ssteit) *n* Estado *m*; estado *m*; *v* declarar; **the States** Estados Unidos

statement (*ssteit*-mönt) *n* declaración *f*

statesman (*ssteitss*-mön) *n* (pl -men) estadista *m*

station (*sstei*-ʃön) *n* estación *f*; puesto *m*

stationary (*sstei*-ʃö-nö-ri) *adj* estacionario

stationer's (*sstei*-ʃö-nös) *n* papelería *f*

stationery (*sstei*-ʃö-nö-ri) *n* papelería *f*

statistics (sstö-*ti*-sstikss) *pl* estadística *f*

statue (*sstæ*-chuu) *n* estatua *f*

stay (sstei) *v* quedarse; hospedarse; *n* estancia *f*

steadfast (*sstêd*-faasst) *adj* constante

steady (*sstê*-di) *adj* firme

steak (ssteik) *n* biftec *m*

*steal (sstiil) *v* hurtar; robar

steam (sstiim) *n* vapor *m*

steamer (*sstii*-mö) *n* vapor *m*

steel (sstiil) *n* acero *m*

steep (sstiip) *adj* empinado

steeple (*sstii*-pöl) *n* campanario *m*

steer (sstii°) *v* dirigir; conducir; *L.Am.* manejar; gobernar; navigar

steering column (*sstii°*-ring-ko-löm) *n* columna del volante

steering wheel (*sstii°*-ring-ᵘiil) *n* volante *m*

steersman (*sstii°s*-mön) *n* (pl -men) timonel *m*

stem (sstêm) *n* tallo *m*; caña *f*

step (sstêp) *n* paso *m*; peldaño *m*; *v* pisar

stepchild (*sstêp*-chaild) *n* (pl -children) hijastro(a) *m/f*

stepfather (*sstêp*-faa-ðö) *n* padrastro *m*

stepmother (*sstêp*-ma-ðö) *n* madrastra *f*

stereo (*ssti*-ri-ou) *n* equipo *m* de música

sterile (*sstê*-rail) *adj* estéril

sterilize (*sstê*-ri-lais) *v* esterilizar

steward (*sstyuu*-öd) *n* mayordomo *m*; camarero *m*

stewardess (*sstyuu*-ö-dêss) *n* azafata *f*

stick (sstik) *n* palo *m*

*stick (sstik) *v* pegar; clavar; fijar

sticky (*ssti*-ki) *adj* pegajoso

stiff (sstif) *adj* tieso; rígido

still (sstil) *adv* todavía; sin embargo; *adj* quieto

stimulant (*ssti*-myu-lönt) *n* estimulante *m*

stimulate (*ssti*-myu-leit) *v* estimular

sting (ssting) *n* picadura *f*

*sting (ssting) *v* picar

stingy (*sstin*-dʒi) *adj* mezquino

*stink (sstingk) *v* apestar

stipulate (*ssti*-pyu-leit) *v* estipular

stipulation (ssti-pyu-*lei*-ʃön) *n* estipulación *f*

stir (sstöö) *v* *mover; *revolver

stitch (sstich) *n* punto *m*, punzada *f*; sutura *f*

stock (sstok) *n* existencias *fpl*; *v* *tener en existencia; ~ **exchange** bolsa de valores, bolsa *f*; ~ **market** bolsa *f*; **stocks and shares** acciones *fpl*

stocking (*ssto*-king) *n* media *f*

stole¹ (sstoul) *v* (p steal)

stole² (sstoul) *n* estola *f*

stomach (*ssta*-mök) *n* estómago *m*

stomachache (*ssta*-mö-keik) *n* dolor de estómago

stone (sstoun) *n* piedra *f*; hueso *m*; **pumice ~** piedra pómez

stood (sstud) *v* (p, pp stand)

stop (sstop) *v* cesar; dejar de; *n* parada *f*; **stop!** ¡alto!

stopper (*ssto*-pö) *n* tapón *m*

storage (*sstoo*-ridʒ) *n* almacenaje *m*

store (sstoo) *n* tienda *f*; almacén *m*; *v* almacenar

storehouse (*sstoo*-hauss) *n* almacén *m*

stor(e)y (*sstoo*-ri) *n* piso *m*

stork (sstook) *n* cigüeña *f*

storm (sstoom) *n* tormenta *f*

stormy (*sstoo*-mi) *adj* tempestuoso

story (*sstoo*-ri) *n* cuento *m*

stout (sstaut) *adj* gordo, corpulento

stove (sstouv) *n* estufa *f*; cocina *f*

straight (sstreit) *adj* derecho; honesto; *adv* directamente; **~ ahead** todo seguido; **~ away** directamente, en seguida; **~ on** todo seguido

strain (sstrein) *n* esfuerzo *m*; tensión *f*; *v* *forzar; filtrar

strainer (*sstrei*-nö) *n* escurridor *m*

strange (sstreindʒ) *adj* extraño; raro

stranger (*sstrein*-dʒö) *n* extranjero *m*, -a *f*; forastero *m*, -a *f*; desconocido *m*, -a *f*

strangle (*sstræng*-ghöl) *v* estrangular

strap (sstræp) *n* correa *f*

straw (sstroo) *n* paja *f*

strawberry (*sstroo*-bö-ri) *n* fresa *f*

stream (sstriim) *n* arroyo *m*; corriente *f*; *v* *fluir

street (sstriit) *n* calle *f*

streetcar (*sstriit*-kaa) *nAm* tranvía *m*

strength (sstrêngz) *n* fuerza *f*, vigor *m*

stress (sstrêss) *n* esfuerzo *m*; énfasis *m*; *v* acentuar

stretch (sstrêch) *v* estirar; *n* trecho *m*

strict (sstrikt) *adj* estricto; severo

strife (sstraif) *n* lucha *f*

strike (sstraik) *n* huelga *f*

*strike (sstraik) *v* golpear; atacar; impresionar; *estar en huelga; arriar

striking (*sstrai*-king) *adj* impresionante, notable, vistoso

string (sstring) *n* cordel *m*; cuerda *f*

strip (sstrip) *n* faja *f*

stripe (sstraip) *n* raya *f*

striped (sstraipt) *adj* rayado

stroke (sstrouk) *n* ataque *m*; golpe *m*

stroll (sstroul) *v* pasear; *n* paseo *m*

strong (sstrong) *adj* fuerte

stronghold (*sstrong*-hould) *n* plaza fuerte

structure (*sstrak*-chö) *n* estructura *f*

struggle (*sstra*-ghöl) *n* combate *m*, lucha *f*; *v* luchar

stub (sstab) *n* talón *m*

stubborn (*ssta*-bön) *adj* testarudo

student (*sstyuu*-dönt) *n* estudiante *m*; estudiante *f*

study (*ssta*-di) *v* estudiar; *n* estudio *m*; despacho *m*

stuff (sstaf) *n* substancia *f*; cachivache *m*

stuffed (sstaft) *adj* rellenado; **stuffed animal** muñeco de peluche

stuffing (*ssta*-fing) *n* relleno *m*

stuffy (*ssta*-fi) *adj* sofocante

stumble (*sstam*-böl) *v* *tropezarse

stung (sstang) *v* (p, pp sting)

stupid (*sstyuu*-pid) *adj* estúpido

style (sstail) *n* estilo *m*; **stylish** elegante

subject¹ (*ssab*-dʒikt) *n* sujeto *m*; súbdito *m*; **~ to** sujeto a

subject² (ssöb-*dʒêkt*) *v* someter

submarine (ssab-mö-*riin*) *submarino *m*

submit (ssöb-*mit*) *v* someterse

subordinate (ssö-*boo*-di-nöt) *adj*

subalterno; subordinado

subscriber (ssöb-*sskrai*-bö) *n* abonado *m*, -a *f*; suscriptor *m*, -a *f*

subscription (ssöb-*sskrip*-ʃön) *n* abono *f*

subsequent (ssab-ssi-kʷönt) *adj* posterior

subsidy (ssab-ssi-di) *n* subsidio *m*

substance (ssab-sstönss) *n* sustancia *f*

substantial (ssöb-sstæn-ʃöl) *adj* material; real; sustancial

substitute (ssab-ssti-tyuut) *v* *sustituir; *n* sustituto *m*, -a *f*

subtitle (ssab-tai-töl) *n* subtítulo *m*

subtle (ssa-töl) *adj* sutil

subtract (ssöb-*trækt*) *v* restar

suburb (ssa-bööb) *n* suburbio *m*

suburban (ssö-*böö*-bön) *adj* suburbano

subway (ssab-ʷei) *nAm* metro *m*

succeed (ssök-*ssiid*) *v* *tener éxito; suceder

success (ssök-*ssêss*) *n* éxito *m*

successful (ssök-*ssêss*-föl) *adj* exitoso

succumb (ssö-*kam*) *v* sucumbir

such (ssach) *adj* tal; *adv* tan; ~ **as** tal como

suck (ssak) *v* chupar

sudden (ssa-dön) *adj* súbito

suddenly (ssa-dön-li) *adv* repentinamente

suede (ssʷeid) *n* gamuza *f*

suffer (ssa-fö) *v* sufrir

suffering (ssa-fö-ring) *n* sufrimiento *m*

suffice (ssö-*faiss*) *v* bastar

sufficient (ssö-*fi*-ʃönt) *adj* suficiente, bastante

suffrage (ssa-fridʒ) *n* derecho electoral, sufragio *m*

sugar (ʃu-ghö) *n* azúcar *m/f*

suggest (ssö-*dʒêsst*) *v* *sugerir

suggestion (ssö-*dʒêss*-chön) *n* sugestión *f*

suicide (ssuu-i-ssaid) *n* suicidio *m*

suit (ssuut) *v* *convenir; adaptar; *ir bien; *n* traje *m*

suitable (ssuu-tö-böl) *adj* apropiado, apto

suitcase (ssuut-keiss) *n* maleta *f*

suite (ssʷiit) *n* apartamento *m*

sum (ssam) *n* suma *f*

summary (ssa-mö-ri) *n* resumen *m*, sumario *m*

summer (ssa-mö) *n* verano *m*; ~ **time** horario de verano

summit (ssa-mit) *n* cima *f*

sun (ssan) *n* sol *m*

sunbathe (ssan-beið) *v* tomar el sol

sunburn (ssan-böön) *n* quemadura del sol

Sunday (ssan-di) domingo *m*

sunglasses (ssan-ghlaa-ssis) *pl* gafas de sol

sunlight (ssan-lait) *n* luz del sol

sunny (ssa-ni) *adj* soleado

sunrise (ssan-rais) *n* amanecer *m*

sunset (ssan-ssêt) *n* ocaso *m*

sunshade (ssan-ʃeid) *n* quitasol *m*

sunshine (ssan-ʃain) *n* sol *m*

sunstroke (ssan-sstrouk) *n* insolación *f*

suntan oil (ssan-tæn-oil) aceite bronceador

super (ssuu-pö) *adj* colloquial genial, estupendo ; *n* portero *m*, -a *f*

superb (ssu-*pööb*) *adj* grandioso, soberbio

superficial (ssuu-pö-*fi*-ʃöl) *adj* superficial

superfluous (ssu-*pöö*-flu-öss) *adj* superfluo

superior (ssu-*piˀ*-ri-ö) *adj* mejor, mayor, superior

superlative (ssu-*pöö*-lö-tiv) *adj* superlativo; *n* superlativo *m*

supermarket (ssuu-pö-maa-kit) *n* supermercado *m*

superstition (ssuu-pö-*ssti*-ʃön) *n*
supersticion *f*

supervise (*ssuu*-pö-vais) *v* supervisar

supervision (ssuu-pö-*vi*-ʒön) *n*
supervisión *f*

supervisor (*ssuu*-pö-vai-sö) *n*
supervisor *m*, -a *f*

supper (*ssa*-pö) *n* cena *f*

supple (*ssa*-pöl) *adj* flexible, ágil

supplement (*ssa*-pli-mönt) *n*
suplemento *m*

supply (ssö-*plai*) *n* abastecimiento *m*,
suministro *m*; existencias *fpl*; oferta *f*;
v suministrar

support (ssö-*poot*) *v* apoyar,
*sostener, soportar; *n* apoyo *m*; ~
hose medias elásticas

supporter (ssö-*poo*-tö) *n* aficionado
m, -a *f*; partidario *m*, -a *f*; seguidor *m*,
-a *f*

suppose (ssö-*pous*) *v* *suponer;
supposing that dado que

suppository (ssö-*po*-si-tö-ri) *n*
supositorio *m*

suppress (ssö-*prêss*) *v* reprimir

surcharge (*ssöö*-chaadʒ) *n* sobretasa *f*

sure (ʃuᵒ) *adj* seguro

surely (ʃuᵒ-li) *adv* seguramente

surface (*ssöö*-fiss) *n* superficie *f*

surfboard (*ssööf*-bood) *n* tabla para
surf

surgeon (*ssöö*-dʒön) *n* cirujano *m*;
veterinary ~ veterinario *m*

surgery (*ssöö*-dʒö-ri) *n* operación *f*;
consultorio *m*

surname (*ssöö*-neim) *n* apellido *m*

surplus (*ssöö*-plöss) *n* sobra *f*

surprise (ssö-*prais*) *n* sorpresa *f*; *v*
sorprender; extrañar

surrender (ssö-*rên*-dö) *v* *rendirse; *n*
rendición *f*

surround (ssö-*raund*) *v* rodear, cercar

surrounding (ssö-*raun*-ding) *adj*
circundante

surroundings (ssö-*raun*-dings) *pl*
alrededores *mpl*

survey (*ssöö*-vei) *n* resumen *m*;
encuesta *f*

survival (ssö-*vai*-völ) *n* supervivencia
f

survive (ssö-*vaiv*) *v* sobrevivir

suspect¹ (ssö-*sspêkt*) *v* sospechar

suspect² (*ssa*-sspêkt) *n* persona
sospechosa

suspend (ssö-*sspênd*) *v* suspender

suspenders (ssö-*sspên*-dös) *plAm*
tirantes *mpl*

suspension (ssö-*sspên*-ʃön) *n*
suspensión *f*; ~ **bridge** puente
colgante

suspicion (ssö-*sspi*-ʃön) *n* sospecha *f*;
suspicacia *f*, desconfianza *f*

suspicious (ssö-*sspi*-ʃöss) *adj*
sospechoso; suspicaz, desconfiado

sustain (ssö-*sstein*) *v* soportar

Swahili (ssᵘö-*hii*-li) *n* suahili *m*

swallow (*ssᵘo*-lou) *v* tragar; *n*
golondrina *f*

swam (ssᵘæm) *v* (p swim)

swamp (ssᵘomp) *n* marisma *f*

swan (ssᵘon) *n* cisne *m*

swap (ssᵘop) *v* *trocar

***swear** (ssᵘêᵉ) *v* jurar

sweat (ssᵘêt) *n* sudor *m*; *v* sudar

sweater (*ssᵘê*-tö) *n* suéter *m*

Swede (ssᵘiid) *n* sueco *m*

Sweden (ssᵘii-dön) Suecia *f*

Swedish (ssᵘii-diʃ) *adj* sueco

***sweep** (ssᵘiip) *v* barrer

sweet (ssᵘiit) *adj* dulce; lindo; *n*
caramelo *m*; dulce *m*

sweeten (ssᵘii-tön) *v* endulzar

sweetheart (ssᵘiit-haat) *n* amor *m*,
querida *f*

sweetshop (ssᵘiit-ʃop) *n* confitería *f*

swell (ssᵘêl) *adj* estupendo

***swell** (ssᵘêl) *v* hincharse

swelling (ssᵘê-ling) *n* hinchazón *f*

swift (ss^{u}ift) *adj* veloz

***swim** (ss^{u}im) *v* nadar

swimmer (ss^{u}i-mö) *n* nadador *m*, -a *f*

swimming (ss^{u}i-ming) *n* natación *f*; ~ **pool** piscina *f*

swim(ming) trunks (ss^{u}i-ming-trangkss) *n* calzón de baño, bañador

swimsuit (ss^{u}im-ssuut) *n* traje de baño

swindle (ss^{u}in-döl) *v* estafar; *n* estafa *f*

swindler (ss^{u}in-dlö) *n* estafador *m*, -a *f*

swing (ss^{u}ing) *n* columpio *m*

***swing** (ss^{u}ing) *v* oscilar; columpiarse

Swiss (ss^{u}iss) *adj* suizo

switch (ss^{u}ich) *n* interruptor *m*; *v* cambiar; ~ **off** apagar; ~ **on** *encender

switchboard (ss^{u}ich-bood) *n* cuadro de distribución

Switzerland (ss^{u}it-ssö-lönd) Suiza *f*

sword (ssood) *n* espada *f*

swum (ss^{u}am) *v* (pp swim)

syllable (ssi-lö-böl) *n* sílaba *f*

symbol (ssim-böl) *n* símbolo *m*

sympathetic (ssim-pö-zê-tik) *adj* cordial, compasivo

sympathy (ssim-pö-zi) *n* simpatía *f*; compasión *f*

symphony (ssim-fö-ni) *n* sinfonía *f*

symptom (ssim-töm) *n* síntoma *m*

synagogue (ssi-nö-ghogh) *n* sinagoga *f*

synonym (ssi-nö-nim) *n* sinónimo *m*

synthetic (ssin-zê-tik) *adj* sintético

Syria (ssi-ri-ö) Siria *f*

Syrian (ssi-ri-ön) *adj* sirio

syringe (ssi-*rind*3) *n* jeringa *f*

syrup (ssi-röp) *n* jarabe *m*

system (ssi-sstöm) *n* sistema *m*; **decimal** ~ sistema decimal

systematic (ssi-sstö-*mæ*-tik) *adj* sistemático

T

table (tei-böl) *n* mesa *f*; tabla *f*; ~ **of contents** índice *m*; ~ **tennis** tenis de mesa

tablecloth (tei-böl-kloz) *n* mantel *m*

tablespoon (tei-böl-sspuun) *n* cuchara *f*

tablet (*tæ*-blit) *n* pastilla *f*

taboo (tö-*buu*) *n* tabú *m*

tactics (*tæk*-tikss) *pl* táctica *f*

tag (tægh) *n* cabo *m*; etiqueta *f*

tail (teil) *n* cola *f*; rabo *m*

taillight (*teil*-lait) *n* farol trasero

tailor (*tei*-lö) *n* sastre *m*

tailor-made (*tei*-lö-meid) *adj* hecho a la medida

***take** (teik) *v* coger; tomar; llevar; comprender, *entender; ~ **away**

quitar; llevarse; ~ **off** despegar; ~ **out** sacar; ~ **over** encargarse de; ~ **place** *tener lugar; ~ **up** ocupar

take-off (*tei*-kof) *n* despegue *m*

tale (teil) *n* cuento *m*

talent (*tæ*-lönt) *n* talento *m*

talented (*tæ*-lön-tid) *adj* talentoso

talk (took) *v* hablar; *n* conversación *f*

talkative (*too*-kö-tiv) *adj* locuaz

tall (tool) *adj* alto

tame (teim) *adj* manso, domesticado; *v* domesticar

tampon (*tæm*-pön) *n* tapón *m*; tampón *m*

tangerine (tæn-d3ö-*riin*) *n* mandarina *f*

tangible (*tæn*-d3i-böl) *adj* tangible;

palpable

tank (tængk) *n* tanque *m*; depósito *m*

tanker (*tæng*-kö) *n* petrolero *m*

tanned (tænd) *adj* bronceado

tap (tæp) *n* grifo *m*; golpecito *m*; *v* golpear

tape (teip) *n* cinta *f*; **adhesive ~** cinta adhesiva; esparadrapo *m*

tape recorder (*teip*-ri-koo-dö) *n* magnetófono *m*

tar (taa) *n* brea *f*; alquitrán *m*

target (*taa*-ghit) *n* objetivo *m*, blanco *m*

tariff (*tæ*-rif) *n* arancel *m*; tarifa *f*

task (taassk) *n* tarea *f*

taste (teisst) *n* gusto *m*; *v* *saber a; *probar

tasteless (*teisst*-löss) *adj* insípido

tasty (*tei*-ssti) *adj* rico, sabroso

taught (toot) *v* (p, pp teach)

tavern (*tæ*-vön) *n* taberna *f*

tax (tækss) *n* impuesto *m*; *v* *imponer contribuciones

taxation (tæk-*ssei*-ʃön) *n* impuesto *m*

tax-free (*tækss*-frii) *adj* libre de impuestos

taxi (*tæk*-ssi) *n* taxi *m*; **~ driver** taxista *m/f*; **~ rank** parada de taxis; **~ stand** *Am* parada de taxis

taximeter (*tæk*-ssi-mii-tö) *n* taxímetro *m*

tea (tii) *n* té *m*; merienda *f*

***teach** (tiich) *v* enseñar

teacher (*tii*-chö) *n* profesor *m*, -a *f*, maestro *m*, -a *f*; institutor *m*

teachings (*tii*-chings) *pl* enseñanza *f*

tea cloth (*tii*-kloz) *n* trapo de cocina

teacup (*tii*-kap) *n* taza de té

team (tiim) *n* equipo *m*

teapot (*tii*-pot) *n* tetera *f*

tear[1] (ti°) *n* lágrima *f*

tear[2] (tê°) *n* rasgón *m*; ***tear** *v* desgarrar

tearjerker (*ti°*-dʒöö-kö) *n* obra

lacrimosa

tease (tiis) *v* tomar el pelo

tea set (*tii*-ssêt) *n* juego de té

tea-shop (*tii*-ʃop) *n* salón de té

teaspoon (*tii*-sspuun) *n* cucharilla *f*

teaspoonful (*tii*-sspuun-ful) *n* cucharadita *f*

technical (*têk*-ni-köl) *adj* técnico

technician (têk-*ni*-ʃön) *n* técnico *m*

technique (têk-*niik*) *n* técnica *f*

technological (têk-nö-*lo*-dʒi-köl) *adj* tecnológico

technology (têk-*no*-lö-dʒi) *n* tecnología *f*

teenager (*tii*-nei-dʒö) *n* adolescente *m/f*

teetotaller (tii-*tou*-tö-lö) *n* abstemio *m*

telepathy (ti-*lê*-pö-zi) *n* telepatía *f*

telephone (*tê*-li-foun) *n* teléfono *m*; **~ book** *Am* listín telefónico, guía telefónica; **~ booth** cabina telefónica; **~ call** llamada telefónica; **~ directory** guía telefónica, listín telefónico; directorio telefónico *Me*; **~ exchange** central telefónica

television (*tê*-li-vi-ʒön) *n* televisión *f*; **~ set** televisor *m*; **cable ~** televisión por cable; **satellite ~** televisión por satélite

telex (*tê*-lêkss) *n* télex *m*

***tell** (têl) *v* *decir; *contar

temper (*têm*-pö) *n* humor *m*; disposición *f*

temperature (*têm*-prö-chö) *n* temperatura *f*

tempest (*têm*-pisst) *n* tempestad *f*

temple (*têm*-pöl) *n* templo *m*; sien *f*

temporary (*têm*-pö-rö-ri) *adj* provisional, temporal

tempt (têmpt) *v* *tentar

temptation (têmp-*tei*-ʃön) *n* tentación *f*

ten (tên) *num* diez

tenant (*tê*-nönt) *n* inquilino *m*

tend (tênd) *v* *tender a; cuidar de; ~ **to** *tender a

tendency (*tên*-dön-ssi) *n* inclinación *f*, tendencia *f*

tender (*tên*-dö) *adj* tierno, delicado

tendon (*tên*-dön) *n* tendón *m*

tennis (*tê*-niss) *n* tenis *m*; ~ **court** campo de tenis, cancha *f*; ~ **shoes** zapatos de tenis

tense (tênss) *adj* tenso; tieso; *n* tiempo *m*

tension (*tên*-ʃön) *n* tensión *m*

tent (tênt) *n* tienda *f* de campaña

tenth (tênz) *num* décimo

tepid (*tê*-pid) *adj* tibio

term (tööm) *n* término *m*; período *m*, plazo *m*; condición *f*

terminal (*töö*-mi-nöl) *n* estación terminal; *adj* mortal

terrace (*tê*-röss) *n* terraza *f*

terrain (*tê-rein*) *n* terreno *m*

terrible (*tê*-ri-böl) *adj* tremendo, terrible, pésimo

terrific (tö-*ri*-fik) *adj* fantástico; estupendo

terrify (*tê*-ri-fai) *v* aterrorizar; **terrifying** aterrador

territory (*tê*-ri-tö-ri) *n* territorio *m*

terror (*tê*-rö) *n* terror *m*

terrorism (*tê*-rö-ri-söm) *n* terrorismo *m*, terror *m*

terrorist (*tê*-rö-risst) *n* terrorista *m/f*

test (têsst) *n* prueba *f*, ensayo *m*; *v* *probar, ensayar

testify (*tê*-ssti-fai) *v* testimoniar

text (têksst) *n* texto *m*

textbook (*têkss*-buk) *n* libro de texto

textile (*têk*-sstail) *n* textil *m*

texture (*têkss*-chö) *n* textura *f*

Thai (tai) *adj* tailandés

Thailand (*tai*-lænd) Tailandia *f*

than (ðæn) *conj* que

thank (zængk) *v* *agradecer; ~ **you** gracias

thankful (*zængk*-föl) *adj* agradecido

that (ðæt) *adj* aquel, ese; *pron* aquél, eso; que; *conj* que

thaw (zoo) *v* descongelarse; *n* deshielo *m*

the (ðö, ði) *art* el *art*; **the ... the** cuanto más ... más

theater *Am*, **theatre** (*ziᵒ*-tö) *n* teatro *m*

theft (zêft) *n* robo *m*; hurto *m*

their (ðêᵒ) *adj* su

them (ðêm) *pron* les

theme (ziim) *n* tema *m*, sujeto *m*

themselves (ðöm-*ssêlvs*) *pron* se; ellos mismos

then (ðên) *adv* entonces; después; en tal caso

theology (zi-o-lö-dʒi) *n* teología *f*

theoretical (zi*ᵒ*-*rê*-ti-köl) *adj* teórico

theory (*ziᵒ*-ri) *n* teoría *f*

therapy (*zê*-rö-pi) *v* terapia *f*

there (ðêᵒ) *adv* allí; hacia allá

therefore (*ðêᵒ*-foo) *conj* por lo tanto

thermometer (zö-*mo*-mi-tö) *n* termómetro *m*

thermostat (*zöö*-mö-sstæt) *n* termostato *m*

these (ðiis) *adj* éstos

thesis (*zii*-ssiss) *n* (pl theses) tesis *f*

they (ðei) *pron* ellos

thick (zik) *adj* espeso; denso

thicken (*zi*-kön) *v* espesar

thickness (*zik*-nöss) *n* espesor *m*

thief (ziif) *n* (pl thieves) ladrón *m*, ladrona *f*

thigh (zai) *n* muslo *m*

thimble (*zim*-böl) *n* dedal *m*

thin (zin) *adj* delgado; flaco

thing (zing) *n* cosa *f*

*think (zingk) *v* *pensar; reflexionar; ~ **of** *pensar en; *recordar; ~ **over** considerar

third (zööd) *num* tercero

thirst (zöösst) n sed f

thirsty (zöö-ssti) adj sediento

thirteen (zöö-tíin) num trece

thirteenth (zöö-tíinz) num treceno

thirtieth (zöö-ti-öz) num treintavo

thirty (zöö-ti) num treinta

this (ðiss) adj este, esto; pron éste

thistle (zi-ssöl) n cardo m

thorn (zoon) n espina f

thorough (za-rö) adj minucioso

thoroughfare (za-rö-fê⁰) n ruta principal, arteria principal

those (ðous) adj aquellos; pron aquéllos

though (ðou) conj si bien, aunque; adv sin embargo

thought¹ (zoot) v (p, pp think)

thought² (zoot) n pensamiento m

thoughtful (zoot-föl) adj pensativo; atento

thousand (zau-sönd) num mil

thread (zrêd) n hilo m; v enhebrar

threadbare (zrêd-bê⁰) adj gastado

threat (zrêt) n amenaza f

threaten (zrê-tön) v amenazar **threatening** amenazador

three (zrii) num tres

three-quarter (zrii-kᵘoo-tö) adj tres cuartos

threshold (zrê-fould) n umbral m

threw (zruu) v (p throw)

thrifty (zrif-ti) adj económico

throat (zrout) n garganta f

throne (zroun) n trono m

through (zruu) prep a través de

throughout (zruu-aut) adv por todas partes

throw (zrou) n lanzamiento m

*****throw** (zrou) v tirar, arrojar

thrush (zraf) n tordo m

thumb (zam) n pulgar m

thumbtack (zam-tæk) nAm chinche f

thump (zamp) v golpear; aporrear

thunder (zan-dö) n trueno m; v

*****tronar**

thunderstorm (zan-dö-sstoom) n tronada f

thundery (zan-dö-ri) adj tormentoso

Thursday (zöös-di) jueves m

thus (ðass) adv así; por consiguiente

thyme (taim) n tomillo m

tick (tik) n señal f; ~ **off** señalar; fastidiar

ticket (ti-kit) n billete m; multa f; boleto mMe; ~ **collector** revisor m; ~ **office** taquilla f

tickle (ti-köl) v cosquillear

tide (taid) n marea f; **high** ~ pleamar f; **low** ~ bajamar f

tidy (tai-di) adj arreglado; limpio, aseado; ~ **up** arreglar

tie (tai) v anudar, atar; n corbata f

tiger (tai-ghö) n tigre m

tight (tait) adj estrecho; angosto, apretado; adv fuertemente

tighten (tai-tön) v estrechar, *apretar; estrecharse

tights (taitss) pl traje de malla

tile (tail) n azulejo m; teja f

till (til) prep hasta; conj hasta que

timber (tim-bö) n madera de construcción

time (taim) n tiempo m; vez f; hora f; época f; **all the** ~ continuamente; **in** ~ a tiempo; ~ **of arrival** hora de llegada; ~ **of departure** hora de salida

time-saving (taim-ssei-ving) adj que economiza tiempo

timetable (taim-tei-böl) n horario m

timid (ti-mid) adj tímido

timidity (ti-mi-dö-ti) n timidez f

tin (tin) n estaño m; lata f; ~ **opener** abrelatas m; **tinned food** conservas fpl

tinfoil (tin-foil) n papel de estaño

tiny (tai-ni) adj menudo

tip (tip) n punta f; propina f

tire¹ (tai⁰) n neumático m; llanta fMe

tire² (tai°) v cansar

tired (tai°d) adj cansado; **~ of** harto de

tissue (ti-ʃuu) n tejido m; pañuelo de papel

title (tai-töl) n título m

to (tuu) prep hasta; a, para, en, hacia

toad (toud) n sapo m

toadstool (toud-sstuul) n hongo m venenoso

toast (tousst) n pan tostado; brindis m

tobacco (tö-bæ-kou) n (pl ~s) tabaco m; **~ pouch** petaca f

tobacconist (tö-bæ-kö-nisst) n estanquero m; **tobacconist's** estanco m

today (tö-dei) adv hoy

toddler (tod-lö) n niño que empieza a andar

toe (tou) n dedo del pie

toffee (to-fi) n caramelo m

together (tö-ghê-ðö) adv juntos

toilet (toi-löt) n retrete m; **~ case** neceser m; **~ paper** papel higiénico

toiletry (toi-lö-tri) n artículos de tocador

token (tou-kön) n señal f; prueba f; ficha f

told (tould) v (p, pp tell)

tolerable (to-lö-rö-böl) adj tolerable

toll (toul) n peaje m

tomato (tö-maa-tou) n (pl ~es) tomate m; jitomate mMe

tomb (tuum) n tumba f

tombstone (tuum-sstoun) n lápida f

tomorrow (tö-mo-rou) adv mañana

ton (tan) n tonelada f

tone (toun) n tono m; timbre m

tongs (tongs) pl tenazas f

tongue (tang) n lengua f

tonic (to-nik) n tónico m

tonight (tö-nait) adv esta noche

tonsilitis (ton-ssö-lai-tiss) n amigdalitis f

tonsils (ton-ssöls) pl amígdalas fpl

too (tuu) adv demasiado; también

took (tuk) v (p take)

tool (tuul) n herramienta f; **~ kit** bolsa de herramientas

tooth (tuuz) n (pl teeth) diente m

toothache (tuu-zeik) n dolor de muelas

toothbrush (tuuz-braʃ) n cepillo de dientes

toothpaste (tuuz-peisst) n pasta dentífrica

toothpick (tuuz-pik) n palillo m

toothpowder (tuuz-pau-dö) n polvo para los dientes

top (top) n cima f; cumbre f; tapa f; **on ~ of** encima de; **~ side** parte superior

topic (to-pik) n asunto m; tema m

topical (to-pi-köl) adj actual

torch (tooch) n antorcha f; linterna f

torment¹ (too-mênt) v atormentar

torment² (too-mênt) n tormento m

torture (too-chö) n tortura f; v torturar

toss (toss) v lanzar al aire; sacudir

tot (tot) n niño pequeño

total (tou-töl) adj total; completo, absoluto; n total m

totalitarian (tou-tæ-li-tê°-ri-ön) adj totalitario

touch (tach) v tocar; *concernir; n contacto m, toque m; tacto m

touching (ta-ching) adj conmovedor

tough (taf) adj duro

tour (tu°) n excursión f; viaje m; v viajar por; recorrer

tourism (tu°-ri-söm) n turismo m

tourist (tu°-risst) n turista m/f; **~ class** clase turista; **~ office** oficina de turismo

tournament (tu°-nö-mönt) n torneo m

tow (tou) v remolcar

towards (tö-ᵘoods) prep hacia; para con

towel (tau°l) n toalla f

towel(l)ing (tau°-ling) n tela para

toallas

tower (tau⁰) *n* torre *f*

town (taun) *n* ciudad *f*; **~ center** *Am*, **~ centre** centro de la ciudad; **~ hall** ayuntamiento *m*

townspeople (*tauns*-pii-pöl) *pl* ciudadanos *mpl*

toxic (*tok*-ssik) *adj* tóxico

toy (toi) *n* juguete *m*

toyshop (*toi*-ʃop) *n* juguetería *f*

trace (treiss) *n* huella *f*; *v* rastrear

track (træk) *n* vía *f*; pista *f*

tractor (*træk*-tö) *n* tractor *m*

trade (treid) *n* comercio *m*; oficio *m*; *v* comerciar

trademark (*treid*-maak) *n* marca de fábrica

trader (*trei*-dö) *n* comerciante *m*

tradesman (*treids*-mön) *n* (pl -men) tendero *m*

trade union (treid-*yuu*-nyön) *n* sindicato *m*

tradition (trö-*di*-ʃön) *n* tradición *f*

traditional (trö-*di*-ʃö-nöl) *adj* tradicional

traffic (*træ*-fik) *n* tránsito *m*; **~ jam** embotellamiento *m*; **~ light** semáforo *m*

trafficator (*træ*-fi-kei-tö) *n* indicador *m*

tragedy (*træ*-dʒö-di) *n* tragedia *f*

tragic (*træ*-dʒik) *adj* trágico

trail (treil) *n* rastro *m*, sendero *m*

trailer (*trei*-lö) *n* remolque *m*; *nAm* caravana *f*

train (trein) *n* tren *m*; *v* amaestrar, entrenar; **local ~** tren de cercanías; **through ~** tren directo; **~ ferry** transbordador de trenes

trainee (trei-*nii*) aprendiz *m*, -a *f*

trainer (*trei*-nö) entrenador *m*, -a *f*; adiestrador *m*, -a *f*

training (*trei*-ning) *n* entrenamiento *m*

trait (treit) *n* rasgo *m*

traitor (*trei*-tö) *n* traidor *m*

tram (træm) *n* tranvía *m*

tramp (træmp) *n* vagabundo *m*; *v* vagabundear

tranquil (*træng*-kᵘil) *adj* tranquilo

tranquillizer (*træng*-kᵘi-lai-sö) *n* calmante *m*

transaction (træn-*sæk*-ʃön) *n* transacción *f*

transatlantic (træn-söt-*læn*-tik) *adj* transatlántico

transfer (trænss-*föö*) *v* *transferir

transform (trænss-*foom*) *v* transformar

transformer (trænss-*foo*-mö) *n* transformador *m*

transition (træn-*ssi*-ʃön) *n* transición *f*

translate (trænss-*leit*) *v* *traducir

translation (trænss-*lei*-ʃön) *n* traducción *f*

translator (trænss-*lei*-tö) *n* traductor *m*, **-a** *f*

transmission (trænss-*mi*-ʃön) *n* transmisión *f*

transmit (trænss-*mit*) *v* transmitir

transmitter (trænss-*mi*-tö) *n* emisor *m*

transparent (træn-*sspê*⁰-rönt) *adj* transparente

transport¹ (*træn*-sspoot) *n* transporte *m*

transport² (træn-*sspoot*) *v* transportar

transportation (træn-sspoo-*tei*-ʃön) *n* transporte *m*

trap (træp) *n* trampa *f*

trash (træʃ) *n* basura *f*

travel (*træ*-völ) *v* viajar; **~ agency** agencia de viajes; **~ agent** agente de viajes; **~ agency** agencia de viajes; **~ insurance** seguro de viaje; **travel(l)ing expenses** gastos de viaje

travel(l)er (*træ*-vö-lö) *n* viajero *m*, -a *f*; **traveler's check** *Am*, **traveller's cheque** cheque de viajero

tray (trei) *n* bandeja *f*; charola *fMe*

treason (*trii-*sön) *n* traición *f*

treasure (*trê-*ȝö) *n* tesoro *m*

treasurer (*trê-*ȝö-rö) *n* tesorero *m*

treasury (*trê-*ȝö-ri) *n* Tesorería *f*

treat (triit) *v* tratar; convidar

treatment (*triit-*mönt) *n* tratamiento *m*

treaty (*trii-*ti) *n* tratado *m*

tree (trii) *n* árbol *m*

tremble (*trêm-*böl) *v* *temblar; vibrar

tremendous (tri-*mên-*döss) *adj* tremendo

trendy (*trên-*di) *adj* de moda; moderno

trespass (*trêss-*pöss) *v* infringir

trespasser (*trêss-*pö-ssö) *n* intruso *m*

trial (trai[ö]l) *n* proceso *m*; prueba *f*

triangle (*trai-*æng-ghöl) *n* triángulo *m*

triangular (trai-*æng-*ghyu-lö) *adj* triangular

tribe (traib) *n* tribu *m*

tributary (*tri-*byu-tö-ri) *n* afluente *m*

tribute (*tri-*byuut) *n* homenaje *m*; tributo *m*

trick (trik) *n* truco *m*; trampa *f*; estafa *f*

trigger (*tri-*ghö) *n* gatillo *m*

trim (trim) *v* recortar; cortar; podar

trip (trip) *n* viaje *m*

triumph (*trai-*ömf) *n* triunfo *m*; *v* triunfar

triumphant (trai-*am-*fönt) *adj* triunfante

troops (truupss) *pl* tropas *fpl*

tropical (*tro-*pi-köl) *adj* tropical

tropics (*tro-*pikss) *pl* trópicos *mpl*

trouble (*tra-*böl) *n* preocupación *f*; molestia *f*; aprieto *m*; *v* molestar; inquietar

troublesome (*tra-*böl-ssöm) *adj* molesto

trousers (*trau-*sös) *pl* pantalones *mpl*

trout (traut) *n* (pl ~) trucha *f*

truck (trak) *nAm* camión *m*

true (truu) *adj* verdadero; real, auténtico; leal, fiel

trumpet (*tram-*pit) *n* trompeta *f*

trunk (trangk) *n* baúl *m*; tronco *m*; *nAm* portaequipajes *m*; **trunks** *pl* bañador *m*

trust (trasst) *v* confiar en; *n* confianza *f*

trustworthy (*trasst-*[u]öö-ði) *adj* confiable

truth (truuz) *n* verdad *f*

truthful (*truuz-*föl) *adj* verídico

try (trai) *v* intentar; *esforzarse; *n* tentativa *f*; ~ **on** *probarse

tube (tyuub) *n* tubo *m*

tuberculosis (tyuu-böö-kyu-*lou-*ssiss) *n* tuberculosis *f*

Tuesday (*tyuus-*di) martes *m*

tug (tagh) *v* remolcar; *n* remolcador *m*; estirón *m*

tuition (tyuu-i-*ʃön*) *n* enseñanza *f*; *Am* cuota *f* de enseñanza

tulip (*tyuu-*lip) *n* tulipán *m*

tumbler (*tam-*blö) *n* vaso *m*

tumo(u)r (*tyuu-*mö) *n* tumor *m*

tuna (*tyuu-*nö) *n* (pl ~, ~s) atún *m*

tune (tyuun) *n* tonada *f*; ~ **in** sintonizar

tuneful (*tyuun-*föl) *adj* melodioso

tunic (*tyuu-*nik) *n* túnica *f*

Tunisia (tyuu-*ni-*si-ö) Túnez *m*

Tunisian (tyuu-*ni-*si-ön) *adj* tunecino

tunnel (*ta-*nöl) *n* túnel *m*

turbine (*töö-*bain) *n* turbina *f*

turbojet (töö-bou-*dȝêt*) *n* avión turborreactor

Turk (töök) *n* turco *m*

Turkey (*töö-*ki) Turquía *f*

turkey (*töö-*ki) *n* pavo *m*

Turkish (*töö-*kiʃ) *adj* turco; ~ **bath** baño turco

turn (töön) *v* girar; *volver; *n* cambio *m*, vuelta *f*; curva *f*; turno *m*; ~ **back** *volver; ~ **down** rechazar; ~ **into** *convertirse en; ~ **off** *cerrar; ~ **on** *encender; abrir; ~ **over** *volver; ~

round *volver; *volverse
turning (*töö*-ning) *n* vuelta *f*; ~ **point** punto decisivo
turnover (*töö*-nou-vö) *n* volumen de transacciones; ~ **tax** impuesto sobre la venta
turnpike (*töön*-paik) *nAm* autopista de peaje
turpentine (*töö*-pön-tain) *n* trementina *f*
turtle (*töö*-töl) *n* tortuga *f*
tutor (*tyuu*-tö) *n* maestro particular; tutor *m*, -a *f*; profesor *m*, -a *f* particular
tuxedo (tak-*ssii*-dou) *nAm* (pl ~s, ~es) smoking *m*
TV (tii-*vii*) televisión *f*; **on TV** en la televisión
tweed (t^{u}iid) *n* paño *m* de lana
tweezers (*t^{u}ii*-sös) *pl* pinzas *fpl*
twelfth (t^{u}êlfz) *num* duodécimo
twelve (t^{u}êlv) *num* doce

twentieth (*t^{u}ên*-ti-öz) *num* vigésimo
twenty (*t^{u}ên*-ti) *num* veinte
twice (t^{u}aiss) *adv* dos veces
twig (t^{u}igh) *n* ramita *f*
twilight (*t^{u}ai*-lait) *n* crepúsculo *m*
twine (t^{u}ain) *n* trenza *f*
twins (t^{u}ins) *pl* gemelos *mpl*; **twin beds** camas gemelas
twist (t^{u}isst) *v* *torcer; *n* torsión *f*
two (tuu) *num* dos
two-piece (tuu-*piiss*) *adj* de dos piezas
type (taip) *v* escribir a máquina, mecanografiar; *n* tipo *m*
typewriter (*taip*-rai-tö) *n* máquina de escribir
typhoid (*tai*-foid) *n* tifus *m*
typical (*ti*-pi-köl) *adj* característico, típico
typist (*tai*-pisst) *n* dactilógrafa *f*
tyrant (*tai^ö*-rönt) *n* tirano *m*, -a *f*
tire *Am*, **tyre** (tai^ö) *n* neumático *m*; ~ **pressure** presión del neumático

U

ugly (*a*-ghli) *adj* feo
ulcer (*al*-ssö) *n* úlcera *f*
ultimate (*al*-ti-möt) *adj* último
ultraviolet (al-trö-*vai^ö*-löt) *adj* ultravioleta
umbrella (am-*brê*-lö) *n* paraguas *m*
umpire (*am*-pai^ö) *n* árbitro *m*
unable (a-*nei*-böl) *adj* incapaz
unacceptable (a-nök-*ssêp*-tö-böl) *adj* inaceptable
unaccountable (a-nö-*kaun*-tö-böl) *adj* inexplicable
unaccustomed (a-nö-*ka*-sstömd) *adj* desacostumbrado
unanimous (yuu-*næ*-ni-möss) *adj* unánime

unanswered (a-*naan*-ssöd) *adj* sin contestación
unauthorized (a-*noo*-zö-raisd) *adj* desautorizado
unavoidable (a-nö-*voi*-dö-böl) *adj* inevitable
unaware (a-nö-*^{u}ê^ö*) *adj* inconsciente; **be ~ of** ignorar
unbearable (an-*bê^ö*-rö-böl) *adj* insoportable
unbreakable (an-*brei*-kö-böl) *adj* irrompible
unbroken (an-*brou*-kön) *adj* intacto
unbutton (an-*ba*-tön) *v* desabotonar
uncertain (an-*ssöö*-tön) *adj* incierto
uncle (*ang*-köl) *n* tío *m*

unclean (an-*kliin*) *adj* sucio

uncomfortable (an-*kam*-fö-tö-böl) *adj* incómodo; molesto

uncommon (an-*ko*-mön) *adj* insólito, raro

unconditional (an-kön-*di*-ʃö-nöl) *adj* incondicional

unconscious (an-*kon*-ʃöss) *adj* inconsciente

uncork (an-*kook*) *v* descorchar

uncover (an-*ka*-vö) *v* destapar

uncultivated (an-*kal*-ti-vei-tid) *adj* inculto; yermo

under (*an*-dö) *prep* debajo de, bajo

undercurrent (*an*-dö-ka-rönt) *n* tendencia *f* oculta; corriente *f* submarina

underestimate (an-dö-*rê*-ssti-meit) *v* subestimar

underground (*an*-dö-ghraund) *adj* subterráneo; *n* metro *m*

underline (an-dö-*lain*) *v* subrayar

underneath (an-dö-*niiz*) *adv* debajo; por debajo

undershirt (*an*-dö-ʃööt) *n* camiseta *f*

*****understand** (an-dö-*sstænd*) *v* comprender

understanding (an-dö-*sstæn*-ding) *n* comprensión *m*

understatement (an-dö-*ssteit*-mönt) *n*: **that's an ~** ¡y te quedas corto!

*****undertake** (an-dö-*teik*) *v* emprender

undertaking (an-dö-*tei*-king) *n* empresa *f*

underwater (*an*-dö-ᵘoo-tö) *adj* subacuático

underwear (*an*-dö-ᵘêᵒ) *n* ropa interior

undesirable (an-di-*sai*ᵒ-rö-böl) *adj* indeseable

*****undo** (an-*duu*) *v* desatar

undoubtedly (an-*dau*-tid-li) *adv* sin duda

undress (an-*drêss*) *v* desnudarse

unearned (a-*nöönd*) *adj* inmerecido

uneasy (a-*nii*-si) *adj* inquieto; inseguro; intranquilo

uneducated (a-*nê*-dyu-kei-tid) *adj* inculto

unemployed (a-nim-*ploid*) *adj* parado; sin empleo

unemployment (a-nim-*ploi*-mönt) *n* paro *m*; desempleo *m*

unequal (a-*nii*-kᵘöl) *adj* desigual

uneven (a-*nii*-vön) *adj* desigual; irregular

unexpected (a-nik-*sspêk*-tid) *adj* imprevisto, inesperado

unfair (an-*fê*ᵒ) *adj* ímprobo, injusto

unfaithful (an-*feiz*-föl) *adj* infiel

unfamiliar (an-fö-*mil*-yö) *adj* desconocido

unfasten (an-*faa*-ssön) *v* desatar

unfavo(u)rable (an-*fei*-vö-rö-böl) *adj* desfavorable

unfit (an-*fit*) *adj* inadecuado

unfold (an-*fould*) *v* *desplegar

unfortunate (an-*foo*-chö-nöt) *adj* desafortunado

unfortunately (an-*foo*-chö-nöt-li) *adv* por desgracia, desgraciadamente

unfriendly (an-*frênd*-li) *adj* poco amistoso

ungrateful (an-*ghreit*-föl) *adj* ingrato

unhappy (an-*hæ*-pi) *adj* desdichado

unhealthy (an-*hêl*-zi) *adj* enfermizo; insalubre

unhurt (an-*hööt*) *adj* ileso

uniform (*yuu*-ni-foom) *n* uniforme *m*; *adj* uniforme

unimportant (a-nim-*poo*-tönt) *adj* insignificante

uninhabitable (a-nin-*hæ*-bi-tö-böl) *adj* inhabitable

uninhabited (a-nin-*hæ*-bi-tid) *adj* inhabitado

unintentional (a-nin-*tên*-ʃö-nöl) *adj* no intencional

union (*yuu*-nyön) *n* unión *f*; liga *f*,

confederación f; sindicato m

unique (yuu-*niik*) adj único

unit (*yuu*-nit) n unidad f

unite (yuu-*nait*) v unir; **united** unido

United States (yuu-*nai*-tid ssteitss) Estados Unidos

unity (*yuu*-nö-ti) n unidad f

universal (yuu-ni-*vöö*-ssöl) adj general, universal

universe (*yuu*-ni-vööss) n universo m

university (yuu-ni-*vöö*-ssö-ti) n universidad f

unjust (an-*dʒasst*) adj injusto

unkind (an-*kaind*) adj desagradable, arisco

unknown (an-*noun*) adj desconocido

unlawful (an-*loo*-föl) adj ilegal

unlearn (an-*löön*) v desacostumbrar

unless (ön-*lêss*) conj a menos que; a no ser que

unlike (an-*laik*) adj diferente

unlikely (an-*lai*-kli) adj improbable

unlimited (an-*li*-mi-tid) adj ilimitado

unload (an-*loud*) v descargar

unlock (an-*lok*) v abrir con llave

unlucky (an-*la*-ki) adj desafortunado

unnecessary (an-*nê*-ssö-ssö-ri) adj innecesario

unoccupied (a-*no*-kyu-paid) adj desocupado; vacante

unofficial (a-nö-*fi*-föl) adj no oficial

unpack (an-*pæk*) v desempaquetar; deshacer las maletas

unpleasant (an-*plê*-sönt) adj desagradable; antipático

unpopular (an-*po*-pyu-lö) adj impopular

unprotected (an-prö-*têk*-tid) adj indefenso

unqualified (an-k^"o-li-faid) adj incompetente

unreal (an-*ri^öl*) adj irreal

unreasonable (an-*rii*-sö-nö-böl) adj irrazonable

unreliable (an-ri-*lai*-ö-böl) adj no confiable

unrest (an-*rêsst*) n disturbio m; inquietud f

unsafe (an-*sseif*) adj inseguro

unsatisfactory (an-ssæ-tiss-*fæk*-tö-ri) adj insatisfactorio

unscrew (an-*sskruu*) v destornillar

unselfish (an-*ssêl*-fiʃ) adj desinteresado

unskilled (an-*sskild*) adj inexperto; no especializado; no cualificado

unsound (an-*ssaund*) adj defectuoso; erróneo

unstable (an-*sstei*-böl) adj inestable

unsteady (an-*sstê*-di) adj poco firme, inestable

unsuccessful (an-ssök-*ssêss*-föl) adj fracasado

unsuitable (an-*ssuu*-tö-böl) adj inadecuado

unsurpassed (an-ssö-*paasst*) adj sin igual

untidy (an-*tai*-di) adj desaliñado; desordenado

untie (an-*tai*) v desatar

until (ön-*til*) prep hasta

untrue (an-*truu*) adj falso

untrustworthy (an-*trasst*-^öö-ði) adj indigno de confianza

unusual (an-*yuu*-ʒu-öl) adj inusitado, insólito

unwell (an-^"*êl*) adj indispuesto

unwilling (an-^"*i*-ling) adj desinclinado

unwise (an-^"*ais*) adj imprudente

unwrap (an-*ræp*) v *desenvolver

up (ap) adv hacia arriba, arriba

upholster (ap-*houl*-sstö) v tapizar

upkeep (*ap*-kiip) n manutención f

uplands (*ap*-lönds) pl altiplano m; meseta f

upon (ö-*pon*) prep sobre

upper (a-*pö*) adj superior; más alto

upright (*ap*-rait) adj derecho; adv de

pie

upset (ap-ssêt) v trastornar; volcar; perturbar; adj trastornado; perturbado

upside down (ap-ssaid-*daun*) adv al revés

upstairs (ap-sstê°s) adv arriba

upstream (ap-sstriim) adv río arriba

upwards (ap-ᵘöds) adv hacia arriba

urban (öö-bön) adj urbano

urge (öödʒ) v estimular; n impulso m

urgency (öö-dʒön-ssi) n urgencia f

urgent (öö-dʒönt) adj urgente

urine (yu°-rin) n orina f

Uruguay (yu°-rö-ghᵘai) Uruguay m

Uruguayan (yu°-rö-ghᵘai-ön) adj uruguayo

us (ass) pron nosotros

usable (yuu-sö-böl) adj utilizable

usage (yuu-sidʒ) n uso m

use¹ (yuus) v usar; ***be used to** *estar acostumbrado a; ~ **up** consumir

use² (yuuss) n uso m; utilidad f; ***be of ~** *servir

useful (yuuss-föl) adj útil

useless (yuuss-löss) adj inútil

user (yuu-sö) n usuario m

usher (a-ʃö) n acomodador m

usherette (a-ʃö-rêt) n acomodadora f

usual (yuu-ʒu-öl) adj usual

usually (yuu-ʒu-ö-li) adv habitualmente

utensil (yuu-tên-ssöl) n herramienta f, utensilio m

utility (yuu-ti-lö-ti) n utilidad f

utilize (yuu-ti-lais) v utilizar

utmost (at-mousst) adj extremo; último

utter (a-tö) adj completo, total; v emitir; pronunciar; proferir

V

vacancy (vei-kön-ssi) n vacante f

vacant (vei-könt) adj vacante

vacate (vö-*keit*) v vaciar

vacation (vö-*kei*-ʃön) n vacaciones fpl

vaccinate (væk-ssi-neit) v vacunar

vaccination (væk-ssi-*nei*-ʃön) n vacunación f

vacuum (væ-kyu-öm) n vacío m; ~ **cleaner** aspiradora f; ~ **flask** termo m

vague (veigh) adj vago

vain (vein) adj vanidoso; vano; **in ~** inútilmente, en vano

valet (væ-lit) n ayuda de cámara

valid (væ-lid) adj vigente

valley (væ-li) n valle m

valuable (væ-lyu-böl) adj valioso; **valuables** pl objetos de valor

value (væ-lyuu) n valor m; v valuar

valve (vælv) n válvula f

van (væn) n camioneta f

vanilla (vö-ni-lö) n vainilla f

vanish (væ-niʃ) v *desaparecer

vapo(u)r (vei-pö) n vapor m

variable (vê°-ri-ö-böl) adj variable

variation (vê°-ri-*ei*-ʃön) n variación f; cambio m

varied (vê°-rid) adj variado

variety (vö-*rai*-ö-ti) n variedad f; ~ **show** espectáculo de variedades; ~ **theater** Am, ~ **theatre** teatro de variedades

various (vê°-ri-öss) adj varios

varnish (vaa-niʃ) n barniz m; v barnizar

vary (vê°-ri) v variar; cambiar; *diferir

vase (vaas) n vaso m

vaseline (*væ*-ssö-liin) *n* vaselina *f*

vast (vaasst) *adj* vasto

vault (voolt) *n* bóveda *f*; caja de caudales

veal (viil) *n* carne de ternera

vegetable (*vê*-d3ö-tö-böl) *n* legumbre *f*

vegetarian (vê-d3i-*tê⁰*-ri-ön) *n* vegetariano *m*, -a *f*

vegetation (vê-d3i-*tei*-ʃön) *n* vegetación *f*

vehicle (*vii*-ö-köl) *n* vehículo *m*

veil (veil) *n* velo *m*

vein (vein) *n* vena *f*; **varicose ~** varice *f*

velvet (*vêl*-vit) *n* terciopelo *m*

velveteen (vêl-vi-*tiin*) *n* pana *f*

venerable (*vê*-nö-rö-böl) *adj* venerable

venereal disease (vi-*ni⁰*-ri-öl di-*siis*) enfermedad venérea

Venezuela (vê-ni-*sᵘei*-lö) Venezuela *f*

Venezuelan (vê-ni-*sᵘei*-lön) *adj* venezolano

ventilate (*vên*-ti-leit) *v* ventilar; airear

ventilation (vên-ti-*lei*-ʃön) *n* ventilación *f*; aireo *m*

ventilator (*vên*-ti-lei-tö) *n* ventilador *m*

venture (*vên*-chö) *v* arriesgar

veranda (vö-*ræn*-dö) *n* veranda *f*; terraza *f*

verb (vööb) *n* verbo *m*

verbal (*vöö*-böl) *adj* verbal

verdict (*vöö*-dikt) *n* sentencia *f*, veredicto *m*; fallo *m*

verge (vööd3) *n* borde *m*; margen *m*; **on the ~ of** al borde de

verify (*vê*-ri-fai) *v* verificar

verse (vööss) *n* verso *m*

version (*vöö*-ʃön) *n* versión *f*

versus (*vöö*-ssöss) *prep* contra

vertical (*vöö*-ti-köl) *adj* vertical

very (*vê*-ri) *adv* mucho, muy; *adj* preciso, verdadero; extremo

vessel (*vê*-ssöl) *n* embarcación *f*, buque *m*; vasija *f*

vest (vêsst) *n* camiseta *f*; *nAm* chaleco *m*

veterinary surgeon (*vê*-tri-nö-ri *ssöö*-d3ön) veterinario *m*, -a *f*

via (vai⁶) *prep* por

viaduct (*vai⁰*-dakt) *n* viaducto *m*

vibrate (vai-*breit*) *v* vibrar

vibration (vai-*brei*-ʃön) *n* vibración *f*

vicar (*vi*-kö) *n* vicario *m*

vicarage (*vi*-kö-rid3) *n* casa del párroco

vice president (vaiss-*prê*-si-dönt) *n* vicepresidente *m*

vicinity (vi-*ssi*-nö-ti) *n* vecindad *f*

vicious (*vi*-ʃöss) *adj* vicioso

victim (*vik*-tim) *n* víctima *f*

victory (*vik*-tö-ri) *n* victoria *f*

video (*vi*-di-ou) *n* vídeo *m*; *v* grabar en vídeo; **~ camera** videocámara; **~ cassette** videocassette; **~ game** videojuego; **~ recorder** videograbadora

view (vyuu) *n* vista *f*; parecer *m*, opinión *f*; *v* mirar; contemplar; considerar

vigilant (*vi*-d3i-lönt) *adj* vigilante

villa (*vi*-lö) *n* villa *f*; chalet *m*

village (*vi*-lid3) *n* pueblo *m*

villain (*vi*-lön) *n* malvado *m*

vinegar (*vi*-ni-ghö) *n* vinagre *m*

vineyard (*vin*-yöd) *n* viña *f*

vintage (*vin*-tid3) *n* vendimia *f*

violation (vai⁶-*lei*-ʃön) *n* violación *f*

violence (*vai⁶*-lönss) *n* violencia *f*

violent (*vai⁶*-lönt) *adj* violento; impetuoso

violet (*vai⁶*-löt) *n* violeta *f*; *adj* morado

violin (vai⁶-*lin*) *n* violín *m*

VIP (vii-ai-*pii*) *n* (= **very important person**) VIP *m*

virgin (*vöö*-d3in) *n* virgen *f*

virtue (*vöö*-chuu) *n* virtud *f*

visa (*vii*-sö) *n* visado *m*

visibility (vi-sö-*bi*-lö-ti) *n* visibilidad *f*

visible (*vi*-sö-böl) *adj* visible

vision (*vi*-ʒön) *n* visión *f*

visit (*vi*-sit) *v* visitar; *n* visita *f*; **visiting hours** horas de visita

visitor (*vi*-si-tö) *n* visitante *m/f*

vital (*vai*-töl) *adj* esencial

vitamin (*vi*-tö-min) *n* vitamina *f*

vivid (*vi*-vid) *adj* vivo

vocabulary (vö-*kæ*-byu-lö-ri) *n* vocabulario *m*; glosario *m*

vocal (*vou*-köl) *adj* vocal

vocalist (*vou*-kö-lisst) *n* vocalista *m*

voice (voiss) *n* voz *f*

void (void) *adj* vacío

volcano (vol-*kei*-nou) *n* (pl ~es, ~s) volcán *m*

volt (voult) *n* voltio *m*

voltage (*voul*-tidʒ) *n* voltaje *m*

volume (*vo*-lyum) *n* volumen *m*; tomo *m*

voluntary (*vo*-lön-tö-ri) *adj* voluntario

volunteer (vo-lön-*ti*ᵒ) *n* voluntario *m*

vomit (*vo*-mit) *v* vomitar

vote (vout) *v* votar; *n* voto *m*; votación *f*

voter (*vou*-tö) *n* votante *m/f*

voucher (*vau*-chö) *n* recibo *m*, comprobante *m*

vow (vau) *n* voto *m*, juramento *m*; *v* prestar juramento

vowel (vau°l) *n* vocal *f*

voyage (*voi*-idʒ) *n* viaje *m*

vulgar (*val*-ghö) *adj* vulgar; popular, ordinario

vulnerable (*val*-nö-rö-böl) *adj* vulnerable

vulture (*val*-chö) *n* buitre *m*

W

wade (ᵘeid) *v* vadear

wafer (ᵘ*ei*-fö) *n* oblea *f*

waffle (ᵘ*o*-föl) *n* barquillo *m*

wages (ᵘ*ei*-dʒis) *pl* salario *m*; sueldo *m*

wag(g)on (ᵘ*æ*-ghön) *n* vagón *m*

waist (ᵘeisst) *n* cintura *f*

waistcoat (ᵘ*eiss*-kout) *n* chaleco *m*

wait (ᵘeit) *v* esperar; ~ **on** *servir

waiter (ᵘ*ei*-tö) *n* camarero *m*; mesero *mMe*

waiting *n* espera *f*; ~ **list** lista de espera; ~ **room** sala de espera

waitress (ᵘ*ei*-triss) *n* camarera *f*; mesera *fMe*

***wake** (ᵘeik) *v* *despertar; ~ **up** *despertarse

walk (ᵘook) *v* *andar; pasear; *n* paseo *m*; caminata *f*; **walking** a pie

walker (ᵘ*oo*-kö) *n* paseante *m*

walking stick (ᵘ*oo*-king-sstik) *n* bastón *m*

wall (ᵘool) *n* muro *m*; pared *f*

wallet (ᵘ*o*-lit) *n* cartera *f*; monedero *m*

wallpaper (ᵘ*ool*-pei-pö) *n* papel pintado

walnut (ᵘ*ool*-nat) *n* nogal *m*

waltz (ᵘoolss) *n* vals *m*

wander (ᵘ*on*-dö) *v* vagar; *errar

want (ᵘont) *v* *querer; desear; *n* necesidad *f*; carencia *f*, falta *f*

war (ᵘoo) *n* guerra *f*

warden (ᵘ*oo*-dön) *n* guardián *m*

wardrobe (ᵘ*oo*-droub) *n* guardarropa

m, vestuario *m*

warehouse (ᵘé°-hauss) *n* almacén *m*

wares (ᵘé°s) *pl* mercancías *fpl*

warm (ᵘoom) *adj* caliente; *v* *calentar

warmth (ᵘoomz) *n* calor *m*

warn (ᵘoon) *v* *advertir

warning (ᵘoo-ning) *n* advertencia *f*

wary (ᵘé°-ri) *adj* prudente; cauteloso

was (ᵘos) *v* (p be)

wash (ᵘoʃ) *v* lavar; ~ **and wear** no precisa plancha; ~ **up** *fregar

washable (ᵘo-ʃö-böl) *adj* lavable

washbasin (ᵘoʃ-bei-ssön) *n* palangana *f*

washing (ᵘo-ʃing) *n* lavado *m*; ropa sucia; ~ **machine** lavadora *f*; ~ **powder** jabón en polvo

washroom (ᵘoʃ-ruum) *nAm* lavabo *m*

wasp (ᵘossp) *n* avispa *f*

waste (ᵘeisst) *v* *perder; despilfarrar; malgastar; *n* despilfarro *m*; basura *f*; *adj* baldío; desechado, inútil

wasteful (ᵘeisst-föl) *adj* derrochador

wastepaper basket (ᵘeisst-*pei*-pö-baa-sskit) *n* cesto para papeles

watch (ᵘoch) *v* mirar, observar; vigilar; *n* reloj *m*; ~ **for** acechar; ~ **out** *tener cuidado

watchmaker (ᵘoch-mei-kö) *n* relojero *m*, -a *f*

watchstrap (ᵘoch-sstræp) *n* correa de reloj

water (ᵘoo-tö) *n* agua *f*; **iced** ~ agua helada; **running** ~ agua corriente; ~ **pump** bomba de agua; ~ **ski** esquí acuático; ~ **softener** ablandador *m*

watercolo(u)r (ᵘoo-tö-ka-lö) *n* acuarela *f*

watercress (ᵘoo-tö-krêss) *n* berro *m*

waterfall (ᵘoo-tö-fool) *n* cascada *f*

watermelon (ᵘoo-tö-mê-lön) *n* sandía *f*

waterproof (ᵘoo-tö-pruuf) *adj* impermeable

waterway (ᵘoo-tö-ᵘei) *n* vía navegable

watt (ᵘot) *n* vatio *m*

wave (ᵘeiv) *n* ondulación *f*, ola *f*; *v* *hacer señales

wavelength (ᵘeiv-lêngz) *n* longitud de onda

wavy (ᵘei-vi) *adj* ondulado

wax (ᵘækss) *n* cera *f*

waxworks (ᵘækss-ᵘöökss) *pl* museo de figuras de cera

way (ᵘei) *n* manera *f*; camino *m*; lado *m*, dirección *f*; distancia *f*; **any** ~ de todos modos; **by the** ~ a propósito; **one-way traffic** dirección única; **out of the** ~ apartado; **the other** ~ **round** al revés; **back** vuelta *f*; ~ **in** entrada *f*; ~ **out** salida *f*

wayside (ᵘei-ssaid) *n* borde del camino

we (ᵘii) *pron* nosotros

weak (ᵘiik) *adj* débil; flojo

weakness (ᵘiik-nöss) *n* debilidad *f*

wealth (ᵘêlz) *n* riqueza *f*

wealthy (ᵘêl-zi) *adj* rico

weapon (ᵘê-pön) *n* arma *f*

*wear (ᵘê°) *v* llevar; ~ **out** gastar

weary (ᵘí°-ri) *adj* cansado; abatido

weather (ᵘê-ðö) *n* tiempo *m*; ~ **forecast** boletín meteorológico

*weave (ᵘiiv) *v* tejer

weaver (ᵘii-vö) *n* tejedor *m*, -a *f*

web (ᵘêb) *n* tela *f*; **the Web** la Web

wedding (ᵘê-ding) *n* matrimonio *m*, boda *f*; ~ **ring** anillo de boda

wedge (ᵘêdʒ) *n* cuña *f*

Wednesday (ᵘêns-di) *n* miércoles *m*

weed (ᵘiid) *n* mala hierba

week (ᵘiik) *n* semana *f*

weekday (ᵘiik-dei) *n* día laborable

weekend (ᵘii-kênd) *n* fin de semana

weekly (ᵘii-kli) *adj* semanal

*weep (ᵘiip) *v* llorar

weigh (ᵘei) *v* pesar

weighing machine (ᵘei-ing-mö-ʃiin)

n báscula *f*

weight (^ueit) *n* peso *m*

welcome ("*êl*-köm) *adj* bienvenido; *n* bienvenida *f*; *v* *dar la bienvenida

weld (^uêld) *v* *soldar

welfare ("*êl*-fê^ö) *n* bienestar *m*

well¹ ("êl) *adv* bien; *adj* sano; **as ~** también; **as ~ as** así como; **well!** ¡bueno!

well² ("êl) *n* pozo *m*

well-founded ("êl-*faun*-did) *adj* fundamentado

well-known ("êl-noun) *adj* notorio

well-to-do ("êl-tö-*duu*) *adj* acomodado

went (^uênt) *v* (p go)

were (^uöö) *v* (p be)

west (^uêsst) *n* occidente *m*, oeste *m*

westerly ("*ê*-sstö-li) *adj* occidental

western ("*ê*-sstön) *adj* occidental

wet ("êt) *adj* mojado; húmedo

whale ("eil) *n* ballena *f*

wharf ("oof) *n* (pl ~s, wharves) muelle *m*

what (^uot) *pron* qué; lo que; **~ for** para que

whatever ("*o*-tê-vö) *pron* cualquier cosa que

wheat ("iit) *n* trigo *m*

wheel ("iil) *n* rueda *f*

wheelbarrow ("*iil*-bæ-rou) *n* carretilla *f*

wheelchair ("*iil*-chê^ö) *n* silla de ruedas

when ("ên) *adv* cuándo; *conj* cuando

whenever ("ê-*nê*-vö) *conj* cuando quiera que

where ("ê^ö) *adv* dónde; *conj* donde

wherever ("ê^ö-*rê*-vö) *conj* dondequiera que

whether ("*ê*-ðö) *conj* si; **whether … or** si … o

which ("ich) *pron* lo que, lo cual, la cual; cuál?

whichever ("i-*chê*-vö) *adj* cualquiera

while ("ail) *conj* mientras; *n* rato *m*

whilst ("ailsst) *conj* mientras

whim ("im) *n* antojo *m*, capricho *m*

whip ("ip) *n* azote *m*; látigo *m*; *v* azotar; batir

whiskers ("i-sskös) *pl* patillas *fpl*

whisper ("i-sspö) *v* susurrar; *n* susurro *m*

whistle ("i-ssöl) *v* silbar; *n* silbato *m*

white ("ait) *adj* blanco

whiting ("*ai*-ting) *n* (pl ~) merluza *f*

Whitsun ("*it*-ssön) Pentecostés *m*

who (huu) *pron* quien; que

whoever (huu-ê-vö) *pron* quienquiera

whole (houl) *adj* completo, entero; intacto; *n* total *m*

wholesale (*houl*-sseil) *n* venta al por mayor; **~ dealer** mayorista *m*

wholesome (*houl*-ssöm) *adj* salubre

wholly (*houl*-li) *adv* totalmente

whom (huum) *pron* a quien(es)

whore (hoo) *n* puta *f*

whose (huus) *pron* cuyo; de quien(es)

why ("ai) *adv* por qué; para qué

wicked ("i-kid) *adj* malvado

wide ("aid) *adj* vasto, ancho

widen ("*ai*-dön) *v* ensanchar

widow ("i-dou) *n* viuda *f*

widower ("i-dou-ö) *n* viudo *m*

width ("idz) *n* anchura *f*

wife ("aif) *n* (pl wives) esposa *f*, mujer *f*

wig ("igh) *n* peluca *f*

wild ("aild) *adj* salvaje; feroz

will ("il) *n* voluntad *f*; testamento *m*

*****will** ("il) *v* *querer

willing ("i-ling) *adj* dispuesto

willingly ("i-ling-li) *adv* gustosamente

willpower ("*il*-pau^ö) *n* fuerza de voluntad

*****win** ("in) *v* vencer

wind ("ind) *n* viento *m*

*****wind** ("aind) *v* serpentear; *dar cuerda, enrollar

winding (*"ain*-ding) *adj* tortuoso

windmill (*"ind*-mil) *n* molino de viento

window (*"in*-dou) *n* ventana *f*

windowsill (*"in*-dou-ssil) *n* antepecho *m*

windscreen (*"ind*-sskriin) *n* parabrisas *m*; ~ **wiper** limpiaparabrisas *m*

windshield (*"ind*-∫ild) *nAm* parabrisas *m*

windy (*"in*-di) *adj* ventoso

wine (*"ain*) *n* vino *m*; ~ **cellar** cueva *f*; ~ **list** carta de vinos; ~ **merchant** vinatero *m*

wing (*"ing*) *n* ala *f*

winkle (*"ing*-köl) *n* caracol marino

winner (*"i*-nö) *n* vencedor *m*

winning (*"i*-ning) *adj* ganador; **winnings** *pl* ganancias *fpl*

winter (*"in*-tö) *n* invierno *m*; ~ **sports** deportes de invierno

wipe (*"aip*) *v* enjugar

wire (*"ai*) *n* alambre *m*; telegrama *m*

wireless (*"ai*-löss) *adj* inalámbrico

wisdom (*"is*-döm) *n* sabiduría *f*; juicio *m*

wise (*"ais*) *adj* sabio; juicioso

wish (*"i*∫) *v* desear; *n* deseo *m*

wit (*"it*) *n* ingenio *m*; ingenioso *m*, -a *f*; **be at one's wits' end** estar desesperado; **be scared out of one's wits** estar aterrorizado

witch (*"ich*) *n* bruja *f*

with (*"ið*) *prep* con; de

***withdraw** (*"ið-droo*) *v* retirar

within (*"i-ðin*) *prep* dentro de; *adv* de dentro

without (*"i-ðaut*) *prep* sin

wit (uit) *n* ingenio *m*

witness (*"it*-nöss) *n* testigo *m*

witty (*"i*-ti) *adj* ingenioso, chistoso

wolf (*"ulf*) *n* (pl wolves) lobo *m*

woman (*"u*-mön) *n* (pl women) mujer *f*

womb (*"uum*) *n* matriz *f*

won (*"an*) *v* (p, pp win)

wonder (*"an*-dö) *n* milagro *m*; asombro *m*; *v* preguntarse

wonderful (*"an* dö-föl) *adj* estupendo, maravilloso; delicioso

wood (*"ud*) *n* madera *f*; bosque *m*

wooded (*"u*-did) *adj* selvoso

wooden (*"u*-dön) *adj* de madera; ~ **shoe** zueco *m*

woodland (*"ud*-lönd) *n* arbolado *m*

wool (*"ul*) *n* lana *f*; **darning** ~ hilo de zurcir

wool(l)en (*"u*-lön) *adj* de lana

word (*"ööd*) *n* palabra *f*

wore (*"oo*) *v* (p wear)

work (*"öök*) *n* obra *f*; trabajo *m*; *v* trabajar; funcionar; **working day** día de trabajo; ~ **of art** obra de arte; ~ **permit** permiso de trabajo

worker (*"öö*-kö) *n* obrero *m*

working (*"öö*-king) *n* funcionamiento *m*

workman (*"öök*-mön) *n* (pl -men) obrero *m*

works (*"öökss*) *pl* fábrica *f*

workshop (*"öök*-∫op) *n* taller *m*

world (*"ööld*) *n* mundo *m*; ~ **war** guerra mundial

world-famous (*"ööld-fei*-möss) *adj* de fama mundial

world-wide (*"ööld-"aid*) *adj* mundial

worm (*"ööm*) *n* gusano *m*

worn (*"oon*) *adj* (pp wear) gastado

worn-out (*"oon-aut*) *adj* gastado; estropeado

worried (*"a*-rid) *adj* inquieto; preocupado

worry (*"a*-ri) *v* inquietarse; *n* preocupación *f*, inquietud *f*

worse (*"ööss*) *adj* peor; *adv* peor

worship (*"öö*-∫ip) *v* venerar; adorar; *n* culto *m*; adoración *f*

worst (*"öösst*) *adj* pésimo; *adv* peor

worth (^uööz) n valor m; mérito m; ***be ~ *valer; *be worth-while *valer la pena**

worthless (^uööz-löss) adj sin valor

worthy of (^uöö-ði öv) digno de

would (^uud) v (p will) *soler

wound¹ (^uuund) n herida f; v ofender, *herir

wound² (^uaund) v (p, pp wind)

wrap (ræp) v *envolver

wreck (rêk) n pecio m; v *destruir

wrench (rênch) n llave f inglesa; tirón m; v dislocar

wrinkle (ring-köl) n arruga f

wrist (risst) n muñeca f

wristwatch (risst-^uoch) n reloj de pulsera

*write (rait) v escribir; **in writing** por escrito; **~ down** anotar

writer (rai-tö) n escritor m

writing pad (rai-ting-pæd) n bloc m

writing paper (rai-ting-pei-pö) n papel de escribir

written (ri-tön) adj (pp write) por escrito

wrong (rong) adj impropio, erróneo; n mal m; v agraviar; ***be ~** no *tener razón

wrote (rout) v (p write)

X

Xmas (kriss-möss) Navidad f

X-ray (êkss-rei) n radiografía f; v radiografiar

Y

yacht (yot) n yate m

yacht club (yot-klab) n club de yates

yachting (yo-ting) n deporte de vela

yard (yaad) n patio m; jardín m; corral m

yarn (yaan) n hilo m

yawn (yoon) v bostezar

year (yi^ö) n año m

yearly (yi^ö-li) adj anual

yeast (yiisst) n levadura f

yell (yêl) v gritar; n grito m

yellow (yê-lou) adj amarillo

yes (yêss) sí

yesterday (yê-sstö-di) adv ayer

yet (yêt) adv aun; conj pero, sin embargo

yield (yiild) v producir; ceder; n rendimiento m; cosecha f

yoke (youk) n yugo m

yolk (youk) n yema f

you (yuu) pron tú; a ti; usted; a usted; vosotros; os; ustedes

young (yang) adj joven

your (yoo) adj de usted; tu; vuestro, tuyos

yours (yoos) pron el tuyo, la tuya, L.Am. el suyo, la suya; pl el vuestro, la vuestra; **a friend of yours** un amigo tuyo/suyo/vuestro; **yours ...** un saludo

yourself (yoo-*ssêlf*) *pron* te; tú mismo; usted mismo

yourselves (yoo-*ssêlvs*) *pron* se; vosotros mismos; ustedes mismos

youth (yuuz) *n* juventud *f*

Z

zap (sæp) *v colloquial* borrar; liquidar; golpear; enviar

zeal (siil) *n* celo *m*; ardor *m*

zealous (*sê*-löss) *adj* celoso; fervoroso

zebra (*sii*-brö) *n* cebra *f*

zenith (*sê*-niz) *n* cenit *m*; apogeo *m*

zero (*si*°-rou) *n* (pl ~s) cero *m*

zest (sêsst) *n* energía *f*; entusiasmo *m*

zinc (singk) *n* cinc *m*

zip (sip) *n* cremallera *f*; ~ **code** *Am* código postal

zipper (*si*-pö) *nAm* cremallera *f*

zodiac (*sou*-di-æk) *n* zodíaco *m*

zone (soun) *n* zona *f*; región *f*

zoo (suu) *n* (pl ~s) jardín zoológico

zoology (sou-*o*-lö-dʒi) *n* zoología *f*

Léxico gastronómico
Comidas

almond almendra

anchovy anchoa

angel food cake pastel confeccionado con clara de huevo

angels on horseback ostras envueltas en tocino, asadas y servidas en pan tostado

appetizer entremés

apple manzana

~ **charlotte** pastel de compota de manzanas y pan rallado

~ **dumpling** bola de masa hervida de manzanas

~ **pie** pastel de manzanas

~ **sauce** puré de manzanas

apricot albaricoque

Arbroath smoky róbalo ahumado

artichoke alcachofa

asparagus espárrago

~ **tip** punta de espárrago

aspic (en) gelatina

assorted variado

aubergine berenjena

avocado (pear) aguacate

bacon tocino

~ **and eggs** huevos con tocino

bagel panecillo en forma de corona

baked al horno

~ **Alaska** helado cubierto con merengue, dorado en el horno; se sirve flameado como postre

~ **beans** judías blancas en salsa de tomates

~ **potato** patata sin pelar cocida al horno

Bakewell tart pastel de almendras con mermelada de frambuesas

baloney especie de mortadela

banana plátano

~ **split** dos mitades de plátano servidas con helado y nueces, rociadas con almíbar o crema de chocolate

barbecue 1) carne picada de ternera en una salsa a base de tomates, servida en un panecillo 2) comida al aire libre

~ **sauce** salsa de tomates muy picante

barbecued asado a la parrilla con carbón de leña

basil albahaca

bass lubina (pescado)

bean judía, haba, fríjol

beef carne de vaca, carne de res

~ **olive** rollo de carne de ternera

~ **Stroganoff** bistec asado con fideos y crema ágria

beefburger bistec de carne picada, asado y a veces servido en un panecillo

beet, beetroot remolacha

bilberry arándano

bill cuenta

~ **of fare** lista de platos

biscuit 1) galleta (GB) 2) panecillo (US)

black pudding morcilla

blackberry zarzamora

blackcurrant grosella negra

bloater arenque salado, ahumado

blood sausage morcilla

blueberry arándano

boiled hervido

Bologna (sausage) especie de mortadela

bone hueso

boned deshuesado

Boston baked beans judías blancas con tocino y melaza

Boston cream pie torta rellena de nata en capas superpuestas, cubierta de chocolate

brains sesos

braised asado

bramble pudding pudín de zarzamoras (a menudo con manzanas)

braunschweiger salchichón de hígado ahumado

bread pan

breaded empanado

breakfast desayuno

bream brema (pescado)

breast pecho, pechuga

brisket pecho

broad bean haba

broth caldo

brown Betty especie de compota de manzanas, con especias y cubierta de pan rallado

brunch comida que reemplaza el desayuno y el almuerzo

brussels sprout col de Bruselas

bubble and squeak patatas y coles picadas que se fríen, mezcladas a veces con trozos de carne de ternera (especie de tortilla)

bun 1) panecillo dulce confeccionado con frutas secas 2) especie de panecillo (US)

butter mantequilla

buttered con mantequilla

cabbage col, repollo

Caesar salad ensalada verde con ajo, anchoas, cuscurro y queso rallado

cake pastel, torta

cakes galletas, pastelillos

calf ternera

Canadian bacon lomo de cerdo ahumado que se corta en lonchas finas

cantaloupe melón

caper alcaparra

capercaillie, capercailzie urogallo grande

caramel caramelo

carp carpa

carrot zanahoria

cashew anacardo

casserole cacerola

catfish siluro (pescado)

catsup salsa de tomate

cauliflower coliflor

celery apio

cereal cereal

  hot ~ gachas

chateaubriand solomillo de ternera

check cuenta

Cheddar (cheese) queso de textura firme y de sabor ligeramente ácido

cheese queso

  ~ board bandeja de quesos

  ~ cake pastel de queso doble crema, ligeramente azucarado

cheeseburger bistec de carne picada, asado con una loncha de queso, servido en un panecillo

chef's salad ensalada de jamón, pollo, huevos cocidos, tomates, lechuga y queso

cherry cereza

chestnut castaña

chicken pollo

chicory 1) endibia (GB) 2) escarola, achicoria (US)

chili pepper chile, ají

chips 1) patatas fritas (GB) 2) chips (US)

chitt(er)lings tripas de cerdo

chive cebolleta

choice elección, surtido

chop costilla

  ~ suey plato hecho con carne picada de cerdo o de pollo, arroz y legumbres

chopped picado

chowder sopa espesa a base de

mariscos

Christmas pudding pudín inglés hecho con frutas secas, a veces flameado, muy nutritivo y que se sirve en Navidad

chutney condimento indio muy sazonado, con sabor agridulce

cinnamon canela

clam almeja

club sandwich bocadillo doble con tocino, pollo, tomates, lechuga y mayonesa

cobbler compota de frutas cubierta con una capa de pasta

cock-a-leekie soup sopa de pollo y puerros

coconut coco

cod bacalao

Colchester oyster ostra inglesa muy afamada

cold cuts/meat fiambres

coleslaw ensalada de col

compote compota

condiment condimento

cooked cocido

cookie galleta

corn 1) trigo (GB) 2) maíz (US) ~ **on the cob** mazorca de maíz

cornflakes copos de maíz

corned beef carne de ternera sazonada

cottage cheese requesón

cottage pie carne picada que se cuece con cebollas y se cubre con puré de patatas

course plato

cover charge precio del cubierto

crab cangrejo de mar

cracker galletita salada

cranberry arándano agrio
~ **sauce** mermelada de arándanos agrios

crawfish, crayfish 1) cangrejo de río 2) langosta (GB) 3) langostino (US)

cream 1) nata 2) crema (sopa) 3) crema (postre)
~ **cheese** queso doble crema
~ **puff** pastelillo con nata

creamed potatoes patatas cortadas en forma de dados en salsa blanca

creole plato muy condimentado con tomates, pimientos y cebollas; suele servirse con arroz blanco

cress berro

crisps patatas a la inglesa, chips

croquette croqueta

crumpet especie de panecillo redondo, asado y untado de mantequilla

cucumber pepino

Cumberland ham jamón ahumado, muy conocido

Cumberland sauce jalea de grosellas sazonada de vino, jugo de naranja y especias

cupcake pastelillo, hojaldre

cured salado y ahumado

currant 1) pasa de Corinto 2) grosella

curried con curry

custard 1) crema 2) flan

cutlet 1) chuleta 2) escalope 3) fina lonja de carne

dab lenguado

Danish pastry pastelillos hojaldrados

date dátil

Derby cheese queso blando picante, de color amarillo claro

dessert postre

devilled con aliño muy fuerte

devil's food cake torta de chocolate muy nutritiva

devils on horseback ciruelas pasas cocidas en vino tinto, rellenas de almendras y anchoas, envueltas en tocino, asadas y servidas en una tostada

Devonshire cream crema doble muy espesa

diced cortado en daditos
diet food alimento dietético
dill eneldo
dinner cena
dish plato
donut, doughnut buñuelo en forma de anillo, rosquilla
double cream doble crema, nata
Dover sole lenguado de Dover, muy afamado
dressing 1) salsa para ensalada 2) relleno para aves (US)
Dublin Bay prawn langostino
duck pato
duckling anadón
dumpling albóndiga de pasta
Dutch apple pie tarta de manzanas, cubierta con una capa de azúcar negra y mantequilla
éclair pastelillo relleno de crema de chocolate o de café
eel anguila
egg huevo
  Benedict ~ con jamón o tocino y salsa holandesa
  boiled ~ pasado por agua
  fried ~ frito
  hard-boiled ~ duro
  poached ~ escalfado
  salad ~ con cebolla, apio, mayonesa y mostaza
  scrambled ~ revuelto
  soft-boiled ~ poco pasado por agua
eggplant berenjena
endive 1) escarola, achicoria (GB) 2) endibia (US)
entrecôte solomo de ternera
entrée 1) entrada (GB) 2) plato principal (US)
fennel hinojo
fig higo
filet mignon solomillo
fillet filete de carne o de pescado
finnan haddock róbalo ahumado

fish pescado
  ~ **and chips** filetes de pescado y patatas fritas
  ~ **cake** albóndigas, galleta de pescado y patatas
flan tarta de frutas
flapjack hojuela espesa
flounder fleso (pescado)
forcemeat relleno, picadillo
fowl ave
frankfurter salchicha de Francfort
French bean judía verde
French bread pan francés
French dressing 1) vinagreta (GB) 2) salsa cremosa de ensalada con salsa de tomates (US)
french fries patatas fritas
French toast rebanada de pan, mojada en huevos batidos, frita en una sartén y servida con mermelada o azúcar
fresh fresco
fried frito, asado
fritter buñuelo
frogs' legs ancas de rana
frosting capa de azúcar garrapiñado
fruit fruta
fry fritura
galantine trozos de carne y picadillo cocidos en gelatina
game caza
gammon jamón ahumado
garfish anguila de mar
garlic ajo
garnish aderezo
gherkin pepinillo
giblets menudillos de ave
ginger jengibre
gingerbread pastel hecho con melaza y especias
goose ganso
  ~**berry** grosella espinosa
grape uva
  ~**fruit** pomelo, toronja

grated rallado

gravy jugo de carne, salsa

grayling pescado de la familia del salmón

green bean judía verde

green pepper pimiento verde

green salad ensalada verde

greens verduras

grilled asado a la parrilla

grilse salmón joven

grouse urogallo

gumbo 1) legumbre de origen africano 2) plato criollo a base de okra, con carne o pescado y tomates

haddock róbalo

haggis panza de cordero rellena de copos de avena

hake merluza

half mitad, semi

ham jamón

~ **and eggs** huevos con jamón

hamburger hamburguesa

hare liebre

haricot bean alubia blanca

hash 1) carne picada 2) picadillo de carne de ternera cubierto con patatas y legumbres

hash brown potatoes patatas ralladas fritas

hazelnut avellana

heart corazón

herb hierba aromática

herring arenque

home-made de confección casera

hominy grits crema espesa de harina de maíz, especie de polenta

honey miel

~**dew melon** tipo de melón cuya carne es de color verde amarillento

hors-d'œuvre entremeses

horse-radish rábano picante

hot 1) caliente 2) con especias

~ **cross bun** bollito con pasas (que se come durante la Cuaresma)

~ **dog** salchicha caliente en un panecillo

huckleberry especie de arándano

hush puppy buñuelo a base de harina de maíz

ice-cream helado

iced helado

icing capa de azúcar garrapiñado

Idaho baked potato patata sin pelar cocida al horno

Irish stew guisado de cordero con cebollas y patatas

Italian dressing vinagreta

jam confitura

jellied en gelatina

Jell-O postre a la gelatina

jelly gelatina o jalea de frutas

Jerusalem artichoke aguaturma

John Dory especie de dorada

jugged hare estofado de liebre

juice jugo, zumo

juniper berry baya de enebro

junket leche cuajada azucarada

kale cob rizada

kedgeree migajas de pescado aderezadas con arroz, huevos y mantequilla

ketchup salsa de tomates

kidney riñón

kipper arenque ahumado

lamb cordero

Lancashire hot pot guisado de chuletas y riñones de cordero, con patatas y cebollas

larded mechado

lean magro

leek puerro

leg pierna, muslo, corvejón

lemon limón

~ **sole** especie de platija

lentil lenteja

lettuce lechuga, ensalada verde

lima bean haba grande

lime lima (limón verde)

liver hígado
loaf pan, hogaza
lobster bogavante
loin lomo
Long Island duck pato de Long Island, muy afamado
low-calorie pobre en calorías
lox salmón ahumado
lunch almuerzo
macaroni macarrones
  ~ and cheese macarrones al horno con queso
macaroon macarrón (almendrado)
mackerel caballa
maize maíz
mandarin mandarina
maple syrup jarabe de arce
marinade escabeche
marinated en escabeche
marjoram mejorana
marmalade mermelada de naranja u otros sabores
marrow tuétano
  ~ bone hueso con tuétano
marshmallow dulce de malvavisco
marzipan mazapán
mashed potatoes puré de patatas
mayonnaise mayonesa
meal comida
meat carne
  ~ball albóndiga de carne
  ~ loaf carne picada preparada en forma de un pan y que se cuece al horno
medium (done) a punto
melted derretido
Melton Mowbray pie especie de empanada de carne
menu lista de platos
meringue merengue
milk leche
mince picadillo
  ~ pie tarta de frutas confitadas cortadas en daditos, con manzanas y

especias (con o sin carne)
minced picado
  ~ meat carne picada
mint menta
mixed mezclado, surtido
  ~ grill brocheta de carne
molasses melaza
morel morilla
mousse postre de nata aromatizada
muffin mollete; tarta pequeña (US)
mulberry mora
mullet mújol (pescado)
mulligatawny soup sopa de pollo muy picante de origen indio
mushroom champiñón
muskmelon tipo de melón
mussel mejillón
mustard mostaza
mutton carnero
noodle tallarín
nut nuez
oatmeal (porrdige) gachas de avena
oil aceite
okra fruto del gumbo utilizado generalmente para espesar las sopas y guisados
olive aceituna
omelet tortilla
onion cebolla
orange naranja
ox tongue lengua de buey
oxtail cola de buey (sopa)
oyster ostra
pancake hojuela espesa, torta de sartén
paprika pimiento
Parmesan (cheese) queso parmesano
parsley perejil
parsnip chirivía
partridge perdiz
pastry pastel, pastellillo
pasty empanadilla de carne
pea guisante
peach melocotón

peanut cacahuete, maní
~ **butter** manteca de cacahuete
pear pera
pearl barley cebada perlada
pepper pimienta
peppermint menta
perch perca
persimmon caqui
pheasant faisán
pickerel lucio pequeño (pescado)
pickle 1) legumbre o fruta en vinagre 2) pepinillo (US)
pickled conservado en salmuera o vinagre
pie torta a menudo cubierta con una capa de pasta, rellena de carne, legumbres, frutas o crema inglesa
pig cerdo
pigeon pichón
pike lucio
pineapple piña
plaice platija, acedía
plain natural
plate plato
plum ciruela, ciruela pasa
~ **pudding** pudín inglés hecho con frutas secas, a veces flameado, muy nutritivo y que se sirve en Navidad
poached escalfado
popcorn palomitas de maíz
popover panecillo esponjoso cocido en el horno
pork cerdo
porridge gachas
porterhouse steak lonja espesa de solomillo de res
pot roast carne de ternera asada y legumbres
potato patata, papa
~ **chips** 1) patatas fritas (GB) 2) chips (US)
~ **in its jacket** patata sin pelar
potted shrimps mantequilla sazonada, derretida y enfriada,

servida con camarones
poultry ave de corral
prawn camarón grande
prune ciruela seca
ptarmigan perdiz blanca
pudding pudín blando o consistente hecho con harina, relleno de carne, pescado, legumbres o frutas
pumpernickel pan hecho con harina gruesa de centeno
pumpkin calabaza
~ **pie** pastel de calabaza con canela y nuez moscada
quail codorniz
quince membrillo
rabbit conejo
radish rábano
rainbow trout trucha arco iris
raisin pasa
rare poco hecho
raspberry frambuesa
raw crudo
red mullet salmonete
red (sweet) pepper pimiento morrón
redcurrant grosella roja
relish condimento hecho con trocitos de legumbres y vinagre
rhubarb ruibarbo
rib (of beef) costilla (de ternera)
rib-eye steak solomillo
rice arroz
rissole croqueta de pescado o carne
river trout trucha de río
roast(ed) asado
Rock Cornish hen pollo tomatero
roe huevos de pescado
roll panecillo
rollmop herring filete de arenque escabechado con vino blanco, enrollado con un pepinillo en medio
round steak filete de pierna de ternera
Rubens sandwich carne de ternera en pan tostado, con col fermentada,

queso suizo y salsa para ensalada; se sirve caliente

rump steak filete de lomo de ternera

rusk rebanadas tostadas de pan de molde

rye bread pan de centeno

saddle cuarto trasero

saffron azafrán

sage salvia

salad ensalada

~ **bar** surtido de ensaladas

~ **cream** salsa cremosa para ensalada, ligeramente azucarada

~ **dressing** salsa para ensalada

salmon salmón

~ **trout** trucha asalmonada

salt(ed) sal(ado)

sandwich bocadillo, emparedado

sardine sardina

sauce salsa

sauerkraut col fermentada

sausage salchicha

sauté(ed) salteado

scallop 1) venera 2) escalope de ternera

scampi langostino

scone panecillo tierno hecho con harina de avena o cebada

Scotch broth caldo a base de carne de carnero o de buey y legumbres

Scotch woodcock pan tostado con huevos revueltos y crema de anchoas

sea bass róbalo, lubina

sea kale col marina

seafood mariscos y peces marinos

(in) season (en su) época (estación del año)

seasoning condimento, sazón

service servicio

~ **charge** importe que se paga por el servicio

~ **(not) included** servicio (no) incluido

set menu menú fijo

shad alosa, sábalo

shallot chalote

shellfish marisco

sherbet sorbete

shoulder espalda

shredded wheat hojuelas de trigo en croquetas (se sirven en el desayuno)

shrimp camarón, gamba

silverside (of beef) codillo (de ternera)

sirloin steak bistec del solomillo

skewer brocheta

slice loncha, rodaja

sliced cortado en lonchas

sloppy Joe carne picada de ternera con una salsa picante de tomates, se sirve en un panecillo

smelt eperlano

smoked ahumado

snack comida ligera

sole lenguado

soup sopa, crema

sour agrio

soused herring arenque conservado en vinagre y especias

spaghetti espaguetis

~ **and meatballs** con albóndigas

spare rib costilla de cerdo casi descarnada

spice especia

spinach espinaca

spiny lobster langosta

(on a) spit (en un) espetón

sponge cake bizcocho ligero y esponjoso

sprat arenque pequeño, sardineta

squash calabaza

starter entrada

steak and kidney pie empanada de carne de ternera y riñones

steamed cocido al vapor

stew guisado

Stilton (cheese) queso inglés afamado (blanco o con mohos

strawberry fresa
string bean judía verde
stuffed relleno
stuffing (el) relleno
suck(l)ing pig lechón
sugar azúcar
sugarless sin azúcar
sundae copa de helado con frutas, nueces, nata batida y a veces jarabe
supper comida ligera de la noche, cena
swede naba de Suecia
sweet 1) dulce 2) postre
~ **corn** maíz blanco
~ **potato** batata
sweetbread lechecillas
Swiss cheese queso suizo (Emmenthal)
Swiss roll bizcocho enrollado y relleno de mermelada
Swiss steak lonja de ternera asada con legumbres y especias
T-bone steak bistec y filete de ternera separados por un hueso en forma de T
table d'hôte menú fijo
tangerine especie de mandarina
tarragon estragón
tart tarta de frutas
tenderloin filete de carne
Thousand Island dressing salsa para ensalada, sazonada, hecha de mayonesa y pimientos
thyme tomillo
toad-in-the-hole carne de ternera (o salchicha) cubierta de pasta y cocida al horno
toast pan tostado, tostada
toasted tostado
~ **cheese** pan tostado con queso derretido
tomato tomate
tongue lengua

tournedos bistec espeso del filete (ternera)
treacle melaza
trifle pastel con jerez o aguardiente, hecho con almendras, mermelada y crema batida o natillas y crema de vainilla
tripe tripas, callos
trout trucha
truffle trufa
tuna, tunny atún
turbot rodaballo, rombo
turkey pavo
turnip nabo
turnover pastelillo relleno de compota o mermelada
turtle tortuga
underdone poco hecho
vanilla vainilla
veal ternera
~ **bird** pulpeta de ternera
vegetable legumbre
~ **marrow** calabacín
venison caza, corzo
vichyssoise sopa fría preparada con puerros, patatas y crema
vinegar vinagre
Virginia baked ham jamón cocido al horno, adornado con clavos de especia, rebanadas de piña y cerezas; se le baña con el jugo de las frutas
vol-au-vent pastel de hojaldre relleno de salsa con crema, trozos de carne y champiñones
wafer barquillo
waffle especie de barquillo caliente
Waldorf salad ensalada de apio, manzanas, nueces y mayonesa
walnut nuez
water ice sorbete
watercress berro de agua
watermelon sandía
well-done bastante hecho
Welsh rabbit/rarebit queso derretido

sobre una tostada
whelk buccino (molusco)
whipped cream nata batida
whitebait boquerón
Wiener schnitzel escalope de ternera empanado
wine list lista de vinos
woodcock becada
Worcestershire sauce condimento líquido picante a base de vinagre,

soja y ajo
yam camote
yoghurt yogur
York ham jamón de York (ahumado)
Yorkshire pudding especie de pasta de hojuelas que se sirve con el rosbif
zucchini calabacín
zwieback rebanadas tostadas de pan de molde

Bebidas

ale cerveza negra, ligeramente azucarada, fermentada a elevada temperatura
  bitter ~ negra, amarga y más bien pesada
  brown ~ negra de botella, ligeramente azucarada
  light ~ dorada de botella
  mild ~ negra de barril, bastante fuerte
  pale ~ dorada de botella
angostura esencia aromática amarga que se añade a los cócteles
applejack aguardiente de manzanas
Athol Brose bebida escocesa hecha con whisky, miel, agua y a veces copos de avena
Bacardi cocktail cóctel de ron con ginebra, jarabe de granadina y jugo de limón
barley water bebida refrescante a base de cebada y aromatizada con limón
barley wine cerveza negra muy alcoholizada
beer cerveza
  bottled ~ de botella
  draft, draught ~ de barril

bitters aperitivos y digestivos a base de raíces, corteza o hierbas
black velvet champán mezclado con stout (acompaña con frecuencia las ostras)
bloody Mary vodka, jugo de tomate y especias
bourbon whisky americano, a base de maíz
brandy 1) denominación genérica de los aguardientes de uvas y otras frutas 2) coñac
  ~ **Alexander** mezcla de aguardiente, crema de cacao y nata
British wines vino fermentado en Gran Bretaña, fabricado a base de uvas o jugo de uvas importados
cherry brandy licor de cerezas
cider sidra
  ~ **cup** mezcla de sidra, especias, azúcar y hielo
claret vino tinto de Burdeos
cobbler long drink helado a base de frutas, al que se añade vino o licor
coffee café
  ~ **with cream** con nata
  black ~ solo
  caffeine-free ~ descafeinado

white ~ con leche, cortado

cordial licor estimulante y digestivo

cream nata

cup bebida refrescante a base de vino helado, sifón, un espirituoso y adornada con una raja de naranja, de limón o de pepino

daiquiri cóctel de ron con jugo de limón y de piña

double doble porción

Drambuie licor a base de whisky y miel

dry martini 1) vermú seco (GB) 2) cóctel de ginebra con algo de vermú seco (US)

eggnog bebida de ron u otro licor fuerte con yemas de huevos batidas y azúcar

gin ginebra

gin and it mezcla de ginebra y vermú italiano

gin-fizz mezcla de ginebra, jugo de limón, sifón y azúcar

ginger ale bebida sin alcohol, perfumada con extracto de jengibre

ginger beer bebida ligeramente alcohólica, a base de jengibre y azúcar

grasshopper mezcla de crema de menta, crema de cacao y nata

Guinness (stout) cerveza negra, con gusto muy pronunciado y algo dulce, con mucha malta y lúpulo

half pint aproximadamente 3 decilitros

highball whisky o aguardiente diluido con agua, soda o ginger ale

iced helado

Irish coffee café con azúcar y whisky irlandés, cubierto con nata batida (Chantilly)

Irish Mist licor irlandés a base de whisky y miel

Irish whiskey whisky irlandés menos

áspero que el whisky escocés (scotch); además de cebada contiene centeno, avena y trigo

juice jugo, zumo

lager cerveza dorada ligera

lemon squash zumo de limón

lemonade limonada

lime juice zumo de lima (limón verde)

liqueur licor, poscafé

liquor aguardiente

long drink licor diluido en agua o tónica y servido con cubitos de hielo

madeira vino de Madera

Manhattan whisky americano, vermú y angostura

milk leche

~ **shake** batido

mineral water agua mineral

mulled wine vino caliente con especias

neat bebida pura, sola, sin hielo y sin agua

old-fashioned whisky, angostura, cerezas con marrasquino y azúcar

on the rocks con cubitos de hielo

Ovaltine Ovomaltina

Pimm's cup(s) bebida alcohólica compuesta por alguno de los siguientes licores; se mezcla con zumo de fruta y algunas veces con agua de Seltz

~ **No. 1** a base de ginebra

~ **No. 2** a base de whisky

~ **No. 3** a base de ron

~ **No. 4** a base de aguardiente

pink champagne champán rosado

pink lady mezcla de clara de huevo, Calvados, zumo de limón, jarabe de granadina y ginebra

pint aproximadamente 6 decilitros

port (wine) (vino de) Oporto

porter cerveza negra y amarga

punch ponche

quart 1,14 litro (US 0,95 litro)

root beer bebida edulcorada efervescente, aromatizada con hierbas y raíces

rum ron

rye (whiskey) whisky de centeno, más pesado y más áspero que el bourbon

scotch (whisky) whisky escocés, mezcla de whisky de trigo y de whisky de cebada

screwdriver vodka y zumo de naranja

shandy bitter ale mezclada con zumo de limón o con una ginger beer

sherry jerez

short drink todo licor no diluido, puro

shot dosis de cualquier licor espirituoso

sloe gin-fizz licor de endrina con sifón y zumo de limón

soda water agua gaseosa

soft drink bebida sin alcohol

spirits aguardientes

stinger coñac y crema de menta

stout cerveza negra con mucho lúpulo

y alcohol

straight alcohol que se bebe seco, sin mezcla

tea té

toddy ponche hecho de ron, agua, limón y azúcar

Tom Collins ginebra, zumo de limón, sifón y azúcar

tonic (water) (agua) tónica, agua gaseosa, a base de quinina

vermouth vermú

water agua

whisky sour whisky, zumo de limón, azúcar y sifón

wine vino

    dessert ~ de postre

    dry ~ seco

    red ~ tinto

    rosé ~ clarete, rosado

    sparkling ~ espumoso

    sweet ~ dulce (de postre)

    white ~ blanco

Mini-gramática

El artículo

El artículo determinado (el, la, los, las) tiene una sola forma: *the*.

the room, the rooms	el cuarto, los cuartos
the end of the month	el fin del mes

El artículo indeterminado (un, una, unos, unas) tiene dos formas: *a* se usa cuando precede a sonidos consonantes; *an* antes de sonidos vocales.

a coat un abrigo   **an umbrella** un paraguas   **an hour** una hora

Plurales

El plural de la mayor parte de los nombres se forma añadiendo -*(e)s* al singular. Según el sonido final del singular, el plural se pronuncia -*ss* o -*s* o -*is* (que forma una sílaba extra).

cup — cups (taza — tazas)   **dress — dresses** (vestido — vestidos)

Los plurales siguientes son irregulares:

man — men (hombre/s)	**foot — feet** (pie/s)
woman — women (mujer/es)	**tooth — teeth** (diente/s)
child — children (niño/s)	**mouse — mice** (ratón/ratones)

El posesivo

1. Si el poseedor es una persona: los nombres en singular y los plurales que no terminan en -*s* añaden '*s*.

the boy's room	el cuarto del muchacho
the children's clothes	los vestidos de los niños

Los nombres terminados en -*s* (incluyendo la mayoría de los plurales), añaden solamente el apóstrofe (').

the boys' room   el cuarto de los muchachos

2. Si el poseedor no es una persona: se emplea la preposición *of*.

the key of the door   la llave de la puerta

Adjetivos

Los adjetivos preceden normalmente al nombre.

a large brown suitcase   una maleta marrón grande

El comparativo y el superlativo de los adjetivos se pueden formar de dos maneras:

1. Los adjetivos monosílabos y muchos adjetivos bisílabos añaden -(e)r y -(e)st.

small (pequeño) — **smaller** — **smallest**
busy (ocupado) — **busier** — **busiest**

2. Los adjetivos de tres sílabas o más y algunos adjetivos de dos sílabas (los que terminan en -ful o -less, por ejemplo) no sufren inflexión y forman los comparativos y superlativos con las palabras *more* y *most*.

expensive (caro) — **more expensive** — **most expensive**
careful (cuidadoso) — **more careful** — **most careful**

Nótense los siguientes comparativos irregulares:

good (bueno) — **better** — **best**
bad (malo) — **worse** — **worst**
little (poco) — **less** — **least**
much/many (mucho) — **more** — **most**

Pronombres

		Sujeto	Objeto (dir./indir.)	Posesivo 1	2
Singular					
1.ª persona		**I**	**me**	**my**	**mine**
2.ª persona		**you**	**you**	**your**	**yours**
3.ª persona	(m)	**he**	**him**	**his**	**his**
	(f)	**she**	**her**	**her**	**hers**
	(n)	**it**	**it**	**its**	—
Plural					
1.ª persona		**we**	**us**	**our**	**ours**
2.ª persona		**you**	**you**	**your**	**yours**
3.ª persona		**they**	**they**	**their**	**theirs**

Nota: en inglés *you* es tanto singular como plural. No existe la distinción como en español entre «tú» y «usted».
El caso acusativo se usa también para el complemento indirecto y antes de las preposiciones.

Give it to me.   Dámelo.
He came with us.   Él vino con nosotros.

La forma 1 del posesivo se usa antes del nombre, la forma 2 se usa sola.

Where's my key?   ¿Dónde está mi llave?
That's not mine.   Esa no es mía.

Verbos

La misma forma que el infinitivo para todas las personas excepto la 3.ª persona del singular, ésta se forma añadiendo -(e)s al infinitivo.

	to love amar	to come venir	to go ir
I	love	come	go
you	love	come	go
he/she	loves	comes	goes
we	love	come	go
they	love	come	go

Los negativos se forman empleando el verbo auxiliar *do/does* + *not* + infinitivo.

We do not (don't) like this hotel.	No nos gusta este hotel.
She does not (doesn't) smoke.	Ella no fuma.

Los interrogativos se forman empleando el verbo auxiliar *do* + pronombre + infinitivo.

Do you like it?	¿Te gusta?
Does he live here?	¿Vive aquí?

Verbos irregulares

En la siguiente lista damos los verbos irregulares ingleses. Los verbos compuestos o los que llevan un prefijo se conjugan como los verbos simples, por ej.: *mistake* y *overdrive* se conjugan como *take* y *drive*.

Infinitivo	Pret. indefinido	Participio pasado	
arise	arose	arisen	*levantarse*
awake	awoke	awoken	*despertarse*
be	was	been	*ser, estar*
bear	bore	borne	*soportar*
beat	beat	beaten	*batir*
become	became	become	*llegar a ser*
begin	began	begun	*comenzar*
bend	bent	bent	*doblar*
bet	bet	bet	*apostar*
bid	bade/bid	bidden/bid	*pedir*
bind	bound	bound	*atar*
bite	bit	bitten	*morder*
bleed	bled	bled	*sangrar*

blow	blew	blown	*soplar*
break	broke	broken	*romper*
breed	bred	bred	*criar*
bring	brought	brought	*traer*
build	built	built	*construir*
burn	burnt/burned	burnt/burned	*quemar*
burst	burst	burst	*reventar*
buy	bought	bought	*comprar*
can*	could	—	*poder*
cast	cast	cast	*arrojar*
catch	caught	caught	*coger*
choose	chose	chosen	*escoger*
cling	clung	clung	*adherirse*
clothe	clothed/clad	clothed/clad	*vestir*
come	came	come	*venir*
cost	cost	cost	*costar*
creep	crept	crept	*arrastrar*
cut	cut	cut	*cortar*
deal	dealt	dealt	*distribuir*
dig	dug	dug	*cavar*
do (**he does**)	did	done	*hacer*
draw	drew	drawn	*dibujar*
dream	dreamt/dreamed	dreamt/dreamed	*soñar*
drink	drank	drunk	*beber*
drive	drove	driven	*conducir*
dwell	dwelt	dwelt	*habitar*
eat	ate	eaten	*comer*
fall	fell	fallen	*caer*
feed	fed	fed	*alimentar*
feel	felt	felt	*sentir*
fight	fought	fought	*luchar*
find	found	found	*encontrar*
flee	fled	fled	*huir*
fling	flung	flung	*lanzar*
fly	flew	flown	*volar*
forsake	forsook	forsaken	*renunciar*
freeze	froze	frozen	*helar*
get	got	got	*obtener*
give	gave	given	*dar*
go	went	gone	*ir*
grind	ground	ground	*moler*
grow	grew	grown	*crecer*

* presente de indicativo

hang	hung	hung	*colgar*
have	had	had	*tener*
hear	heard	heard	*oír*
hew	hewed	hewed/hewn	*cortar*
hide	hid	hidden	*esconder*
hit	hit	hit	*golpear*
hold	held	held	*sostener*
hurt	hurt	hurt	*herir*
keep	kept	kept	*guardar*
kneel	knelt	knelt	*arrodillarse*
knit	knitted/knit	knitted/knit	*juntar*
know	knew	known	*saber*
lay	laid	laid	*acostar*
lead	led	led	*dirigir*
lean	leant/leaned	leant/leaned	*apoyarse*
leap	leapt/leaped	leapt/leaped	*saltar*
learn	learnt/learned	learnt/learned	*aprender*
leave	left	left	*marcharse*
lend	lent	lent	*prestar*
let	let	let	*permitir*
lie	lay	lain	*acostarse*
light	lit/lighted	lit/lighted	*encender*
lose	lost	lost	*perder*
make	made	made	*hacer*
may*	might	—	*poder*
mean	meant	meant	*significar*
meet	met	met	*encontrar (personas)*
mow	mowed	mowed/mown	*segar*
must*	—	—	*tener que*
ought (to)*	—	—	*deber*
pay	paid	paid	*pagar*
put	put	put	*poner*
read	read	read	*leer*
rid	rid	rid	*desembarazar*
ride	rode	ridden	*cabalgar*
ring	rang	rung	*sonar*
rise	rose	risen	*ascender*
run	ran	run	*correr*
saw	sawed	sawn	*aserrar*
say	said	said	*decir*
see	saw	seen	*ver*
seek	sought	sought	*buscar*

* presente de indicativo

sell	sold	sold	*vender*
send	sent	sent	*enviar*
set	set	set	*poner*
sew	sewed	sewed/sewn	*coser*
shake	shook	shaken	*agitar*
shall*	should	—	*deber*
shed	shed	shed	*desprenderse*
shine	shone	shone	*brillar*
shoot	shot	shot	*tirar*
show	showed	shown	*mostrar*
shrink	shrank	shrunk	*encogerse*
shut	shut	shut	*cerrar*
sing	sang	sung	*cantar*
sink	sank	sunk	*hundir*
sit	sat	sat	*sentarse*
sleep	slept	slept	*dormir*
slide	slid	slid	*resbalar*
sling	slung	slung	*lanzar*
slink	slunk	slunk	*escabullirse*
slit	slit	slit	*rajar*
smell	smelled/smelt	smelled/smelt	*oler*
sow	sowed	sown/sowed	*sembrar*
speak	spoke	spoken	*hablar*
speed	sped/speeded	sped/speeded	*apresurarse*
spell	spelt/spelled	spelt/spelled	*deletrear*
spend	spent	spent	*gastar*
spill	spilt/spilled	spilt/spilled	*derramar*
spin	spun	spun	*girar*
spit	spat	spat	*escupir*
split	split	split	*rajar*
spoil	spoilt/spoiled	spoilt/spoiled	*estropear*
spread	spread	spread	*extender*
spring	sprang	sprung	*saltar*
stand	stood	stood	*estar de pie*
steal	stole	stolen	*robar*
stick	stuck	stuck	*hundir*
sting	stung	stung	*picar*
stink	stank/stunk	stunk	*apestar*
strew	strewed	strewed/strewn	*esparcir*
stride	strode	stridden	*andar a pasos largos*
strike	struck	struck/stricken	*golpear*
string	strung	strung	*atar*

---

* presente de indicativo

strive	strove	striven	*esforzarse*
swear	swore	sworn	*jurar*
sweep	swept	swept	*barrer*
swell	swelled	swollen	*hinchar*
swim	swam	swum	*nadar*
swing	swung	swung	*balancearse*
take	took	taken	*tomar*
teach	taught	taught	*enseñar*
tear	tore	torn	*desgarrar*
tell	told	told	*decir*
think	thought	thought	*pensar*
throw	threw	thrown	*arrojar*
thrust	thrust	thrust	*impeler*
tread	trod	trodden	*pisotear*
wake	woke/waked	woken/waked	*despertar*
wear	wore	worn	*llevar puesto*
weave	wove	woven	*tejer*
weep	wept	wept	*llorar*
will*	would	—	*querer*
win	won	won	*ganar*
wind	wound	wound	*enrollar*
wring	wrung	wrung	*torcer*
write	wrote	written	*escribir*

---

* presente de indicativo

Abreviaturas inglesas

AA	*Automobile Association*	Asociación Automovilística
AAA	*American Automobile Association*	Asociación Automovilística de los Estados Unidos
ABC	*American Broadcasting Company*	Sociedad Privada de Radiodifusión y Televisión (EE.UU.)
A.D.	*anno Domini*	año de Cristo
Am.	*America; American*	América; americano
a.m.	*ante meridiem (before noon)*	de la mañana (de 00.00 a 12.00 h.)
Amtrak	*American railroad corporation*	Sociedad Privada de Compañías de Ferrocarriles Americanos
AT & T	*American Telephone and Telegraph Company*	Compañía Americana de Teléfonos y Telégrafos
Ave.	*avenue*	avenida
BBC	*British Broadcasting Corporation*	Sociedad Británica de Radio-difusión y Televisión
B.C.	*before Christ*	antes de Cristo
bldg.	*building*	edificio
Blvd.	*boulevard*	bulevar
B.R.	*British Rail*	Ferrocarriles Británicos
Brit.	*Britain; British*	Gran Bretaña; británico
Bros.	*brothers*	hermanos
¢	*cent*	1/100 de dólar
Can.	*Canada; Canadian*	Canadá; canadiense
CBS	*Columbia Broadcasting System*	Sociedad Privada de Radiodifusión y Televisión (EE.UU.)
CID	*Criminal Investigation Department*	Oficina de Investigación Criminal
CNR	*Canadian National Railway*	Ferrocarriles Canadienses
c/o	*(in) care of*	al cuidado de
Co.	*company*	compañía
Corp.	*corporation*	compañía
CPR	*Canadian Pacific Railways*	Compañía Privada de Ferrocarriles Canadienses
D.C.	*District of Columbia*	Distrito de Columbia (Washington, D.C.)
DDS	*Doctor of Dental Science*	Dentista
dept.	*department*	departamento, división adminis-trativa
EEC	*European Economic Community*	Comunidad Económica Europea
e.g.	*for instance*	por ejemplo, verbigracia
Eng.	*England; English*	Inglaterra; inglés
excl.	*excluding; exclusive*	no incluido

ft.	*foot/feet*	pie/pies (medida: 30,5 cm.)
GB	*Great Britain*	Gran Bretaña
H.E.	*His/Her Excellency; His Eminence*	Su Excelencia; Su Eminencia
H.H.	*His Holiness*	Su Santidad
H.M.	*His/Her Majesty*	Su Majestad
H.M.S.	*Her Majesty's ship*	navío de guerra británico
hp	*horsepower*	caballos de vapor
Hwy	*highway*	carretera principal
i.e.	*that is to say*	a saber, es decir
in.	*inch*	pulgada (medida: 2,54 cm.)
Inc.	*incorporated*	Sociedad Anónima
incl.	*including, inclusive*	incluido
£	*pound sterling*	libra esterlina
L.A.	*Los Angeles*	Los Angeles
Ltd.	*limited*	Sociedad Anónima
M.D.	*Doctor of Medicine*	médico
M.P.	*Member of Parliament*	Miembro del Parlamento
mph	*miles per hour*	millas por hora
Mr.	*Mister*	Señor
Mrs.	*Missis*	Señora
Ms.	*Missis/Miss*	Señora/Señorita
nat.	*national*	nacional
NBC	*National Broadcasting Company*	Sociedad Privada de Radiodifusión y Televisión (EE.UU.)
No.	*number*	número
N.Y.C.	*New York City*	Ciudad de Nueva York
O.B.E.	*Officer (of the Order) of the British Empire*	Caballero de la Orden del Imperio Británico
p.	*page; penny/pence*	página; 1/100 de libra
p.a.	*per annum*	por año
Ph.D.	*Doctor of Philosophy*	Doctor en Filosofía
p.m.	*post meridiem (after noon)*	de la tarde/noche (de 12.00 a 24.00 h.)
PO	*Post Office*	Oficina de Correos
POO	*post office order*	giro postal
pop.	*population*	población
P.T.O.	*please turn over*	vuelva la página, por favor
RAC	*Royal Automobile Club*	Real Club Automóvil (Gran Bretaña)
RCMP	*Royal Canadian Mounted Police*	Policía Montada de Canadá
Rd.	*road*	carretera
ref.	*reference*	referencia

Rev.	*reverend*	Reverendo (pastor de la Iglesia Anglicana)
RFD	*rural free delivery*	distribución del correo en el campo
RR	*railroad*	ferrocarril
RSVP	*please reply*	se ruega contestación
$	*dollar*	dólar
Soc.	*society*	sociedad
St.	*saint; street*	santo(a); calle
STD	*Subscriber Trunk Dialling*	teléfono automático
UN	*United Nations*	Organización de las Naciones Unidas
UPS	*United Parcel Service*	Compañía Privada de Expedición de Paquetes (EE.UU.)
US	*United States*	Estados Unidos de América
USS	*United States Ship*	navío de guerra (EE.UU.)
VAT	*value added tax*	tasa al valor añadido
VIP	*very important person*	persona importante que beneficia de ventajas particulares
Xmas	*Christmas*	Navidad
yd.	*yard*	yarda (medida: 91,44 cm.)
YMCA	*Young Men's Christian Association*	Asociación Cristiana de Muchachos
YWCA	*Young Women's Christian Association*	Asociación Cristiana de Muchachas
ZIP	*ZIP code*	número de distrito postal

Numerales

Cardinales

0	zero
1	one
2	two
3	three
4	four
5	five
6	six
7	seven
8	eight
9	nine
10	ten
11	eleven
12	twelve
13	thirteen
14	fourteen
15	fifteen
16	sixteen
17	seventeen
18	eighteen
19	nineteen
20	twenty
21	twenty-one
22	twenty-two
23	twenty-three
24	twenty-four
25	twenty-five
30	thirty
40	forty
50	fifty
60	sixty
70	seventy
80	eighty
90	ninety
100	a/one hundred
230	two hundred and thirty
500	five hundred
1,000	a/one thousand
10,000	ten thousand
100,000	a/one hundred thousand
1,000,000	a/one million

Ordinales

1st	first
2nd	second
3rd	third
4th	fourth
5th	fifth
6th	sixth
7th	seventh
8th	eighth
9th	ninth
10th	tenth
11th	eleventh
12th	twelfth
13th	thirteenth
14th	fourteenth
15th	fifteenth
16th	sixteenth
17th	seventeenth
18th	eighteenth
19th	nineteenth
20th	twentieth
21st	twenty-first
22nd	twenty-second
23rd	twenty-third
24th	twenty-fourth
25th	twenty-fifth
26th	twenty-sixth
27th	twenty-seventh
28th	twenty-eighth
29th	twenty-ninth
30th	thirtieth
40th	fortieth
50th	fiftieth
60th	sixtieth
70th	seventieth
80th	eightieth
90th	ninetieth
100th	hundredth
230th	two hundred and thirtieth
500th	five hundredth
1,000th	thousandth

La hora

Los británicos y los americanos utilizan el sistema de 12 horas. La abreviatura *a.m.* (*ante meridiem*) designa las horas anteriores al mediodía, *p.m.* (*post meridiem*) las de la tarde o de la noche. Sin embargo, en Gran Bretaña existe la tendencia, cada vez más acentuada, a indicar los horarios como en el continente.

I'll come at seven a.m.   Vendré a las 7 de la mañana.
I'll come at two p.m.   Vendré a las 2 de la tarde.
I'll come at eight p.m.   Vendré a las 8 de la noche.

Los días de la semana

Sunday	domingo	*Thursday*	jueves
Monday	lunes	*Friday*	viernes
Tuesday	martes	*Saturday*	sábado
Wednesday	miércoles		

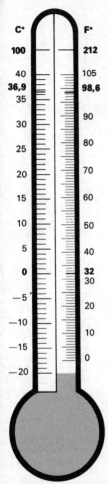

Conversion tables/
Tablas de conversión

Metres and Feet

The figure in the middle stands for both metres and feet, e.g. 1 metre = 3.281 ft. and 1 foot = 0.30 m.

Metros y pies

Los números de la columna del centro son válidos tanto para los metros, como para los pies, p.ej.: 1 metro = 3,281 pies, 1 pie = 0,30 metros.

Metres/Metros		Feet/Pies
0.30	**1**	3.281
0.61	**2**	6.563
0.91	**3**	9.843
1.22	**4**	13.124
1.52	**5**	16.403
1.83	**6**	19.686
2.13	**7**	22.967
2.44	**8**	26.248
2.74	**9**	29.529
3.05	**10**	32.810
3.66	**12**	39.372
4.27	**14**	45.934
6.10	**20**	65.620
7.62	**25**	82.023
15.24	**50**	164.046
22.86	**75**	246.069
30.48	**100**	328.092

Temperature

To convert Centigrade to Fahrenheit, multiply by 1.8 and add 32.
To convert Fahrenheit to Centigrade, subtract 32 from Fahrenheit and divide by 1.8.

Temperatura

Para convertir de grados Celsius a Fahrenheit, se multiplica la cantidad de grados Celsius por 1,8 y luego se añade 32.
Para convertir de Fahrenheit a Celsius, se resta 32 y luego se divide por 1,8.